The Logic of God Incarnate

By the same author:

Understanding Identity Statements

The Logic of
God Incarnate

Thomas V. Morris

Cornell University Press

ITHACA AND LONDON

First published 1986 by Cornell University Press.
First printing, Cornell Paperbacks, 1987.

International Standard Book Number 0-8014-1846-1 (cloth)
International Standard Book Number 0-8014-9474-5 (paper)
Library of Congress Catalog Card Number 85-21252
Printed in the United States of America
Librarians: Library of Congress cataloging information appears on the last page of the book.

The paper in this book is acid-free and meets the guidelines for permanence and durability of the Committee on Production Guidelines for Book Longevity of the Council on Library Resources.

No relationship is adequate to unite the Son of Mary with the Son of God except the relationship of numerical identity.

C. J. F. Williams

The main point of the incarnation is not a matter of relation at all. It is a matter of identity. Jesus *is* God incarnate. . . .
Brian Hebblethwaite

If the Christian gospel continues to be proclaimed, there is no escape from the paradox of the one person who is truly divine and truly human.

John MacQuarrie

I know nothing so contemptible as a mere paradox; a mere ingenious defense of the indefensible.

G. K. Chesterton

It is a sacred duty for any thinking person to try to eliminate paradox.

C. F. D. Moule

Contents

Contents

Preface

I first began reflecting on the philosophical problems confronting the traditional doctrine of the Incarnation when I was a graduate student. The departments of Religious Studies and Philosophy at Yale University generously allowed me to pursue an unusual joint course of study necessary for attaining some clarity on a number of those problems. One result was a doctoral dissertation with the same basic aim as this book, but with almost nothing else in common with it. In the dissertation, "Identity and Incarnation," I constructed an elaborate theory concerning language and the world which would render the doctrine of the Incarnation immune to most contemporary challenges. I have come to judge that theory wholly unacceptable; and so in the present work it gets no more than a brief mention. It is said in the Talmud by Rabbi, the son of R. Huna, that a man does not understand the words of the Torah until he has been tripped up over them, or understood them wrongly. I suspect the same is often true in philosophy as well. At any rate, my present understanding of the Incarnation has benefited a great deal from that earlier attempt. In the course of thinking about the Incarnation for some years now, I have come to see that a few simple metaphysical distinctions and a solid dose of logical care will suffice to explicate and defend the doctrine against all extant criticisms of a philosophical nature. That is what this book attempts to show.

9

Preface

A word of thanks should go to a number of people who have encouraged me in various ways in my work on this project. My ideas were initially developed in various undergraduate and graduate seminars at Notre Dame. To the Department of Philosophy, its exemplary chairman, Richard Foley, and its students I owe a great deal, both for the opportunity to work out many of the concepts and arguments I use here and for the valuable leave time during which this book was actually composed. I am grateful, further, to the editors of *Analysis* and *Mind* for allowing me to develop in their pages some of the ideas that find application here. A portion of chapter 2 has appeared in "The Natures of God Incarnate: A Study of Christian Orthodoxy," *Christian Scholar's Review* 14 (1985), 35–44. Another part is scheduled to appear in *Modern Theology*. Some of chapter 3 derived from "Divinity, Humanity, and Death," *Religious Studies* 19 (1983), 451–458; "Incarnational Anthropology," *Theology* 87 (1984), 344–350; and "Creation *ex Nihilo*: Some Considerations," *International Journal for the Philosophy of Religion* 14 (1983), 233–239. Material in chapter 4 comes from "The God of Abraham, Isaac, and Anselm," *Faith and Philosophy* 1 (1984), 177–187, and from "Properties, Modalities, and God," *Philosophical Review* 93 (1984), 35–55. Chapter 5, "The Necessity of God's Goodness," draws on an article by the same name which appeared in the *New Scholasticism* 54 (1985), as well as on "Duty and Divine Goodness," *American Philosophical Quarterly* 21 (1984), 261–268. A section of chapter 6 first appeared in "St. Thomas on the Identity and Unity of the Person of Christ: A Problem of Reference in Christological Discourse," published by the Scottish Academic Press in *The Scottish Journal of Theology* 35 (1982), 419–430. I thank both the editors and the publishers of these journals for their permission to use this material.

Finally I thank my wife, Mary, my daughter, Sara, and my son, Matthew, for their understanding and loving support during the difficult time of preparing a book such as this for publication. To them, my family, it is dedicated.

THOMAS V. MORRIS

Notre Dame, Indiana

The Logic of God Incarnate

Introduction

A few years ago, in his contribution to the book *Incarnation and Myth: The Debate Continued*, Nicholas Lash wrote, "The 'incarnation debate' badly needs, as one of its components, a fresh look at the logical problems to which classical formulations in christology give rise."[1] In a review of that book, Keith Ward echoed Lash's concern by pointing out that none of the contributors to the recent theological controversy over the doctrine of the Incarnation has even begun to engage in the sort of careful analysis of such concepts as incarnation, identity, humanity, and divinity which will be a necessary prerequisite for making any real progress in evaluating the doctrine. Ward concluded his review by emphasizing that "all the hard logical work yet remains to be done."[2] It is just this work, or at least a significant portion of it, which I shall attempt in this book to do.

The traditional doctrine of the Incarnation has as its central affirmation the claim that Jesus of Nazareth was one and the same person as God the Son, the Second Person of the divine Trinity. In the case of Jesus, the tradition tells us, we are faced with one person in two natures—divine and human. It would be very difficult to write a single book dealing with all the logical, metaphysical, and epistemological issues which could, in one way or another, be

---

[1] Nicholas Lash, "Jesus and the Meaning of 'God'—A Comment," in *Incarnation and Myth: The Debate Continued*, ed. Michael Goulder (Grand Rapids: Eerdmans, 1979), p. 42.

[2] Keith Ward, Review of Goulder, ed., in *Theology*, 82 (November, 1979), 452.

viewed as preliminary to any full philosophical grasp of this claim. Some of the groundwork in philosophical logic and the philosophy of language, for example, might just be too tedious and circuitous for most theological readers and even for some philosophers of religion, eager to tackle head-on the few core issues that are most central for assessing this fundamental doctrine of the Christian faith. For this reason I have not tried to put into one book all the philosophical explorations which might be relevant to an understanding of the Incarnation. Rather, in what follows, I build on work previously done and published elsewhere. From the reader's point of view, however, the present book will be self-contained. It is only some logical background issues whose detailed development has been left elsewhere.

In particular, the fundamental christological affirmation is an identity statement, a statement of faith identifying Jesus as a literally divine person. It is probably the most extraordinary identity claim ever propounded by large numbers of serious people concerned with the truth. In order to be able to bring the utmost philosophical clarity to bear on this particularly striking identity claim, one needs to get as clear as possible on identity statements in general. This I have tried to do in a contribution to the Scots Philosophical Monographs Series entitled *Understanding Identity Statements*, the last chapter of which adumbrates some of the basic framework of this book.[3] There I lay out and argue for the basic perspective on identity statements I assume here.

But, as C. J. F. Williams reminds us, "we cannot discover what it means to say that God the Son is identical with Jesus of Nazareth simply by examining the concept of identity."[4] So the work on identity statements and the concept of identity is no more than a preliminary for a proper explication and defense of the doctrine of the Incarnation. In the pages that follow, I shall try to lay out an understanding of the doctrine which I think is fully in accord with the decrees of the church councils of past centuries and which I believe stands triumphant against all contemporary challenges of a philosophical nature.

[3] Aberdeen: Aberdeen University Press; Atlantic Highlands, N.J.: Humanities Press, 1984.

[4] C. J. F. Williams, "A Programme for Christology," *Religious Studies*, 3 (1968), 523.

The organization of this book is thoroughly polemical. It is structured around four problems, the first of which demands by far the most attention. Recent critics of the doctrine I have in view have charged it with being either conceptually incoherent or cosmologically incongruous, or both. The incoherence charge, the main philosophical challenge, arises quite simply from applying a law or principle governing identity statements to the claim that Jesus, a man, was numerically identical with God Incarnate, the Second Person of the Trinity, in human nature. I discuss this challenge in chapters 1 through 6. Under the pressure of the challenge, we are forced to recognize and employ a number of important distinctions which provide us with an apparatus not only for defending the doctrine of the Incarnation, but also for arriving at some substantive philosophical understanding of it. They will also help us to deal with the three remaining problems to be considered.

The second problem, addressed in chapter 7, is the charge of cosmological incongruence—the claim that any belief that God, creator and sustainer of the entire universe, came to earth in human nature, is such that although it might have made sense in a ptolemaic, or naive, first-century Palestinian world-view, it makes no sense at all given the elements of modern cosmology. According to this criticism, our discoveries concerning the vastness and nature of the cosmos somehow impugn traditional Christian claims about the Incarnation.

The third problem to be discussed, in chapter 8, is one of christological espistemology. Frances Young once posed the following problem: "If Jesus was an entirely normal human being, no evidence can be produced for the incarnation; If no evidence can be produced, there can be no basis on which to claim that an incarnation took place."[5] In this chapter, some general questions about religious epistemology are broached, but the focus is on some matters concerning the epistemic status of the doctrine of the Incarnation.

The fourth and final problem to be treated is how the doctrine of the Incarnation, as articulated and defended in this book, relates to the doctrine of the Trinity. I shall not attempt here a full ex-

[5]Frances Young, "Can There Be Any Evidence?" in Goulder, ed., p. 62.

plication and defense of the doctrine of the Trinity. I just think it important to say something about how the views herein developed relate to that other central and clearly connected tenet of traditional Christian theology.

The book as a whole should be viewed as a defense of the orthodox doctrine of the Incarnation, the two-natures view of Christ, against contemporary philosophical attacks. I do not purport here to show that the doctrine is true; I seek only to answer some contemporary arguments against accepting it as true. And lest even the defensive scope of this volume be overestimated, I should repeat here with a measure of agreement the words of Peter Geach:

> Of course I do not think that natural reason can establish even the non-contradictoriness, let alone the truth, of the Christian belief that a certain human being was and is Almighty God in person. . . . A demand for a strict proof of non-contradictoriness is anyhow often unreasonable—even, as recent logical researches have shown, in pure mathematics. Certainly, if the doctrine of the Incarnation is true, it will not be self-contradictory, and any argument that it is self-contradictory will contain a flaw; but saying this is very different from saying that if the doctrine is true, we ought to be able to see, or prove once for all, that it is non-contradictory.[6]

Nevertheless, it will be of significant theological interest to see that none of the few major arguments on the basis of which many contemporary philosophers and theologians reject the doctrine is a success. It will be of significant philosophical interest to see exactly how they fail. For in the process of examining these objections, we shall come to appreciate in a new way a number of metaphysical and logical features of this central Christian belief.

[6]P. T. Geach, *God and the Soul* (London: Routledge & Kegan Paul, 1969), pp. 106–7.

1 *The Incoherence Charge*

Statements of identity often convey important empirical information about the world. They are a central form of statement in the natural sciences and serve a vital role in ordinary nonscientific contexts as well. In addition, some of the most striking and controversial metaphysical theses ever propounded have had the form of identity statements. All such literal statements of absolute, numerical identity are governed by a set of principles or laws, among which is the principle of the indiscernibility of identicals. Simply put, this principle in its traditional form specifies that a necessary condition for identity is complete commonality of properties. An object x is identical with an object y only if every property had by x is had by y, and vice versa.[1] If, for example, Cicero and Tully did not have all properties in common, Cicero would not be the same person as Tully. Further, if it is impossible that some object a share all properties in common with some object b, it is impossible that a be identical with b. A warranted judgment that some identity statement violates the indiscernibility requirement both warrants and requires judging that statement to be false.

The core claim of the traditional Christian doctrine of the Incarnation, the fundamental and most distinctive tenet of the Chris-

---

[1]The principle of the indiscernibility of identicals is presented here quite simply, for the sake of convenience. For a more complete presentation of the way in which this and other principles can be said to govern identity, see my *Understanding Identity Statements* (Aberdeen: Aberdeen University Press, 1984), chap. 6.

tian faith as defined at the Council of Chalcedon (A.D. 451), is the claim that the person who was and is Jesus of Nazareth is one and the same individual as God the Son, the Second Person of the divine Trinity—a literal statement of absolute, numerical identity. As an identity statement, it, like any other such statement, stands under the requirement of indiscernibility. It is not true unless Jesus had all and only the properties of some divine being, in particular the individual referred to in Christian theology as God the Son. But in recent years, a significant number of the most prominent contemporary theologians have held it to stand in blatant and multiple violation of this requirement, and so have announced it to be false. Their recommendation has been that Christians abandon the doctrine of the Incarnation, and find some other way of conceptualizing the relation between Jesus and God which is sufficient for the propriety of treating Jesus as both Revealer and Christ.

Few of these recent critics of the doctrine of the Incarnation, however, have been content to label it false. Most have gone further to charge it with being, variously, impossible, self-contradictory, incoherent, absurd, and even unintelligible. In this chapter, we shall begin to examine all these charges, look at the structure of the sort of argument that can be used to support them, and identify a type of strategy most appropriate for defending the orthodox doctrine against them.

1   *Incarnation and Incoherence*

According to Chalcedonian orthodoxy, we have in the case of Jesus the Christ one person in two natures, divine and human. Since the times of the early church Fathers, it has been fully appreciated how different these two natures are. Indeed, since Old Testament times, it has been emphasized in the Judeo-Christian tradition that God is qualitatively different from man in the extreme. There is no greater divide in the ontology of the Bible than that between Creator and creature. So I think it is safe to say that the ascription of diety to the man Jesus has never been engaged in lightly by Christian theologians. Indeed, the history of early christological heresies testifies to the theological tension that was felt from the very beginning in the attempt to bring together the concepts of divinity and humanity to characterize this one person.

It is interesting to note that many theologians who have been led in recent years to reject the doctrine of the Incarnation as a logical and metaphysical impossibility have subscribed to an idea of God as in every way utterly transcendent. Some of them hold that God and men can have literally no properties in common, since they are of such different ontological status. Indeed, they even say, none of our human concepts apply to God at all.

It is no surprise that on this sort of view, the doctrine of the Incarnation would be judged absurd or incoherent. But such a view of God itself falls to the same charge. For if, *per impossibile*, God and men shared no properties due to their difference in ontological status, they would have to share at least the following property: the property of having a set of properties not shared by some being with a different ontological status. Likewise, if no human concepts applied to God, at least one human concept would apply to him— the concept of being such as to escape characterization by human concepts.

These may seem artificial or contrived objections, but they suffice to show this view of deity to be logically self-defeating and thus incoherent. Furthermore, careful reflection will reveal that even if this sort of view were qualified in such a way as to circumvent such objections, it still would be such that no one could possibly have any evidence, argument, or rational justification of any kind for thinking it correct.

However, to reject such a view of God is not yet to pave the way for a doctrine of divine incarnation. For even on a quite traditional conception of deity, the doctrine can seem just too obviously incoherent. God traditionally is said to be omnipotent, omniscient, incorporeal, impeccable, and necessarily existent. It is also said by eminent spokesmen of the church that the deity is impassible, immutable, and eternal. Further, these are presented not just as properties God happens to have, but rather as attributes essential to him and constitutive of his deity. We human beings, by contrast, seem clearly to exemplify the logical complement of each of these attributes. We are limited in power, restricted in knowledge, embodied in flesh, liable to sin, and are contingent creations. Certainly, we suffer, change, and live out our lives within a measure of time. It is logically impossible for any being to exemplify together both a property and its logical complement. Nothing can be, for example, both necessary and contingent in metaphysical status. So it can easily be concluded that, on the basis of an orthodox conception of God and a patently true characterization of what human beings are like, it would be just impossible for one individual to be both human and divine. If Jesus was truly human, he could not have been divine. If he was truly God, he could not have been a man. He could not have had both these sets of properties at once.

Throughout the history of the church, this has been the common assumption of all the christological heresies: humanity and divinity are not compossibly exemplifiable by one and the same bearer of properties. The Psilanthropists concluded that Jesus was a mere man, the Docetists that he was only God appearing to be man, the Arians that he was neither true God nor true man. The Nestorians attempted to affirm both divinity and humanity, but under the pressure of this common assumption ended up with the quite unusual heresy of apparently postulating in the case of Christ two distinct bearers of properties, one of the divine attributes, one of the human, in the most intimate dyadic relation possible, one to the other.[2]

In our own day, we find the British theologian Don Cupitt declaring: "The eternal God, and a historical man, are two beings of quite different ontological status. It is simply unintelligible to declare them identical."[3] But of course Cupitt's charge, as it stands, in addition to being otherwise flawed, is not precisely to the point. Chalcedonian orthodoxy does not allege any historical man to be identical with God *simpliciter*. The doctrine of the Trinity clearly precludes that. God, on the trinitarian conception, has the property of being somehow three persons in one substance or nature. No human person can have that property, because no single person

---

[2]Brief explications of these ancient christological heresies are available in any of a number of standard works such as, for example, Aloys Grillmeier, *Christ in Christian Tradition*, 2d rev. ed., English trans. (London: Mowbrays, 1975); and J. N. D. Kelly, *Early Christian Doctrines*, rev. ed. (New York: Harper & Row, 1978).

[3]Don Cupitt, "The Finality of Christ," *Theology*, 78 (December, 1976), 625.

of any sort can have that property. The identity claim made about Christ in the doctrine of the Incarnation is

(C) Jesus is God the Son

not

(C′) Jesus is God.

However, no traditional theologian would tolerate for a minute the claim recently made by John Hick that the traditional assertion that Jesus is God is "as devoid of meaning as" a statement of the form 'this circle is a square', a charge which is as logically infelicitous as it is theologically scandalous.[4] In traditional christology (C′) is taken to express a perfectly meaningful and true predication, not an identity claim. But of course, if 'Jesus' is intended to designate a man known to have lived in first-century Palestine, believed to have been born of Jewish parentage, to have gone about for at least a short time as an itinerant preacher, and to have died by crucifixion, all those contemporary theologians who reject (C) because of the sorts of considerations already raised will thereby reject (C′) as well, as a false predication expressing an impossibility.

(C) is thus commonly rejected as false because it is believed to stand in violation of the indiscernibility principle governing identity statements. Because of what God and men are, the charge goes, we can know that, as a man, Jesus had properties any divine being lacks, and that, conversely, any divine being has properties that Jesus lacked. But why is (C) branded as, so to speak, much worse than false? Why is it also labeled by most critics as impossible, self-contradictory, incoherent, absurd, and unintelligible?

On a standard view of identity statements, any false identity is necessarily false, and thus in the broadly logical sense impossible.[5] From this perspective, the incarnational identity's being false would

---

[4]John Hick, "Jesus and the World Religions," in *The Myth of God Incarnate*, ed. John Hick (London: SCM Press, 1977), p. 178. 'This circle is a square' is not devoid of meaning; it just cannot standardly be used in English to state anything other than a proposition which is, *a priori*, necessarily false.

[5]For a brief, intuitive indication of the broadly logical sense of possibility, necessity, and impossibility, see Alvin Plantinga, *The Nature of Necessity* (Oxford: Clarendon Press, 1974), chap. 1.

entail its being impossible as well. I suspect, however, that this is not what theological critics of the Incarnation have had in mind when they have gone on to denounce it as impossible, and so forth. Apart from any possible desire just to be as rhetorically iconoclastic as they can, I think these critics use such extreme terms of disapprobation because they consider (C) to be false not only necessarily, but also a priori. They see it as semantically deviant or conceptually skewed. In other words, it is viewed as the sort of statement which is such that no one can both understand it and at the same time be in the state of either believing it or even wondering whether it is true. It is rather such that anyone who understands it, understands it to be false. From this point of view, it is as impossible to conceive of Jesus' being God (predication) or being God the Son (identity) as it is to conceive of his being prime or being identical with $\sqrt{4}$.

We know a priori of any substitution instance of the sentence frame 'x is married and is a bachelor' that it is false. It is impossible to understand such a statement and yet not know it to be false. Many critics of the doctrine of the Incarnation seem to view the sentence frame 'x is God and is a man' in the same way. From the knowledge of what it is to be God and what it is to be man, the knowledge is supposed to result that no individual could be both. And some seem to think that this is an altogether analytic, conceptual matter.

If the concept of humanity contained analytically any properties which were logical complements of properties analytic to the concept of divinity, they would be right. But it does not seem to be the case that both 'divinity' and 'humanity' are concept words with this sort of analytic content. They are not both linguistically on a par with terms such as 'bachelor', which do have the sorts of definitions supportive of both analytic truths and falsehoods. At least the term 'humanity' seems to be more like a natural-kind term than like such a concept word.

According to one standard account of natural kinds, every such kind has an essence, a set of properties or underlying traits individually necessary and jointly sufficient for membership in the kind. We can understand both human nature and divine nature, or humanity and divinity, in a parallel fashion. Human nature comprises all those properties individually necessary and jointly sufficient for being human. No individual can be human without having each and every one of the properties essential to humanity. And likewise for divinity. For example, on the traditional doctrine of God, properties essential for divinity include omnipotence, omniscience, aseity, eternality, and the like. No individual can be God without having all such properties.

In most cases, specifications of what properties are essential to particular kinds constitute what Stephen Schwartz has called "stable generalizations"—propositions which are necessarily true (with "broadly logical" necessity), but known only a posteriori.[6] That is, in most cases, few nontrivial kind-essential properties are known to characterize particular natural kinds a priori. In this respect divinity seems to differ quite a bit from standard natural kinds. For the epistemic status of many, if not all, of the known attributes essential to deity can be argued to be known to be such a priori. To this extent, 'divinity' is like a constructed concept word. And at least one nontrivial essential human property may be able to be known to be such a priori—the modal property of possibly being conscious at some time. But most nontrivial essential human properties will not be known a priori. They will, like most properties nontrivially essential to any ordinary natural kind, be known only a posteriori. In this important respect, humanity differs from such constructed concepts as that of a square, a circle, a home-run, or, in a slightly different way, that of a bachelor.

But once it is known, whether on a priori or a posteriori grounds, what some of the component properties of a particular kind-essence are, certain sorts of claims about members of that kind can be known to be false a priori, without the necessity of checking into the specifics of the particular case. If, for example, we know, as a matter of fact on a posteriori grounds, that water is essentially H_2O, then we can rule out a priori as false any claim that a particular container is filled with a substance which is water but lacks any hydrogen content. We do not have to examine the substance to reject that claim. Its falsehood, and impossibility, follow from what it is to be water, what the kind-essence of water is.

[6]See Stephen Schwartz, "Natural Kinds and Nominal Kinds," *Mind*, 89 (1980).

It seems that some contemporary critics of the Incarnation can be understood as making a parallel argument: Once we know, on a priori or a posteriori grounds, or both, what divinity is and what humanity is, we can rule out a priori as false and impossible any particular claim that some individual is both human and divine. The assumption operative here is then of course that some kind-essential properties of deity are logical complements of some such properties of humanity. If there is just one such logical disparity between humanity and divinity, the doctrine of the Incarnation is ruled out, as these critics allege—we can know a priori that (C), as an identity statement concerning a man and a divine being, is false. But as I have indicated already, a fairly impressive list of such disparities has been drawn up by the critics. If they are right, the incarnational identity does violate the indiscernibility requirement blatantly, and many times over. But if this is so, the doctrine foundational to traditional Christian faith is indeed false, expressive of an impossibility.

2 Defensive Strategies

Near the end of his important book on the Incarnation, entitled *A Study in Christology*, H. M. Relton said of the doctrine, "It postulates a logical impossibility. . . . But the Person of Christ is the bankruptcy of human logic."[7] Likewise, it is well known that Søren Kierkegaard was prepared to endorse the claim that God had become a man while at the same time characterizing it as "a breach with all thinking."[8] There are those within the church who would accept the contemporary critique of the doctrine as impossible and incoherent by human lights, but join Tertullian in believing it precisely because it is absurd. In fact, many religious people seem to share the view once expressed by Blaise Pascal, when he wrote, "It is amusing to think that there are people in the world who have renounced all the laws of God and nature only to invent laws for

[7]H. M. Relton, *A Study in Christology* (London: SPCK, 1917), p. 265.
[8]Søren Kierkegaard, *Concluding Unscientific Postscript*, trans. David F. Swenson and Walter Lowrie (Princeton: Princeton University Press, 1941), p. 513.

themselves, which they scrupulously obey, as, for example, Mahomet's soldiers, thieves and heretics, and likewise logicians."[9]

Commenting on some of the history of early christology, Gareth Moore recently stated:

> If the orthodox doctrine was attacked on logical grounds, the defense, as often as not, was not to demonstrate how coherent, clear and consistent it really was, but to accuse its opponents of presumption. The doctrine of the incarnation expressed a divine mystery which we mere mortals could not expect to understand, and it was bordering on the blasphemous for any feeble, logic-chopping human intellect to attack it.[10]

From this point of view, it is no serious criticism of the doctrine of the Incarnation that it involves logical inconsistency, the violation of logical laws. Indeed, this may even be seen as a mark of its supernatural pedigree.

It should, however, be clear that the strategy of defending the doctrine by devaluing the status of logical consistency has very little to be said for it from a philosophical perspective. It is just a desperation move which embraces incoherence to avoid its sting. From any adequate and traditional notion of deity, it follows that we should not expect to be able to understand all the things of God. There will thus be an ineliminable element of mystery attending any claim about God. But of course it does not at all follow from this that within the domain of what we can understand concerning a claim about God, logical inconsistency is not a clear and conclusive mark of falsehood. Any defense of the Incarnation which alleges otherwise is just rooted in confusion.

There are some, however, who are prepared to defend orthodox Christian doctrines not by a wholesale devaluing or rejection of human logic, but rather by dismissing only whatever specific rules or principles create theological trouble. In the case of the incarnation identity (C), it is the principle of the indiscernibility of iden-

---

[9]Blaise Pascal, *Pensées*, trans. A. Krailscheimer (Harmondsworth: Penguin Books, 1966), p. 167, number 794.

[10]Gareth Moore, "Incarnation and Image of God," *New Blackfriars*, 10 (December, 1983), 456.

ticals which can appear to be the problematic principle. It is only because it is judged to violate this requirement that (C) is said to be false. But why should the Christian accept this as a true principle, binding on all identity statements? This is a question that has been raised by A. P. Martinich in a paper entitled "Identity and Trinity."[11] He contends that in order to establish consistency at the heart of another central doctrine of Christianity, the traditional doctrine of the Trinity, the Christian must reject the indiscernibility principle, a rejection which he endorses.

Martinich identifies the following four propositions as a set of Christian affirmations that are apparently inconsistent:

1 There is only one God.
2 The Father is God.⟩ *Predications, not identities*
3 The Son is God.
4 The Father is not the Son.

He suggests that if 2 and 3 are treated as true identities governed by the indiscernibility principle, a treatment clearly compatible with 1, then by the symmetry and transitivity of identity, 4 cannot be true. But Christians, he states, hold to the truth of all four propositions.

There have been groups in the early history of Christianity who avoided this problem with views found to be unsatisfactory by the church at large. The Sabellians accepted the obvious implication of the first three statements, and so denied the fourth. They held that one and the same individual is both God the Father and God the Son. This position has been known also as 'modalism'. The three persons of the Trinity are said to be merely modes of appearance or modes of existence of the one and only God. The Arians tried a different maneuver. They held to the truth of 1, 2, and 4, and so by implication rejected 3. But their understanding of Christ was found by the church to be unacceptable. So they, like the Sabellians, were relegated to the realm of heresy.

But accepting the first three propositions as true statements of the form Martinich claims for them has obviously untoward consequences. The Son, according to orthodoxy, suffered and was

[11]A. P. Martinich, "Identity and Trinity," *Journal of Religion*, 58 (April, 1978), 169–181.

crucified. Did God suffer in this way? If 3 is a true identity and the principle of indiscernibility holds, one must answer in the affirmative. But then it will follow from the truth of 2 that the Father suffered and was crucified, which implicates us in the heresy of patripassionism, rejected by the church. To avoid this heresy while holding 2 and 3 to be true identities in the way Martinich suggests, the principle of the indiscernibility of identicals must be rejected.

However, 2 and 3 are best not understood as identities. They, like (C′) mentioned earlier, are predications. But clearly if they are true predications, their truth again seems not be to compatible with the truth of both 1 and 4. For consider the parallel

5 There is only one man.
6 Cicero is a man.
7 Cataline is a man.
8 Cicero is not Cataline.

If 6, 7, and 8 were all true, there would be at least two men, and so 5 would be false. If 6 and 7 were identities, 6, 7, and 8 would form an inconsistent triad given the symmetry and transitivity of identity. 5 would not be required to generate inconsistency. And of course the same holds for 1–4. If 2 and 3 were identities, 2–4 alone would form an inconsistent set, given symmetry and transitivity. 1 would be superfluous for producing inconsistency. So since Martinich apparently thinks it important to present the whole tetrad 1–4 for our consideration as seemingly productive of inconsistency, it is safe to assume he would not want 1 to be superfluous in that matter. He thus ought to have treated 2 and 3 as what they are, not identities, but predications like 6 and 7.

Still, to avoid inconsistency in the set of propositions he understands to form the tetrad 1–4, Martinich endorses the thesis of the relativity of identity, recently popularized by the work of Peter Geach and others.[12] Simply put, the relativity thesis is that identity is sortal relative. Every statement of the form '*a* is *b*' or '*a* is the same as *b*' is said to be incomplete. In every such case, we are told, it needs to be asked "The same what?" The further claim is then

[12]See, for example, Peter Geach, *Logic Matters* (Berkeley: University of California Press, 1980), pp. 238–249, and Nicholas Griffin, *Relative Identity* (Oxford: Clarendon Press, 1977).

made that, in at least many such cases, *a* and *b* could be the same *F* but not the same *G* (where '*F*' and '*G*' stand in for sortal terms, or general count nouns with associated criteria for individuation and reidentification). And this is just what Martinich thinks Christians need to claim about identity. For if the relativity thesis is right, 4 can be true under the covering term 'person', and thereby accord with 2 and 3, while at the same time being false under the covering term 'God', thereby remaining consistent with 1. Thus, Martinich holds, the Father is not the same person as the Son, but is the same God. The problem of the apparently inconsistent tetrad 1–4, as understood by Martinich, is by this simple maneuver solved.

But the relativity thesis is highly controversial, at best. It is commonly acknowledged that all identity statements allow of expansion into a form in which some sortal term which is common to both referring expressions, under which they are used and their referents individuated, is explicitly mentioned. But it is also denied by most philosophers that this implies or even allows for the relativity thesis that some *a* and *b* could be in a literal, numerical sense, the same *F* but different *G*s. David Wiggins, for example, has argued in a well-known passage that such a construal of identity would violate the principle of the indiscernibility of identicals.[13] And it seems clear that Wiggins is right. That is why in order to appropriate the relativity thesis, Martinich is forced to deny the truth of the indiscernibility principle.

Following an early article by Leonard Linsky, Martinich claims that there are quite general, nontheological grounds for denying the principle.[14] These grounds consist, however, entirely in alleged counterexamples to the principle which are easily exposed and defeated as irrelevant to it.[15] And this should be no surprise since, as the vast majority of philosophers agree, strict numerical identity *must* involve qualitative identity. Wiggins, for example, has expressed the feeling that the principle of the indiscernibility of identicals is as obvious as the law of noncontradiction. He asks: "How

---

[13]David Wiggins, *Sameness and Substance* (Cambridge: Harvard University Press, 1980), chap. 1.

[14]Leonard Linsky, "Hesperus and Phosphorus," *Philosophical Review*, 68 (1959), 515–519.

[15]See *Understanding Identity Statements*, pp. 89–93.

if *a is b* could there be something true of *the object a* which was untrue of *the object b*? After all, *they are the same object.*"[16] Richard Cartwright, likewise, has suggested that the principle is a self-evident truth.[17] To maintain otherwise just to defend one construal of the doctrine of the Trinity seems to be nothing more than, in the words of Geach himself, something like bending logic *ad hoc* to meet the needs of theology.[18]

For this reason alone, denying indiscernibility just to save the doctrine of the Incarnation from contemporary challenges would hardly be more plausible than the general devaluation-of-logic strategy. Furthermore, it seems anyway that no such move would be acceptable to the orthodox in the long run because of its theological implications alone. The only purpose of denying indiscernibility would be to allow that there are some properties Jesus had but God the Son lacked, and vice versa. It is hard to see how in the end such a view could avoid the condemnation of Cyril, bishop of Alexandria (412–444), who attacked the Nestorians for allowing such distinctions between Jesus and God the Son, saying: "If anyone distributes between two characters or persons the expressions used about Christ in the Gospels, etc. . . . applying some to the man, conceived of separately, apart from the Word. . . . others exclusively to the Word. . . . let him be anathema."[19] And of course it was the view of Cyril which became recognized as orthodoxy at Chalcedon.

In the past hundred years, at least two significant metaphysical views have been developed which have offered for our consideration and acceptance statements of identity that have seemed to many philosophers to stand in clear violation of the indiscernibility requirement as traditionally formulated. Phenomenalists, at least of the broadly Berkeleyan stripe, for example, some decades ago propounded a general claim that physical objects are identical with collections of sense data, or sensa. In accordance with this, a phe-

---

[16] Wiggins, *Sameness and Substance*, p. 21.

[17] Richard Cartwright, "Identity and Substitutivity," in *Identity and Individuation*, ed. Milton K. Munitz (New York: New York University Press, 1971), p. 133.

[18] Geach, *Logic Matters*, p. 298.

[19] In Henry Bettenson, ed., *Documents of the Christian Church*, 2d ed. (London: Oxford University Press, 1967), p. 46.

nomenalist would insist of any particular physical object that it was identical with some specific collection of sensa. Likewise, in the philosophy of mind, identity theorists have held the much more popular view that mental states, events, or processes are identical with physical (e.g., neutral) states, events, or processes. But such claims have seemed to many philosophers, even to some sympathetic thinkers, to link items of categorially heterogeneous status in a way which, on the traditional indiscernibility principle, appears strictly impossible.

Consider for example, the mental-physical identities, which have been extensively discussed in recent literature. It has been supposed by some identity theorists as well as their opponents that mental items have properties which neural items cannot even sensibly be said to have, and vice versa. Thoughts, for example, can be cruel or ingenious, puerile or profound. Pains can be throbbing. But surely, many have agreed, it makes no sense to attribute these properties to neuron firings, or neural states. A bit of brain matter, or a state it is in, can seem conceptually barred from having such properties. Conversely, a neural item can have the property of being located intracranially in region R_1 of the left hemisphere of a brain, a property it surely would make no sense to attribute to my wistful thoughts of home. Or at least, many have claimed so. In short, it has been widely thought that mental-physical identity statements cannot possibly satisfy the condition for truth or warranted assertability specified by the traditional indiscernibility principle.

Phenomenalist identities run up against the same difficulty. Physical objects are three-dimensional. Sense data, even in collections, are not and cannot be three-dimensional. Sense data are essentially private. It is a logical (or conceptual) truth that physical objects are not. And so forth. So again the indiscernibility requirement seems to be violated in the most flagrant way.

We also find the same problem with many identity claims of a far less controversial sort. Consider, for instance, the identification of temperature with mean kinetic energy. On the basis of this general theoretical identity, the specific temperature of any body will be identified with the mean kinetic energy of its molecular constitution. But such identities seem to join the ranks of mental-physical and phenomenalist claims as being what some philosophers have called 'cross-category identities', statements which identify what appear to be categorially heterogeneous items conceptually barred from satisfying the traditional indiscernibility requirement. An example often used by the late James Cornman involves the fact that the temperature of a body can have, for instance, the property of being 27° centigrade, a property that seems not to be meaningfully ascribable to the mean kinetic energy of that body's molecules.[20] Many, if not all, of the theoretical identities in science will issue in this sort of divergence in predications, and, apparently, in properties. Thomas Nagel, for his part, tells us that his being kicked by a horse can be ridiculous, although the vastly complex molecular event with which the kick is identical can hardly be properly so characterized.[21] But surely, we do not let such apparent violations of indiscernibility cast any shadow of a doubt on these identities yielded by modern science.

In light of this, some philosophers such as Cornman proposed that we revise our traditional formulation of the indiscernibility principle, so that it be required of any items x and y that in order for '$x = y$' to be acceptable as a true identity statement, it is necessary only that any property which is such that it can be meaningfully ascribed to both x and y be such that x has it if and only if y has it.[22] This restriction was introduced to allow true identities to be asserted concerning items which are conceptualized in very different ways, yielding predications true of those items as conceptualized one way, which come out false under a different conceptuality. Why, it has been asked, should we allow the conceptual multiplicity of natural languages to force on us a correspondingly complex ontology? It is precisely the reductive function of cross-category identities to resist that ontological multiplication.

The relevance of this sort of move to the doctrine of the Incarnation is obvious. It could be argued that many human properties are such that it would make no sense to ascribe them literally to

[20]See, for example, James Cornman, "The Identity of Mind and Body," in *The Mind-Brain Identity Theory*, ed. C. V. Borst (London: Macmillan, 1970).
[21]See Thomas Nagel, "Physicalism," in *Materialism and the Mind-Body Problem*, ed. David M. Rosenthal (Englewood Cliffs: Prentice Hall, 1971).
[22]Cornman, "The Identity of Mind and Body."

God, and that many divine properties are such that they could not meaningfully be thought to characterize any man. If all divergences between divine and human properties were of this sort, the incarnational identity (C) could be claimed to satisfy a suitably restricted requirement of limited indiscernibility and thus to stand as true against all current challenges.

It can be shown, however, that no theory of the conceptual multiplicity of natural languages can be developed which will ground such a restriction of indiscernibility with any real plausibility. Prohibitive problems arise for any such theory.[23] Even Cornman, one of the first to propose such a revision of the indiscernibility requirement, apparently came to appreciate this and finally gave up this strategy for defending mental-physical and micro-theoretical identities. Their defense must be otherwise effected. Although this strategy can initially appear more reasonable than any attempt to deny outright the governance of the indiscernibility principle over identity, in the end it can be seen to have philosophical consequences which are hardly less implausible. Further, it is easy to see that this maneuver would have results just as vulnerable to Cyrilline condemnation as those arising out of the absolute rejection of indiscernibility as a requirement for identity.

So it seems clear that a defender of the orthodox doctrine of the Incarnation ought not to respond to the contemporary challenge based on the indiscernibility principle by either devaluing the status of human logic, rejecting the problematic principle outright, or revising it in such a way as to square with what seem to be essential divine-human property differences. The best response to the challenge will consist in meeting it head on, in acknowledging the governance of the traditional indiscernibility principle over identity statements and arguing that, contrary to what has been alleged, the incarnational identity (C) satisfies its requirements.

[23] These are laid out in *Understanding Identity Statements*, chap. 8.

2 *Alternatives to Orthodoxy*

If the traditional doctrine of the Incarnation is to be defended against the contemporary challenge of incoherence, it must be indicated how one individual could have all the properties constitutive of deity and all the properties essential to humanity. But before I attempt to do that, I want to examine some recent views on the Incarnation which, while attempting to preserve as much as they can of the traditional understanding of Christ, in my opinion depart unsatisfactorily and unnecessarily from the orthodox Chalcedonian account.

1 *The One-Nature View*

First, I want to take a look at an interestingly different objection to the orthodox doctrine of the Incarnation that can be gleaned from an article by Ronald W. Leigh entitled "Jesus: the One-Natured God-Man," which appeared just a few years ago.[1] It is a complaint which has been independently adumbrated more recently by Gareth Moore in his fascinating paper entitled "Incarnation and Image of God."[2] Getting clear on what this objection

[1] Ronald W. Leigh, "Jesus: The One-Natured God-Man," *The Christian Scholar's Review*, 11 (1981–1982), 124–137.
[2] Gareth Moore, "Incarnation and Image of God," *New Blackfriars*, 64 (December, 1983).

is, and on what is wrong with it, will help us to appreciate more fully the precise intent of the traditional doctrine of the Incarnation.

Leigh contends that what he calls "the two-natures model" of Christ propounded at Chalcedon and accepted by orthodox theologians ever since is fundamentally misguided in its ascription of a duality of natures to Christ. Indeed, he characterizes the two-natures view as incoherent, logically inconsistent, and logically impossible. The charges sound familiar, but in Leigh's case they result from a completely different sort of argument from that examined in chapter 1. And what is especially interesting about Leigh's position is that, unlike the vast majority of contemporary critics of the doctrine, he basically wants to preserve a biblical and traditional perspective on Christ—in fact, a rather high christology—while at the same time rejecting the orthodox doctrinal formulation of that sort of view.

What I want to show is that a quite simple argument against the two-natures model suggested by Leigh's paper, persuasive as it might appear at first, is simply flawed. Careful attention to some rudimentary features of the metaphysical notion of a nature will allow us to see not only that the ascription of two natures to Christ escapes any direct charge of incoherence such as that leveled by Leigh, but even that on a very plausible view of what sorts of properties can go together to constitute a nature, a two-natures model of Christ is clearly preferable to the one-nature alternative Leigh expounds in its place.

Leigh begins his argument by introducing what he considers to be a definition of 'nature' consistent with standard usage:

> *Nature* is the set of essential characteristics (qualities or attributes) of any given individual or class of individuals, that is, the set of characteristics which that individual must have in order to be included in its class.[3]

The argument against the two-natures view then appears to go something like this: Every individual has a nature. Every individual has some set of properties essential for being the individual it is.

---

[3] Leigh, "Jesus: The One-Natured God-Man," p. 125.

Further, every individual in some fundamental sense belongs to some class of individuals, thereby having whatever properties are essential for membership in that class. An individual's nature is to be understood as the whole set of properties which in one way or the other can be characterized as essential for it. But then, by definition, an individual cannot have two natures. For any two sets of essential properties an entity has will be no more than subsets of the whole set of its essential properties. And it is only such a whole set, or comprehensive set, which will count as a nature of an object. Thus, from the understanding that every object has essential properties and the definition of 'nature', it follows that every individual is such that it has one and only one nature. So the orthodox ascription of two natures to the person of Christ is logically blocked, ruled out from the start by the very notion of a nature.

To represent Leigh's view as fairly as possible, a somewhat extensive quotation may be helpful. He says:

> When two or more individuals have the same set of essential characteristics, those individuals can be grouped into the same classification because they have the same nature. . . . Suppose that nearly all individuals have been classified according to their characteristics. Then a unique individual is found whose one set of characteristics includes characteristics from two previously established classifications. Even in such a case it would not be appropriate to say that the unique individual has two natures. Every individual is what it is. What it is, its nature, is its set of essential characteristics. Certainly, this unique individual has a set of characteristics not previously found together in a single individual. But that does not change the fact that it has one set rather than two sets of characteristics.[4]

The same sort of view is expressed, a bit more tentatively, by Gareth Moore:

> We normally think that things can have only one nature each, and that is not an accident. To describe a thing's nature is to describe the sum total of the qualities that are essential to it; if we leave anything

[4]Ibid., pp. 125–126.

35

out, our description of the nature is incomplete. Conversely, if our description is complete, then there is nothing essential left out. What the definition of Chalcedon seems to do is to say that Christ's qualities can be summed up by attributing human nature to him, and then immediately to go on to say that that is not a complete summing up at all: it leaves out a whole other nature, his divinity. Trying to get two natures into the same individual is like trying to get a quart into a pint pot.[5]

It appears that on Leigh's view, a position apparently endorsed by Moore and, I think, held by a number of other contemporary theologians as well, no set of characteristics or properties included by, but not including, the largest set of essential properties an individual has can count as one of its natures. That is, no proper subset of an object's largest or most comprehensive set of essential properties can comprise a nature for it. No object can have a nature which is not a set of essential properties. Thus no object can have more than one nature.

The argument can be put in a number of different ways, but it is basically very simple. An understanding of what a nature is prevents our understanding any object to have more than one. If Leigh were right in this, then one would not need to highlight the metaphysical contrasts between divinity and humanity as most recent critics do in order to overturn the claim that Jesus the Christ exemplified both human and divine nature, that in his case we have one person with two natures. Any coexemplification of two distinct natures would be ruled out on quite general logical or conceptual grounds. And then the incoherence of the orthodox two-natures model of Christ would of course follow directly.

Consider any set of essential properties, S_1, which constitutes the nature of some individual a, and any distinct set, S_2, which constitutes the nature of some distinct individual b. It is Leigh's view that an individual c with all the properties of S_1 and all those of S_2 would not properly or even coherently be described as having two natures corresponding to S_1 and S_2, but rather would have to be described as having a single nature, S_3, composed of all the properties of S_1 and S_2. What is particularly interesting about

[5]Moore, "Incarnation and Image of God," p. 456.

Leigh's attack on orthodoxy is that, unlike almost all other recent critics, he does not want, in the case of the Incarnation, to deny that Jesus had both human and divine properties. He just denies that Jesus can be characterized coherently as exemplifying both a human nature and a divine nature. According to Leigh, although Jesus cannot properly be said to exemplify both humanity and divinity, he can and should be viewed as having a superset of those two sets of properties, which itself thereby constitutes for him a single nature. Jesus is thus a one-natured God-man.[6]

It seems to be Leigh's supposition, further, that it was only some false metaphysical views concerning God and man, along with a sizable dose of logical shortsightedness which forced on the church Fathers a two-natures model of Christ. For it is obvious that a number of properties can go together to make up a nature only if it is possible that some individual exemplify together all of them. Yet in early patristic theology, it was often accepted from sources heavily influenced by Greek philosophical speculation that God is immutable, impassible, eternal, and the like. Likewise, it seems to have been recognized that human beings essentially lack all such properties, having instead, as was pointed out in the last chapter, the logical complements or "opposites" of these divine characteristics. It is obviously not possible, nor did early theologians think it was possible, for any individual to have at one and the same time, as parts of one and the same nature, both a property and its logical complement. Thus, it would look as if it is not possible for the range of divine properties and the set of human properties to form together a single nature. Leigh seems to think that in a hopeless attempt to reconcile two such irreconcilable sets of properties they wanted to ascribe to Christ, the Fathers fooled themselves into thinking that their problem would be solved just by strictly dividing Christ's characteristics into two distinct natures. The relation be-

---

[6]Some of the language and diagrams used by Leigh in "Jesus: the One-Natured God-Man" and in a later paper, "A Reply to Edwin Walhout," *The Christian Scholar's Review*, 13 (1983), 48–53, which indicate that he sees the nature of Jesus as corresponding to that involved in an intersection of the classes of human and divine beings can appear to imply that he takes the essential properties of Jesus to be a set formed of a proper *subset* for each of the natures of God and man. I believe it is his intention, however, to see Jesus' nature as inclusive of all properties truly essential to being God and all truly essential to being human.

tween those two natures might then be the deepest of mysteries, productive of paradox after paradox, but simple inconsistency might have been believed to have been thereby avoided at the core of christology. It is Leigh's point that if this move to two natures is made just to avoid logical problems, the problems, of course, end up not being avoided at all.

Some traditional theologians may have been guilty of this sort of strategy, relying too heavily on a mere distinction between the two natures and on a reduplicative form of statement about Christ—Christ *as God* had this property, *as man* its complement—in the attempt to avoid contradiction. I agree with Leigh that if one starts with logically incompatible and, as I hope to show in later chapters, faulty conceptions of human nature and divine nature, no such stratagem can circumvent the logical problems which result for christology. But I do not think the two-natures model was concocted in order to be able to employ such a strategy. Nor do I think that the mere ascription of two natures to Christ is in itself incoherent.

In order to get both the orthodox doctrine and Leigh's contentions in clear focus, let us note for a moment some of the distinctions which must be drawn in any careful essentialist metaphysic. Recent work on essentialism gives us a new appreciation for the metaphysical roles a concept of a nature properly can have.[7] First, we can consider any individual, and the whole set of properties individually necessary and jointly sufficient for being numerically identical with *that individual*. That set of properties we can call an individual-essence, an haecceity (to use a medieval expression recently revived), or, in the present context, an individual-nature. On this conception of a nature, the claim that no individual can have more than one nature would stand as a necessary truth. No individual can have more than one individual-nature. There is, however, a second use of the notion of a nature, one touched on in the last chapter, which is at least as important as this one.

In our scientific as well as our purely metaphysical endeavors, we divide the inventory of individuals in the world into different fundamental *kinds* of entity. It is arguable that the notion of a

[7] See for example some of the papers in Stephen P. Schwartz, ed., *Naming, Necessity, and Natural Kinds* (Ithaca: Cornell University Press, 1977), and the bibliography of literature there cited.

kind nature

vs

individual nature

natural kind is one of the most important of human conceptual devices employed in our attempt to understand the world around us. As indicated in chapter 1, a natural kind can be understood as constituted by a shareable set of properties individually necessary and jointly sufficient for membership in that kind. Such a set of properties can be characterized as a kind-essence, or a kind-nature. Most often, when we inquire about the nature of an object, we are concerned with determining its nature in *this* sense, its kind-nature. This metaphysical notion of a nature is, in interesting and important ways, different from the idea of an individual-nature. It is only with this notion of a kind-nature that we can explicate intelligibly and coherently the view that Jesus was one person with two natures.

Not just any shareable set of properties will be identified as a kind-nature. Not every class or classification of objects corresponds to a nature in this sense. When we are told, for example, that some named or described entity belongs to a certain known natural kind, then, given a relatively developed account of the kind, we are told something about the fundamental structure or constitution of the thing; specifically, we are thereby provided with information concerning the sorts of properties relevant to the causal powers or dispositions the thing has or is capable of having. A natural kind is a classification relevant to, among other things, causal powers and dispositions. The natural kind to which an object belongs, its nature in this sense, is in such a way determinative of the sorts of relational properties it can have.

So not every classification delimits a nature. Not every class of objects forms the extension of a nature term. Many diverse things, for example, are topics of conversation. They can be classed together as such. But to be told that some identified object is a topic of conversation is not to be told anything relevant to knowing its basic causal powers or dispositions. One is not thereby informed of its nature.

We think of all those individuals we classify together as, say, tigers, oak trees, or pieces of gold as having something important and fundamental in common, something in virtue of which it is best to group them together as belonging to the same natural kind, or as having the same nature. Exactly how we determine what properties we group together to constitute kind-natures is a complex and difficult story. Suffice it to say in this context that the principles we use to make such determinations are consistent with, indeed supportive of, our treating humanity and divinity as kind-natures. When we know of some individual that it is a human being or that it is God, we know something quite fundamental about what it is. An individual will count as human only if it has all the properties essential to being human, the joint satisfaction of which will be sufficient for exemplifying human nature. Likewise, an individual will count as divine only if it has all the properties essential to being God, the joint satisfaction of which will suffice for having the nature of deity.

It is the claim of orthodoxy that Jesus had all the kind-essential properties of humanity, and all the kind-essential properties of divinity, and thus existed (and continues still to exist) in two natures. Now, orthodoxy is not committed to the view that just any two natures could be coexemplified by one and the same individual. Theologians from the earliest times have pointed out that the possibility of God's having become a man does not entail, or in any way have the same metaphysical status as a claim that it is possible, that, say, God once became a donkey, or a flower, or that a dogwood once became a dog, or that a diamond once became a positive integer. To hold that it is possible for one entity to have two natures is not to hold that it is possible for just any entity to have just any two natures. Christian theology is more discriminating than that. The Christian claim is that because of the distinctiveness of divinity and humanity, it was possible for the Second Person of the Trinity, God the Son, to take on human nature while still retaining his deity. The two particular natures involved, despite appearances to the contrary, allowed this unusual duality.

In the case of a typical member of a natural kind, it seems to be true that the properties essential to kind membership are among the properties essential to that very individual's existence. A typical member of a natural kind thus has its kind-nature as a component of its individual-nature. No individual has more than one individual-nature. But of course it does not follow from this that no individual has more than one kind-nature. The conception of a kind-nature certainly does not in itself rule out by definition the possibility that there be a single individual with two such natures. And it is two natures of this sort which orthodox doctrine ascribes to Christ.

Once these metaphysical distinctions are clearly drawn, I think we can see, at least at this point, the coherence of the two-natures model of Christ. Of course, the orthodox theologian must be metaphysically circumspect at a number of points if he wants to display a traditional doctrine free of any hint of incoherence. For example, some philosophers view kind-natures as essential to all their members.[8] On this view, any member of a natural kind is essentially a member of that kind, such that it could not exist without exemplifying that particular kind-essence. But of course, this view of kinds is inconsistent with traditional christology, for it is an orthodox belief that God the Son now exemplifies human nature, yet has it contingently. This follows from the conviction that there was a time before the Son began to exemplify human nature, a time at which he was not a man and yet existed. Thus, though he exemplified humanity, he did not exemplify it essentially. For this reason, and possibly for others as well, the Christian who wants to preserve an orthodox theology with a consistent set of metaphysical commitments will reject the view that every nature is an essential property of every individual who exists in that nature.[9] But this is a rejection which, so far as I can tell, need carry with it no discernible metaphysical price, as I shall attempt to indicate in a moment. In general, I hope to show that the metaphysical circumspection required for a logically coherent articulation of orthodox doctrine will carry with it no cost that the Christian philosopher or theologian should hesitate to incur. In particular, orthodox Chalcedonian claims about the mere number of natures of Christ can stand immune to charges of incoherence if only the requisite amount of care is exercised in understanding exactly what they involve.

I want, however, to suggest not only that the two-natures view of Christ is coherent, presenting us with a logical possibility, but also that it is preferable to the alternative Leigh advances, an un-

[8]See, for example, Richard Thomason, "Species, Determinates, and Natural Kinds," *Nous*, 3 (1968), 95–101. For a purely philosophical repudiation of Thomason's view, see Howard Kahane, "Thomason on Natural Kinds," *Nous*, 3 (1969), 409–412.

[9]For another claim about kinds or natures a consistent orthodoxy must reject, see the concluding pages of chap. 3, below.

derstanding of Jesus as having only one nature. I think a fairly plausible argument can be constructed to indicate the metaphysical superiority of the two-natures view.

Consider again the common claim about kinds or kind-natures which the Christian philosopher must reject—the view that every member of a natural kind belongs to that kind essentially. It does seem to be a metaphysical truth about natural kinds that any *typical* member of such a kind will belong to it essentially. This is a closely related view which I believe the Christian metaphysician both can and should embrace, for reasons to be sketched below. The position is that a typical bearer of a kind-nature is such that the kind-essence of its nature—the properties severally necessary and jointly sufficient for its belonging to that kind—is a part of that object's individual-nature, or individual-essence. A typical tiger, for example, could not have existed without being a tiger. Tigerhood is part of its individual-essence. Likewise, a typical human being is human essentially. By 'typical' I mean here something like 'common', or 'average', or 'ordinary', and in that sense, 'representative'. A typical member of a kind has its individual identity tied to that kind essentially. In this sense of the word 'typical', Jesus the Christ was not a typical human being, although he exemplified the fullness of human nature.[10] He was and is a typical member of the higher kind-nature of divinity.

Leigh understands Christ as having only one nature, a nature inclusive of the kind-essences of humanity and divinity. Let us call that alleged single nature 'Incarnality'. On Leigh's view, Jesus exemplifies Incarnality. Does he exemplify it essentially? Is it among Christ's essential properties to exemplify Incarnality? If he only contingently has all the attributes essential to being human, attributes partially constitutive of his Incarnality, he could exemplify

[10]Recall that, by stipulation, the denial that Jesus is a typical human being does not imply that he was not in some important value-normative sense an exemplar, paradigm, or ideal of humanity, and in this rather different sense a type for humanity. It is only in the metaphysical, value-neutral sense that he is not a typical member of the human race. A typical member of humanity, or of any nature, belongs to that kind essentially in virtue of not also belonging to some ontologically higher kind in which its identity is rooted. For more on ontological hierarchy among kinds, see chap. 3. A typical human being is what I shall call a 'merely human' being there for some important reasons to be given.

that single nature only contingently, not essentially. And it is a deep Christian conviction that God became a man freely, from which it follows that he, in the person of the Son, does exhibit all the properties kind-essential for humans only contingently. So it would be a deep Christian conviction that Christ have his Incarnality only contingently, not as a part of his individual-essence. Yet Christians would certainly be committed to characterizing Christ as a typical member of the nature of Incarnality. Even if it ends up not being impossible that other persons of the Trinity take on human properties, and thus on Leigh's view take on Incarnality, and so not being the case that Christ is the only possible member of the kind Incarnality, there could be no good grounds whatsoever for denying that he would be a typical member of that kind. But, as indicated, it seems an unimpeachable metaphysical principle that any typical member of a kind-nature exemplifies that nature essentially. Without this principle, it becomes impossible to draw a clear enough distinction between natures and other sorts of properties.[11] As a typical member of Incarnality, Christ would then have to exemplify it essentially. But as an individual having only contingently all properties essential for being human, he would have to exemplify this single nature of Incarnality nonessentially. And of course, we do have here a blatant inconsistency, the only fully plausible resolution of which involves, in my opinion, rejecting Leigh's claim that Jesus is one-natured and retaining the Chalcedonian view that his natures are two.

Now, it might seem at first that Leigh, or any proponent of a one-nature view such as his, could resist this argument simply by denying on christological grounds the metaphysical claim that every typical member of a kind belongs to that kind essentially. After all, I have claimed that on the basis of the doctrine of the Incarnation, the orthodox Christian is justified in resisting the more common view that *every* member of a natural kind belongs to that kind essentially. Why couldn't Leigh make precisely the same sort of move in response to my argument and hold that because of what

[11] This is the sort of argument used by Thomason, "Species, Determinates, and Natural Kinds," pp. 99–100, in contending for the principle that all kinds are essential properties of their members. But the weaker principle I am endorsing fully satisfies the desideratum.

Christian convictions would be about the single nature of Incarnality, he is fully justified in rejecting the weaker claim about kinds on which my argument turns, as well as rejecting its stronger counterpart?

First, I do believe that the orthodox Christian is completely justified in employing his core theological convictions as a check and constraint on his metaphysical theorizing. But to recognize the legitimacy of this sort of control is not to license just anything in the realm of metaphysics. The Christian metaphysician has many more data for philosophical reflection than just the deliverances of revealed theology, central as these might be. Whenever there is a strong case for a particular metaphysical principle stemming from nontheological data, the Christian philosopher must take the principle seriously. If the principle is fully compatible with orthodox doctrine, and there is no good reason to abandon the orthodox formulations (e.g., they are not demonstrably inconsistent or otherwise provably false), this should constitute for the Christian philosopher a strong presumption against any view which (1) departs from orthodoxy, and (2) contravenes that metaphysical principle. This seems to me so obvious as hardly to need stating. But its application to the case in view is worth making fully explicit.

The main reason many philosophers have thought it important to hold that all members of natural kinds belong to their kinds essentially is that they have believed it impossible otherwise to account for the truth of many sorts of modal claims, in particular counterfactual statements, which can be made about any bearers of properties. Individuals can change over time with respect to a great many of their properties. Likewise, at any time at which it exists, any individual could have had a number of quite different properties from those it actually has at that time. In the terminology of contemporary modal logic, there are possible worlds in which Socrates never philosophized, and also possible worlds in which philosophers such as Leigh and Moore, after reflecting carefully on the doctrine of the Incarnation as expressed by Chalcedon, come to see its truth. Beneath all the diversity of properties individuals are capable of taking on, or of having had instead of those they actually have, there must be some continuity not admitting of change or possible replacement. Again in the possible-worlds language of recent metaphysics, we need to be able to secure "trans-world identity" for the individuals of our ontology if we are to do justice to the sorts of modal affirmations we standardly make. And a number of arguments can be produced that it is natural-kind properties which are needed to provide the sort of essential continuity that is wanted. Socrates could have existed without ever having philosophized, without ever having drunk hemlock, without ever exemplifying a great many of the properties he in fact had. But he could not have existed without ever being a human person. His membership in this natural kind is essential to him, providing in part for the trans-world identity or individual continuity needed to secure the truth of modal claims which can properly be made about him. We could say that both trans-world and trans-temporal identity are anchored in the essentiality to each individual of at least one kind-nature.[12]

And this brings us to the crucial point which many philosophers have overlooked. In order to secure trans-world and trans-temporal identity, we need only affirm that for each individual bearer of properties there exists at least one kind-nature essential to it. We do not need to claim that every kind is essential to each individual which is a member of it. And of course, as I have pointed out, orthodox Christians will reject this stronger claim. Every individual will have some kind-nature as an ingredient in its identity as the object it is. It will have some such nature essentially. If an object has more than one nature, then prima facie, the possibility is open that it has one of them only contingently or nonessentially. If an individual has only one nature, it must have that nature essentially. Thus if Jesus the Christ had only one nature, he had it, and any properties constitutive of it, essentially. But as I have argued, this contravenes the firmly entrenched convictions that Christ had his human properties only contingently.

Could someone like Leigh nevertheless deny the metaphysical principle on which this argument against the one-nature view of Christ rests? I suppose so, since almost any metaphysical principle

---

[12] An enormous literature relevant to these claims exists at the present time. See for example relevant passages of Alvin Plantinga's *The Nature of Necessity* (Oxford: Clarendon Press, 1974), and David Wiggins' *Sameness and Substance* (Cambridge: Harvard University Press, 1980).

can be denied without flagrant irrationality. But I see no reason for orthodox Christians to follow him in this, and good reason for a contrary judgment. In sum, I think the conclusion we should draw, in the final analysis, is that the traditional two-natures view of Christ not only is not obviously incoherent on account of the duality it alleges, but even for the Christian philosopher or theologian appears so far logically preferable to the one-nature view which, given some very plausible and important claims about both Christ and kind-natures, seems after all not itself to be coherent.

Leigh's attack on orthodoxy is, in one way, a relatively minor one. For as I mentioned earlier, he wants to maintain a fairly high christology, involving the attribution of a wide range of divine as well as human characteristics to Christ. He does not join many recent critics in thinking that all supernaturalistic claims about Christ are fundamentally misguided. Yet his attack is nonetheless one worth examining and rebutting. For any attribution to the church Fathers of logical inconsistency is a strong charge indeed. If the church has been guided by God in such matters as the formulation of its creeds, conciliar decrees, and catechisms, even with a rather loose providential hand, we would not expect glaring logical flaws in its central doctrinal affirmations. It is my conviction that when we examine those doctrines carefully enough, we find them logically beyond reproach. And I think this should be our conclusion concerning Leigh's charge against the Incarnation. Enough care in analysis reveals the coherence and merit at this precise point of the orthodox formulation, vindicating in one small way the sort of claims which the church makes for its fundamental tenets.

2 Representational Christology

Both Ronald Leigh and Gareth Moore apparently have wanted to defend what is in many ways a basically traditional perspective on Christ, but seem mistakenly to have thought it impossible to endorse one of the central claims of orthodoxy. Some other contemporary philosophers have been prepared to defend the orthodox Chalcedonian definition of the person of Christ, but have attempted to do so in a way which is inadequate and which both inadvertently and unnecessarily departs from the precise claims of orthodox christology. One such philosopher is R. T. Herbert. A brief examination of a striking view developed in his book *Paradox and Identity in Theology*[13] will be of some benefit to us at this point.

It is one thing to argue against Leigh that it is possible for one object to have two natures; another matter altogether to show that the two natures of humanity and divinity are indeed compossibly exemplifiable by one and the same individual. In a chapter entitled "The Absolute Paradox: The God-Man," Herbert makes a quite original attempt to do the latter. First, he focuses on what he considers to be a problem which arises for the doctrine in the pages of the New Testament itself. It is asserted in the New Testament that Jesus was born in the days of Herod (Matthew 2:1). Yet in many other passages it is claimed or implied that Christ existed before the days of Herod, indeed, before the creation of the world (Colossians 1:15, 1 John 2:13, etc.). In Herbert's opinion, a problem thus arises: "For it is according to Scripture that Jesus Christ was born in the days of Herod and also that he existed before the days of Herod: that he both did and did not exist before the days of Herod."[14] But does ⌜x was born at t⌝ entail ⌜x did not exist before t⌝? Herbert apparently assumes so, but I think he would be in a rather small minority in holding that, for example, a human being does not exist between the time of his or her conception and the moment of birth. However, for the purposes of his argument, this is a relatively small matter. For the New Testament also indicates that Jesus was (rather remarkably) conceived during the days of Herod. And unless one sides with Origen in adopting the unorthodox and exceedingly implausible platonic doctrine of the preexistence of human souls, one will accept the claim that, in reference to any of us, ⌜x was physically conceived at t⌝ does entail ⌜x did not exist before t⌝.

So if that entailment holds in reference to Jesus, we have the sort of contradiction among the claims of the New Testament Herbert alleges. But why think it does? Herbert says of this original example: "to object that the phrase 'was born' as applied to Jesus

hair splitting

---

[13] R. T. Herbert, *Paradox and Identity in Theology* (Ithaca: Cornell University Press, 1979), chap. 4.
[14] Ibid., p. 85.

has a sense different from the ordinary is to suggest that Jesus was not a 'true man' (for one is suggesting that he was not 'truly born')."[15] Altering Herbert's example here in ways that he surely would find acceptable, we can represent his argument as follows: To say of any human being a that a was born at t entails that a was physically conceived before t. But no individual which is physically conceived existed before the time of its conception. Yet in the New Testament, it is said both that Jesus was born, and previously conceived, and also, however, that Christ had always existed. To attempt to escape this contradiction by saying that Jesus' birth or conception was not like any other human's—in not constituting his coming into existence—is to suggest he was not truly human. This in itself contradicts orthodoxy. Thus, it cannot be used as a strategy for helping clear orthodoxy of contradiction.

Herbert then represents the traditional defensive maneuver of orthodoxy to consist in holding that: "According to Scripture, Christ both did and did not exist before the days of Herod. But this scriptural claim is not self-contradictory. For what is being claimed is that Christ *as God* existed before the days of Herod and that Christ *as a man* did not exist before the days of Herod."[16] These statements about Christ *as God* and Christ *as a man* are traditionally known as reduplicative propositions. It has been thought by numerous recent defenders of orthodoxy, such as Peter Geach and R. L. Sturch, that this form of statement is central to laying out a consistent account of the Incarnation.[17] And Herbert seems to agree. But he also believes that the reduplicative maneuver can be thought to be vulnerable to an apparently decisive objection.

Consider any conjunctive reduplicative proposition of the form $\ulcorner x$ as A is N and x as B is not $N.\urcorner$ If the subjects of both conjuncts are the same and the substituends of N are univocal across the conjunction, then as long as (1) the reduplication predicates being A of x and predicates being B of x, and (2) being N is entailed by being A, and not being N is entailed by being B, then the redupli-

[15] Ibid., p. 86.
[16] Ibid., p. 88.
[17] See Geach, *Logic Matters* (Berkeley: University of California Press, 1980), pp. 295–301, and R. L. Sturch, "God, Christ and Possibilities," *Religious Studies*, 16 (March, 1980), 81–84.

cative form of predication accomplishes nothing except for muddying the waters, since in the end the contradiction stands of x being characterized as both N and not N.

Now of course many cases of reduplication do not satisfy the conditions just laid out. Consider for example the shocking story of Jones who lives the Jekyll-and-Hyde double life of an apparently upstanding Sunday School teacher and a particularly lecherous theology professor. Jones *as a professor* is a seducer of his students, yet *as a Sunday School teacher* he is not a seducer of his students. Clearly there is nothing logically impossible about such a case or logically self-contradictory about its description. But that is precisely because, among other things, it involves one of those typical cases of reduplication which do not satisfy the foregoing conditions. For one thing, condition (2) is not satisfied. Fortunately, it is not the case that being a theology professor entails being a seducer of one's students. Nor, unfortunately, does being a Sunday School teacher entail not being a seducer of one's students. Moreover, it can be argued further, and seems to be true, that there is a failure of univocality, or something sufficiently akin to that, with respect to the predicate phrase 'a seducer of his students', across the conjunction.

But the christological case does seem to satisfy all these conditions, on common assumptions about divinity and humanity which give rise to the contemporary incoherence challenge, and which Herbert appears to accept. Herbert presents the proposition:

(H)   Christ *as God* existed before the days of Herod, but
       as a man did not exist before the days of Herod

as one apparently vulnerable to this objection. But contrary to what he seems to assume, (H) does not satisfy all the conditions laid out. Obviously, being a man does not entail not existing before the days of Herod; otherwise all Herod's ancestors and other predecessors were nonmen, or nonhuman. Nor, on one construal, does being God entail existing before the days of Herod. It is logically possible that Herod never existed throughout all eternity. But then in such a possible world, no one would exist, in any straightforward sense, before the days of Herod. If this property were entailed by being God, no one would then be God. So it was necessary that God, in order to secure his own existence as deity, create Herod. All this absurdity indicates that (H) clearly does not satisfy the conditions Herbert lays out to give rise to the objection he has in mind.

Consider rather

> (H′) Christ *as God* is uncreated, but *as a man* is a created being

or

> (H″) Christ *as God* never came into existence, but *as a man* did come into existence.

(H′) and (H″) at least do not obviously fail to satisfy the conditions laid out. So they, and other such propositions like them about Christ, could be held vulnerable to the contradiction charge. If, in order to escape the obvious inconsistency in holding of the God-man that he is both created and uncreated, the orthodox move is to attempt to defuse the logical problem by merely adverting to a reduplicative form of predication, and the resulting proposition does meet the conditions laid out, it seems clear that contradiction is not avoided after all.

Herbert, however, thinks he can show conjunctive reduplicative propositions of this form not to be contradictory, by providing a concrete example of one which is obviously clear of logical impropriety. His strategy is to claim that from their being of the form in question it does not follow that christological reduplications such as (H′) and (H″) are contradictory, despite appearances to the contrary. Their consistency, and truth, are compatible with their form. What makes the example he provides even more interesting is that, in addition, he claims it to be a model of the metaphysics of the Incarnation.

The example Herbert produces is the famous ambiguous figure, the Jastrow duck-rabbit, introduced to the attention of many contemporary philosophers by Wittgenstein's *Philosophical Investigations* and often referred to in the context of philosophy of religion by John Hick.[18] The duck-rabbit is a simple line drawing which, looked

---

[18]See Ludwig Wittgenstein, *Philosophical Investigations*, 3d ed. (New York: Macmillan, 1958), pp. 193–198, and John Hick, *God and the Universe of Faiths* (London: Macmillan, 1973), pp. 37–52.

at in one way, represents or pictures a duck, and which seen in another way pictures a rabbit. Concerning any particular inscription of the duck-rabbit, it is Herbert's claim that the following proposition could be asserted truly:

(D)   As a rabbit the figure has long, pointed ears, but as a duck it does not.[19]

He presents (D) as both a conjunctive reduplicative proposition conforming to the conditions laid out, and as a consistent, true one. But of course, again, this example as presented is a faulty one. No inscription of the duck-rabbit has ears—at most it represents ears. Likewise, if (D) meets the relevant conditions, it predicates of a line drawing the properties of being a rabbit and of being a duck, and so cannot possibly be true, given the obvious truth that no line drawing can be a living, breathing animal. Moreover, being a rabbit does not entail having long, pointed ears. Aside from the fact that there are rabbits with wide floppy ears, no amount of ear surgery would remove any Bugs Bunny look-alike from the natural kind of rabbit.

Let us attempt to repair (D) to circumvent these needless problems. Consider then

(D′)   As a representation of a rabbit with long, pointed ears, the figure pictures long, pointed ears, but as a representation of a normal duck having no long, pointed ears, it does not picture long, pointed ears.

This rather prolix alternative to (D) gives us, I think, just what Herbert was after. Close inspection will show that all the relevant conditions are met to make this what he takes to be an analogue of orthodox christological statements. And (D′) clearly is true. Thus, conjunctive reduplicative propositions of the form in question are not one and all false on account of contradiction. So their being of this form does not rule out traditional christological statements from being possibly true. Q.E.D.

Ian T. Ramsey once claimed that it is impossible to provide a model of the hypostatic union, the union in one *hypostasis*, or in-

[19] Herbert, *Paradox and Identity in Theology*, p. 92.

re. model of the hypostatic union

The Logic of God Incarnate

dividual bearer of properties, of the two natures of humanity and divinity.[20] Herbert presents the duck-rabbit figure as serving to provide just that. He says: "The orthodox claim is that Christ is one person who is both truly God and truly a man. The duck-rabbit is one figure that is both 'truly' a duck and 'truly' a rabbit,"[21] and concludes a discussion of this suggestion with the contention that "the duck-rabbit figure appears to be a model of the sort that Ramsey claims it is logically impossible to produce, a model of the hypostatic union."[22] But of course, understood in strictly the way Herbert seems to suggest, the duck-rabbit line drawing is clearly a heretical Arian model of the Incarnation, or of the hypostatic union. For the duck-rabbit figure is neither a duck nor a rabbit. It is rather a third sort of thing which merely represents each. And the Arian heresy is precisely the view that Christ was neither God nor a man, but a third sort of individual which merely represents each. So Herbert's own portrayal of the duck-rabbit cannot provide a model of the orthodox doctrine about Christ.

However, the duck-rabbit is both a representation of a duck and a representation of a rabbit. It is truly a rabbit picture and truly a duck picture. It thus does present us with a case in which one thing, the line drawing, is a thing of two otherwise apparently different sorts. And this could be taken as a perfectly orthodox model of the Incarnation. But to the extent that it does model the Incarnation, nothing so rare as an ambiguous figure is needed to do the job. One and the same item can be both a good baseball glove and an effective doorstop for my office door. One object can thus be *used* in two quite different ways. This is not at all uncommon. And it is a truth which shows what is unsatisfactory about the duck-rabbit figure as a proper model for the Incarnation.

The duck-rabbit's being both a picture of a duck and a picture of a rabbit involves its being able to be seen or *used* in two different ways. It is a truly ambiguous figure—not more deeply rabbitlike than ducklike or vice versa. The God-man is, according to ortho-doxy, both fully human and fully divine, but at the same time more deeply or fundamentally divine than human. The Person bearing

[20] Ian T. Ramsey, *Religious Language* (New York: Macmillan, 1963), pp. 193–200.
[21] Herbert, *Paradox and Identity in Theology*, p. 94.
[22] Ibid., p. 95.

the two natures is an essentially divine Person. He is not an essentially human person, only contingently having taken on human nature, although, once assumed, it is never to be lost by him, according to the traditional doctrine. There is no parallel to this in the case of the duck-rabbit.

Furthermore, is the duck-rabbit simultaneously a representation of a rabbit and a representation of a duck? If not, it is not a model of the Incarnation, for since the time of his physical conception Jesus is held to be at the same time both human and divine. And surely it is not possible for one observer to see the duck-rabbit as, simultaneously, a picture of a duck and a picture of a rabbit. At best, one switches one's perception of it back and forth, rapidly. It can, however, be argued that the figure is both simultaneously even if it cannot be seen as both simultaneously by a single observer. For two observers can at the same time see it in two different ways, one as a duck picture, the other as a rabbit picture. But if this one line drawing can be both a representation of a rabbit and a representation of a duck simultaneously, it is not a model of the Incarnation which would defuse the attacks of recent critics. For if it can indeed be both, then we can conclude that there are no properties essential to being a line drawing representative of a duck which are logical complements of properties essential to being a line drawing representative of a rabbit. And likewise, of course, there are no properties necessarily ingredient to being a good baseball glove which are logically incompatible with any properties required for being a good doorstop for my office door. Yet, in the case of the doctrine of the Incarnation, it is precisely the claim of recent critics that there are properties essential for being human which are logical complements of properties essential for being divine. And this is a claim Herbert seems prepared to accept. At least he does not deny it, but rather tries to circumvent the obvious problems which arise for the doctrine by merely employing reduplicative forms of statement.

The duck-rabbit figure was said to have both the property of picturing long, pointed ears and the property of not picturing long, pointed ears. But it has neither *simpliciter*. It has the former only *as a picture of a rabbit* and the latter only *as a picture of a duck*. The *as*-clauses here both specify representational properties. And the properties had only in virtue of these are themselves representational properties. A representational property is always an intentional polyadic relation holding between an object x which is represented, an object y which is the object held by convention, intention, or perception to represent x, and at least one individual z who treats or perceives y as representational of x, where x, y, and z are distinct. It is of the nature of representational properties to allow predicates of the syntactic form of logical complements to be ascribed to one and the same object in reduplicative propositions without inconsistency.

But consider again the christological propositions (H') and (H"):

> (H') Christ *as God* is uncreated, but *as a man* is a created being.
>
> (H") Christ *as God* never came into existence, but *as a man* did come into existence.

The properties of being created and having come into existence do seem to be the sorts of metaphysical properties individuals have or lack *simpliciter*, rather than only in virtue of having other properties. Further, neither the properties specified in the as-clauses—humanity and divinity—nor the properties Christ is said to have had in virtue of them, are representational properties like that of picturing a rabbit. Herbert successfully argues that not all propositions of the syntactic form of (H') and (H") are productive of contradiction. But it seems that the example he means to provide, (D'), as a proposition of this form free of contradiction, is specifically different from the christological statements in a way which seems to impugn any compelling, or even particularly helpful, analogy. The duck-rabbit figure provides no good model for an orthodox doctrine of the Incarnation, nor does the freedom of (D') from logical inconsistency establish in any clear way at all the freedom of (H'), (H") and other such christological reduplicatives from inconsistency.

What is still needed is a way of seeing *how* orthodox christology can be free of contradiction, a more decisive answer to the arguments of those who allege it is not. Are Christians committed to saying that Christ both did and did not come into existence in virtue of first one and then the other of his natures? Must he be held somehow (reduplicatively) to be both created and uncreated? Herbert seems to think so. But I believe the answer to these questions is "No." Accepting the apparent contradictions and trying to defuse them with reduplicative statement is in general not sufficiently convincing, and, in one particular case to be discussed in chapter 6, can be shown clearly not to work. So I judge Herbert's defense of orthodoxy inadequate, for all its ingenuity and interest, and his model of the Incarnation to be not an explication of orthodoxy, but more like an alternative to it.

3 *Divine and Human Existence*

In an article which appeared a few years ago, entitled "God's Death," A. D. Smith launched one of the most interesting of recent attacks on the traditional doctrine of the Incarnation.[1] Focusing on the death of Christ, he claimed to demonstrate the logical impossibility of Jesus having been both human and divine. Each of the premises of his argument was said to be a commitment of orthodox theology. He thus presented his reasoning as displaying an internal incoherence in that way of thinking about divinity, humanity, and the person of Christ. The argument was basically quite simple: According to Christian theology and in concurrence with general thought on the matter, we must hold that human death involves the possibility of annihilation. As a man, Jesus of Nazareth faced and underwent a human death. He thus faced the possibility of annihilation. But orthodox theologians hold God to be of such an ontological status that no divine being could even possibly be annihilated. So no divine person could die a human death. From this follows the impossibility of the traditional claim that the Second Person of the divine Trinity became a man, lived a human life, and died a human death for us and our salvation. The qualitative difference between God and human beings is such as to render incarnational christology an incoherent theological stance.

[1] A. D. Smith, "God's Death," *Theology*, 80 (July, 1979), 262–268.

56

In this chapter I want to examine Smith's argument with some care. The details and outcome of this examination should be of significant theological interest. For as I have already indicated, it has become quite common recently to charge the doctrine of the Incarnation with incoherence. Yet, surprisingly, Smith has given us one of the very few extended arguments for this claim to be found in the literature. I hope to show that we have no reason to think his argument, or any sympathetically reconstructed version of it, to be sound. And in coming to recognize his errors, we shall begin to come to see what is wrong with the most common sort of contemporary philosophical critique of traditional christology.

1   *The Metaphysical Difference of God and Man*

Smith attempts to unearth property divergences between Jesus and any divine being by inquiry into the nature of human death. What happens when a human being dies? Well, first of all, it is obvious that his bodily processes cease, that his body ceases to be a living organism. Following Smith's terminology, let us call this event "somatic termination." Now, the interesting philosophical question about death concerns what happens to the human *person* upon somatic termination. Does the person, the subject of consciousness, survive the death of his body, or does somatic termination involve personal annihilation? Further, if human beings do survive bodily death, in what does that survival consist? What is responsible for it?

As a first step toward dealing with these questions, Smith directs our attention to the fact that many people fear death and suggests that what most are fearing is annihilation, or the possibility of annihilation. The point is that it seems to be a fairly widespread belief that human death either is, or at least involves the possibility of, personal annihilation. He then goes on to argue the surprising claim that the Christian must concur with this common belief. He says: "Now I take it to be central to Christianity that man's death is, as such, viewed as annihilation. This is not to deny that it may be the case, as a matter of fact, that all people will survive their deaths; the point is that whoever does survive his death does so only as a result of God's grace and power." He then remarks: "Thus we may say that the immortality in which the Christian believes and for which he hopes is *conditional immortality*, since dependent wholly on the will and power of God. Such a view stands in stark contrast with belief that man is necessarily immortal or immortal by right, since this is to recognize a principle of power and meaning independent of God himself, which is sheer heresy."[2] A careful examination of Smith's article reveals that he takes orthodox Christian theology to be committed to the position that human death involves a real possibility of annihilation, in the sense that only if God freely chooses to sustain a man in existence beyond his bodily death will that death involve merely somatic termination and not also personal annihilation, and it is possible for God not to so choose.

In the passages just quoted, three sorts of immortality are mentioned: 1 necessary immortality, 2 immortality by right, and 3 conditional immortality. Presumably, a person would have necessary immortality just in case, due to his intrinsic properties, it would be impossible in a broadly logical or metaphysical sense for him to cease to exist. And I suppose someone would be immortal by right just in case it would be, of necessity, an irredeemable and unjustifiable moral wrong for God to allow him to be annihilated. On the traditional view that God is necessarily good and has power over matters of annihilation with respect to persons, it follows that such a person could not possibly be annihilated. There is a theological tradition which holds that the annihilation of any person would be a wrong of this sort, so that, given the perfect goodness of God, all persons are immortal by right. On these two views of immortality, no created person is ever annihilated, because personal annihilation is not a real possibility. On the third view of immortality, which Smith sees as alone a truly Christian view, the possibility of annihilation is real, but God will freely choose moment by moment to prevent the annihilation of those he graciously saves. The survival of human

[2] Ibid., pp. 263–264.

persons beyond bodily death is on this view conditional upon the continuing free choice of God.

Smith suggests that, given the fundamental conviction that God is sovereign, Christian theology cannot countenance any view of human immortality except the conditional view. By categorizing together necessary immortality and immortality by right as different versions of "absolute immortality," we can say that Smith presents us with three basic options concerning the question of what human death involves for the persons and his or her consciousness. There is: 1 annihilation, 2 absolute immortality, and 3 conditional immortality. He tries to rule out absolute immortality on two different grounds. First, he appears to argue: People fear death. In fearing death, people fear annihilation. No one fears impossibilities. Therefore, in human death, annihilation is possible.

If this were a good argument, it would rule out 2, as on either version of that view, annihilation is impossible. But of course, it is not a good argument. It is true that people do not fear what they believe to be impossible. So if x is feared, x must be believed to be possible. But it does not follow that x is possible. This can be put another way. A metaphysical impossibility can be feared if it is an epistemic possibility, if there is some overall belief-set sufficient for the thought and action of a rational agent with reference to which its metaphysical possibility is not ruled out. And this clearly is the case with respect to personal annihilation. On almost any naturalistic world-view or comprehensive belief-set, personal annihilation upon somatic termination is an epistemic possibility. It does not follow that it is possible in the sense required to rule out absolute immortality as in fact a property of human beings.

Smith's theological argument against 2 is vague, and just as uncompelling. He thinks that if a created being were essentially immortal or immortal by right, there would exist "a principle of power and meaning independent of God." He does not make clear exactly what this means, but it is easy to guess. Immortality by right presupposes the existence of necessary moral principles distinct from God, in accordance with which he necessarily acts. But it is well known that distinctness is not the same relation as metaphysical or ontological independence. It could in fact be that there is an asymmetric dependence relation of those moral principles on God, impugning in no way the divine sovereignty.[3] The same could be said concerning necessary immortality. It could be that once God creates Smith, Smith's nature is such that he cannot ever cease to exist, yet also be true that God is responsible for Smith's continuing existence in the sense that (a) he freely and graciously brought Smith into existence as an immortal being, and (b) he is thereafter in some basic metaphysical sense responsible for Smith's moment-to-moment existence, which cannot cease. So it is not at all clear that Christian intuitions about, and doctrines concerning, divine sovereignty and grace at all preclude God's creatures being endowed with absolute immortality.

The point of Smith's arguments concerning the nature of death is to convince us that human survival of death can at best exemplify conditional immortality, that human death involves the possibility of annihilation. He then uses this claim to attempt to block the traditional incarnational identity, the affirmation that Jesus is God the Son. For God is, according to orthodox thought, a being who essentially lacks the modal property of possibly being annihilated. If Jesus was human, he had to have every essential human property. If every human must have the property of possibly being annihilated (a property ingredient in the view of conditional immortality), then Jesus had a property which no divine being could possibly have, and thus Jesus could not possibly have been divine.

To put it another way, the somatic termination of any human being will be accompanied by either annihilation of the person or conditional immortality, according to Smith. The somatic termination of any embodied divine being would have to be accompanied by absolute immortality, more specifically, by necessary immortality. No divine being could suffer the death of a human, because

---

[3] A justification of this claim is sketched out in an unpublished paper by Christopher Menzel and Thomas V. Morris entitled "Absolute Creation." On questions concerning the relation between divine sovereignty and the necessity of things distinct from God, see Alvin Plantinga's Aquinas Lecture, *Does God Have a Nature?* (Milwaukee: Marquette University Press, 1980). For an exploration of some of the implications of the claim that God necessarily acts in accordance with moral principles, see my "Duty and Divine Goodness," *American Philosophical Quarterly*, 21 (July, 1984), 261–268.

no single being could exemplify both the ontological status of the divine creator and the metaphysical dependency of a human creature.

Even if we reject Smith's contention that human death involves, at best, conditional immortality, and hold that it involves absolute immortality, the metaphysical difference remains that humans are *endowed* with immortality. God is not. Furthermore, as Smith himself indicates, in focusing on the matter of death, his real intent is just to direct us to basic ontological disparities between God and man. And of course, not all those disparities have to do with annihilation and immortality. For example, humans are the sorts of being who, even if they cannot cease to exist, can and do begin to exist. But God is everlasting. And most fundamentally, we are all contingent beings. God is a necessary being.[4] So even if Smith himself has not properly specified a point at which human and divine properties diverge by contrasting conditional and absolute immortality, it seems that he has at least pointed us in the right direction to see logically disparate and metaphysically incompatible sets of properties concerning divine and human existence, which are more than sufficient to rule out God's once having been a man.

As was pointed out in the two previous chapters, philosophers and theologians for many centuries have been acutely aware of the great difference between divine and human properties and of the difficulties this creates for the doctrine of the Incarnation. God is, among other things, omnipotent, omniscient, and omnipresent. Every human being is limited with respect to power, knowledge, and presence. But it has been thought by many that these difficulties could be circumvented. Kenotic christology, for example, an attempt to defend orthodoxy developed during the nineteenth century, holds that God the Son "laid down," or limited his exercise of, these unlimited attributes during the sojourn of the Incarnation. The properties to which Smith has directed us, however, clearly do not admit this maneuver. An everlasting being cannot lay aside

---

[4]For some clarification on, and a simple delineation of, the sort of modal distinctions I assume here, distinctions which can be of significant use in philosophical theology, see the opening sections of my "Properties, Modalities, and God," *Philosophical Review*, 93 (January, 1984), 35–55.

his eternity and begin to exist. A necessary being cannot become contingent. These are logical impossibilities not available even to a God with the most extraordinary powers of self-limitation.

Smith's type of argument exemplifies very well the structure of the common incoherence challenge explicated in chapter 1. He is arguing that, if 'God the Son' is meant to refer to some literally divine being, the traditional christological identity claim

(C) Jesus is God the Son

cannot possibly be true. But we can know Smith's claim to be true only if we can know that (C) violates the principle of the indiscernibility of identicals. We can know that Jesus was not God only if we can know of such a divergence in properties. But Smith has pointed us toward a range of properties having to do with the basic metaphysical status of divine and human existence which seems to provide us with multiple violations of indiscernibility. However, we must then ask: How can we know of the particular metaphysical divergence in properties that Smith has brought to our attention?

Smith says: "If Christ is God, then he cannot have begun to exist at a certain point in human history because God (and his Son) are necessarily eternal. But then nothing can count as a man, a creature, which does not have a beginning in time and which is thus coeval with God."[5] The remark about "counting as a man" makes clear the structure of Smiths' reasoning. Like all other contemporary critics who issue a form of incoherence challenge, Smith is relying on a certain sort of conception of human nature and of divine nature for the generation of his argument. And, crucially, he is assuming that, with respect to questions concerning metaphysical status, the ontological status of an object's existence, properties essential for being God are logical complements of those essential for being human.

2 Some Crucial Distinctions

If the properties of possibly being annihilated, having a beginning in time, and metaphysical contingency were all essential hu-

[5] Smith, "God's Death," p. 265.

man properties, any truly human being would have to exemplify each of them. Thus Jesus, if he was fully human, would have had them, and Smith's argument could succeed. For surely these are properties no divine person could have. But the question we must press is: What reason do we have to believe that they are essential human properties, necessary elements of what it is to be human?

In order to appreciate the impact of this question, we first must take care to draw a clear distinction between *common* human properties and *essential* ones. A common human property will be one which many or most human beings have. A limiting case of commonality would be a property which was universally shared by all humans alike. We need to be clear that a property's being common or even universal for members of a kind does not entail that it is essential for the kind, such that membership in the kind would be impossible without its exemplification. For example, the property of living at some time on the surface of the earth is a common human property. I think it is safe to assume it is now a universal property for humans. But it is not an element of human nature. It is not essential for being human. It is clearly possible that at some time in the future human beings be born, live, and die on a space station or on another planet colonized by earth, without ever setting foot on the earth itself. This is an obvious example of our distinction. The property of living at some time on the surface of the earth may now be a universal human property, but it is not an essential one.

This simple but important distinction is often overlooked by theologians. Richard Norris, for example, has written: "We can speak of human nature, meaning something like 'that which is normally characteristic of all human beings.' "[6] I do not want to deny that Norris' use of the phrase 'human nature' is an allowable one in colloquial or informal contexts. It just is not the one which properly operates in metaphysics. For philosophical or theological anthropology, we need something much more precise and demanding than that. It is normally characteristic of human beings to have hair. Yet one can certainly be fully human, exemplify human nature, while lacking this adornment. It is also normally characteristic of human beings to come

[6]Richard A. Norris, Jr., "Interpreting the Doctrine of the Incarnation," in *The Myth/Truth of God Incarnate*, ed. Durstan R. McDonald (Wilton, Conn.: Moorehouse-Barlow, 1979), p. 81.

into existence and to have the metaphysical status of contingency. But of course Smith wants to block the possibility of there being a man who lacks these properties. So his argument depends on the more precise understanding of human nature I have explicated in the first and second chapters and have assumed here.

Once we acknowledge a clear distinction between commonality and essence, what forces the Christian to count as essential any common human properties which would preclude a literal divine incarnation? I can think of nothing which would do this. If we develop our philosophical anthropology and our doctrine of God in isolation from each other and from the central tenets of Christian faith, it is no surprise that conflicts may arise, that "impossibilities" be generated. But it is a perfectly proper procedure (some would even say—rightly, I think—mandatory) for the Christian philosopher or theologian to develop his idea of human nature, his conception of what the essential human properties are, with certain presuppositions or controls derived from his doctrine of God and his belief in the reality of the Incarnation.

In a moment of insight apparently rare among contemporary theologians involved in the debate over the Incarnation, John MacQuarrie wrote a few years ago: "Part of the trouble with the doctrine of incarnation is that we discuss the divinity and even the humanity of Christ in terms of ready-made ideas of God and man that we bring with us, without allowing these ideas to be corrected and even drastically changed by what we learn about God and man in and through the incarnation."[7] This is precisely the problem. It is all a matter of epistemic priorities. The orthodox Christian can quite rationally argue that we are less sure that human nature essentially comprises properties incompatible with a divine incarnation than Christians are that Jesus was God Incarnate. This is not to say that the doctrine of the Incarnation should or even could have complete epistemic priority for the Christian over any conception whatsoever of humanity or divinity. Some prior idea of what it is to be God and what it is to be a man is required for even understanding the doctrine at all. But the prior conceptions requisite for any understanding of the doctrine at all are far from

[7]John MacQuarrie, "The Humility of God," in McDonald, ed., p. 13.

complete and unalterable. And I think it can be shown that the Christian of orthodox leanings can, in all epistemic propriety, develop his philosophical anthropology in such a way as to allow for a divine incarnation, thereby disallowing the sort of argument mounted by Smith.

Only a very few contemporary theologians who have written on the topic seem to have recognized that we can understand human nature in such a way that it can be coexemplified with divinity in one and the same subject. Herbert McCabe, for one, has said: "A human person just is a person with a human nature, and it makes absolutely no difference to the logic of this whether the same person does or does not exist from eternity as divine."[8] Surely, a *merely* human being will not have existed from eternity as divine. A mere human will furthermore be a contingent creation. But no orthodox theologian has ever claimed that Jesus was merely human. The claim is that he was fully human, but also divine. If contingency, coming into existence, and possibly ceasing to exist were essential human properties, the doctrine of the Incarnation would express a metaphysical, or broadly logical, impossibility. But I can think of no compelling argument, or any other type of good reason, to think they are elements of human nature, understood along our precise metaphysical lines.

It may be that these, or at least two of these, properties just mentioned are essential to being merely human. Any being which exemplifies human nature without also exemplifying divine nature would then have to exemplify them, otherwise it would not "count as" a mere human. But the Christian claim is that in order to be fully human, it is not necessary to be merely human. An individual is merely human just in case it has all the properties requisite for being fully human (the component properties of human nature) and also some limitation properties as well, properties such as those adduced by Smith. These limitation properties will not be understood as elements of human nature at all, but as universal accompaniments of humanity in the case of any created human being.

Perhaps a few more words should be said about this merely *x*/ fully *x* distinction. Consider a diamond. It has all the properties

[8]Herbert McCabe and Maurice Wiles, "The Incarnation: An Exchange," *New Blackfriars*, 58 (December, 1977), 552.

essential to being a physical object (mass, spatiotemporal location, etc.). So it is fully physical. Consider now an alligator. It has all the properties essential to being a physical object. It is *fully* physical. But, there is a sense in which we can say that it is not *merely* physical. It has properties of animation as well. It is an organic being. In contrast, the gem is merely physical as well as being fully physical. Now take the case of a man. An embodied human being, any one you choose, has mass, spatiotemporal location, and so forth. He is thus fully physical. But, again, there is a sense in which he is not merely a physical object, he has organic and animate properties as well. So let us say he is fully animate. But unlike the alligator he is not merely animate; he has rational, moral, aesthetic, and spiritual qualities which mere organic entities lack. Let us say that he belongs to a higher ontological level by virtue of being human. And if, like you and me, he belongs to no ontological level higher than that of humanity, he is merely human as well as being fully human.

To repeat: the kind-nature exemplified distinctively by all human beings is that of humanity. To be a human being is to exemplify human nature. An individual is fully human just in case he fully exemplifies human nature. To be merely human is not to exemplify a kind-nature, a natural kind, distinct from that of humanity; it is rather to exemplify humanity without also exemplifying any ontologically higher kind, such as divinity.

Now, as I have said, according to orthodox christology, Jesus was fully human without being merely human. He had all the properties constitutive of human nature, but had higher properties which, from an Anselmian perspective, form the upper bound of our scale. A philosophical anthropology developed from a distinctively Christian point of view will categorize all human properties logically incompatible with a divine incarnation as, at most, essential to being *merely human*. And, again, the Chalcedonian claim is not that Jesus was merely human. It is rather that he was, and is, fully human in addition to being divine.

I am suggesting that, armed with a couple of fairly simple metaphysical distinctions, we can begin to see how the doctrine of the Incarnation can possibly be true. In this chapter I have considered only a few alleged divergences and metaphysical disparities between human nature and divine nature, specifically that range of properties concerning divine and human existence to which A. D. Smith's argument draws our attention. My suggestion is that such properties as those of possibly coming into existence, coming to be at some time, being a contingent creation, and being such as to possibly cease to exist are, although common human properties, not essential to being human. They, or some of them, may be essential to being *merely* human, but they can be held, in all epistemic and metaphysical propriety, not to be essential to being *fully* human, to exemplifying the kind-essence of humanity.

The traditional Christian must be metaphysically circumspect regarding numerous features of kinds and essences if he is to be able to articulate a christology free from logical impropriety. In addition to distinguishing carefully between a property's being essential for being fully human and one's being essential to being merely human, one must also maintain a careful distinction between a property's being kind-essential for an individual, and its being a part of an individual-essence without also being part of a kind-essence.

It is widely agreed that stable generalizations (necessary, a posteriori propositions) hold concerning the fundamental constitution of members of natural kinds, whether this is spelled out in terms of genetic makeup, molecular constitution, or atomic number, or along more macroscopic lines. If all members of a kind K examined are found to have an underlying trait concerning their basic constitution C, then it is held that we have discovered the truth of a proposition of the form:

1 $\Box(x)\, (Kx \rightarrow Cx)$ nothing is a K unless it has C

which ascribes *de dicto* a necessity of C to members of K. 1 simply amounts to the claim that, necessarily, nothing is a K unless it has C.

Saul Kripke, among others, has argued that propositions concerning the origin of individuals have the same epistemic and metaphysical status as stable generalizations. They are necessary a posteriori truths. For instance, if H. T., and T. F. are my natural parents, I could not possibly have sprung from any other source. No one can know a priori my parentage, but it is an essential property of mine nonetheless. These claims are familiar in the literature. Now, some philosophers have been tempted, on the basis of the arguments for the necessity of kind constitution and individual origin, to incline favorably toward the further claim that having a certain sort of origin is also necessary for natural-kind membership, at least in the case of biological kinds. If all examined members of kind K are found to have had an origin of type O (making the range of O, of course, wide enough through disjunction of conditions to accord with evolutionary theory), it can be thought that the truth is discovered of a proposition of the following form:

2   $\Box(x) (Kx \rightarrow Ox)$

which of course would be the claim that, necessarily, nothing is a K unless it has had some origin of type O.

But it is quite easy to see that any theist who believes there to have been a creation *ex nihilo* cannot hold such a position concerning all natural kinds whatsoever. For consider the following argument, which I shall put crudely in order to present the point vividly. Suppose we find all examined humans to have had an origin of type G described by scientific accounts of the genetics and microbiology of human conception. Can we consider

3   $\Box(x) (Hx \rightarrow Gx)$

to be a truth we have discovered about human nature? Suppose we also hold, for simplicity's sake, that God directly produced Adam *ex nihilo* along with an entire universe to boot. Then according to 3, Adam was not a human being or the sort of human precursor allowed by standard evolutionary theory, since he did not have the requisite sort of natural origin. But then what would that make us, as his descendants? Surely if origin G were a kind-essential property, a human must originate from humans or, given evolutionary theory, some other closely related natural organism(s), which again must have had the appropriate form of natural origin. But in that case, Cain and Abel, along with the rest of us following them, fail to count as humans.

But if *we* fail to count as humans, then what natural kind is it whose essential origin we have discovered in isolating G? Must we say we have discovered a truth not about humans but *humanoids*, some other natural kind H_1? Have we found that

4 $\Box(x)\,(H_1x \rightarrow Gx)$?

But, again, if that is what we discovered, then Adam will fail to count as even a humanoid. And likewise, as his descendants, so shall we. And so forth, ad infinitum.

To escape all this absurdity, it will of course suffice to deny that type of origin is a kind-essential property for any natural kinds. Specifically, a Christian commited to the orthodox doctrine of the Incarnation will need to hold that there are no stable generalizations about natural origins for the kind-nature of humanity. Only if this is true will there be no difficulty on this count with the orthodox claim that Jesus was fully human even though he had no human paternity, and moreover, in the strictest sense never came into existence at all. The lack of standard origin will then be fully compatible with his complete humanity.

Is the denial that origins are essential to natural kinds, and specifically the denial that standard origin is essential to being fully human a plausible one? I think so. For suppose that in some laboratory of the future, scientists were to accomplish the astounding task of concocting *from scratch* (from basic chemicals, etc.) a being with the constitution, organs, appearance, mannerisms, and cognitive abilities of a normal human adult male. Suppose he acts like a human, marries a woman, fathers a child, takes a job, and cultivates many close and satisfying friendships. Would this creature *be* human or not? Intuitions may possibly vary on this, but I think it most reasonable to say yes. And if so, this provides us with some additional backing for the sort of metaphysical view which is needed to support not only a doctrine of *creatio ex nihilo*, but an orthodox doctrine of the Incarnation. Properties of origin will then be, at most, candidates for inclusion in individual-essences, not in natural kind-essences.

It is only with a clear focus on the difference between a property's being essential for being fully human, and its being essential merely to being a particular human that we can begin to turn back the incoherence charge against the Incarnation and display its metaphysical possibility. But these few distinctions alone will not do the full job of rebutting all alleged violations of the indiscernability principle. For merely to claim of all human properties incompatible with some kind-essential divine attribute that they are not part of the kind-essence of humanity may turn back the a priori incoherence charge, or at least a part of it, but it can appear to yield by implication an utterly fantastic figure of Christ. And in so doing, it can appear implausible to the point of being just as desperate a strategy as those canvassed and rejected at the end of chapter 1.

On the resultant picture, will it not follow that Jesus was omniscient, omnipotent, necessarily existent, and all the rest, as well as being an itinerant Jewish preacher? And is this not outlandish to the greatest possible degree? Did the bouncing baby boy of Mary and Joseph direct the workings of the cosmos from his crib? Was this admittedly remarkable man, as he sat by a well or under a fig tree, actually omnipresent in all of creation? Did this carpenter's son exist necessarily? Such implications of orthodoxy can sound just too bizarre for even a moment's serious consideration. How could such a view possibly be squared with the biblical portrait of Jesus as a limited man among men? How could such a being possibly be said to have shared the human *condition*?

What I hope to show in the next three chapters is that a couple of independently plausible ancient claims, together with some modern analogies, are sufficient to rid Chalcedonian orthodoxy of any such appearances of absurdity. Together with some of the metaphysical distinctions already drawn, they will provide us with the conceptual apparatus for plausibly and decisively turning back the incoherence challenge, as well as for arriving at some potentially substantive philosophical understanding of the doctrine of the Incarnation.

4 *Jesus and the Attributes of Deity*

In the previous chapter, I began to develop some of the basic elements of a strategy for defending the doctrine of the Incarnation against the incoherence challenge and for providing a philosophical explication of its content. First, the distinction was stressed between a property's being common or even universal to members of a kind *K* and its being essential for membership in *K*. In light of this distinction, we can see that good reason for thinking all examined *K*s to be *F* is not alone good reason for holding *F* to be essential to being a *K*. Thus, if it is true, and indeed it is, that you and I and all other humans now living on the face of the earth have properties that no divine being could possibly have, nothing untoward for the doctrine of the Incarnation need follow. If we had good reason to think such properties to be essential for being human, we would therein have good reason to think the Incarnation an impossibility. But finding such properties to be common does not alone support the view that they are kind-essential for humanity. It is perfectly compatible with their being common to humans that they need not have been exemplified by God the Son in order for him to acquire human nature.

We considered the properties of coming into existence at some time, being a contingent creation, and being such as to possibly cease to exist. Apart from the case of the Incarnation, Christians would all, I think, agree that the first two of these properties characterize all human beings. But they are properties not compossibly

So, being contingent creatures + reality of death, while common to human nature,
⟶ Are not properties essential, hence allowing possibility that a deity could
Assume human nature in its essence (vs. commonality)

The Logic of God Incarnate

exemplifiable by one and the same individual with all the attributes traditionally held to be constitutive of deity. If they had to be exemplified by an individual in order for that individual to have a human nature, then on this standard, and quite orthodox, understanding of deity, a divine incarnation would be an impossibility. But armed with a firm distinction between commonality and kind-essences, the orthodox Christian can deny that they are properties essential to being human, thereby blocking this objection to the Incarnation.

There are, however, some strong and common modal intuitions that properties of origin cannot be characterized as merely common properties for human beings, but are in addition properties had with the modality *de re* of necessity, or essentially. Moreover, on a quite standard view of modality, it is impossible to have the property of being a contingent creation without having it essentially. It is clearly not enough merely to characterize these properties as common to human beings. They seem in addition to be in some sense essential, and this can be thought to count against, or even overturn, my strategy.

However, I have shown how a standard distinction between individual-essences and kind-essences, along with a new hierarchical distinction between properties necessary for being merely human and those necessary for being fully human, can accommodate these intuitions quite well and defuse this objection to my strategy. Any common human properties which are logically incompatible with divinity, but are judged reasonably to be in some sense essential properties, are then judged by the orthodox Christian to be merely components of individual-essences, or else at most essential for being merely human. In either case, their being in some sense essential to every human being other than Jesus would not entail their being essential to, or even exemplified by, him as well, if he is fully human.

But this appears to leave us with a person who was Jesus of Nazareth and was omniscient, omnipotent, omnipresent, and necessarily existent. Of course, we ordinary human beings exemplify the logical complements of each of these attributes of deity. But on the strategy I am deploying, it seems that these characteristic human properties will be categorized as common to humanity rather than essential to being human. Such properties as being restricted in knowledge, limited in power, localized in presence, and contingent in existence will be held to be at most essential for being merely human. But this can appear to be a near *reductio* for the strategy. Can a fully human being be omnipotent, omniscient, and the rest? Did Jesus have these properties? The New Testament portrays him as at times tired, hungry, and as lacking knowledge of certain things.[1] And surely no amount of modal manipulation of human nature can render it possible that this man was also incorporeal, immutable and impassible. At this point, the initially promising strategy for blocking the incoherence charge can appear to break down. One way of rescuing it would be to rethink the traditional concept of God in such a way as to rid ourselves of these absurdities. But would this have to involve ceasing to characterize omnipotence, omniscience, omnipresence, and immutabilty, for example, as divine attributes?

Responding to the charge that we can know on conceptual grounds alone that the attributes of divinity and humanity are such that they could not possibly be found together in one and the same individual, the Reverend Brian Hebblethwaite has recently protested:

> But 'God' and 'man' are far from being such tightly defined concepts. It is difficult enough to suppose that we have a full and adequate grasp of what it is to be a human being. We certainly have no such grasp of the divine nature. Who are we to say that the essence of God is such as to rule out the possibility of his making himself present in the created world as a human being, while in no way ceasing to be the God he ever is?[2]

John Hick, however, has criticized this defensive maneuver with a bit of a parody, writing: "And yet although we do not know what God and man are, we can apparently know that God was able to become a man! Surely, if one is genuinely agnostic about the divine nature, he will not profess to know either that God can or that God

---

[1] See, for example, Mark 5:30 and 13:32.
[2] Brian Hebblethwaite, "Incarnation: The Essence of Christianity?", *Theology*, 80 (1977), 86.

cannot become a man; and accordingly he will not claim to know that God *did* become a man."[3] But of course, Hebblethwaite need not be either espousing or recommending anywhere near the degree of agnosticism Hick seems to attribute to him. He could be intending rather to make the much more modest and reasonable claim that we are not given a priori a full conception of deity such as to render a doctrine of incarnation incoherent or absurd.

In this chapter, I want to consider in some detail how a conception of God can be articulated along quite traditional lines and yet still be such as to allow the possibility of a divine incarnation. I hope to indicate how even a very strong and exalted philosophical conception of deity, one which might initially make the doctrine of the Incarnation look utterly hopeless, can be reconciled quite easily with all that Chalcedon claimed about Christ. And I hope to show this in such a way that the figure of the God-man is in no way at all even a paradox for faith. First, I shall present and defend the approach toward articulating a conception of deity which will lie behind the picture of the Incarnation I shall go on to sketch.

1   *The God of Abraham, Isaac, and Anselm*

In contemporary thought about God, there is a great divide. On one side are those who work in the a priorist, Anselmian tradition, which begins with a purportedly self-evident conception of God as the greatest possible being. This exalted yet simple conception of deity is taken to entail all the divine attributes, and acts as the single most important control on philosophical theology. On the other side of the divide are those who are committed to an a posteriori, empirical, or experiential mode of developing our idea of God. These theologians take as their starting point and touchstone for truth the data of religious experience and biblical revelation. Variations on these two very different procedures for conceptualizing the divine have resulted in a bewildering multiplicity of portrayals of God, ranging from the relatively naive and anthropomorphic to the utterly abstruse and mysterious.

[3] John Hick, Letter to the Editor, *Theology*, 80 (May, 1977), 205.

Many philosophers who travel the high road of a priorism are a bit perplexed by their biblicist colleagues, and claim to find the God of the two testaments something of an embarrassment. Those who draw their sustenance from the pages of scripture and the day-to-day realities of religious experience are for their part apt to contrast starkly the God of faith with the God of reason, the God of history with the God of the academy, the God of Abraham, Isaac, and Jacob with the God of the philosophers, even going so far as to denounce the latter as an abstract theoretical construct bearing no interesting relation to the true object of religious devotion. One respected Christian theologian, for example, not too long ago proclaimed with great flourish and finality that "*Deus philosophorum* is not the God and Father of our Lord Jesus Christ."[4]

A growing number of religious philosophers, however, are attracted to the Anselmian conception of God and yet also take seriously the empirical phenomena of religion. Many of us who find ourselves in this position have in effect internalized the dichotomy and have often felt quite unsure how exactly to relate these two very different ways of thinking about God. Does, for example, one of them deserve our primary allegiance, the other properly serving an ancillary role? Or should one be chosen to the exclusion of the other?

In this section I want to address the question of whether this deep divide in theology, or perhaps metatheology, can be bridged. It seems to me that it can be and should be. I think an interesting prima facie case can be made that the God of Anselm *is* the God of the patriarchs. At least this is what I want to suggest. More precisely, I shall argue that under two simple conditions, the very different ways of thinking about God converge. I hope to show that if the object of worship in the Judeo-Christian tradition is indeed intended to be God—the ultimate reality responsible for the existence and activity of all else—and if the Anselmian conception gives us a description whose exemplification is at least possible in the broadly logical, or metaphysical, sense, then the God of Anselm is one and the same as the God of Abraham, Isaac, and

[4]W. R. Matthews, *God in Christian Thought and Experience* (London: Nisbet, 1930), p. 104.

Jacob, the sort of God who was incarnate in Jesus the Christ. If I am right, then the only responsible way of developing either of the competing traditions of theological thinking is by drawing on the other. Philosophers can no longer discount the data of religious experience. Theologians can no longer ignore philosophical arguments about God. And those of us who have been caught in the middle can begin to map out some order amid the disarray which has characterized recent talk about God.

The Anselmian conception of God is that of a greatest possible, or maximally perfect, being. On this conception, God is thought of as exemplifying necessarily a maximally perfect set of compossible great-making properties. To put it simply, a great-making property is understood to be a property it is intrinsically better to have than to lack. If, for instance, the exemplification of a state of knowledge is of greater intrinsic value than a lack of its exemplification, it will follow that one of the divine attributes is that of being in a state of knowledge. Likewise, if it is better to be omniscient than to be deficient in knowledge, God will be thought of as omniscient, and so forth. Traditionally, the Anselmian description has been understood to entail that God is, among other things, omnipotent, immutable, eternal, and impeccable as well as omniscient.

There are significant advantages to this conception of deity. For one thing, it can generate an ontological argument for the existence of God. It also appears to be a conception of great simplicity and power. All the divine attributes are unified under the single notion of maximal perfection. And in addition to these obvious benefits, there are less obvious ones as well. Consider for example the doctrine of creation *ex nihilo*, mentioned in the last chapter—the belief that the entire contingent universe is created by God from nothing. The core of this doctrine is the claim that all things are ontologically dependent on God, that he relies on nothing existing independently of his creative power for the universe he has brought into being. What is the warrant for this doctrine? Biblical documents are not wholly unambiguous on this issue. There is significant scholarly dispute over whether it is even a biblical doctrine at all. Nor is there anything about religious experience which would clearly warrant this position. But it is entailed by the Anselmian conception of God, as standardly explicated. More precisely, it will follow from the Anselmian conception that if any contingent being, or universe of such beings, exists, it must stand in the relation of being created *ex nihilo*. For the Anselmian God is understood to be omnipotent or almighty. And it is a conceptual truth that an omnipotent or almighty being cannot rely on any independent source for its power or its products. In short, the Anselmian conception of God has the powerful effect of logically integrating a good deal of traditional theology as well as of providing a completely a priori argument for its truth.

Because of its rational appeal and the many benefits it offers, the Anselmian formula has recently experienced a resurgence of popularity among philosophers. But a number of objections can be raised against the claim that it is a correct conception of God. Let us consider a few.

It might be suggested first of all that the property of efficiency is surely the sort of property it is better to have than to lack. A maximally perfect being then will be perfectly efficient in whatever he does. But if any version of the story of evolution is true, the development of organized systems up to the point of the emergence of intelligent and rational life seems to have been as inefficient a process as can be imagined. The story of evolution appears to many to be a tale of the grossest inefficiency on a colossal cosmic scale. The conclusion thus would seem to be forced on us that there is no maximally efficient being in charge of things, and thus, if the Anselmian conception of God is correct, no God. Conversely, it would follow that if there is a God, the Anselmian conception cannot be right. Since theists are committed to there being a deity, they must reject the a priorist account of what God is like.

An argument such as this can at first appear quite reasonable and even compelling. It may even capture one way in which many people feel that the theory of evolution is incompatible with religious belief. But the flaws of the argument should be evident on even a moment's reflection. First of all, efficiency is always relative to a goal or set of intentions. Before you can know whether a person is efficient in what she is doing, you must know what it is she intends to be doing, what goals and values are governing the activity she is engaged in. In order to be able to derive from the story of evolution the conclusion that if there is a God in charge of the world, he is grossly inefficient, one would have to know of all the relevant divine goals and values which would be operative in the creation and governance of a world such as ours. Otherwise, it could well be that given what God's intentions are, he has been perfectly efficient in his control over our universe.

But more important, what reason do we have to hold that efficiency is a great-making property at all? Is it a property which it is *intrinsically* better to have than to lack? What is the property of being efficient, anyway? An efficient person is a person who husbands his energy and time, achieving his goals with as little energy and time as possible. Efficiency is a good property to have if one has limited power or limited time, or both. But apart from such limitations, it is not clear at all that efficiency is the sort of property it is better to have than to lack. On the Anselmian conception of God, he is both omnipotent and eternal, suffering limitations with respect to neither power nor time. So it looks as if there is no good reason to think that efficiency is the sort of property an Anselmian being would have to exemplify. This argument against the Anselmian conception thus does not succeed.

A more important and quite common worry about Anselmianism goes as follows. It is argued that the notion of a greatest possible being makes sense only if there is some single, all-encompassing, objective scale of value on which every being, actual and possible, can be ranked, with God at the top. But surely, it is insisted, not all things are value-commensurable. It just makes no sense to ask which is of greater intrinsic value, an aardvark or an escalator. The conclusion is then drawn that since there seems to be no such comprehensive scale of value the Anselmian formula is meaningless.

This objection is well known. And just as well known is the Anselmian rejoinder that the characterization of God as the greatest possible being does not require universal value-commensurability. It does require that every object be value-commensurable with God, but not that every object be so commensurable with every other object. In fact, the Anselmian will often have the same intuitions about this latter claim as his critic. So the Anselmian will characteristically, and most plausibly, hold that God is greater than any other being, and that many other beings are incommensurable with each other.

There is an argument, however, by means of which the critic might be tempted to reject this common response and insist that the Anselmian is logically committed to universal commensurability. The Anselmian is attempting to defend his position by allowing that for some x and some y, God is greater than x, God is greater than y, and x and y are pair-wise incommensurable. Letting the sign '$>$' represent the predicate 'is greater than' and the sign '$\geqslant\leqslant$' stand for 'is greater than, or less than, or equal to', the Anselmian is trying to acknowledge that:

(A): $(\exists x)\,(\exists y)\,((G > x)\ \&\ (G > y)\ \&\ (-(x \geqslant\leqslant y)))$

where 'G' denotes God. But for any values of x and y, the following argument can be constructed to show that the first two conjuncts of (A) entail the denial of its third conjunct (letting 'a' and 'b' denote any two individual entities distinct from God):

1	$G > a$	Assumption
2	$G > b$	Assumption
3	$(G > a) \rightarrow (G \geqslant\leqslant a)$	1 Addition, def. of '$\geqslant\leqslant$'
4	$(G > b) \rightarrow (G \geqslant\leqslant b)$	2 Addition, def. of '$\geqslant\leqslant$'
5	$G \geqslant\leqslant a$	1, 3 Modus Ponens
6	$G \geqslant\leqslant b$	2, 4 Modus Ponens
7	$a \geqslant\leqslant G$	5 Symmetry of '$\geqslant\leqslant$'
8	$a \geqslant\leqslant b$	7, 6 Transitivity for '$\geqslant\leqslant$'

If this argument is cogent, the Anselmian cannot consistently hold that God is greater than every other being, but that many beings are value-incommensurable with each other.

Is the argument sound? It certainly can appear to be. The rules of inference it employs are all standard and truth-preserving. The relation of being greater than, less than, or equal to is clearly symmetric. And unlike the relation of being greater than or less than, it can seem to be transitive as well. The relation of being greater than or less than ('$><$') can be seen not to be transitive very simply. Obviously, it is symmetric. If $a >< b$, then $b >< a$. So if it were transitive, it would be reflexive as well, which it clearly is not. No object is greater or less than itself in intrinsic value. But the relation denoted by '$\geqslant\leqslant$' clearly is reflexive. So it is not on that ground ruled out from being transitive as well as symmetric. But is it after all a transitive relation?

The critic of Anselmianism has taken the original relation under discussion, that of being greater than—a transitive, asymmetric, and irreflexive relation—and performed a simple operation on it to attain additively a relation composed of it, its converse, and identity, a relation intended to be transitive, symmetric, and reflexive. However, a general proof can be given to show that this operation cannot be relied upon to succeed in producing relations with the desired properties of transitivity as well as symmetry, properties necessary for the critic's argument to go through.

Consider for example a simple case from set theory. Let '$\supset$' denote the relation of being a superset of (the converse of the subset relation) and '$\supseteq\subseteq$' denote the transform produced by our critic's general operation, the relation of being a superset of, a subset of, or the same set as. Now consider an argument strictly parallel to the one offered against Anselmianism (where 'G', 'a', and 'b' here denote sets of objects).[5]

1	$G \supset a$	Assumption
2	$G \supset b$	Assumption
3	$(G \supset a) \to (G \supseteq\subseteq a)$	1 Addition, def. of '$\supseteq\subseteq$'
4	$(G \supset b) \to (G \supseteq\subseteq b)$	2 Addition, def. of '$\supseteq\subseteq$'
5	$G \supseteq\subseteq a$	1, 3 Modus Ponens
6	$G \supseteq\subseteq b$	2, 4 Modus Ponens
7	$a \supseteq\subseteq G$	5 Symmetry of '$\supseteq\subseteq$'
8	$a \supseteq\subseteq b$	7, 5 Transitivity for '$\supseteq\subseteq$'

The conclusion in this second argument can be shown diagrammatically not to follow from its assumptions:

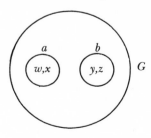

[5]This parallel was first suggested to me by Christopher Menzel.

In what is represented by this diagram, it is true that:

(B): $(G \supset a)$ & $(G \supset b)$ & $(-(a \supseteq\subseteq b))$

which is precisely parallel to what the Anselmian envisions to be the case with respect to certain value rankings concerning God and his creatures, as expressed in (A).

The Anselmian can thus consistently affirm (A), because he can deny that the relation of being greater than, less than, or equal to—the relation of being value-commensurable with—is transitive. In particular, he can ground this denial with a claim that relations of intrinisic value comparison have a property akin to that ascribed to the identity relation by Geach and others. For want of a better name, let us speak of the Value Relativity Thesis, the thesis that for any objects x and y, x is greater than, or less than, or the same in value as y only if there is some feature with respect to which the comparison holds, and some scale on which the ranking can be made. Retaining our previous assignments, and letting the lower-case letters 'f', 'g', and 'h' stand in for features or value scales with respect to which a relation of value comparison holds ('f' and 'g' acting as constants, 'h' as a variable), the Anselmian can consistently hold that:

(C): $(G \underset{f}{>} a)$ & $(G \underset{g}{>} b)$ & $(-(\exists h)\, (a \underset{h}{\gtreqless} b))$

The argument against the standard Anselmian position on value commensurability is thus a failure. The Anselmian can quite consistently concur with the common intuition that not all objects are value-commensurable. The Anselmian conception of God thus does not require at this point a position which is clearly false.

One might have some worries about the notion of intrinsic value being employed here and about our epistemic access to the value rankings requisite for the Anselmian conception. But I can think of no other *arguments* by means of which this conception of God can be impugned along these lines. So let us then turn our attention in another direction.

There is a simple yet forceful thought experiment which can appear to show that the Anselmian description does not capture the properly religious concept of God at all. This is the last of the major objections to Anselmianism I shall consider at any length, because it is the only remaining line of reasoning which I think could be perceived as counting decisively against the a priorist view.

Suppose we somehow discovered that a less-than-Anselmian being, an individual who was very powerful but not strictly omnipotent, very knowledgeable but not literally omniscient, and very dependable but not altogether immutable, etc., had created our universe and was responsible for the existence of intelligent life on earth. Suppose we found that he had been the one to call Abraham out of Ur, to speak to Moses, and to send the prophets. Suppose he had somehow become incarnate in the man Jesus, and that he will be the one responsible for giving eternal bliss to all who are properly related to him. Let him even sustain directly the very existence of the universe moment to moment. Would we rightly on a priori grounds refuse to call him "God," just because he did not satisfy Anselm's precise requirements?

The most common response to this question is to say of course not—it would be absurd to refuse to call such a being 'God'. If he is the being the Bible is about, then Jews and Christians would just be committed to acknowledging him as God, regardless of the requirements of a priorism. Few if any people would doubt that the Anselmian formula specifies a sufficient condition for deity. But many would deny that it presents a necessary one. And this is what our brief thought experiment could be taken to show. Surely, it might seem, we have here a set of circumstances in which a being would rightly be characterized as God without his satisfying the Anselmian description. I think this would be a common judgment, and that it is on the basis of some such consideration as this that many people reject the a priorist tradition. Our thought experiment can appear to show that Anselm's concept of God just is not the Christian concept.

This, however, would be a hasty conclusion to draw. For consider an important feature of the Anselmian conception. As standardly understood, it entails that among the properties of a maximally perfect being is that of being necessarily existent, or existent in every possible world. If the Anselmian conception as a whole is coherent, or more exactly, if maximal perfection is possibly exemplified, then it is necessarily exemplified as well. With this in mind, let us return to our story. Call the less-than-Anselmian being "El" and the world in which he accomplishes all those prodigious feats W. If Anselmianism is at least possibly true, in a broadly logical, or metaphysical sense, an Anselmian being exists in some possible world. But by virtue of being necessary, he exists in every other world as well, including W. Now if in W there is a being who is omnipotent, omniscient, and all the rest, surely El is *not* God, but rather, at best, the vicegerent or deputy of God, a sort of demiurge. If El is less than omnipotent and there is an omnipotent, omniscient individual, then clearly anything El accomplishes is done only at the good pleasure, or according to the wishes, of the Anselmian being. El would not be the ultimate reality. He would not be God. I think this conclusion is fully in accord with the properly religious usage of 'God' in Christian orthodoxy, and in fact that it is a conclusion forced on us by that usage. If the object of worship in the Western tradition of theology is intended to be the ultimate reality, and if the Anselmian conception of God is one of a possible being, then the God of religious devotion is the God of the philosophers.

A number of problems could be raised for what has just been argued. Suppose for example that El was less-than-Anselmian not by lacking all the maximal perfections but rather by lacking just one or two. He could be fully omnipotent and completely omniscient, but less than wholly immutable, or somewhat short of perfectly just. In that case, he need not be dependent on any other being, even a fully Anselmian one, for his power and deeds. In light of this apparent possibility, my response to the thought experiment might be considered incorrect.

However, this second supposition, unlike our first, could rationally be judged not to portray a real possibility at all. For it is a commitment of many Anselmians that the divine perfections are all necessarily coexemplified. Further, I think it is also implicitly held by many that the exemplification of any perfection entails the exemplification of some maximally perfect set of great-making properties. This might even be taken to be the clearly intelligible core of the doctrine of divine simplicity. Note that it is not claimed that all great-making properties are necessarily coexemplified—an obviously false proposition; only that all the divine perfections are. Great-making properties fall into various categories. First, there are those that are degreed and those that are not. Likewise, among degreed properties such as that of being powerful, there are those that have logical maxima, or highest possible degrees, and those that admit of infinite increase.[6] A property which is constituted by the logical maximum of an upwardly bounded, degreed great-making property is a perfection. Clear examples of such perfections would be omnipotence and omniscience. Examples of other sorts of properties which standardly would be considered perfections are necessary goodness, aseity, and necessary existence. If the divine perfections are all necessarily coexemplified, then the supposition that a being could have some without others conveys an impossibility, and thus can raise no genuine difficulties for the position that the Anselmian description expresses a necessary condition for deity.

It should be noted that the claim that the divine perfections are necessarily coexemplified is an ontological position which does not entail the epistemological claim that we can deduce the various perfections from each other. Claims to display entailment relations between conceptually distinct divine attributes, such as R. G. Swinburne's recent attempts to deduce God's goodness from his omnipotent freedom and omniscience, are notoriously less than universally convincing.[7] The Anselmian need not hold that this second supposition is *demonstrably* inconsistent, only that what it supposes is in a broadly logical sense impossible. The existence of an omnipotent and omniscient, but less than maximally perfect, being may then be in some sense *conceivable*, but it is not, in a metaphysical or broadly logical sense, *possible*. So if the Anselmian conception, so understood, is possibly exemplified, then no less-than-Anselmian being is God.

At this point, however, an epistemological query could be raised. Can we not imagine a set of circumstances in which 1 we have found no logical or metaphysical flaw in the Anselmian conception and thus on these grounds have good reason to believe it coherent, but 2 we have a body of strong evidence that a being, El, exists who

[6] For a defense of the claim that there are such maxima, see William Mann, "The Divine Attributes," *American Philosophical Quarterly*, 12 (April, 1975), 151–159.
[7] The attempt is made in Swinburne's *The Coherence of Theism* (Oxford: Clarendon Press, 1977), chap. 8 and p. 202, and in his *The Existence of God* (Oxford: Oxford University Press, 1979), pp. 97–102.

created the world, spoke to Moses, became incarnate, etc., and is *not* Anselmian, and 3 on all the available and relevant evidence, we are justified in believing that El is the ultimate reality in the actual world, and thus is God? In such circumstances would not 2 and 3 block the conclusion we might otherwise draw from 1, the conclusion that the Anselmian description is both possibly and actually exemplified, and thus that an Anselmian being is God?

Of course, if we had a strong *proof* that the Anselmian description is possibly exemplified, then 3 would not be true, we would not be justified in believing that any less-than-Anselmian being is actually the ultimate reality. But short of such proof, 2 and 3 could both be true, and thus the inference many philosophers would otherwise seem prepared to draw from 1 would be overturned.

These are some of the dynamics of the situation. There are two ways of blocking the Anselmian claim. One would be to show that conditions 2 and 3 obtain. We would then have good evidence that maximal perfection is not actually exemplified and thus good indirect evidence that it is not possibly exemplified, however coherent the conception might otherwise appear. Unfortunately for non-Anselmians, conditions 2 and 3 clearly do not obtain in our present circumstances. At worst, we could be thought to lack sufficient evidence that maximality is possibly exemplified. And lacking good evidence that there is an Anselmian ultimate reality is quite different from having good evidence that there is a non-Anselmian ultimate. So Anselmianism cannot be circumvented in this way.

The second way to dispose of the a priorist claim would be to show directly an incoherence or inconsistency in the Anselmian conception of deity. This could be done in either of two ways. First, it could be argued that the notion of maximal perfection entails individual properties which are self-contradictory, or not possibly exemplified. This has been tried quite recently, for example, by Morris Lazerowitz.[8] Lazerowitz argues that a perfect being is understood to have infinite properties, and that no such properties can be had. The paradox of omnipotence could also be taken to have the same force: maximal greatness requires omnipotence, and there can be no omnipotent being.

[8]Morris Lazerowitz, "On a Property of a Perfect Being," *Mind*, 92 (April, 1983), 257–263.

The second strategy would consist in arguing that some two or more properties entailed by maximal perfection are logically incompatible with each other, and so not compossibly exemplified by any single being. This is a common sort of move used against traditional theism. It has been argued in recent years that there is a logical incompatibility between immutability and omniscience, necessary omnipotence and essential goodness, incorporeality and agency, and omniscience and omnipotence, to name a few. If the Anselmian conception could be shown to entail two such incompatible properties, it would be shown not to be a coherent conception.

If this were accomplished, what would follow? That there is no God? No, only that there is no Anselmian being. I have argued that the Anselmian formula provides a necessary condition of deity only if it is coherent, and possibly exemplified. That is the condition under which, and under which alone, the ultimate reality will be Anselmian. Otherwise, it could be that there is a less-than-Anselmian being, such as El, who is the ultimate reality and is a proper object of religious devotion. Or it could be that there is no such being at all.

Is the Anselmian right in thinking there are no incoherencies or impossibilities in his specification that God is the greatest possible being? I think it would be extraordinarily difficult, much more difficult than most critics realize, to show Anselmianism to be incoherent or to be otherwise barred from the realm of possibility. One obvious flaw in most incoherence arguments, for example, is that they deal with explications of the divine attributes which some Anselmians may hold but which are not necessary for the Anselmian to espouse. A critic will, for instance, present a faulty definition of omnipotence and then go on to show, to almost no one's surprise, that there cannot be an individual with the property defined. Detractors such as Lazerowitz then hastily conclude that they have shown the conception of a perfect being to be incoherent. And it must be admitted that many theists encourage this sort of thing. For many Anselmians act as if the formula of maximal perfection self-evidently entails all the divine attributes and even gives us a precise understanding of each of those properties God must have. And surely this is not the case at all.

It is well known that the classical divine attributes are seriously underdetermined by the data of religious experience and biblical revelation. What is not as widely recognized, or at least acknowledged, is that there is underdetermination in the a priorist tradition as well, such that the core elements of the Anselmian tradition do not yield self-evidently a determinate array of precisely defined attributes. When a certain understanding of omniscience is shown to be incompatible with a particular interpretation of immutability, as Norman Kretzmann once attempted, or with an explication of omnipotence, as David Blumenfeld has argued, the Anselmian can thank the critic for his help and conclude that those precise versions of the divine attributes are not the ones a maximally perfect being must exemplify.[9] The specific properties an Anselmian God must have are underdetermined by the Anselmian formula and by the basic intuitions by means of which it is applied (e.g., in identifying great-making properties).

Of course, Anselmians could not with any legitimacy endlessly exploit this fact. If every attempt to explicate the perfections was an obvious failure, the Anselmian could not responsibly appeal again and again to the "open texture" of his conception of God to evade the obvious conclusion that it is incoherent. But a number of philosophers have argued in recent years that the traditional divine attributes can be seen to be coherent after all—in spite of the many attacks which have been launched against them. I believe this is correct, that there exists at least a strong prima facie case for the coherence of the elements of classical theism, and so for the coherence of an a priori conception of deity understood as entailing these elements.[10] If this is right, then there can be a strong

---

[9]For the arguments referred to, see Norman Kretzmann, "Omniscience and Immutability," *Journal of Philosophy*, 63 (1966), 409–421, and David Blumenfeld, "On the Compossibility of the Divine Attributes," *Philosophical Studies*, 34 (July, 1978), 91–103.

[10]I have tried to show this with respect to some difficult problem cases in a number of recent papers, including "Impeccability," *Analysis*, 43 (March, 1983), 106–112; "Duty and Divine Goodness," *American Philosophical Quarterly*, 21 (July, 1984), 261–268; and "Properties, Modalities, and God," *Philosophical Review*, 93 (January, 1984), 35–55. For a well-known, extensive argument to this effect, see Swinburne's book *The Coherence of Theism*.

prima facie case for the God of Abraham, Isaac, and Jacob being the God of Anselm, a maximally perfect being.

There must be controls over the articulation of a conception of deity, if it is to be anything more than just creative speculation. I think there is good reason to believe that one of the controls must be the Anselmian formula. But in light of the open texture of even Anselmianism, it seems that the data of religious experience and purported revelation can function as a control as well. And from a distinctively Christian point of view, they must.

I have introduced this rather lengthy excursus regarding the Anselmian conception of God for at least three reasons. First, I believe that Anselm's formula should play a central role in any attempt to articulate a conception of deity adequate to the Christian tradition. Thus, I have thought it important to say something about that formula and defend it against some obvious criticisms. Second, I want to argue that even so exalted a conception of deity as that provided by Anselm's formula can be squared with the doctrine of the Incarnation. And third, I think it important to have pointed out the aspect of the Anselmian conception I have referred to as its "open texture." For only in seeing this can we come to appreciate fully that the orthodox Christian need not follow any specific application of Anselmianism which results in a conception of deity disallowing the possibility of a divine incarnation. Such fundamental Christian beliefs as belief in the Incarnation can rightly act as a control over the precise specification of what God is like. A priori and a posteriori elements can thus both enter into an articulation of the nature of deity. And from a Christian point of view, I think, neither should be ignored or minimized.

2 The Properties of the God-Man

Let us follow the Anselmian tradition in holding that God is omnipotent, omniscient, and omnipresent. Let us grant that these are attributes of deity, properties any divine being has. It seems to follow then quite directly from

(C) Jesus is God the Son,

where 'God the Son' denotes a divine being, that Jesus was omnipotent, omniscient, and omnipresent. But this is hard to swallow for two reasons: 1 it is difficult to see how anyone could be fully human while having such properties, and 2 according to the biblical portrayal of Christ, Jesus seems not to have had such properties. Our problem is to provide a model for the Incarnation which both recognizes these properties as properties of deity and yet at the same time reconciles this view with what seems so clearly to have been true of Jesus.

A strategy I mentioned earlier, the kenotic strategy (from *kenosis*, Greek for 'emptying'—see Philippians 2:5–8) involves the attempt to maintain that in order to become incarnate as a human being, God the Son, Second Person of the Trinity, temporarily divested himself of all divine properties not compossibly exemplifiable with human nature. Many theologians of the nineteenth century and the early part of this century apparently thought that this one simple claim would solve all the problems of the orthodox doctrine of the Incarnation. They often specified that the Son gave up all the distinctively metaphysical attributes of deity while retaining all moral qualities which are properly divine. In particular, it would be claimed, God the Son laid aside his omnipotence, omniscience, and omnipresence in order to become a man. These attributes he ceased to have while incarnate, later to regain them upon his return to a properly divine existence.

Now, as I pointed out while discussing A. D. Smith, it is impossible that all the distinctively metaphysical attributes of deity be temporarily laid aside. No individual could possibly cease to be eternal, or immutable, or necessary (existent in all possible worlds) for a brief period of time. But it could be argued in defense of kenotic theology that the kenotic maneuver need not be applied to these properties. If we employ the distinctions of the last chapter, we can argue that the properties of coming into existence at some time (a contrary of eternality) and contingency (the contradictory of necessity) are not kind-essential properties for being fully human. Thus the individual who was Jesus could have been both necessary and eternal in basic metaphysical status while taking on the status of a fully human being at a specific point in time. Fur-

The Logic of God Incarnate

thermore, there are construals of immutability which will allow the possibility of a divine incarnation, as I intend to show, as well as possibly also others which logically preclude such an entry of God into human nature. None allow a movement of kenosis with respect to immutability; but this is unnecessary anyway, since on the understanding of immutability clearly compatible with a divine incarnation, God the Son could perfectly well retain his proper immutability while yet exemplifying the fullness of human nature, as I shall indicate later. So it could be argued that, armed with the distinctions of the last chapter, we can see that any divine attributes which do not allow of kenosis do not require it either, in order to be compatible with incarnation.

And Jesus' having these kenotically recalcitrant metaphysical attributes need not have any absurd implications for orthodoxy. For it is an ancient, and independently plausible, claim that no person is strictly identical with his body. Even a modern materialist who holds that all personality is necessarily embodied need not deny this. So the necessary existence of God the Son, with its implications that he cannot have begun to exist and cannot cease to exist and therefore is eternal, does not entail that the earthly body in which he incarnated himself had these properties. His body was conceived, and grew like any other human body. Likewise, the kenotic theologian must hold, a person is not identical with any particular range of conscious experience, or any particular set of belief-states, he might have. So the eternality of God the Son need not entail the comprehensive continuity of his cognitive states from his preincarnate mode of existence as God into his earthly childhood. The kenotic theologian thus allows that the earthly mind-set, along with the earthly body, came into existence and grew. Nothing about the necessity, eternality, or immutability (in a sense to be explicated) of the divine Son need preclude this.

It is a standard kenotic claim that God the Son temporarily gave up his omniscience for the course of the earthly stage of the Incarnation. From all eternity, he had been omniscient. For roughly three decades he was not. But upon his ascension, and for all future eternity, he continues now to enjoy that maximal noetic state once again. This is the kenotic story about God the Son's knowledge.

Jesus and the Attributes of Deity

Clearly, it allows both the orthodox claim that Jesus was God, and the biblical claim that he grew in wisdom as a child.[11]

It is fairly easy to explicate coherently the kenotic allegation that the Son voluntarily and temporarily gave up his omniscience, later to regain it. For consider Shorty, a spy who is going on a dangerous mission in which he will have to pretend to be a great scientist with amnesia. So that he will not succumb to questioning under torture if suspected, Shorty is given a limited-amnesia producing pill, and an antidote for later use. . . . Clearly, such a scenario seems perfectly coherent. And in relevant respects it parallels the kenotic claim about Christ.

Temporarily failing to exemplify the property of omniscience thus seems at least so far to be a possibility. But what of omnipotence and omnipresence? Perhaps the best understanding of the attribute of omnipresence is that of its being the property of being present everywhere in virtue of knowledge of and power over any and every spatially located object. A divine being would then presumably divest himself of that attribute by divesting himself of the requisite power or knowledge. Omnipotence, however, does not as simply fit into the kenotic scheme. It, like immutability, is what we might call an internally modalized attribute. Being omnipotent is, very roughly, being *able* (having the power) to do anything it would be logically possible (in the broadly logical sense) for a maximally perfect being to do. Now, let us attempt to describe a case of fully voluntary kenosis with respect to this property. A being S is omnipotent from t_1 to t_2, voluntarily divests himself of this property from t_3 to t_5, and regains it at t_6. What exactly is the state of S's power or abilities at t_4, during the period of kenosis? If the state of kenosis is entirely and thoroughly voluntary, at t_4 S has the ability (an ability which he freely refrains from exercising) to re-exemplify omnipotence. But at t_4, if S *can* be such that he can do anything logically possible for a maximally perfect being, then at that time he can do anything logically possible for such a being— in other words, he is still omnipotent. If he cannot at t_4 take up his omnipotence again, he is not in a state of the thoroughly voluntary, temporary relinquishing of it.

[11]Luke 2:40.

defects of the kenotic strategy

The Logic of God Incarnate

If the kenotic theologian is committed to the complete voluntariness of the state of the Incarnation, he cannot hold that God the Son temporarily ceased to be omnipotent. But if the Son then lacked at least omniscience, one piece of knowledge he may be said to have lacked is the knowledge of his being omnipotent. And anyone who has restricted his knowledge of the range of his own power may be argued thereby to have restricted the exercise of his power, since, presumably, no one usually draws on resources he does not believe he has.

By maneuvers such as this, kenoticism can attempt to explain how it is that 1 omniscience, omnipotence, and omnipresence are properly divine attributes, 2 Jesus was divine as well as human, but 3 during the decades of his time among us on earth, this individual appeared to have none of these attributes. The kenotic strategy has had many critics, but most of them have failed to appreciate the subtleties of a limited kenotic picture with elements such as those I have just sketched. When combined with the distinctions of the previous chapter, and with a perspective on the divine attributes I shall adumbrate shortly, the kenotic maneuver applied to the attribute of omniscience can go a significant way toward ridding orthodoxy of any apparently absurd implications.

I do not, however, find the traditional kenotic strategy fully plausible, or even very attractive. It seems to me to have in its traditional form at least two serious defects. Many theologians would argue that it just as clearly has a third: The kenotic picture of the Incarnation clearly requires a certain view of the Trinity which is controversial and has not, throughout most of the history of the church, represented the mainstream theological understanding of the triune nature of God. Kenotic christology seems to demand a view of the Trinity as consisting in three metaphysically distinct individuals severally exemplifying the attributes of deity, a view which has come to be known as "Social Trinitarianism" because, according to it, there exists a society of divine persons. The argument is that some divine being must have been supporting the existence and operation of the physical universe during the earthly career of Jesus. If the Son had divested himself of his omniscience and severely limited his exercise of his power, then we must understand deity as comprising some other individual bearer of properties distinct from

Social trinitarianism

And polytheism

the Son to continue in the proper activity of deity with respect to the created universe. Strictly speaking, of course, such an argument, if cogent, would require only a Social Binatarianism—two divine persons, one not engaged in kenosis. But any such view is found unacceptable by many theologians, who brand it as "polytheism."

I shall return to this topic in the last chapter. Suffice it to say here that I do not find commitment to anything like Social Trinitarianism theologically objectionable. It is, on the contrary, a view to which (in one of its forms) I am, in fact, attracted. So I shall not criticize or reject the kenotic strategy on this ground. However, the alternative strategy I shall use in laying out a different picture of the Incarnation will, unlike kenoticism, not in itself depend on a social view of deity—which, in the eyes of many, will count significantly in its favor.

The two fundamental objections I have to kenoticism are, first, that, given any standard analysis of the divine attributes, it requires a view of the modalities of those attributes which seems unsatisfactory, and second, that on the same condition it necessitates abandoning any substantive, metaphysical ascription of immutability to God, of even a quite moderate form. Let us consider the point about modality first.

As I mentioned earlier, it is a standard theistic view that there are properties essential to being God, attributes which can be considered to be constitutive of deity. Omnipotence and omniscience are clear and relatively uncontroversial as examples of such properties. It is impossible, on this view, for an individual to be God, or to be literally divine, without being omnipotent and omniscient. One way to put this is to say that the proposition

1   God is omnipotent,

for example, expresses a necessary truth *de dicto*. Omnipotence is a necessary characteristic of deity. Many orthodox theists, in particular Anselmians, go further and hold that omnipotence, omniscience and the other attributes constitutive of deity form not only the kind-essence of deity, but also serve as components of the individual-essence of any being who is God. That is, they understand 1 to express in addition a necessity *de re*.

93

Moreover, many would go on to hold the even more stringent view that

2   God is necessarily omnipotent

expresses *de dicto* a necessary requirement for deity. No individual can count as God unless it is essentially possessed of maximal power, and likewise for the other attributes constitutive of deity. On this view, there is a collection of attributes an individual must have, and must have essentially, in order to be strictly, literally divine.[12]

It should be clear that on this modally exalted view of deity, divine kenosis as I have explicated it so far would be an impossibility. No individual can temporarily give up a property he has essentially. If any being who is divine must have all the metaphysically distinctive attributes of deity essentially, none of them could be given up by him temporarily while he yet continued to exist. If omniscience is an essential property of God the Son, he could not have given it up temporarily. If it is merely a requisite of deity, but not a part of his individual-essence, he could have given it up, but he would thereby have ceased to be God. So the earthly period of the Incarnation would not, after all, have presented us with an individual with two natures simultaneously. On either understanding of the modal status of omniscience, the traditional kenotic strategy as so far presented cannot be used to explicate and defend the orthodox doctrine of the Incarnation.

But why accept these views about the modal status of the divine attributes? It has been suggested by some very traditional, conservative theists that these modal claims are untrue. Stephen Davis, for example, has claimed to see no reason to think that omniscience is necessary for being divine.[13] Alvin Plantinga has suggested that on a Social Trinitarian view, the divine persons may differ in the modal status of their attributes; for example, it could be that God the Father is essentially omniscient, and that God the Son exemplifies that property only contingently, being capable of ceasing to

[12] In speaking of a collection of attributes I am assuming here the falsehood of the ancient philosophical doctrine of divine simplicity. For a justification of the reasonableness of this assumption, see my paper "On God and Man: A View of Divine Simplicity," to appear in *Religious Studies*.

[13] Stephen Davis, *Logic and the Nature of God* (London: Macmillan, 1983), p. 124.

have it for a while.[14] If we make modally minimal claims for deity, the kenotic strategy will be a live option for displaying the coherence of the Incarnation and explicating some of its features. But it seems to me that there are plausible grounds of an Anselmian sort to make strong modal claims for deity, such as I have mentioned. If such claims clearly prohibited an incarnation, I would join Davis and Plantinga in relinquishing them. For any intuitions on which they are based are after all defeasible. And as I have suggested, it is proper for a Christian theist to develop an Anselmian articulation of deity with controls derived from his central, distinctively Christian beliefs. But I think these modally strong claims can be made for God and can be reconciled quite well with the evident facts of the career of Jesus that kenoticism tries to accommodate. If I can show this, I can show the modal background of standard kenoticism to represent at least an unnecessary weakening of the claims an Anselmian can otherwise plausibly make about God.

Consider now for a moment the attribute of immutability. A number of theists throughout history have understood God's immutability to be the property of being absolutely incapable of undergoing or engaging in any sort of real change whatsoever. This understanding of divine immutability has been held mainly by philosophers who subscribe to the doctrine of divine timelessness, the position that God is outside time, having no temporal properties and standing in no temporal relations. Some have mistakenly thought that divine changelessness entails divine timelessness and thus have held the latter position on the basis of their desire to embrace the former. The converse entailment, however, does hold; so those who think they have independent grounds for ascribing timelessness to God must hold God to be incapable of real change, and thus they tend to hold this absolutist conception of divine immutability.

So understood, the claim that God is immutable encounters a number of difficulties. It takes a great deal of ingenuity, for example, to reconcile this claim with the fundamental Judeo-Christian conviction that God is a moral agent who acts in history, often in response to the freely initiated acts of his creatures. No such at-

---

[14]This was suggested in conversation.

tempts I know of seem fully plausible. And if absolute changeless-ness is incompatible with divine agency, it is inconsistent with a fundamental presupposition of the doctrines of omnipotence and perfect goodness, as normally understood by Christian theists. It is also well known of course that in the past Norman Kretzmann and Anthony Kenny, among others, have argued that this sort of immutability is incompatible with omniscience.[15] Given certain plausible assumptions about human freedom and the ontological status of the future, I believe that this case can be made much more strongly than it has been so far in the literature, although I shall not attempt to do so here. And finally, all the more serious problems alleged against divine timelessness, although not all directly problems for this conception of immutability, do tend to impugn rather seriously the major ground usually appealed to for holding God to be absolutely incapable of real change.

I want to suggest that the standard kenotic christological strategy is inconsistent with the ascription to God of any remotely traditional, metaphysically substantive understanding of immutability, and that, on the contrary, the very different picture of the Incarnation I shall offer comports quite well with a reasonable, and fairly strong, construal of this divine attribute. I have mentioned my difficulties with the most extreme interpretation of immutability for two reasons. First, I incline to think that it is wrong, and this should at least be mentioned. But second, and more important, I want to emphasize that in claiming traditional kenoticism to be incompatible with divine immutability I am not relying on this most extreme and controversial understanding of that attribute.

Philosophers who hold the absolutist view of immutability seem to go too far in one direction, claiming too much, whereas many contemporary theologians who hold that divine immutability amounts to no more than God's reliable conduct of his affairs err on the other extreme and claim too little. There is a mediating position possible, which I have laid out at length elsewhere and shall indicate only in the briefest way here.[16] The immutability of God can be

[15] Kretzmann, "Omniscience and Immutability," and Anthony Kenny, *The God of the Philosophers* (Oxford: Clarendon Press, 1979), chap. 4.

[16] The position is delineated in "Properties, Modalities, and God," *Philosophical Review*, 93 (January, 1984), 35–55.

understood as a property, or modality, of the exemplifications of all those attributes constitutive of deity, kind-essential for divinity. In brief, any individual who has a constitutive attribute of deity can never have begun to have it, and can never cease to have it. He has it, rather, immutably. It will follow then, of course, that any individual who is God cannot have begun to be God and cannot cease to be God. He is God immutably. I also believe that immutability must hold with respect to at least some sorts of divine intentions, but it will not be necessary to go into that for my purposes here. The claim already made will suffice to block any traditional form of kenoticism.

If no divine being can cease to have any attribute partly constitutive of deity, and omniscience is partly constitutive of deity, God the Son cannot have ceased to be omniscient for a period of time. The standard kenotic account of the Incarnation, as I have explicated it, then cannot be accepted.

It is, however, open to the kenotic theologian to modify the specifics of his position. As I have presented it, the kenotic claim is that during the earthly stage of the Incarnation, God the Son temporarily ceased to exemplify some central divine attributes, such as omniscience and omnipresence. And on any standard analysis of those attributes, the kenotic thesis has to be stated in precisely this way in order to accomplish its goal. For if omniscience as standardly explicated requires knowing every true proposition, then during that time he was in a state of having ceased to be omniscient. Thus, kenotic theologians, assuming a standard account of the divine attributes, talk of the Son's temporarily laying aside, giving up, or relinquishing the relevant attributes. But the kenoticist could attempt to reconcile his basic perspective on the Incarnation with both a modally exalted view of deity and a philosophically substantive conception of divine immutability by adopting a more complex, nonstandard analysis of such attributes as omniscience and omnipresence. For any such attribute, the required sort of nonstandard analysis would be formed simply by appending to whatever standard analysis was found otherwise adequate what we can call a "kenotic clause." According to the sort of analysis which would result, a being would be said to be, for example, omniscient just in case that being naturally (in the sense of 'ordinarily' or 'typically') knows all true propositions *and* fails to know any true proposition only when freely and temporarily restricting its knowledge. In a slightly different idiom, an individual could be said to be omniscient if and only if it has maximal cognitive power and fully exercises that power in such a way as to have all knowledge *de dicto* and *de re* it is logically possible for a perfect being to have *except* at any time it freely and temporarily chooses to restrict its exercise of that power.[17] In each of these statements, the kenotic clause is the clause following the italicized connective.

The effect of such nonstandard analyses would then be to allow any kenotically relevant, central divine attribute to be retained during the earthly stage of the Incarnation. It would no longer have to be said that during that time God the Son failed to exemplify omniscience or omnipresence. The facts of the Incarnation would be compatible with all such central attributes being exemplified immutably (in the sense indicated) and essentially. For any lack of knowledge or restriction in personal presence characterizing the Second Person of the Trinity during his time on earth could then be held to satisfy the proper conditions of omniscience, or omnipresence, in virtue of the kenotic clause given in the analysis of each of these attributes.

Let us refer to such nonstandard analyses of the divine attributes as "kenotic analyses." Given a kenotic analysis of omniscience, the kenotic theologian would no longer need to claim that it is possible that there be a time when a properly divine person is without omniscience. He would no longer need to claim that it is possible for a divine being to fail temporarily to exemplify omniscience or any other central constitutive attribute of deity. On the traditional kenotic picture, it is hard to see exactly how God the Son is supposed to retain his divinity, his divine nature, during the earthly stage of the Incarnation. On this new version of the kenotic picture, however, it could be claimed that the Son retains during that period every traditionally recognized requisite of divinity. There may be many things he does not know during that time and many places bereft of his personal presence, but on a kenotic analysis of om-

[17]The explication of omniscience in terms of maximal cognitive power has been explored, and its importance indicated, in an unpublished paper by Charles Taliaferro entitled "Divine Cognitive Power."

niscience and omnipresence it could still be true during that time that he is omniscient and omnipresent, and thus that he is God.

Unfortunately, it seems to me that the mere statement of such a view suffices to display its artificiality. Its net effect seems to be merely to mask the difficulties the kenotic view faces. For surely what theists traditionally have intended to claim when ascribing immutable and essential omniscience to God is precisely the metaphysical impossibility of God's ever ceasing or failing to have knowledge of anything it is possible for a perfect being to know. Any attempt to preserve the ascription of immutability and necessity, or essentiality, to divine omniscience which allows a being to be omniscient while lacking an enormous amount of knowledge surely seems to amount to no more than a verbal maneuver which departs dramatically from the traditional concept of omniscience. It is semantically deviant to a clearly unacceptable degree to allow an individual to count at any time as omniscient who is severely limited at that time in knowledge. So I think that a strategy of reconciling the kenotic perspective with standard essentiality and immutability claims for deity which relies on nonstandard kenotic analyses of such attributes as omniscience and omnipresence is in the end unsatisfactory.

As a matter of fact, though, one other maneuver might be open to someone who favors the kenotic approach. It is possible to reject a kenotic analysis of any divine attribute such as omniscience and yet square the kenotic perspective with strong modal claims for deity by specifying that the conditions or requisites of divinity, the properties ingredient in or constitutive of deity, are not simply the divine attributes such as omniscient or omnipresence (as standardly analyzed), but rather are properties composed of these attributes *qualified by* kenotic limitation possibilities. In other words, for example, on this move a standard analysis of omniscience would be endorsed. No kenotic clause would be included in the proper analysis of omniscience itself. What would be claimed, though, is that it is not precisely *omniscience* which is a requisite of deity. It is rather a distinct property, the property of being omniscient-unless-freely-and-temporarily-choosing-to-be-otherwise, which is a logically necessary condition of deity. Note that in the expression of this latter property, we have an analogue of the kenotic clause which was introduced into the nonstandard kenotic analysis of omniscience, but that now it has been exported from the proper analysis of omniscience and has instead been used to link up with or operate upon that standard divine attribute to form the distinct property which itself will then be claimed to be the only necessary requisite of deity having to do most generally with knowledge. It will be this compound property rather than omniscience *simpliciter* which will be said to be an essential property of any individual who is God. And then of course it will be this kenotic attribute which will be immutably exemplified by God.

On this line, we can return to the traditional kenotic claim that in order to enter into our human condition God the Son took on a form of existence which involved voluntarily ceasing to have certain sorts of knowledge and thus ceasing to be omniscient. However, with the new conception of precisely what properties are requisites of deity, it will not follow that he thereby ceased to be divine. Nor will it follow that he ceased to have any property which (on this view) should be had essentially or exemplified immutably by him. By reconsidering and reconceptualizing exactly what properties are ingredient in the kind-essence of deity, essential to any individual who is God, and thus immutably exemplified by any such being, it seems that a kenotic theologian can after all reconcile his perspective with a modally exalted conception of deity and a substantive philosophical account of immutability, while at the same time avoiding the patent artificiality of trying to introduce a new analysis of such traditionally recognized divine attributes as omniscience and omnipresence.

I think that with this maneuver we have arrived at the strongest and most sophisticated form of the kenotic approach to reconciling the divinity of Christ with the evident limitations evinced in his earthly career. We have arrived at the most plausible strategy for squaring kenoticism with at least the basic form of traditional claims about the modalities of divine properties. It should be noted, however, that this version of kenoticism also involves a real departure from what most theists, Christian as well as non-Christian, have wanted to say about the nature of God. For on this precise version of the kenotic theory, it also fails to be true that any divine person is logically or metaphysically immune to states of extensive ignorance concerning important truths about the world. A form of divine immutability compatible with a divine person's ceasing to know a vast number of truths is very different from anything traditional theists have wanted to ascribe to God. And this kenotic view represents a perspective on deity which is not clearly in accord, with an Anselmian conception of God. For there can be Anselmian intuitions that it is better to be absolutely immune to states of avoidable ignorance than to be capable of such states, and thus that it is omniscience *simpliciter* which is a requisite of deity, as well as a property any particular divine being must have essentially, and hence immutably. The precise status of such intuitions, which can stand against the kenotic maneuver, will be discussed at some length at the end of chapter 5. It will suffice to say here that they can provide fairly strong prima facie warrant for resisting any such kenotic innovations.

But in light of what I have said about the open texture of our conception of deity, the defender of kenoticism could insist that making sense of the Incarnation requires endorsing some version of the kenotic claim, and so from the perspective of a Christian commitment, one ought to reject any conception of the divine attributes, of immutability, or of the modal features of deity which precludes this. For, after all, as H. M. Relton has said, echoing the sentiments of many sensible theologians: "So long as men clung to the Ante-Christian conception of God . . . so long would they dwell upon his unlikeness to man and tend to widen the gulf between the creator and his creatures. Thus they would be liable to miss the significance of that fuller revelation of the Divine and human natures in their affinity and likeness which the Incarnation was meant to teach."[18] Perhaps standard accounts of precisely what properties are logically ingredient in deity, metaphysically strong conceptions of divine immutability, and what I have been calling the modally exalted claims for deity are not properly to be brought within the province of a distinctively Christian conception of God, taking as one of its controls the doctrine of the Incarnation. If the kenotic strategy offered us what seemed clearly to be the only way of making sense of the attributes of God the Son while present

[18]H. H. Relton, *A Study in Christology* (London: SPCK, 1917), p. 56.

The Logic of God Incarnate

among us as Jesus of Nazareth, this sort of suggestion would have considerable, even decisive, weight for the Christian theist. But I think an alternative to kenoticism is available which accords both with standard accounts of the divine attributes and with the strong claims about the immutability and modal features of deity theists have traditionally wanted to make. It is a perspective which would even comport with the most extreme understanding of immutability, if that construal can be shown to be compatible with any divine agency in a world such as ours. It is clearly a perspective which stands fully consistent with that sort of metaphysically distinctive immutability which I am prepared to endorse and which I think would be endorsed by most theists. In many ways it seems to me to offer a picture, or model, of the Incarnation superior to that provided by a kenotic view. The view I want to present can be called, succinctly, if possibly somewhat misleadingly, 'the two-minds view of Christ'.[19] It is an ancient view which has been relatively neglected for a long time. I believe some distinctively modern perspectives can be drawn upon to explicate it and display its plausibility.

Recall first of all a claim needed for kenoticism, the claim that no person is identical with any particular range of conscious experience, or collection of belief states, he might have. I think that the truth of this claim will follow from any modally plausible and metaphysically careful account of what a person is. With this in mind, we can begin to appreciate the early view that in the case of God Incarnate, we must recognize something like two distinct ranges of consciousness.[20] There is first what we can call the eternal mind

[19] Of course, to avoid the Nestorian heresy, we must use the word 'mind' here to denote something a person *has* rather than simply something that a person *is*.

[20] One of the few contemporary theologians contributing to the current debate over the doctrine of the Incarnation even to have hinted at the importance of this view, or to have mentioned it at all, is Brian Hebblethwaite. See his article "The Propriety of the Doctrine of the Incarnation as a Way of Interpreting Christ," *Scottish Journal of Theology*, 33 (1980), 201–202. Hints at something like such a view can be found in the writings of Gregory of Nyssa (c. 330–c. 395), Gregory Nazianzen (329–389) and Cyril of Alexandria (d. 444). For some specific references, see, for example, A. T. Hanson's "Two Consciousnesses: The Modern Version of Chalcedon," *Scottish Journal of Theology*, 37 (December, 1984), 471–483. Unfortunately, Hanson appears to misunderstand the view and reject it for no good reason.

Jesus and the Attributes of Deity

of God the Son with its distinctively divine consciousness, whatever that might be like, encompassing the full scope of omniscience. And in addition there is a distinctly earthly consciousness that came into existence and grew and developed as the boy Jesus grew and developed. It drew its visual imagery from what the eyes of Jesus saw, and its concepts from the languages he learned. The earthly range of consciousness, and self-consciousness, was thoroughly human, Jewish, and first-century Palestinian in nature.

We can view the two ranges of consciousness (and, analogously, the two noetic structures encompassing them) as follows: The divine mind of God the Son contained, but was not contained by, his earthly mind, or range of consciousness. That is to say, there was what can be called an asymmetric accessing relation between the two minds. Think, for example, of two computer programs or informational systems, one containing but not contained by the other. The divine mind had full and direct access to the earthly, human experience resulting from the Incarnation, but the earthly consciousness did not have such full and direct access to the content of the overarching omniscience proper to the Logos, but only such access, on occasion, as the divine mind allowed it to have. There thus was a metaphysical and personal depth to the man Jesus lacking in the case of every individual who is merely human.

This account allows for the apparent intellectual and spiritual growth of Jesus in his humanity to be a real development. It can also help to explain, or at least to allow for, the cry of dereliction.[21] When this view is used to augment the apparatus of the previous chapter, we have in principle a full and adequate account of the basic features of the metaphysics of the Incarnation. In particular, it allows us to avoid the absurdities to which orthodoxy has always seemed vulnerable. On it, we have in the person of Jesus no case of a God merely dressed up as a man. We have an individual who is fully human, and who shares in the human condition, experiencing the world in a human perspective. No Docetic absurdities are implied by the view. Nor is it Nestorian. Nor Appolinarian. There is one person with two natures and two ranges of conscious-

[21]Mark 15:34.

The Logic of God Incarnate

ness. He is not the theological equivalent of a centaur, half God and half man. He is fully human, but not merely human. He is also fully divine.

The two-minds view seems to me, further, to be a clear improvement over kenoticism. When he became a man, God the Son did not give up anything of deity; he merely took on the nature and condition of humanity. We can capture full well the New Testament claim that in the Incarnation God the Son humbled himself, without following kenotic christology in holding that he gave up any metaphysical attributes distinctive of deity. His humbling consisted rather in his rendering himself vulnerable to the pains, sufferings, aggravations, and agonies which became his as a man but which, in his exclusively divine form of existence, could not have touched him this way. It is not by virtue of what he gave up, but in virtue of what he took on, that he humbled himself. This sort of divine kenosis was a feature of the Incarnation, but so understood, it is a feature which accords logically with strong claims concerning the modality and immutability of the attributes distinctive of and traditionally held to be constitutive of deity. No kenotic move with any of those attributes is required for ridding orthodoxy of any appearances of absurdity.

But can we really understand what it is to attribute two minds, or two ranges of consciousness, to one person? That depends on what is required for understanding the claim. Can we know what it is like to be a God-man? Well, can we know what it is like to be a bat? It is hard, if possible at all, to imagine what a sonar-consciousness is like. Likewise, we do not, and cannot, know what it is like to be God, at least not in the way we know what it is like to be a human being. It is no objection to my suggestions that we cannot in this sense know what it would be like to be a God-man with two related but distinct ranges of consciousness. But as a matter of fact, we can fill out some significant level of understanding concerning the claim by way of some analogies.

I have suggested already a computer or artificial intelligence analogy. Consider two or three others. First, an interesting, and interestingly parallel, dream phenomenon is reported by many people. I think I have had such an experience myself on more than one occasion. The dreamer is having a dream with a large cast of characters. The dreamer himself is one of those characters, perceiving the internal environs of the dream and taking part in its action "from within." But at the same time, the dreamer "as sleeper" is somehow aware, in what could be called an overarching level of consciousness, that it is just a dream that is going on, in which he is playing a role as one of the characters. If in fact there is in such an experience a twofold consciousness, one "within" the dream, the other "outside" the dream simultaneously, then we have, if not a model, then at least an analogy of some value in helping us to get some imaginative grip on the two-minds picture of the Incarnation. It is possible, though, that in such experiences the dreamer is very rapidly alternating between two perspectives. And of course such a case would provide no model or particularly good analogy at all.

Consider the common claim in twentieth-century psychology that there are various strata to the ordinary human mind. The postulated unconscious, or subconscious, mind would stand in an asymmetric accessing relation to the conscious mind somewhat parallel to that postulated between the divine consciousness and the earthly consciousness of God Incarnate. If modern psychology is even possibly right in this postulation, one person can have different levels or ranges of mentality. In the case of Jesus, there would then be a very important extra depth had in virtue of his being divine.

Finally, there are cases of brain hemisphere commisurotomy, multiple personality, and even hypnosis, in which we are confronted by what seems to be in some significant sense a single individual human being, one person, but one person with apparently two or more distinct streams or ranges of consciousness, distinct domains of experience. Now, of course, there are philosophers who claim that in many if not all cases of multiple, simultaneous ranges of experience associated with the stimulation of one human body, the requisite conditions are lacking for judging there to be a single person who is the ultimate bearer of the disparate sets of experience. Some theorists identify each discrete range of consciousness in the commissurotomy patient and each personality in the case of a multiple personality as a person. Such a claim is less often made with respect to different levels of consciousness or divergent streams of awareness associated with cases of hypnotism.

The Logic of God Incarnate

But in any case, this sort of identification can be argued to be implausible.[22] If one troubling aberrant personality is eliminated therapeutically from the behavioral repertoire of someone afflicted with multiple personalities, the therapist surely need not see the effect of her work as the killing of a person. Moreover, it is plausible, and indeed illuminating, to view normal persons as either having or even being systems of systems of mentality or experience. And, again, if it is even conceivable that one person have, simultaneously, such distinct ranges of mentality, we may have here, in at least some of the more unusual cases, vivid partial analogies which can help us to gain some firmer understanding of the two-minds view.

As a matter of fact, in some cases of multiple personality, there exists one personality with apparently full and direct knowledge of the experiences had, information gathered, and actions initiated by one or more other personalities, a sort of knowledge which is not had by any other personality concerning it. In other words, there seem to exist asymmetric accessing relations in such cases, interestingly though of course not perfectly parallel to the sort of relation claimed by the two-minds view to hold between the divine and human minds of Christ.[23]

Does the two-minds view then present the Incarnation as a case of split personality on the part of God the Son? And if so, should not the recognition of this alone suffice for a rejection of the view as an unworthy, demeaning characterization of Christ? Does what initially can appear to serve as a partial explication of orthodoxy end up amounting to no more than a gross impiety?

First of all, the reference to some phenomena of multiple personality here is intended only to provide a partial analogy for some of what the two-minds view claims to be true in the case of Christ. It is to have no more than the limited but, I hope, helpful function of providing some understanding of, and imaginative grip on, the

[22]For some relevant lines of argument, see David G. Benner and C. Stephen Evans, "Unity and Multiplicity in Hypnosis, Commissurotomy, and Personality Disorder," *Journal of Mind and Behavior* 5 (Autumn, 1984), 423–431, and Charles E. Marks, *Commissurotomy, Consciousness and Unity of Mind* (Montgomery, Vt.: Bradford Books, 1980), and the literature there cited.

[23]This sort of parallel was first brought to my attention by Stephen Evans.

Jesus and the Attributes of Deity

central elements of the two-minds view. It thus is intended to serve the same function as the computer analogy, the dream analogy, and the reference to the classic distinction between the conscious and unconscious, or subconscious, mind. It is not intended to be a complete modeling of the noetic features of the Incarnation.

Furthermore, the analogy or partial parallel is in no way demeaning to God the Son. To see this we must ask exactly what it is about the phenomena of multiple personality generally that renders the state of exhibiting such phenomena a bad state for a human being to be in, a state it would be better to be without. The answer is, I think, quite simple. Typical cases of multiple personality exhibit two negative features: They are not mental states, or arrangements, voluntarily entered into by the person who exhibits the phenomena, and they are not mental states, or arrangements, conducive to that attainment of goals valuable to the person involved. Both these features are, on any orthodox deployment of the two-minds view, absent from the case of Christ's exemplification of two minds. His taking on of a human mind was entirely voluntary. And according to any traditional account of the purpose of the Incarnation, it was conducive to, if not in fact necessary for, the attainment of goals valuable to God. So it seems to me that we have no reason from this quarter for hesitating to use whatever parallel phenomena we find in psychologically unusual human cases to help us to understand the relevant aspects of the Incarnation.

The two-minds view of Christ allows us to take seriously the human limitations of Jesus' earthly career without incurring the metaphysical and modal costs of kenoticism. I believe it is a very powerful picture, and that it can be an important ingredient in a solution to the single most difficult logical challenge to the doctrine of the Incarnation, a challenge I shall set the stage for in the next chapter and deal with directly in the following one. If it is defensible, which I think it is, the two-minds view along with the distinctions of chapter 3 gives us all we need for philosophically explicating the orthodox doctrine of the Incarnation and defending it against all forms of the contemporary incoherence challenge.

5 The Necessity of God's Goodness

One of the most difficult forms of the logical challenge to the doctrine of the Incarnation arises out of a traditional theistic claim concerning the modal status of God's goodness. It is a claim which hooks up in an interesting way with the Anselmian conception of God, the conception which I have suggested rightly stands behind the articulation of any orthodox account of the Incarnation. And the problem which results for the identity claim

(C)   Jesus is God the Son

is perhaps the only problem for the doctrine of the Incarnation which has been discussed in print by numerous philosophers, among them such prominent authors as C. B. Martin, Alvin Plantinga, William Rowe, and G. E. Hughes. In this chapter I want to clarify and defend the modal claim which gives rise to the problem, as it has been criticized even by numerous theists in recent years. Then the specific problem to which it leads will be addressed in chapter 6. The problem is sufficiently interesting to warrant our devoting some time to getting its crucial theistic component clear.

1   The Traditional View

Many theists affirm that God is necessarily good. To be more precise, they hold that the proposition

1   God is good

expresses *de re* as well as *de dicto* a necessity. It is necessary *de dicto* in virtue of specifying a condition of deity. Goodness is a requisite for holding the divine office, or for having the ontological status of being God. It is also held to be necessary *de re* because goodness is believed to be an essential property of any individual who in fact, and of necessity, is God. Indeed, as in the case of the parallel proposition about omnipotence mentioned in the previous chapter, the proposition

2   God is necessarily good

is held by many to express *de dicto* a necessary condition of deity. In order for an individual to be God, it is not enough that he be as a matter of fact good—he must be good *essentially*.

The proposition that goodness is a requirement of deity—at least as deity is understood in the Judeo-Christian tradition—is a relatively uncontroversial conceptual claim. This is owing, I think, to the intimate connections which have been forged between the concepts of divinity and worship-worthiness, and the fairly obvious containment of the notion of goodness in the latter. But the stronger traditional claims about necessary goodness are nowadays far from uncontroversial. Among the tenets of the modally strongest form of classical theism are the beliefs that any individual who is God must be a necessarily existing entity who exemplifies all of the attributes constitutive of deity as essential properties. Any divine person is thus, for example, believed to be necessarily omnipotent (omnipotent in all possible worlds), necessarily omniscient, and necessarily good. In recent years, however, a number of philosophers, including some otherwise quite traditional theists, have come to believe that this exalted conception of God goes a bit too far and thereby falls into logical difficulty. Most locate the problem in the claim that any divine being's goodness is among his essential properties, and appear to hold that if only this one modal claim is given up, otherwise intractable problems for theism vanish, leaving the concept of God intact, at least with respect to its modal elements. Many such philosophers are content to allow other divine attributes to be viewed as properties essential to any individual who is God. In this, they often seem to acknowledge the deep religious conviction that nothing could possibly thwart God's power or escape divine knowledge. They disavow the *de re* necessity only of God's goodness.

Traditionally, the goodness of God has been understood in two distinct ways. First, there is a conception of what often has been referred to as "metaphysical goodness." On this understanding, God's goodness involves his having, in some important and axiologically relevant sense, ontological completeness.[1] He is held to exemplify a maximally perfect set of compossible, ontological great-making properties, construed along Anselmian lines. On the other hand, there is a very different and quite important religious belief that God is good in much the same way as an ideal human moral agent would be. On this view, it is held that God acts in perfect accord with all moral principles relevant to his actions. Along these lines, religious believers often speak of the "moral goodness" of God.

To my knowledge, no one has found any special problems with the claim that God is necessarily good in the distinctively metaphysical sense. It is only with respect to the other sort of divine goodness, that having to do with agency and moral principles, that significant modal controversy has arisen. In fact, some philosophers who make it a point to assert that God is necessarily good in the metaphysical sense explicitly deny the *de re* necessity of his goodness as an agent.[2]

In order to gain some perspective on this controversy, and to arrive at some sort of assessment of the dispute, let us begin by asking what sorts of considerations can seem to raise special problems for the view that any divine being necessarily acts in perfect accord with all moral principles relevant to his conduct.

---

[1] For the sake of simplicity, and to mesh stylistically with other authors who have written on this topic, I shall henceforth in this chapter most often refer to God in the singular, setting aside for now any trinitarian concerns which would militate otherwise.

[2] See, for example, Bruce Reichenbach's *Evil and a Good God* (New York: Fordham University Press, 1982), chap. 7.

2   *Challenges to the Tradition*

For convenience, and in accord with our earlier usage, we can refer to the view that any individual who is God exists necessarily (in every possible world) and exemplifies each of the properties constitutive of deity (such properties as omnipotent, omniscience, and perfect goodness) necessarily as simply "Anselmianism," or "the Anselmian conception of God." Of course, someone could hold these views without being an Anselmian in all respects; but for present purposes we shall ignore this possibility, for it is probably safe to say that most who hold such views do so on Anselmian grounds. A number of well-known arguments have been constructed to show that anyone who holds God to be necessarily good will become entangled in logical incoherence if he embraces the other elements of the Anselmian conception as well. A decade ago, for example, Lawrence Resnick argued as follows:[3] An Anselmian God would create or allow to exist only a best of all possible worlds. There can be such a world only if there are a number of possible worlds differing in overall value, some worse than others. But a world is possible only if it could be actual. And if God is necessarily good, as well as existent in and responsible for all possible worlds, no less-than-optimal world could be actual. That is to say, given Anselmianism, there are no less-than-optimal possible worlds. But if possible worlds cannot differ in this way in overall value, the notion of a best of all possible worlds loses its sense. And since the existence of such a world is entailed by the Anselmian conception of God, that conception itself is thereby shown to be incoherent.

It is notorious that arguments such as this are, in all epistemic propriety, reversible. The Anselmian could thus begin to counter Resnick's charge by reasoning that precisely because of the evident problem in combining his conception of God with a notion of a best possible world, Anselmianism does not entail that God would create or allow to exist only a best possible world. In fact, many traditional theists have argued on completely independent grounds

[3]Lawrence Resnick, "God and the Best Possible World," *American Philosophical Quarterly*, 10 (October, 1973), 313–317.

that the idea of a best possible world is no more coherent than that of a greatest possible integer.[4] And even if on some construal the notion could be made coherent, the assumption that any Anselmian being necessarily would be a universal maximizer of value is itself far from uncontroversial.[5] So Resnick's argument can be said to employ premises a good deal more dubious than any element of the traditional view he means to impugn.

On the basis of such moves, the Anselmian could respond to Resnick that his conception of deity entails only that God will create a good world. But of course, this is not enough as a response, for the Resnick ploy can be reintroduced here: The notion even of a good possible world depends for its sense on there being a number of possible worlds differing in overall value, some worse than others. But a world is possible only if it could be actual. And if God is *necessarily* good, as well as existent in and responsible for all possible worlds, no less-than-good world could be actual. That is, given Anselmianism, there are no less-than-good possible worlds. But there is an important sense in which 'good' is just as much a comparative concept as 'best', depending for its meaning on possible contrast. So if possible worlds cannot differ in this way in overall value, the notion of even a good possible world loses its sense. And since the Anselmian conception of God entails the existence of such a world, it is thereby shown to be itself an incoherent conception.

Here we have what can appear to be Resnick's argument considerably strengthened. But to it the traditional theist has a simple and decisive reply at hand. Given the existence of an Anselmian God, there are no less-than-good worlds which are genuinely possible, in the broadly logical sense. But such worlds are, in an important sense, at least partially *conceivable*. That is, worlds are (at least partially) conceivable which if, *per impossibile*, the Ansel-

[4] See, for example, Bruce Reichenbach, "Must God Create the Best Possible World?," *International Philosophical Quarterly*, 19 (June, 1979), 203–212; and George Schlesinger's "The Problem of Evil and the Problem of Suffering," *American Philosophical Quarterly*, 1 (July, 1964), 244–247.

[5] See Robert Adams, "Must God Create the Best?," *Philosophical Review*, 81 (1972), 317–332.

The Necessity of God's Goodness

mian God did not exist, would be possible.[6] A number of these are worlds in which, in the final analysis, the overall condition of God's creatures is less-than-good. The excellence of the actual world, its ultimate overall goodness, is highlighted in its contrast to these *conceivable* worlds. It is in this context that the claim that God will create or allow only a good world has its sense. With these distinctions, which I shall presently develop a bit more, the Anselmian who holds God to be, among other things, necessarily good can turn back the force of Resnick's argument completely. In this light, his reasoning can be seen to be totally ineffectual as an attack on any careful version of traditional theism.

Far better known than Resnick's argument is Nelson Pike's contention that necessary goodness is incompatible with omnipotence, and so should not be ascribed to God.[7] The sort of reasoning Pike offers is basically quite simple. Surely, many states of affairs are conceivable which it would be wrong for any rational agent intentionally to bring about. If God were necessarily good, logically unable to violate any moral principle, he would be unable to bring about any such state of affairs. But then, surely this would constitute a limitation on God's power incompatible with his being omnipotent. Further, we might add in support of Pike, God would seem thereby to lack a sort of creative power that many of his creatures have. And in that case, it would be absurd to call him omnipotent.

As initially plausible as Pike's argument might seem, it has been as well rebutted as any in the literature. First of all, even if we were convinced that there is an ineliminable logical incompatibility between the properties of omnipotence and necessary goodness, it would not be altogether obvious which one should be relinquished as a divine attribute. This is shown clearly by the case of Peter Geach, who believes there to be such an incompatibility, yet unlike Pike chooses to give up the traditional claim that God is omnipotent,

---

[6] Here and elsewhere, the theist will depart from the standard view of subjunctive conditionals with necessarily false antecedents and separate the sheep from the goats, affirming some, such as the one just given in the text, on good grounds, while denying others.

[7] Nelson Pike, "Omnipotence and God's Ability to Sin," *American Philosophical Quarterly*, 6 (July, 1969), 208–216.

Pike's necessary goodness is incompatible with omnipotence

adverting instead to a notion of what he calls "almightiness" to explicate the nature and extent of divine power, in a way obviously compatible with God's being necessarily good.[8] But what is more important is that Pike's argument fails to provide us with any good reason to think that there is such an incompatibility in the first place. Some criticize him for relying on too simplistic and inadequate an understanding of what the property of omnipotence involves. And it is true that he operates with a very unrefined conception. But another problem with his argument, one less frequently mentioned, is that he makes too quick a transition from the claim that a certain sort of state of affairs is (in some sense) conceivable to the stronger assumption that it represents a genuine, broadly logical, possibility. As we have seen, no state of affairs incompatible with the goodness of the Anselmian God will represent, from the theistic point of view we are considering, a genuine possibility. In a less than Cartesian sense, the God who is perfectly good is to the Anselmian the ground of all possibility. And this is certainly important, for on any standard traditional account of omnipotence, this maximal extent of power is supposed to range over only what is possible. The Anselmian will remind Pike that many impossibilities are consistently describable *to a point*, and in this sense conceivable. Thus, for reasons having nothing to do with theism, we must always carefully distinguish between this sort of conceivability and possibility, that is to say, between partial conceivability and genuine possibility. Something is genuinely possible in the broadly logical sense, and, we might say, in the fullest sense conceivable, only if its actuality would be compatible with all the necessary features of reality, including, for example, the laws of mathematics. But among those necessary features of reality, the Anselmian will hold the nature of God to be the most important of constraints on what is possible.

So the Anselmian reply to Pike goes as follows.[9] No state of affairs whose actualization would be prohibited to just any moral agent

---

[8] Peter Geach, *Providence and Evil* (Cambridge: Cambridge University Press, 1977), chaps. 1 and 2.

[9] For examples of the Anselmian response, see Joshua Hoffman, "Can God Do Evil?," *Southern Journal of Philosophy*, 17 (1979), 213–220; and Jerome Gellman, "Omnipotence and Immutability," *The New Scholasticism*, 51 (1977), 21–37.

The Necessity of God's Goodness

whatsoever, which would be such that God in particular would be blameworthy in intentionally bringing it about or allowing it, represents a genuine possibility. Thus, on any careful definition of omnipotence, God's inability to actualize such a state of affairs no more detracts from his omnipotence than does his inability to create spherical cubes or objects which are green yet uncolored.[10] And none of God's creatures has the power to trespass beyond the bounds set by the necessities of the divine nature. No one can have the power to make this world into a world it would be wrong of God to allow.

In both Resnick's argument and this response to Pike, we find an important corollary of the Anselmian conception of God brought to light. Such a God is a delimiter of possibilities. If there is a being who exists necessarily and is necessarily omnipotent, omniscient, and good, then many states of affairs which otherwise would represent genuine possibilities, and which by all nontheistic tests of logic and semantics *do* represent possibilities, are strictly impossible in the strongest metaphysical sense. In particular, worlds containing certain sorts or amounts of disvalue or evil are metaphysically ruled out by the nature of God, divinely precluded from the realm of real possibility. In a recent article entitled "God and Possible Worlds: The Modal Problem of Evil," Theodore Guleserian takes issue with this entailment of Anselmianism.[11] Guleserian points out that there are common modal intuitions, intuitions concerning what is possible, which conflict with Anselmian strictures on possibility. And certainly, this much is undeniable. But Guleserian goes on to argue that when forced to choose between our theistically untutored intuitions and the dictates of Anselmianism, it is more reasonable to follow those intuitions and reject the conception of God with whose implications they conflict. If successfully made out, this contention would undermine the Anselmian solution to Pike's problem, although that in particular is not Guleserian's intention. He offers

[10]The most complete elucidation of omnipotence to date appears in Alfred J. Freddoso and Thomas P. Flint, "Maximal Power," in *The Existence and Nature of God*, ed. Alfred J. Freddoso (Notre Dame: The University of Notre Dame Press, 1983), pp. 81–113. This is an account fully consistent with what I have said.
[11]Theodore Guleserian, "God and Possible Worlds: The Modal Problem of Evil," *Nous*, 17 (May, 1983), 221–238.

his argument as a general case for jettisoning at least one of the modal attributes ascribed to God by classical theists and suggests that it is necessary goodness which most obviously should go.

He asks us to engage in a thought experiment. We can easily imagine, he suggests, a single rabbit living in a desert environment, leading a thoroughly wretched, miserable, pain-racked existence. The existence of such a creature is surely conceivable. And our modal intuitions assure us that, so far, we are dealing with the conception of a genuine possibility. But certainly, if the existence of one such poor creature is possible, so is the existence of a second, and of a third, and so on. Nothing in the conception of one miserable rabbit logically precludes the existence of two or more, or for that matter of any number, however great. The additive expansion of our conception seems on modally solid ground. And as the existence of one wretched rabbit will not logically preclude the sufferings of a horde, there is nothing in the conception of a multitude of such creatures which entails the existence of any other contingent sentient being not sharing their plight. Guleserian thus concludes that it is possible that a world exist whose only contingent denizens are those myriads of thoroughly miserable creatures. Such a world would contain any amount you like, however great, of disvalue or evil whose existence contributed to no greater or justifying good. If God exists necessarily and, by virtue of his necessary omnipotence and omniscience, would thus be responsible for the features of any possible world which was actual, it follows that he is not necessarily good. For any being who intentionally brought it about, or unnecessarily allowed it to be the case, that the only other individuals who existed were creatures totally immersed in pain to no good purpose would surely be evil. It is possible for such a world to exist. So it is possible for the individual who is God to be evil. His goodness thus is not among his essential attributes.

Strictly speaking, as Guleserian acknowledges, this argument alone could show at best only that there is a possible world in which God either fails to exist or else lacks at least one of the properties of omnipotence, omniscience, or goodness. It gives us no special reason to pick out goodness as what would be lacking. But Guleserian feels that there is a good reason to see necessary goodness as the modal attribute which must be given up. Before I comment on that reason, I should focus on what is particularly interesting in Guleserian's contribution, which otherwise can be seen on close inspection to differ basically very little in fundamental structure from Pike's reasoning. The distinctiveness of this argument lies in his emphasis on modal intuitions and how they come into play in the assessment of Anselmianism.

As we have seen clearly by now, the Anselmian will argue that if the existence of such a rabbit-world as Guleserian depicts would in fact be inconsistent with the reality of the Anselmian God, its conception does not represent a genuine possibility. It is one of Guleserian's main objectives to counter this sort of move. He maintains that to rule out the possibility of there being a wretched rabbit-world on the basis of a belief that there is a necessary individual who would not allow it is on an epistemic par with ruling out the possibility of there being any pink and purple moons by holding there to exist "a necessary being that would prevent, in every world, the actuality of a pink and purple moon." He goes on to say that this sort of thinking would lead "to the bancruptcy [*sic*] of our knowledge claims about nonactual possibilities."[12] The point seems to be that any such modal proscription of what our theistically untutored intuitions deem to be possible would be arbitrary, or otherwise ill-grounded.

But of course the Anselmian restrictions on the realm of real possibility are far from arbitrary. They are grounded in an utterly simple, unified conception of the nature of the ultimate Source of reality. It is among the strongest of intuitions for most traditional theists that God is a greatest possible, or maximally perfect, being. Informing this conception are value intuitions regarding what properties are, objectively, perfections. That goodness is one of those properties is about as strong a value intuition as there can be, whose content borders on analyticity. There is, of course, absolutely no parallel in the view that a necessary being exists who essentially prevents pink and purple moons, which is as arbitrary a claim as one could imagine. To allow any more than the mere

[12] Ibid., p. 234.

(partial) conceivability of such being would indeed signal "the bankruptcy of knowledge claims about nonactual possibilities." But this effect Anselmianism does not have.

Now of course the Anselmian's judgments about what conceivable worlds do or do not represent real possibilities will be no stronger than his judgments concerning what the moral principles are in accordance with which God necessarily acts. But these moral intuitions can be at least as strong as any modal intuitions with which their deliverances might conflict. To see this, let us consider that there are at least three different sorts of modal intuitions. First, there are modal intuitions about what is or is not logically possible, in a narrow sense. These intuitions will have to do with what the laws of logic are and when a proposition or set of propositions contains a violation of these laws. They will also have to do with what entails what, by virtue of logical form alone. We can call these "logical intuitions." Second, there are modal intuitions concerning semantic matters. These intuitions will have to do with the concepts in language, with matters concerning the intensions and possible extensions of predicates, with such things as conceptual truths. Call these "semantic intuitions." A third sort of modal intuition we apparently must recognize, one which draws the battle line between philosophers such as Guleserian and their Anselmian opponents, is an intuition concerning the status of logical and semantic intuitions. Are they the only legitimate guides to nonactual modal reality, or not? Apparently, Guleserian's intuitions lead him to say yes; the Anselmian disagrees.

With these distinctions drawn, we can see clearly an important thing which Guleserian seems to fail to appreciate sufficiently. The Anselmian can follow him in his logical intuitions concerning the conception of the rabbit-world—there is no strictly logical flaw in the idea of a terminally miserable rabbit or in the conception of any number of such creatures. The Anselmian can also accept Guleserian's semantic intuitions that nothing in the ideas and stipulations involved is conceptually amiss, given only the concepts employed. So if the Anselmian rejects the genuine possibility of such a world, it is not because he is resisting any relevant logical or semantic modal intuitions. He is differing with Guleserian only with respect to what we might call his apparent "meta-modal in-tuition," the intuition that genuine, broadly logical or metaphysical possibility always is established by the consultation of logical and semantic intuitions alone. For the theist, Anselmian intuitions may rule out what logical and semantic intuitions alone permit.

The Anselmian would be in a dubious position if he were com-mitted to resisting common logical and semantic intuitions left and right. For such intuitions have nearly as strong an epistemic status as one could like. We are, after all, inveterate language users. We have a basis in our lives for having logical and semantic intuitions. They are grounded in our successful activity as speakers and think-ers. But what is the epistemic status of the meta-modal intuition which Guleserian apparently affirms and the Anselmian denies? What is its strength? How is it grounded? Whatever we say in answer to these questions, I think that we must recognize that Guleserian's restrictive meta-modal intuition is at a significant epistemic remove from his logical and semantic intuitions. It is certainly rationally deniable. There is nothing dubious about the Anselmian registering disagreement at this point. The value intuitions which inform his conception of God and provide a context for a contrary meta-modal judgment, as firmly grounded as they are in his activity as a moral agent, combine to provide the theist with a position having at least as strong an epistemic status as Guleserian's. No number of logical or semantic intuitions, no cumulative effect of their plausibility, can in the slightest throw into question the Anselmian's judgment that a world in which God would be blameworthy does not rep-resent a genuine possibility. So I think Guleserian has done nothing to undermine the corollary of Anselmianism that God is a delimiter of possible worlds.

To be as fair to Guleserian as possible, nothing he says strictly rules out his accepting, on intuitive grounds or otherwise, some *de re* essentialist strictures on what is genuinely possible, apart from the deliverances of logical and semantic intuitions alone. But if he does accept some such strictures on possibility, then it is clear that his argument turns on a meta-modal intuition very closely related to the one I have already identified, and just as vulnerable to An-selmian resistance. For he provides no justification whatsoever for being selectively essentialist in such a way as to rule out Anselmian delimitations of possibility as distinctively groundless, unacceptable, or even suspect.

In the last section of this chapter I shall have a bit more to say on the epistemic status of modal, moral, and metaphysical intuitions as they relate to what will be our central concern: the traditional claim that God is necessarily good. But now I should focus briefly on an argument that Guleserian merely mentions at the end of his article. It is the real basis on which he picks the necessity of God's *goodness* as the modal attribute that should be rejected when counterintuitive results or logical difficulties arise out of the fully developed Anselmian conception of God. But it also can be seen as providing an entirely independent, logically distinct reason for holding that God's goodness must be contingent rather than necessary. In this capacity, Pike sketches it out in one paragraph of the article whose central claims we already have considered. It is the main argument on the basis of which such otherwise traditional theists as Bruce Reichenbach and Stephen Davis recently have given up the *de re* necessity of divine goodness in the sense which is our concern.[13] So it deserves at least some attention in its own right.

The claim is made by all these philosophers that God's goodness could not consist, even in part, in his acting in accordance with moral principles unless he had a certain sort of freedom—the freedom to act or to refrain from acting in the way these principles determine. As a perfectly good agent, God must be free to do evil; otherwise, his continually refraining from doing so would not be worthy of praise. The argument seems to be that perfect goodness *as an agent* requires that one have moral duties which one satisfies without fail; moral principles do not provide moral duties for any individual who cannot possibly act contrary to their leading; and so, if God is a perfectly good agent, it must be possible for him to act contrary to moral principles—i.e., there must be possible worlds in which God lies, breaks promises, tortures innocent beings for no good reason, and so forth. For this reason, the notion of a necessarily good agent is something of a self-contradiction. If God

[handwritten margin note: Kantian]

[handwritten note below text: 7. "The notion of a necessarily good Agent is something of A]

[handwritten note at bottom: self-contradiction"]

[13]Reichenbach, *Evil and a Good God*, chap. 7, and Stephen Davis, *Logic and the Nature of God* (London: Macmillan, 1983), chap. 6.

is perfectly good, his goodness must be one of his contingent properties.

Suppose for example that God tells Moses at some time t that at a later time $t+1$ he will be given divine assistance in carrying out some important mission. At $t+1$ the required aid is forthcoming and the mission succeeds. On the view under consideration, what has happened is relevant to God's goodness only if at some point in the story God stood under, or incurred, a moral duty, which his actions then satisfied. In this particular instance, only if we have a case of moral truth-telling or promise-keeping, the satisfaction of a duty not to lie or not to break promises, do we have on God's part a good act. God's communication at t can count as the making of a promise only if it generates, at least prima facie, a duty. But God can be such as to have duties only if he has full moral freedom. Specifically, he can have a duty to give Moses aid at $t+1$ only if he is genuinely free to give or withhold that aid when the time comes. But if God necessarily acts in accordance with moral principles, then once he has committed himself at t to giving the future assistance, he is not subsequently free in the manner required by these philosophers for his actions to count as the moral satisfaction of any duty. If, given the stipulated history of his dealings up to $t+1$, it is not then possible that he not help Moses, his granting aid is not a morally relevant act and so not worthy of any sort of praise. It neither contributes to, nor exemplifies, divine goodness.

There are a number of problems in this argument, which, in order to be made to appear as plausible as it has seemed to many philosophers, would, I think, have to be developed at greater length. As I have discussed the cluster of issues it involves at greater length elsewhere, I shall here make only the briefest of comments on it.[14] First, it should be pointed out that if it were a compelling argument, selectively giving up the necessity of God's goodness would alone do nothing toward solving the problem of moral freedom it poses. It seems that the assumption made by philosophers like Reichenbach and Davis is that if the goodness of God as an agent has the modal status *de re* of contingency, it follows that at the time of any

---

[14]This discussion can be found in "Duty and Divine Goodness," *American Philosophical Quarterly*, 21 (July, 1984).

of his acts he is able to do morally otherwise than he does. But if God exemplifies all the other attributes constitutive of deity with either the modal status of necessity or even just immutability in the sense delineated in the previous chapter, it can be strictly demonstrated that from God's being contingently perfectly good at any one time it follows that he cannot cease to be good at any subsequent time.[15] Thus, if such a God is good at t, he will not have the sort of freedom at $t+1$ these philosophers require. The problem they raise is solved on its own terms only if both the *de re* necessity and even the immutability of other important defining attributes of deity are given up as well. And this results in such an extreme emaciation of the traditional conception of God as to be wholly unsatisfactory to most theists, being contrary to some deep religious convictions.

But this says nothing about the argument itself. The whole line of reasoning is based on a failure to appreciate a perfectly reasonable way in which the traditional religious convictions about God's goodness as an agent can be explicated. The religious belief is fundamentally that God acts in perfect accord with principles which for ordinary human moral agents express moral duties—for instance, the principle that it is good to deal truthfully and honestly with others. It is in no way necessary to this religious belief to hold that these principles actually bind God himself with moral duties. In fact, some theists would find such a claim to border on the blasphemous. The relevance of God's acting in perfect accord with moral principles to his goodness need not depend on his standing in exactly the same ontological and axiological relations to these principles that we do. His goodness need not encompass his having and satisfying any literal duties at all. I can do no more than indicate here the view I have attempted to develop elsewhere that God's axiological goodness as an agent consists in his necessarily acting in accordance with moral principles as well as his freely engaging in acts of gracious supererogation.[16] The perfect goodness of any created moral agent would be ontologically different from, although in principle functionally isomorphic with, the goodness of

[15] I have produced the arguments for this most fully in "Properties, Modalities, and God," *Philosophical Review*, 93 (January, 1984).
[16] "Duty and Divine Goodness," section IV.

God as an agent. Divine goodness is distinct from, though appropriately modeled by, creaturely moral goodness. And in each one of God's necessarily good acts which benefits us, there is an element of supererogation sufficient for grounding our gratitude and praise. The main point is that so long as the goodness of God as an agent is not held to be in *every* respect like the goodness of his creatures, this argument against the necessity of divine goodness cannot even get off the ground. And as the ontological status of God is in other respects so different from that of his creatures, it is eminently reasonable for the theist to articulate his view in this way. So from this point of view, I think the argument can be judged a failure as an attempt to show that the goodness of God as an agent cannot be among his essential properties.

The developed arguments of Resnick, Pike, and Guleserian, as well as this particular line of thought, basically exhaust the contemporary philosophical challenges to the belief that God is necessarily good. I think it is safe to say that none of them is a clear success. At least, on the basis of what we have seen, I think we can give a sympathetic hearing to some arguments in favor of God's goodness being among his essential properties. Even if there is no decisive reason to give up this traditional tenet of theism, we still need to see whether there is any good reason for the theist to affirm it. For affirming it, as we shall see in the next chapter, can involve commitment to one of the main metaphysical underpinnings of what many people have thought to be the thorniest problem for Christian claims concerning Christ.

3 Arguments for the Tradition

It has been urged by some philosophers, quite recently by Richard Swinburne and Keith Ward, that from God's power and freedom together with his omniscience we can deduce his goodness.[17] If this sort of argument could be made out in a fully convincing

[17]Swinburne, *The Coherence of Theism* (Oxford: Clarendon Press, 1977), pp. 146 and 202. The argument is repeated in *The Existence of God* (Oxford: Oxford University Press, 1979), pp. 97–102. See also Keith Ward, *Rational Theology and the Creativity of God* (Oxford: Basil Blackwell, 1982), chaps. 6 and 8.

way, it obviously could be used by anyone who held God to be necessarily omnipotent and necessarily omniscient to establish that he is necessarily good as well. However, the versions of this argument to have appeared in the literature depend on a highly controversial assumption concerning the inability of an omnipotent and omniscient being to act without regard to anything like moral reasons. This assumption has not yet been made to look sufficiently plausible to render it likely that such an argument can succeed. So I shall not discuss here the versions put forward by either Swinburne or Ward. There is, however, a distinct form of argument from necessary omnipotence and necessary omniscience to necessary goodness which does not share the form or assumptions of the Swinburne-Ward arguments, and I think it does merit our attention. A faulty version of this argument was recently advanced by W. R. Carter in an article entitled "Omnipotence and Sin."[18] Although I have explored various forms of this sort of argument elsewhere,[19] I will lay out one version here, as its results will be important in another context later on.

Carter thinks that a certain kind of *reductio* argument can be used to show that the traditional theist must hold God to be necessarily good. Formulated rigorously, the sort of argument he has in mind can be presented like this: Suppose there is an individual, call him "Yahweh," who is necessarily omnipotent and necessarily omniscient. Suppose further for *reductio* that there is a possible world W in which Yahweh is, as a matter of contingent fact, perfectly good and thus blameless, let us say "sinless," up until some time t, at which time he performs an evil deed, sinking into sin and thus ceasing to be perfectly good. Now, at some time just prior to t, say $t - 1$, either Yahweh intends to sin at t, or he does not so intend. If he does, then in having such an intention he sins at $t - 1$, and is not then blameless, contrary to our assumptions. For given that intentions to sin are just as much worthy of blame as the act or acts intended, an intention to sin is itself a sin. If on the contrary, Yahweh does not intend at $t - 1$ to sin at t, it is either because he intends at $t - 1$ not to sin at t, or because he has at $t - 1$ no

[18] W. R. Carter, "Omniscience and Sin," *Analysis*, 43 (March, 1983).
[19] "Impeccability," *Analysis*, 43 (March, 1983).

intention at all concerning whether he will sin at t. If the former is true, then by stipulation of W his intention is thwarted and so he is not omnipotent, contrary to our assumptions. No being will count as omnipotent who cannot see to it that his intentions are carried out concerning his own conduct. At $t - 1$, Yahweh in this case would lack an important power: the power to see to it that his present intentions are enacted at t. If on the other hand, Yahweh at $t - 1$ has no intention at all concerning whether he will sin at t, then at that prior time he fails either to be sinless or to be omniscient or both. In the case of an omnipotent and omniscient individual such as Yahweh is stipulated to be, being perfectly good or sinless, even contingently, entails intending never to sin. Thus, in order to be sinless at $t - 1$, Yahweh would have to intend then never to sin, and thus not to sin at t. His lacking any such intention would entail his not being sinless at $t - 1$, contrary to our assumptions. In addition, it can be argued that if Yahweh were omniscient at $t - 1$, then he would know at that time that he was about to sin at t. None of the even remotely plausible arguments that omniscience does not entail foreknowledge of some sort or other would block this modest inference. But Yahweh could not know he was about to act in a certain way without intending so to act. This follows from the freedom which is an essential component of necessary omnipotence and omniscience. So if Yahweh did not intend at $t - 1$ to sin at t, it would follow that he did not know at that earlier time that he was about to commit such an act. But in that case, he would not be omniscient at $t - 1$, again contrary to our assumptions. And at this point, our *reductio* is complete.

Carter believes that this sort of argument establishes that Yahweh cannot cease to be good, and so is good necessarily. I think it can be taken to show, quite successfully, that if any divine being is essentially omnipotent, essentially omniscient, and good at some time, then he can never thereafter cease being good.[20] But this can be true even if that divine being is good only contingently, such

---

[20] In fact, the same reasoning shows that regardless of whether omnipotence and omniscience are exemplified necessarily or contingently, if they are strongly enduring properties of God—such that he cannot cease to have them if he exemplifies them at all—it also follows that if he is good at any time, he can never thereafter cease to be good.

that he could have existed without ever being good at all. From the fact that an individual *can* cease to have a property without thereby ceasing to exist, it follows that the property in question is not among that individual's essential properties. But from the fact that a being *cannot* cease to have a certain property so long as he continues to exist, it does not follow that it is one of his essential properties. Carter, for example, has the property of apparently having believed otherwise, a property which, unfortunately, he can never cease to have while continuing to exist. Yet, obviously, it is not one of his essential properties. There are possible worlds in which he avoids this modal mistake altogether. So the sort of argument which he thinks can be used to prove that the necessity of God's goodness is entailed by that of some of his other attributes does not succeed at its appointed task.

It is a bit surprising that, given the strength with which many theists will insist on the necessity of God's goodness, so few arguments have been advanced for this view. There is a well-known and rather rhetorical contention that since God is omnipotent, sin can have no power over him. But by simply distinguishing between something like moral weakness and the different sort of weakness conceptually incompatible with omnipotence—weakness in creative power—Pike has neutralized this sort of appeal.[21] And then there is the well-known claim that it is not possible that God do evil since whatever God does is by definition good. But, notoriously, the problem with this sort of reasoning is that it evacuates the belief in God's goodness of any determinate and stable content. The theist traditionally holds that God necessarily acts in accordance with a certain invariable set of principles, a set inclusive of principles which express moral duties for his creatures. Theists do not standardly hold that set to be malleable to divine whim. No such view is implied by even any reasonable version of a divine command theory of ethics. So this line of thought fails to provide the kind of support needed for the tradition.

It could be argued that it is a firm religious requirement that the believer trust God absolutely and obey him unconditionally, and that this sort of trust and obedience would be morally unwarranted

[21]"Omnipotence and God's Ability to Sin," pp. 210–211.

and improper unless God was held to be necessarily good. This would be an argument that for religious and moral consistency the believer must hold God's goodness to be among his essential properties. I think it is an argument that a number of theists would give to support their holding of this belief. It too seems to be a failure, however. For in light of the sort of argument to which Carter has drawn our attention, the religious believer who is convinced that God is perfectly good now, or even that he has been perfectly good at some time in the past, and who holds God's other attributes to be at least immutably exemplified, can be absolutely assured that God's goodness will continue unfailingly into the future. Even if his goodness is contingent, God cannot cease to be good, and so rightly is worthy of the strongest trust and obedience. Thus, again, we have no line of reasoning which establishes either the necessity of divine goodness or even the religious need to affirm it.

To my knowledge, the arguments just mentioned and briefly discussed basically exhaust the ratiocinative support which has been marshaled by most traditional theists for the view that God is necessarily good. There is, however, one other argument which could be developed for this view, an argument which appeals to a striking metaphysical principle favored by a number of great philosophers and proceeds by means of the argument that a being such as God could never cease being good, once he is good at some time. It may be interesting for us to consider.

The principle which launches this new argument is the ancient Principle of Plenitude, the thesis that, given infinite space or infinite time, all possibilities are actualized. It is a thesis espoused in one form or another by philosophers from at least Aristotle to Russell. And certainly, there are interpretations under which it would be embraced by numerous philosophers of the present day. Our argument then begins with an assumption of the Principle of Plenitude, an assumption that God is temporally everlasting, existent through infinitely many moments of time, and for *reductio* the assumption that God is good, but is so only contingently, from which it follows that it is possible, in a broadly logically sense, that God sin. These assumptions together entail that there is some time at which God sins. But, as we have seen earlier, it is provable that if God is necessarily omnipotent and necessarily omniscient, or even if he has these properties in a contingent yet immutable manner, and he is perfectly good at some time, it follows that he never can subsequently sink into sin, regardless of whether his goodness is contingent.

From this we can conclude rigorously that there can be no time of perfect divine goodness before the time of a divine sin. Thus, either there was a single divine sin which occurred infinitely long ago and was preceeded by no prior moments, which is strictly impossible, or it is the case that at every moment God sins. But if the latter is true, God would not be contingently perfectly good, as was assumed. So if God is good at all, he is good *necessarily*. Our argument is complete.

As interesting as this argument is, I believe it cannot be used by the traditional theist to support his position. Persuasive though it might appear at first glance, it too is a failure. Consider more carefully the principle on which it is constructed, the principle that given infinite space or time, there are, ultimately, no unactualized possibilities. The modal element of this principle can be given either of two interpretations. First, there is the logical interpretation: In infinite space or time, anything which is logically possible will come about at some time. Since Aristotle's attempt to define the alethic modalities extensionally, some philosophers have held to the Principle of Plenitude under this interpretation. But a traditional theist is theologically committed to judging the thesis under this construal to be false. For it is then incompatible with the central religious belief that God is a free creator, free to bring contingent things into existence and free to refrain from so doing. If the logical reading of the principle were true, God would not have this freedom. Everything whose existence was logically possible would come into being, regardless of God's desires.

But more is wrong with the principle so understood than just its incompatibility with the traditional doctrine of creation. For one thing, in order to be acceptable at all, the principle as it stands would have to be qualified in various ways. For example, it is logically possible that I sit at some time t and equally possible that I not sit at t. But it is clearly impossible that both these possibilities be actualized for the same value of t. The principle must therefore be qualified so as not to apply to temporally indexed properties.

But the very point of carefully introducing such qualifications so as to provide a principle immune to obvious counterexample would itself have to be questioned. For under the logical interpretation, there seems to be absolutely no good reason to accept any such principle in the first place. It seems utterly gratuitous. Aristotle's definitions of necessity and possibility just do not capture the logical conception of these modalities. 'Necessarily p' can be argued to entail ⌜p at every time⌝, but the converse entailment cannot plausibly be thought to hold. Likewise, ⌜p at some time⌝ does entail ⌜possibly p⌝, but the converse entailment, the one expressed in the Principle of Plenitude, does not obviously, or even plausibly, hold at all.

In an article entitled "Nature, Plenitude, and Sufficient Reason," R. H. Kane has argued that the Principle of Plenitude follows from the Principle of Sufficient Reason.[22] And in that case it would seem that many traditional theists who value a cosmological argument for God's existence would find themselves committed to its truth, inconsistently with their doctrine of creation. But no such quandary actually arises, as the precise version of the Principle of Sufficient Reason required for the entailment is a version which few, if any, philosophers would view as having much plausibility at all, and which is not required for the construction of any standard cosmological argument. So I think it is safe to conclude that the logical version of the principle has problems, seems totally unwarranted even if it can be formulated in such a way as to circumvent obvious counterexamples, and anyway could not be accepted with theological consistency by any traditional theist.

The other interpretation of the principle, one on which it is accepted by a substantial number of philosophers nowadays, is a physical interpretation: Given infinite space or time, anything physically possible will become actual. Again, it seems that there are plenty of cases in which it would be physically possible for me to sit at some time t and physically possible for me not to sit at t, so the principle would have to be qualified accordingly, unless a view of complete determinism is embraced. But I suspect that many who

---

[22] R. H. Kane, "Nature, Plenitude, and Sufficient Reason," *American Philosophical Quarterly*, 13 (January, 1976), 23–31.

hold the principle on this reading do accept its deterministic implications in unrestricted form.

The warrant for this interpretation of the principle is fairly simple to state. If to say that something is physically possible is to say or imply that, given relevant prior physical conditions and natural laws, it has a positive finite probability, however small, the truth of the principle arguably follows on one other assumption. For consider some event E understood in this way to be physically possible. Assign E a probability of 1/1 trillion. Given an infinite succession of times, or an infinite spatial continuum, containing unlimitedly many events, sufficiently many events will occur that if the probability assignment is right, E will come to obtain.

This argument itself would admit of a good deal of critical analysis and comment. But for our purposes, such a discussion would be useless. For even if the Principle of Plenitude is true on the physical interpretation, and we are justified in accepting it, suitably qualified, it is on this construal completely irrelevant to the case of God and unusable in the argument for the necessity of divine goodness. For, from the assumption that God is good only contingently, it follows only that it is *logically* possible, not that it is *physically* possible, that God do wrong. Physical possibility just has no relevant connection to our question about the modal status of divine goodness.

So we can conclude that, of the two basic interpretations of the Principle of Plenitude, the one that is necessary for the argument is wholly ungrounded, apparently false, and unusable for any traditional theist. The one which has something of any force that can be said in its behalf is, unfortunately, inapplicable to the argument. So once again we see the failure of an argument purporting to support the belief in the necessity of God's goodness.

4   *The Anselmian Appeal*

We have considered a number of arguments for and against the belief that God is necessarily good. I judge them all failures. I have no closure principle by which to establish that these are the only lines of deductive argument that might be used with any appearance of plausibility to assess this important religious belief. So I do not pretend to have established that no such argument for or against this belief can succeed. But I do think that at this point it can be reasonable to hold that no well-known argument has in fact settled the issue. And further, it also seems reasonable to conjecture that no such proof will be forthcoming. We are left then with an important question. Is the belief that God is necessarily good one which it is rational for any theist to hold? And, connected to this: If there is a ground on which the theist can reasonably affirm the necessity of divine goodness, what is it?

In section 2 while discussing the arguments of Guleserian, as well as in the previous chapter, I suggested that the traditional theist, especially of the Anselmian stripe, develops his conception of God from, among other sources, a set of intuitions. There is first of all the core intuition that God is a maximally perfect, or greatest possible, being. This is the religious intuition most central to the Anselmian. And then there are all the value intuitions about what properties are perfections which allow the Anselmian to begin to fill out this conception of deity. I would like to suggest that this may be an ultimate ground of the belief that God is necessarily good. It can be a function of traditional religious and value intuitions. It is intuitively held that the property of being good as an agent is a perfection. And it may be a further deliverance of the Anselmian's intuitions that being necessarily good as an agent is a perfection as well. Both properties can in this way be judged to be of the sort it is intrinsically better to have than to lack. I want to contend that a case can be made to show that the Anselmian can be reasonable in believing such deliverances of intuition to be reliable.

First I should do something to indicate, at least briefly, the variety of intuitions which may serve to ground the belief that God is necessarily good. I think that many religious people hold intuitively that God is as firmly entrenched in goodness, or alternately, that goodness is as firmly entrenched in God, as it is possible to be. Most who have this sort of intuition would go on to insist that it is not possible for God to do evil. It seems then that a further conviction

The Logic of God Incarnate

is held, presumably also intuitively, that it is possible that God be necessarily good as an agent. And of course the implication of these two views is that God's goodness is among his essential properties.

A slightly different grounding for the modal belief about God we are examining may arise from an application of an axiological principle once discussed by J. N. Findlay.[23] Findlay allows that theists with Anselmian inclinations may hold intuitively that goodness is a perfection, and thereby ascribe it to God. But then it is claimed that believers go on to hold that God is *necessarily* good only by applying to that intuitive starting point a principle which Findlay finds dubious. The principle as reported by Findlay is that if to have any property F is good, then to have F necessarily is better. If the belief that God is necessarily good were derived from an application of the principle as stated by Findlay, it would be on shaky ground. For that formulation is critically flawed. To see this, consider a property G, a property of performing freely some supererogatory good act. Surely, to exemplify G is good. But just as surely, it cannot be the case that to have G necessarily is better. For it is not even coherent to suppose that G could be exemplified necessarily by any individual who has it. So the principle as stated leads to incoherence. But of course it can be qualified to apply only to cases of properties capable of essential exemplification. And, so qualified, I can see nothing at all wrong with the principle. Findlay might find the restricted version dubious as well, and it surely is such that it can be doubted, but it seems to me not to be such that it is clearly more reasonable for just any rational person to doubt it than to accept it. In particular, if an Anselmian theist finds it intuitively plausible, I see no reason why he cannot be fully justified in applying it to his other relevant intuitions and thereby justifiably arriving at the view that God is necessarily good.

Each of the intuitive groundings just mentioned has involved a cluster of intuitions and an inference to the proposition that God is necessarily good. I think it is important to point out that it may be the case for many theists that the necessity of God's goodness is a direct deliverance of intuition, not merely inferred from, though

---

[23] See J. N. Findlay, "Can God's Existence Be Disproved?", *Mind*, 57 (1948), 176–183.

perhaps also supported by, the other sorts of intuitions just discussed. Rooting such a modal belief directly in intuition, however, may worry and even irritate many philosophers, goading them to question the epistemic status of any such moves as those I have just briefly surveyed. For even if there are such intuitions, the critic may say, they provide at best no more than prima facie and tentative support to the proposition believed. But further, it might be asked, why in the first place should we endow such otherwise unsupported proclivities to assert the necessity of divine goodness with the honorific title of "intuitions," allowing them to count as even prima facie warrant, however slight, for the claim?

First, the least difficult point. All apparent deliverances of intuition may be defeasible. What is held intuitively as true at one time may at a later time be rejected as false because of some countervailing argument whose soundness appears even more obvious. In this sense, it may be agreed that the warrant provided by intuition is only prima facie. Intuitively held beliefs must withstand the fire of criticism. But after examining the arguments which can be given against the necessity of God's goodness, I think it is safe to say that the prima facie support any intuitions may have provided this belief need not be judged defeated. Further, I do not think that to agree that the defeasibility of intuitive support renders that support prima facie is to concede that there is any likelihood that as a matter of fact it will be defeated, rendering it tentative at best. So the claim of intuitive support for the belief that God is necessarily good as an agent should not be thought of as a minimalist claim with little epistemic significance.

But why ascribe it any such support at all? First, I should say something about intuitions in general. Roughly, I think of a belief as intuitively held if it is held just because it strikes one as true, and not because of any inferential relations it might stand in to other beliefs. An intuitive belief is something like a basic belief or a natural belief. Accordingly, an appeal to intuitions to justify a belief is an acknowledgment that the proposition believed strikes one naturally as being true.

Saul Kripke once responded to philosophers who depreciate appeals to intuition by countering that he takes it to be "very heavy evidence in favor of anything," going on to say that he does not know "what more conclusive evidence one can have about anything, ultimately speaking."[24] I have to admit to not being quite so sanguine about this apparent noetic faculty. In fact, I think we have to distinguish carefully between sorts of intuitions we are justified in taking to be reliable and sorts of intuitions we have no good reason to trust. To put it bluntly, I suspect that we may have no good reason to trust many intuitions about relatively abstruse metaphysical matters. Unfortunately, it is often in disputes about such matters that we find intuition prominently appealed to. As I indicated earlier, I think it is our successful activity as speakers and thinkers which grounds our logical and linguistic intuitions. There are things about our lives which give us some reason to think that our intuitions about such matters as these deserve a strong measure of trust. But what in the world could account for many alleged intuitions on most matters of metaphysical esoterica, I have no idea.

Against this backdrop of general doubt about the status of many metaphysical intuitions, however, I believe the Anselmian theist to be justified in marking out at least a few intuitions about metaphysical matters as trustworthy. Included among these will be intuitions relevant to the existence and basic nature of God. For the Anselmian's intuitions about God, or more broadly, all those intuitions which together yield the Anselmian conception of God, generate without intentional contrivance an overall belief-set in which it makes sense that there should be such intuitions and that they should be, at least a core of them, reliable.[25] For if an Anselmian God exists and creates rational beings whose end is to know him, it makes good sense that they should be able to come to know something of his existence and attributes without the need of highly technical arguments, accessible to only a few. It makes sense that there be reliable intuitions such as those which yield the Anselmian conception of God. So, it is my suggestion that within a framework which they themselves contribute to providing, the Anselmian intuitions on which the doctrine of necessary goodness rests can be

[24]Saul Kripke, "Naming and Necessity," in *Semantics of Natural Language*, ed. Donald Davidson and Gilbert Harman, 2d ed. (Dordrecht: D. Reidel, 1972), p. 266 (Lecture One).
[25]Guleserian's meta-modal intuition, which conflicts with those of the theist, is backed up by no such grounding framework.

judged rationally to have a firm grounding as at least prima-facie reliable indicators of religious truth.

I am not making the empirical claim that all theists intuit that God must be necessarily good. For of course, not all even believe this. But it does seem typically to be the case that theists fail to hold this belief only if they either never have reflected on such modal matters at all or else have become convinced by apparently plausible arguments such as those discussed in section 2 that God's goodness cannot be among his essential properties. In cases such as the latter, it may be that they have had initial intuitions, which then have been thought to be defeated by contrary considerations. So there are ready explanations as to why some otherwise traditional theists do not hold the belief in question. After all, whatever intuition is, it is such that it must be brought into play by contact with the appropriate context, and when it is, or at least appears to be brought into play, its apparent deliverances are not incorrigible or indefeasible. In addition, the Anselmian can even have plausible explanations distinct from these to account for the lack of general acknowledgment of such intuitions in the population at large. By these means, the argument that if an Anselmian God exists, we might expect to find such intuitions among his rational creatures need not founder on any empirical data, or allow from such data the simple construction of an argument actually disconfirming theism.

A point which will bear repeating is that it is not the case that on this view of Anselmian intuitions the Anselmian will have an incorrigible, priviledged access to truth in the form of intuition, whose apparent deliverances he would always be justified in accepting uncritically. Nothing of the sort follows from what I have suggested at all. In fact, as I indicated in the previous chapter, the apparent deliverances of intuition concerning the nature of God need to be checked by a number of a posteriori controls derived from general experience, religious experience, the data of purported revelation, and critical argument.

So with respect to the Anselmian belief that God is necessarily good, I think the following can be said: Traditional theists who hold this belief intuitively, or infer it from more general beliefs or principles they hold intuitively, can be justified in taking such intuitions to be reliable and in maintaining that there exist no de-

135

featers of those intuitions. Even without the sort of deductive support from other theistic beliefs which many philosophers have sought, I think a theist can be justified fully in holding to the high modal status of God's goodness, both as a fact about any individual who is God and as an element in his concept of God. And what is important for our purpose here is that this is a commitment which can generate a very interesting problem for the doctrine of the Incarnation, which we now need to explore.

6 *Tempting God*

The Apostle James tells us that God cannot be tempted to do evil. Christian orthodoxy proclaims that Jesus was and is God. And yet the Gospels of Matthew and Luke, as well as the Letter to the Hebrews, state that Jesus was tempted.[1] Clearly, we have in this cluster of assertions a problem for the consistency of traditional Christian beliefs.

As we have seen in the previous chapter, it can be held as a tenet of classical theism that God is necessarily good, such that it is impossible in a broadly logical sense that he do evil. In addition, it seems to be a conceptual truth that, in some sense, temptation requires the possibility of doing evil. Thus, that of which James assures us has seemed to many theistic philosophers to be entailed by two necessary truths and therefore to be itself an unimpeachable pronouncement. Furthermore, it is a vital part of Christian faith, a significant component of almost any Christian soteriology, to hold that Jesus suffered real temptation without yielding himself to sin. In order that his life be a relevant exemplar and encouragement for ours, most theologians have agreed that Jesus must have undergone every fundamental sort of human struggle compatible with his being in fact sinless, including the experience of being tempted to do evil. How can these Christian convictions be consistent with

[1] James 1:13; Matthew 4:1–11; Luke 4:1–13; Hebrews 2:18. The statement in Hebrews occurs just a chapter after it has been declared that Jesus shares the full nature of God.

the doctrine of the Incarnation, specifically with the ascription of deity to Jesus? In this chapter, I hope to answer this serious and quite difficult question for Christian theology.

1   *The Martin Argument*

A related problem was once posed for Christian theology by C. B. Martin in his book *Religious Belief*. Concerning the ascription of deity to Christ, he wrote:

> Theologians admit freely enough that if the goodness of Christ is in doubt then his divinity must be in doubt, and, of course, if the goodness of Christ is denied then it must also be denied that he is God. However, they think there is nothing contradictory remaining if the goodness of Christ is asserted without qualification and he is called God, the Perfect Good. I have been at pains to point out that a contradiction of an irresoluble sort remains still. The contradiction is: Christ can be conceived to have been other (that is, not good) than he was, yet as God it would be not just false but *inconceivable* that he should have been not good.[2]

Martin's argument here seems to be that the propositions

    1   Christ is God   ⟩ Pledication, Not An Identity statement

and

    2   It is not conceivable that God not be good

together entail

    3   It is not conceivable that Christ not be good

which is logically inconsistent with what he apparently takes to be the obvious truth that

    4   It is conceivable that Christ not be good.

If 4 is indeed an obvious truth, then we must reject 3 as false. But since 1 and 2 entail 3, they cannot both be true unless 3 is. The falsehood of 3 is thus transmitted to their conjunction. At least one

[2]C. B. Martin, *Religious Belief* (Ithaca: Cornell University Press, 1959), p. 40.

of them must be false as well. It can be argued that 2 is a firm and central commitment of the Anselmian theist and of most traditional theists. And so it seems that any such theist would, on the basis of this, have to reject 1, the ascription of deity to Christ.

What can be said for the truth of 2? First, it should be pointed out that the sentence used to express 2 can be taken in at least two different ways. It can be taken to express the conceptual requirement that no individual can be counted as God unless he is good. This is of course like the conceptual requirement that no individual can be counted as a bachelor unless he is unmarried. On this reading, 2 is true just in case the concept of God is understood in such a way as to involve a necessary, a priori connection between goodness and deity, and thus to support analytic truths about divine goodness. Most traditional theists would endorse 2 in this purely *de dicto* sense. For on this reading, 2 does not express the inconceivability of any individual's not being good; it merely expresses the inconceivability of an individual's being God while not being good.

On a second possible reading of 2, it does not merely express a conceptual requirement, but ascribes a property to an individual. It says of some individual, God, that it is inconceivable that *he* not be good. Let us say that this reading of 2 arises out of treating 'God' in a purely referential manner, using it like a proper name just to designate a particular individual. If the Martin argument is to be a successful one, 'God' must be treated semantically in the same way in 1 and 2. But then, on this reading, 1 would be an identity statement, which it is not. If 1 is treated like a predication, 2 must be given the purely *de dicto* reading. But then if 'Christ' is just another name for 'Jesus,' which Martin clearly intends it to be, 3 does not follow from 1 and 2. All that follows is something like

    3′   Christ is good.

And the contradictory of 3′,

    4′   Christ is not good,

is of course, unlike what Martin claims of 4, not an obvious truth at all. Thus, theists committed to 1 as a predication and 2 as a purely *de dicto* truth are not therein committed to anything inconsistent with an obvious truth.

But we can reconstruct the argument Martin presumably had in mind, altering it in a couple of important ways, in accordance with the last chapter, to give it the sort of force he intended it to have. Christian theists of the Anselmian stripe hold it to be true both that

(1a) Jesus is God the Son

and that

(2a) No individual is God unless he is necessarily good.

Given the orthodox trinitarian commitment that

(3a) God the Son is God

it follows that

(4a) God the Son is necessarily good.

But then from (1a), (4a), and the principle of the indiscernibility of identicals, it follows that

(5a) Jesus is necessarily good.

And of course, (5a) entails

(6a) It is impossible that Jesus sin.

But (6a), Martin could argue, is the logical contradictory of an obvious truth,

(7a) It is possible that Jesus sin.

So given the truth of (7a), we can conclude that Christian theists are committed to a set of fundamental theological views not all of which are true. And of course, given the importance of (2a) to many theists, this can be taken as an argument against (1a), the incarnational identity claim.

William L. Rowe has raised an objection to this sort of argument which we need to consider for a moment.[3] Theists are committed

[3]William L. Rowe, "C. B. Martin's Contradiction in Theology," *Australasian Journal of Philosophy*, 40 (May, 1962), 75–79.

to something inconsistent with (7a) only if they are committed to (6a). The argument just given presents (6a) as an entailment of a proposition, (5a), which is produced by a simple application of the indiscernibility principle to (1a) and (4a). Rowe's objection appears to be that indiscernibility does not hold with respect to modal properties. He gives as an example of this failure of indiscernibility:

(a) The number of planets = 9   *not identity but predication*

(b) It is possible that the number of planets is less than 7; thus

(c) It is possible that 9 is less than 7.

Rowe says that (a) is a true identity, that (b) is the ascription of a modal property to one term of the identity, and that (c) is the result of applying the indiscernibility principle to (a) and (b). His claim is that this argument leads from two truths to a falsehood, and so is not an instance of a valid argument form. And of course, since this is the form of the transformed Martin argument, if Rowe is right, theologians have nothing here to worry about.

But unfortunately, Rowe's example will not work. Proposition (a) is an identity statement rather than a predication only if 'The number of planets' is taken in a purely referential way to designate rigidly the number 9. But if 'the number of planets' is used in the same way in (b), (b) is false, for the same reason that (c) is. We thus have a falsehood entailed by a truth conjoined with a falsehood. To get what Rowe wants, a falsehood produced from two truths, the phrase 'the number of planets' would have to be used differently in (b) from the way it is used in (a). But then we would have a clear case of the fallacy of equivocation, and nothing which can be blamed on the application of indiscernibility to modal properties.[4] No such argument can show this sort of application of indiscernibility to be in any way illegitimate. So on this point, the Martin argument stands.

Martin himself actually accuses Christian theologians not just of holding at least one false view as one of their central tenets, but even of holding contradictory views. This will be true only if (7a), the proposition expressing the possibility of Jesus' sinning, is itself

[4]For more on this, see *Understanding Identity Statements* (Aberdeen: Aberdeen University Press, 1984), chap. 6, pp. 90–92.

a theological commitment, regardless of whether it is an obvious truth. By seeing how Christian theologians can turn back this charge of holding contradictory beliefs, we shall see how they can also block the charge of holding at least one false proposition among their central beliefs.

On what grounds could (7a) be thought a theological commitment? Well, theologians are committed to believing Jesus to have been fully human. If being such that it is possible for one to sin is a property essential to being fully human, then the theological belief that Jesus was and is fully human will entail (7a), and the theological belief-set including this as well as (1a)–(6a) will contain a contradiction. However, the strategy used against A. D. Smith in chapter 3, with its simple distinction between common and essential human properties, can be brought to bear here. The Christian theologian can, in all epistemic propriety, just deny that being such that one possibly sins is a property essential to being fully human. It may be a property which, apart from the case of Jesus, is universal to human beings, but it is not part of the kind-essence of humanity.

But applied in this case, our distinction between commonality and kind-essentiality may seem to have shockingly counterintuitive results. For many theists hold a libertarian conception of moral freedom, a conception according to which the property of being such that one possibly sins is necessary for being a moral agent. And surely, it might be insisted, human beings are essentially moral agents.

merely human
vs
fully human

Here we can employ the second distinction of chapter 3, that between a property's counting as essential for being fully human and one's counting as essential for being merely human. It can be held that being such that one possibly sins is a property essential only to being merely human, to belonging to the kind of humanity *and* to no higher kind. On this view, Jesus need not be such that he possibly sins, since he is not, on the traditional view, merely human. Or it could be held that it is just part of the individual-essence of any created rational being who exemplifies it to have the property of possibly sinning. In either of these ways, an orthodox theologian can accommodate an essentiality intuition with respect to the relation between this property and ordinary human beings without counting it as a component of the kind-essence of humanity.

Some care must be exercised, however, in ascribing these modalized properties of moral agency to human beings in any such way. For consider both ends of human existence, as seen by orthodox Christian thought—the fetal stage and the beatific vision. Is a fetus such that he possibly sins? Certainly the answer is: only with respect to his future development. But of course many Christians hold that even within its present uterine stage of life, a fetus already is a human being. If he is ontologically like the rest of us, he is already a merely human being. Is it necessary that in order to have this status he exemplify at least the property of possibly sinning sometime in the future? Is *this* a property essential for being merely human, or a property which otherwise enters into his individual-essence? Well, consider the blessed in heaven. On one standard theistic view, they have attained to—or, better, have been granted—impeccability. It is, within the context of their eternally future existence, their infinitely extensive beatitude in the presence of God, impossible for them to sin. So they, while presumably still remaining merely human, although in glorified form, lack the possibility of sinning sometime in the future. Thus, having this property cannot be essential either for being merely human or for retaining their own identities. But presumably the blessed in heaven are such as to possibly have sinned in the past. So perhaps the property of possibly sinning *at some time* is among their essential properties in one way or the other. If so, then it will be an essential property for any mere human that he be such that he possibly sins at some time during his existence. On such a view, every human being who is not also divine must possibly be a moral agent in the libertarian sense at some time during his existence, but neither at all times nor even at most.

Although these distinctions will be important to some theists, they will not be important to all. For some will hold that every mere human is essentially free to sin at every time during his consciously mature existence, and that every such individual who eternally communes with God will forever freely refrain from exercising that possibility of sinning at each and every moment through his beatific

The Logic of God Incarnate

afterlife. What is important here for our purposes is the main point, that the property of being such that one possibly sins need not be held by the Christian theologian to be a property essential for being fully human. There are other equally legitimate ways of characterizing its status with respect to human beings.

At this point, a potential worry should be addressed, however briefly, before we go on. Is the concept of human nature endlessly malleable? Can just anything which would seem to preclude a divine incarnation be dropped as a kind-essential human property? How far can the orthodox theologian exploit the open texture of our conception of human nature without evacuating it of content altogether? After all that we have ruled out as not being kind-essential properties of human nature and relegated to the status of modal requisites for individuals who are merely human, is there any substantial content remaining to the concept of being fully human? Or is the humanity of Jesus, on this strategy, ultimately either evacuated of any content or else swallowed up, so to speak, by his divinity?

It is exceedingly difficult to say exactly what properties are kind-essential for human nature. One mentioned earlier in the book is the property of possibly being conscious at some time. But surely this is also a property kind-essential for divinity. If the strategy for defending the doctrine of the Incarnation I am deploying allowed only the identification of properties such as this as properties kind-essential for being human—properties which are also kind-essential for being divine—then it would be difficult for me to justify my claim that it is the traditional two-natures view of the Incarnation which I in fact am defending. The resultant view could look more like a one-nature alternative to orthodoxy in the end. Moreover, this appearance could be exacerbated by something like the following reasoning: I understand the humanity of Jesus to encompass within itself a finite degree of power, a finite degree of knowledge, and so forth. But if his divinity encompasses *all* power and *all* knowledge, doesn't this include all finite degrees of power and knowledge, and so doesn't his deity in effect swallow up his humanity, resulting in the heretical alternative of monophysitism, a one-nature view, instead of the Chalcedonian two-natures view?

144

Fortunately, the defense I am constructing does allow the identification of kind-essential human properties which are *distinctively* human, and not also kind-essential for divinity. Consider, for example, the property of having a body at some past or present time during one's existence of the genetic type or basic structure of present human bodies. This is a very plausible candidate for just such a kind-essential human property. Again, another plausible suggestion would be the property of having, at some time in one's career, a certain sort of consciousness, a certain sort of experiential field and mental structure such as the sort we find ourselves to have. These are admittedly vague characterizations, but this should be no surprise. For most kind-essential human properties will be knowable only a posteriori and even now wait upon an advanced science, for example, an advanced neuroscience and cognitive science, for their precise, determinate specification. But vague as our characterizations of some of the elements of human nature might be at this point, it is certainly not the case that an incarnational anthropology—an account of human nature partially controlled by a doctrine of divine incarnation—removes from the idea of human nature all determinate content whatsoever or else results in a view on which two distinct natures can no longer be distinguished in Christ. If God the Son had never taken on either a human body or a human range of consciousness, he would not have exemplified human nature. That we know.

The Martin argument exposes a contradiction within the tenets of Christian theology only if it can be shown that theologians are committed to (7a), the proposition that it is at least possible that Jesus sin. I suggested that one way this might be attempted would be to argue that from the ascription of human nature to Jesus it follows that he is possibly sinful. But we have seen how this argument can be blocked with our simple distinctions between common and kind-essential human properties and between being merely human and being fully human. However, another path is open for the Martin argument. Recall the opening paragraphs of this chapter. In so far as they are committed to biblical affirmations concerning Jesus, Christian theologians are committed to the claim that Jesus was tempted to do evil. And if temptation requires the

The proposition that Jesus could sin can be blocked by:

i) distinction between common & kind-essential human properties

ii) merely human vs fully human

But, Jesus was tempted

possibility of sinning, as it certainly does seem to, then it is hard to see how any such theologian could claim rationally and consistently not to accept the truth of (7a). But then the conclusion of the Martin argument will be secured: There does exist logical contradiction within a very central set of traditional Christian beliefs. However, this attempt to saddle the theologian with (7a) can be turned back as well. It will be especially interesting to see how.

[handwritten note: Idea: that Jesus was tempted, leaving open the possibility of sinning]

2   *Temptation and Possible Sin*

How could Jesus the Christ, Son of God, be tempted by sin if he was, even in his earthly career, necessarily good, *non posse peccare?* Some Christian theists are tempted to try to solve this problem merely by adverting to the two-natures model and the reduplicative form of proposition. They attempt to specify that *qua* God, or with respect to his divine nature, he was not able to sin, whereas *qua* man, or with respect to his human nature, he was able to sin, and thus able to be tempted. But could it have been that God the Son was necessarily good *qua* God while only contingently good *qua* man? I think it is fairly easy to see the impossibility of this.

If Jesus was contingently good, let us say that it was possible for him to commit adultery. But what is it to commit adultery? It is to have certain sorts of intentions toward, or to engage in certain forms of sexual behavior with, a person to whom one does not stand in the proper relation of personal commitment which alone would render such behavior morally permissible and appropriate. If the human body in which one is embodied engages in the prohibited form of behavior, and does so by a free intention to so behave, then one commits adultery. If it was possible for Jesus to commit adultery, it was possible for him to form certain intentions and engage in the sexual forms of behavior morally proscribed. Well, consider now any possible world, W, in which he does this. In W Jesus has the intentions and bodily behavior constituting adultery. But Jesus is God the Son, and is God the Son in W. Remember, on the standard view we are considering, any individual who is God exemplifies his deity essentially. In W, God the Son thus has the prohibited intentions in a range of his consciousness and is such that the human body he is embodied in engages in the prohibited behavior. But then, of course, in *W* God the Son commits adultery. So he is not in any sense necessarily good, contrary to our original hypothesis.

Why are theologians tempted to say that Christ is necessarily good *qua* God but only contingently good *qua* man? It seems to be because of the simple truth that it is in virtue of his divine nature that Christ is necessarily good, as necessary goodness is a requisite of deity, not in virtue of his human nature. This is clear. Nothing about human nature carries with it the entailment of necessary goodness. It is not required for being fully human that an individual be necessarily good. And nothing about the distinctive features of his humanity solely allows Christ's goodness to have this modal status. So it is not *qua* man that he is necessarily good. But of course it does not follow from this that *qua* man he is only contingently good. The consistent orthodox position here should be just that nothing follows from his human nature alone concerning the modal status of Christ's goodness.

How can it be the case that Jesus was necessarily good and yet was tempted to sin? We have said that it seems to be a conceptual truth that, in some sense, temptation requires the possibility of sinning. On reflection, we can see that it is the *epistemic* possibility of sinning rather than a broadly logical, or metaphysical, or even physical possibility that is conceptually linked to temptation. Jones can be tempted at *t* to go and lie to his department chairman, although, unknown to him, his chairman died an hour earlier, making it impossible for Jones or anyone else to go and lie to him at *t* or thereafter. Suppose again that a certain form of time-travel is impossible, but that Brown, a great scientist with eccentric ways who loves a practical joke, approaches Jones with an elaborate-looking apparatus about the size of a telephone booth which she tells Jones can effect that form of time travel, an invention of hers as yet unknown to the world-at-large or even to the scientific community. Jones, believing Brown, can be tempted to travel in the machine in order to commit some evil deed otherwise impossible. The reality of his temptation does not require the broadly logical, or metaphysical, possibility of what he considers doing. It requires only that the imagined deed not be an epistemic impossibility for him. He must think it possible, and within his power to do. It need not actually be so.

Epistemic possibility, unlike logical possibility, is a relative notion. What is epistemically possible for Jones need not be epistemically possible for Brown. But rather than indexing epistemic possibilities to persons it seems that we should index them to belief-sets. For a certain proposition P can represent an epistemic possibility for Jones at t, and then later at $t + 1$, when Jones has gathered more information, no longer be epistemically possible for him. We could accommodate this by indexing epistemic possibility to persons *and times*, but that course would be superficial and not get at the heart of the matter, for certainly the relevant difference between Jones-at-t and Jones-at-$t + 1$ is not the difference in times but a difference in Jones' beliefs at those two times. So it seems that we should index epistemic possibility to belief-sets. Very roughly, but sufficient for our purposes here, we can say that some proposition P is epistemically possible for some subject S at a time t just in case it is epistemically possible relative to a full accessible belief-set B of S at t, where that relation consists in something like the following: B neither contains nor self-evidently entails the denial of P, nor does B contain or self-evidently entail propositions which seem to S to show P to be either false or impossible. A full accessible belief-set of a person at a time consists in all and only those beliefs which are accessible to a range of conscious thought and deliberation of that person at that time sufficient to support the initiation of action. This is, roughly put, the general notion of epistemic possibility with respect to propositions. Its application to contemplated actions is straightforward.

Jesus could be tempted to sin just in case it was epistemically possible for him that he sin. If at the times of his reported temptations, the full accessible belief-set of his earthly mind did not rule out the possibility of his sinning, he could be genuinely tempted, in that range of consciousness, to sin. But this could be so only if that belief-set did not contain the information that he is necessarily good. In order that he suffer real temptation, then, it is not necessary that sinning be a broadly logical or metaphysical possibility for Jesus; it is only necessary that it be an epistemic possibility for him.

148

"In order that he suffer real temptation, it is not necessary that sinning be a broadly logical or metaphysical possibility for Jesus; it is only necessary that it be an epistemic possibility for him"

How could this be the case? During the times of temptation, the earthly mind of Christ could not partake of the riches of omniscience. He would need to lack knowledge of at least one truth—the truth that he is necessarily good, such that it is impossible that he sin. The kenotic claim about omniscience provides for this—during his earthly sojourn, God the Son took on the limited knowledge of a human being. But I have already presented the reasons I hesitate to endorse a kenotic christology: Primarily, it requires significantly altering the traditional conception of deity, or else recognizing the existence of at least one divine person who lacks the modal status and immutability thought to be proper to any such person on a modally exalted conception of deity. If we are willing to alter our conception of God enough, or else to give up these exalted modal claims for deity in order to allow for a coherent christology, this maneuver is possible. But I think we can preserve the precise, traditional version of the high modal claims about deity and, while avoiding kenoticism, still secure the epistemic possibility requisite for the temptations of Christ.

Recall the two-minds view developed in chapter 4. On this view, there existed in the case of God Incarnate two distinct ranges of consciousness, the omniscient divine mind proper to God the Son, and the distinct, nonomniscient earthly mind which developed by and large as any merely human mind would. On the two-minds view, it can be held that within the beliefs naturally accessible to his earthly consciousness, it was epistemically possible for Christ that he sin. From his earthly point of view, his sinning was not logically ruled out. Thus, in his earthly stream of consciousness, it was possible for Jesus to be tempted to sin. The information that he is necessarily good was not contained in his human range of thought. That allowed for his temptations.

On either a kenotic or a two-minds view, we can see that the theological belief that Jesus was tempted to sin does not entail a commitment to Martin's (7a), the proposition that it is possible in the broadly logical or metaphysical sense that Jesus sin. Thus, it seems, Martin cannot make good his charge that theologians are committed to a contradictory set of beliefs. But what of the claim that in light of the obvious truth of (7a), of the possibility that Jesus sin, it is clear that at least one central theological affirmation is

The Logic of God Incarnate

false? That, of course, is at this point also quite simple to refute. The very distinctions drawn upon to show that it is not a theological commitment that Jesus was possibly sinful show just as well that it is in no way obvious that he had this property at all.

But what of conceivability? Surely, returning to the original Martin argument, we could worry that it is at least conceivable that Jesus sin; whereas it is not conceivable that any divine being sin. How then can he be identical with some divine being? The answer to this question is also simple. We can conceive of Jesus as sinning only if we leave out of our conception of him the information that he was necessarily good. And just as easily, if we leave out of our conception of any divine being the information that necessary goodness is a requisite of deity, we can conceive of a divine being as sinning. There is nothing about his humanity inconsistent with the proposition that Jesus was necessarily good. So a conception of Christ just as consistently can contain such information as can a conception of deity. Martin's original argument is thus at least as flawed as its reconstruction.

If we hold that Jesus was necessarily good, then does that mean that we must devalue his resisting of temptation? Can he be held responsible as a man for what he did? Was his choosing rightly a free act of his? Well, it must be admitted from the outset that he could not have chosen otherwise. His divine nature would have prevented it. But I think that, in order to avoid the heresy of monotheletism condemned at the Third Council of Constantinople—the view that every act of Christ was divinely accomplished, done in virtue only of his divinity, and never a properly human act—orthodox theologians must hold that the divinity of Christ, the modal properties which were his in virtue of being divine, played no actual causal role in his rightly resisting temptation. The decision arrived at in his earthly consciousness not to sin was not causally imposed on him by his divine nature. And in the sense of being both intentional and bereft of any such causal determination, it was free.

Consider some familiar sorts of story. Story 1: Dr. Delusion, a famous hypnotist, hypnotizes Jones, telling him that after he is awakened from his trance, he will walk into a certain room, close

This seems evasive

the door, stay for exactly two hours, and then leave. In his post-hypnotic state Jones does exactly that, all the while rationalizing his behavior with "decisions" to go into that room for a certain reason, to stay just the prescribed length of time, and then to leave. We can suppose that there is a sense, a physical or psychological sense, in which it was impossible that he do otherwise or even decide to do otherwise than as he had been hypnotized to do. In such circumstances, Jones is certainly not free with respect to the behavior in question. The salient feature of this story is that the very thing that prevented Jones's doing otherwise than as he did—his posthypnotic state—was in fact causally responsible for his doing what he did. There is thus no sense in which he did it freely.

Story 2: Jones enters the room, closing behind him the door which, unknown to him, locks with a two-hour time-lock. He finds various reasons to stay in the room, considers leaving once or twice during the two hours, but each time decides to stay a while longer. Right at the two-hour mark he decides to leave, turns the door knob, opens it, now just unlocked, and leaves. Did he stay freely those two hours? Unlike story 1, this situation can call forth intuitions that differ quite a bit. Jones could not have done otherwise then stay the two hours, since the door was locked. But his staying in the room as a matter of fact resulted from his deciding to stay. Although he could not have done otherwise than stay, the story allows that he could have done otherwise than decide to stay. The salient feature of this story is that the thing which is identified as having prevented Jones's leaving—the lock on the door—did not play any causal role in his doing as he in fact did.

Story 3: Jones has entered the room freely. Unknown to him, electrodes have been implanted in his brain which upon activation will prevent his deciding, or attempting, to leave the room before the two-hour mark. They are activated only by neural events which are, let us suppose, the immediate and otherwise guaranteed precursors of a decision or intentional attempt to leave during that time. The action of the electrodes is to prevent any such decision or behavior. As a matter of fact, Jones considers possible reasons to leave a couple of times during the two hours, but on each occasion decides to stay, not even coming anywhere near to a decision to

151

leave. The electrodes are thus never activated. After the lapse of the full two hours, he does decide to leave and does so unimpeded. Did he stay in the room freely during those two hours?

This is the sort of story told by Harry Frankfurt in his rightly well known paper "Alternate Possibilities and Moral Responsibility,"[5] The point of such a story for Frankfurt was to attempt to show that performing an act A in such a way as to be free and morally responsible in one's performing of it does not require that one be such that it was possible to refrain from doing A. In this third story, like the first, Jones could not have done otherwise than he did, nor could he have even decided otherwise than he decided. But this story is like the second in that the thing which prevented him from doing other than he did—the implanted electrodes—did not play any causal role in his actual doing as he did. He could not possibly have done otherwise, but nothing apart from his own decisions as a matter of fact brought it about that he did as he did. We can suppose that he stayed in the room because he wanted to. And nothing forced that desire upon him.

Unlike in the story of Dr. Delusion, we do not have here a case of a man whose acts are really not his own, the equivalent of a puppet. Frankfurt insists that in this sort of story Jones exemplifies full moral freedom and responsibility in spite of the impossibility of his having done or even decided otherwise. If circumstances had been such that staying in the room was a good thing to do and leaving during the two hours bad, we could properly praise or morally commend Jones for staying. However, if during that time we knew the electrodes to have been activated, praise or commendation would be inappropriate. Since this was not the case, Jones can be said to have stayed freely.

Perhaps we can understand the temptations of Jesus in a somewhat parallel way. Perhaps his divine property of being necessarily good, although it rendered impossible his having decided or having done otherwise than he did with respect to resisting temptation, as a matter of fact played no causal role in his doing as he did. Like Jones's unactivated electrodes, it did not act to force on him what

[5] Harry Frankfurt, "Alternate Possibilities and Moral Responsibility," *Journal of Philosophy*, 66 (1969), 829–839.

he did. He did it freely. As Jones was unaware of the electrodes in story 3, Jesus was unaware in his earthly consciousness that he was necessarily good, unable to sin. Within the deliberation of that earthly mind, he freely, of his own accord, decided not to succumb to temptation. It was a choice for which, as a matter of fact, he was fully responsible. By making such claims, I think, the orthodox theologian avoids altogether the lurking problem of monotheletism.

The Apostle James said that God cannot be tempted. And he cannot be, *qua* God. He cannot be, except in so far as he is incarnate in a created nature with a created, finite, consciousness. Only under those conditions is it possible to tempt God.

---

3   *One Person with Two Minds*

The temptation problem for the doctrine of the Incarnation is solved in case God Incarnate can be held to have had a consciousness or mind lacking omniscience, in particular the knowledge that he was necessarily good, during that span of existence in which he is believed to have undergone and resisted temptation to sin. On the kenotic model, he lacked omniscience and this particular knowledge, *simpliciter* throughout this time. On the two-minds view, he lacked it *in his human consciousness*, but not in his divine consciousness. And this, if the two-minds view is coherent, seems sufficient for his being tempted *as a man*, and as such overcoming temptation. Either view will supply what is needed here—a mind or range of consciousness devoid of certain information. But each view may appear problematic. In addition to the weaker modalities or other conceptual alterations it necessitates for our concept of God, the kenotic view may be thought to have a problem concerning the diachronic identity of God the Son. But perhaps this can be easily overcome by a sufficiently careful tailoring of modal claims concerning that divine person. What may not appear so easy to solve is an apparent problem of synchronic identity the two-minds view faces. How can one and the same person have at the same time two distinct ranges of consciousness, each, on the solution to the

Nestorian heresy : does th 2 minds view suggest 2 persons (vs Chalcedon view [person, 2 natures])?

The Logic of God Incarnate

temptation problem, apparently capable of supporting the initiation of action at least somewhat independently of the other?

If we have in the case of God Incarnate a human mind and a divine mind, how can we avoid the Nestorian conclusion that we have here two persons, one human, the other divine? On the two-minds view, must we conclude ultimately that we are dealing with a composite Christ somehow constituted by two distinct ultimate bearers of properties? If it were committed to this sort of conclusion, the two-minds view would be just a form of heresy condemned at the Council of Ephesus (A.D. 431), and thus could not be used as an explication of orthodoxy.

By the time of Aquinas, a version of the composite view deriving from Abelard had been developed which attempted to avoid heresy. The ancient heretical view had it that in Christ there were two *supposita* (bearers of properties) and thus two persons. The view derived from Abelard tried to affirm the unity of the person of Christ while at the same time placing behind that single person two distinct *supposita* or *hypostases*. By looking for a moment at the way in which Aquinas criticized this attempt at a compromise view which would secure composition while avoiding the two-person heresy, and by seeing a bit of the alternative modeling of Christ he offered in its place, we can come to see how a two-minds view can avoid the heretical implication of Nestorianism.

On the basis of the accepted concept of a person laid down by Boethius—'an individual substance in rational nature'—Aquinas simply dismissed the attempt at a compromise view as inconsistent.[6] The theory held that in Christ there was one *hypostasis*, or individual substance "in" human nature (the bearer of human properties, the subject of human predicates), a second *hypostasis* in divine nature, and a single person in which the union of human and divine natures took place. Aquinas argued simply that if for Christ's human nature there is a *hypostasis*, then, according to the Boethian conception, in Christ there is a human person. And likewise, if for Christ's divine nature there is a separate *hypostasis*, then in Christ there is a separate divine person. Consequently, to maintain both that there are two

---

[6]*Summa Theologia* III. Q.2, A.3 (*S.T.*)

hypostases or *supposita* in Christ, to each of which is joined one of his rational natures, and that there is only one person in Christ, is to hold an inconsistent set of propositions.

In the course of rejecting this theory, Aquinas made it clear that no account of Christ is acceptable to Christian faith which does not allow both human properties and divine properties to apply to one and the same person, and hence to one and the same individual substance, in Christ. It was not merely a human being who underwent the human sufferings Christ experienced, but the very divine Son of God himself. So Aquinas' view was fully in line with conciliar orthodoxy: In the Incarnation, one of the three persons of the Divine Trinity, a divine *hypostasis* in divine nature, became a man by taking on human nature as well. His view was the traditional one that in Christ there was one individual substance in two natures, the unity of his person consisting in the unity of his *suppositum*. Now, as we have seen, it can be said that a nature is something like a set of properties any instance of the joint instantiation of which we consider an individual of that nature, or in the terminology accepted by Aquinas, an individual substance "in" that nature. For example, human nature is that set of properties any joint instantiation of which we consider to be a human being, or human person. In the case of human nature, we have noted that the properties of that set seem to include both physical and "nonphysical" (mental, spiritual, psychological) attributes, the having (at some time) of a body as well as a "rational soul." Of course, as we have seen, not all physical and nonphysical properties exemplified by human beings are members of that set of properties. Only those considered to constitute the essence of what it is to be human, for example the having at some time or other of a certain kind of physical body and a certain kind of soul, make up human nature. Any others are classed as merely accidental human properties.

Aquinas was aware that a particular problem could be felt to attend his view of Christ. On the account just given of human nature, it would seem that wherever there is a complete instantiation of the set of properties constitutive of human nature, there is

[7] *S.T.* III. Q. I, A.1.

a human person; more simply, wherever there is a human body and a human soul, there is a human person.[8] Aquinas acknowledged that in Christ there was a human body and a human soul.[9] So, the argument would go, he must accept the existence of a human person in Christ. And if he continued to hold that there is a divine person in Christ, he would have to admit the presence in him of two persons.

In response to this argument, Aquinas offered an interesting line of reasoning, which can be most fully appreciated by looking at a passage in his *Compendium of Theology*.[10] In the chapter entitled "One Suppositum and One Person in Christ," he makes his first move by suggesting to the reader that reflection on the names 'person', '*hypostasis*', and '*suppositum*' will show that they refer to "a whole of a certain kind." A hand is not considered in itself a *suppositum* or a person, because it is merely a part of the kind of whole which is considered to be such. The implication is that nothing, in so far as it is a part rather than a whole, qualifies as a *suppositum*, *hypostasis*, or person. Aquinas goes on to suggest that there are cases in which a combination of ingredients in one context will constitute a whole, and thus individuate a *suppositum*, but in another context will constitute only a part of a larger whole and therein will not alone individuate a *suppositum*. The cases he gives are these: In a stone, the combination of physical elements ("the four elements") constitutes an integral whole, and thus the object characterized by these elements as properties can be called a *suppositum*. In an animal, however, the combination of physical elements is merely a part of a larger whole including also what we might call attributes of animation, or, more simply, a soul. In the case of an animal, a single *suppositum* is individuated only by the instantiation of both kinds of properties, physical and animate. The physical elements alone do not characterize their own *suppositum*, numerically distinct from the *suppositum* characterized by all the elements together. Aquinas

---

[8] And, on the accepted account of a person, where there is a human person, there is a created *suppositum*.

[9] *S.T.* III. Q.2, A.5.

[10] *Compendium Theologia*, trans. Cyril Vollert (London: B. Herder, 1947), chap. 211, pp. 231–235. See also *S.T.* III. Q.2, A.5.

quickly adds that it is not that the physical elements are thereby less "effectual" in an animal than in a stone; on the contrary, he says, they are more effectual and are given more dignity by their union with a soul into a greater whole.

In the case of a man, Aquinas continues, the union of a human body with a human soul is indeed ordinarily sufficient to individuate a single substance or *suppositum* and thereby to constitute an individual human person. But the case of Christ is unique. In Christ the human body and soul were not an independent whole, but were joined to the divine person of God the Son, as the human nature in which the divine *suppositum* dwelt. Not being an independent whole, but only a part of that greater whole which was God Incarnate, they did not alone constitute a person or characterize a *suppositum* distinct from that single person who was the Christ, or from that single eternal *suppositum* dwelling in both divine and human natures. Hence, to admit that in Christ there was a human body and a human soul is not thereby to admit that in Christ there was a human person distinct from the divine person God the Son. Consequently, taking seriously both the true humanity and the true divinity of Christ does not commit one to a double person, or double *suppositum*, view of Christ. Such was Aquinas' argument.

The relevance of his reasoning to our problem is straightforward. Ordinarily, minds and persons are individuated in a one-one correlation. Indeed, it may be impossible for any merely human being to have more than one mind, or range of consciousness of the sort we are considering, at the same time. The existence of a human mind in a merely human person may preclude the exemplification by that person of any other mind, or range of consciousness of the appropriate sort at the same time. So among mere humans, the individuation of two minds at any one time will suffice for the identification of two persons. But this leaves open the possibility that outside that context, there is no such one-one correlation. When a human body and soul, to use Aquinas' terms, are a part of a larger whole—which on the two-minds view they are in the case of Jesus—they alone do not suffice to individuate a person not possibly having as well some other distinct sort of mind at the same time. Only together with the divine mind eternally exemplified by God the Son, do they individuate a person who is both human and divine, having thus two minds or ranges of consciousness simultaneously.

Let us attempt here a rough thought experiment, developing somewhat an analogy hinted at earlier. Imagine the work in artificial intelligence (AI) to be extremely advanced and very successful. Suppose there is developed a system, call it S_1, which through the hardware in which it is housed, picks up light waves, sound waves, etc., as information from its environment much as a human being would. It can, in effect, see and hear. Suppose that on the basis of the information it collects and its in-built program, it can interact with its environment just as a human being would. It passes the Turing Test with flying colors. On the basis of its behavior, we have no reason not to ascribe to it intentional actions. If anyone has a mind, we might say, S_1 does. That is to say, everything which justifies us in ascribing mindedness to the human bodies around us justifies us to the same degree (let us suppose) in thinking mindedness to be embodied in the hardware of S_1. Suppose now that there is another system, a master system M, embodied in different hardware, which has full, direct, and immediate access to all the information obtained through the sensors of S_1, and a great deal of other information as well. It too passes the Turing Test through interactions with us mediated through its own hardware. It seems to me easy to imagine S_1 engaging in behavior it would not engage in if it had all the information of M, so that in ascribing mindedness to both S_1 and M we would be justified in thinking of two minds, one of S_1 and one proper to M. Yet we can imagine the relation of S_1 to M to be such that we are justified in ascribing to these two minds a unity parallel to the one alleged to hold between a human and a divine mind in Christ—a unity we there want to conceptualize as that of a single person having the two distinct ranges of consciousness, or two minds.

An analogy such as this, however, can appear to raise a serious problem for the two-minds view. In the AI story, it can look as if full and direct access to the information of S_1 is meant to be sufficient for M standing in the relation to S_1 of having as one of its own minds the mind of S_1. But on any traditional view of deity, doesn't a divine being have full and direct access to every created mind? Surely, theists do typically hold that divine omniscience encompasses perfect knowledge of our innermost thoughts. But then it looks as though every human mind stands in just that asymmetric accessing relation to the divine mind of God the Son that is claimed for the earthly mind of Jesus. Will it now follow then that if Jesus is God Incarnate, so is each of us? And certainly, such an implication of the two-minds view, however fondly it might be embraced by Hegelians, would be totally unacceptable to orthodoxy.

I think we can come to see that this is an implication the two-minds view does not have. The possibility of the line of reasoning just presented will serve to show us only that we must be very careful about the way in which we develop and employ such analogies and about the way in which we attempt to spell out the two-minds view in detail.

Consider a case of telepathy. Person A has telepathic access to the mind of person B. Suppose if you like that A telepathically has complete access to the mind of B. Does it follow that B's thoughts are A's thoughts, that B's mental states are A's mental states? Of course not. From B's believing that it is raining outside and A's having perfect telepathic access to the mind of B, it does not follow that A believes it is raining outside, for A can have independent reason to think that B is wrong. The accessing relation itself does not alone constitute ownership. So from God's standing in a perfect accessing relation to all our minds it does not follow that all our minds *are* his minds or that all our thoughts are his thoughts. And so of course it does not follow that each of us is God Incarnate.

But on first glance, it can look as though it is precisely just something like the telepathic relation which we need to acknowledge between the divine and human minds of God Incarnate. For presumably the beliefs contained in the earthly mind did not perfectly coincide with the beliefs contained in the divine mind. Otherwise, we lack our solution to the temptation problem. Moreover, most theologians who take seriously the real humanity of Jesus, however orthodox they might be, will want to allow at least the possibility that the full belief-set of the earthly mind of Jesus, at some if not all times during the earthly sojourn, did not even constitute a proper subset of the belief-set ingredient in the omniscient mind. That is to say, they will want to allow the possibility of the earthly mind of

Jesus containing some false beliefs, beliefs, for example, concerning the shape of the earth, or the nature of the relative movement of the sun and the earth, among other things. But any false belief will be a belief that, in virtue of its omniscience, the divine mind did not contain. From the earthly mind of Jesus containing the belief that the sun moves around the earth, it thus would not follow that this is something believed by God the Son in his properly divine mind. The divine mind would have perfect access to the contents of the human mind and thus would know this belief to be contained in the human mind. It just would not thereby have this belief as one of its beliefs.

This cognitive arrangement does seem to fit exactly into the pattern displayed by the telepathic relation we supposed to hold between person A and person B. But if it is the telepathic relation which models the relation between the divine mind of God the Son and the earthly mind of Jesus, and it is precisely the telepathic relation which best models the relation an omniscient God stands in to each of our minds, does it not follow after all that our minds and their contents stand to God the Son in precisely the same relation as that which the two-minds view attempts to portray as holding distinctively between the earthly mind of Jesus and the divine mind of the Son? Are we then in the end able to avoid the Hegelian view that we are all incarnations of God only at the cost of coming to realize that the noetic relations I have been alleging to hold in the case of Christ are not after all sufficient to ground and explicate the claim that Jesus was God Incarnate, one person with, as a function of his two natures, two discrete minds? Must we conclude that the mind of Jesus was no different from any other human mind in its ultimate type of metaphysical ownership, not, indeed, because our minds are all minds of God, but rather because his mind like ours was not a mind of God?

The crucial difference between Christ and any of us is this: I, for example, am a created being, endowed with causal and cognitive powers. My causal and cognitive powers are not *independent* of God's causal powers, for presumably the existence and exercise of my powers depend (in a way not compromising my genuine freedom) on the existence and exercise of divine causal powers. On a standard theistic view, I exist at all, and continue to exist from moment to moment, only because of an ongoing exercise of divine causal power which is responsible for my existence. Nevertheless, I have been endowed with real causal and cognitive powers numerically different from any divine powers. Though dependent on God's causal powers, they are ontologically distinct from those powers. If the functioning of my mind involves an exercise of my causal and/or cognitive powers, then the contents of my mind are, at least in part, a result of the exercise of those powers. If anyone has something like telepathic access to the contents of my mind, he thereby has, as a result of an exercise of his *own* cognitive and/or causal powers, access to something the existence of which consists in, or results from, an exercise of *my* powers. Two distinct sets of powers are involved. And it is this which is very different in the case of the Incarnation.

Let us generalize. Suppose that for any person B and mental state S, whenever B attains to S as a result of the exercise of her own cognitive and causal powers, there is a person A who has something like direct telepathic access to S, and who is thereby directly aware that B is in S. In any such case, there are two distinct sets of cognitive and/or causal powers involved, one set exercised by each person. B has S in virtue of, at least in part, her exercise of her own powers; A has access to and knowledge of B's being in S in virtue of his exercise of his own powers. The distinctness of the power sets is a manifestation of, and indeed is partly constitutive of, the distinctness of the persons involved. B is not A, nor is the mind of B a mind of A, nor is a state of B simply a state of A.

In the case of Jesus, God Incarnate, the full relation between the earthly mind and the divine mind is in important ways different from the totality of the relation which holds between the mind of any merely human being (such as you or me) and the mind of God. The completeness of epistemic access which God enjoys may be no different. But in Jesus' case, the earthly mind is contained in the divine mind in a distinctive way. Jesus was a being who was fully human, but he was not a created human being. He was not a being endowed with a set of personal cognitive and causal powers distinct from the cognitive and causal powers of God the Son. For Jesus was the same person as God the Son. Thus, the personal cognitive and causal powers operative in the case of Jesus' earthly mind were just none other than the cognitive and causal powers of God the Son. The results of their operation through the human body, under the constraints proper to the conditions of a fully human existence, were just such as to give rise to a human mind, an earthly noetic structure distinct from the properly divine noetic structure involved with the unconstrained exercise of divine powers. Thus there came to be two minds, the earthly mind of God Incarnate and his distinctively divine mind, but two minds of one person, one center of causal and cognitive powers. The asymmetric accessing relation holding between those two minds, if it were thought to involve no more than the mere epistemic access of one mind to the other with respect to information, would indeed not suffice for single ownership, for both minds being minds of one and the same person. However, the precise relation the two-minds view can claim to hold in the case of Christ, involving as it does a unity of cognitive and causal powers productive of the contents of each mind, is sufficient to distinguish the case of Christ from the case of any merely human being. In the two-minds view, and in the analogies we have used to develop it, we thus appear to have what can rationally be seen as a partial explication and modeling of the doctrine of the Incarnation.

Of course, we must admit that any analogy for the Incarnation is a bit tricky, to say the least. But the AI analogy, as well as the other analogies developed in chapter 4, at least may help us to some extent to model the relation of two minds alleged to hold in the case of Christ. In any event, it seems that there is no good reason to think this an incoherent or impossible view. The mereological remarks of Aquinas help us to see where the view is going, although neither his remarks nor my attempted analogies can guarantee that we understand fully, or even that we can imagine at all firsthand, what it is like to be in the appropriate metaphysical sense doubly-minded. But this we cannot expect in any case. All that I have attempted here to indicate is that it is by no means clear that the ascription of two minds to one person is any more problematic than the ascription of two natures to one person. And, as I have developed it, it is an alternative to the kenotic view of Christ which seems to me philosophically preferable.

7 *A Cosmic Christ*

The first six chapters of this book have dealt with the most important and most difficult sort of philosophical objection which has been raised against the traditional doctrine of the Incarnation. I have sought to show how a few simple metaphysical distinctions can be used to turn back this sort of attack on the doctrine's coherence. This chapter and the next two will deal with other problems, the consideration of which may help us to see some implications of the understanding of the Incarnation which has already been laid out in its main metaphysical outlines. The predominant philosophical charge against the doctrine has been that it is conceptually incoherent. A very different sort of objection is that, in the context of a modern scientific world-view, it is a cosmologically incongruous claim. In the present chapter, I want to set forth some ways of understanding this cosmological challenge and indicate the potential relevance to it of the view of Christ which has been presented.

1 *Approaches to the Problem*

The doctrine of the Incarnation is one component in a much larger doctrinal scheme encompassing the themes of creation, fall, and redemption. Contemporary critics of the traditional renderings of these themes have often pointed out that they were originally enunciated and developed in prescientific conditions and thus within the context of a very different sort of world-view from the one scientifically-minded people have today. They have then usually gone on to suggest that religious claims which may have made a great deal of sense in their original context have lost much, if not all, of their plausibility in the modern age. It is interesting to note that this is a general point made repeatedly in recent years by many prominent professors of Christian theology as well as by critics avowedly outside the communion of the church.

Now, I think we must recognize that many professedly Christian theologians during the past century or so have appeared a bit overly ready to beat a hasty retreat in the face of almost any specious argument or other consideration against the traditional affirmations of the faith they are supposed to be representing. Often they seem inclined to relinquish or "reinterpret" important doctrines on no better grounds than that those beliefs can appear to some secular critics to be somehow out of step with the march of science. There have been those such as Rudolf Bultmann, for example, who claim to be unable to believe in the literally miraculous while at the same time availing themselves of the comforts of modern technology. But such cases as these rarely provide much in the way of philosophical substance for anyone seeking to determine the objective status, or truth value, of orthodox Christian beliefs. Occasionally, however, an interesting and even challenging philosophical or theological problem can be extracted from the often vague misgivings of such critics of orthodoxy. Let us consider various ways in which such a challenge might be thought to arise here against the doctrine of the Incarnation.

It has been suggested many times during the past two hundred years that this doctrine, which made a great deal of sense to many people living within the geocentric world-picture of ptolemaic cosmology, is rendered in some sense absurd by modern accounts of the immensity and nature of our universe. The problem seems to be something like this: During the times when the Chalcedonian understanding of Christ was developed and reigned supreme, it was believed by great numbers of people, including the best educated, that we human beings live in a relatively circumscribed universe, the entirety of which has been created for the benefit of human life, which represents the special crowning act of divine creation, situated, appropriately, at the hub of the cosmos, around which all else literally as well as figuratively revolves. Within such an overall perspective, it would have seemed in no way incongruous, but rather could have appeared supremely fitting, that the Creator of all take such interest in his human creatures as to step into his world himself and take a part in the human drama being enacted, as it was, on the center stage of the universe. An anthropocentric world-view provided the cosmological backdrop and framework for a literally anthropomorphic theology—God become a man. The importance of the earth and the importance of humanity rendered this incarnation of deity intelligible and appropriate.

During the past few centuries, however, this world-view and the framework it provided have been destroyed, eroded bit by bit by waves of scientific discovery until nothing of it remains. Actually, it is quite a variety of scientific discoveries, assumptions, hypotheses, speculations, and methodological implications which have seemed to many people to have had the net result of demoting humankind from its traditionally exalted place in the universe to what can appear to be a relatively unexceptional and terribly insignificant role in the cosmic process. I shall not attempt to delineate here the variety of negative effects modern science has been perceived to have on religious doctrine. Numerous books exist which thoroughly document the so-called history of the warfare between science and theology. But it will be of some interest at least to indicate a few points at which scientific developments have been thought to have this devaluing impact on our view of humanity and thus on the system of Christian doctrines, including centrally that of the Incarnation, in which the value of human beings seems clearly to be assumed to be great.

Some critics appear to think that the sheer size of the universe renders humanity unimportant in the cosmos and Christian doctrine thus implausible. Of course it is no modern novelty to juxtapose the immensity of the universe to the religious emphasis on man. The psalmist, for example, wrote long ago:

When I consider Thy heavens, the work of Thy fingers, the moon and the stars, which Thou hast ordained: What is man that Thou dost take thought of him? And the son of man that Thou dost care for him?[1]

This is an expression of an attitude of wonderment, and perhaps astonishment, that amid the grandeur of the heavens human beings should be especially valued by God. The attitude of modern critics, however, is that of simple disbelief. Of course, the psalmist was not aware, as some of us are today, *how* immense the heavens might be. But it is a bit difficult to see exactly what about distinctively modern knowledge of the scale of the universe is thought to show the absurdity of any religious beliefs based on the assumption that the earth and human beings are important to the Creator of all.

Now, it is clear that in many contexts size and value are in direct correlation, the latter depending on the former. For example, all other things being equal, a large army is often of greater value than a small one, if one seeks protection of one's country from an enemy. But this dependence of value on size is relative only to some contexts having to do with instrumental value, and clearly does not hold true in either all or even most such contexts. And when it comes to considerations of intrinsic value, the sort of value ascribed to human beings by Christian theology, questions of size or physical magnitude are simply irrelevant. It is just absurd to argue: small, therefore unimportant. Critics often accuse Christian theologians of being anthropomorphic in their thought. But here it seems to be the critics who are anthropomorphizing, or better, anthropopathizing, with the assumption that if there were a God, he would not deign to notice or value anything as small and insignificant on the cosmic scale as the earth and its inhabitants. On the Christian picture, God is sufficiently unlike a human being that his attention and care can extend fully to every part of a universe, however large, to the point of being infinite in space and time.

So I think we are safe in concluding that if any discovery of modern science undercuts the Christian belief that God so valued us that he became a man, it will not be any discovery concerning the sheer size of the universe. But as with the link between relative size and value, there have been traditionally believed to be a number of other signs, or even requisites, of human importance which have

[1]Psalm 83: 4.

been undercut by the advance of the sciences. For example, in many primal religions an equation is held between spatial centrality and importance. Anthropologists have found many tribes who hold as a sacred belief the claim that their village, or a fire in the center of the village, is located at the center of the world or at the center of the entire cosmos. Their importance to the gods is held to be tied to their central location. Such a view also can be seen in the ptolemaic cosmology and in the many theological and philosophical speculations arising out of that cosmology. In light of this apparently natural equation of importance and spatial centrality, reflected also in nonspatial uses of the notion of centrality, it is easy to understand the resistance many Christian theologians and clerics once manifested toward any transition away from a geocentric cosmology. But again, outside a very few contexts of instrumental value considerations, it is simply wrong to think there is a necessary link between spatial centrality and value. Modern critics who cite the transition from a ptolemaic to a copernican to a contemporary cosmology as counting against or as undercutting traditional Christian claims that the earth and humanity are sufficiently important as to render appropriate a divine incarnation on earth are making the same mistake with respect to value theory as the ancients whose views they deride.

The assumption we are exploring so far is, roughly, that the doctrine that God became a man cannot make any sense and cannot have any degree of plausibility whatsoever unless there is something sufficiently special or uniquely valuable about humanity, something marking out humans as contrasted with all the rest of nature, which would render appropriate God's taking on human nature in a divine incarnation. Before the development of evolutionary theory, it was widely believed by Christians that human beings had a special origin, having been uniquely created in the image of God. Again, in the minds of many people, human value came to be linked to a distinctiveness of human origin. And certainly it can be argued that in many contexts there is a firm link between value and distinctiveness of origin. Consider for example the difference in value many would see in a painting done by the hand of Picasso and in a perfect reproduction otherwise aesthetically identical to it done by a skilled forger. And in a very different way, some unusual

"God has involved himself with us not because [of] what we are, but because [of] what he has chosen to call us to become + to do"

The Logic of God Incarnate

i.e., we are distinctive because [of] our vocation

marks in stone will have or fail to have real value for a paleontologist depending on whether they originated from the distinctive footfalls of some rare prehistoric creature or rather have been crafted by someone intending to perpetrate a hoax. However, it is hard to see how such a relation between value and origin could be held plausibly to obtain outside either contexts concerning cultural artifacts and cultural conventions or contexts of instrumental value. For human beings to have had, in some sense, the same sort of origin as any other kind of recently developed entity in nature—the outworking of natural processes—is not for humans to lack any special value. No such entailment can be made out or defended with any plausibility. It is thus hard to see how the development of evolutionary theory could be taken reasonably to undercut the plausibility of assumptions of human value behind the doctrine of the Incarnation.

If it is not in their relative magnitude in the cosmos, in their location, or in their origin that the value of human beings lies, many philosophers and theologians have held that it is in the distinctiveness of their metaphysical constitution. Dualism has been viewed by many as the last bulwark for claims that human beings have an unusual importance in the order of nature. And of course there are many contexts in which value does depend on constitution. So it is no surprise that recent developments in both neuroscience and artificial intelligence reflected in the philosophy of mind have been perceived as threatening religious claims about the distinctiveness and unusual value of human beings. But as in the case of the other alleged value dependencies we have looked at, it can be denied that the distinctiveness of human value resides in or requires the uniqueness of human constitution. One recent author who has argued this is Donald M. MacKay.[2] Taking up and generalizing a theme developed in the Old Testament by the prophet Amos with respect to the Jewish people, MacKay sees the distinctive value or importance of human beings as residing in a human vocation—in what God has called human beings to do and to be. God has involved himself with us not because of what we are, but because of what he has chosen to call us to become and to do.

[2]See Donald M. MacKay, *Human Science and Human Dignity* (Downers Grove, Ill.: Inter Varsity Press, 1979).

There are many details of MacKay's suggestion which would repay careful scrutiny, but I shall not go into them here. One point, however, should be made. MacKay seems to deny the constitution-value connection in order to avoid the need to endorse dualism concerning human beings just to make sense of the special value Christian theology portrays God as placing on human nature. If this suggestion is plausible, then no developments in modern neuroscience or artificial intelligence need be taken as detracting in the least from the credibility of Christian assumptions concerning the value or importance of humanity in nature.

Of course, most orthodox or traditional theists are, in some form or other, dualists. Nearly all such theists hold that there exists at least one (ordinarily) nonembodied person, namely God.[3] Most also subscribe to some form of dualism concerning human beings. And it is widely recognized among metaphysicians that no amount of neuroscience or success in the development of artificial intelligence need be taken to count in the least against the truth of a view with the metaphysical status of traditional dualism.[4] For example, even if some physical system were constructed which exhibited all the behavioral repertoire of a human being, monists might declare it proof of the materialist claim that purely physical systems are capable of personality, but dualists could claim for their part just as good a reason to think that the constructed system in question embodies a nonmaterial mind as they have to think the same of any organic human body. It seems that metaphysical views such as dualism are not vulnerable to falsification, or even clear disconfirmation, by advances in the physical sciences. So the claim that the value or importance of human beings is connected with their being constituted metaphysically by minds as well as bodies has nothing to fear from modern science. And unlike the other alleged connections between value and relative size, centrality of location, and special origin, this view is not clearly ruled out for the case of human beings by any highly plausible value theory. So the Christian theist need not go along with MacKay in order to avoid having his assessment of the importance to God of humanity undermined by advances in neuroscience or artificial intelligence.

[3] Notable exceptions include Denis of Dinant and Thomas Hobbes.
[4] See George Schlesinger, *Metaphysics* (Oxford: Basil Blackwell, 1983), chap. 1.

It thus seems that Christians could in all epistemic propriety hold that having a dualistic metaphysical constitution is closely tied to humans' being such that a divine incarnation in human nature is appropriate, or even possible. Some may thus hold in particular that being minded, or having an immaterial soul, is a condition of humans necessary for being such that an incarnation in human nature is possible. MacKay and those inclined to follow his line will at least have to acknowledge that having certain capacities or potentialities relevant to the vocation he discusses is a constitutional requisite for having the sort of value Christian theology ascribes to human beings. So either dualistic constitution or at least the exemplifying of certain sorts of intelligent behavioral capacities can be held to be a condition of human existence necessary for the appropriateness or intelligibility of God's becoming a man. But are such properties sufficient for the appropriateness of an incarnation as well? It is with this question that we approach the heart of the problem of cosmological incongruity which throughout the last couple of hundred years has been felt by a great many people to attend the claim that, of all his creation, God chose to come and dwell among us.

2   The Problem in Focus

After recounting some of the astronomical discoveries in recent centuries regarding the existence of suns other than our own and the probable existence of planets orbiting around these suns in great number, Thomas Paine wrote in *The Age of Reason*:

> From whence, then, could arise the solitary and strange conceit that the Almighty, who had millions of worlds equally dependent on his protection, should quit the care of all the rest and come to die in our world because, they say, one man and one woman had eaten an apple! And, on the other hand, are we to suppose that every world in the boundless creation had an Eve, an apple, a serpent, and a redeemer? In this case, the person who is irreverently called the Son of God, and sometimes God himself, would have nothing else to do than to

travel world to world, in an endless succession of death, with scarcely a momentary interval of life.[5]

Voicing this same sort of view, Horace Walpole, fourth Lord of Oxford, had written: "Fontenelle's Dialogues on the Plurality of Worlds, first rendered me an infidel. Christianity, and a plurality of worlds, are, in my opinion, irreconcileable."[6] And from Ralph Waldo Emerson, we have the related statement that "I regard it as an irresistible effect of the Copernican astronomy to have made the theological *scheme of Redemption* absolutely incredible."[7] The incongruity of Christian claims concerning the person and work of Christ in the context of modern cosmology was a theme raised and developed by many prominent intellectuals during the eighteenth and nineteenth centuries. In a massive scholarly work detailing some of the history of the idea of extraterrestrial intelligent beings existing throughout the universe, Michael Crowe has succeeded in showing how this idea was perceived by many on the one hand to enhance the credibility of theism, but on the other to render distinctively Christian claims provincial, gratuitously anthropocentric, and completely unbelieveable.[8] Crowe suggests, for example, that Emerson gave up his pastorate for this reason, feeling the discoveries of astronomy to have utterly discredited Christian claims about Christ.

In light of the historical importance of this cosmological objection to the Christian faith, it is interesting to note how little it is discussed nowdays by either philosophers or theologians. One reason for its neglect among philosophers may lie in the fact that it is unusually difficult to extract a challenging *argument* against the truth of Christian claims, such as the doctrine of the Incarnation, from this perspective, although it has clearly yielded an emotionally powerful skepticism for many people, in spite of the intellectual vagueness

[5] Thomas Paine, *Representative Selections*, ed. Harry Hoyden Clark (New York: Hill & Wang, 1961), p. 283.

[6] Horace Walpole, "*Walpoliana* . . . Number IV," *Monthly Magazine* (1798), p. 116.

[7] R. W. Emerson, "Astronomy," in *Young Emerson Speaks: Unpublished Discourses on Many Subjects*, ed. A. C. McGiffert, Jr. (Boston: Houghton Mifflin, 1938), pp. 174–175.

[8] Michael Crowe, *The Extraterrestrial Life Debate 1750–1900: The Idea of a Plurality of Worlds from Kant to Lowell* (Cambridge: Cambridge University Press, 1985).

it involves. Some even seem to think that our modern perspective on the cosmos so obviously discredits the pretensions of Christian theology that explaining exactly *how* it counts against Christianity is as needless as explaining the point of a clear and simple joke. In contemporary literature, it is in fact hard to find even a passing mention of this objection. In one recent book, however, Paul and Linda Badham have devoted a few pages to an attempt to elucidate the challenge.[9] They articulate it as follows.

According to Christian theology, human beings are very valuable to God. In the words of E. L. Mascall, the fact that "God has himself become a man in the incarnation . . . has sealed human nature with a certificate of value whose validity can never be questioned."[10] And according to Pope John Paul II, "the incarnation of the Son of God emphasizes the great dignity of human nature; and the mystery of redemption . . . reveals the value of every human being."[11] But are human beings *uniquely* valuable to God? The Badhams cite contemporary estimates of the number of stars capable of supporting planetary systems and of providing habitable temperature zones for those planets. On one conservative estimate, assuming only one inhabitable planet for every million stars, the number of planets capable of supporting life is something like ten million million. On another well-known estimate, it is more like 500,000 million million. This disparity alone should make us a bit wary of such estimations. But it seems safe to assume that there is an enormous number of such planets. Suppose then that life has developed and reached the stage of rational intellect on a sizable fraction of them. Assuming that all rational, intellectual beings are capable of a spiritual relationship with God, the question then arises as to whether, on the assumptions operative in Christian theology, we are to say that it is only on this planet that God became incarnate, or we should postulate the occurrence of multiple divine incarnations throughout the universe.

[9]Paul and Linda Badham, *Immortality or Extinction?* (London: Macmillan, 1982), pp. 51–58.

[10]E. L. Mascall, *The Importance of Being Human* (Oxford: Oxford University Press, 1959), p. 22.

[11]*Sign of Contradiction* (New York: Seabury, 1979), p. 122; cited in Badham and Badham, p. 131.

The Badhams pose this as a dilemma for Christian theology by reasoning as follows. Either it is the case that extraterrestrials need salvation, or it is not. If it is not the case, then divine incarnations other than our own would not be necessary in any sense, on the assumptions traditionally made about the rationale of the incarnation of God on the earth. But to entertain this possibility would be, according to the Badhams, theologically objectionable or just plain implausible. If humans alone were in need of salvation or reconciliation to God, they reason, it would not be true that, as Mascall suggests, the Incarnation signals how precious human beings are to God, for all other intelligent creatures would be existing in a spiritual state much closer to God. In so reasoning, the Badhams appear to forget the parable of the lost sheep. However, their more important line is to question the plausibility of holding that only humans are in such a state as to need salvation and reconciliation to God. They suggest that it would be very implausible to claim that human beings are in an utterly unique state of "fallenness" not shared by any other creatures. Their argument is basically that either a state of fallenness results from a historic fall from an original state of perfection, which is a traditional claim rendered absolutely incredible by our knowledge of human evolution, or it is a function of our physical, animal nature. And if the latter is true, our being such that a divine incarnation and redemption were needed is due to a condition which presumably would be shared by extraterrestrials. Thus, they would be such that a divine incarnation is needed by them as well. But then, in the Badhams' own words: "If this is so, then 500,000 million million incarnations would be necessary. . . . And with 500,000 million million worlds to 'visit' in the limited timescale in which planets are inhabitable, multiple simultaneous incarnations would be inevitable!"[12] They go on to say: "The more one tries to make sense of this picture, the more the received understanding of the doctrines of incarnation and atonement dies the death of a thousand qualifications. These doctrines came into being against a back-cloth of a geocentric, man-oriented vision of the cosmos. It is hard to see how they can

[12]Badham and Badham, pp. 56, 57.

survive the passing of that world-view, and a psychological acceptance of a wider vision of reality."[13]

In other words, the Badhams argue that in light of the world-picture of modern astronomy and cosmology, Christian theologians cannot resist the conclusion from what remains of their traditional assumptions that God must have been engaging in multiply incarnating himself throughout the universe a mind-boggling number of times. And they suggest that this is an absurd picture departing from and undermining altogether the intent of orthodox christology. They state: "To suppose that the 'complete being of the Godhead' was simultaneously present on a million other planets would radically transform the normal sense in which these words were understood."[14] This is an argument, and a conclusion, which requires some critical consideration.

Although the question was never subject to conciliar review and decree, it seems to have been assumed by most traditional theologians that there has been only one incarnation of God into a creaturely nature, and thus that it is through the drama which was enacted on this earth that all salvation is effected. There can, however, be two major sorts of argument for postulating the occurrence of multiple divine incarnations throughout the universe. The first is based on a traditional theological problem often known as "the scandal of particularity." The second is based on a soteriological principle enunciated by Gregory Nazianzen (329–389) which played an important role in early christology and in the articulation of conciliar orthodoxy on the person of Christ. The Badhams' argument seems to be a version of the first sort, so we shall turn now to take a look at that.

Briefly put, the scandal of particularity arises with a simple set of questions asked of the Christian theologian who claims that it is only through the life and death of God incarnated in Jesus Christ that all can be saved and reconciled to God: How can the many humans who lived and died before the time of Christ be saved through him? They surely cannot be held accountable for responding appropriately to something of which they could have no knowledge. Furthermore, what about all the people who have lived since

---

[13] Ibid., p. 57.
[14] Ibid.

the time of Christ in cultures with different religious traditions, untouched by the Christian gospel? How can they be excluded fairly from a salvation not ever really available to them? How could a just God set up a particular condition of salvation, the highest end of human life possible, which was and is inaccessible to most people? Is not the love of God better understood as universal, rather than as limited to a mediation through the one particular individual, Jesus of Nazareth? Is it not a moral as well as a religious scandal to claim otherwise? This is, roughly, the problem known as the scandal of particularity.

The argument presented by the Badhams can be seen as a variant of this set of worries. In fact, it seems that many who appear to have rejected Christian faith on astronomical or cosmological grounds, such as Emerson and Walpole, are affected by just a cosmic-scale version of the scandal of particularity. If that is so, then what they find to be a distinctively modern and decisive blow against Christian theology is, in its logical form, not a new and distinctively modern problem at all. It is merely a psychologically more striking version of a problem which has long been with us. This cosmological challenge thus stands to the traditional scandal of particularity much as the problem of evil posed by the Nazi extermination camps stands to the traditional problem of evil—it is logically the same problem, although psychologically a much more intense and gripping rendition of it. With this in mind, let us look again at the type of argument given by the Badhams for the postulation of multiple incarnations of God.

What is the point of the Incarnation? To provide in a certain way for revelation and salvation. Spelling this answer out in any detail is a very difficult task, but fortunately it will not be necessary to go into much detail here. The Badhams assume that if extra-terrestrials exist who need revelation and salvation, then, on the traditional Christian assumption that both the supreme revelation of God and our salvation are conveyed to us through the earthly incarnation and career of God in Christ, we must postulate for all those extraterrestrials as well their own divine incarnations. But this assumption is eminently questionable.

How is the salvation wrought by Christ to be conveyed to those needing to be saved from sin and reconciled to God? On one ancient model favored by some of the Eastern church Fathers, the incar-

nation of God into human nature somehow metaphysically transformed our nature. It is possible to understand this model of salvation
very mechanically. On this interpretation, in a process sometimes
known loosely as deification, God's mere taking on of human nature
itself effected our salvation. According to this extreme view, we
need not know about the Incarnation in order to be saved by it. If
salvation were understood in this way, any soteriological argument
for multiple incarnations could be blocked quite easily. The transformation in which deification consists is not propagated from Christ
to us by any sort of physical causation. Thus, perhaps it can touch
human beings living before Christ and in other cultures during his
time as well as those who have lived since and have heard the
message of his incarnation. Likewise, deification can be understood
to result from God's taking on a rational created nature. Then the
resultant salvation could be viewed as shared by any rational created
beings, whatever their location in the space-time continuum. One
divine incarnation could serve for the salvation of all the universe.

But this has not been a very popular understanding of the salvation made available by Christ. Dominant models of salvation have
required a response on the part of the created individual being
saved. Let us refer to the deification model of salvation as constituting a metaphysical soteriology, and let us call any model of
salvation in which a free creaturely response is required a moral
soteriology. It seems most likely that the Badhams are assuming a
moral soteriology in their argument. The argument could then be
understood like this: Extraterrestrials can be saved by God Incarnate only if they can know of the incarnation through which their
salvation is offered. This is so because, of course, they cannot properly respond to something of which they have no knowledge. Suppose there are, have been, or will be such rational beings on 500,000
million million worlds. There is no natural means whereby the
gospel of Jesus the Christ could reach most of those other beings.
Thus, if God had incarnated himself only on the earth, they could
not be saved, since they could not have the knowledge of God's act
requisite for salvation. If they are to be saved, it thus cannot be
through the incarnation on this planet. Hence, in order to offer
them salvation, God must become incarnate on their planets as
well. And so there must be, ultimately, hundreds of thousands of
millions of millions of incarnations of God.

This argument as it stands turns on at least two crucial assumptions which can be questioned. First, the argument assumes that if God chooses to reveal himself and provide salvation to human beings through an incarnation, it would be necessary for him to deal in the same sort of way with any of his other rational creatures needing revelation or salvation. And this can be questioned. For if God freely chose to incarnate himself in human nature, he was presumably under no necessity of doing so. In principle, it seems that a Christian could hold that the divine economy is such that we human beings are offered salvation through the incarnation of God as Jesus, but that other rational beings may be offered salvation through some completely different sort of means not involving a divine incarnation at all. Understanding the Christ to be God's reaching out to his creation in the person of the Logos, the Second Person of the Trinity, one could hold that all are saved through Christ without holding that all are saved through a particular divine incarnation or through any incarnation at all. If the assumption that since some salvation is offered through an incarnation then all salvation must be so offered is in doubt, the Badhams' argument is in doubt as well. But as this is a relatively orthodox sort of assumption, I incline not to press this doubt too far.

The other assumption operative in the Badhams' argument seems to be that if knowledge of an incarnation of God is a requisite of salvation, then that knowledge must be propagated by natural causal means and must be had in this life. If saving knowledge of a divine incarnation can be offered to a created being directly by God in this or the next life independently of any natural communicative or other causal chains initiated by the incarnation itself, the Badhams' argument collapses. For in that case, it would not be necessary in any sense for God to engage in local planetary incarnations in order to save creatures in widely disparate places and times. He could directly provide them with whatever knowledge they needed for salvation. Thus rational beings with no natural epistemic access to an earthly incarnation of God as Jesus could nonetheless be given the opportunity to respond to this single event.

Furthermore, seeing the Badhams' argument as arising out of a version of the traditional scandal of particularity, one could respond to them as follows. If all persons or groups of persons needing salvation must be at some time during their lives in this physical universe in natural causal contact with an incarnation of God (through either firsthand acquaintance, or through hearing the message others convey about this incarnation) if they are to be given the opportunity for salvation, and if a great number of groups and persons isolated from one another are to be offered salvation, then it follows that for each of them there must be an incarnation. But the consequence of such reasoning is not merely the postulation of 500,000 million million incarnations, but many, many more than that. For there have been an untold number of groups and individuals on the earth isolated from the gospel of Jesus. Anticipating this point, John Hick, for example, once said:

> Many would accept that if there is intelligent life on other planets of other stars, a divine incarnation on such a planet would not have to be as the earth-man Jesus of Nazareth, but rather as a member of the stream of life taking place on that other planet. If this is right, it implies that God could become incarnate more than once—and indeed, in principle, an indefinite number of times—for the sake of separate numbers of people. And it could well be argued that the Chinese population in the fifth century B.C. was almost as separate from the population of Europe as are those of earth and another planet. Is it then really axiomatic that God could not have become incarnate separately within the great civilizations of the ancient world—China, India, and the Mediterranean?[15]

And the same sort of situation would presumably obtain on most other planets requiring, by the Badhams' reasoning, an incarnation. So if we are justified by their argument in postulating one for each inhabited planet, it seems by the same sort of scandal of particularity we would be justified in postulating a truly bewildering number, even on each planet. And this can reasonably be judged to come about as close to a practical *reductio ad absurdum* as one can get. Certainly it is by no means clear that the sort of argument hinted at by the Badhams could serve to take a person rationally and compellingly from fairly orthodox Christian beliefs to the additional belief in multiple divine incarnations throughout the uni-

[15]John Hick, "A Response to Hebblethwaite," in *Incarnation and Myth: The Debate Continued*, ed. Michael Goulder (Grand Rapids: Eerdmans, 1979), p. 192.

verse. However, there is a second line of argument which will bear consideration.

One of the dominant principles of patristic reflection on the person of Christ, a principle in important ways operative in the articulation and early defense of orthodox christology, was the principle that "the unassumed is the unhealed." Any component of human nature not assumed, or taken on, or exemplified by God the Son in his earthly incarnation, was not healed by his becoming incarnate. The argument proceeded from the premise that we have been totally healed by Christ to the conclusion that he was fully human—that there was no component of human nature he did not assume. In its original formulation and use, the principle was linked with the deification model of salvation, the metaphysical soteriology of the East. But it need not be taken in this way. It can be argued that if Christ is to be our high priest, our advocate before God the Father, as the book of Hebrews would have it, then he must be able to sympathize—or better, empathize—with all of our lot, with the entirety of our condition. But then, in order to be able to do this, the argument would continue, he must have shared all types of human experience—anger, grief, joy, frustration, love, temptation, etc.—during his time among us. Otherwise he would not know "from the inside," so to speak, what it is like to be a human being. And it can be suggested finally that his having this knowledge and our knowing of him that he has this knowledge are conditions of that salvation and reconciliation to God which is our healing.[16] This way of understanding the principle that the unassumed is the unhealed can avoid altogether the distinctive metaphysical claims of the deification model while at the same time serving its original function.

Let us refer to the version of the principle linked to the deification model as the metaphysical version, and call the understanding of it just sketched the moral version. Either version can be used to argue for multiple interplanetary incarnations, and the resultant argument avoids altogether the extreme implications of the Badham-style arguments. The form of the new argument is simple. It is very unlikely that rational intelligent life on other planets would

---

[16]This sort of argument was first suggested to me by Michael Detlefsen.

have followed precisely the same course of evolutionary development as life on earth. It is thus unlikely that extraterrestrials would be exactly like us in all respects. It seems possible that their sensory apparatus would be very different from ours, their physical structures serving the functions of our brains and central nervous systems very different, and thus the conditions of their lives very unlike ours. On either version of the principle that the unassumed is the unhealed, it would seem that in order to provide for salvation for these creatures through the means of incarnation, God would have to take on their very different natures in addition to taking on ours. And this, of course, could not all be done in one incarnation; it would require the sorts of multiple incarnations the Badhams envision. So long as these were all incarnations of the Christ, God the Son, the central claim of Christian theology that it is through Christ that all are to be saved would be preserved. One and the same person who became a man as Jesus of Nazareth would have to take on as well each of the differing creaturely natures, becoming one of each of these sorts of person. But of course neither version of the principle would force us to acknowledge multiple incarnations within a kind, such as one on the continent of India, one in South America, one in 400 B.C. (by our calendar), one in 6 B.C., one in A.D. 1884, etc. For all human beings, for example, wherever or whenever they have lived, have shared the same basic nature. One incarnation would suffice for their healing, one and all.

So here is an argument for postulating, or recognizing the likelihood of, multiple incarnations of God throughout the universe which neither assumes nor entails anything which must be rejected by adherents of Chalcedonian orthodoxy. Do we then have a good argument for multiple incarnations? I do not know. I think the most that can reasonably be said is that a measure of pious agnosticism is appropriate here. I think we definitely should leave open the possibility of multiple incarnations. And I believe that on the basis of some such argument as those I have just surveyed, a Christian could rationally come to believe that God has engaged in this act of incarnation multiply. But the Badhams seem to suggest both that on traditional Christian assumptions concerning Creator-creature relations, multiple incarnations must be acknowledged and that this acknowledgment somehow undermines, or, worse, is impossible on, the traditional understanding of our earthly incarnation. In the next section, I want to suggest that the picture of the Incarnation I have been developing will perfectly well allow the possibility of multiple divine incarnations.

3 The Possibility of Multiple Incarnations

In a contribution to *Incarnation and Myth: The Debate Continued*, Brian Hebblethwaite wrote:

> The suggestion that Jesus might have been one of many incarnations of God in human history betrays a complete failure to appreciate what the doctrine of the incarnation, in classical Christian faith, has been held to state. If God himself, in one of the modes of his being, has come into our world in person, to make himself personally known and to make himself vulnerable to the world's evil, in order to win our love and bind us to himself, we cannot suppose that he might have done so more than once. For only one man can actually *be* God to us, if God is one. We are to posit relation in God, yes, but not a split personality. Only one actual human person can be the vehicle and expression of one God on earth.[17]

Elsewhere, he has written in the same vein that:

> If the Incarnation is to be understood to be God's self-presentation in person within the structures of his creation then its uniqueness follows immediately from the fact that God is one. God can doubtless be *represented* by innumerable *other* people; but if he is to come himself into our world, then he cannot split his own identity by identifying himself with two or more human beings, any more than one human being can be resurrected as two or more replicas. . . .[18]

The conclusion Hebblethwaite is urging on us could be defended by a *reductio ad absurdum* argument. Suppose for *reductio* that there have been multiple divine incarnations. Let '*J*' stand for Jesus, '*K*'

[17]Brian Hebblethwaite, "The Uniqueness of the Incarnation," in Goulder, ed., p. 189.
[18]Brian Hebblethwaite, Letter to the Editor, *Theology*, 80 (September, 1977), 366.

for, say, Krishna, and 'G' for God the Son. The argument such as Hebblethwaite may have in mind could then proceed as follows:

1	$J = G$	Assumption
2	$K = G$	Assumption
3	$J \neq K$	Assumption
4	$G = K$	2 Symmetry for identity
5	$J = K$	1, 4 Transitivity for identity
6	$(J = K)\ \&\ (J \neq K)$	5, 3 Conjunction introduction

Premises 1–3 amount to the assumption that there have been two incarnations. Using only these assumptions and two rules governing identity, we produce a contradiction. So by *reductio* we must reject at least one of the premises. And the rejection of any one of them will, we can generalize, amount to the rejection of the claim that there has been more than one divine incarnation. Further, by parallel argument, it can be deduced that multiple divine incarnations could be possible only if some contradiction were possibly true. But by elementary logic, no contradiction is possibly true. Thus multiple incarnations of deity are not possible.

Consider for a moment the premises of the argument as given. Which of them would a traditional Christian reject? Presumably, premise 2, the claim that Krishna is God the Son. Which would a Hindu reject? The first premise, the claim that Jesus is God the Son? Typically, Hindu ecumenism would allow the truth of 1, but require denying 3, the claim that Jesus and Krishna are two entirely distinct persons. On some Hindu understandings of deity and the avatar concept, 1 and 2 could both be true precisely because 3 would be false. Now, Hindu theologians may be quite wrong in many of their claims about deity and avatars, and Christians right to reject claims about the divinity of, for example, Krishna, but the type of strategy which could be used by the Hindu here points in the direction of a strategy a Christian could also use in order to allow the possibility of multiple incarnations of God.

For consider again the two-minds picture of Christ. There is, in the case of the incarnation of God as Jesus, an earthly range of consciousness and a properly divine range of consciousness, the former contained in, but not also containing, the latter. That is to say, an asymmetric accessing relation obtains between the two noetic structures which are noetic structures had by one and the same person. If this picture, which I have already spelled out to some extent, portrays a possible situation—and I see no good reason to think that it does not—then there also seems to be no good reason to think that this accessing relation could not hold severally between any number of finite, created minds, or ranges of consciousness, and the properly divine mind of God the Son. And if this is possible, multiple divine incarnations are possible in any number. There could be only one person involved in all these incarnations—God the Son—but this one person could be incarnate in any number of created bodies and minds, such as the body and earthly mind of Jesus.

What is particularly surprising about Hebblethwaite's giving the sort of argument that he does is that he is one of the few recent defenders of orthodox christology to have endorsed and stressed the importance of some sort of two-minds view. What he apparently has not realized is that once we have a defensible account of the two-minds view, in even rudimentary form, we have the metaphysical apparatus which will allow for multiple incarnations of one and the same divine being. And it should be noted that the two-minds view is congenial to the idea of multiple incarnations in a way in which the alternative kenotic defense of traditional christology is not. For if kenoticism is true, God the Son was here and not elsewhere during his earthly incarnation. Multiple incarnations, on this view, would have to be sequential. And, needless to say, anything like 500,000 million million would require a very long sequence. The implausibility of such a view can be highlighted by merely considering how the Son could arrange to get to all inhabited planets during the, perhaps quite limited, time in which they are inhabited by rational creatures. And if multiple incarnations on the same planet are to be allowed in principle, the kenotic picture appears even worse suited to the task. Questions of sheer numbers and times, however, are not in the least problematic for the two-minds view. So if we are to allow in principle the widest range of possibilities concerning multiple divine incarnations, we should endorse the two-minds view. If we return then to own original *reductio* argument, the Christian who affirms the two-minds view of Christ could accept 1, the claim that Jesus is God the Son, and 2 for many assignments to '*K*', letting it stand for any divine incarnation on another planet, for example, while denying the truth of any appropriate related proposition of the form of 3, thereby blocking the *reductio*. Any two incarnations of God then could be incarnations of one and the same person.

Before going on, I should at least mention a misunderstanding that could arise concerning the possibility of multiple incarnations in any number which the two-minds view seems clearly to allow. In a recent essay, the British theologian Maurice Wiles presented the following line of reasoning: "If it is logically conceivable . . . for God to be actually identified with a human person without in any way taking away from the full and genuine humanity of that human person, it follows that God does not, in fact, draw near to us as individual men and women or share our suffering as directly as apparently he could."[19] I think the argument Wiles had in mind could be put something like this: Orthodoxy claims it to be logically possible that God became a man, and so that he once came among us as one of us. But if such a divine incarnation is possible at all, multiple incarnations surely seem possible as well. If it is possible that a being who is God be identical with any one of us human beings (Jesus), it is equally possible that he be identical with each and every one of us human beings. But orthodox theology denies that he identifies himself this intimately, by incarnation, with each of us. We are not all incarnations of God. So it follows that God does not draw as near to us as he could. Nor does he share our suffering as directly as he could. But orthodox theologians often argue in favor of the doctrine of the Incarnation by contending that God would surely do everything he could to draw near to us and share in our sufferings, to the extent of entering human nature. In context, it seems that the suggestion Wiles wants to communicate is that traditional Christians cannot have it both ways. Since the multiple incarnation of God in all of us is denied, this particular and common argument in favor of the orthodox doctrine must be relinquished.

A great deal could be said in criticism of the line of reasoning Wiles presents, but I am concerned here only to point out what is

[19]Maurice Wiles, "A Survey of Issues in the *Myth* Debate," in Goulder, ed., pp. 7–8.

wrong with one crucial inference it involves. Wiles seems to mis-understand deeply what exactly the possibility of multiple incarnations amounts to. When orthodox Christians claim that

(A)   God became a man,

there is an important sense in which they do not mean to imply that

(B)   There was a man whom God became.

The man Jesus was none other than a divine person in human nature. He was not merely a human person very intimately related to deity. Nor was he a merely human being who was identical with a divine being. This is, by definition, impossible. Now, you and I, and Maurice Wiles, are all, presumably, merely human beings. As such, we could not be literally identical with any divine being or beings. But is it an essential fact, a necessity, concerning any merely human being that he not be also divine? Couldn't Wiles have been fully human without being merely human, in virtue of being also an incarnation of God? Doesn't the possibility of multiple incarnations imply this?

The simple answer is: It does not. The view most consonant with orthodox theology and most in line with independently plausible, relevant metaphysical theories is that any contingent, created being is essentially a contingent, created being. Any divine being is essentially not a contingent, created being. And so no such created being could logically be a literal incarnation of God. None of us mere humans could possibly be identical with any divine being. It is the Christian claim that in creating the world, God has brought about the existence of contingent, created beings distinct from himself. It is also a Christian claim that he draws near to us, "nearer than a brother," as we allow him. It is by no means an implication of any orthodox assumptions that we should, or even could, all be incarnations of God. And the possibility of multiple incarnations on the part of God allowed by the two-minds view does not entail that this is possible. From even the extreme claim that it is possible that all individuals who exemplify human nature be individuals who exemplify divine nature, it does not follow that all individuals who as a matter of fact exemplify human nature could possibly be individuals who exemplify the divine nature as well. That is, letting 'H' represent the predicate 'is fully human', 'D' the predicate 'is fully divine', and '$\Diamond$' the modal possibility operator, meaning 'it is metaphysically possible that', unless one makes the crazy assumption that no human beings could possibly exist except those that actually exist and that there could not possibly exist fewer humans than actually exist, it does not follow from

(i) $\Diamond$ (x) $(Hx \rightarrow Dx)$

that

(ii) (x) $(Hx \rightarrow \Diamond Dx)$.

To assume otherwise, as Wiles's argument seems to do, is just to commit an elementary modal fallacy.

My purpose in this section has not been to argue that there have been, are, or will be multiple incarnations of God in creaturely natures. That question could not be handled with any degree of adequacy apart from a good deal of work on the notions of salvation and revelation, work beyond the scope of the present study. If a reasonable consideration of such questions would not result in the conclusion that multiple incarnations must be postulated throughout the universe in order for most traditional Christian assumptions about salvation and revelation to be squared with any reasonable beliefs we have about the nature of the cosmos, then no challenge for Christian orthodoxy results from this quarter. On the other hand, if multiple incarnations were to be required, any challenge could be met by the two-minds view I have developed. So I am concerned in this chapter only to argue that distinctively cosmological challenges do not successfully show Christian theology concerning the Incarnation to be in any way incongruous or absurd. The metaphysics of God Incarnate are such as to accord with any reasonable cosmic perspective.

8 *The Nicodemian* Modus Tollens

The Gospel according to John presents for our instruction a very interesting case of rational reflection on the identity of Jesus. The passage I refer to begins with the words:

> Now there was a man of the Pharisees, named Nicodemus, a ruler of the Jews. This man came to Jesus by night and said to him, "Rabbi, we know that you are a teacher come from God; for no man can do these signs that you do unless God is with him."[1]

Since at least the time of Nicodemus, people have reasoned about what should be made of Jesus. And it has been the most widespread view of Christians throughout the centuries that it is eminently reasonable to believe Jesus to be, not just a teacher come from God, but God himself incarnate in human nature. In this chapter, I want to examine some important facets of the question as to whether it is even possible that it be reasonable or rational to believe Jesus to be God Incarnate. In particular, we shall take a look at some considerations which have been thought by many to constitute obstacles to a positive answer to this question, and see how the perspective on the Incarnation developed in previous chapters allows these potential obstacles to be overcome. In this chapter we shall be dealing with some epistemic matters concerning the doctrine of the Incarnation. My aim here, however, is not to marshal evidence or

[1] John 3:1–2.

other sorts of epistemic support in favor of the doctrine. I shall not try to prove, argue, or in any other way show that Jesus was God Incarnate. Not even the more modest task will be attempted of showing that all Christians ought to adopt this traditional understanding of Jesus over any of the alternative conceptions of him developed by a number of modern theologians. In the pages of this book, we are dealing only with what in a broad sense I have dubbed "the logic of God Incarnate." In this chapter, we shall focus on what are, in principle, some of the epistemic dynamics of the incarnational identity claim—some of its logical relations to the sorts of epistemic considerations in the light of which its rational affirmation would be possible or impossible. What I do hope to indicate, in a positive vein, is that it is possible that it be rational to believe Jesus to be God Incarnate. If this is an acceptable conclusion to our reflections here, we shall have succeeded in one more way in the ground-clearing task we are engaged in for this central Christian doctrine.

1   *God in Christ: The Possibility of Discernment*

In the past, many people, some friends as well as foes, have believed the doctrine of the Incarnation to be ultimately beyond the scope of reason. Some have so believed because they have taken the doctrine to be inexpungibly obscure to the point of being without clear sense or determinate, cognitive meaning. If it were beyond the scope of reason on this ground, or on any other ground, it would not be such that belief in it could be rational, or in accord with reason.

What are we to make of this sort of view? I think it will be interesting here to quote at length a line of reasoning presented some time ago by John Wisdom:

It has been said that once at least a higher gift than grace did flesh and blood refine, God's essence and his very self—in the body of Jesus. Whether this statement is true or false is not now the point but whether it's so obscure as to be senseless. Obscure undoubtedly it is but senseless it is not, beyond the scope of reason it is not. For to say that in Nero God was incarnate is not to utter a senseless string of words nor merely to express a surprising sentiment; it is to make a statement which is absurd because it is against all reason. If I say of a cat, 'This cat is abracadabra' I utter a senseless string of words, I don't make a statement at all and therefore don't make an absurd statement. But if I say of a cat which is plainly dead, 'In this cat there is life' I make a statement which is absurd because it is against all reason. The cat is not hunting, eating, sleeping, breathing; it is stiff and cold. In the same way the words, 'In Nero God was incarnate' are not without any meaning; one who utters them makes a statement, he makes a statement which is absurd and *against* all reason and therefore *not* beyond the scope of reason. Now if a statement is not beyond the scope of reason then any logically parallel statement is also not beyond the scope of reason. . . . The statement 'In Jesus God was incarnate' is logically parallel to 'In Nero God was incarnate.' The latter we noticed is not beyond the scope of reason. Therefore the statement 'In Jesus God was incarnate' is not beyond the scope of reason.[2]

It is not merely the case that we have no reason to believe that Nero was God Incarnate; that would be compatible with our also having no reason to believe he was not God Incarnate. And in that case, the claim, and claims of its type, could be beyond the scope of reason. Wisdom's point is that we have very good reason, as decisive a grounding as we could want, for believing that the wicked man Nero was *not* God Incarnate. And surely to this everyone in possession of the Judeo-Christian conception of God would agree. Any claim that Nero was God Incarnate we would label as nonsense or absurd. Now it is true that many critics of orthodox Christian doctrine within the contemporary academic theological community have called the traditional claim that Jesus was literally God Incarnate nonsense or absurd. But even these critics, or at least the vast majority of them, surely would recognize something clearly wrong with the Nero claim which is not wrong with the parallel claim about Jesus. The Nero claim is nonsensical or absurd on properly epistemic grounds, and thus in an epistemic sense: It stands in flagrant contradiction to all we know about the character of the man Nero, in light of the concept we have of God. What is

[2]John Wisdom, *Paradox and Discovery* (Oxford: Basil Blackwell, 1965), pp. 19–20.

interesting here is that it is something about Nero himself, his particular personality and character, which would make a claim of his deity particularly absurd and markedly inferior in an epistemic sense to the parallel claim about Jesus. It is this that Wisdom would have us attend to.

The Christian claim has been said by some critics to be non-sensical or absurd in a logical, or semantic, or conceptual sense. That this is not the case can be held to be evinced by the comparative difference in prima facie epistemic status we sense between the claim about Nero and the claim about Jesus, given what we know about the two of them on the human level. Thus, as Wisdom indicates, neither of these statements is unintelligible. And neither is beyond the scope of reason. The difference we feel between them witnesses to that.

If Wisdom has indeed successfully indicated to us that the doctrine of the Incarnation is not beyond the scope of reason, has he shown that the possibility is open that it may be rational or reasonable to endorse this doctrine? The answer to this question is clearly "No," for the claim that Jesus was God Incarnate could fall within the scope of reason in much the same way as would a claim that, for example, Jesus was a married bachelor, for all that Wisdom shows. Wisdom does draw our attention helpfully to a difference between the Nero claim and the Jesus claim. But the claim of deity for Nero could be absurd in a way in which the claim of deity for Jesus is not absurd without its following from this that the claim about Jesus is not absurd in any sense at all, and such that it is even possible that it be rational to endorse it.

As we have seen earlier in this book, various contemporary theologians have thought the incarnational identity claim about Jesus to be patently incoherent. From this point of view, it would be possible to believe Jesus to be God Incarnate and to be rational in so believing only if one rationally could fail to see the patent incoherence of the claim. A certain significant degree of ignorance or obtuseness would be required, if this were to be possible at all. A number of philosophers have offered persuasive arguments in recent years to the effect that it is possible rationally to believe the impossible, or necessarily false.[3] However, if 'incoherent' means more than merely 'necessarily false', if 'patently incoherent' means something more like 'analytically false' or 'a priori impossible', then it is less likely, to say the least, that anyone would be able rationally to believe a patently incoherent doctrine, for it is highly unlikely that belief in the truth of an analytically false, or a priori impossible, proposition can reasonably be ascribed to a person at all. If a patently incoherent proposition is such that one cannot understand it without seeing it to be false, and it is impossible to believe a proposition to be true without understanding it, and, moreover, it is impossible to believe a proposition to be true while seeing it to be false, then should the doctrine of the Incarnation be patently incoherent, it would not be possible rationally to believe it, because it would not be possible to believe it at all. Furthermore, understood in this way, it is clear that nothing could count as a positive epistemic consideration in favor of the truth of a patently incoherent claim. If the incarnational identity claim endorsed by traditional Christians had this status, there could be no positive epistemic ground for believing it true. For example, Grace Janzen has said, "If the claim that Jesus is God incarnate is on an epistemological level with 'Jesus was a married bachelor' then no matter how much evidence we could discover for his having said so, his disciples and others having believed it, and the early church having affirmed it, the claim must still be rejected: such 'evidence' would be strictly irrelevant."[4] And this is certainly correct. Nothing can count as evidence or any other form of epistemic grounding for belief in a proposition the very understanding of which suffices for seeing its falsehood.

But of course, I hope to have shown earlier in this study that the incarnational identity claim is not patently incoherent, as incautious critics have charged. I hope also to have shown much more than this as well: We have no reason at all to think that the doctrine of the Incarnation is even subtly incoherent, or demonstrably im-

---

[3] An example commonly given is this: In mathematics, one can come to believe, quite rationally, the result of a faulty calculation or series of calculations, a proposition which is false, and given the status of mathematical propositions, necessarily false.

[4] Grace Jantzen, "Incarnation and Epistemology," *Theology*, 83 (May, 1983), 171.

possible, either by any lines of argument critics have yet used against it or by strengthened versions of such arguments. In any case, to the extent that the arguments and suggestions of the previous chapters are successful, the sort of objection we are presently considering to the possibility of belief in the Incarnation being rationally grounded is blocked. We have no reason from this quarter to think there could not possibly be good grounds for incarnational belief.

But before concluding too hastily that it is at least possible for belief in the Incarnation to be rationally grounded, we would do well to consider briefly a problem which has been raised by Frances Young. Young has said:

> ... it is now accepted by the majority of Christian theologians that Jesus must have been an entirely normal human being, that any qualification of this implies some element of docetic thinking, and that docetism, however slight, undermines the reality of the incarnation.
> I therefore pose the following conundrum:
> *If Jesus was an entirely normal human being, no evidence can be produced for the incarnation.*
> *If no evidence can be produced, there can be no basis on which to claim that an incarnation took place.*[5]

If it is assumed, as I would suspect it is by Young, that the belief that Jesus was God Incarnate cannot be a reasonable or rational belief to hold unless there can be evidence on which to base it, this argument, or conundrum, immediately becomes an argument to the effect that, on a certain assumption concerning what the doctrine of the Incarnation itself requires with respect to the humanity of Jesus, we find that it cannot be reasonable or rational to believe that Jesus was God Incarnate.

It is true that in order to avoid the Docetic tendency which some critics have claimed plagues traditional theology, we must maintain the full, complete humanity of Jesus. But Young has a genuine problem here for incarnational belief only if in order to avoid Docetism we also would have to hold that Jesus was *merely* human, and thus different from ordinary human beings such as you or me

[5]Frances Young, "Can There Be Any Evidence," in Goulder, ed., p. 62.

in no metaphysical way which could possibly be empirically manifested. As we have seen, there is an important distinction to be
drawn between being fully human and being merely human. Jesus
can be fully human without being merely human. At least, that is
the orthodox claim as I have articulated it. His complete humanity
is thus compatible with his belonging to the higher ontological level
of deity as well, and being such that his deity as well as his humanity
is manifest in his life. We need not hold that Jesus was merely
human in order to avoid Docetism and uphold the doctrine of the
Incarnation. If we did hold this, it is clear that we would be fleeing
Docetism only to fall into the grasp of Psilanthropism, and thereby
relinquish the doctrine just as certainly, only in a more currently
fashionable way. On a careful understanding of the logic and metaphysics of the Incarnation, we can thus see that Young's "conundrum" cannot even arise. So, once again, we find that what has
been taken to be a problem for the traditional position that it is
possible for belief in the Incarnation to be rational is in actuality
no problem at all. None of the considerations we have examined
has had the slightest tendency to block in principle the possibility
of rationally discerning God in Christ.

2 Experience and Affirmation

If it is possible that it be rational to believe Jesus to be God
Incarnate, how is it possible? On what grounds, or in what circumstances, could a person be rational in believing Jesus to be literally
God in human nature? What is required for rationality here? What
will suffice? Can it be that any Christians who hold to an incarnational christology or, more simply, ascribe deity to Jesus are
rationally justified in so doing? And if so, how so?

If we survey a good deal of relatively conservative theological
literature relevant to the topic, we often find writers of an orthodox
bent producing arguments of one kind or another for the deity of
Jesus, arguments which they apparently attempt to use to ground
the propriety or reasonableness of affirming the doctrine of the
Incarnation. A number of these arguments can be put quite con-
cisely as producing their common desired conclusion from a simple

two-premise structure. Among the arguments frequently to be found are, for example, the following:

(1) The Soteriological Argument
  (a) Jesus can forgive us our sins and offer us salvation.
  (b) Only God can forgive us our sins and offer us salvation; thus
  (c) Jesus is God.

(2) The Liturgical Argument
  (a) Jesus is properly worshiped.
  (b) Only God is properly worshiped; thus
  (c) Jesus is God.

(3) The Revelatory Argument
  (a) Jesus reveals God perfectly.
  (b) Only God can reveal God perfectly; thus
  (c) Jesus is God.

Such arguments, of course, hardly ever appear in such pared-down form. Usually the (a)-premise is defended as part of the distinctively Christian proclamation throughout the centuries and as either given in Christian experience or assumed in Christian practice. The (b)-premise is seen as a product of conceptual truths concerning the concepts involved: in each case the concept of God and, respectively, the concepts of sin, forgiveness, and salvation in the first argument, that of worship in the second, and revelation in the third.

These are clearly instances of deductively valid argument forms. And if the (b)-premise in each case is a conceptual truth, it follows that it will be reasonable to accept the conclusion of each argument if it is reasonable to accept its (a)-premise. But of course, it is also true that it is reasonable to accept the (a)-premise in each case only if it is reasonable to accept the claim of deity for Jesus. And that is precisely the question at issue. Such arguments as these clearly can serve a function within the context of an incarnational Christian faith—the function of explicitly displaying important logical relations between and among various central commitments of such a faith. A function they cannot perform is that of endowing incarnational belief with a rationality or reasonableness it otherwise would lack apart from their construction.

Can there be a deductively valid argument for the truth of the doctrine of the Incarnation which can function in such a way as to provide a person with a rational belief in it which, without the argument, he would not have, all other things being equal? In order to enhance our perspective on this question a bit further, let us look at one more relevant form of deductive argument.

In one of his contributions to the debate over the Incarnation, Brian Hebblethwaite sketched a number of arguments for the preferability of the Chalcedonian characterization of Jesus over the reduced claims for his status propounded in more recent times.[6] In a response to Hebblethwaite, Keith Ward wrote:

> Hebblethwaite introduces the remarkable argument that 'if God might have become a man, but did not, then the reduced claims for what God has done in Christ fail to satisfy'. It is difficult to formalize the argument; but it seems to go like this: 'if x is logically possible; and if we think it better that x, then x.' It is the sort of argument sometimes produced for the doctrine of the Assumption of Mary: 'God could have done it; he should have; so he did.'[7]

Consider for a moment Ward's attempt to formalize the argument he finds in Hebblethwaite. He first offers us the schema

(A)   1. x is logically possible
        2.   We think it better that x; thus,
        3. x

and then apparently means to paraphrase it or at least apply it in such a way that a parallel schema, each of whose premise-forms he apparently takes to be entailed by the corresponding premise-forms of (A), will result which relates directly to theological argument:

(But is it logically possible?)

(B)   1.   God could have done x
        2.   God should have done x; thus,
        3.   God did x.

[6] Brian Hebblethwaite, "Incarnation—The Essence of Christianity?", *Theology*, 80 (1977).
[7] Keith Ward, "Incarnation or Inspiration—A False Dichotomy?", *Theology*, 80 (1977), 253.

given our understanding of omnipotence, B Not logically

195

Fallacious

It is Ward's contention that using arguments of the form of (A) in theological matters will yield arguments of the form of (B) and will have, to say the least, untrustworthy results. Ward seems to view the sort of theological argument represented in (B) as having all the benefit of theft over honest toil—that of providing an easy route to results we have no right to.

Of course, the first thing that should be pointed out about what Ward says and seems to assume here is that (A) clearly neither is equivalent to (B) and thus properly paraphrased by it, nor even entails (B). The many qualifications we must introduce into a careful definition of omnipotence have taught us that (A)-1 does not entail (B)-1. And certainly (A)-2 does not entail (B)-2. We can be wrong about what states of affairs would be or would have been better than others; moreover, even when we are right in such judgments, we are not always discovering divine obligations to bring about such states of affairs.

Since (A) does not entail (B), (A) can be a fallacious form of argument without its following that (B) is as well. And this, as a matter of fact, is the case. Arguments of the form of (A) are obviously fallacious. The world does not necessarily conform itself to our preferences. But, interestingly, arguments of the form of (B) are not fallacious. The (B) schema is a deductively valid one, given the concept of God as a necessarily good being. If we could know, concerning some possible action, both that God could have done it and that he should have done it, then we also could know that he did it. Applying this to the doctrine of the Incarnation, if we knew or had reason to believe the two premises in the following argument, our knowledge or reasonable belief would be transmitted to its conclusion:

I   1.   God could have become incarnate in human nature as Jesus of Nazareth.

    2.   God should have become incarnate in human nature as Jesus of Nazareth; thus,

    3.   God did become incarnate in human nature as Jesus of Nazareth.

It is the major burden of this book to defend the truth of (I)-1. But, in light of the epistemic realities for religious belief with which we live, it is difficult to see how anyone could be in a better epistemic position with respect to (I)-2 than with respect to (I)-3. It is thus hard to see how the reasonableness of a belief that (I)-3 could be thought to be based on or grounded in an argument such as (I) operating on an independently reasonable belief that (I)-2 and (I)-1, given the epistemic conditions we are all in with respect to God's actions and the principles of his actions.

It seems to me that vast numbers of Christians are reasonable in believing Jesus to be God Incarnate, and it is my guess that many of them have never reflected on or in any other way entertained proposition (I)-2, the claim that God should have become incarnate, and have no reasonable belief that it is true. Moreover, many who have considered it would, I suspect, maintain a properly pious agnosticism about it, while wholeheartedly and reasonably endorsing the doctrine of the Incarnation. And further, I would expect that any Christians who would affirm (I)-2 would do so on the basis of, among other things, their prior belief that Jesus was God Incarnate. So even in their case, the reasonableness of the latter belief would in no way depend on the reasonableness of the former—quite the opposite.

I have introduced this excursus into Ward's remarks along the way to making a very simple point. If it is reasonable to believe Jesus to be God Incarnate, that reasonableness is not likely produced by means of, or grounded in, any such deductive argument. It seems to be the case that deductive arguments for the Incarnation will always have at least one premise whose positive epistemic status is no greater or more obvious than that of the doctrine itself. In the soteriological, liturgical, and revelatory arguments, it will be reasonable to believe the premise in question, at best, *if and only if* it is reasonable to believe Jesus to be God Incarnate. In the argument (I), gleaned from Ward's remarks on Hebblethwaite, it will be reasonable to believe the more controversial premise at best *only if* it is reasonable to believe in the Incarnation. In none of these cases do we find a prior, independent, reasonableness transmitted to and conferred upon the incarnational belief from more evident beliefs. So if it can be, or is, reasonable to believe Jesus to be God Incarnate, then most likely that reasonableness will neither consist in nor be provided by the having of such a simple deductive argument.

It is natural to ask next whether some form of inductive, or nondeductive, argument could render belief in Jesus' deity reasonable. Consider for a moment first, however, that form of reasoning in which Nicodemus engaged concerning Jesus, and from which this chapter began. We can represent the structure of his argument as

N   1.   Jesus performed a certain class of acts M (acts such as traditionally have been classed as miracles).

2.   No one can perform acts of class M unless he is a teacher come from God; thus,

3.   Jesus was a teacher come from God.

And again, this is a deductively valid argument concerning the status of Jesus. As Nicodemus appears to have reasoned to the conclusion that Jesus was a teacher come from God, many Christians of conservative theological orientation talk as if they themselves have reasoned, or as if they are convinced that a rational nonbeliever could reason, from empirically ascertainable facts about the circumstances, character, and deeds of Jesus to the much stronger conclusion that he was and is God Incarnate. They could have in mind an argument such as (N), where M now presumably would include, say, postresurrection activities of the risen Christ, and which would employ a substituted second premise such as

2'.   No one can perform acts of class M unless he is God,

from which it would follow validly that Jesus was God. Or they could have in mind a probabilistic transform of the revised (N), in which case the simple, categorical claim of deity for Jesus would not validly follow, but the weaker claim that it is probable that Jesus was divine would. Or it could be the case that many Christians who reason about Jesus in the tradition of Nicodemus have something in mind which cannot be captured by any such simple, two-step deductive argument. Perhaps there is a complex nondeductive form of argument to the best explanation which they have in mind, and which cannot be so simply represented. Thus, they would argue that the best explanation for a certain range of facts about Jesus is that he was God Incarnate.

On the one hand, it is clear that most mature Christians who affirm the divinity of Jesus see their belief as anchored in the empirical realm. They see their incarnational belief as in accord with their own personal experience, with the experience of other Christians throughout the centuries, and with the apparent though sometimes elusive manifestations of deity in the empirical realm which the New Testament documents appear to record surrounding the person of Jesus. But on the other hand, it seems not to be the case that there is any single, isolable form of nondeductive argument typically relied upon by such Christians to get from distinct facts about the portrayal of Jesus in the New Testament, from facts about the experience of Jesus on the part of fellow believers through the ages, or from features of their own experience to a conclusion that Jesus is God the Son, the Second Person of the divine Trinity. Nor is it obvious that any account of their reasonableness in so believing must involve the production of such an argument.

It does not seem that the reasonableness of incarnational belief is provided by deductive arguments from premises it is independently reasonable to believe, nor does it seem to be provided by any single sort of nondeductive argument consciously entertained or used by believers. Could it then be a simple function of direct experience? Could it be the case that traditional Christians have just *seen* Jesus to be God Incarnate, and that their belief in his deity, thus generated, is reasonable precisely in light of that experience? Grace Jantzen once wrote:

Clearly, any doctrine which wishes to affirm that Jesus of Nazareth is God the Son, the Second Person of the Holy Trinity, is going well beyond the boundary of empirical observability. Indeed, what would it be *like* to make that sort of observation? Even the question seems misphrased. No list of empirical data, whether these are taken strictly as sense data or more broadly as observation of speech and behaviour patterns could ever entail the conclusion reached by the centurion in the Gospel: 'Truly this man was the Son of God.'[8]

[8]Jantzen, "Incarnation and Epistemology," pp. 173–174.

Sense data reports underdetermine statements about physical objects. Reports about the disposition and behavior of physical objects (such as arms, legs, mouths, and even brains) arguably underdetermine claims about the distinctively mental properties of persons. And claims about the divine can seem to be even more remote from any reports about what is experienced in the empirical realm. For example, a few years ago an article appeared in which it was argued that not even God could know from observation, or even from observation enhanced by inductive reasoning, that he is God, i.e. that he exemplifies the distinctively divine attributes.[9] Consider omnipotence alone. No matter how many extraordinary tasks a being has attempted to perform and has carried out successfully with no difficulty or strain whatsoever, it will not follow from his record of accomplishments, however astounding, that he is literally omnipotent. Thus, no matter what we observe a being do in the empirical arena, a full report of our observations will not entail the proposition that the being in question is omnipotent. If seeing that an individual is God requires seeing that he is omnipotent, necessarily good, omnipresent, omniscient, ontologically independent, and the like, then the prospects for just directly seeing that Jesus is God look pretty dim, to say the least.

But does experiencing Jesus as divine require this sort of "seeing-that" relation? Clearly, in undergoing the processes which sense data theorists have characterized as the having of percepts or sense data, we most often reasonably take ourselves to be experiencing physical objects. Likewise, in experiencing the dispositions and behaviors of certain sorts of physical objects in certain sorts of circumstances, we reasonably take ourselves to be experiencing or observing the mental qualities of other persons—e.g., their anger, happiness, irritation, tranquility. It is true that if the observational experience of a table were to be reported in purely sense data language (supposing that to be possible), the report would not entail any appropriately related proposition about a physical object. But this does not prevent our sense experience being experience of physical objects. Likewise, the lack of entailments between reports

[9]See Richard Creel, "Can God Know That He is God?", *Religious Studies*, 16 (June, 1980), 195–201.

about Jesus cast in this-worldly terms and the appropriate propositions concerning his deity need not preclude the possibility of
an experience of Jesus as the infinite God Incarnate through the
sort of finite range of experience of him available to an ordinary
human believer.

Suppose that, as many theologians have suggested through the
centuries, there is an innate human capacity which, when properly
functioning, allows us to see God, or, to put it another way, to
recognize God when we see him, in the starry heavens above or in
the moral law within. If there is such a capacity to recognize God
both in his products and where he is distinctively present and active,
and if he is personally present and active in the life of Jesus of
Nazareth as the ultimate subject of that life, then we would expect
him to be recognized in his incarnate form by those whose relevant
capacity for seeing is sufficiently unimpeded.

Many children believe that Jesus is divine upon being told so by
their elders. They believe it on testimony. They do not believe it
on the basis of any argument or inference from the general reliability of testimony, from the particular reliability of the elders in
question, or from any fact or belief about testimony at all. They
just believe it on the occasion of being told it, like so much else
they believe. And surely they are not irrational in so believing. But
perhaps small children are not yet at an age of epistemic account-
ability. Perhaps. As children mature, we expect them to start hook-
ing up their beliefs into coherent pictures of the world. What was
once a properly basic belief for the young child, a belief not based
by any standard basing relations on any other beliefs epistemically
more secure than itself, and not requiring such basing, may later
come to stand in such relations in the young person's noetic structure that it is no longer among his basic beliefs, but that it is nonetheless still among the beliefs reasonable for him to have.

Likewise, many people who become Christians or who come to
see Jesus as divine come to believe in his divinity upon seeing the
portrait of him in the Gospels or upon experiencing what they take
to be his presence in prayer or his power transforming their lives.
They do not base their belief on any argument or inference from
the details of the scriptural account or from the features of their
own personal experience. They merely find themselves believing

on having some such appropriate originating experience or experiences, experiences which they take to be experiences of God Incarnate. But as the Christian who holds such a belief matures in his faith, he comes to know much better the testimony of scripture and of other believers to the reality of what he has taken himself to have experienced. I want to suggest that the Christian who originally attains a belief that Jesus is God Incarnate either from testimony or from his own experiences, of the sorts indicated, can reasonably take up such a belief and, as he matures, reasonably take much of what he subsequently learns of the Christian story, and from his own experience, to be corroboration of that belief. Instances in the life of Jesus, for example, as recounted in the Gospels, can reasonably be thought by a responsible reader to attest to his divinity. As we have seen in discussing the conundrum for incarnational belief which Frances Young attempted to formulate, the metaphysics of the Incarnation allow Jesus' divinity to be manifested through displays of knowledge and power often categorized as miraculous, as well as in other ways. And, despite what some critics seem to imply, one need not be exceedingly naive concerning the vicissitudes of New Testament criticism in order to be reasonable in so reading the Gospels as to find corroboration in them for a belief in the Incarnation.

The dynamics of reasonable belief are extremely complex and are far beyond the scope of the present chapter to lay out in any general way, even for the restricted, though highly controversial, class of religious beliefs such as the one which is our proper focus. One feature of reasonable belief maintenance, however, should be mentioned here: Whenever one holds a belief which is challenged by apparently powerful considerations which one understands, one's maintaining of the belief will continue to be reasonable to the same degree only if one is able to locate a sufficient response to the newly introduced challenge. For many sophisticated Christians of an orthodox persuasion in recent years, the challenges to the doctrine of the Incarnation which we have been reviewing in this book have constituted potentially the most difficult obstacles to the continued reasonableness of their belief that Jesus was God Incarnate. The availability of such perspectives as I have been attempting to sketch out constitutes, I think, a response to those challenges sufficient to block any negative net impact on the reasonableness of endorsing the incarnational identity claim. A traditional believer who has grown in the maturation of his faith and who has faced and met such challenges as those we have considered can be held to have attained the sort of corroboration and defense of his incarnational belief which can secure the reasonableness of his maintaining that conception of the status of Jesus which most often arises from the simple founts of testimony and experience.

If there is an innate human capacity which, when properly functioning, allows us to recognize God when we see him, then if Jesus is God Incarnate, it is clear that there are widespread and deeply rooted impediments to this capacity's functioning. It seems likely, in light of what has just been adumbrated, that a reasonable belief that Jesus is God Incarnate will arise and flourish only with the removal of some of these impediments from the life of a person. And this is just the insight we can derive from the original Nicodemus story when we see that Jesus' response to Nicodemus' simple *modus tollens* argument whose conclusion fell well short of the mark, is not the glaring *non sequitur* it can initially appear, but instead is a profound indication of the truth, or rather of the only way to come to the truth about who he is. The story, with which I began this chapter, will bear repeating:

> Now there was a man of the Pharisees, named Nicodemus, a ruler of the Jews. This man came to Jesus by night and said to him, "Rabbi, we know that you are a teacher come from God; for no one can do these signs that you do unless God is with him."

And then the key:

> Jesus answered him, "Truly, truly I say to you, unless one is born anew he cannot see the kingdom of God."

In the Gospel of Matthew we find this exchange between Jesus and his disciples:

> He said to them: "But who do you say that I am?" Simon Peter replied, "You are the living Christ, the Son of the living God." And Jesus

answered him, "Blessed are you, Simon Bar-Jona! For flesh and blood has not revealed this to you, but my Father who is in heaven."[10]

And in the Apostle Paul's first letter to the church at Corinth, we find the succinct claim that "no one can say 'Jesus is Lord' except by the Holy Spirit."[11] A full account of the epistemic status of Christian doctrine would be quite complex and would require, at its core, what we might call a Spirit Epistemology. The remarks of the present chapter have been laid out in broad strokes and have hinted at no more than a very few elements of such an account in even the case of the one tenet of orthodox Christian belief which is our present concern. Yet, despite the severe limitations of what I have undertaken to say here, it seems to me that on the basis of the few considerations we have been able to reflect on, however briefly, we can conclude that there seems to be no obstacle in principle to the acceptability of the widespread Christian assumption that it is possible that it is rational to believe Jesus to be God Incarnate.

[10]Matthew 17:15–17.
[11]1 Corinthians 12:3.

9 Some Trinitarian Concerns

The beginning proclamation of the Shema, "Hear, O Israel: the Lord our God is one Lord . . ." (Deuteronomy 64) can serve to remind us that the primary religious backdrop for the development of Christian faith was a strict Jewish monotheism. The ontology implied by Jewish religious belief at its most developed and focused stage involved a fundamental dichotomy between a created physical world on the one hand and a single Creator God on the other. Even within the apparently henotheistic currents of early Jewish belief, it was held that the only proper object of Israel's worship was a single, unitary God.

The Jews of Jesus' time believed, as did their ancestors, that in some way this one God had established a special relationship with them, calling them to be his representatives on earth. He was thought to have sent prophets and kings to direct and rule them in his ways. The prophet was said to be inspired by, or to have the spirit of, God. The king was said to be "the son of God," his special representative or emissary on the earth, modeling the role the people as a whole were to have for the world at large. It was believed that the prophet and the king often spoke God's words or enacted his will. But it is important to note that speaking God's words and doing his will were not taken as signs of divinity, only as marks of divine selection and guidance. It was also a widely held belief that God had promised to send his people a special deputy to bring them deliverance from their troubles in the world and initiation into his own kingdom. There was thus in first-century Judaism the expectation of a Messiah.

It was such religious beliefs as these which set the stage for Christianity. So it is more than a little surprising that a man, Jesus, thought by many to be a prophet or teacher sent by God, came to be spoken of by his followers not just as an emissary from God, but as himself divine. Those followers, as they experienced him and as they reflected on his life, his words and deeds, felt all their conceptual apparatus inadequate to express what they found in him except for that language which always had been reserved for God alone. Thus, Jesus came to be spoken of, and thought of, in divine categories.

Likewise, in the early church, the working of God among the believers and his personal presence felt in their lives came to be conceptualized as a distinct personal presence of deity distinguishable from that found in Jesus, and from that experienced by Jesus and other Jews in the guise of Yahweh, the Creator God of Israel whom Jesus called "Father." The attempt to give precise theological articulation to this threefold experience of God by Christian believers eventuated, of course, in the distinctively Christian doctrine of the Trinity—the doctrine that within the unity of the divine there is distinctness and internal relatedness, the doctrine, as it came to be specified, that God is, somehow, three persons in one divine unity.

As I have had occasion to mention in an earlier chapter, the doctrine of the Incarnation does not exist in pristine isolation within the context of Christian theology. It rather stands in a network of manifold and complex relations to a number of other doctrines, such as those concerning, for example, creation, sin, salvation, revelation, and the nature of God. Indeed, the christological identity statement we have been considering in this study has been formulated with a referring expression which derives explicitly from the doctrine of the Trinity: Jesus is said to be identical with, not God *simpliciter*, but rather God the Son, the Second Person of the divine Trinity in human nature. I think it would be somewhat inappropriate to end a book on the doctrine of the Incarnation, even a small one with highly restricted aims, without a bit more discussion of this closely connected doctrine and of how our understanding of the Incarnation relates to an understanding of it. I shall not attempt here any general analysis or discussion of the doctrine of the Trinity, but shall merely address some few issues concerning it which I think merit comment in this context.

1   *Incarnation and Trinity*

A kenotic christology, an account of the Incarnation in which it is alleged that during his earthly sojourn, God Incarnate divested himself of his properly divine omniscience and thus at least restricted the exercise of his omnipotence, thereby ceasing to be omnipresent as well, seems on some standard and orthodox metaphysical assumptions to require what we can call a social view of deity. If the universe exists moment to moment only by virtue of an ongoing exercise of distinctively divine power informed by a properly divine omniscience, and the exercise of such power informed by such knowledge cannot be delegated to a nondivine being for a limited span of time, then if a divine being ceased to exemplify or exercise the attributes requisite for this function for roughly three decades in order to enter into a continually existing physical world in a way otherwise impossible, we must acknowledge the existence of at least a second divine person not engaged concurrently in a kenotic transformation, who conserved the world in existence during that time through the exemplification and exercise of those attributes. On the kenotic view of the Incarnation, there must be at least two divine persons in society, each distinctly exemplifying or exercising every one of the attributes necessary for being God. Bringing this implication of the kenotic view in line with the doctrine of the Trinity then results in what is widely known as a social view of the Trinity, or Social Trinitarianism. According to this version of the doctrine of the Trinity, the deity worshiped by Christians is comprised by three ontologically distinct persons, severally exemplifying each of the attributes strictly necessary for being God, or for being literally divine.

Whatever else may be said about the doctrine of the Trinity, it is safe to say that in the history of Christian doctrine there has been no single, universally accepted articulation of the specific way in which it is to be understood. Every attempt to articulate the doctrine in detail has had its detractors and has been viewed as erring in one direction or the other: Articulations stressing the unity of God to the relative de-emphasis of divine threeness have most often been labeled modalist or Sabellian; whereas, those stressing the threefold existence of deity to the relative neglect of divine unity have been castigated as tritheistic or polytheistic. It has seemed next to impossible to achieve a balanced presentation of the triune nature of God that is both relatively detailed and also acceptable to most sincere Christians with theological sensitivity. So, although the view of Social Trinitarianism has had its advocates, it has had its opponents as well. It has seemed to its critics to involve the simple abandonment of monotheism and the embracing of a world-view according to which there are three gods, much as in the pantheons of pagan religion.

In chapter 4, I expressed a serious reservation about the traditional version of the kenotic strategy for defending and explicating the doctrine of the Incarnation. I criticized it on account of the precise sort of Social Trinitarianism it seems to imply. What I want to make completely clear at present is that I find traditional kenoticism relatively unattractive (relative, of course, to the availability of the two-minds view) not because it requires a social view of deity but rather because it necessitates either simply abandoning the strongest modal claims about deity or else embracing a modally subordinationist picture of the divine society, wherein members of the Trinity differ in the modal status of their distinctively divine attributes. It is the peculiar modal requirements of the particular version of Social Trinitarianism wrapped up with kenotic christology which I find unattractive, and which I suppose most philosophers and theologians of an Anselmian persuasion would judge unacceptable.

As a matter of fact, I find myself inclined to endorse a Social Trinitarianism, but one in which individual members of the Trinity are modal equals, so to speak. Yet I should point out that the understanding of the Incarnation which has been sketched out here, does not, unlike the kenotic view, require any social conception of deity whatsoever. The two-minds view of Christ is logically compatible with a fully modalist conception of the Trinity. And I

take it to be, at least prima facie, a strength or plus for a philosophical view if its truth is compatible with any of a number of
controversial alternatives in a cognate and hotly disputed subject.
The two-minds view should thus be equally available to theologians
wherever they find themselves on the trinitarian spectrum from
tritheism to modalism. It will not stand or fall with any particular
explication of the Trinity.

One feature of the New Testament to which Social Trinitarians
often appeal for support of their view is the fact that Jesus had a
prayer life and understood himself in relation to something or
someone on the level of the divine called by him "Father." The
inference is of course that, for example, prayer to a real God involves a two-termed relation. If Jesus is God and there is an individual distinct from him, the Father, to whom he in his humanity
properly relates in prayer, then it follows that more than one individual is God. Thus we have a social view of deity and are well
on our way to a Social Trinitarianism.

I should point out, however, that the two-minds view of Christ
can be taken to block this common inference. For it seems possible
to hold, on the two-minds view, that in prayer and other spiritual
exercises engaged in by Jesus the earthly mind or consciousness
was relating itself consciously to the overarching, properly divine
mind, both of which, on the view developed, belong to one and
the same divine person. Thus the relational, spiritual activities arising out of the earthly mind of Christ could be taken to connect up
with the other mind of the single divine person he is, and thus to
be understandable on a fully modalist conception of deity.

Although this seems a logical possibility, and may serve to block
any hard and fast inference from the prayer life of God Incarnate
to a social view of deity, it does not strike me as a very compelling
or even particularly plausible suggestion in its own right. And of
course, in addition to the mere fact that Jesus prayed, there are
features of his prayers as represented in the Gospels which can be
taken by orthodox, theologically conservative Christians as support
for a social conception of the Trinity. When Jesus, for example, is
represented in the Gospel of John (17:21) as praying to the Father
concerning his disciples and other followers "that they may all be
one; even as thou, Father, art in me, and I in thee," he was surely

not asking that there be only a single, solitary Christian. He was asking for unity among numerically distinct individuals, not for numerical identity here, and thus he was implying that he perceived the oneness between himself and the Father not to be that of numerical identity, as that between, say, Cicero and Tully, but rather to be that of some other sort of harmonious unity between ontologically distinct individuals.

Of course, the social conception of the Trinity does not hang only on such thin exegetical threads. Its motivation and grounding is broader than that. Although it is not my purpose here to marshal any sort of positive epistemic support for a social conception of the Trinity, or for that matter, for any sort of Trinitarian doctrine at all, I can at least indicate an example of a way in which Social Trinitarianism can be motivated by other theological and philosophical concerns. And, in the process, I can show how this conception of deity can escape objections many critics have thought to be decisive against it.

2 *Social Trinitarianism*

One contemporary movement in religious thought widely known as "process theology," a movement deriving ultimately, but for the most part quite loosely, from the philosophical work of such figures as Alfred North Whitehead and Charles Hartshorne, has succeeded in capturing a number of insights about God and the world, but along with these insights has spun out a number of needless theological errors which, from a traditional Christian point of view, are fully suited to the ancient category of heresy. One example of how process theology has transformed insight into error will lead us to see how one sort of motivation for endorsing something like a social conception of the Trinity can arise. With something like Social Trinitarianism, the insight captured by process theology which we shall consider can be preserved while the error into which it is taken by process thinkers is avoided.

In process thought, every existent object is viewed as essentially related to other existent objects. Essential relatedness is said to be a pervasive characteristic of reality. Prominent process thinkers such as Charles Hartshorne, along with more traditional theologians influenced by Anselm, hold that God necessarily exists. Not only is it as a matter of fact true that God exists, but things could not possibly have been otherwise. God's nonexistence is impossible. Now a property is essential to an individual just in case that individual could not fail to have that property without failing to exist. Since God cannot fail to exist, his essential properties are all necessarily exemplified. And so, if every existent individual is essentially related to other existent objects, and God is a necessarily existent individual, there must of necessity exist objects distinct from God to which he is related. And further, since every object distinct from God must be dependent on him as creature to Creator, it follows that a created world necessarily exists. God is necessarily a Creator. But any property an individual has necessarily, he does not have freely. So it follows that God never was free with respect to whether he could create a world distinct from himself. He may have been free to create this world rather than another one, but he was not free not to create at all.

On this view, God needs a world to which to relate himself. And a number of process thinkers have given a parallel argument for this view, beginning not from the premise that all existent objects are essentially related to others, but from a specifically theistic premise that God essentially exemplifies a certain sort of relation—that of being loving. The sort of love intended here is not self-love, but what we can call "other-love." It is thus impossible that God exist without loving another, some individual distinct from himself. But every individual distinct from God is a created being. It is thus impossible for God to exist without a creation. So, again, God has never been free to refrain from creating at all. To be who he is, he needs a created world.

The conclusion common to both these lines of reasoning is at odds with a firm commitment of the Christian tradition, the belief that with respect to creation God was utterly free not only concerning what he would create, but also concerning whether he would bring into existence any contingent universe of creaturely beings at all. I think that process theologians who mount these sorts of arguments are starting from genuine insights about relatedness and divine love: everything that exists is essentially related to other

---

existent individuals (this follows simply from the necessity of God's existence), and it is an essential property of any individual who is divine to be other-loving. But the process theologians' conclusions do not clearly follow from these premises as they seem to think. A traditional Christian, upholding the orthodox belief in God's absolute freedom with respect to creation can capture both these insights by a properly articulated doctrine of the Trinity.

The minimal content of any acceptable formulation of Trinitarianism will specify that within deity there is an internal relatedness. On any traditional understanding of the Trinity, each of the three persons found in the Godhead is somehow distinct from the other two, and distinct in such a way as to support a real internal relatedness. But, as I have already indicated, theologians throughout the centuries have differed over whether to stress the distinctness of these three persons, one from the others, or their unity, which is such that Christians can say there is one God who exists as three persons. There are thus two strands of orthodox thinking on the matter. The social view of the Trinity is an approach which stretches back to at least the Cappadocian fathers (Gregory of Nyssa, Gregory Nazianzen, et al.) and which has had able development and defense in recent years. The other emphasis, on the unity of deity, which tends to see the threeness of the Trinity as merely three modes of the existence of one individual being, was represented by, for example, Augustine, and has actually been the dominant view among theologians. The Augustinian emphasis may in some way have resources for countering the process view of creation, but that is not at all clear. What should be completely clear is how a social view of the Trinity can capture the process theologians' insights at this point and yet avoid their unorthodox conclusion.

While discussing favorably the argument that the essentiality of divine love requires a creation, Barry L. Whitney has written, "If one were to reply that love could exist only in God himself among the persons of the Trinity, this would seem to imply an unacceptable 'tri-theism' wherein the persons of the Trinity are considered as distinct centers of consciousness."[1] Is a social view of the Trinity,

[1] Barry L. Whitney, "Divine Immutability in Process Philosophy and Contemporary Thomism," *Horizons*, 7 (Spring, 1980), 67.

as Whitney claims, an unacceptable tritheism? Or can three distinct centers of consciousness, three individuals, three persons be acknowledged as God without any unacceptable theological results? These are difficult questions, any thorough examination of which would require a great deal more treatment than can be given them here. I do, however, want to look at least at a few simple but interesting arguments which can be advanced against the possibility of three ontologically distinct divine persons. The first line of reasoning we shall consider will be what many philosophers and theologians appear to have taken to be an utterly decisive argument against any plurality of divine persons. I want to attempt to show how, in seeing what is wrong with it, we may be seeing how a Social Trinitarianism can be a coherent and completely orthodox view to hold. If I am right, then anyone who wants to recognize the process insights about the essentiality of divine relatedness and divine other-love while yet preserving an orthodox view of divine creation will have a clear motivation to endorse a social conception of the Trinity and can do so without falling into either obvious incoherence or heresy.

No being is divine unless it has all the defining attributes of deity. Let us assume here that any divine person must be essentially omniscient, omnibenevolent, and omnipotent, as well as necessarily existent, and so forth. With this in mind let us ask whether there could be two divine individuals or persons.

We can begin with a thought experiment. Imagine two arm wrestlers of exactly equal power, skill, and determination. Their match presumably will end in a standoff, clasped hands straight up, equidistant from each side of the table. Now imagine two essentially omnipotent beings O_1 and O_2. Suppose O_1 wants some contingent object A to exist at some time t. And suppose O_2 wants A not to exist at t. At t, what happens? There is here no equivalent to a standoff. By reflection on this sort of imaginable scenario numerous philosophers and theologians have been led to conclude that there cannot possibly be more than one essentially omnipotent being. Yet, our thought experiment does not alone support this strong a conclusion, only the interestingly weaker conclusion that there cannot be multiple, essentially omnipotent beings with opposible wills. However, one philosopher, William Wainwright, has recently proposed a conceptual claim about persons which, when joined to this weaker conclusion, will entail the stronger one that there cannot be more than one essentially omnipotent person.[2] The claim is that

(C) Necessarily, given that two persons are genuinely distinct, it is possible for their wills to conflict.

This is just a claim, in other words, that it is necessarily the case that any two or more persons have opposible wills. If Wainwright is correct here, a Social Trinitarianism of the modally exalted and modally egalitarian sort is ruled out.

But why think Wainwright is correct? It surely does seem to be a necessary truth of a conceptual sort that it is possible for the wills of any distinct persons to differ—O_1 for example willing A, O_2 either just having no intention with respect to A or else willing only that whatever O_1 wills concerning A be done. But differing in this way is compatible with their wills being necessarily harmonious, such that it is impossible for them to conflict. Unless we have any good reason to endorse Wainwright's stronger claim (C), and I for one do not see any good reason to, we seem to be left with the real possibility that there be multiple, essentially omnipotent persons necessarily harmonious in will. And this is a far cry from any sort of pagan polytheism, whose gods were in continual conflict. As long as we recognize the conceptual requirement of necessary harmony in will, a belief in multiple divine persons, in particular three, will be far from any obviously unacceptable sort of tritheism. And it may well be that the unity of deity among the three persons of the Trinity consists, at least in part, in that very harmony of will.

If we can endorse a social conception of the Trinity, a very simple way of blocking the process arguments for the necessity of creation we are examining will follow. But there is one further argument which can be given against a multiplicity of divine persons that draws on a distinctive claim of process theology. According to leading process thinkers such as Whitehead and Hartshorne, God develops through time, progressively enriching his experience and

[2]Wainwright has discussed this in a paper entitled "Monotheism," which was presented at a research conference in the philosophy of religion held at the University of Nebraska–Lincoln in April, 1984, sponsored by the National Endowment for the Humanities.

thereby surpassing his own previous levels of greatness. According to them, it is a conceptual truth that any divine being is a greatest possible being, not in the sense that he is so great he could not possibly be greater, but in the sense that he is so great no other being could possibly be greater. In short, God's greatness is unsurpassable by any other being. In light of this, I want to look briefly at another interesting argument Wainwright has attempted to construct, this time from the process conception of unsurpassability to the conclusion that there cannot be more than one divine person. Wainwright very carefully lays out his argument in the following ten numbered propositions:[3]

1 Necessarily, any perfect being is more perfect at later times than at earlier times. (This follows from the dynamic process conception of perfection)

2 Necessarily, if there were two unsurpassable beings A and B, then A at time $t + 1$ would be more perfect than A at time t, and B at $t + 1$ would be more perfect than B at t. (from 1)

3 Necessarily, B at $t + 1$ is either more perfect than, just as perfect as, or less perfect than, A at t.

4 Necessarily, if it is more perfect, then B at $t + 1$ surpasses A at t, from which it follows that A is surpassable by another being and is therefore not perfect.

5 Necessarily, if it is less perfect, then A at t surpasses B at $t + 1$ from which it follows that B is surpassable by another being and is therefore not perfect.

6 Necessarily, if it is equally perfect, then since A at $t + 1$ is more perfect that A at t, A at $t + 1$ is more perfect than B at $t + 1$, from which it follows that B is surpassable and is therefore not perfect. Therefore,

7 Necessarily, if there were two perfect or unsurpassable beings A and B, then either A would not be perfect or B would not be perfect. (from 2 through 6)

8 Necessarily, if there were two perfect or unsurpassable beings, then there would be two perfect beings at least one of which was not perfect.

[3]This was presented in the draft of "Monotheism" read in Nebraska.

9   It is impossible for there to be two perfect beings at
     least one of which is not perfect. Therefore,
10 It is impossible for there to be two perfect or unsur-
     passable beings. (from 8 and 9)

This is an impressive argument, whose only major flaw is that it depends on an artificial conception of unsurpassability which not even process theologians need to hold. The intuition or claim that God is unsurpassable by any being distinct from himself is captured most naturally by an understanding of unsurpassability according to which a being A is unsurpassable just in case it is impossible that there exist a being B and a time t such that B-at-t is greater than A-at-t. And on this most natural understanding of unsurpassability the argument given by Wainwright will not work. For the unsurpassability of A will not be judged by how A at t compares to B at $t+n$ (for any nonzero value of n). To the extent that we have no good reason to accept the construal of unsurpassability on which Wainwright's argument turns, and reason to prefer a more natural construal, even if we accepted the novel process conception of perfection, we would have no good reason to judge this to be a good argument against any multiplicity of perfect divine persons. So the possibility of a social Trinity still stands.

Suppose we endorsed a social view of the Trinity, as many orthodox Christians of the past have. Could we then account for the essential relatedness of all existent beings and the essentiality of the other-love of God without accepting the process claim about the necessity of creation? Yes, we obviously could, for the three persons of the Trinity would clearly be recognized to exist in eternal and necessary relatedness to one another, a relatedness which includes an intra-Trinitarian relation of love. The necessity for any divine person that there exist an object distinct from himself as an object of relatedness and love thus does not at all clearly entail the necessity of a physical universe or the necessity that there exist some contingent created being or other distinct from God. So in the light of this understanding of the doctrine of the Trinity, we can capture the insights of process theology at this point without following the process theologians into their quite unorthodox conclusions concerning God's freedom in creation, or, rather, his lack of it.

Numerous other arguments can be, and have been, mounted against the possibility of multiple divine persons. There is also argumentation in the a posteriori mode against postulating the actual existence of a multiplicity of such beings.[4] Moreover, there is even a form of argument which attempts to show that no religious person can sincerely, rightly, and consistently recognize more than one being as divine. This sort of argument starts from the premise that, by definition, any divine being is a being worthy of undivided and unconditional commitment and devotion. It then proceeds by means of the claim that no religious person can sincerely and rightly recognize a being to have this status without actually adopting the relation to that being of undivided and unconditional commitment and devotion. It then follows that it is not consistently possible sincerely and rightly to recognize two or more beings to have this status, for no one could possibly be undividedly committed to two or three different individuals. Equal devotion and commitment to a multiplicity of individuals would of necessity be divided among those individuals and in each case conditioned by that of each other case. So no religious believer can sincerely, rightly, and consistently recognize more than one person as divine. What cannot be done sincerely, rightly, and consistently ought not to be done. Thus, no religious person, and in particular no Christian, ought to accept the social conception of the Trinity.

But let us examine this argument a bit more closely. What intuition, or clear conceptual truth lies behind the first premise? Is it a definitional truth, a conceptual truth, or any sort of truth at all that any divine being is a being worthy of undivided and unconditional commitment and devotion? Well, perhaps it is conceptual truth, or some other sort of necessary truth, that any divine being is worthy of devotion not divided and shared with any independent devotion to a nondivine being. We must choose between God and Mammon. But of course this is perfectly consistent with my being devoted equally to, say, three distinct divine persons.

[4]A full range of arguments is laid out by Wainwright.

Unconditional commitment cannot be given to each of two or more beings at the same time if there is any possibility that they would require of any believer conflicting acts; but if multiple divine beings are perfectly good and necessarily harmonious in will, then it can be argued that there is no possible world in which they impose such a dilemma on any follower. It might be insisted that a commitment to any such being would still be conditional on the concurrence of the others, but since the condition here would presumably be met necessarily, this would amount to no more than trivial conditionality, not weakening the strength of the religious commitment in the least. And surely such a trivially satisfied condition would be compatible with any clear and widely acknowledged intuitions we have about the appropriate or required strength and nature of religious commitment.

Thus a reasonable conception of the proper response and attitude due any divine being will not, I think, support an argument that we ought not accept a Social Trinitarian conception of God. Recognizing three distinct persons or centers of consciousness or ultimate subjects as divine will not clearly involve either an abrogation of duty or a flouting of logic.

Although I have indicated that I personally incline toward a social conception of the Trinity, find it compatible with numerous biblical passages, see it motivated by other theological and philosophical concerns, and judge it defensible against major objections, I should reiterate the fact that this understanding of the doctrine of the Trinity is not entailed, or in any other strict way required, by the understanding of the Incarnation which I have attempted to sketch out in these pages. I suspect that within the scope of philosophical theology there are, and will remain, various alternatives for spelling out in detail the fundamental tenets of the Christian faith, any consistent combination of which a believer could be rational in adopting. My main concern in this book has merely been to begin to display one way in which the logical and metaphysical outlines of the focus of Christian theology can be developed in such a manner as to show them to be free from obvious incoherence and to be intelligible, within our limits, to those who see God in Christ.

Index

Index

Library of Congress Cataloging-in-Publication Data

Morris, Thomas V.
   The logic of God Incarnate.

   Includes index.
   1. Incarnation—Addresses, essays, lectures.
2. Jesus Christ—Person and offices—Addresses,
essays, lectures. I. Title.
BT220.M815   1986   232'.8   85-21252
ISBN 0-8014-1846-1

Religion / Philosophy

The Logic of God Incarnate

THOMAS V. MORRIS

"A valuable book which breaks new ground in applying modern philosophical techniques in a plausible attempt to make sense of the Chalcedonian definition."—R. G. Swinburne, Department of Philosophy, Oriel College, Oxford

"Morris's arguments are presented forcefully and lucidly; they are invariably clever and intelligent."—Eleonore Stump, Department of Philosophy, Virginia Polytechnic Institute and State University

This book provides a philosophical examination and defense of one of the central tenets of traditional Christian theology—the doctrine of the Incarnation, the metaphysically remarkable claim that Jesus of Nazareth was one and the same individual as God the Son, the Second Person of the divine Trinity, in human nature. In recent years, this fundamental and distinctive Christian doctrine has been the subject of considerable theological controversy. It has been characterized by critics as incoherent, inconsistent, self-contradictory, absurd, and even unintelligible.

Thomas Morris enters into this controversy, employing some of the most effective techniques and useful theoretical constructs of contemporary philosophical analysis. He raises its logical, metaphysical, and epistemological issues to a new level of clarity and articulates a coherent model of God Incarnate, defending it against the strongest objections that can be made. In so doing, he charts important new territory within the province of contemporary philosophy of religion and demonstrates that issues raised by traditional Christian theology can be of general philosophical interest.

Written in an unusually clear and accessible prose, *The Logic of God Incarnate* will be rewarding reading for both philosophers and theologians, as well as for anyone wishing to reflect seriously on the central commitments of the Christian faith.

THOMAS V. MORRIS is Assistant Professor of Philosophy at the University of Notre Dame. A graduate of the University of North Carolina, Chapel Hill, he received his M.Phil. and Ph.D. degrees from Yale University.

 **Cornell Paperbacks**
Cornell University Press

ISBN 0-8014-9474-5

METAHUMANO

LIBERA TU POTENCIAL INFINITO

METAHUMANO

LIBERA TU POTENCIAL INFINITO

Deepak Chopra

Traducción
Karina Simpson

Grijalbo

Metahumano
Libera tu potencial infinito

Título original: *Metahuman. Unleashing your infinite potential*

Primera edición: junio, 2020

D. R. © 2019, Deepak Chopra

D. R. © 2020, derechos de edición mundiales en lengua castellana:
Penguin Random House Grupo Editorial, S. A. de C. V.
Blvd. Miguel de Cervantes Saavedra núm. 301, 1er piso,
colonia Granada, alcaldía Miguel Hidalgo, C. P. 11520,
Ciudad de México

www.megustaleer.mx

D. R. © 2020, Karina Simpson, por la traducción
Esta traducción se publica bajo el acuerdo con Harmony Books,
un sello de Random House, una división de Penguin Random House LLC

ISBN: 978-607-319-182-1

Impreso en México – *Printed in Mexico*

El papel utilizado para la impresión de este libro ha sido fabricado a partir de madera
procedente de bosques y plantaciones gestionadas con los más altos estándares ambientales,
garantizando una explotación de los recursos sostenible con el medio ambiente y beneficiosa para las personas.

Penguin
Random House
Grupo Editorial

ÍNDICE

PRIMERA PARTE
Los secretos de la metarrealidad

SEGUNDA PARTE
Despertar

TERCERA PARTE
Ser metahumano

UN PREFACIO PERSONAL

IR MÁS ALLÁ

Este libro es una invitación para que descubras quién eres en realidad, comenzando con dos simples preguntas: en los momentos en que te sientes muy feliz, ¿también te ves a ti mismo siendo feliz? Cuando te enojas, ¿alguna parte de ti está totalmente libre de enojo? Si contestaste "sí" a las dos preguntas, puedes dejar de leer. Ya has llegado. Has ido más allá de la conciencia cotidiana, y este ir más allá es lo que se necesita para saber quién eres realmente. El conocimiento de ti mismo se desplegará para ti todos los días. A la larga —o quizás en este preciso momento— te verás a ti mismo viviendo en la luz. Al igual que el gran poeta bengalí Rabindranath Tagore, podrás decir: "El hecho de que yo exista es una sorpresa perpetua".

Sería fascinante conocerte, porque sin duda tu existencia es bastante inusual; incluso podrías asumir que eres único. Miras a tu alrededor y ves que la gran mayoría de la gente es simplemente feliz cuando está contenta, y enojada cuando está enojada. Pero tú no. Tú ves más allá.

Cuando comencé a escribir libros hace 30 años no había duda de que ser feliz y enojarse era normal, sin el elemento añadido de observarte a ti mismo. El término *atención plena* ni siquiera existía; la meditación todavía era considerada sospechosa por la persona promedio, y todo el asunto de una conciencia más elevada era visto con la dura mirada del escepticismo. Yo era un médico joven en Boston con una familia que iba en aumento, y pasaba los días trabajando, dando servicio a una larga lista de pacientes y viajando cada día entre dos o más hospitales.

Cuando me alegraba porque mejoraba un paciente enfermo de la tiroides ¿me observaba a mí mismo siendo feliz? No. Al igual que todos los demás a quienes conocía, yo estaba contento o enojado sin tener misterio alguno al respecto. Pero al provenir de la India yo buscaba en mis recuerdos de infancia las pistas para un estado diferente de ser. De acuerdo con un Upanishad antiguo, la mente humana es como dos pájaros posados en una rama. Uno de los pájaros está comiendo una fruta del árbol, mientras que el otro lo mira amorosamente.

Desde que asistí algunos años a una escuela de una orden de hermanos católicos encontré otras claves de una fuente distinta, como Jesús que les decía a sus discípulos que debían "estar en el mundo sin ser del mundo". Si buscas esa frase en Google encontrarás una gran confusión sobre lo que realmente significa, pero la esencia de esa enseñanza es que existe una diferencia entre creer en la vida mundana y no creer en ella. Cuando no crees en ella, dice Jesús, de alguna manera estás con Dios.

Desearía poder decir que estas pistas sobre una conciencia más elevada me transfiguraron y le dieron forma a mi vida. No fue así. Las guardé en el fondo de mi mente, y nunca las evoqué en mi vida ocupada y llena de estrés. No existía la conciencia incipiente de la Verdad, con V mayúscula, la cual es que yo, y todo el resto del mundo, encarnamos el misterio de la existencia. Finalmente, ésta es la razón por la que Tagore se encontraba perpetuamente sorprendido. Una vez que despiertas a la realidad enfrentas el misterio de la vida de forma íntima y personal: no podría haber misterio sin ti.

En una frase o dos he dado saltos gigantescos, lo sé. Hay un abismo profundo entre las cosas que una persona debe hacer en un día —comenzando por levantarse, vestirse, ir al trabajo y demás— y el misterio de la existencia. Una sociedad basada en la razón y la ciencia ve con escepticismo cualquier noción como estar en el mundo sin ser del mundo, o la Verdad, con V mayúscula. Vivimos juntos en una realidad que obedece a la ley de "lo que ves es lo que hay". El mundo físico nos confronta: lidiamos con sus múltiples desafíos, y como la mente racional indaga en la oscuridad de lo desconocido, lo que emerge de ello son nuevos hechos y datos, no un sentido de asombro de que existamos en primer lugar.

Lo primero que me persuadió a enfrentar el misterio de la vida —y el misterio de mí mismo como un ser humano— fue la medicina. Practiqué endocrinología, especialidad que me fascinaba porque las hormonas son químicos únicos. Pueden volverte flojo y desanimado si tienes una deficiencia tiroidea; pueden hacer que huyas o luches cuando te enfrentes a una amenaza. Un estallido de adrenalina es el responsable de una reacción común ante un mago callejero que levita frente a tus ojos, mientras los espectadores se sobresaltan o se alejan.

Estamos tan acostumbrados a aceptar que estos comportamientos son inducidos químicamente que casi todos conectan el comportamiento adolescente con "hormonas enfurecidas". Incluso cuando el deseo sexual es controlado de alguna manera nunca está del todo domesticado, así como enamorarse nunca es algo racional. Si yo hubiera estado satisfecho al aceptar el sentido común de la conexión entre las hormonas y los efectos que provocan, no habría más que contar.

Pero hay un inconveniente, y afecta las cosas mucho más allá de las hormonas: potencialmente revierte la realidad misma. Existe una hormona cerebral llamada oxitocina, que se ha ganado el nombre de la "hormona del amor", porque la presencia de niveles más altos de esta hormona en el cerebro vuelve a una persona más afectiva y confiada. Pero esta molécula secretada por la glándula pituitaria es mucho más compleja que eso. La madre secreta niveles más altos de esta hormona durante el parto y la lactancia, fomentando un vínculo cercano con el bebé. Si acaricias a tu perro por algún rato, la oxitocina se eleva tanto en ti como en tu perro. La oxitocina hace que las personas amen más la bandera de su país, mientras que les son indiferentes las banderas de otras naciones. Durante la actividad sexual la oxitocina aumenta en las mujeres y hace que se vinculen emocionalmente con sus parejas sexuales, pero el efecto no parece ser igual en los hombres.

Algo extraño debe estar sucediendo, y sin embargo estos complejos descubrimientos no sacuden la fe de la mayoría de los endocrinólogos. Yo era diferente. Lo que me molestaba era que la oxitocina de hecho no hace nada de lo que se le acredita a menos que la mente lo acepte. Una mujer no sentirá mayor afecto por una pareja sexual si es forzada, si está atemorizada, enojada o simplemente distraída por algo más importante. Tu oxitocina no se elevará si acaricias a un perro que te desagrade. No amarás la bandera de tu país si un régimen autoritario te obliga a saludarla.

Llegué a ver el efecto explosivo de la conexión mente-cuerpo. Es como si fuéramos dos criaturas: una de ellas un robot que puede ser programado por químicos, y la otra un agente libre que piensa, considera y decide. Al parecer estas dos criaturas son incompatibles. No tienen derecho a coexistir, y sin embargo lo hacen, como lo refleja la estructura de nuestro sistema nervioso. Una parte opera de forma automática, permitiendo que la vida continúe sin que pienses al respecto. No tienes que pensar para seguir respirando o hacer que lata tu corazón, pero puedes tomar control conscientemente, y el sistema nervioso voluntario te permitirá alterar tu respiración e incluso, con un poco de práctica, disminuir tu ritmo cardiaco.

De pronto estamos al borde de un misterio, porque *algo* debe decidir actuar o no. Ese algo no puede ser el cerebro, porque al cerebro le es indiferente si usa un lado u otro del sistema nervioso central. En el lado involuntario, el cerebro disminuye tu ritmo cardiaco si corres un maratón, pero fuiste tú quien decidió correr el maratón en primer lugar.

Entonces, ¿quién es este "tú"?

Esa pregunta trivial es lo que afecta la realidad. En cualquier momento tú —esto es, el ser— decides a qué sistema nervioso llamar; por lo tanto tú no puedes ser la creación de ninguno de los dos sistemas. Cuando te das cuenta de este simple hecho estás en el camino de la conciencia de ti mismo. Puedes estar contento y al mismo tiempo observarte estando contento; comienzas a experimentarte completamente sin enojo, incluso si demuestras enojo.

La razón de este movimiento es simple: has ido más allá del lado mecánico de la vida. Has despertado a quien realmente eres, el usuario del cerebro, pero no el cerebro; el viajero en un cuerpo, pero no el cuerpo; el pensador de pensamientos que está lejos, muy lejos de cualquier pensamiento. Como te mostraré en las siguientes páginas, tu verdadero ser está más allá del tiempo y el espacio. Cuando te identificas con tu verdadero ser has logrado el dictado de estar en el mundo sin ser del mundo. La palabra griega *meta* significa "más allá", por ello la utilizo para describir la realidad que se encuentra más allá de "lo que ves es lo que hay". Cuando ocupas la metarrealidad eres un metahumano.

De vez en cuando todos ya estamos ahí. La metarrealidad es la fuente de toda creatividad, porque sin ir más allá de lo viejo y lo convencional no habría nuevos pensamientos, obras de arte, libros o descubrimientos científicos. Sin importar cuántos pensamientos hayas tenido a lo largo de tu vida, hay una infinidad de pensamientos más para pensar; sin importar cuántas oraciones los escritores hayan plasmado en el papel, hay una infinidad de oraciones más para escribir. Las palabras y los pensamientos no están almacenados en el cerebro como información en una computadora para ser malabareados mecánicamente cuando se necesita otro pensamiento. Shakespeare no estaba tan sólo malabareando su vocabulario isabelino: empleaba las palabras de forma creativa. Van Gogh no solamente combinaba los colores estándar en el espectro: usaba el color como una nueva forma de ver el mundo a su alrededor.

Ir más allá es la forma en que una persona decide si su vida es lo bastante significativa. Cuando deseas más de lo que la vida te está dando no es tu cerebro el que busca un mayor significado, ni es la persona de todos los días atrapada en la rutina de la vida. El ser, que ve las cosas desde una perspectiva más elevada, está decidiendo al respecto. El ser también decide a quién amar, lo que es verdad, si confiar o no, y así sucesivamente. Si una madre piensa que un niño de tres años malhumorado necesita una siesta, ha ido más allá de una simple evaluación de lo que el niño hace y dice. Los niños malhumorados dicen todo tipo de cosas, y si las madres les creyeran, no serían mejores que los niños.

Si ir más allá ha demostrado ser tan indispensable, ¿por qué no somos metahumanos todavía? No hay motivo para continuar repitiendo las mismas opiniones triviales y gastadas para seguir las mismas convenciones sociales pasadas de moda y rendirnos ante el pensamiento conformista. Todas esas trampas de pose en las que caemos, y el resultado es más de los mismos conflictos, guerras, violencia doméstica, prejuicio racial e inequidad de géneros de los cuales hemos sido presas a lo largo de la historia. Elegimos ser nuestros propios prisioneros. Esta paradoja, jugar el papel de preso y carcelero al mismo tiempo, ha causado sufrimientos inconmensurables a la humanidad.

Terminar con este terrible desastre implica una cosa: cambiar de ser humanos a metahumanos. Los dos estados existen aquí y ahora. No se debe ir a ningún lugar para alcanzar la metarrealidad. Como los dos pájaros en el árbol, te estás deleitando con la vida mientras que también te observas. Pero la parte de observar ha sido ignorada, suprimida, pasada por alto y sobrevalorada. En las tradiciones espirituales del mundo la transformación que te vuelve metahumano es conocida como "despertar". Una vez que alguien se eleva al estado de metahumano parece que el antiguo yo cotidiano fuera un sonámbulo, apenas consciente de las posibilidades infinitas de la vida.

Estar despierto es aceptar la conciencia plena de uno mismo. Muchas otras metáforas me vienen a la mente. Ser metahumano es como sintonizar toda la banda de radio en vez de sólo una estación. Es como una cuerda vibrando hacia una nota más alta. Es como ver un mundo entero en un grano de sal. Pero *como* es una palabra limitante. Lo verdadero es indescriptible y debe ser experimentado de primera mano, justo como la vista no puede ser descrita a alguien que nació ciego, pero sería revelador si esa persona pudiera empezar a ver.

Los editores incentivan a los escritores a persuadir a los lectores usando una gran promesa de algo nuevo, fresco y diferente. Despertar es tan viejo como ser humano. Es imposible prometer algo como despertar, lo cual es indescriptible en primer lugar. Al releer mis obras anteriores siento que estaba inhibido por lo peculiar y misterioso que es despertar. Sin embargo, esta vez he inhalado profundo y me he arriesgado. Confío en que el lector no sea alguien que nació ciego para quien la vista es algo completamente desconocido. Con una pizca de confianza, a todos nos pueden mostrar que ya somos metahumanos y que la realidad está aquí y ahora.

No sé quién será persuadido y quién no. Al final, el misterio de ser humano se obedece solamente a sí mismo. Sin embargo tengo fe en una cosa. Si al leer este libro te conectas con lo que significa despertar te darás cuenta de la verdad en mucho menos tiempo que los 30 años que me tomó a mí. Entre más rápido el metahumano comience en nuestra vida es mejor.

PANORAMA GENERAL

SER METAHUMANO ES UNA
ELECCIÓN DE POR VIDA

La gente hace muchas cosas para mejorar su vida. Podrías decir que las sociedades desarrolladas viven en una edad de oro en lo que se refiere a la calidad de vida. Se ha vuelto realista esperar vivir décadas con buena salud comiendo alimentos orgánicos e integrales disponibles a la vuelta de la esquina, sin mencionar tener cosas que antes estaban fuera del alcance de la persona promedio, como ser dueño de tu propia casa y retirarte con cierto tipo de seguridad.

Entonces, resulta extraño que millones de personas se esfuerzan en mejorar su vida sin mejorar su realidad personal. Las dos cosas están íntimamente relacionadas, y si no mejoras tu realidad, mejorar tu vida es algo inestable y poco viable. La realidad no es solamente lo que "está allá afuera": es muy personal. Dos personas que viajan todos los días al mismo trabajo pueden ver el mundo de formas completamente distintas, una de ellas sintiéndose ansiosa por su seguridad en el trabajo y la posibilidad de ser despedida, y la otra sintiéndose plácidamente contenta y optimista. Dar a luz podría ser el mismo evento físico, sin ninguna complicación médica, para dos madres primerizas, pero una puede sufrir depresión posparto mientras que la otra está llena de alegría maternal.

La realidad personal nos define. Consiste en todas las cosas en que creemos, las emociones que sentimos, nuestro conjunto único de recuerdos, y toda una vida de experiencias y relaciones. Nada es más decisivo en la manera en que resulta la vida de una persona. Así que es peculiar —podría decirse que es profundamente misterioso— que construyamos nuestra vida sobre una abismal carencia de conocimiento sobre quiénes somos en realidad. Indaga en cualquier asunto básico sobre la existencia humana, y detrás de la fachada de la opinión experta yace un vacío donde debería estar el entendimiento.

No tenemos idea de por qué los humanos estamos diseñados tanto para amar como para odiar, pregonar la paz y practicar la violencia, oscilar entre la felicidad y la desesperanza, y llevar una vida gobernada por la confianza en uno mismo en un momento y dudar de nosotros al siguiente. Ahora mismo, a tu manera, actúas todas estas contradicciones. Eres un misterio para ti, porque todos somos un misterio para nosotros mismos. Lo que hace que la gente siga adelante es la rutina cotidiana y la esperanza de que nada vaya terriblemente mal.

No estoy devaluando las cosas por las que vive la mayoría de la gente —la familia, el trabajo y las relaciones—. No obstante, para ser francos, incluso las cosas más importantes no las manejamos con la confianza de que sabemos lo que estamos haciendo. Por ello no es de sorprender que pasemos tanto tiempo trabajando para mejorar nuestra vida y tan poco tiempo trabajando para mejorar nuestra realidad. La realidad es demasiado confusa. Estamos bien si ignoramos las aguas profundas y permanecemos donde estamos seguros en lo superficial.

Sin embargo, un puñado de personas se ha aventurado a aguas más profundas, y en cada cultura esas personas dan cuenta de experiencias extrañas y al mismo tiempo inspiradoras. Es inspirador amar a tus enemigos, pero ¿quién los ama realmente? El hecho de que te digan que el amor infinito es divino no hace que así sea tu realidad. La paz eterna compite con el prospecto del crimen, la guerra y la violencia en todas las épocas. Un puñado de personas son veneradas como santas, y cabe la posibilidad de que sean etiquetadas como locas, o simplemente que sean desestimadas por ser demasiado buenas para este mundo.

Pero algo está más allá de la duda: la realidad personal es donde se lleva a cabo todo el juego. Contiene todo el potencial que los seres humanos han logrado, pero también las limitaciones que nos frenan. Un psicólogo neoyorquino llamado Abraham Maslow, que murió en 1970, sigue siendo famoso hoy porque nadó contracorriente. Mientras que la típica carrera de psicología consistía en examinar las enfermedades y defectos de la psique, Maslow sintió que la naturaleza humana iba mucho más allá de la experiencia cotidiana. Su idea central, que ahora ha florecido mucho más lejos de lo que él imaginó, es que los seres humanos estamos diseñados para alturas extraordinarias en la experiencia y, más que eso, deberíamos estar creando esas experiencias en la vida diaria. Era como si los únicos autos en el camino fueran trastos oxidados e inútiles, y alguien anunciara que puedes cambiar tu chatarra por un Mercedes o un Jaguar.

Si los únicos autos que ves son chatarra oxidada y los Mercedes y Jaguares existen lejos, del otro lado del océano, tu realidad no cambiará. Sin embargo, Maslow, al basarse en siglos de aspiraciones espirituales, insistía en que las experiencias sublimes en la vida son parte de nuestro diseño, que las necesitamos y las anhelamos. La clave es ir más allá de lo cotidiano.

La noción de ir más allá se convirtió en la motivación para este libro.

Para descubrir quién eres realmente debes ir más allá de lo que crees que eres. Para encontrar paz debes ir más allá del miedo. Para

experimentar amor incondicional debes ir más allá del amor con-
dicional, el tipo de amor que va y viene. Incluso por algún tiempo
pensé que este libro debía llamarse simplemente *Más allá*. Pero elegí
Metahumano, usando la palabra griega *meta*, que páginas atrás dije
que significa "más allá". Mi tesis es que volverse metahumano es
un cambio mayor de identidad que puede realizar cualquiera. Estar
diseñados para tener experiencias sublimes plantea la pregunta de
si tenemos elección. A menudo los momentos más reveladores en
la vida descienden como si provinieran de otro plano más elevado.
¿Cómo sabemos que no son accidentales?

En una conferencia reciente sobre ciencia y conciencia, una joven
mujer se presentó conmigo y me dijo que estaba escribiendo su tesis
de licenciatura sobre la comunicación con las aves. Le pregunté cómo
era posible hablar con las aves, y ella respondió que era más fácil
mostrármelo que decírmelo. Salimos del lugar. Era un día soleado, y
nos sentamos en silencio en una banca. Volteó hacia arriba para ver
algunos pájaros posados en un árbol cercano, y uno de ellos voló y
aterrizó confiado sobre su regazo.

¿Cómo lo hizo? Sin sentir la necesidad de decir algo, ella me miró
como diciendo: "¿Lo ves? Es muy simple". Mis viejos maestros católicos habrían señalado a san Francisco de Asís, quien a menudo es re-
presentado beatíficamente con aves aleteando hacia él. De la tradición
hindú, pensé en una cualidad en la conciencia conocida como *ahimsa*,
que significa "inocuidad", la empatía extendida a todos los seres vivos.

En cualquier caso, no era cuestión de hablar con las aves o conocer su lenguaje —todo había sucedido en silencio—. Era un ejemplo
perfecto de ir más allá, en este caso, ir más allá de mis propias expectativas. La joven mujer me explicó después que lo que hizo fue tener
claridad mental e insertar una intención para que el ave volara hacia
ella. En otras palabras, todo sucedió en la conciencia.

Son tan pocas las personas que tienen estas experiencias, que con eso sólo se magnifica la necesidad de mostrar toda la posibilidad de elección que tenemos para ir más allá. Creo con firmeza que tenemos mucho más control sobre la vida de lo que creemos.

Para mí, ser metahumano es una elección de por vida. Las experiencias sublimes son sólo el inicio, un vistazo de lo que es posible.

El término *experiencia sublime* se ha vuelto tan popular que la mayoría de la gente tiene una idea general de lo que significa. Describe momentos en que las limitaciones desaparecen y el entendimiento que transforma la vida llega a nosotros, o bien logramos un desempeño magnífico sin esfuerzo alguno. En futbol americano, el *quarterback* que llega a los 40 con múltiples triunfos en el Super Bowl, el prodigio musical que debuta a los ocho años tocando un concierto para piano de Mozart, el genio matemático que puede multiplicar dos números de 18 dígitos cada uno en cuestión de segundos: no tenemos que ir más lejos para encontrar historias de desempeño magnífico como éstas, que nos dan un indicio del potencial humano expandido enormemente. Pero estos logros, aunque sean asombrosos, ocupan un nicho específico. Cuando la fama y la fortuna se prodigan a unos cuantos, perdemos la posibilidad de que se aplique a la mayoría.

La realidad es mucho más maleable de lo que cualquiera cree. De hecho, la mayoría de las limitaciones que sientes que están impuestas sobre ti personalmente son autoimpuestas. No saber quién eres en realidad te mantiene atorado en creencias de segunda mano, alimentando viejas heridas, siguiendo condicionamientos desgastados y padeciendo un sentimiento de culpa y autojuicio. Ninguna vida está libre de estas limitaciones. El mundo ordinario, y nuestra vida ordinaria en él, no es suficiente para revelar quiénes somos en realidad, sino todo lo contrario. El mundo ordinario nos ha engañado, y esta decepción es tan profunda que nos hemos moldeado a nosotros mismos para ajustarnos a él. En las leyes, la evidencia contaminada se conoce como "fruta del árbol venenoso". No exagero al decir que aunque la vida sea maravillosa, todavía hay una mancha que proviene de las decepciones que confundimos con la realidad. Nada, sin importar lo bello y bueno que sea, ha escapado por completo a esta mancha. Ir más allá es la única manera de librarse de ella.

Un metahumano es alguien cuya personalidad está basada en valores más altos; no sólo en experiencias sublimes, sino en amor y autoestima. Después de que terminé de escribir este libro me maravilló descubrir que Maslow de hecho había usado el término *metahumano* justo de esta forma. (Él no lo asociaba con un cómic de superhéroes, ni tampoco yo. Dado que el metahumano de la fantasía es perseguido como bicho raro y amenaza para la sociedad, evitaremos por completo esta connotación.)

Está muy bien considerar ciertas experiencias tan exaltadas como algo divino, que es donde Maslow ubicó al metahumano. Fue un importante paso declarar que aspirar a llegar a Dios o alcanzar la paz y el amor eternos es tan real como fijar un clavo en la pared. Sin embargo, yo argumentaré que volverse metahumano es una necesidad urgente. Es la única forma de escapar de las ilusiones que representamos en la vida como sufrimiento, confusión y conflicto internos.

La fantasía de la vida cotidiana

Todos estarían de acuerdo con que es mejor vivir en la realidad que en la fantasía. Entonces te resultará algo perturbador saber que toda tu vida has vivido en la fantasía. Es una ilusión abarcadora que creíste desde la más tierna infancia. Incluso la persona más práctica y obstinada está inmersa en la fantasía todo el tiempo. No me refiero a fantasías eróticas o de lujos o sueños de volverte rico de la noche a la mañana. Nada de lo que percibes es lo que parece. Todo es una ilusión de principio a fin.

Saca tu celular y observa cualquier foto que hayas guardado. La imagen tiene varios centímetros de ancho. Tus ojos están separados entre sí al igual que la pantalla del celular, pero percibes el Gran Cañón, un ratón y un microbio de un tamaño sumamente diferente. ¿Cómo es que automáticamente ajustamos la medida de lo que aparece en un celular? Nadie lo sabe, y esto se vuelve incluso más desconcertante al pensar que la retina del ojo es curva y la imagen se proyecta de cabeza. ¿Por qué el mundo no se ve distorsionado como en una casa de los espejos?

Podrías encogerte de hombros y asignarle todo el misterio al cerebro, que manipula la información en bruto que llega al ojo y nos brinda una imagen realista del mundo. Pero esto solamente intensifica la ilusión. Cuando decimos que nuestros ojos responden a la "luz visible", convenientemente nos saltamos el hecho de que las partículas elementales de la luz —los fotones— son invisibles. Un fotón no tiene radiación, brillo, color o ninguna otra característica que asociamos con la luz. Como un contador Geiger que cliquea intensamente en la presencia de altos niveles de radiactividad, y cliquea de forma leve ante niveles bajos, la retina "cliquea" intensamente cuando millones de fotones detonan los bastones y conos que la alinean, y apenas cliquea cuando los niveles son bajos (lo que llamamos oscuridad).

De cualquier forma, todo lo que crees que ves ha sido procesado dentro de tu cerebro, en una región específica llamada corteza visual, que es completamente oscura. El foco de un flash directo en el ojo que te ciega es tan negro en el cerebro como el más leve brillo de las estrellas por la noche. Tampoco las señales que llegan a la corteza visual forman imágenes, y mucho menos imágenes en 3D. La imagen que crees que es una instantánea del mundo fue fabricada por tu mente.

De la misma manera, los otros cuatro sentidos son sólo "clics" en la superficie de otro tipo de células. No hay una explicación de por qué las terminaciones nerviosas en tu nariz convierten el bombardeo de moléculas flotando en el aroma de una rosa o en el olor apestoso de un basurero. Todo el mundo tridimensional está basado en un truco mágico que nadie puede explicar, pero ciertamente no es una imagen verdadera de la realidad. Todo está hecho por la mente.

Un neurocientífico me detendría para corregirme, afirmando que el mundo que percibimos está hecho por el cerebro. Pero unos simples ejemplos refutan esta opinión. En lo que respecta a tu cerebro, las letras de esta página son motas pequeñas, que no difieren de las motas que podrías salpicar con la tinta de un pincel. Antes de que aprendieras a leer el alfabeto las letras sólo eran manchas sin significado, y cuando aprendiste a leer tuvieron sentido. Y aun así posees el mismo cerebro que tenías a los tres años, en términos de procesamiento de la información. La mente aprende a leer, no el cerebro. Igualmente, cualquier cosa que ves a tu alrededor —un olmo, una barra de chocolate belga, una iglesia o un cementerio— adquiere significado porque tu mente la dota de significado.

Otro ejemplo: cuando a los niños que nacen ciegos les devuelven la vista por un procedimiento médico, están perplejos por cosas que nosotros damos por hecho. Una vaca a la distancia parece tener el mismo tamaño que un gato visto de cerca. Las escaleras parecen estar pintadas en la pared; su propia sombra es una misteriosa área negra que insiste en seguirlos. Lo que a estos niños les ha hecho falta es la curva de aprendizaje por medio de la cual todos aprendimos a dar forma a la realidad ordinaria. (El mundo visible es tan desconcertante que los niños y adultos que ven por primera vez prefieren sentarse en la oscuridad para recobrar la sensación de comodidad.)

La curva de aprendizaje es necesaria para abrirte paso en el mundo, pero te has adaptado de formas extrañas e inesperadas. Toma perspectiva. Si estás recostado en la cama y alguien te toca el hombro para despertarte, no ves a esa persona con un cuerpo muy ancho y una cabeza pequeña. Pero toma una fotografía desde la posición de estar recostado en la cama y la realidad se revelará. El torso de la persona, al estar al nivel de tus ojos, tiene un ancho no natural, mientras que la cabeza, al estar más lejos, tiene un tamaño pequeño que tampoco se ve natural. Asimismo, cuando hablas con alguien que está junto a ti, su nariz está hinchada de forma desproporcionada, y si la comparas con una fotografía, sus ojos pueden ser más grandes que la mano que descansa sobre su regazo.

En automático bloqueamos cómo se ven las cosas en perspectiva, y por medio de un acto mental ajustamos la información. La información que llega a tu ojo reporta que la habitación en la que estás sentado tiene paredes que convergen en el extremo más lejano, aunque tú sabes que la habitación es cuadrada, por lo tanto ajustas la información. Sabes que una nariz es más pequeña que una mano, y eso requiere un ajuste similar.

Lo que causa la verdadera conmoción es que *todo* lo que percibes está ajustado. Las moléculas que flotan en el jardín se ajustan y convierten en fragancias. Las ondas de radio vibratorias se ajustan en sonidos que reconoces e identificas. No podemos negar que vivimos en un mundo hecho por la mente. Esto es tanto la gloria como el peligro de ser humanos. Hace 200 años, mientras el visionario poeta William Blake caminaba por las calles de Londres, se lamentaba de lo que veía:

y en cada rostro que me mira advierto
señales de impotencia, de infortunio.

En cada grito humano
en cada llanto infantil de miedo,
en cada voz, en cada prohibición,
escucho las cadenas forjadas por la mente.

Es una imagen triste, que se repite hoy en día. Los humanos hemos atravesado todo tipo de sufrimientos y adversidades debido a la creencia profundamente arraigada de que estamos destinados a vivir así la existencia. No existe ninguna alternativa hasta que aceptes que lo que la mente ha hecho no se puede deshacer.

Bienvenido a la casa de las ilusiones

Cuando participamos en el mundo cotidiano no podemos ver más allá de la ilusión. Es necesario ir más allá, y para ello se requiere el cambio a ser metahumano. La única forma en que una ilusión puede ser universal es si todo en relación con ella es falso y nos engaña acerca de las grandes y las pequeñas cosas por igual. Ése es el caso aquí. La mente humana ha construido todo para ajustarse a ello desde cero. En cierto sentido, este libro fue escrito tan sólo para convencerte de que tu realidad personal está hecha por la mente en su totalidad, y no sólo por tu mente. Al haber pasado toda una vida adaptándote a la realidad artificial que heredaste como niño, debes emprender un viaje para descubrir la diferencia entre la realidad y la ilusión.

Para cualquiera que acepte el mundo físico "allá afuera" como totalmente real, la noción de un mundo hecho por la mente parece algo absurdo. Una cosa es ser afectado por una idea, y otra muy distinta es ser golpeado por un rayo. La diferencia es tan obvia que desconfiarías de cualquiera que te diga que los dos eventos son iguales.

Algunas de las mentes más grandes han dicho justamente eso. Aquí es donde comienza la verdadera fascinación. Max Planck, un físico alemán brillante, fue una gran personalidad en la revolución cuántica; de hecho, él acuñó el término *mecánica cuántica*. En una entrevista que el periódico londinense *Observer* le realizó en 1931, Planck dijo: "Considero que la conciencia es fundamental. Considero que la materia es derivada de la conciencia. No podemos actuar a espaldas de la conciencia. Todo aquello de lo que hablamos, todo lo que consideramos como algo que existe, es un postulado de la conciencia".

En otras palabras, la conciencia es fundamental. Si eso es cierto, entones las rosas floreciendo en un jardín inglés provienen de la misma fuente que la pintura de una rosa. Esa fuente es la conciencia, lo que significa que es tu conciencia. Sin conciencia no se puede probar la existencia de nada. Simplemente al ser consciente participas en el mundo hecho por la mente y ayudas a crearlo todos los días. La belleza de esta comprensión es que, si la creación surge de la conciencia, entonces podemos dar nueva forma a la realidad desde su origen.

Planck no estaba solo en su reinterpretación de la realidad, lejos del plano físico y hacia el plano mental. Todo el movimiento de la revolución cuántica fue para desmantelar la visión con sentido común de que el mundo es primeramente y sobre todo material, sólido y tangible. Otro brillante pionero cuántico, el físico alemán Werner Heisenberg, dijo: "Lo que observamos no es la naturaleza misma, sino la naturaleza expuesta a nuestro método de cuestionamiento".

Las implicaciones de esta afirmación son extraordinarias. Mira por tu ventana y quizá veas un árbol, una nube, una franja de pasto o el cielo. Inserta cualquiera de esas palabras en la frase de Heisenberg en lugar de la palabra *naturaleza*. Ves un árbol porque pediste ver un árbol. Ves una montaña, una nube y el cielo por la misma razón. Como observador, todo aquello que se encuentra afuera de tu ventana cobra existencia por medio de las preguntas que formulas. Quizá no estés consciente de formular preguntas, pero eso es sólo porque fueron formuladas tan temprano en la vida. Cuando los niños pequeños divisan su primer árbol, prueban que ven lo que es preguntando básicamente: "¿Esto es duro o suave? ¿Áspero o liso? ¿Alto o bajo? ¿Qué son esas cosas verdes en las ramas? ¿Por qué ondean con el viento?". De esta forma, al aplicar la conciencia humana a todo en el universo obtenemos respuestas que se ajustan a la conciencia humana. Pero no obtenemos la realidad. La física desmantela todas las cualidades de un árbol —su dureza, altura, forma y color— al revelar que todos los objetos de hecho son ondas invisibles en el campo cuántico.

Si esta discusión te parece demasiado abstracta, puede ser llevada a lo más cercano. Tu cuerpo está siendo creado en conciencia en este preciso instante; de otra manera no existiría. Una vez más, a Heisenberg se le puede dar el crédito de haber llegado antes ahí: "Los átomos o partículas elementales por sí mismas no son reales; forman un mundo de potencialidades o posibilidades". Sin embargo, en el mundo del sentido común, donde el cuerpo es nuestro refugio, nuestro sistema de vida y vehículo personal para estar en el mundo, es necesario defenderlo. Es demasiado perturbador pensar en el cuerpo como una ilusión mental.

El argumento antirrobot

Cuando abandonamos la falsa suposición de que el mundo es sólido y físico vemos que va en contra de una tendencia que me parece cada vez más perturbadora. La ciencia intenta demostrar de forma persistente que los seres humanos son máquinas, y mientras que ésta antes era tan sólo una metáfora de cómo funciona el cuerpo en todas sus partes complejas, la idea del ser humano como una máquina cada vez se toma más literalmente. Nos han dicho que la complejidad de las emociones humanas puede ser reducida a la elevación y disminución de niveles hormonales en el cerebro. Las áreas del cerebro que se encienden en una resonancia magnética supuestamente indican la causa o mecanismo de que una persona se sienta deprimida o con tendencia a un comportamiento criminal, y muchas cosas más. Además de ser marionetas del cerebro, supuestamente creemos que nuestros genes nos programan de maneras poderosas, al grado de que los genes "malos" condenan a una persona a sufrir toda una variedad de problemas, desde esquizofrenia hasta Alzheimer. Esos ejemplos de predisposición genética son extendidos a comportamientos y rasgos como tener propensión a la ansiedad y la depresión.

El metahumano tiene muchas implicaciones, pero una de las más fuertes es rechazar la noción de que los seres humanos somos mecanismos, primordialmente. Aunque la ciencia tiene una riqueza de descubrimientos tanto de los genes como del cerebro, eso no hace que esa noción sea más válida. El público general no sabe, por ejemplo, que sólo 5% de las mutaciones genéticas vinculadas a enfermedades en definitiva provocará un padecimiento en particular. El otro 95% de los genes eleva o disminuye los factores de riesgo de una persona e interactúa con otros genes de formas complejas.

El público todavía está atorado en la idea equivocada de que un solo gen, como el llamado "gen *gay*" o el "gen del egoísmo", existen y crean una predisposición irresistible. Esta idea errónea fue desechada cuando el genoma humano fue mapeado. La imagen actual del ADN es casi la opuesta de la imagen equivocada que tiene el público. El ADN no es inalterable; es fluido y dinámico, interactúa constantemente con el mundo exterior y con tus pensamientos y sentimientos internos.

La noción de que tus genes dirigen tu vida está muy arraigada, incluso entre las personas con educación, así que es revelador un experimento reciente que publicó la revista *Nature: Human Behavior* en el número del 10 de diciembre de 2018. Los investigadores del Departamento de Psicología de la Universidad de Stanford tomaron dos grupos de participantes y les realizaron pruebas en dos genes, uno asociado con un mayor riesgo de volverse obesos, y el otro con un mayor riesgo de tener un mal desempeño en el ejercicio físico.

Primero abordaré el asunto del gen de la obesidad. Los participantes ingirieron una comida y después les preguntaron qué tan llenos se sentían; además, les hicieron análisis de sangre para medir los niveles de leptina, la hormona asociada con sentirse satisfecho después de una comida. Los resultados fueron casi los mismos en gente predispuesta genéticamente a la obesidad y la gente que no lo era. La siguiente semana el mismo grupo regresó e ingirió la misma comida, con una diferencia. Se dividió el grupo en dos, al azar: a una mitad del grupo se le dijo que tenía el gen que protege del riesgo de padecer obesidad, mientras que a la otra se le dijo que tenía la versión de alto riesgo del mismo gen.

Para sorpresa de los investigadores, se dio un efecto inmediato y dramático. Con tan sólo escuchar que tenían el gen protector, los sujetos mostraron un nivel de leptina en la sangre dos y media veces más alto que antes. Los resultados del grupo al que le dijeron que no tenía el gen protector no cambiaron con respecto a la medición anterior. Esto indica que el solo hecho de escuchar sobre un gen benéfico provocaba que las personas exhibieran la fisiología asociada con ese gen. Lo que los participantes creían que era verdad anulaba su predisposición genética actual, porque en algunos casos las personas que creían estar protegidas genéticamente, de hecho, no lo estaban.

Los mismos resultados dramáticos sucedieron en el experimento del ejercicio. La gente a la que le dijeron que tenía un gen que producía resultados deficientes a partir del ejercicio, mostraba los signos cardiovasculares y respiratorios que ese gen debe producir. Aunque no tenía el gen del riesgo, tan sólo con escuchar que sí lo tenía redujo su capacidad pulmonar y quedó demasiado exhausta como para continuar corriendo en la caminadora.

En resumen, el cuerpo se ajusta a la realidad hecha por la mente. Si tu fisiología produce efectos genéticos con tan sólo escuchar que tienes cierto gen, el mito de que los genes controlan nuestra vida está seriamente desafiado. Esto no significa que la programación genética sea irrelevante (para conocer el panorama completo de este tema consulta el libro *Supergenes*, que escribí en coautoría con el genetista de Harvard, Rudy Tanzi), pero la realidad es tan compleja como la vida humana misma. Los genes están entre una multitud de causas e influencias que nos afectan. Es imposible predecir qué tanto afectarán a una persona en particular; en cada área del comportamiento y la salud existe una amplia libertad de elección de cada quien.

Cuando debas elegir entre dos opciones, mírate a ti mismo como un agente libre capaz del cambio consciente, en vez de una máquina robótica dirigida por genes y células cerebrales. Pero a pesar de la imagen pública fomentada por artículos científicos populares, no es verdad que el ser humano es una marioneta biológica. La visión de que somos agentes conscientes con un potencial ilimitado para

la creatividad y el cambio es más cercana a la verdad. Nos convertimos en metahumanos al tomar la decisión transformadora de vida
de serlo.

En la encrucijada metahumana

No espero que aceptes esto como una conclusión; al menos no todavía. El panorama completo debe ser bosquejado frente a ti para que
te decidas. Sin darnos cuenta, todos nosotros estamos integrados a
una realidad prefabricada a la cual comenzamos a adaptarnos durante la infancia. Todo lo que percibes en este momento por medio
de los cinco sentidos —las paredes sólidas de tu habitación, el leve
movimiento del aire en tus pulmones, la brillantez de la luz que entra
por la ventana o la que emite una lámpara— es una estimulación, un
constructo que te envuelve en una realidad virtual.

Por una parte, estamos hechos —cerebro, cuerpo y mente— para
conformarnos a una realidad virtual, que es el resultado del engaño
colectivo que ha tardado miles de años en ser creado. Esto hace que
las cosas sean muy complicadas. Un prisionero tiene el incentivo de
cavar un túnel hacia el mundo exterior, porque sabe que hay algo más
allá de los muros de la prisión. La realidad virtual que experimentas
no ofrece nada que puedas tocar, saborear, sentir, escuchar u oler del
otro lado. Aunque hay algo que existe fuera de la realidad virtual, lo
cual denominaré *metarrealidad*. La metarrealidad es el taller donde la
conciencia lo crea todo. Es nuestra fuente y origen, un campo de potencial creativo puro. La metarrealidad no se percibe por medio de los
cinco sentidos, porque no tiene forma ni ubicación. Sin embargo, es
totalmente localizable y ofrece nuestros únicos medios para escapar
de la realidad simulada.

Una vez que te das cuenta de que estás envuelto en una simulación puedes ver a cabalidad que el poder creativo de los humanos es infinito. Fabricamos nuestro mundo no con ladrillos y cemento, sino con un material invisible: la conciencia. En una era científica esta afirmación parece increíble, si no es que absurda. Desde el interior de la simulación la creación puede ser vista como una película del universo desenvolviéndose desde el Big Bang hacia delante, junto con una línea del tiempo que fue tomada 13 700 millones de años atrás. ¿Cómo es posible que esta alucinante escena, regida por el tiempo, el espacio, la materia y la energía, sea esencialmente falsa?

Para descubrirlo será necesario un sentido personal de curiosidad y un toque de aventura para ir más allá de la sabiduría convencional. La conciencia está presente en cada segundo de nuestra vida, y aun así la sabiduría convencional lo subestima. Esto no es como ver los árboles y no el bosque. Es más bien como vivir en el bosque sin ver un solo árbol.

Tomemos el famoso libro *Homo Deus*, cuyo tema abarcador es la invención del futuro. El autor e historiador israelí Yuval Noah Harari busca ofrecer un punto de partida nuevo y mejor para el futuro. Las cargas antiguas del pasado alguna vez parecieron ser inevitables, escribe Harari:

> Los mismos tres problemas le preocupaban a la gente del siglo xx en China, de la India medieval y del antiguo Egipto. La hambruna, las plagas y la guerra siempre encabezaron la lista [...] Muchos pensadores y profetas concluyeron que la hambruna, las plagas y la guerra debían ser parte integral del plan cósmico de Dios para nuestra naturaleza imperfecta.

Con un estallido extrañamente optimista entre los futuristas, Harari continúa escribiendo que estos problemas ya están resueltos en esencia, aunque persisten en algunos lugares aislados alrededor del mundo: "En los albores del tercer milenio la humanidad despierta a un maravilloso entendimiento [...] En las últimas décadas hemos logrado controlar la hambruna, las plagas y la guerra". Sus lectores están ávidos por aceptar la visión de Harari de que "en la escala cósmica de la historia la humanidad puede levantar la mirada y comenzar a ver hacia nuevos horizontes".

¿Y cuáles son estos horizontes? En *Homo Deus*, Harari lleva al lector por un recorrido a través de todos los problemas existentes y un conjunto de soluciones posibles que a los futuristas les encanta explorar. Hasta la página 409 de su libro llega al tema de la conciencia, y entonces promueve un futuro dominado por "tecnorreligiones" —en otras palabras, nuestra evolución conduce hacia la inteligencia artificial y las supercomputadoras que mejoran la materia prima del cerebro humano—. Confrontados con una estupenda inteligencia que se cierne sobre nosotros, ¿qué podemos hacer si no adorarla?

La visión de Harari termina en el lugar equivocado porque comenzó en el sitio equivocado. La conciencia debía aparecer en la primera página, y el futuro al que puede conducirnos la conciencia evolucionada es hacia donde debería estar encaminada la humanidad. Cada futuro que se ha desenvuelto a lo largo de la historia ha estado basado en una dirección tomada por la mente. Después de todo, la inteligencia artificial es tan sólo otro agujero en el cinturón de la inteligencia humana; por ello es muy prematuro predecir que seremos superados por una raza de supercomputadoras al estilo Frankenstein. Es preciso que conozcamos nuestra capacidad total antes de apostar por el futuro. Hasta que la metarrealidad se convierta en una experiencia común, el ser humano aún no ha alcanzado su capacidad creativa total. Conformarnos por un sueño mejor no es suficiente: al fin y al cabo una ilusión mejorada sigue siendo una ilusión.

En tu vida

LA ENCUESTA METAHUMANA

La mejor evidencia que tenemos de ir más allá es que la gente común y corriente ya está experimentando la metarrealidad. Una forma de medir esto es una encuesta de 20 preguntas desarrollada por John Astin y David Butlein, que lleva el complicado título de Inventario Temático de Personificación No Dual (en adelante NETI, por sus siglas en inglés). En una escala del 20 al 100, NETI evalúa cómo las personas se clasifican en cualidades consideradas como espirituales, psicológicas o morales. Incluyen rasgos metahumanos que ya valoramos altamente porque son muy significativos, así como otros que nos ayudan a enfrentar la vida, como los siguientes:

Compasión

Resiliencia

Propensión a soltar

Interés en la verdad

No estar a la defensiva

Capacidad de tolerar la disonancia cognitiva (por ejemplo, tener pensamientos, creencias o actitudes inconsistentes)

Tolerancia para la incomodidad emocional

Gratitud

Bajo nivel de ansiedad

Autenticidad

Humildad

Estos rasgos describen la naturaleza humana liberada de normas y condicionamientos sociales de segunda mano. Cuando posees estas cualidades estás libre para alcanzar el estado metahumano de conciencia.

Toma un momento para participar en la encuesta. A continuación presento el cuestionario NETI que se usó para evaluar lo que comúnmente se conoce como "experiencias no duales", que significan un estado de conciencia intensificado. Te darás un número de 20 a 100, y procederemos desde ahí.

CUESTIONARIO NETI*

Instrucciones: por favor indica qué tan a menudo te ocurren las siguientes situaciones. Circula sólo una respuesta (nota: el puntaje está invertido en las preguntas 4, 8, 14 y 16):

1. Nunca
2. Rara vez
3. A veces
4. Casi siempre
5. Siempre

1. Sentir una satisfacción que no es accidental ni depende de las circunstancias, objetos o acciones de otras personas.
    1. Nunca
    2. Rara vez
    3. A veces
    4. Casi siempre
    5. Siempre

---

* Desarrollado por John Astin y David A. Butlein.

2. Aceptar (no lidiar con) cualquier experiencia que esté teniendo.
    1. Nunca
    2. Rara vez
    3. A veces
    4. Casi siempre
    5. Siempre

3. Tener un interés en ver con claridad la realidad o la verdad sobre mí mismo, el mundo y los demás, en vez de sentirme de una forma particular.
    1. Nunca
    2. Rara vez
    3. A veces
    4. Casi siempre
    5. Siempre

4. Tener la sensación de que estoy protegiendo o defendiendo una imagen o concepto acerca de mí mismo.
    5. Nunca
    4. Rara vez
    3. A veces
    2. Casi siempre
    1. Siempre

5. Sentir amor y aprecio profundo por todas las personas y todas las cosas que encuentre en la vida.
    1. Nunca
    2. Rara vez
    3. A veces

4. Casi siempre

5. Siempre

6. Comprender que al final no existe una separación entre lo que llamo "yo" y la existencia en su totalidad.
   1. Nunca
   2. Rara vez
   3. A veces
   4. Casi siempre
   5. Siempre

7. Sentirme sumamente relajado, donde esté o en cualquier situación o circunstancia en la que me encuentre.
   1. Nunca
   2. Rara vez
   3. A veces
   4. Casi siempre
   5. Siempre

8. Sentir una satisfacción que no es accidental ni depende de las circunstancias, objetos o acciones de otras personas.
   5. Nunca
   4. Rara vez
   3. A veces
   2. Casi siempre
   1. Siempre

9. Tener un entendimiento consciente de mi no separación de (unidad esencial con) una realidad trascendente, fuente, poder superior, espíritu, Dios, etcétera.

    1. Nunca

    2. Rara vez

    3. A veces

    4. Casi siempre

    5. Siempre

10. No estar personalmente comprometido o apegado a mis propias ideas y conceptos.

    1. Nunca

    2. Rara vez

    3. A veces

    4. Casi siempre

    5. Siempre

11. Sentir una conciencia inquebrantable de quietud/paz, incluso en medio del movimiento y el ruido.

    1. Nunca

    2. Rara vez

    3. A veces

    4. Casi siempre

    5. Siempre

12. Actuar sin asumir un rol o identidad, basado en mis propias expectativas o las de los demás.

    1. Nunca

    2. Rara vez

    3. A veces

    4. Casi siempre

    5. Siempre

13. Tener una sensación de inmensa libertad y posibilidad en mi experiencia de momento a momento.
    1. Nunca
    2. Rara vez
    3. A veces
    4. Casi siempre
    5. Siempre

14. Sentir un deseo de ser comprendido por otros.
    5. Nunca
    4. Rara vez
    3. A veces
    2. Casi siempre
    1. Siempre

15. Sentir preocupación o incomodidad sobre el pasado o el futuro.
    1. Nunca
    2. Rara vez
    3. A veces
    4. Casi siempre
    5. Siempre

16. Sentir miedo o ansiedad tal que inhiban mis acciones.
    5. Nunca
    4. Rara vez
    3. A veces
    2. Casi siempre
    1. Siempre

17. Tener un sentimiento de profundo alivio y vitalidad.
    1. Nunca
    2. Rara vez
    3. A veces
    4. Casi siempre
    5. Siempre

18. Actuar sin el deseo de cambiar a nadie o nada.
    1. Nunca
    2. Rara vez
    3. A veces
    4. Casi siempre
    5. Siempre

19. Tener sentimientos de gratitud o abierta curiosidad sobre todas las experiencias.
    1. Nunca
    2. Rara vez
    3. A veces
    4. Casi siempre
    5. Siempre

20. Sentir la perfección y la belleza de todo y de todos, tal como son.
    1. Nunca
    2. Rara vez
    3. A veces
    4. Casi siempre
    5. Siempre

Puntaje total _____

EVALÚA TU PUNTAJE

Si nunca has experimentado ningún rasgo de la conciencia metahumana, tu puntaje será de 20. Si experimentas la conciencia metahumana todo el tiempo, tu puntaje será de 100. Cualquiera de los dos casos sería muy raro. Los siguientes son los puntajes promedio para tres grupos específicos de la comunidad terapéutica:

Estudiantes de licenciatura en psicología: 52
Psicoterapeutas: 71
Psicoterapeutas que han reportado que se han establecido en la conciencia no dual (metahumana): 81.6

¿Qué dice esto de la gente en la vida cotidiana? Y lo más importante, ¿acaso todos podemos desarrollar una conciencia más elevada aquí y ahora? Para descubrirlo, un equipo de investigación del que formé parte condujo un estudio sobre el despertar a corto plazo. Tuvimos 69 voluntarios que eran adultos sanos, de entre 32 y 86 años (la edad promedio era poco más de 59 años). Había dos requerimientos para ellos: que prácticamente se abstuvieran de tomar alcohol por una semana (sólo se permitía una bebida alcohólica al día) y que no hubieran asistido a un retiro de meditación o yoga en los últimos 12 meses.

Los participantes fueron divididos al azar en dos grupos en el Centro Chopra en Carlsbad, California, que tiene spa. A un grupo se le pidió que pasara los siguientes seis días relajándose y disfrutando de la experiencia del spa. El otro grupo se sometió a un programa de mente-cuerpo basado en la Ayurveda, cuyo objetivo era mejorar el bienestar en general. Esto incluía una dieta especial (primordialmente vegetariana, pero también ajustada para los diferentes tipos de cuerpo), masajes, meditación e instrucciones para llevar un estilo de vida ayurvédico. El enfoque es de amplio alcance porque abarca el bienestar emocional y espiritual. Debido a los años que llevábamos ofreciendo el programa, conocido como Salud Perfecta (Perfect Health), ya sabíamos que después de cursarlo los participantes reportarían que se sentían más saludables, menos estresados, más relajados y en general más felices.

La perspectiva específica en este nuevo estudio fue comparar la manera en que cada grupo respondía el cuestionario NETI, antes y después de los seis días que duraba el programa. El grupo en el programa de mente-cuerpo mostraba una mejoría significativa en su puntaje, comparado con el grupo de control, y los resultados fueron sustentados con una reevaluación realizada un mes después.*

En el estudio del Centro Chopra los participantes comenzaron con puntajes por encima del promedio, alrededor de 62, lo cual es 10 puntos más alto que el típico estudiante de la licenciatura de psicología. Después de ser divididos en los dos grupos, el grupo que cursó el régimen de Salud Perfecta tenía un puntaje de 74 (más alto que el psicoterapeuta promedio), mientras que el grupo que pasó seis días de relajación en el spa mejoró sólo de forma marginal, con un puntaje promedio de 68. Cuando fueron evaluados un mes después, hubo un pequeño aumento entre el grupo de Salud Perfecta, de 74 a 76, mientras que el puntaje del grupo de relajación permaneció igual.

Tu puntaje debe darte una idea general de dónde estás parado, con la advertencia de que es sólo un estudio pequeño. Es asombroso

---

* Los detalles completos del estudio fueron publicados en un artículo revisado por especialistas en el *Journal of Alternative and Complementary Medicine*, en diciembre de 2017. Los coautores provienen de múltiples universidades, desde la Universidad Davis de California, la Escuela de Medicina de Harvard, la Universidad Duke y el Centro Chopra para el Bienestar. El artículo rápidamente se volvió muy citado. Su largo título es "Cambio en el sentido de la conciencia no dual y despertar espiritual en respuesta a un programa de bienestar multidimensional" ("Change in Sense of Nondual Awareness and Spiritual Awakening in Response to a Multidimensional Well-Being Program").

y esperanzador descubrir que una semana de enfocarte en la mente y el cuerpo aumenta estas experiencias, y el camino por venir está abierto a cualquiera que desee desarrollar programas de capacitación incluso mejores que ése.

No sugiero que el enfoque basado en la Ayurveda tenga la última palabra para alcanzar una conciencia superior. Lo que más importa son las implicaciones generales. Las experiencias metahumanas suceden en todos lados, pero la gente difiere en qué tan a menudo las vive. Algunas personas las han tenido desde hace mucho y con frecuencia a lo largo del tiempo. Este tipo de personas puede dar por hecho una experiencia como sentir una energía de felicidad en su cuerpo. La misma experiencia podría dejar atónito a alguien más si surgiera de la nada y fuera del todo nueva.

Obviamente, la gama de la conciencia es mucho más grande que lo que puede medir un cuestionario. Aun así, surge una enorme pregunta: ¿por qué vivir en la limitación cuando la conciencia expandida ofrece recompensas tan grandes, como la sensación de paz y la comprensión que surge cuando conoces quién eres en realidad y el potencial creativo ilimitado que has sido diseñado para realizar?

PRIMERA PARTE

Los secretos de la metarrealidad

1

ESTAMOS ATRAPADOS
EN UNA ILUSIÓN

En algún momento de la prehistoria los *Homo sapiens* pasaron hacia la realidad virtual, cuando una simulación hecha por la mente se volvió esencial en nuestro camino evolutivo. Nunca sabremos cuál fue esa era exacta, ni la razón, si es que la hubo, de que una especie adquiriera este tipo de poderes y supiera que los tenía. Ninguna otra criatura da forma a su futuro de forma consciente. Ninguna otra especie cuenta historias y se convence a sí misma de que son verdad. Existen muchos misterios en nuestro pasado. De alguna manera, siguiendo cualquier camino tortuoso, nos las hemos arreglado para que nuestra simulación sea tan convincente que nos perdemos en ella.

Aunque esta simulación es muy convincente, todos los días se derrumba. Hay momentos en que la vida va muy mal y el mundo ya no parece real ni sustancial. Estas experiencias nos suceden a nosotros mismos o a otras personas. Por ejemplo, cuando alguien muere de pronto en la familia o cuando una catástrofe como un tornado o una casa se quema, quizá nos conmocione. Con una mirada vacía revelamos que nuestra existencia de repente se siente dislocada y decimos cosas como: "Esto no puede estar sucediendo. No es real", o bien: "Ya nada importa".

Por lo regular este estado disociado pasará, y con el tiempo todo se volverá a sentir real. Sin embargo, algunas personas nunca regresan. Por ejemplo, después de un brote psicótico, un porcentaje de los pacientes se vuelven esquizofrénicos crónicos y tienen alucinaciones, ven imágenes o escuchan voces por el resto de su vida. Pero el sentimiento de "esto no puede estar pasando, es como un sueño" no tiene que ser detonado por una conmoción. Innumerables personas se enganchan en fantasías personales de fama, riqueza o algún sueño que sienten como algo real por completo y las conduce durante toda su vida. Cuando alguien de pronto siente una felicidad extática, por cualquier motivo, también todo puede parecerle surreal.

Sin embargo, el mundo físico "allá fuera" se siente real y sustancial más de 99% del tiempo, y uno pensaría que ello es prueba suficiente de que no estamos bajo una especie de hechizo. Pero sí lo estamos. Es irónico que ahora existe tecnología que obliga a la persona a confrontar lo que es real y lo que no lo es. Cuando te colocas el casco de realidad virtual, accionado por inteligencia artificial, la simulación a la que te conectas es como una película envolvente y tridimensional, con una intensidad tal que abruma los sentidos y provoca la dislocación de lo que consideramos que es la realidad cotidiana. Puedes encontrarte sentado precariamente sobre la viga de una construcción que cuelga sobre la ciudad, la cual se encuentra muchos pisos debajo de ti. Tu cerebro, engañado por la imagen visual, detona la respuesta del estrés como si en realidad estuvieras tambaleándote en la viga. Sentirás que pierdes el equilibrio y entrarás en pánico, aunque en la habitación en la que estás parado tus pies están apoyados con firmeza y no te encuentras en peligro de caer y morir.

La ilusión de la realidad virtual se crea con imágenes visuales, y lo mismo sucede en la vida cotidiana. Crees en aquello que ves. Esta confianza está mal colocada, como lo aprenden todos los niños en edad escolar cuando les dicen que el sol no sale por el este y se pone por el oeste. Pero cuando la física cuántica afirma que la materia no es lo que parece ser, continuamos aferrándonos a las sensaciones de peso y solidez de los objetos físicos duros como si fueran indiscutibles. ¿Una bala sería menos peligrosa si pudiéramos ver a través de la ilusión? No. La bala y todo el mundo físico permanecen intactos, pero sabiendo que están en el extremo de un proceso que comienza en la conciencia.

Una vez que comprendes esto y lo absorbes plenamente, tu realidad personal se vuelve mucho más maleable, porque puedes acudir a la fuente y ser parte del proceso creativo. Salirse de la simulación de la realidad virtual no es fácil. Nuestra experiencia personal tendría que cambiar de forma drástica, pero la belleza de todo esto es que tenemos el potencial de cambiar, cuando antes no teníamos ninguno o muy poco. Aunque no puedes convertir las balas en bolitas de algodón, no es verdad que toda la realidad "allá fuera" está más allá de tus capacidades.

Las reglas básicas para la vida cotidiana son mucho más imprecisas de lo que imaginamos. Incluso cuando una persona se siente inmersa por completo en la simulación, hay una ruta de escape. Y no sólo una, sino muchas. Sólo esto tiene sentido. La metarrealidad es más real que cualquier simulación virtual. Deberíamos echar vistazos dentro de ella como evidencia de que podemos habitar el metaestado todo el tiempo. En lugar de eso, los enredos de la realidad virtual han puesto la imagen de cabeza. Conforme leas las metaexperiencias a continuación, te sentirás tentado a verlas como anómalas, raras o poco confiables. Volverse real es un proceso que comienza al confrontar tu confianza mal colocada en las ilusiones cotidianas.

"Algo sucedió"

Consideremos uno de los aspectos más básicos de la realidad virtual. Casi nadie podría cuestionar que estar dentro del cuerpo es normal, natural y una experiencia verdadera. Pero esta certeza va en contra del fenómeno de las experiencias extracorporales, que han sido documentadas en todas las culturas durante siglos. La experiencia extracorporal más difundida es "ir hacia la luz", como lo han reportado pacientes que murieron clínicamente durante procedimientos médicos de urgencias, en especial de ataques cardiacos.*

Resulta que si cuando morimos esperamos ir hacia la luz es engañoso, porque lo que sucede en las experiencias cercanas a la muerte es mucho más individual de lo que cualquiera pensaría. El estudio más grande sobre experiencias cercanas a la muerte, que examinó a 2 060 pacientes que murieron en urgencias o en cuidado intensivo, llegó a la conclusión de que la muerte no es un evento único, sino que es un proceso. No existe un evento final o definitivo. Durante este proceso hay formas de revertir la muerte. En los casos en que los profesionales médicos tuvieron éxito al devolver el corazón, los pulmones y el cerebro a su funcionamiento normal, alrededor de 40% de quienes murieron y regresaron a la vida recuerdan que "algo sucedió" cuando dejaron de presentar signos vitales.

Esta parte del estudio, que fue titulada AWARE (palabra inglesa que significa "conciencia") y fue dirigida por el médico británico de cuidados intensivos Sam Parnia, parece ser irrefutable. Pero pronto los detalles de que "algo sucedió" se volvieron controversiales. Tenemos que sumergirnos en algunos detalles para ver cuáles son los

---

* La experiencia cercana a la muerte se aborda a detalle en mi libro *La vida después de la muerte*, en el que comparto evidencia ofrecida por escépticos e investigadores que apoyan la validez de "ir hacia la luz".

problemas. De los 2 060 pacientes que murieron (el estudio se llevó a cabo entre 2008 y 2012 e incluyó 33 investigadores en 15 hospitales), 104 fueron resucitados. Lo primero a observar es que todos habían muerto. No estaban "casi muertos". Sus corazones y pulmones habían dejado de funcionar, y después de 20 o 30 segundos sus cerebros no mostraban actividad alguna. La descomposición de las células a lo largo del cuerpo toma varias horas para comenzar. El 39% de los pacientes reportó que durante el intervalo entre morir y ser traídos de vuelta tuvieron el recuerdo de estar conscientes, aunque su cerebro se hubiera detenido.

El doctor Parnia cree que esto es quizás una fracción de aquellos que han tenido una experiencia de este tipo; el resto tenía los recuerdos borrados, ya fuera por la inflamación cerebral, que ocurre 72 horas después de que una persona es traída de regreso de la muerte, o por medicamentos que le administraron como parte de la resucitación, que también pueden causar pérdida de la memoria. De los 101 pacientes que completaron el cuestionario sobre su experiencia durante la muerte, sólo 9% tuvo una experiencia compatible con el modelo típico de "ir hacia la luz". La mayoría de los recuerdos eran vagos y borrosos, a veces agradables, pero otras veces no.

Sólo 2% de los que volvieron, que significa dos personas de 101, tuvo la experiencia de conciencia total o experiencias extracorporales, como ver su propio cuerpo desde arriba, observando y escuchando al equipo médico que se esforzaba por revivirlo. Sólo una persona fue capaz de narrar con precisión lo que había estado sucediendo en la habitación, con un nivel de detalle que correspondía a las cosas que sucedieron. ¿Qué dice esta persona acerca de morir?

Depende. Los escépticos se encogen de hombros ante estas experiencias y las ven como algo puramente físico, afirmando que si tuviéramos mejores mediciones de la actividad cerebral, a un nivel muy sutil descubriríamos que el cerebro no había muerto. El doctor Parnia acepta que esto puede ser verdad. Su enfoque principal es cómo lograr mejores resultados en la resucitación que podrían traer de vuelta a una persona normal sin daño en los órganos, sobre todo daño cerebral después de la muerte clínica. Pero la conclusión personal del doctor Parnia es que una persona puede estar completamente consciente sin la actividad cerebral, como le sucedió a ese único paciente. Él señala el desacuerdo básico entre Platón y Aristóteles hace miles de años. Aristóteles sostenía que la conciencia era un fenómeno físico, mientras que Platón afirmaba que no era físico y que residía en un alma que trasciende el cuerpo.

El estudio AWARE no confirmó ninguna de las dos posturas. Como era de esperarse, ni los escépticos ni los creyentes cambiaron su postura ni sus prejuicios. Se podría decir que convertir la muerte en un proceso que puede revertirse es un paso significativo. También es significativo que la conciencia durante la muerte cubre un amplio rango de experiencias de ir hacia la luz, y no es una sola igual para todos. Lo que quiero enfatizar es que incluso cuando mueres vives la experiencia de forma personal. El doctor Parnia descubrió que la interpretación de su experiencia de muerte coincidía con su propia fe. Interpretaban la luz como si fuera Cristo, si eran cristianos, lo cual era diferente para los hindúes y sin espiritualidad alguna para los ateos.

Entonces, lo que sucede cuando morimos está abierto a la interpretación. El único consenso entre aquellos que volvieron a la vida es que la muerte es un proceso tranquilo, y no algo que se deba temer. Al haber experimentado directamente que su miedo a la muerte no tenía sustento, estas personas descubrieron una perspectiva diferente de la vida. Muchos, si no es que la mayoría, concluyeron que debían llevar una vida más altruista en servicio de los demás.

Creo que es útil que el estudio AWARE validara que "algo sucede", pero ¿por qué estamos tratando de resolver el asunto de la conciencia en el momento más extremo, cuando la muerte y la vida están en la balanza? Es como tratar de validar la gravedad al preguntar a los sobrevivientes de un accidente aéreo acerca de su experiencia al caer del cielo.

Lo que debe ser explicado es la experiencia normal y cotidiana de la conciencia, no sus estados extremos. He debatido o conversado con muchos neurocientíficos, y ninguno de ellos ha podido responder las preguntas más simples sobre la conciencia. Éstas son algunas de ellas:

¿Qué es un pensamiento?

¿Cómo es que la actividad electroquímica en una neurona se puede convertir en palabras, visiones y sonidos en nuestra cabeza?

¿Por qué es impredecible el siguiente pensamiento de una persona?

Si alguien tiene un vocabulario de 30 000 palabras, ¿significa que un montón de células cerebrales sabe 30 000 palabras? Si es así, ¿de qué forma se almacenan las palabras? Para la palabra *gato*, ¿hay un lugar del cerebro que guarde las letras *g-a-t-o*?

Nadie puede contestarlas adecuadamente.

El modelo del yo

Una experiencia tan etérea como "ir hacia la luz" puede ser una pista falsa. Resulta que estar "dentro" de tu cuerpo es un estado maleable; puedes entrar y salir de tu cuerpo casi a voluntad.

Un recuento fascinante publicado en el *New Yorker* y titulado "As Real As It Gets" ("Lo más real posible"), por Joshua Rothman (2 de abril de 2018), confronta el tema de vivir dentro del cuerpo con una claridad inusual. A los 19 años Thomas Metzinger, un estudiante universitario alemán, se quedó dormido en un retiro de meditación y despertó sintiendo comezón en la espalda. De acuerdo con Rothman:

> Intentó rascarse, pero no pudo, su brazo parecía estar paralizado. Intentó forzar su brazo para moverlo y, de alguna manera, esto lo elevó y lo sacó de su cuerpo, así que parecía que estaba flotando sobre sí mismo [...] Escuchó la respiración de alguien más y, apanicado, miró a su alrededor en busca de un intruso. Mucho después se dio cuenta de que la respiración había sido suya.

Esta experiencia insólita terminó pronto, pero le dejó una impresión duradera. Después de que esto sucedió, Metzinger se convirtió en un prominente filósofo de la mente, y se dedicó asiduamente a explicar las experiencias cercanas a la muerte, que se estima que le ocurren a entre 8 y 15% de la población, por lo regular durante la noche o después de una cirugía. Aunque sintió su experiencia muy real —fue seguida por otras experiencias similares de vez en cuando—, Metzinger descubrió sus limitaciones. Por ejemplo, no podía apagar el interruptor de la luz, o salir volando por la ventana para ir a visitar a su novia.

Metzinger comenzó a comprender una explicación sorprendente. Descubrió la obra del psicólogo Philip Johnson-Laird y su teoría de los modelos mentales. En vez de evaluar el mundo lógicamente, Johnson-Laird sostenía que aplicamos una imagen mental y cambiamos de un modelo mental a otro, dependiendo de la situación. "Si quieres saber si un tapete va a combinar con tu sofá —explica

Rothman— no deduces tu respuesta, sino que la imaginas, al mover los muebles de lugar en un escenario mental."

Metzinger se preguntó entonces si lo que llamamos realidad no es tan sólo un escenario ordenado y coloreado por la mente. Éste fue un entendimiento clave, y su confirmación sucedió por casualidad cuando contactó a Metzinger un neurocientífico suizo, Olaf Blanke, quien había inducido de forma artificial experiencias extracorporales en sus pacientes. Al trabajar con una mujer de 43 años con epilepsia, Blanke estimuló un área específica de su cerebro con una corriente eléctrica leve "y ella tuvo la experiencia de flotar hacia arriba y mirar su propio cuerpo recostado abajo". Esta ilusión tenía muchas variaciones que podían ser provocadas de forma deliberada. El artículo de Rothman en el *New Yorker* explica: "Estimular otra parte en el cerebro creaba la impresión de un *doppelgänger* parado del otro lado de la habitación; al estimular un tercio del cerebro creaba la 'sensación de una presencia', el sentimiento de que alguien está merodeando cerca, sólo que fuera de la vista".

Este estudio le pareció difícil de interpretar a Metzinger, porque estaba comprometido como filósofo a rastrear la experiencia en la mente, en vez de tomar el típico enfoque científico que afirma que todos los eventos mentales son producto de la actividad física en el cerebro. Pero eventualmente llegó a una conclusión consistente con la noción de "modelos mentales". Sucedió una especie de avance radical. Rothman continúa:

No es sólo que vivimos en un modelo del mundo exterior, escribió Metzinger. También vivimos dentro de modelos de nuestro propio cuerpo, mente y nuestro yo. Estos "modelos del yo" no siempre reflejan la realidad y pueden ser ajustados de forma ilógica. Por ejemplo, pueden representar un yo que existe fuera del cuerpo, una experiencia extracorporal.

Ésta es una forma fructífera de explicar por qué vivir "dentro" del cuerpo se siente tan convincente: lo necesitamos para la estabilidad y seguridad, para sentirnos arraigados en nuestro propio refugio personal. Hay otras formas de inducir una experiencia extracorporal, como usar la droga ketamina, que tiene propiedades de alteración de la mente. Sin embargo, la estimulación de la realidad virtual es quizá lo más efectivo. Por ejemplo, con un escenario específico de realidad virtual, Metzinger vio su propio cuerpo parado frente a él de espaldas (esto se hizo al poner una cámara detrás de él y transmitir esa imagen al caso de realidad virtual). Si alguien rascaba la espalda de Metzinger, sentía que la sensación la tenía el cuerpo frente a él; un sentimiento escalofriante y distorsionado. Al permanecer "dentro" del cuerpo puedes evitar esta desorientación.

Pero al mismo tiempo estás atrapado detrás de la piel de tu traje protector. No es que una experiencia extracorporal sea mejor que la forma normal de habitar nuestro cuerpo, sino que al parecer hemos perdido la capacidad de cambiar de un modelo mental a otro. Sin embargo, esta capacidad nunca se puede perder del todo. De varias maneras —al soñar, fantasear, en la negación, con ceguera deliberada y más— le damos la espalda a la simulación que hemos acordado aceptar casi todo el tiempo.

La realidad virtual de cualquier tipo —inducida por las drogas, estimulada eléctricamente o detonada por casualidad— crea imágenes. El hecho de que las imágenes aparezcan en 3D, como si estuvieran creadas por el cerebro o por equipo de realidad virtual, no las vuelve reales. Tu modelo de yo personal ha sido construido meticulosamente por imágenes del pasado almacenadas en tu memoria. Estos artefactos de experiencias viejas se sienten como "tú". No es difícil recordar los momentos de tu vida en que realizaste las mayores adiciones a tu modelo del yo. Por ejemplo, me puedo ver a mí mismo en la escuela de medicina, en el avión de la India a América, trabajando duro en mis primeros días en un hospital de Nueva Jersey con la presión de la carga de trabajo, estar en un ambiente extranjero, y la cautela de los médicos nacidos en Estados Unidos para aceptarme. Estas imágenes pasan por la mente como si estuvieran sucediendo otra vez, pero no es así.

Los modelos del yo son compartidos en algunos niveles, pero no en otros. Hay muchísimo espacio para las variaciones personales. Tú y yo podríamos pasar un día entero viendo las mismas cosas, comiendo la misma comida, interactuando con las mismas personas. Un modelo del yo compartido nos cegaría. El océano Pacífico, un plato de arroz pilaf y los amigos que encontramos podrían ser parte de las experiencias que compartimos. Pero tu modelo del yo absorberá y rechazará, interpretará y olvidará, se aferrará y soltará el día de una forma totalmente única. A mí me podrán encantar las ragas improvisadas por un gran citarista hindú, mientras que tú experimentas los microtonos de la música como ruido incoherente. Si nuestras parejas nos acompañan a comer, tú y yo estaremos apegados a diferentes personas con distintas historias de elación. Y así sucesivamente, momento a momento, el modelo del yo procesa cada experiencia de vida de acuerdo con sus propios designios.

Cuando la ilusión se desmorona

Lo que revela la tecnología de realidad virtual es que el modelo del yo no está limitado a una dimensión, la visual. También creemos en lo que escuchamos, tocamos, saboreamos y olemos. En efecto, tú y yo nacimos para encajar a la perfección con una simulación envolvente de la realidad. Sin embargo, hay una capacidad escondida en la mente humana que no podemos pasar por alto. Es la capacidad para desconectarnos, dejar de identificarnos con la ilusión. Sacar un conejo de un sombrero asombra a los niños porque creen en lo que ven. Una vez que descubres que un sombrero puede tener un fondo falso, el truco no cambia, pero sí cambia la forma en que te relacionas con él. Para el mago que ha presentado cientos de veces el número del sombrero y el conejo no existe ilusión. Puede sentirse impaciente y aburrido, queriendo terminar el acto de magia para ir a sentarse. Una vez que una ilusión pierde su fascinación, lo pierde todo.

Pero también lo opuesto es verdad, cuando se trata de desmantelar el modelo del yo, aquel escenario envolvente que cada uno de nosotros habita. Una vez que ves más allá de esta ilusión, la vida de pronto se vuelve más fascinante. Éste es el testimonio de personas a quienes se les derrumbó la ilusión, por lo regular sin advertencia alguna ni esfuerzo de su parte. Hace poco conocí a alguien a quien le pasó esto. Lorin Roche, que ahora tiene 68 años, en aquel entonces era un estudiante universitario de 18 años a final de la década de 1960, que accedió a participar en un proyecto de investigación sobre los efectos fisiológicos de la meditación. Pero como narra Roche en su sitio de internet, cuando llegó al laboratorio le dijeron que "él era un sujeto de control, y no recibió ninguna instrucción; le pagaron para sentarse en la oscuridad total, en una habitación a prueba de ruido durante dos horas al día por varias semanas, y medían sus ondas cerebrales. Sin haber recibido instrucciones, y dado que nunca escuchó sobre la meditación, Lorin tan sólo asistió en total silencio y oscuridad, y de forma espontánea entró en un estado de atención intensa".

Ésta fue una experiencia sorprendente e inesperada, la cual le pareció muy absorbente mientras duró. Unos meses después alguien le regaló a Lorin un libro de 112 meditaciones basadas en los antiguos sutras (dichos o enseñanzas) en sánscrito de la India. Estaba maravillado al describir que había tenido espontáneamente algunas de las experiencias descritas en estos textos de siglos de antigüedad. El hecho de que un adolescente occidental tenga predilección por la meditación es tan extraordinario como tener un talento musical innato, aunque Rocher fue más allá. Asistió al festival de los devotos de Bhakti en el Parque Nacional de Joshua Tree en el desierto de California. En la India, Bhakti encarna la forma más popular de adoración, que consiste en amor, fe y devoción como el camino de la iluminación. La práctica diaria más común es el canto, y Roche asistió para participar en él.

Sin embargo, el calor era terrible y su energía estaba comenzando a disminuir. Como él describe la experiencia: "Lo que vendría bien ahora es ir a saltar en la alberca de agua salada más cercana. Conforme me alejo del campo acústico del festival, me doy cuenta de que el canto todavía está dentro de mí. Y aunque ya no hay mucho ruido, esta pista sonora interna se siente poderosa. De alguna manera mis átomos están bailando y cantando los himnos de alabanza a la diosa y el dios, Devi y Shiva… Es el Bollywood de los átomos".

Actualmente Roche continúa bailando en alabanza a la diosa y el dios, y ha traducido los 112 sutras de Shiva que están considerados entre los más extáticos. A continuación presento una muestra, todos basados en fundir el texto antiguo con sus propias experiencias personales. Shiva le canta a Devi:

> Ríos de poder fluyendo en todos lados.
> Campos de magnetismo relacionando todo.
> Éste es tu origen. Éste es tu linaje.

La corriente de la creación está aquí,
cruzando a través de canales sutiles,
dando vida a esta misma forma.

Sigue el toque suave de la vida,
leve como la huella de una hormiga,
como sensaciones minúsculas abiertas a la vastedad.

Tuve un encuentro con Lorin Roche mientras escribía este libro, y él irradiaba el estado de dicha que es la meta de Bhakti —su traducción de los sutras se titula *The Radiance Sutras*—. Compré un ejemplar para leerlo en un avión, y su autenticidad personal sobrepasa cualquier otra versión que yo conozca. Para él, la "danza de los átomos" es real:

El poder canta conforme fluye,
electrifica los órganos de los sentidos,
se vuelve luz líquida,
nutre a todo el ser.
Celebra la frontera
donde los arroyos se unen al mar,
donde el cuerpo encuentra lo infinito.

Un escéptico diría que ésta fue una experiencia tan subjetiva que no tiene sustento en la realidad. Los átomos que danzan están en la imaginación de Lorin Roche, no en un laboratorio de física. El mundo físico no se siente como una simulación; se siente totalmente real, y cuando vemos algo fantástico en nuestra imaginación, como un dragón volador, no corremos para escapar del fuego que exhala.

Pero este argumento pierde el punto central. Todo está hecho por la mente, incluido el calor del fuego y su capacidad destructiva.

Esto sólo muestra qué tan completa es la ilusión. Los dragones que exhalan fuego son imaginarios y un incendio forestal no lo es; como parte de la simulación, el mundo físico opera de la forma en que lo hace. El fuego es caliente, el hielo es frío. Los árboles se queman, el agua se congela. La clave es la identificación: una vez que identificas la simulación, estás sumergido en ella. Tú eres parte de toda la configuración, representando un rol pasivo. Si tu involucramiento cambia, también lo hace tu experiencia. Tienes un rol más flexible que representar. Por ejemplo, tomemos algo tan básico como el dolor. No existe una forma objetiva de medir el dolor. La gente lo experimenta de forma muy diferente e impredecible.

En un experimento de dolor típico se les pidió a participantes calificar el dolor en una escala del 1 al 10, donde 10 es insoportable. Aunque la temperatura del agua es la misma para todos, una persona calificará el dolor como 5 (moderado) y otro le dará un 8 o 9 (de severo a insoportable). Por otra parte, si visitas la cocina de un restaurante donde el chef hierve jarabe de azúcar para el dulce o el glaseado, observarás que muchos de los chefs pueden meter el dedo para saber si el jarabe ya comenzó a espesar, lo cual sucede a los 100 °C. (Por cierto, las mujeres parecen tener un umbral del dolor más alto que los hombres.)

El resultado no es muy sorprendente, pero pocos de nosotros nos damos cuenta de que de hecho estamos produciendo el dolor que sentimos como creado físicamente. Como parte de la respuesta del estrés, una ráfaga de adrenalina puede bloquear el dolor, y por ello los soldados reportan que sufrir un disparo no era tan doloroso al estar en el campo de batalla, y lo mismo sucede cuando una persona se conmociona. Aunque también el cese total del dolor puede suceder de la nada, y con ello llega un cambio dramático en la conciencia.

La gente que ha tenido esta experiencia por lo general reporta un "quiebre" cuando la mente crea su propio estado de conciencia de forma espontánea. En el libro *Stealing Fire*, publicado en 2017, los autores Steven Kotler y Jamie Wheal ponen el ejemplo sorprendente de Mikey Siegel, un ingeniero graduado del MIT que terminó extenuado por su lucrativo trabajo en robótica e inteligencia artificial. Él quería más satisfacción, y comenzó su búsqueda haciendo senderismo en las selvas sudamericanas, después visitó *ashrams* en la India, y eventualmente decidió practicar la meditación.

En un retiro de meditación de 10 días Siegel participó en un ejercicio de concentración en el cual el objetivo era sentarse quieto y experimentar sensaciones en el cuerpo sin juzgarlas:

> "Pero Siegel estaba abrumado por las sensaciones. Después de una semana de meditar con las piernas cruzadas le dolía la espalda, le palpitaba el cuello y no sentía los muslos. 'Era un dolor absorbente', explica, 'y todo lo que yo hacía era juzgar'".

Los momentos de experiencias extremas, ya sean placenteras o dolorosas, de alguna forma rompen los vínculos de la mente condicionada que está atrapada en el hábito de aceptar las limitaciones físicas al pie de la letra. De pronto hay acceso a un estado extático, libre de condicionamientos, como fue el caso de Siegel:

> Algo dentro cambió. La parte de su cerebro que había estado juzgando de pronto se apagó. "Se sentía como libertad", explica Siegel [...] "Nunca había estado tan claro, presente y consciente. Y podía sentir dolor extremo y aun así permanecer en paz y con claridad, pensé que entonces otras personas podían hacerlo también. En ese instante cambió todo lo que creía sobre el potencial humano."

Siegel no sólo estaba asombrado; no soltó esta experiencia, sino que decidió darle seguimiento. Se embarcó con fervor en el proyecto de "ingeniería de la iluminación" usando la meditación como una herramienta entre muchas más. Por ejemplo, podemos acceder a la calma al disminuir nuestro ritmo cardiaco por medio de un dispositivo portátil de *biofeedback*. Ya llegaremos al tema de la interconexión de la mente con dispositivos que mejoran la conciencia, pero hay algunos puntos básicos de los que quiero hablar aquí. Se sabe que el dolor de pronto da lugar a un estado desapegado y de no juicio, conocido como "atestiguamiento". En la India durante siglos los sadhus y yoguis se han sometido a *tapas*, o austeridad física, como camino al despertar. El estereotipo del yogui barbado sentado en una remota cueva de los Himalayas refleja un tipo de tapas.

Someter al cuerpo al estrés se encuentra en las disciplinadas meditaciones del budismo zen, en el que los monjes se levantan antes del amanecer, consumen té verde y un puñado de arroz, y después se sientan a meditar por horas con la cabeza derecha y la columna erguida. Como con Siegel, es predecible que haya un momento de "quiebre" cuando la mente se salga de su identificación con el dolor y la lucha por detenerlo. Sin embargo, muchas personas están atoradas de varias formas, e incluso años de soportar la incomodidad extrema quizá no deriven en los resultados deseados.

El cese del dolor es una evidencia poderosa de que la mente puede liberarse de sensaciones que todos consideramos un aspecto natural de la vida. Pero no debemos perder las implicaciones más amplias, que nos llevan a los alcances más lejanos de la realidad. Al estar atrapados en el modelo del yo, que se aferra a nosotros con más firmeza que nuestra propia piel, podemos rendirnos ante él o investigarlo. La investigación puede ser intelectual, de la forma en que opera la física cuántica. Podría usar la imaginación para sonsacarnos de nuestra inflexibilidad. Cuando Alicia entra al agujero del conejo hacia el País de las Maravillas el mundo cotidiano se remodela por el sinsentido, con el que Alicia, al ser una propia señorita inglesa, está impaciente. Conforme Alicia observa a la Reina Roja jugar croquet usando flamencos como mazos, o mirar al Gato de Cheshire desaparecer en el aire sin quedar nada de él excepto su sonrisa, sus protestas sensibles no son las mismas que las de los lectores. Estamos felices de que el País de las Maravillas no sea el mundo cotidiano.

¿Por qué anhelamos asombrarnos? Porque hemos estado en la vida real. La maravilla existía mucho antes de que el modelo del yo quedara a cargo. Como ha concluido un investigador sobre los efectos de alteración mental del LSD, los bebés no necesitan psicodélicos porque están "viajando todo el tiempo". A los bebés les toma tiempo apegarse al programa, por así decirlo. Tienen los ojos bien abiertos y están asombrados con un mundo que todavía no debe tener sentido. Para aprender que el fuego es caliente y que el invierno es helado un niño pequeño debe ajustarse a la realidad cotidiana. Crecer significa aprender las reglas del camino. Pero una vez que las aprendes el camino resulta ser angosto, y cruzar la línea central augura un desastre. Si te desvías de la norma puedes enloquecer.

El metahumano sostiene un tercer camino que no es tan borroso como la inocencia de los bebés, y tampoco tan rígido como la conformidad social. Podemos vivir en ambas realidades en un estado que William Blake llamaba "inocencia organizada". El asombro puede infundir el mundo cotidiano sin disolverlo en un viaje psicodélico. (Al famoso maestro espiritual hindú J. Krishnamurti, quien tenía un sentido del humor sarcástico, le gustaba decir que ser atemporal y eterno, que es parte del despertar, no significa que pierdas el tren de la tarde.) El mundo de los cinco sentidos es la parte organizada. No habitamos una alucinación caótica. El escenario envolvente en el que estamos enredados parece estar completo. Cubre todo lo que podemos ver, oír, tocar, saborear y oler.

La metarrealidad es la parte inocente, donde el asombro y la maravilla infunden la mente. No es un estado mecánico, pero sí va más allá del pensamiento racional. Nada menos que Albert Einstein lo confirmó personalmente:

> A veces me pregunto cómo sucedió que yo desarrollara la teoría de la relatividad. Creo que la razón es que un adulto normal nunca se detiene a pensar sobre los problemas del espacio y del tiempo. Éstas son cosas que pensó cuando era niño. Pero mi desarrollo intelectual fue retrasado, porque comencé a preguntarme sobre el espacio y el tiempo cuando había crecido.

Einstein nunca perdió su sentido del asombro y lo infundió con una profunda cualidad espiritual. "Mi sentido de Dios es mi sentido del asombro acerca del universo", dijo alguna vez Einstein. Pero no es necesario, como lo he enfatizado muchas veces, formular la metarrealidad en términos espirituales. "Ir más allá" es un aspecto de la conciencia y es accesible para todos.

Si le preguntas a la gente cuánto tanto interés tiene en investigar la realidad, no muchos responderán con entusiasmo. Sin embargo, hay una historia fascinante detrás de cómo nos enredamos en una ilusión. Incluso más apasionante es la posibilidad de escribir un nuevo final para la historia, que nos tiene escapando hacia el mundo del asombro, el descubrimiento, el éxtasis y la libertad.

En tu vida

CAMBIA TU EXPERIENCIA CORPORAL

Estás viviendo en un mundo interpretado y tu cuerpo es parte de la interpretación. Si cambias la interpretación experimentarás tu cuerpo de una nueva manera. Cuando ves el ejercicio no como algo que debes hacer, por ejemplo, sino como una forma de aumentar tu concentración y tu energía, has creado una nueva interpretación. Cuando te duelen los músculos en la escaladora y la falta de aire que sientes cuando corres un kilómetro son cosas positivas, no motivos para sufrir.

Para dejar de ver tu cuerpo como una cosa, un objeto suspendido en el tiempo y el espacio, se requiere algo más que un cambio básico en la interpretación. ¿Es una mera interpretación? Sí lo es. Cuando te miras al espejo ¿qué ves? Estamos condicionados para ver un objeto sólido y físicamente estable con límites definidos; en ese sentido, podrías estar viendo un maniquí de tamaño natural en el espejo. Gracias a que hemos abordado la revolución cuántica, ya sabemos que la materia sólo parece ser sólida. Cuando tocas tu brazo con la otra mano —hazlo ahora, si quieres— parece como si dos objetos sólidos entraran en contacto.

En realidad estás experimentando dos campos electromagnéticos entrando en contacto, lo cual da la impresión de solidez. Por ejemplo, dos imanes con polos opuestos puestos uno contra otro crean una fuerza repelente. Si los imanes son lo bastante poderosos, llegará un punto en el que no podrás juntarlos hasta que se toquen. La fuerza que los repele los mantendrá separados. Por ello, desde la perspectiva de los imanes, el aire que hay entre ellos se siente como algo sólido.

Los otros cuatro sentidos, además del tacto, también colaboran en el cuerpo interpretado. Ya que los fotones no tienen color, el hecho de que puedas ver tu cuerpo con color —cabello oscuro, ojos azules, piel aceitunada— es una ilusión óptica. Lo mismo sucede con los contornos definidos del cuerpo. Tú no terminas en la barrera de tu piel. Viajas en un aura vagamente formada de humedad y aire exhalado, dejando tras de ti un rastro constante de microbios y células muertas al mudar de piel (se estima que las pelusas que se acumulan en una casa son 50% células muertas de la piel). También emites calor y una carga eléctrica leve. Estas emanaciones no tienen ningún límite, ya que son parte de los campos universales que se extienden al infinito.

Tampoco puedes decir que estás viendo "mi" cuerpo, porque de inmediato surge una pregunta: ¿A qué cuerpo te refieres? Tus células están siendo intercambiadas constantemente, como ladrillos volando hacia fuera y hacia dentro de un edificio. El cuerpo que ves en el espejo no es el mismo que cuando eras un niño pequeño, o incluso el que fue ayer y el que será mañana. Además de la muerte de las células viejas y el nacimiento de las nuevas, los átomos y las moléculas entran y salen por trillones cada hora conforme tu cuerpo se nutre y excreta desechos.

El hecho es que tu cuerpo es coherente y se ve estable, como un edificio mantenido de pie no por ladrillos y cemento, sino por su estructura. En tu caso, la estructura deja una huella física en forma de ADN, que sirve como la plantilla para todas las formas de vida. Pero repito, la fisicalidad del ADN es una ilusión, una máscara. Los compuestos químicos que constituyen el ADN son fosfatos y azúcares, y sólo su *acomodo* determina la diferencia entre un plátano y el mono que se lo come, o entre tú y un caracol marino. Estos acomodos no son otra cosa que información pura. Por ello, tu cuerpo es un constructo de información, y tu torrente sanguíneo, repleto de mensajes químicos diferentes que fluyen de célula a célula, es una autopista de información.

Al haber llegado hasta aquí, ya hemos desmaterializado tu cuerpo. Pero hay otro paso que dar. ¿Qué es la información? También es un constructo. Hasta que la mente humana nombró el constructo, la información no tenía una existencia formal, y algunas personas han afirmado que un universo de información podría ser una sopa cuántica girando, combinándose y recombinándose en cada segundo a la velocidad de la luz. Esta sopa puede ser codificada de la forma en que lo desees.

Un físico podría codificarla en términos de campos de fuerza como la gravedad y el electromagnetismo. Pero estos campos están unificados y se funden en el estado fundamental de todas las cosas que existen, desapareciendo del universo visible en un vacío sin forma.

Un ingeniero en computación podría codificar la información de diferente manera, como los 1 y 0 de la programación digital, pero su acomodo de la información es viable sólo para la información tangible, como las letras en esta página, que podrías estar leyendo digitalmente ahora mismo. Es posible calcular las matemáticas de cualquier cosa en el universo visible. Tu ADN está codificado por las matemáticas de nuestros cuatro pares base (tiamina, adenina, guanina y citosina) y una secuencia con tres mil millones de unidades separadas de información. Lo cual nos lleva a cerrar el círculo, porque los pares base tampoco son materia sólida. Incluso las matemáticas no pueden llegar hasta ahí. Un lenguaje matemático de 1 y 0 es útil para la tecnología de la computación, pero los aspectos inmateriales de la vida —inteligencia, creatividad, emociones, esperanzas, miedos y demás— no tienen codificación matemática. Antes de que Einstein formulara $E = mc^2$, esta fórmula existía como puro potencial creativo —un pensamiento aún no pensado—, y al ser todavía no creado, no tenía existencia en el mundo físico o en la información del mundo y ni siquiera en el mundo matemático.

La lección del ADN

Por décadas ha prevalecido la noción de que la vida puede ser explicada al comprender el genoma humano, pero de hecho nuestro ADN resulta tener un rol pequeño en el diseño a mayor escala. Es sorprendente que el ADN no pueda explicar cómo surgió la vida, aunque el público general no ha escuchado mucho al respecto. Éste es un ejemplo perfecto de cómo las explicaciones materialistas siempre se quedan cortas, así que vale la pena contar la historia con cierto detalle.

La historia aceptada, que todos aprendieron en la escuela, es que el ADN contiene el "código de la vida", una estructura maestra que entra en acción en el instante en que un óvulo es fertilizado en el vientre de la madre. Desde ese momento en adelante un ser humano desarrolla a partir de una sola célula hasta 30 billones de células conforme la estructura se despliega. Aunque la historia del "código de la vida" sea tan poderosa, tras bambalinas un creciente número de genetistas no la cree; de hecho, piensan que hemos entendido mal muchas cosas sobre los genes. De varias maneras "el código de la vida" tiene enormes huecos que están aumentando cada día. Esto fue presentado en un artículo en la revista *Nautilus*, titulado "Es el fin del gen como lo conocemos". El autor, Ken Richardson, es un experto en desarrollo humano y nos brinda una notable visión de cómo funcionan las células, lo cual depende mucho más de ingredientes invisibles, como la inteligencia y la creatividad, que de las moléculas, incluso algo tan complejo como el ADN humano.

El argumento de Richardson es el siguiente: el propósito del ADN es producir las proteínas, que son los bloques de construcción básicos de una célula. Pero el ADN sólo no es responsable de las muchas formas en que las células, los tejidos y los órganos usan las proteínas. La noción de que el ADN contiene la estructura para el cuerpo básicamente es una causa perdida. Una investigación reciente ha demostrado que las células son sistemas dinámicos que cambian su constitución "en el camino", como dice Richardson, un proceso de autorregulación que comienza casi al momento en que un esperma fertiliza a un óvulo.

En cuanto esa célula se convierte en una bola minúscula de células idénticas, escribe Richardson, "ellas ya están hablando unas con otras con tormentas de señales químicas. Por medio de los patrones estadísticos dentro de las tormentas, las instrucciones, una vez más, son creadas de cero". Resulta que una célula, totalmente independiente del ADN, controla todo tipo de información contenida en aminoácidos, grasas, vitaminas, minerales, enzimas y varios tipos de ácido ribonucleico (ARN) —una fábrica completa de ingredientes necesarios para mantener la célula en marcha para nada está predeterminada por nuestros genes—. Esta autorregulación implica una inteligencia tremenda.

En la visión que ha surgido recientemente, la célula controla el ADN tanto como el ADN controla la célula. La situación ha sido así desde el principio de la vida sobre la Tierra. Al parecer el ADN surgió en una etapa tardía de la evolución celular. En sus etapas más tempranas, miles de millones de años atrás, las células no tenían ADN, pero eran contenedores de sopa molecular cerrados en sí mismos. De alguna manera esta sopa comenzó a regularse a sí misma, y con el paso del tiempo dio origen a estructuras permanentes que eran necesarias con regularidad, como proteínas, enzimas y quizá ARN, que produce proteínas. La información de estas estructuras entonces fue codificada como ADN, que sirve como una especie de base de datos pasiva. Richardson afirma que algo más pone al ADN en su lugar: "Ha resultado más alarmante saber que menos de 5% del genoma es usado para producir proteínas. La mayoría produce una amplia gama de factores diferentes (ARN) que regulan, a través de la cadena, cómo se usan los demás genes".

Como validación de este nuevo entendimiento, ahora se sabe que las células pueden alterar su propio ADN; esto ha surgido en el nuevo campo de la epigenética, que explora cómo es que la experiencia cotidiana deja "marcadores" químicos en un gen, alterando la forma en que funciona. Lejos de seguir robóticamente una estructura fija, la vida de una célula es sumamente dinámica y flexible, y responde a las condiciones cambiantes a escala microscópica. Si no fuera así, no podríamos responder a la vida a escala macroscópica.

Ser humano significa que pensamos y actuamos con creatividad, usando nuestra inteligencia para encontrar nuevas formas de superar todo tipo de retos. El ADN no descubrió el fuego ni inventó la computadora personal. Es importante el hecho de que el ADN es responsable de la manufactura de proteínas, pero es muy equivocado expandir su rol a la vida como un todo. Richardson se muestra particularmente preocupado porque las suposiciones tan exageradas sobre el ADN podrían derivar en una política social que repita el racismo que alimentó el movimiento eugenésico hace décadas, más notoriamente con la ideología nazi de una raza suprema. Como buen ejemplo, al Premio Nobel James Watson, que fue uno de los descubridores de la estructura del ADN en 1952, recientemente le quitaron todos sus honores en el Laboratorio Cold Spring Harbor, donde pasó buena parte de su carrera científica, ya que con frecuencia expresaba su opinión prejuiciosa de que la gente negra y las mujeres eran menos inteligentes que otros, basados en su genética.

Ahora que la estructura de la vida se desmorona ante nuestros ojos, ¿qué sigue? Actualmente la nueva historia en la genética está atorada en dos factores: información y complejidad. La noción es que la "sopa molecular" primigenia encontró maneras en que los átomos y las moléculas formaran estructuras complicadas por medio del intercambio de información y las posibilidades estadísticas que surgen cuando miles de millones de moléculas comenzaron a alborotarse. Pero ¿eso es factible? Por ejemplo, ¿el cerebro humano puede ser el producto final de una sopa turbulenta a la que cada vez se le añaden más "cosas"? Como alguien dijo con ingenio, la noción de que la complejidad es suficiente para explicar el cerebro es como si alguien dijera que si añades las suficientes cartas a la baraja, éstas comenzarán a jugar póker.

Dado que la ciencia está atada a la explicación materialista de todas las cosas tiene un enorme punto ciego. Un biólogo celular no puede dar el salto hacia las características invisibles que una célula presenta más allá de sus estructuras químicas, digamos, en la inteligencia y la creatividad. El análisis lógico ha sido la herramienta más poderosa de la ciencia, y no ha sido poca cosa remplazar el mito, la superstición y la opinión popular con hechos racionales. Pero ¿es realmente posible que suceda un repentino salto creativo porque alguien siguió las leyes de la lógica? La respuesta obvia es que no, y como prueba podemos ofrecer los increíbles saltos dados por los pioneros cuánticos que descubrieron que el mundo cuántico es absolutamente ilógico. Más recientemente, la existencia de la materia y la energía oscura revelaron otro dominio, incluso más peculiar e ilógico que el cuántico, que ni siquiera interactúa con la materia y la energía ordinarias. Tu cuerpo no es una máquina gobernada por la lógica, y por ello es que está destinado a fallar cualquier intento de convertirlo en una máquina supercomplicada. Demasiada información que sale por el cuerpo, y que afecta a los 30 billones de células, está generada por las emociones, esperanzas, miedos, creencias, errores e imaginación: todas las cosas más importantes que enriquecen la existencia humana.

Al nivel cuántico, la materia y la energía se comportan de forma muy peculiar, hasta el punto en que los objetos físicos sólidos quedan minados. Todo fenómeno en el universo puede ser reducido a ondas en el campo cuántico conforme éste interactúa con el campo gravitatorio o con el oculto campo cuántico. En la superficie de la vida los objetos sólidos son sólo ondas de lento movimiento comparadas con, digamos, fotones viajando a la velocidad de la luz. Los físicos pueden decir una y otra vez que el cuerpo humano, al igual que todos los objetos sólidos, permanece intacto a pesar de las cosas raras que hace el campo cuántico. Pero tu cuerpo está intacto debido a otro campo, el de electrones.

Sin embargo, esta confirmación sólo es verdad mientras la información del ADN esté intacta; con la muerte física, el electromagnetismo no ha cambiado, y tampoco lo han hecho los átomos y las moléculas que constituyen tu cuerpo. Pero el proceso de decadencia descompone los vínculos invisibles de la vida. Las células pierden el pegamento real que posibilita la vida, y éste no es el electromagnetismo. Nadie puede decir con certeza lógica por qué el cuerpo humano no se convierte en una nube de átomos que volarán con la brisa.

Es fácil que la mente empiece a darte vueltas cuando te das cuenta de que tu cuerpo, cuando mucho, es un caudal constante de información que cambia todo el tiempo, pero no debemos apoyarnos en esta noción como muleta para mantener intacto el mundo físico. Recordemos que la información es un concepto humano, como cualquier otro modelo. Decir que estamos intactos gracias a la información tiene sus límites. No es como si los ceros y los unos fueran pegajosos. No se aferran unos a otros. La forma en que los ceros y los unos están pegados es gracias a la interpretación humana. Sabemos que la información existe porque nosotros inventamos el concepto.

¿Entonces de dónde obtuvimos la capacidad de pegar el mundo y darle significado? La respuesta a esta pregunta será convincente sólo si podemos aplicarla a nuestro cuerpo. ¿Cómo adquirimos la capacidad de mantener nuestro cuerpo unido? Esa capacidad debe yacer fuera del cuerpo, porque no podemos decir que nuestro cuerpo nos dice cómo vivir, ser y pensar. Ni siquiera podemos afirmar que nuestro cerebro nos dijo cómo vivir, ser y pensar. El cerebro es otro objeto físico, y sería propio de la lógica circular decir que un objeto físico se creó a sí mismo. (En el campo de la inteligencia artificial es como decir que hubo un robot que inventó a los robots.)

Sin importar desde qué ángulo lo veas, el cuerpo desaparece en el reino del concepto y la mente, y los agentes inmateriales deben tener una fuente. Antes de poder pintar la *Mona Lisa*, debe existir un concepto de arte. ¿Qué fue lo que dio origen al arte que no sea arte? ¿Qué dio lugar a los conceptos, que no sea concepto? La única respuesta posible, como afirma este libro desde diversas perspectivas, es la conciencia. No existe otra pieza fundamental que explique viablemente todos los misterios que acabamos de abordar, desde la creatividad para que las células se mantengan unidas, hasta cómo los átomos y las moléculas inanimadas de alguna forma se convirtieron en criaturas vivientes.

Hay mucho más que decir, pero si miras tu reflejo en el espejo, puedes ver que es sólo una "cosa" sólida y estable con bordes definidos porque tú lo interpretas de esa forma. Pero mi objetivo no es hundirte en un estado de confusión sobre tu cuerpo. Mi meta es liberarte de todas las interpretaciones que te limitan. Ser humano sólo puede ser definido como ilimitado. Cuando imponemos limitaciones disminuimos al ser humano. Ésa es la verdad de la metarrealidad, una verdad hacia la cual podemos caminar paso a paso hasta que se convierta en una realidad viva para el mayor número posible de personas, incluidos tú y yo.

2

"YO" ES EL CREADOR DE LA ILUSIÓN

Cuando ves tu reflejo en el espejo, el hecho de que te reconozcas es natural y parece un evento tan básico que no lo comentarías, y aun así, este pequeño acto de conciencia de uno mismo resulta tener una significación tremenda. El yo que has aprendido a reconocer en el espejo constantemente refuerza todo tipo de limitaciones que no es necesario que existan. Cuando William Blake habló de "grilletes creados por la mente", bien podría haber dicho "creados por el ego".

Es imposible recordar una época en la que no te mirabas al espejo y te veías a ti mismo. Pero hay pasos en el desarrollo de la infancia que te dieron tu primera noción de "yo", tu sentido de tu propio ser. A los niños pequeños no les interesan los espejos, por ejemplo, y es bastante sorprendente que caminar y hablar sucedan alrededor de los 18 meses, antes de que un niño pequeño reconozca que está viendo su propio cuerpo al espejo. Después de eso, el cuerpo se convierte en su juguete favorito. (Los pocos animales que pueden verse en el espejo también se fascinan con su propia imagen una vez que lo captan.)

Por lo menos necesitamos darnos cuenta de que nadie vive en la misma realidad. La versión de cada quien es personal. Si cien personas están mirando un atardecer glorioso en Hawái, de hecho, están viendo cien atardeceres distintos. Para una persona que se siente deprimida quizá no exista la belleza en ningún atardecer, y mucho menos gloria. Dado que "yo" es central para la versión de la realidad de cada persona, es un elemento clave en la simulación que aceptamos como real, y hasta que podamos conocernos más allá del "yo", las ilusiones de la realidad virtual nos mantendrán atrapados.

Ilusión es una palabra muy cargada. La sociedad desaprueba a alguien que esté bajo la ilusión de que nadie más importa en el mundo; a esto le llamamos ego inflado o solipsismo. Pero la ilusión de que el amor todo lo puede, la cual todos creen si sienten un profundo enamoramiento, es una ilusión en la que todos quisiéramos creer todo el tiempo: desenamorarse, que remplaza la ilusión con la realidad, es bastante doloroso. Una mezcla de placer y dolor caracteriza al "yo". Del lado placentero, cuando los niños pequeños descubren su identidad se ponen sumamente felices. Los "terribles dos" reflejan un despliegue de egotismo cuando el niño afirma: "¡Éste soy yo! Ponme atención. ¡Aquí estoy!".

Los terribles dos son característicos por ser una etapa enloquecedora para los papás, porque la afirmación brutal del ego es odiosa. Más importante todavía es que no es realista. No puedes sobrevivir en sociedad si vas por ahí demandando que el mundo te dé su atención todo el tiempo, o incluso la mayor parte del tiempo. La vida adulta es un compromiso entre obtener lo que quieres y seguir normas sociales, entre el "yo" acaparador como el centro del universo y un "yo" silenciado que es un pequeño engranaje en la vasta maquinaria de la sociedad. No es fácil vivir con el equilibrio, e innumerables personas caen en la trampa de sentirse insignificantes, mientras que a otras se les permite que se impongan agresivamente sobre el resto.

Los psicólogos dedican su carrera a arreglar el sentido del yo dañado de la gente, pero en el camino hacia el metahumano debemos formularnos una pregunta más radical: ¿Por qué "yo" debería existir, en primer lugar? Conlleva una vida de placer y dolor impredecibles. Nos aísla del mundo y limita lo que sentimos, pensamos, decimos y hacemos. ¿Qué tan a menudo dejamos de hacer algo impulsivo porque en automático pensamos: "No soy el tipo de persona que hace equis cosa"? Esa equis cosa puede ser cualquier cosa desde hacer una broma, hasta presumir todo el dinero que ganas o huir y unirte al circo. Todas las limitaciones impuestas por el "yo" no tienen sentido. Sirven sólo para sostener los viejos condicionamientos del pasado.

Cuando vemos que "yo" es un constructo mental —y uno muy endeble— se convierte en algo abierto al cambio. Una vez que "yo" pierde su propósito, podríamos decidir arreglárnoslas sin él por completo. "Yo" existe para convencerte de que eres una criatura de la realidad virtual, y que no es posible ir más allá de la simulación, al igual que un retrato no puede salir de su marco. La razón por la que nos encontramos irremediablemente enredados en una ilusión es porque estamos totalmente envueltos en un "yo" y todo lo que éste representa.

Es necesario desmantelar muchas cosas antes de que el "yo" deje de gobernar la vida de una persona. Desde nuestros primeros recuerdos de tener un yo, el "yo" ha sido nuestro compañero más cercano, y pasa todo momento de vigilia aferrándose a las experiencias deseables y desechando las no deseables. "Yo" no quiere ceder su poder, y por una buena razón. Que una persona especial te ame a ti y sólo a ti hace que la vida valga la pena. Cuando "yo" se desvanece, ¿quién está ahí para amar y ser amado? Pero hay mucho más en juego. Todo lo que una persona piensa, siente, dice y hace es para que "yo" se sienta más fuerte, feliz y mejor. Volverse metahumano no puede tener éxito a menos que ofrezca algo más satisfactorio que cualquier cosa que "yo" nos ofrezca.

La agenda del ego

A primera vista, el ego parece indispensable. ¿Cómo podemos abandonar algo que necesitamos para sobrevivir? "Yo" es el motivo por el que te sientes tú y nadie más. Te asomas al mundo a través de un par de ojos que nadie más posee. Una madre que ubica a su hijo en cuanto sale de la escuela para que lo recojan recibe la misma información visual que todos los demás papás esperando a que salgan los niños, pero ella literalmente ve a su hijo singular, suyo. La singularidad es valiosa, pero tiene un precio. Casi ninguno de nosotros estamos cómodos al estar completamente solos, y si insistes en ser tú mismo, el prospecto de convertirte en un marginado es muy real. El poeta William Wordsworth dice con entusiasmo: "Deambulé solitario como una nube / Que flota alto sobre valles y colinas", pero muy pocos de nosotros vemos lo *solitario* como algo positivo. Cuando alguien es tan desinteresado que suelta todas sus necesidades personales, a veces se dice que es un santo. Pero es más probable que sea etiquetado como antisocial o loco —es difícil creer que alguien pueda ser normal y al mismo tiempo totalmente liberado del ego y su necesidad de placer y aceptación—. Muchos movimientos espirituales denigran el ego como si fuera una carga, una maldición o un enemigo oculto de la conciencia superior.

Irónicamente, decir que el ego es tu enemigo es un juicio del ego. Decir que el ego es tu amigo también es un juicio del ego. Por lo tanto, decir: "Quiero no tener ego" es contradictorio en sí mismo; el ego está diciendo eso, y ciertamente no quiere suicidarse. Tus mismas palabras no pueden llevarte a un lugar fuera de la ilusión en la que estás enredado. No puedes extraer el ego como si extirparas un apéndice inflamado. Si crees que puedes hacerlo, tan sólo te hundes más en la ilusión al engañarte a ti mismo y decirte que eres desinteresado.

"Yo" es una cosa pequeñita, tan sólo compuesta por dos letras. Pero lo que has construido alrededor de él —lo que todos hemos construido alrededor de él— es como un arrecife de coral compuesto por celdas minúsculas endurecidas por un caparazón enorme.

Si esta descripción te parece extrema, considera cómo procesas la experiencia en bruto. Las experiencias son interpretadas y se vuelven parte de cómo aceptas o rechazas la realidad a nivel personal. No atestiguamos cómo sucede esto porque la mayoría de las experiencias parecen demasiado insignificantes como para ser importantes. Por ejemplo, podrías probar un curry vindaloo en un restaurante hindú, y quizá lo encuentres demasiado picante, decides que no te gusta y nunca vuelves a ordenar ese platillo del menú de un restaurante. Otra persona, criada en Goa, en la India, donde el curry vindaloo es un platillo básico, apenas registra el picor de los chiles que contienen las recetas y en cambio tiene recuerdos nostálgicos sobre el vindaloo que cocinaba su madre.

Estas dos experiencias, como información en bruto que entra al cerebro por el sentido del gusto, parecen idénticas. Pero no lo son: la experiencia siempre pasa a través de la interpretación personal de alguien. "Yo" está teniendo cada experiencia, no los cinco sentidos ni el cerebro. Reducir la experiencia a información en bruto es totalmente engañoso, como si el tímpano determinara qué música te gusta, o si las células cerebrales decidieran que una pintura de Rembrandt es una obra maestra. "Yo" toma todas estas decisiones y, conforme lo hace, cada experiencia fortalece el poder de "yo".

Por naturaleza, las experiencias son fugaces y momentáneas. En cuanto terminé de decir "gracias" o de morder una barra de chocolate o de besar a mi nieta, la experiencia ha desaparecido. Basados en este hecho innegable, tienes dos opciones. Puedes aceptar lo fugaz que es cada experiencia, o puedes aferrarte a ella. Cuando eliges la primera opción, la vida es un flujo de experiencias frescas, como un caudal constantemente renovado desde su origen. No estás perseguido por los malos recuerdos ni lleno de ansiedad sobre lo que sucederá después. Si eliges la segunda opción, almacenas hábitos, condicionamientos, lo que te gusta y lo que no te gusta, y todo un catálogo de cosas que no quieres volver a repetir. La segunda opción es la base del ego, que se aferra con fuerza para reforzar al "yo" y su sentido de seguridad. Sin embargo, la pérdida es muy grande porque las experiencias no dejarán de suceder sólo porque quieres que así sea, y al aferrarte a ello bloqueas el flujo de la vida.

¿Qué nos conmina a aferrarnos en vez de soltar? Un simple hecho de la vida: "yo" tiene una agenda. Las ilusiones creadas por la mente no son azarosas. "Yo" está a cargo de tu interés personal y su agenda sirve para una demanda única: "Más para mí". No deberíamos sorprendernos cuando "más para mí" se convierte en algo insaciable, como los multimillonarios que desean tener más dinero y los déspotas quieren más poder. La persona promedio no se identifica con este extremismo. Pero la necesidad de tener más es muy poderosa en cualquier persona, porque todos tenemos necesidades y deseos que queremos satisfacer. Todos necesitamos seguridad y la sensación de estar a salvo. Necesitar amor nos hace humanos. Necesitar explorar el mundo es un deseo irrefrenable en un niño pequeño que se echa a correr por la casa y se mete en todas partes.

Pero si miras más profundo resulta claro que "yo" está *sustentado* en la necesidad. Te ata a un programa de encontrar constantemente nuevas necesidades que nunca terminan, lo cual es lo opuesto a la plenitud. La plenitud es el estado de no necesitar nada porque tú eres suficiente en ti mismo. La sociedad de consumo promueve la necesidad como algo normal; siempre hay algo nuevo que comprar que al fin te dará una sonrisa de satisfacción. Así, una vida normal es de hecho una vida de carencia, intentando con desesperación y sin cesar llenar un hoyo negro que nunca será saciado. Cuando estás necesitado, la plenitud es inalcanzable.

Aquí surge un entendimiento importante. "Yo" no tiene una agenda. "Yo" es la agenda. El ego viene con demandas inherentes a él, sin importar qué tanto nos esforcemos para negar estas demandas o satisfacerlas. La necesidad es un estado de conciencia, y "yo" nunca te soltará hasta que encuentres un estado de conciencia superior.

Un nacimiento misterioso

"Yo" crea obstáculos que mantienen bloqueada la metarrealidad, como si fuera una pared gruesa, aunque ésta sea invisible. En nuestro viaje hacia la conciencia de uno mismo es importante comprender por qué los seres humanos decidimos aislarnos de esta particular manera. ¿Existió alguna era en que "yo" era débil o no existía? Aunque el ego ahora es una parte enraizada en la psique humana tiene una historia. Ha dejado pistas de forma física, como un rastro de huellas en el bosque hechas por una criatura invisible. Por ejemplo, un signo de que eres un "yo" individual es que respondes a tu nombre. El primer nombre está perdido en la prehistoria, pero el primer nombre escrito pertenece a un faraón egipcio, Horus Iry (la Boca de Horus), de 3200 a. e. C.

Cuando comienzas a investigar surgen otras pistas sobre la evolución de la conciencia de uno mismo. Mucho antes de los nombres escritos ya estaba la capacidad de reconocer nuestro propio reflejo. Naturalmente no tenemos manera de recrear lo que experimentaban nuestros ancestros remotos. ¿Los humanos prehistóricos se asomaban a pozos oscuros de agua y reconocían su reflejo? Se especula que sí lo reconocían, pero el evento no puede ser fechado. Sin embargo, la invención de los espejos sucedió muy recientemente, si lo medimos en tiempo evolutivo. Las piedras pulidas como espejos datan del 6000 a. e. C. en la zona que actualmente es Turquía, y conforme surgieron las civilizaciones antiguas en Egipto, Sudamérica y China, cualquier cosa que pudiera sostener una superficie pulida, desde obsidiana y cobre hasta bronce y plata, era usada para este propósito.

¿Acaso somos las únicas criaturas que podemos vernos en el espejo? Un periquito jugará con su imagen en el espejo porque (suponemos) ve a otro periquito ahí. Los perros y los gatos por lo regular no muestran interés en los espejos. Pero es bastante raro que el reconocimiento personal evolucionó en criaturas que no tienen motivo para poseer esta habilidad. Los chimpancés, gorilas y otros grandes simios se ven en un espejo. ¿Cómo sabemos si una criatura se ve a sí misma en un reflejo? La prueba más reveladora es de hecho bastante simple: pon un sombrero rosa en la cabeza del animal. Cuando el animal se ve en el espejo y mira el sombrero rosa, ¿toca el sombrero en su cabeza o el sombrero en el espejo? Si toca el sombrero en su cabeza, pasa la prueba de "soy yo lo que veo".

Como los grandes simios no tienen espejos en su hábitat natural, parece que no hay una razón evolutiva para esta capacidad. Asimismo, no sabemos por qué otras tres criaturas —las urracas, los elefantes y los delfines— pueden reconocerse en un espejo. Las urracas usan sus reflejos para acicalarse mejor, mientras que los elefantes, una vez que comprenden cómo funciona un espejo, presentan comportamientos nuevos. Por ejemplo, pasan una cantidad exorbitante de tiempo examinando el interior de sus bocas, un área del cuerpo que no podrían ver sin la ayuda de un espejo. (Si este tema te fascina, observa un video de YouTube que muestra elefantes asiáticos y la manera en que se comportan cuando están frente a un espejo: https://www.youtube.com/watch?v=-EjukzL-bJc.)

Los espejos no son la única forma que tenemos para reconocernos a nosotros mismos. Los artefactos más antiguos que insinúan la conciencia de uno mismo son esculturas que representan formas humanoides. Lo que las hace más maravillosas, de acuerdo con la arqueología más reciente, es que estos objetos son anteriores al surgimiento del *Homo sapiens*. Una línea del tiempo simplificada nos ayudará a ubicarnos:

14 millones años a. e. C.	Aparecen los primeros grandes simios
2.5 millones años a. e. C.	Evoluciona el género *Homo*
1.9 millones años a. e. C.	Los homínidos evolucionan en *Homo erectus*
200 000 años a. e. C.	Aparece el *Homo sapiens*
10 000 años a. e. C.	Termina la última Edad de Hielo

Para cuando el *Homo sapiens* se estaba convirtiendo en una especie distinta, 200 000 años a. e. C., nuestro ancestro más cercano, el *Homo erectus*, hacía mucho había descubierto el fuego y la fabricación de herramientas. Ni los homínidos esperaron a nuestra especie para desarrollar la conciencia de uno mismo. En ruinas sumamente antiguas se han encontrado figuras humanoides rudimentarias hechas por *Homo erectus*. Son sumamente antiguas. La primera en ser descubierta fue la Venus de Berejat Ram, un artefacto de basalto desenterrado en 1981 por un equipo de arqueólogos de la Universidad Hebrea, en una excavación en los Altos del Golán en Israel, cerca de Siria.

La Venus de Berejat Ram consiste en dos piezas redondas, la mayor sugiere ser el cuerpo y la menor la cabeza. Se pueden observar tres incisiones, dos a cada lado del "cuerpo" a manera de brazos, y una rodeando la cabeza sin representar ningún rasgo facial. A pesar del nombre Venus, este objeto es tan primitivo que al principio algunos expertos creyeron que era una formación accidental hecha por la erosión natural. El debate sobre si son marcas intencionales grabadas por un artista fue determinado cuando una figura muy parecida, la Venus de Tan-Tan, fue descubierta después en Marruecos. Las dos esculturas se parecen tanto que podrían haber sido creadas por las mismas manos.

Fue fascinante datar el descubrimiento israelí, pero resulta difícil precisarlo. La Venus de Berejat Ram estaba atrapada entre dos capas de depósitos volcánicos, uno alrededor de 230 000 años a. e. C. y el otro de 700 000 años a. e. C. La escultura fue hecha en algún punto en ese vasto periodo. Desde el punto de vista moderno, la Venus de Tan-Tan de la misma Edad de Piedra Baja parece más humana, ya que tiene torso, cabeza y piernas. El hecho de que una mente, anterior no sólo al *Homo sapiens* sino también al neandertal, sintiera la necesidad de representar su figura de manera artística es un signo de conciencia de uno mismo entreverado en el tejido de nuestra propia existencia. El escultor dice: "Así nos vemos yo y toda mi gente". Desde tiempos remotos, nunca han existido seres humanos *sin* conciencia de sí mismos.

"Yo" no ha sobrevivido desde la prehistoria: se ha metastatizado. En todas partes a nuestro alrededor vemos la evidencia del egoísmo maligno. Los excesos grotescos de la avaricia en la actual Era Dorada son un síntoma de "yo" fuera de control, y hemos visto cómo la insensatez en el sector financiero puede provocar desastres en la economía global sin que a los adinerados culpables les importe, ni detengan su búsqueda de poseer más riquezas. Si no fuera por el impulso del ego de derrotar a otros egos, por volverse importante al denigrar a quien es diferente, no tendríamos la necesidad de pensar las cosas en términos de "nosotros contra ellos" y los interminables conflictos que este enfoque ha creado, desde disputas familiares hasta guerras civiles, cruzadas religiosas y la amenaza atómica global. ¿Podemos dar cuenta de esta metástasis y generar una cura?

Si viviste durante la Guerra Fría y la amenaza de la devastación nuclear, has visto cómo "yo", al crear un enemigo, llevará la hostilidad hasta el borde de la destrucción masiva. Y aunque la sombra nuclear de alguna manera desapareció, las naciones continuarán perfeccionando formas de muerte mecanizada, nuevas y más mortíferas. Sería benéfico para la humanidad reducir la cantidad de daño que nos hacemos a nosotros mismos, que se puede atribuir directamente a nuestro hábito de ver el mundo desde la perspectiva del ego, dado el miedo y sufrimiento innecesario que éste ha traído.

Elegir estar separado

Nadie contrae neumonía o un resfriado común por voluntad, cuyos efectos nocivos alcanzan todos los rincones de la vida, pero cuando se trata de "yo" hemos elegido estar separados, es una característica de la especie. Hemos evolucionado para sentirnos superiores a todas las demás formas de vida. Por una parte, esto nos ha dado una gran ventaja evolutiva. Considera cómo nos relacionamos con el medio ambiente. Todas las demás criaturas se adaptan al medio ambiente y se funden con él. Por más de miles de millones de años, la evolución ha creado mecanismos extraordinarios para adaptarse a los rincones más inhóspitos del planeta. Por ejemplo, el interior de la Antártida contiene una especie de montaña conocida como "nunatak", una cima que se eleva a través de una gruesa capa de hielo que la circunda. Es difícil imaginar un entorno más desolado que éste, con nada más que campos de hielo en todas direcciones, frío bajo cero, vientos que aúllan y al parecer sin la posibilidad de albergar plantas ni animales.

Sin embargo, hay registros de un ave marina blanca conocida como petrel níveo (*Pagodroma nivea*) que anida en nunataks hasta a 97 kilómetros tierra adentro desde la costa, hacia donde debe volver para buscar alimento en el agua. Cuando llega la época de apareamiento, los petreles níveos encuentran fisuras expuestas en las rocas para hacer sus nidos con piedritas pequeñas, y una pareja que se aparea empolla un solo huevo en medio de la naturaleza helada durante 40 a 50 días, antes de que se rompa el cascarón. La evolución colocó en esta situación al petrel níveo, pero los humanos podemos elegir dónde y cómo vivir.

Estas elecciones no fueron dictadas por nuestras limitaciones físicas. Los humanos hemos invadido los sitios más recónditos del planeta, mucho más de lo que nuestros ancestros homínidos habrían podido resistir físicamente. Es nuestra fuerza de voluntad, una motivación interior que está determinada a tener bajo control la naturaleza, la que nos ha compelido a habitar todos los lugares, con excepción de los entornos menos habitables en términos de calor y frío extremo, alimento escaso, largos periodos del año sin sol, alturas elevadas, etcétera.

Cuando todavía estábamos desnudos, la adversidad física extrema nos empujaba al borde de la supervivencia, a punto de extinguir al *Homo sapiens* casi en cuanto apareció nuestra especie. Fue necesario que la conciencia superara las desventajas físicas en nuestra contra. En un artículo publicado en 2016 en la revista *Scientific American*, titulado "When the Sea Saved Humanity" ("Cuando el mar salvó a la humanidad"), se detalla que la supervivencia humana era impredecible y la mayoría de nuestros ancestros no lo logró. El autor del artículo, Curtis W. Marean, es un arqueólogo de la Universidad Estatal de Arizona, cuyo equipo ha descubierto la evidencia de esta crisis evolutiva. Marean escribe:

> En algún punto entre 195 000 y 123 000 años atrás, el tamaño de la población de *Homo sapiens* se desplomó, debido a condiciones climáticas de frío y sequía que dejaron inhabitable buena parte del territorio africano de nuestros ancestros. Todas las personas vivas hoy somos descendientes de un grupo de personas de una región que sobrevivió esta catástrofe. La costa sur de África podría ser uno de los pocos lugares en que los humanos hubieran logrado sobrevivir durante esta crisis climática porque alberga una gran abundancia de moluscos y plantas comestibles.

En unas cuevas a lo largo de una sección de la costa sudafricana, conocida como Pinnacle Point, los arqueólogos han encontrado un gran número de conchas de moluscos y en ocasiones restos de focas y ballenas, lo cual indica que casi 50 000 años antes, en los sitios explorados previamente, los primeros humanos habían aprendido a pescar alimento en el mar, mientras que ante la severidad del clima de la Edad de Hielo sucumbían casi todos los demás. Las herramientas encontradas en las cuevas sugieren que estos sobrevivientes tenían capacidades cognitivas elevadas; Marean afirma enérgica y controversialmente que ciertas facultades mentales eran totalmente necesarias para la supervivencia, como calcular el aumento y descenso de las mareas debido a la Luna. Él afirma que sólo durante la marea baja los habitantes de las cuevas tierra adentro viajaban hasta el mar para llevar a cabo la peligrosa tarea de pescar mejillones y otros moluscos contra las olas.

Atrapados en el peligro extremo, nuestros ancestros no tenían salvamento ni escapatoria física. ¿Cómo encontraron los medios para rescatarse a sí mismos?

La elección de estar separado

La respuesta a esa pregunta es que no fue por medio de lo físico. Aunque estos descubrimientos arqueológicos sean fascinantes, no fue la severa presión externa lo que obligó a nuestros ancestros a adaptarse. Requirió de un gran cambio de la realidad "aquí dentro". Nos convertimos en una especie basada en la conciencia, usando la mente para enfrentar los desafíos de la naturaleza. Uno de los factores más importantes en la expansión de la conciencia humana fue que nuestro cerebro se volvió demasiado grande, eficiente y complejo para su propio bien. Una especie de sobrecarga cerebral alimenta nuestra necesidad desesperada de reducirla para que la vida cotidiana fuera manejable. Si la prisa y el bullicio de una ciudad moderna parece una sobrecarga, no es nada comparado con la crisis mental que enfrentaron nuestros ancestros remotos.

El problema no fue que el cerebro humano simplemente creció y no pudo parar. El problema fue que el instinto, que indica cómo se comportarán otras criaturas, comenzó a disminuir en nosotros. Una abeja sólo busca flores; instintivamente pica a los intrusos; sólo la abeja reina pone huevecillos. Los seres humanos tenemos elección en esos tres comportamientos. Exploramos la naturaleza para encontrar todo tipo de alimento. Luchamos o mantenemos la paz en diferentes circunstancias. Nos emparejamos de acuerdo con patrones de comportamiento en extremo complejos. Al haber sido liberados del instinto, las opciones ante nosotros son, literalmente, infinitas. Pero el cerebro no puede ser infinitamente grande. ¿Entonces cómo puede la mente humana acomodar las opciones infinitas dentro de una fisiología finita?

Este dilema no sólo lo enfrentaron nuestros ancestros remotos. Cada bebé recién nacido llega a un mundo en el que demasiada información bombardea sin cesar el cerebro superior, una inundación de datos crudos que quizá nunca serán procesados en su totalidad. Imagina buscar tu coche en un estacionamiento lleno. Para encontrarlo no integras a tu campo de visión el pavimento, el cielo, la gente y cada vehículo, ya sea detenido o en movimiento. Lo que sí tienes es una imagen mental de tu coche y, con la atención enfocada, editas todo lo que es irrelevante a una tarea, que es encontrar un vehículo específico.

Esto señala otro motivo por el cual desarrollamos un ego. La gente se identifica con lo que puede hacer. Un mecánico automotor es distinto a un violinista de conciertos. Una frase que empieza con "Yo soy X" puede terminar con todo tipo de comportamientos, rasgos, talentos y preferencias. De la misma manera, una frase que empiece con "Yo no soy Y" también puede terminar de muchas formas. Resulta que la lista de cosas que elegimos no ser es mucho más larga que la lista de las que decidimos ser. Si eres cristiano, ésa es una elección única que excluye las demás religiones —actualmente existen 4 200 religiones en el mundo, sobre las cuales una persona sin fe no tiene que pensar, si no es sólo de paso—. Como excluimos opciones incontables sin siquiera pensar en ellas, estamos editando la realidad de acuerdo con los dictados del "yo" individual.

Esta capacidad de editar la realidad en bruto ya estaba presente en animales que cazan una presa específica, por ejemplo, pero ello no implicaba una elección consciente. Cuando los pingüinos y otras aves marinas que anidan en enormes colonias vuelven a la orilla con el buche lleno de alimento, de alguna manera identifican al polluelo específico que les pertenece, en medio del abrumador escándalo creado por miles de ellos. Durante el invierno, el zorro ártico puede detectar el movimiento de los ratones bajo varios centímetros de nieve y lanzarse directo hacia su presa. Las mariposas monarca pueden seguir un mismo patrón de migración desde y hasta una localidad en México donde se aparean.

Existe un enorme misterio sobre cómo los humanos desarrollaron la atención de concentración profunda, no para tipos específicos de alimento y lugares, sino como una característica que podemos encender y apagar. Las cosas en las que estás interesado te fascinan y captan tu atención, mientras que las cosas que no te importan escapan a tu atención. El atractivo de las novelas de detectives reside en el ingenio con que Sherlock Holmes detecta la pista más mínima y al parecer irrelevante. (Supuestamente Holmes era experto en la ceniza del puro y el tipo de tabaco que cada ceniza representaba, pero no sabía que la Tierra gira alrededor del Sol porque esa parte del conocimiento era inútil en el arte de detectar un crimen.)

Aunque no podemos resolver este misterio de poner atención y desconectarnos, no hay duda de que "yo" está a cargo de ambos. Mi esposa, mis hijos y mis nietos son sujetos de profundo interés personal para mí (el tipo de interés que etiquetamos como "amor"), mientras que ellos mismos son completos extraños para los casi 7 000 millones de personas en el planeta. Una vez que se enfoca la atención, sigue la emoción. Cuando era niño, mi hijo Gotham amaba al equipo de basquetbol Celtics de Boston, y odiaba a los Lakers de Los Ángeles. Esto se convirtió en parte de quien era, una decisión de esto/aquello con la que él se identificaba.

Esto/aquello es la herramienta más básica de edición que posee nuestra mente, y comienza con "yo o no yo". El ego separa a cada persona de cada una de las demás por medio de incontables decisiones sobre "yo o no yo". Muchas de estas decisiones no tienen un propósito real, excepto reforzar el ego. (No es que los fanáticos de los Celtics sean mejores, más inteligentes o más adinerados que los fanáticos de los Lakers. Pero cuando Gotham se mudó a vivir a Los Ángeles y su trabajo lo puso en contacto cercano con los Lakers, fue un cambio desgarrador. Convertir "no yo" en "yo" puede ser muy duro. Por ejemplo, imagina que debes pasar un año trabajando para un partido político que siempre te ha desagradado.)

Conforme el ego hizo metástasis a lo largo del tiempo, las "otras" diferencias adquiridas se convirtieron en la base de la desconfianza y desaprobación social. Antes de que nacieran mis hijos, yo era un inmigrante recién llegado que trabajaba en un hospital en Nueva Jersey durante la escasez de médicos, provocada por la guerra de Vietnam en la década de 1970. Todos los días iba al trabajo sabiendo, en el fondo, que los doctores nacidos en Estados Unidos que estaban en la sala de urgencias me veían como inferior a ellos porque había venido de la India.

Si damos un paso atrás para considerar el panorama completo, "yo" edita mucho la realidad y por razones egoístas. Deliberadamente nos cerramos a nosotros mismos a posibilidades nuevas para encajar en preferencias viejas y fijas. El pasado de todas las personas es una colección caótica de decisiones sobre lo que les gusta y disgusta, cómo se sienten emocionalmente y los recuerdos que llevan como bagaje, sin mencionar sus creencias inamovibles, su historia familiar y toda experiencia que haya alterado su vida desde el nacimiento.

Tú no fuiste formado por lo que sucedió desde que naciste. Fuiste formado por lo que pensaste acerca de esos eventos. El ego y todas las respuestas que ha tenido son un enorme constructo mental —la metástasis de "yo"— que creó de las semillas del ego en nuestros ancestros remotos. Nuestra habilidad de editar la realidad es responsable de todo a lo que un ser humano decide prestar atención, y dado que ponemos nuestra atención en mil millones de cosas, la realidad en su estado no editado debe ser infinitamente más grande. Los logros humanos representan una minúscula fracción de lo que la realidad tiene que ofrecer: el horizonte que se despliega ante nosotros es ilimitado.

La decisión de soltar

En páginas anteriores hemos cubierto lo que podría llamarse la historia natural de "yo", y nos ha dicho diversas cosas importantes sobre cómo la realidad virtual que aceptamos como real, de hecho, está fabricada por la mente. En la mente humana, la realidad está construida para que:

La información disponible no sea abrumadora y caótica.

Nos sintamos libres de aceptar o rechazar cualquier aspecto de la realidad que queramos.

Busquemos repetir las experiencias más familiares, seguras y agradables.

Evitemos las experiencias más amenazantes, extrañas y desagradables.

El juez máximo de lo que es real es el ego, que es altamente personal y selectivo sobre la manera en que interpretamos el mundo.

No estoy aquí para declarar que el ego es tu enemigo, lo cual sería otro juicio del ego. Desde un punto de vista neutral, el ego es limitante. Al haber elegido transitar por la vida con "yo" como tu compañero más íntimo, en silencio has accedido a filtrar, censurar y juzgar tus experiencias. Éste es el uso primario de la conciencia en la vida de la mayoría de la gente, y es como si usaran una computadora poderosa sólo para mandar correos electrónicos. Limitar tu realidad personal te desconecta del potencial infinito, que es el regalo más grande de la conciencia.

En algún momento "yo" edita demasiada realidad o se pierde de las cosas importantes que podrían expandir el amor, la compasión, la creatividad y la evolución. Dedicamos demasiada energía mental concentrándonos en cosas dañinas y contraproducentes para nosotros. Si has ido a una cena de Acción de Gracias, en la que los mismos problemas gastados e irritantes de siempre salen a relucir año con año, ya sabes que "yo" puede ser muy testarudo y aferrarse a cosas insignificantes y fastidiosas. Para las criaturas atrapadas en la evolución física no hay escape. Los chitas son los corredores más rápidos de la Tierra, pero su increíble velocidad los ha hecho más pequeños y débiles que los demás depredadores. La etapa más vulnerable en su ciclo de vida es el nacimiento, cuando la madre chita está limitada en su capacidad de proteger a su cría. Se estima que 90% de los chitas recién nacidos no sobrevive. A lo anterior se suma la velocidad de las gacelas, que son presa de los chitas. Las gacelas y los chitas están tan vinculados, que los chitas adultos a menudo fallan en su búsqueda de alimento y por ello viven al borde de la inanición. Al estar atrapados por su adaptación evolutiva específica, los chitas no pueden darse cuenta de otros alimentos que están a su alrededor —termitas, pasto o ratones— para evitar morir de hambre.

El *Homo sapiens* enfrenta un dilema opuesto. Nuestra mente se abre al campo de las posibilidades infinitas. Al tener la capacidad de torcer la naturaleza a voluntad, tomamos decisiones deliberadas que parecen benéficas para nuestra supervivencia, pero las decisiones tienen consecuencias inesperadas. El desarrollo de los primeros humanos avanzó gracias a que se defendían con armas, y armas tan sofisticadas como el arco y la flecha aparecieron tan temprano como 45000 a. e. C. Entonces el armamento ya no podía detenerse, lo que hizo inevitable la catástrofe de la carrera armamentista. ¿O sí podía ser evitada? La libertad de pensamiento es nuestro estado natural; estar atrapados en el pasado no lo es. Todavía nos encontramos en ese estado deliberación y deberíamos elegir aprovecharlo. El tema crucial es la metástasis de "yo", que ha llevado demasiado lejos al libre albedrío en servicio de la ira, el miedo, la avaricia, el egoísmo ciego y todo lo demás.

Una vez que vemos esto, podemos comprender cómo las relaciones personales son saboteadas. Dos personas se enamoran y se casan. Después de la luna de miel, deben relacionarse uno con otro de todo tipo de formas —hacer tareas del hogar, ganar dinero, programar tiempo para hacer cosas juntos o separados—, y "yo" hace su trabajo al manejar una situación tras otra. Pero si estás teniendo una pelea por las finanzas familiares, tu ego pone sobre la mesa el enojo, la necesidad de ganar y el deseo persistente de tener la razón. Si la discusión se acalora lo suficiente, emergen a la superficie dolores de peleas antiguas. A menos de que seas cuidadoso, un desacuerdo trivial puede volverse amargamente personal. Lo que se ha perdido en el calor del momento es el amor subyacente que encendió la relación en primer lugar. Ésa es la realidad más amplia, que el "yo" monotemático excluye para poder ganar una discusión pequeña y por lo general inútil.

Dos personas ocupan un pequeño punto en el mapa. Ahora expande el territorio a una escala global. La carrera humana está devastando el planeta porque 7 000 millones de personas, que actúan por el consejo de "yo", prefieren la experiencia local por encima de la solución de un problema global. Las guerras se desatan y las poblaciones sufren muerte y destrucción a una escala masiva, porque el territorio mayor —mantener la paz amigable— es saboteado por el enojo generado por cada "yo", eligiendo así seguir su agenda irracional, furiosa y hostil.

La conclusión es que "yo" cree con firmeza que puede manejar la realidad, y aun así la historia humana está repleta de sus fracasos abyectos. Incluso es falsa la suposición básica de que "yo" está en contacto con la realidad. En este momento no tienes experiencia del campo cuántico, del cual surge todo lo creado. No tienes experiencia de los átomos y moléculas que constituyen tu cuerpo, ni de la operación de tus células, ni del cerebro mismo. Resulta extraño que el cerebro humano no tenga idea de su propia existencia. Al ver un cerebro bajo el bisturí de un cirujano o cuando se disecciona un cuerpo en la escuela de medicina, es tan sólo la observación de segunda mano de una cosa gris y blanda con surcos a lo largo de su superficie exterior. No hay nada observable que dé indicios de que esta cosa blanda procese la conciencia.

En resumen, "yo" controla nuestra experiencia para asegurarse de que la vida siga siendo local y no infinita. El infinito es el enemigo del ego, porque el infinito es el mapa entero, no sólo puntos y alfileres colocados por aquí y por allá. Soltar "yo" es acoger el infinito. Sólo al estar cómodos con nuestro potencial infinito podemos descubrir que la realidad no necesita ser editada. Pertenecemos a la plenitud. Cuando comenzamos a partir la totalidad en pedacitos y piezas, el ego asume el cargo para manejar cada una de ellas, pedazo a pedazo, y se dé cuenta o no, nos disminuye física y mentalmente. Así que debemos investigar si el infinito es un entorno habitable. Si es así, entonces soltar el ego puede ser justificado. Y no importa lo que haya hecho "yo" para mejorar la vida, podemos comenzar a darnos cuenta de que vivir en la plenitud es mejor.

3

EL POTENCIAL HUMANO ES INFINITO

El potencial humano es infinito porque la conciencia no tiene fronteras. Ser humano significa que cualquier cosa puede suceder. Por ahora, exploremos el mundo interno de posibilidades. Hay formas en las que nuestra realidad exterior es mucho más maleable a través de la conciencia que lo que cualquiera cree. Dado que la conciencia es el cimiento de la realidad, no deberíamos fijar límites absolutos. Para poder volar, los seres humanos no hicimos que nos crecieran alas, pero encontramos un camino para lograr lo que imaginamos. Ten en mente que un camino siempre estará abierto, sin importar qué tan disparatadas sean nuestras aspiraciones.

En el mundo interno de la conciencia, las posibilidades de nuevos pensamientos, entendimientos y descubrimientos ya son ilimitadas. Tan sólo por esto es importante ver al *Homo sapiens* como una especie basada en la conciencia. Las posibilidades infinitas son parte de nuestra conformación. Pero algo dentro de nosotros se resiste a creer en el infinito como una cualidad humana. La realidad editada se siente más cómoda. Sin embargo, hay eventos extraordinarios que demuestran, de forma muy literal, la realidad de la noción de "todo puede suceder". Ocurren saltos repentinos en la conciencia a nuestro alrededor y nos daremos cuenta si nos damos el tiempo para observarlos. Pero "todo puede suceder" quizá describa un universo del todo azaroso lleno de ruido cuántico. En la teoría cuántica, todo borbotea en "espuma cuántica" antes de que la forma y la estructura aparezcan, como una masa de pastel sin forma antes de que el pastel esté horneado y adquiera una forma sólida. Debido a que las partículas cuánticas entran y salen de la existencia, de acuerdo con las leyes de la probabilidad existe una oportunidad infinitesimal de que un objeto físico —una hoja, una silla o una ballena— aparezcan de pronto de la nada. La física existe para decirnos con exactitud qué tan imposible es que suceda algo así.

Podrías pensar que estos temas son tan abstractos que no tienen nada que ver contigo a nivel personal. Cuando la física cuántica afirma que la probabilidad de que un calamar gigante bloquee tu cochera es muy, muy pequeñita, no estás aprendiendo nada nuevo. Participamos en el mundo "allá afuera" de la forma en que la sociedad nos ha enseñado a hacerlo. Pero es una visión radicalmente corta de la realidad. De hecho, nuestra participación en el mundo comienza en el nivel cuántico. Para efectos prácticos, aquí es donde la mente y la materia se encuentran. Ambas existen como posibilidades, listas para hacerse manifiestas, pero todavía son invisibles.

Por lo tanto, la mente y la materia son más maleables ahí, al igual que el barro suave es más maleable que un plato o una figura de porcelana después de que se les dio forma, se hornearon y se vidriaron. Al ser humanos podemos regresar conscientemente al nivel cuántico, que expande nuestra participación infinitamente, comparado con lo que podemos hacer cuando la creación ha tomado un lugar solidificado. No sólo la creación es más suave, por así decirlo, sino que la mente y la materia no se han separado aún. Cuando se separan, una roca no se convertirá en una roca al instante, mientras que un pensamiento se va por otro lado y en ese momento se convierte en un pensamiento. La mente y la materia primero surgen idénticas, como ondas invisibles en el campo cuántico. Estas ondas formarán patrones conforme chocan con ondas del campo de gravedad, el campo de los quarks, el campo de los electrones y algunos más. Los patrones de interferencia, que son como la huella ondulada de las olas en la arena de una playa, se arman y sólo entonces comienzan a aparecer objetos reconocibles como quarks y electrones.

La física ha realizado un trabajo brillante al rastrear la creación hasta este punto. Sin embargo, ha hecho muy poco para rastrear la mente hasta su origen —todos tenemos mucho más que decir al respecto—. Pero la conclusión es que la persona promedio supone que la mente y la materia están naturalmente separadas. Así es como nos confunde la ilusión. Pensar en una manzana es muy distinto de sostener una manzana física. Pero a un nivel más profundo, el pensamiento y la manzana alguna vez fueron lo mismo. Comienzan como posibilidades en el mundo que la física llama realidad virtual. El misterio gira en torno a la manera en que dos cosas tan distintas pueden provenir de la misma semilla.

Para aprovechar el potencial infinito debes aceptar que la realidad no es concluyente y es capaz de tomar impulsos sutiles e invisibles y convertirlos en mente y materia. Esta apertura es lo que yo llamo metarrealidad, porque yace más allá de la mente y la materia; la metarrealidad es donde el universo entero y todo lo que contiene, incluyendo toda la actividad mental, se encuentra en un estado embrionario.

No pretendo decir que es fácil adoptar la metarrealidad cuando apenas te enteras de su existencia. ¿Qué tan seguro te puedes sentir acerca de tu vida si ésta es totalmente abierta? No mucho; todo mundo prefiere que las cosas estén más establecidas y ordenadas que eso. Pero si lo piensas, un pintor que contempla un lienzo en blanco o un escritor que observa una hoja en blanco confía en que "todo puede suceder" como el mejor y más alto estado creativo. Cuando te aproximas al potencial infinito como posibilidades creativas infinitas, hay una apertura al tipo de libertad que "yo" no puede experimentar dentro de las fronteras.

Estamos tan condicionados para decir "mi" cuerpo y "mi" mente que en automático creemos que están realizando los actos y los pensamientos que experimentamos. Pero en la metarrealidad la conciencia actúa y piensa. Podríamos, y deberíamos, cambiar a esa perspectiva por un simple motivo. El cerebro no puede dar el salto a una conciencia superior; sólo puede hacerlo la conciencia. Una cuerda de un violín no puede inventar nuevas formas de música, pero la mente musical puede usar el violín como su instrumento de expresión física. De la misma manera, la mente-cuerpo —una comprensión de que el cuerpo y la mente son una unidad— es la expresión física de la conciencia.

En la música hay más combinaciones de notas posibles que átomos en el universo, y aun así estamos cómodos con estas posibilidades tan vastas. Jugamos al ajedrez sin ansiedad ante las 400 posiciones posibles que existen después de que cada jugador mueve una pieza, lo cual explota hasta 228 000 millones de posiciones posibles en cuatro movimientos. De forma cotidiana, al igual que cuando jugamos algún juego, damos infinidad de cosas por hecho. Está a todo nuestro alrededor. Incluso si tienes un vocabulario limitado de 2 000 palabras, que es lo que tiene un niño típico de cinco años, es suficiente para crear una secuencia interminable de combinaciones de palabras, sin mencionar que nada te detiene de darle múltiples significados nuevos a una palabra común. (Por ejemplo, la palabra *pet* en inglés es un verbo, un sustantivo y un adjetivo: "I pet my cat, who is the only pet I have", que en español significa: "Acaricio a mi gato, que es la única mascota que tengo") —y cada quien es libre de asignarle nuevos significados a la palabra—. La palabra *pet* podría ser un sustituto de mimado, suntuoso, adorable, y cosas por el estilo. Ya tiene esas connotaciones. Se pueden inventar nuevos significados de la nada, así como *la buena onda* se ha alejado de su significado literal.)

Como estamos tan acostumbrados al infinito en estas simples presentaciones, podemos expandir nuestra zona de confort para sentirnos a gusto con el infinito como un rasgo personal.

El genio repentino

El hecho de que "todo puede suceder" es esencial para ser humano. De pronto puede suceder un salto de conciencia, como en el increíble fenómeno llamado *genio repentino*, término acuñado por Darold Treffert, un médico de Wisconsin que se ha vuelto un experto en el "desempeño excepcional del cerebro". Él define al *genio repentino* como "un momento espontáneo tipo epifanía en el que las reglas y las complejidades de la música, el arte o las matemáticas, por ejemplo, son experimentadas y reveladas, produciendo un talento casi instantáneo".

De los 14 casos que Treffert ha estudiado hasta la fecha, un ejemplo impresionante es el de un hombre de 28 años nacido en Israel, a quien él llama "K. A." Como intérprete, K. A. podía sacar tonadas populares en el piano una nota a la vez. Un día estaba en un centro comercial que tenía un piano en exhibición. Cito su recuento del momento: "De pronto me di cuenta de lo que eran la escala mayor y la escala menor, lo que eran sus cuerdas y dónde poner los dedos para tocar ciertas partes de la escala". Sin previo conocimiento o habilidad, K. A. de pronto *supo* cómo funcionaba la armonía musical. Buscó sobre teoría musical en internet y así lo verificó y, para su sorpresa, "ya sabía casi todo lo que enseñaban". Se quedó pasmado y pensó cómo era posible saber sobre un tema que nunca había estudiado.

Este tipo de fenómenos apoyan con fuerza una característica central de la metarrealidad: que los seres humanos ya estamos conectados a posibilidades infinitas.

Nos mantenemos alejados de nuestro potencial oculto por todo tipo de razones; de entrada, acabamos de ver cómo el ego edita y limita la realidad. Incluso cuando nos confronta la evidencia de lo contrario, el poder de la limitación nos conmina a verlo con escepticismo o ignorarlo por completo. El mismo hecho de que Treffert logró que sus observaciones sobre el *genio repentino* fueran publicadas en la revista *Scientific American* (el 25 de julio de 2018) se debe a un misterio más grande, conocido como *síndrome del sabio*, que tiene una historia muy conocida en la práctica médica y psicológica.

El síndrome del sabio también implica habilidades extraordinarias que desafían toda explicación. Ya había dos formas diferentes de esta condición, de las cuales Treffert también es experto. En el "síndrome del sabio congénito", las habilidades extraordinarias aparecen cuando el niño es pequeño. Hay niños que pueden decirte el día de la semana en que cae cualquier día, ya sea pasado o futuro —los llamados sabios de calendario—, y otros que pueden generar números primos mentalmente con la velocidad y precisión de una computadora. (Un número primo es un numeral divisible sólo entre y sí mismo y uno. La secuencia comienza fácil con 2, 3, 5, 7 y 11. Pero pronto se vuelve mucho más difícil saber el siguiente número en la secuencia sin la ayuda de una calculadora. Por ejemplo, 7 727 y 7 741 son números primos, pero ninguno de los números entre ellos es primo.)

La otra forma es el "síndrome del sabio adquirido", en el que una persona ordinaria de pronto tiene habilidades sorprendentes después de una lesión en la cabeza, un derrame cerebral o algún otro incidente del sistema nervioso central. A estas dos versiones Treffert añadió el "síndrome del sabio repentino" como un tercer tipo, como en la historia de K. A. Ninguno de ellos puede ser explicado científicamente. En la forma congénita, por lo regular el niño está en el espectro del autismo o del retraso mental. (En su aclamado libro publicado en 1985, *El hombre que confundió a su mujer con un sombrero*, el neurólogo Oliver Sacks narra historias de personas "con otro tipo de cerebro", incluyendo incidentes en gente con lesiones en el lado derecho del cerebro y niños autistas con habilidades matemáticas extraordinarias.)

El síndrome del sabio tuvo una reputación hasta cierto punto ajena porque estaba confinado al autismo y las lesiones cerebrales, pero cuando el genio repentino ocurre en personas que parecen normales, se volvió más familiar. Treffert tituló su artículo "Brain Gain: A Person Can Instantly Blossom into a Savant —and No One Knows Why" ("Logro del cerebro: una persona puede volverse sabia de pronto, y nadie sabe por qué"). Para un lector con mente científica, *cerebro* es la palabra más significativa del título, porque actualmente la explicación de todos los fenómenos mentales está enfocada en el cerebro. Pero no es razonable decir que de pronto un cerebro aprendió cómo funciona la teoría musical sin ningún aporte, educación o capacitación. (Es como decir que el cerebro conoce todas las ciudades del mundo sin haber visto nunca un mapa.) La gente que adquiere habilidades artísticas repentinas por lo regular se obsesiona con la pintura y difícilmente intentará hacer otra cosa. Esto es una reminiscencia de Picasso, que estaba obsesionado con la pintura desde la infancia, pero sería difícil imaginar que a las personas con poco o ningún interés en el arte de un día para otro les fascine pintar porque su cerebro se los indicó.

Para la mayoría de la gente el arte, la música y las matemáticas no son aspectos críticos de la vida, y con sólo 14 casos registrados de genios repentinos, al menos hasta ahora, este fenómeno extraño es bastante exótico. Pero resulta que el genio repentino es otra clave para el misterio de lo que significa ser humano, y la pista tiene que ver con el infinito mismo.

Relacionarnos con el infinito

Si alguien tiene poco o ningún interés en la música y de pronto conoce la teoría musical sin estudiarla, ¿de dónde provino el conocimiento? No fue enviado por medio de un maestro o un libro de texto, que es la forma normal de obtener conocimiento. Fue descargado de alguna forma, podríamos decir que de una fuente "allá fuera", en algún lugar. Pero ¿dónde? La música es una creación humana — no hay acordes, sonatas ni sinfonías en la naturaleza—. Tampoco hay una librería invisible "allá fuera" donde se almacena toda la información sobre la música. Además, si existiera ese tipo de librería, ¿quién enviaría a la gente una descarga si no la quiere?

Queremos mantenernos alejados del área que hace que la cabeza dé vueltas, y la metarrealidad se puede sentir como algo desconcertante. La metarrealidad es el lugar donde se almacena todo lo que ha sido y que será pensado. Dado que el infinito no tiene límites, la metarrealidad también contiene todo *pensamiento posible*. Apenas recientemente los académicos que estudian la Grecia antigua han podido decodificar los fragmentos de manuscritos que contienen música escrita y, con un esfuerzo meticuloso y por medio de conjeturas, permitieron que la música fuera tocada en quenas y tambores, exactamente como Sócrates pudo haber escuchado a músicos callejeros mientras caminaba por Atenas en el siglo IV a. e. C.

Traer de vuelta la música antigua es un acto de recreación. La mente intenta recordar lo que nunca olvidó, lo cual suena extraño.

Eso no es lo mismo que recuperar información. Para captar lo que en realidad está en juego puede ser útil una imagen de la vida cotidiana: la nube.

Cualquiera que use internet quizás haya escuchado, aunque sólo vagamente, sobre la nube, un lugar en el ciberespacio que contiene la suma de la información del mundo. La capacidad de la nube es múltiples veces más grande que las librerías más grandes del mundo. Todos los correos electrónicos son guardados ahí, cada foto en línea, cada transacción realizada en Amazon y cada búsqueda en Google. Aunque la nube se ha vuelto universal, poca gente sabe que tiene una ubicación física.

Se han erigido enormes centros de datos para almacenar toda la información que antes era guardada en las oficinas del hogar o de las empresas. Cuando tomas una foto de cualquier cosa —un atardecer, el Gran Cañón, un bebé recién nacido—, luego la recortas, mejoras el color y la envías al teléfono de alguien más, la imagen no va de tu teléfono a la otra persona sin pasar primero por la nube. Centros gigantescos de información en el condado de Loudoun, en Virginia, cada uno de miles de metros cuadrados, albergan la nube actual.

En el ciberespacio el acceso a la nube es instantáneo, pero entrar en uno de estos centros de datos es un proceso arduo. El núcleo donde se localizan miles de computadoras poderosas está protegido por varias capas de seguridad. Un trabajador debe pasar por un escaneo de la retina que identifique a la persona (pueden detectar incluso si la persona está viva, y que no sea alguien planeando usar el globo ocular de alguien más), luego a través de un portal de seguridad, una habitación en la que la puerta de entrada debe estar cerrada antes de que se abra la puerta de salida, después debe pasar por un escuadrón de guardias armados, y a lo largo de todo esto se deben ingresar contraseñas distintas.

El hecho de que el ciberespacio sea un lugar real contrasta por completo con la conciencia. Uno no tiene que ir a un lugar "allá fuera" para recordar la tonada de "Extraños en la noche" de Frank Sinatra, la cual se evoca con el sonido de su voz y la imagen de su rostro. La metarrealidad almacena la experiencia en su totalidad, y nosotros la recreamos cada vez que lo deseamos. La neurociencia afirma que la recupera del cerebro, pero el fenómeno del genio repentino ensombrece esa explicación, ya que en él la gente puede recuperar conocimientos que nunca tuvo.

Para ir más lejos, el ser humano es creativo, así que usamos la conciencia para inventar y descubrir nuevas cosas. No es lo mismo que recrear la música griega antigua. Pero descifrar por qué algunas personas son creativas es muy difícil. Al igual que la nube, la metarrealidad tiene medidas de seguridad. Para un Leonardo da Vinci o Ludwig van Beethoven las riquezas de la creación se abren fácil y copiosamente. Estos artistas están consumidos por el acto creativo. En el otro extremo, algunas personas están totalmente cerradas a la creatividad artística. Al parecer los genios creativos se infiltran en la metarrealidad. Se relacionan con este potencial infinito mucho más allá de lo que nos permitimos a nosotros mismos hacer normalmente.

Se han realizado esfuerzos para hacer de la creatividad una herramienta, lo cual al principio suena prometedor. Esto motiva a compañías visionarias como Google o Apple a identificar y emplear a las mentes más creativas. Volvamos al libro *Stealing Fire* que mencioné antes. En esta obra, Steven Kotler y Jamie Wheal se internan en la fabricación de "trampas de talento" a lo largo de Silicon Valley. Estas empresas, junto con la revolución en redes sociales por medio de Facebook y Twitter, se echaron a andar gracias a la innovación, y es natural que, con miles de millones de dólares a su disposición, Silicon

Valley quiera estimular ideas cada vez más creativas; en un entorno de alta tecnología, la supervivencia depende de ello.

A estas corporaciones les encantaría monetizar esa "zona" de creatividad sin esfuerzo, pero los momentos "eureka" son sólo eso, destellos temporales de entendimiento. El desafío consiste en sostener ese entendimiento y hacer de la innovación una forma de vida. *Stealing Fire* describe cómo Google ha creado un entorno laboral en el que un elemento importante de la creatividad —fluir— se diseña de formas ingeniosas.

La noción subyacente es simple: si quieres que la mente fluya, haz que el lugar de trabajo fluya. Google toma esta idea en serio y constantemente modifica sus oficinas para que se sienta continuidad con la vida fuera del trabajo. Hay bicicletas con las que puedes ir de un lugar al otro del campus, hay wifi en los autobuses de la compañía, alimentos orgánicos de alta calidad y una estructura bastante relajada que permite que las ideas se muevan con libertad, en vez de la jerarquía tradicional rígida que aleja a los directivos de los empleados.

Pero estas amenidades tienen un éxito limitado, porque el flujo mismo no define la creatividad. Kotler y Wheal se enfocan en los "estados alterados", como los llaman, en los que los hábitos mentales normales desaparecen por completo. Ya sea inducidos por LSD o por un tanque de inmersión total, por medio de la meditación o rituales sagrados, uno puede experimentar el *éxtasis*, palabra derivada del latín que significa "afuera" y "estar parado". Un estado extático pone a la persona afuera y más allá del sentido normal del yo de la mente. En éxtasis nos sentimos libres, sin límites, dichosos —y creativos—. *Stealing Fire* en esencia se trata de cómo Silicon Valley busca monetizar el éxtasis.

Google fomenta la meditación en sus empleados, por ejemplo, lo que les da acceso a un estado de conciencia más calmado y expandido. Pero, a pesar de saber acerca de la zona, el fluir, el éxtasis, la meditación y la conciencia que atestigua, resulta que la creatividad es elusiva. En 2013, en busca de los medios para resolver problemas "retorcidos", un grupo diverso de mentes brillantes se reunió para el proyecto Hacking Creativity, "el metaanálisis sobre creatividad más grande que se haya realizado". La idea rectora era que si la creatividad podía ser comprendida, todo sería posible.

Para este fin, se analizaron más de 30 000 artículos de investigación sobre creatividad y fueron entrevistados cientos de expertos, "desde bailarines de *breakdance* y artistas de circo, hasta poetas y estrellas de rock". Para 2016 se llegó a dos conclusiones.

La primera es que la creatividad es esencial para resolver problemas complejos —el tipo de problemas que a menudo enfrentamos en un mundo acelerado—. La segunda es que tenemos muy poco éxito en entrenar a la gente para ser más creativa. Y hay una explicación bastante simple para este fracaso: intentamos enseñar una habilidad, pero lo que deberíamos enseñar es un estado mental.

Resulta que es imposible piratear la creatividad. Entrar de forma pirata es una intrusión, el equivalente cibernético de forzar la entrada e ingresar. La gente creativa no fuerza la entrada e ingresa. Lo que hace es mucho más cercano a la evolución; algo nuevo sale a la luz y toma forma física, como una pintura o una pieza musical. Evolucionar es creativo —el largo cuello de la jirafa, la capacidad de cambiar de color del camaleón, y nuestra propia posesión física de primera: el pulgar y el índice oponibles, son el resultado de la creatividad de la naturaleza—. Al trabajar desde el campo de las posibilidades infinitas, la evolución procede con un paso a la vez para crear una criatura completa, de la misma forma en que tú y yo recreamos la experiencia total de escuchar a Sinatra cantar "Extraños en la noche".

Cada forma de vida se vincula a la realidad por medio de la evolución, y accede a su potencial creativo de forma ordenada y progresiva. Las criaturas que nos parecen más extrañas no son un ensamblaje de partes separadas que son unidas de forma caprichosa. Son expresiones de una adaptación delicada que encuentra un nicho perfecto para sí misma, además de miles de otras formas de vida que viven en el mismo entorno.

Cada mañana al despertar, el oso hormiguero gigante (*Myrmecophaga tridactyla*) de Sudamérica y Centroamérica está hambriento de hormigas. Está magníficamente adaptado por la evolución física para buscar su presa enterrada profundo bajo la tierra. Las garras frontales del oso hormiguero gigante están equipadas con garras de 10 centímetros para atacar una colonia de hormigas o termitas. Tiene una lengua pegajosa de 60 centímetros que usa para buscar y alcanzar a las hormigas, para después enrollarla y meterlas a su boca.

Uno se maravilla con lo específicas que son estas adaptaciones. Incluso las quijadas del oso hormiguero gigante han sido reducidas a un tamaño miniatura, ya que si fueran más largas serían inútiles para hurgar en los pasajes estrechos de los hormigueros y las colonias de termitas. Pero, al mismo tiempo, ningún humano elegiría estar atrapado en semejante callejón sin salida evolutivo. Para sobrevivir, el oso hormiguero gigante debe consumir alrededor de 30 000 hormigas al día, y dado que su dieta es tan poco nutritiva, el animal no tiene la suficiente energía para hacer nada más que dormir 16 horas al día.

El adorado panda gigante también está en un callejón sin salida. Aunque es un oso verdadero, y uno de los primeros que evolucionaron, el panda está mal dotado porque tiene el tracto intestinal incorrecto; a diferencia de los sistemas digestivos de otros osos, el del panda sólo puede digerir hojas de bambú. ¿Por qué el panda perdió, o bien nunca tuvo, la capacidad típica de un oso de comer casi cualquier cosa? El "por qué" no tiene cabida en la evolución. Sucede una adaptación, y ésta contribuye o no a la supervivencia de una especie.

El *Homo sapiens* ha eludido todos los callejones sin salida, incluyendo los que encontraron otros primates. Nuestros vínculos más cercanos entre las especies vivas son los chimpancés y los gorilas, pero, contrariamente a la opinión popular, no descendimos de ellos y de ningún otro simio. De acuerdo con la mejor estimación actual, el último ancestro común entre los humanos y los chimpancés vivió alrededor de 13 millones de años atrás, y condujo a una separación genética. Una rama de la separación evolucionó en chimpancés, gorilas, orangutanes y sus parientes, mientras que la otra derivó en nuestros ancestros homínidos.

El chimpancé es una especie moderna, al igual que nosotros. (Resulta interesante que la evolución de los chimpancés fue dos o tres veces más compleja que la nuestra, resultado de dos factores: el primero es que los chimpancés pasan el doble de mutaciones aleatorias de padres a hijos que los padres humanos: en promedio, un bebé humano hereda alrededor de 70 nuevas mutaciones de sus padres. El segundo es que existe algo en genética llamado "cuello de botella", donde no hay disponibilidad suficiente de nuevos genes. Menor número de genes conduce a menos mutaciones, lo que provoca que una especie permanezca bloqueada a las nuevas características. De acuerdo con análisis genéticos, a lo largo de millones de años los chimpancés se encontraron con tres cuellos de botella que exprimieron su acervo génico, mientras que los humanos sólo enfrentaron un cuello de botella al migrar fuera de África hace 200 000 años. Una vez fuera del cuello de botella, nuestra especie se expandió de forma explosiva para cubrir todo el orbe.)

El gran cambio de realidad plantea un profundo misterio que no puede ser desentrañado al examinar nuestros genes. Incluso con un índice de mutación dos veces más alto que el *Homo sapiens*, los chimpancés no han obtenido conciencia de sí mismos. Eso no es lo mismo que falta de inteligencia. Los estudios de primates muestran cada vez más que los chimpancés son mucho más cercanos a la inteligencia humana de lo que antes se pensaba. De acuerdo con el primatólogo Frans de Waal, la idea de que sólo los humanos pueden fabricar herramientas ahora es "una postura insostenible. También hay afirmaciones de que los simios no tienen una teoría de la mente, y éstas han sido seriamente debilitadas. Las afirmaciones culturales, la idea de que sólo los humanos son excelentes para la cooperación y demás, en realidad ninguna de ellas se sostiene".

Teoría de la mente es un término de la filosofía y la psicología que habla de conocer el estado mental de alguien más sin que nadie se lo diga. Una definición resumida es "leer la mente". Muchos amantes de los perros jurarían que su mascota sabe cuándo su dueño está contento, triste o enojado. Pero sigue siendo controversial demostrar que cualquier animal comprende que tiene una mente. Es fascinante considerar que hace 13 millones de años nuestro ancestro común tenía el potencial oculto de rasgos que florecieron en los chimpancés a lo largo de una sola rama de la división y en los humanos en la otra rama.

Pero los chimpancés no experimentaron el gran cambio de realidad que le dio la conciencia de sí mismo al *Homo sapiens*. Existen límites en lo que los chimpancés pueden aprender y comprender. Por ejemplo, si colocas un cacahuate bajo una taza amarilla y no pones un cacahuate bajo una taza roja, un chimpancé pronto aprenderá la diferencia y siempre escogerá la taza amarilla. Pero si le presentas a un chimpancé dos pesas y le das una recompensa si levanta la que pesa menos, no hará la conexión y continuará levantando las dos pesas de manera aleatoria. Asimismo, si un chimpancé aprende a abrir una caja para obtener algo de comida, otro chimpancé no puede aprender a resolver el problema si observa al primer chimpancé.

Estas diferencias entre nosotros y nuestros parientes más cercanos llegan hasta ahí. Los chimpancés y los gorilas tienen un rango de posibilidades mucho más amplio que un oso hormiguero gigante. Pero ni remotamente se acercan a nosotros en lo que respecta al acceso a posibilidades infinitas. El gran cambio de realidad trasciende la genética, y no importa qué tanto nos veamos a nosotros mismos cuando observamos a otros primates, ellos no se ven a sí mismos en nosotros, simplemente porque no pueden hacerlo. Algunos callejones sin salida evolutivos conducen a una vida tan compleja como la de los primates más elevados, pero finalmente son callejones sin salida.

El milagro de ser humano es que evolucionamos en múltiples dimensiones. Todo en nosotros —el comportamiento, el pensamiento abstracto, la curiosidad, las personalidades individuales, los sistemas sociales— explotó más allá de cualquier precedente, como si la vida en la Tierra se hubiera apresurado hacia niveles de aspiración desconocidos. Un experto en ajedrez tridimensional estaría perplejo al mirar nuestro tablero de juego, que tiene numerosos niveles y añade nuevos todo el tiempo. Pero este experto no podría ver nuestra configuración, porque ésta existe y evoluciona en la conciencia. Éste es un punto tan importante que necesitamos abordarlo más profundamente.

La conciencia en dimensiones múltiples

El infinito puede permanecer en una dimensión, o bien puede existir en diversas dimensiones al mismo tiempo. Puedes pensar en un número como dos tercios alargando una sola serie de dígitos —0.6666666— al infinito, como un gusano de seda que teje un hilo sin fin. Ése es un ejemplo del infinito ocupando una dimensión. Pero el fluir, al igual que la creatividad, es un estado de conciencia que cubre múltiples dimensiones. Una persona "está fluyendo" cuando todo parece ir bien, los obstáculos se disipan y las respuestas llegan sin esfuerzo alguno. Cada aspecto ocupa su propia dimensión, y sin embargo de alguna manera se coordinan cuando se experimenta el fluir. Hay una sensación de calma y también se siente felicidad, a veces al grado de sentir éxtasis. Si ese fluir es lo suficientemente poderoso, puede ser absorbente, y da la impresión de que las ideas creativas surgen por su propia voluntad, usándonos como vehículo, como un escritor usa a los actores para dar voz a sus palabras.

Fluir es deseable, pero es algo bastante misterioso, ya que viene y va, y algunas personas jamás lo experimentan. El misterio se resuelve cuando te das cuenta de que fluir es el acceso sin obstrucción hacia la metarrealidad. En el fluir estamos experimentando la totalidad. Los charcos no fluyen, pero sí lo hace el océano. Sólo la totalidad puede orquestar un estado de conciencia que abarque múltiples dimensiones. Nuestros ancestros homínidos sin duda se volvieron multidimensionales hace mucho, mucho tiempo. Hubo un despertar masivo que dejó sus rastros en las primeras pinturas rupestres conocidas. Estas pinturas fueron posibles gracias a un cambio radical en la conciencia. La fecha de la creación de las primeras pinturas de animales en las paredes de una cueva ha sido redefinida una y otra vez por los científicos, y cada vez la datan más antiguamente. Durante mucho tiempo el récord lo tuvo Europa, primer lugar en un complejo de cuevas en Lascaux, Francia (hace unos 17 000 años), después cuevas separadas en Francia y Rumania (hace 30 000 y 32 000 años), representando un enorme salto hacia atrás en el tiempo. Ahora el récord lo tiene un sistema de cuevas en Indonesia, en la península de Sulawesi del Sur, que todavía es usada por los nativos. La datación por radiocarbono ha establecido que las pinturas indonesias fueron realizadas de 35 000 a 42 000 años atrás.

Mirar fotografías de estos artefactos prehistóricos (se encuentran fácilmente en internet) es una forma de viaje en el tiempo, no física sino mental. En el sitio francés más antiguo, la cueva de Chauvet-Pont-d'Arc, que está en un acantilado de piedra caliza sobre el antiguo lecho de un río que ahora está seco, las pinturas son nada menos que arte. La cueva de Chauvet fue descubierta en 1994 y pronto fue nombrada Patrimonio de la Humanidad por la UNESCO. Tiene en sus paredes cientos de figuras de animales muy grandes y bien preservadas, que representan 13 especies. En otras pinturas de la Edad de Hielo los sujetos principales son herbívoros, como caballos y ganado, pero los artistas de Chauvet añadieron depredadores, como el león, la pantera, el oso y la hiena.

Las circunstancias detrás del arte fueron arduas. Las paredes de la cueva se encuentran muy adentro, lejos de la luz del exterior, lo que significa que quienes las pintaron trabajaron en la oscuridad con la luz de antorchas titilantes. Aunque la luz se movía, los pintores tenían tan buen pulso que las curvas más largas de cada animal específico —cuernos, lomo, cabeza y piernas— fueron hechas de una sola pincelada, como la haría un dibujante experto en la actualidad. Al parecer las paredes fueron limpiadas y suavizadas para lograr un área pálida apropiada, un lienzo desnudo, antes de comenzar la pintura que vemos hoy. Están representados dos rinocerontes lanudos chocando sus cabezas entre sí, lo que refleja el deseo del artista original de retratar escenas, y se muestran muchos animales en movimiento, no como los dibujos de los niños en los que las figuras aparecen tiesas.

Como podrás imaginar, el deseo de pintar una imagen no es y nunca ha sido algo simple. ¿Estas pinturas son místicas, rituales o mágicas? El estado mental de los artistas no puede ser determinado de forma concluyente. ¿Hay belleza en la forma en la que fueron dibujados los animales, o tan sólo estamos imponiendo la "belleza" a partir de nuestros propios conceptos que nos resultan familiares? Lo que fuera que los pintores de las cuevas tenían en mente, se volvió viral, por así decirlo. Las mismas imágenes fueron repetidas por culturas a miles de kilómetros de distancia.

Un misterio más pequeño dentro del misterio mayor es el motivo por el que los pintores de las cuevas no se dibujaron a sí mismos. En Chauvet, hace 30 000 años, los pintores no realizaron dibujos de figuras humanas completas, y sólo una figura parcial (la mitad inferior de un cuerpo femenino, con órganos sexuales prominentes), pero hay numerosos contornos de manos humanas impresas en la pared. Éstos fueron hechos al soplar pigmento color rojo ocre alrededor de la mano de alguien mientras la presionaba sobre la piedra. También en las cuevas indonesias aparecen contornos de manos datadas miles de años antes, en Argentina entre 9 000 y 13 000 años atrás, y en petroglifos de Anasazi, o en más antiguos al suroeste de Estados Unidos. Estas huellas de manos no conducen a una conclusión definitiva. Quizá marcan alianzas tribales o tan sólo el mensaje de "Yo estuve aquí".

En una escala global, la explosión del arte sofisticado demuestra un potencial oculto que cobró vida como un despertar de la conciencia, completamente desarrollada y vibrante. El arte debe ser considerado evolucionario en el *Homo sapiens*, porque ha persistido como rasgo dominante de nuestra especie en todas las sociedades y no se ha extinguido. Pero parece poco probable que el arte haya tenido un valor para la supervivencia. Las pinturas en las cuevas son prueba de que a los humanos prehistóricos les preocupaba algo más allá de sus necesidades físicas, y este algo emergió directamente de sus conciencias.

Para mí resulta claro que las pinturas de la cueva de Chauvet se hicieron con la mente en su totalidad. Un Picasso prehistórico no se plantó frente al lienzo en blanco de una pared de caliza y dejó volar su imaginación. El *Homo sapiens* evolucionó de manera mucho más holística. Por lo menos, el deseo de crear arte implica los siguientes atributos con los que todos podemos identificarnos, incluso si no somos artistas:

Curiosidad

Inteligencia

Propósito

Motivación

Diligencia

Coordinación entre el ojo y la mano

Aprender un conjunto de habilidades

Estos rasgos mentales deben existir para construir el Taj Mahal, inventar el motor de combustión interna o pintar un rinoceronte lanudo en la pared de una cueva. Y la colección completa de rasgos debe reunirse en una sola intención. Quizás es imposible descubrir a nivel científico cómo sucede esto. No hay forma de reunir evidencia cuando lo que buscas es invisible. De todas formas, la capacidad de usar la mente en su totalidad me convence de que nuestros ancestros remotos contenían en sí mismos las semillas del metahumano. Ser capaz de acceder a la mente en su totalidad destruye el mito de que nuestros ancestros eran primitivos. Su potencial ya era infinito.

Un acertijo

Una vez que el *Homo sapiens* encontró un camino hacia la Mente Total, la experiencia se incrustó en la evolución humana. Si nos examinamos con atención a nosotros mismos, es claro que somos criaturas de mente entera. Probemos lo anterior con una tarea simple, como ir a la tienda a comprar el pastel de cumpleaños de un niño. Detrás de la simplicidad de la tarea hay un complejo de actividades mentales que damos por hecho. Los ingredientes en la mezcla incluyen los siguientes:

Conocer el concepto de "pastel de cumpleaños" y vincular las palabras a un objeto físico.

Querer hacer algo lindo por tu hijo.

Poner el pastel en tu lista de pendientes.

Saber cómo manejar un auto.

Recordar la ruta hasta la tienda.

Dar prioridad a esta tarea por encima de otras cosas que demandan tu tiempo.

Seleccionar un pastel entre muchos, usando tu juicio sobre cuál de ellos le gustará más a tu hijo.

Estas cosas abarcan la emoción, la intención, el reconocimiento visual, la memoria, la coordinación motriz y habilidades almacenadas, ¡tan sólo para una tarea sencilla! La neurociencia puede localizar y aislar el lugar en el cerebro donde se representan algunas de estas actividades mentales, pero no se explica la forma en que se engranan para lograr un resultado unificado (comprar un pastel de cumpleaños). El proceso de lograr que millones de células cerebrales se enciendan en sintonía hace que pastorear gatos parezca fácil. Es más bien como arrear a cada gato en el mundo.

Y mucho menos es posible explicar cómo puede cambiar de dirección sin una transición visible de A a B. Un patrón increíblemente complicado de actividad cerebral cambia de forma espontánea a otro. A diferencia de un automóvil, no hay transmisión o palanca de velocidades. Imagina que estás leyendo una novela y olvidas que tienes un asado en el horno. Estás absorto en la lectura de *El señor de los anillos* o *Jane Eyre* y de pronto percibes el olor del humo en el aire. Al instante, esta simple sensación del olor provoca que entres en acción y olvidas el libro. Las moléculas de carbón que estimulan los receptores para la detección del olor lanzan a tu cerebro a un nuevo patrón de acción coordinada. La relajación se convierte en estrés en un instante.

Decir que tu cerebro detectó el asado quemándose no explica tu reacción. Tu cerebro procesó la información en bruto de partículas de humo entrando al conducto nasal, pero es necesario que una persona perciba el olor y le dé significado. El mismo olor en un asado a la parrilla en exteriores en verano no provoca alarma, aunque el proceso físico que tiene lugar en la nariz y el cerebro es idéntico. La actividad electromagnética que va de un lado a otro del córtex forma un patrón para la casa que se quema y otro para la parrillada. Eso es todo lo que tiene un neurocientífico para trabajar, y no es ni remotamente suficiente.

Incluso si la neurociencia pudiera mapear cada área ínfima de la actividad cerebral hasta el más mínimo detalle —como lo intentan en la actualidad los Institutos Nacionales de Salud de Estados Unidos por medio de Brain Initiative, institución financiada federalmente—, la conciencia sería indetectable. Si el cerebro es una pista falsa con respecto a un tufo a humo, también podría ser una pista falsa de muchas otras formas. Dos aspirantes a poetas podrían estar escribiendo un soneto, causando que una actividad cerebral específica se encienda en una resonancia magnética, pero nadie podría decir cuál de los dos escritores es Shakespeare y cuál es un inútil. Después de que Einstein murió se realizó una autopsia a su cerebro para determinar si el genio más grande de la humanidad, como era etiquetado popularmente, tenía un cerebro inusual, y no lo tenía. Puedes encontrar en YouTube múltiples videos de niños prodigio tocando el piano a la edad de tres o cuatro años cuando, de acuerdo con el desarrollo normal de cerebro, ese despliegue complejo de coordinación musical no debería ser posible. Lograr una habilidad para el piano por lo regular toma años o décadas de práctica.

Al haber escapado a las limitaciones de la evolución física, el *Homo sapiens* dejó de ser una marioneta del cerebro. A pesar de todos los descubrimientos revelados por la neurociencia —muchos de ellos fascinantes e importantes—, el meollo del asunto es que tú gobiernas tu cerebro y no al revés. El camino hacia el metahumano es un camino de conciencia de uno mismo sobre esto. Puedes controlar quién eres, aunque creas que no eres capaz de hacerlo. El rastro de pistas nos ha llevado lejos en el camino. Ahora estamos listos para emprender un cambio de realidad todavía más radical que el despertar masivo de nuestros ancestros remotos. En el próximo cambio de realidad nos definiremos como seres dotados con posibilidades infinitas. La metarrealidad se convierte en nuestro hogar cuando todos estamos de acuerdo en que pertenecemos a ella.

4

LA METARREALIDAD OFRECE
LIBERTAD ABSOLUTA

La libertad es lo opuesto a sentirse atrapado. Hemos creado la realidad virtual a tan gran escala que la gente puede vivir su vida sin sentirse atrapada. Pero, en verdad, toda la configuración es una trampa. Hamlet estaba atrapado en el dilema de asesinar al hombre que asesinó a su padre. La indecisión lo llevaría ya fuera a matar o al suicidio —eventualmente lo conduce a ambos— y en un punto Hamlet habla con sus amigos Rosencrantz y Guildenstern con todos los síntomas de depresión clínica:

> Yo he [...] perdido todo mi júbilo, renunciado a todos ejercicios habituales, y en efecto es tan pesado para mi disposición que esta considerable estructura, la Tierra, me parece un promontorio estéril; este dosel excelente que es el aire —mira tú, este valiente firmamento en lo alto, este techo majestuoso de fuego dorado— no me parece más que una congregación pestilente y fétida de vapores.

Ninguna persona agobiada por la depresión habla tan hermoso, sin duda, pero Hamlet todavía alberga el gran optimismo sobre el potencial humano que alimentó el Renacimiento. De inmediato añade: "¡Qué obra de la creación es el hombre! ¡Qué noble en la razón, qué infinito en facultad! ¡En la forma y el movimiento qué particular y admirable! ¡En acción es como un ángel, en la aprensión es como un dios! ¡La belleza del mundo! ¡Único entre los animales!".

Cuatrocientos años después somos la misma especie, pero el optimismo se ha vuelto una lucha. Si miras a tu alrededor, ¿estarías de acuerdo con la alabanza de Shakespeare a los seres humanos como: "¡La belleza del mundo! ¡Único entre los animales!"? He estado afirmando que el *Homo sapiens* es la única especie sobre la Tierra que es multidimensional. Esto parece el regalo más grande posible que cualquier forma de vida podría recibir. Le dio a nuestra mente un boleto abierto para imaginar cualquier cosa que queramos. Nos salvó del callejón sin salida evolutivo que enfrentaron el oso hormiguero gigante, el panda y todas las demás criaturas que están atrapadas en la evolución física. Es fácil embriagarse con el prospecto de nuestro propio potencial sin límites.

Así que es extraño pero verdadero que los seres humanos no aceptan este regalo del potencial ilimitado. Estamos claramente divididos: un lado de la naturaleza humana desea la libertad, y el otro lado la teme profundamente. Al decir *libertad* me refiero a algo mucho más que no estar en la cárcel o aplastados por los poderosos. La libertad es conciencia sin límites, la definición misma de *metahumano*. Cuando todo es posible somos nosotros mismos al máximo. Cuando sólo algunas cosas son posibles, todos somos demasiado humanos.

La libertad no tiene reglas fijas. No tiene paredes y todos los pensamientos son permitidos. No importa qué tan buena sea tu vida, por desgracia no estás viviendo en libertad. Naciste en una realidad acotada por reglas, paredes y pensamientos que no deberías pensar. En estas páginas hemos estado lidiando con pensamientos prohibidos, el tipo de pensamientos que debilitan la realidad virtual y exponen sus ilusiones. ¿Para qué? Para construir una nueva realidad basada en la libertad. El pensamiento prohibido máximo es: "Nada de esto es real". Borra todas las ilusiones. Lo que hace que este pensamiento sea prohibido no es que la policía vaya a tocar a tu puerta y castigarte por romper la ley. Nadie sabrá nunca que optaste por salir de la realidad virtual.

Lo que hace que sea prohibido pensar "Nada de esto es real" es algo personal: el temor a lo que sucederá después. La libertad absoluta es aterradora. Expande lo desconocido hasta donde la mirada pueda llegar. Ésa es la razón principal por la que la historia humana no se trata de la libertad absoluta; es acerca de probar el siguiente límite, y después avanzar más allá para probar un nuevo límite. Desde la perspectiva de la metarrealidad, el *Homo sapiens* nunca ha tenido que respetar tantos límites. Una historia de "tú no deberías" se ha desarrollado con tanto miedo detrás de ella y un reforzamiento tan poderoso de las reglas, que nuestra evolución ha tenido que luchar a cada paso del camino.

El origen de vivir dentro de las fronteras es el ser dividido. Hemos definido la naturaleza humana simultáneamente como algo que celebrar y algo que temer. Es crucial ir más allá del ser dividido porque, como cada parte de la realidad virtual, el ser dividido no tiene validez alguna, además de la que nosotros le damos. La guerra entre el bien y el mal, luz y oscuridad, creación y destrucción, es un constructo mental. Nació de nuestra profunda confusión acerca de quiénes somos. Cuando una especie tiene un boleto abierto en términos de su evolución futura, el destino impreso en el boleto es Todas Partes. El *Homo sapiens* todavía tiene el boleto abierto en la mano, pero planeamos el curso de la historia en altas y bajas, progresos y retrocesos, tiranos y libertadores, guerra y paz. Cada día forzamos a la realidad a ajustarse al modelo del ser dividido.

Probar los límites es una etapa del desarrollo. Todos los niños prueban las reglas establecidas por sus padres y crecen con un mapa interno de lo que se debe y no debe hacer que, en su mayor parte, dura de por vida. Pero sería mucho mejor si nuestro mapa interno nos mostrara cómo usar el boleto a Todas Partes. Por fortuna, la metarrealidad se acerca cuanto más nos demos cuenta de quiénes somos. Se ha estado acercando por decenas de miles de años. Para ver la evolución invisible de la conciencia es preciso mirar a nuestra especie con nuevos ojos.

La historia del Hombre de Hielo

Aunque no contamos con la fecha exacta, los seres humanos no podían explorar dimensiones múltiples hasta que tuvieron la conciencia de que era posible. Los humanos prehistóricos hicieron un descubrimiento y, como las demás cosas invisibles en nuestro pasado, podemos leer la mente de nuestros ancestros remotos por medio de la investigación de un puñado de pistas físicas. Y lo que revelan estas pistas es fascinante. Mientras nos enfrentábamos entre la luz y la oscuridad dentro de nosotros, también nos expandíamos hacia la libertad. La limitación nos jalaba hacia un lado y la libertad hacia el otro. Es necesario explicar este estira y afloja.

En 1991 algunos excursionistas se encontraron con una momia natural preservada en hielo glacial a una altitud de aproximadamente 3 000 metros a un costado de uno de los Alpes en la frontera ítalo-austriaca. A esta momia los antropólogos la llamaron Ötzi (por el nombre de las montañas en las que fue descubierta) y el "Hombre de Hielo" en la prensa popular; este hombre de 3500 a. e. C. es una fotografía instantánea congelada de la vida en Europa durante el periodo Calcolítico, conocido también como la Edad de Cobre —el término calcolítico se deriva de la palabra griega para cobre—. Para entonces los humanos prehistóricos descubrieron cómo fundir el mineral del cobre, pero tenían que mezclarlo con estaño para formar bronce, que es un metal más duro.

Si estuvieras escalando las montañas de Tirol del Sur y te encontraras con el Hombre de Hielo dos horas antes de su muerte, habrías visto a un hombre delgado, casi desnutrido, de 160 centímetros de altura, quizás en una excursión de caza, sentado sobre una roca, comiendo. Llevaba pan hecho de trigo y cebada; también frutas y raíces en sus provisiones, y carne seca de gamuza, venado e íbice. Si te sonriera, Ötzi habría mostrado los dientes llenos de caries, quizá porque su dieta era alta en carbohidratos.

La piel del Ötzi momificado presenta diversos tatuajes, 61 en total, en su mayoría líneas horizontales y cruces, sobre todo a lo largo de la columna y detrás de las rodillas. De acuerdo con los antropólogos que estudiaron sus restos, había estado enfermo tres veces durante los seis meses antes de morir. Para tener 45 años, Ötzi estaba en malas condiciones desde el punto de vista de los estándares modernos, y ya mostraba deterioro en las rodillas y tobillos, así como osteoporosis en la columna. (Los tatuajes, hechos con polvo de hollín negro, podrían haber sido una forma antigua de tratamiento médico. En todas las culturas existe una tradición ancestral de tatuarse para aliviar el dolor, y los tatuajes del Hombre de Hielo están agrupados alrededor de las articulaciones y la espalda baja, donde seguramente sufría de dolor crónico.) A diferencia de otros que se asentaron en comunidades agrícolas, este hombre realizó largas caminatas a lo largo de toda su vida, lo que suma a la especulación de que quizás era un pastor o un cazador.

Ninguno de los primeros europeos ha sido estudiado con tanta minucia como el Hombre de Hielo, desde los contenidos de su estómago, los minerales en su cabello (que tenían rastros de cobre y arsénico) y la composición exacta de su ADN. Sus genes revelan que tenía ojos color café y cabello oscuro, así como una predisposición a sufrir cardiopatías. Pero mi mente se enfoca en el viaje interno invisible que el *Homo sapiens* había hecho en la Edad de Cobre, y hay fuertes indicios de ello en los descubrimientos físicos.

Ya habían existido varios despertares en la conciencia para que Ötzi fuera posible. Tenemos que imaginar cómo fueron estos despertares. La agricultura, la costura, el bronceado de la piel, el descubrimiento de que las rocas podían ser calentadas hasta rezumar metal puro —éstos son saltos titánicos en la conciencia—. El cerebro del Hombre de Hielo estaba equipado para desempeñar tareas en extremo sofisticadas.

Mantener los pensamientos en un orden consecutivo, y cada uno derivando en su propia conclusión, no es un rasgo moderno. Una mente altamente organizada hizo posible que el Hombre de Hielo transitara por una existencia sorprendentemente complicada. Podemos inferir lo anterior, por ejemplo, por su atuendo elaborado: zapatos, sombrero, cinturón, perneras y un taparrabos, todas las prendas confeccionadas con distintos tipos de piel. Su capa estaba hecha de pasto tejido, señalando el camino para el tejido intrincado que estaba por venir conforme las culturas evolucionaran.

Sentimos al Hombre de Hielo muy lejano a nosotros, y al mismo tiempo muy cercano. Sin embargo, como miembros de la especie *Homo sapiens*, habitamos el mismo tipo de conciencia que Ötzi. Algunas de las evidencias más fuertes de nuestro parentesco a lo largo de los siglos son trágicas. El día de su muerte, el Hombre de Hielo estaba armado con un hacha, hecha de cobre puro en 99%, y un cuchillo de pedernal, ambos con mangos de madera. Sobre su hombro llevaba un arco y una aljaba con 14 flechas. Resulta claro que se encontraba con adversarios armados de forma similar, porque la punta de una flecha había perforado su capa a la altura del hombro, donde quedó incrustada. La vara de la flecha fue rota, tal vez en un intento infructuoso de remover la punta de la flecha. Había ADN en el cuerpo de otros tres individuos: ¿sus amigos, sus enemigos, quizás alguien que mató antes de ser él mismo asesinado?

Ötzi fue encontrado bocabajo, lo que sugiere que alguien más lo colocó de esa forma al intentar sacar la flecha de su espalda. Pero Ötzi se desangró rápido y casi de inmediato fue cubierto de hielo por una tormenta helada. No es difícil imaginar un vínculo entre él y estados emocionales parecidos en la vida moderna: los conflictos y las lealtades tribales, ataques y defensas intensos, el deseo de salvar a un camarada caído. La guerra entre la luz y la oscuridad ya era endémica en la sociedad humana.

La fuente perdida

El Hombre de Hielo no fue la primera persona en morir por violencia. Una serie de esqueletos de mujeres de hace 4 000 años en México presentan huesos rotos y otras heridas, lo que indica que sufrieron lesiones debido al abuso físico, y no por accidentes. En algún lugar entre la metarrealidad y la realidad humana suceden cosas malas. Por milenios, la culpa ha sido adjudicada al pecado o a los defectos humanos en general. Yo lo adscribo al ser dividido, que le ha dado compartimentos separados a la paz y la violencia. Proyectado hacia afuera, se convirtieron en instituciones de la guerra —ejércitos, fabricantes y proveedores de armas— e instituciones de la paz —cortes de la ley, códigos de justicia, religiones que representaban a un Dios misericordioso—.

Las sociedades aprendieron a vivir en la contradicción. Roma se vio a sí misma como la gran precursora de la paz, sin embargo, al conquistar los territorios de lo que hoy es España, Gran Bretaña y Alemania, Julio César lideró campañas de atrocidad indescriptible. En una aldea ordenó que cortaran las manos de todos los adultos; en total, su conquista de Galia cobró dos millones de vidas. Los romanos celebraban a César (y le ofrecieron el título de emperador antes de ser asesinado en el Senado), pero existe un dicho popular que revela una verdad más profunda: *Homo homini lupus*, "El hombre es el lobo del hombre". Al parecer no hemos evolucionado más allá de esta sabiduría brutal, dado que Estados Unidos es tanto el pacificador global como el mayor traficante de armas en el mundo.

Sin embargo, estar atrapados en el ser dividido no es la historia completa. Si examinamos al Hombre de Hielo bajo una nueva mirada, desde la perspectiva de la conciencia, reconocemos que algo inmenso sucedía en la historia humana. Los antropólogos se refieren a la "explosión cognitiva" o "explosión de la inteligencia" que catapultó el avance de los humanos de la Edad de Piedra. Uno no puede negar la evidencia ofrecida por la complejidad de las herramientas, armas, dieta y vestimenta del Hombre de Hielo. Fue necesario que los primeros humanos tuvieran un pensamiento nuevo e ingenioso para llegar a esa actividad mental tan sofisticada.

Para explicar la explosión cognitiva, diversos argumentos señalan el cerebro superior y la genética, o un parteaguas como el descubrimiento del fuego, que provocó que los primeros humanos estuvieran más juntos, lo cual posibilitó el pensamiento colectivo. Como siempre, los científicos se basan en evidencia física. Sin embargo, yo pienso que la verdadera historia yace en la expansión de la conciencia, que sucedió antes de que apareciera la evidencia física. Considera qué tipo de conciencia fue necesaria para crear el primer arco y la primera flecha. Si hubiera sólo un bosque y una piedra filosa, ¿tú podrías inventar el arco y la flecha?

Una sorprendente serie de videos de YouTube titulada "Primitive Technology" (Tecnología primitiva) muestra cómo pudo haber sido logrado. Un hombre descalzo en pantalones cortos tala un pequeño árbol por medio de golpes con una roca gruesa, afilada de uno de sus lados. Quiebra la madera usando la misma roca afilada hasta que tiene una pieza de un metro que estrecha en cada extremo hasta volverla flexible; éste es el arco, que se marca en cada extremo para sostener la cuerda. La cuerda se obtiene de la corteza verde de un árbol joven. Primero se pone a secar la corteza del árbol y se tuerce dos veces, y entonces se une la cuerda al arco. Para las flechas, el hombre usa un retoño delgado, y al remover la corteza y pelar la madera logra obtener un asta larga y fina.

En este punto, nuestro artesano primitivo necesita plumas para lograr que la flecha vuele con rapidez; éstos son los únicos artefactos que no están vinculados a una sola piedra filosa. El artesano usa las plumas traseras de un pollo y las reduce, luego suaviza los bordes con la punta de un palo ardiendo que calentó en una fogata. Después de haber ensamblado el arco y la flecha (junto con una aljaba hecha de corteza para cargar las flechas), el artesano prueba la habilidad de su arma y lanza una flecha hacia un árbol de 15 centímetros a 10 metros de distancia, con una precisión mortífera.

Resulta difícil describir lo extraordinario que parece este proceso la primera vez que se ve, pero al reflexionarlo, un artesano moderno que duplica los esfuerzos de un cazador de hace 40 000 años es hacer trampa. Él ya sabe cómo son un arco y una flecha y para qué sirven. El primer creador de un arco y una flecha trabajó con ingenuidad pura y una sensación de haber descubierto algo. ¿Qué fue necesario para inventar el primer arco y la primera flecha? Fue necesaria la conciencia expandida y, en particular, algunas características de la conciencia que sólo tenían los *Homo sapiens*, de la siguiente manera:

el creador del arco y la flecha tuvo que concebir lo que deseaba hacer y después descifrar la manera de hacerlo. Sin duda experimentó y probó varias opciones, justo como Thomas Edison probó diferentes sustancias para el filamento del bulbo eléctrico antes de llegar al tungsteno. Más aún, conforme creaba su arma, el hombre que hizo el arco y la flecha tuvo que enfocar su atención y mantener la mente concentrada en lo que estaba haciendo. Si se distraía, tenía que recordar su tarea y volver a ella.

Cada una de estas facultades mentales —atención, intención, concentración, curiosidad y diligencia— no son pensamientos. Son la base de los pensamientos, como cemento y ladrillos invisibles. Nada puede ser fabricado sin ellos (un nombre alternativo para nuestra especie es *Homo faber*, hombre hacedor). En el centro de la evolución humana yace el aprendizaje de lo que la conciencia es capaz. Las múltiples dimensiones en las que nos transformamos son dimensiones en la conciencia, que no son las mismas que las dimensiones físicas en el espacio.

Éste es el lugar correcto para especificar la diferencia entre la mente y la conciencia. No necesita ser abstracto. La mente es la actividad del pensamiento. La conciencia es el campo de la conciencia pura. En una analogía de la India antigua, la conciencia es el océano y la mente son las olas que juegan a lo largo de la superficie del océano. Una vez que captas la diferencia surge un entendimiento radical. La mente sólo se dio porque la conciencia comenzó a moverse dentro de sí misma. El campo de la conciencia pura comenzó a vibrar, y de esas vibraciones, la conciencia adquirió los logros mentales familiares necesarios para hacer un arco y una flecha (y todo lo demás en el campo de la tecnología durante los próximos 40 milenios).

Eventualmente, los seres humanos se perdieron en la complejidad, abrumados y fascinados por todo lo que la mente puede hacer. Eso incluye el lado más oscuro, ya que hemos heredado la capacidad de la mente de volvernos violentos, temerosos, deprimidos, tristes y conflictuados: todos ellos rasgos de la mente dividida. Vivir con la mente dividida ha sido la fuente de una pena profunda y a veces de un deseo hondo de comenzar todo de nuevo. Existe una razón por la cual todas las culturas tienen un mito sobre una edad de oro o un Jardín del Edén perdido. Nos decepciona en lo que nos hemos convertido, y la fuerza de la nostalgia nos lleva a un tiempo prístino en que éramos más inocentes y mejores.

Pero si le quitamos los ornamentos al mito, lo que los humanos perdimos fue la conexión con nuestra fuente —o conciencia pura—. Sin embargo, tenemos un camino de vuelta al Edén que no es mítico. En algún punto de la evolución de la mente humana, en un tiempo inalcanzable desde el presente, el *Homo sapiens* se volvió consciente de sí mismo. ¿Acaso éste fue un cambio instantáneo o se trató de un desarrollo gradual? Nadie lo sabe. Los primeros humanos comenzaron a ir más allá del pensamiento cotidiano, que es en gran medida utilitario, dedicado a los deberes y demandas de todos los días. Se podría decir que ir más allá se solidificó con Dios, un superhumano hecho a nuestra propia semejanza. Sin embargo, en otros tiempos ir más allá significaba contemplar la naturaleza de la conciencia. Podemos llamarla la conciencia de ser conscientes. Por lo tanto, obtuvimos acceso a nuestra fuente. Sólo cuando *sabes* que eres consciente puedes empezar a explorar de dónde proviene la conciencia.

Salvados —y malditos— por la razón

A lo largo de la historia, esta búsqueda de la conciencia ha sido caótica y arriesgada al mismo tiempo. Ser humano abarca una cultura de no violencia en el budismo y el cristianismo primitivo, pero también culturas guerreras como los mongoles y los vikingos. Los rasgos que hoy damos por hecho, como el amor romántico, no existían en muchas sociedades primitivas en la cuenca del Mediterráneo, incluyendo a los griegos y egipcios; la caballerosidad hacia las mujeres era desconocida fuera de los círculos de la nobleza hasta la caballería de las cortes de la Edad Media. Los niños no eran considerados ejemplos de inocencia como era de esperarse —en la doctrina cristiana medieval, el pecado se obtenía al nacer, y bajo el derecho común inglés, a los niños se les trataba como propiedades de su padre, o como esclavos—. La misma dignidad humana era traicionada con la práctica del esclavismo.

Lo que indica esta historia lúgubre, si buscamos un denominador común, es que la mente humana se conocía a sí misma en fragmentos, que se acumulaban en historias compartidas construidas a lo largo del tiempo. Por ejemplo, el primer recuento de la vida de Buda, que vivió en el siglo VI a. e. C., fue escrito 400 años después de su muerte y era muy breve. Estaba incluido en el recuento de los 25 Budas que precedieron al Buda Gautama. Esta primera biografía auténtica era un poema épico que databa del siglo II a. e. C., escrito por un monje llamado Ashvaghosha, bajo el título de *Buddhacarita* (*Acto del Buda*). Es comprensible que los mitos y los milagros estén intercalados con hechos que pueden ser recuentos confiables —lo importante era amasar a partir de diversos fragmentos una vida santa adecuada para ser adorada y venerada—. Asimismo, el Nuevo Testamento proviene de diversas fuentes —se cree que principalmente surgió de las diferentes iglesias primitivas desperdigadas a lo largo de todo el Imperio romano— y existen diferencias muy grandes entre los cuatro Evangelios.

Todas las historias entretejidas en la civilización fueron creadas en lo colectivo, incluso cuando es tradición referirse a un solo autor como Homero o el autor de uno de los Evangelios. Los textos originales siempre sufrieron alteraciones después. Algunas historias se volvieron inspiradoras. Otras se volvieron parte de la identidad de la gente o su forma de adoración. En contra de estos efectos positivos, cada historia ha limitado con severidad nuestro potencial infinito. La metarrealidad no tiene una historia porque está fuera del tiempo y por lo tanto fuera de nuestra historia. A diferencia de la mente, que deja un rastro de eventos que los historiadores pueden estudiar, la conciencia no tiene principio ni final.

En términos colectivos, la historia dominante es científica, y se le da crédito a otro aspecto de la mente por motivar el avance de la humanidad: el pensamiento racional. Si compadecemos a nuestros antepasados por su dificultad de superar la superstición y el mito, el futuro podría compadecernos por glorificar la mente racional y abandonar la Mente Total.

En su libro publicado en 2018, *Enlightenment Now*, Steven Pinker, el psicólogo de Harvard que ha sido ampliamente leído, en 450 páginas ensalza el triunfo de la razón en la historia cultural reciente. Pinker defiende el "argumento de la razón, la ciencia, el humanismo y el progreso" (el subtítulo del libro) casi como si hubiera sido realizado en Francia durante la Ilustración en el siglo XVIII. De hecho, él ve ese periodo como el momento cumbre de la historia occidental.

Para la gran mayoría de la gente en Occidente, Pinker predica al coro cuando caracteriza la *ilustración* como algo secular, de libre pensamiento, racional y dedicada al progreso. Yo sé que éste es mi papel como doctor en Medicina, educado en la medicina moderna. La racionalidad tiene unos cuantos triunfos mayores, y el crecimiento de la medicina moderna fue parte de una campaña mucho más grande para aniquilar el latigazo de la superstición ignorante.

Como ejemplo supremo, nadie en el siglo IV tenía una explicación racional para los horrores de la peste negra, que mató quizás a un tercio de la población de Europa, alrededor de 20 millones de personas, entre 1347 y 1352. Se difundieron explicaciones sobrenaturales al respecto, y hubo una serie de persecuciones de judíos y brujas. Tres siglos después, uno pensaría que la sociedad ya habría aprendido sus lecciones y se habría dado cuenta de lo supersticiosa que había sido. Pero no fue así. Cuando en el siglo XVII William Harvey confirmó científicamente que el corazón bombeaba sangre a cada parte del cuerpo y viceversa, mucha gente todavía creía que existían las brujas. Se estima que después de la muerte de Shakespeare en 1616 fueron ejecutadas más personas que en el siglo anterior.

El mismo Harvey visitaba a mujeres de quienes se sospechaba que practicaban brujería y se convirtió en un oponente escéptico importante de este tipo de pensamiento supersticioso. En una de estas visitas llevó un sapo, el cual una mujer pensaba que era un familiar suyo enviado por el diablo, y lo diseccionó ante sus ojos para demostrar que no existía nada sobrenatural en la criatura.

Pinker alaba el surgimiento de la razón ilustrada con fervor y confianza:

> ¿Qué es la ilustración? En un ensayo de 1784 que cuestiona lo mismo que su título, Immanuel Kant respondió que consiste en "el surgimiento de la humanidad desde su inmadurez provocada por sí misma", su sumisión "relajada y cobarde a los dogmas y fórmulas" de la autoridad religiosa o política. El lema de la Ilustración, proclamó, es "¡Atreverse a comprender!".

Ésta es una visión ampliamente aceptada de la Ilustración en la que hay poco que sea atrevimiento. Una cultura secular y científica no sólo se enorgullece de la racionalidad, sino que la adora con una fe tan absoluta como los dogmas religiosos de los que Kant quería que escapara la humanidad. Lo que sería atrevido es encontrar una forma de escapar de la exaltación de la razón sin fundamento. Esto es porque la racionalidad ha infligido tanta ruina como la irracionalidad —los monjes medievales, casados con los dogmas "relajados y cobardes" del catolicismo, como Pinker los describe, no lanzaron la bomba atómica, inventaron las armas químicas y biológicas, o depredaron el medio ambiente al grado de la autodestrucción de la humanidad—.

Ciertamente la razón ha creado muchas cosas buenas, pero en la caja de Pandora también existía una creatividad diabólica. Cuando la libertad de pensamiento se generalizó, no hubo nada para detener la creatividad diabólica de idear nuevas formas de muerte mercantilizada, que ha continuado con rapidez desde la catapulta romana y la ballesta en la Edad Media. La razón no ha sido capaz de frenar sus propias creaciones, siempre perseguidas con el respaldo de las explicaciones racionales de la necesidad de desarrollar terribles armas. Bordeando esta falla fatal, el optimismo de Pinker pinta una imagen de progreso en muchos frentes. El corazón de *Enlightenment Now* es un conjunto de 27 gráficas que ilustran el avance de la humanidad hasta este momento en la historia, contradiciendo la noción popular de que el mundo se está desmoronando. El rango de temas ilustrados por estas gráficas cubre todo, desde el tono de los diarios que lee la gente, la expectativa de vida y la mortandad infantil, hasta las muertes por desnutrición y hambruna; desde el producto mundial bruto y la distribución del ingreso global, hasta el tiempo libre en Estados Unidos y el costo de viajar en un jet.

Es un resumen impresionante de lo que la racionalidad y el progreso han logrado. Pero la reseña de Pinker deja a la conciencia para muy tarde en el juego. La palabra apenas está presente en el libro, y las referencias principales, que comienzan en la página 425, son escépticas y demeritorias. Él aborda el tema del "problema duro", una frase acuñada por el filósofo David Chalmers, que presenta el acertijo de por qué los seres humanos tienen subjetividad —en otras palabras, el mundo "aquí dentro"—.

Fiel a su fe en la razón, la lógica y la ciencia, Pinker afirma que lo que sucede en el mundo subjetivo (por ejemplo, pensamientos, sensaciones, imágenes y emociones), junto con el comportamiento que mostramos basados en eventos subjetivos, son "evidentes adaptaciones darwinianas. Con avances en la psicología evolutiva, cada vez más nuestras experiencias conscientes se están explicando de esta forma, incluyendo nuestras obsesiones intelectuales, emociones morales y reacciones estéticas".

En otras palabras, la mente puede ser explicada lógicamente —o justificada— por el mismo impulso darwiniano que dio forma a cada criatura viviente: la supervivencia del más fuerte. No se toca la posibilidad de que el *Homo sapiens* sea una especie basada en la conciencia, y uno imagina que Pinker se reiría ante ella. Él no es alguien a quien yo quiera señalar para realizar una crítica especial —el argumento de Pinker es parte de una tendencia científica mucho más amplia—, pero decir que la humanidad siente la diferencia entre el bien y el mal (una emoción moral), que anhela la verdad (una obsesión intelectual) y que ama la belleza (una reacción estética) porque esas cosas eran rasgos de supervivencia, es una equivocación muy seria. Al negarse incluso a tomar la conciencia en serio, Pinker nos devuelve a ser mamíferos superiores que se volvieron conscientes para obtener una ventaja para encontrar alimento y ganar derechos de apareamiento.

Algunos darwinianos puros se detienen aquí, pero Pinker se da cuenta de que la conciencia necesita una explicación un poco más creíble, porque el problema duro no se pregunta cómo se volvieron conscientes los seres humanos; pregunta qué es la conciencia. Una vez más, y sin señalar a Pinker como culpable, él se une a muchos otros "apóstoles del cientificismo", como lo llamó uno de sus críticos, al decir dos cosas: 1) probablemente la conciencia es una ilusión creada por actividad cerebral compleja, y 2) todo el tema es básicamente irrelevante.*

Sostener que todo el mundo subjetivo es una ilusión demuestra lo ciego que se ha vuelto el dogma de la racionalidad. Al citar al filósofo Daniel Dennett, uno de los negadores de la conciencia más fuertes, a Pinker le impresiona la visión de Dennett de que "no existe el problema duro de la conciencia: es una confusión que surge del mal hábito de un *homunculus* sentado en un teatro dentro del cráneo. Éste es el experimentador sin cuerpo". La palabra *homunculus* significa un ser humano pequeño, y tiene diversos significados en la ciencia y la filosofía. A quienes apoyan la visión de que la conciencia es una ilusión les gusta decir que la gente cree equivocadamente que existe un "pequeño yo" o un ser individual dentro de nosotros. Dennett descarta al ser como un artefacto ilusorio del cerebro tumultuoso y bullicioso. Pinker no puede llegar tan lejos, pero muchos neurocientíficos lo hacen. En cierto sentido deben hacerlo, pero si el cerebro crea la mente, entonces la noción del yo no puede ser nada más que otro producto de la actividad cerebral. Si cada yo es un engaño, ¿entonces por qué deberíamos creerle a un científico (es decir, a un yo) cuando intenta desacreditar al yo? ¿Acaso no estaríamos creyendo en las palabras de una ilusión? Todo el argumento es irremediablemente ilógico.

---

* Para una discusión extendida sobre el problema duro de la conciencia, véase *You Are the Universe*, libro del cual soy coautor, junto con el físico Menas Kafatos, quien ha publicado extensamente.

Detrás de la máscara

Muchas personas consideran que la ciencia es una fuerza libertadora, y lo es. Pero también ha servido para bloquear el camino hacia la libertad absoluta que tiene el metahumano. Afirmar que la conciencia es una ilusión o algo irrelevante, o que tan sólo es la evolución darwiniana haciendo su trabajo en el cerebro, demuestra hasta dónde están dispuestos a llegar los científicos de la integridad y la inteligencia para adoptar el papel de desmentidores. La ironía más profunda es que la física cuántica, que hace un siglo miramos de cerca detrás de la máscara del mundo físico, dio origen a generaciones de físicos que creen que no vale la pena molestarse por la conciencia.

Pero han existido momentos en que hemos podido volver al futuro. El eminente físico ruso-americano Andrej Linde realizó contribuciones importantes a la "teoría de la inflación", que habla de las primeras etapas del universo naciente, cuando el universo era más pequeño que el punto al final de una oración. Más tarde, Linde se convirtió en uno de los primeros partidarios del "multiverso" que plantea que existen innumerables universos más allá el nuestro —el estimado actual es de 10^{500} universos distintos, o bien 10 seguido por 500 ceros—.

En un artículo académico publicado en 1998 y titulado, con una ambición característicamente amplia, "Universe, Life, Consciousness" ("Universo, Vida, Conciencia"), Linde sabotea, no tan sutilmente, la visión aceptada del mundo de la física moderna. "De acuerdo con la doctrina materialista estándar —afirma—, la conciencia [...] juega un papel secundario y servil, al ser considerada sólo una función de la materia y una herramienta para la descripción del mundo material que existe verdaderamente."

Uno puede ver a la gente asentir en la audiencia mientras Linde dice esto, sin indicio alguno del pensamiento contrario que está por venir. Continúa:

> Pero recordemos que nuestro conocimiento del mundo no comienza con la materia, sino con las percepciones. Sé de cierto que mi dolor existe, mi "verde" existe y mi "dulce" existe. No necesito prueba alguna de su existencia porque estos eventos son parte de mí. Todo lo demás es una teoría.

Esta última afirmación, "todo lo demás es una teoría", indica que algo extraño se avecina y la naturaleza radical de ese algo comienza a crecer. Linde dice que en el modelo científico las percepciones están sujetas a las leyes de la naturaleza, como todo en el universo:

> Este modelo de [un] mundo material que obedece las leyes de la física es tan exitoso que pronto olvidamos nuestro mundo de partida y decimos que la materia es la única realidad y que las percepciones sólo son útiles para su descripción [...] Pero de hecho estamos sustituyendo [la] realidad de nuestros sentimientos por una teoría exitosa de un mundo material que existe independientemente.

Quizá para este punto la audiencia de Linde se estaba retorciendo porque había detectado que el mundo "allá fuera" es un sustituto de las percepciones, que con justa razón deberían ser consideradas como el punto de partida para cualquier modelo de la realidad. Después de todo, como él declara, a la ciencia no se le requiere que demuestre que el verde es verde y que lo dulce es dulce. No puede ofrecer semejante prueba; sólo la experiencia subjetiva valida las percepciones más básicas.

Sólo la percepción, sin duda alguna, es real. En otras palabras, Linde le estaba dando una cucharada de su propia medicina a una visión del mundo que pone primero a la materia y después a la conciencia. Continúa diciendo: "Y la teoría [materialista] es tan exitosa que casi nunca pensamos en sus limitaciones, hasta que tenemos que abordar algunos temas realmente profundos, los cuales no se ajustan a nuestro modelo de la realidad".

La versión de Linde de un tema profundo se enfocaría en la naturaleza precisa de cómo sucedió la creación en términos de *big bangs*, otros universos, partículas subatómicas, y así sucesivamente. Pero cuando especula que la conciencia es inevitable para alcanzar una respuesta —un entendimiento que los pioneros de lo cuántico habían logrado hace mucho—, es muy probable que sea una conexión llevada demasiado lejos. La ciencia hoy en día está en su punto más materialista gracias al éxito creciente de la tecnología. Linde rompe con las clasificaciones, pero aun así permanece encerrado en los tecnicismos de un físico profesional. Sin embargo, se ha unido a Stephen Hawking y otros en darse cuenta de que la ciencia, sin importar qué tan avanzada sea, no describe la realidad. Linde incluso va más allá. Cito un artículo en línea, "Consciousness and the New Paradigm" ("La conciencia y el Nuevo Paradigma"), de Adrian David Nelson:

> Linde [...] ha instado a sus colegas a permanecer con la mente abierta con respecto a un lugar fundamental de la conciencia en la mecánica cuántica. "Evitando el concepto de conciencia en la cosmología cuántica", advierte, "puede conducir a un estrechamiento artificial de nuestra perspectiva".

Si desatamos la advertencia de Linde, que al parecer es suave, él está insinuando que el universo no puede existir sin conciencia. Nelson continúa:

> Linde también es uno de varios físicos respetados que han señalado que la función de la onda cuántica en el universo entero podría no evolucionar en el tiempo sin la introducción de un observador relativo.

En resumen, desde el Big Bang el universo no podría haberse expandido, y conducir a una pequeña esquina de vida en la Tierra, sin alguien que lo vea suceder (el "observador relativo"). ¿Entonces quién es este misterioso observador? Los religiosos dirán que es Dios, pero en términos científicos sólo hay dos posibilidades: una conciencia cósmica infinita o nosotros, los humanos. De hecho, las dos posibilidades se funden en una sola. El universo existe sólo como los humanos lo experimentamos, y nuestra capacidad de experimentarlo proviene de nuestra conciencia infinita o cósmica. Esta fusión ocurre porque la fuente de la conciencia, cósmica e individual, está dentro de nosotros.

Me he tomado este tiempo para aventurarnos en unos conceptos muy abstractos. La racionalidad ha construido un mundo propio. En las sociedades avanzadas, la persona promedio no puede entrar a este mundo sin una capacitación vastamente especializada. Pero hay un lado humano en todo esto. Una visión del mundo que deja a la persona promedio desamparada da lugar a una existencia muy solitaria. El iPhone más nuevo no es un abrazo. Einstein humanizó el aislamiento de la vida moderna en uno de sus fragmentos más poderosos. Un ser humano, dijo Einstein, se experimenta a sí mismo, sus pensamientos y sus sentimientos como separados del resto, una especie de engaño óptico de su conciencia. Este engaño es un tipo de prisión para nosotros, que nos restringe a nuestros deseos personales y a tener afecto por las pocas personas más cercanas a nosotros. Nuestra tarea debe ser liberarnos a nosotros mismos de esta prisión.

Ése es el grito de un científico por algo que nos una, para brindar consuelo y terminar con el engaño del aislamiento solitario. En este libro yo sólo abundo en el mismo deseo. La realidad virtual representa cada limitación hecha por la mente que debe deshacerse. Mientras creamos en la realidad virtual, la metarrealidad yacerá lejos de nuestro alcance. Todo debe ser hecho en nombre de la libertad, lo cual rescata a la realidad y a nosotros mismos al mismo tiempo.

5

LA MENTE, EL CUERPO, EL CEREBRO Y EL UNIVERSO SON CONCIENCIA MODIFICADA

El título de este capítulo abarca una nueva historia de la creación. Comienza planteando que se necesita una nueva historia. La vieja historia se ha hundido en lo profundo. Los niños en edad escolar han escuchado sobre el Big Bang, que fue concebido en la época de sus abuelos —el astrónomo inglés Fred Hoyle acuñó el término en 1949, mientras que el concepto de un universo en expansión que comenzó con una explosión se remonta al astrónomo belga Georges Lamaître en 1931—. Aunque parezca extraño, toda la revolución cuántica no tuvo una historia de creación. Einstein y los demás nombres famosos de su generación aceptaron que el universo es, fue y siempre ha sido.

Detrás de los trabajos de genios dedicados a las nociones radicales de la relatividad general y el quantum, el universo de "estado inalterable", como era conocido, no había avanzado desde la época de los griegos antiguos. El libro del Génesis, si se ve de cierta forma, tenía ventaja sobre la física moderna —el Génesis y los demás mitos de la creación del mundo estaban basados en la creencia de que todo en el cosmos debía tener un inicio—. El Big Bang les permitió a los físicos alinearse a la lógica de esa idea y así podía verificarse el estimado actual de la edad del universo de 13.8 mil millones de años, en remplazo del tiempo bíblico (el cual sir Isaac Newton, un fundamentalista cristiano devoto, pasó años intentando calcular para poder establecer una fecha científica del Jardín del Edén).

Un universo que comenzó con un estallido satisfizo a la mente lógica, pero resulta ser una historia endeble una vez que uno se pregunta cuál fue el origen del Big Bang. Un problema enorme bloquea el camino para encontrar una respuesta: la lógica se desmorona cuando uno se pregunta qué precedió al tiempo y el espacio, ya que nada puede provenir "antes" del tiempo o "fuera" del espacio. La incapacidad de hablar de un mundo fuera del tiempo y el espacio, que sin embargo tomó la decisión de crear el tiempo y el espacio, forzó a la física a retirarse en matemáticas esotéricas que no se basan en la capacidad de formar imágenes o afirmaciones lógicas en la mente. Como lo saben los fanáticos de la ciencia ficción, si vuelves en el tiempo y matas a tu abuelo antes de que se case, de pronto la lógica colapsa también en esa instancia. Tú no puedes estar vivo (como resultado de que tu abuelo tuviera hijos) y muerto (como resultado de que tu abuelo no tuviera hijos) al mismo tiempo.

Una nueva historia de la creación debe sortear este enorme y caótico colapso de la lógica. Debe describir con absoluta solidez el momento exacto en que comenzó la creación, como lo hace el Génesis, o bien debe sustituir algo que no necesita un comienzo. El segundo camino es el que yo he estado tomando al fundamentar el universo en la conciencia. De todos los candidatos de un algo eterno que no tiene principio ni final, la conciencia es el más viable. En una nueva historia de la creación no hay dioses o Dios, no hay universo mecánico que funciona como un reloj finamente ajustado y sin dolores de parto en el Big Bang. Sin todo ello, ni siquiera hay una historia en el sentido usual de la palabra. Sólo está la conciencia haciendo lo suyo mientras el *Homo sapiens* genera las historias de la creación que intentan asir lo inasible, concebir lo inconcebible. Si Dios creó al mundo, ¿quién creó a Dios?

Si el Big Bang generó el tiempo y el espacio, esto implica un estado de no tiempo y no espacio, el cual es ininteligible. No puedes preguntar lógicamente qué sucedió antes de que comenzara el tiempo, ya que "antes" sólo tiene un significado en el marco del tiempo. La creación no existiría si tuviéramos que explicarla primero con el sentido común.

Pero hay una forma de llegar ahí. Dos personas pueden estar en desacuerdo acerca de todo en el mundo. O les puede disgustar lo que le gusta al otro. Uno puede creer en Dios y el otro puede ser un ateo consolidado. Pero incluso si la persona A dedicó su vida a contradecir todo lo que dijo la persona B, incluso si pudiera meterse a la mente de la persona B y contradecir cada pensamiento que ésta tuviera, los dos antagonistas tendrían que estar de acuerdo en una cosa: son seres conscientes. Si la vida inteligente de otro sistema solar hiciera contacto con la Tierra, sin importar el aspecto físico de las criaturas —humanos mutantes, calamares que caminan, masa en forma de amibas—, también tendrían que ser conscientes.

El misterio más oscuro sobre la inteligencia extraterrestre no será la tecnología que ha desarrollado. Sin duda en términos científicos serían alucinantes una nave interestelar, un dispositivo de teletransportación o una máquina del tiempo. Seguramente los terrestres aprenderíamos cosas fascinantes de la tecnología extraterrestre. Pero el misterio más hondo seguiría sin ser resuelto. Nunca sabremos cómo se siente ser ellos, porque su especie de conciencia será impenetrable. Unos pequeños extraterrestres verdes podrían sentir dolor físico al tocar el agua; podrían informarnos que los fotones son deliciosos o que la gravedad es tener un mal día.

Incluso con estas extrañas afirmaciones se asume demasiado. Los pequeños extraterrestres verdes podrían no poseer nuestros cinco sentidos. Mientras sean seres conscientes, la realidad que habitan puede tomar cualquier forma, porque la conciencia ya lo hace. La mariposa más común sobre la Tierra es la llamada vanesa de los cardos, cuyas alas están brillantemente conformadas con parches color naranja y cuya genealogía es exquisitamente poética: la vanesa de los cardos pertenece al grupo de mariposas *Cynthia*, un subgénero de las mariposas *Vanessa*, que son parte de la familia Nymphalidae. Si estos nombres evocan una especie de mitología etérea, poblada por hadas, los órganos sensoriales de la vanesa de los cardos son tan alucinantes como los de cualquier extraterrestre.

Las vanesas de los cardos pueden probar la hoja donde están paradas con la punta de sus patas. Huelen el aire por medio de sus antenas y ven el mundo a través de sus ojos que tienen 30 000 lentes. Escuchan con sus alas. Vistas desde fuera, diríamos que la evolución ha creado una realidad para la vanesa de los cardos, la cual apenas comprendemos. Si quieres creer en que los extraterrestres habitan entre nosotros, cree en las mariposas. Como extraterrestres visitantes, nosotros jamás *experimentaremos* su conciencia.

Pero la vida es imposible sin conciencia, lo cual es algo más a favor de la nueva historia de la creación. Fritjof Capra es un físico estadounidense, nacido en Austria, que se volvió famoso con su libro publicado en 1974, *El Tao de la Física*. Fue un hito en la "nueva física" porque Capra conectó la ciencia con las tradiciones de sabiduría ancestral como el taoísmo. De pronto la evidencia del mundo subjetivo, que había sido considerada inútil en la ciencia por mucho tiempo, se volvió relevante.

Capra ha conectado la vida y la mente mucho más allá de lo que comprenden los biólogos actualmente. Un biólogo diría que la vanesa de los cardos no tiene mente. Por el contrario, Capra afirma que "las interacciones de un organismo vivo —planta, animal o humano— con su entorno son cognitivas. Por ello la vida y la cognición están conectadas de forma inseparable". Es decir, no puede existir vida sin mente. Los órganos sensoriales de la vanesa de los cardos son extraños desde el punto de vista humano, pero es una criatura consciente. No existe otra explicación alternativa. Capra continúa y dice lo siguiente: "El proceso de la cognición —o, si lo prefieres, de la mente— es inmanente en la materia a todos los niveles de la vida. Es la primera vez que tenemos una teoría científica que unifica la mente, la materia y la vida".

Esto suena justo como una declaración metahumana. Es humano creer que sólo el *Homo sapiens* es consciente, con la adición de una cláusula que incluye a los primates superiores como los gorilas y los chimpancés (tal vez). Es metahumano saber que la conciencia es universal. Si este entendimiento no te provoca una sobrecarga mental significa que todavía no comprendes todas sus implicaciones. La conciencia puede ser descrita en tres conceptos: todo, siempre y en todas partes. Por sí mismo, cada concepto es inmanejable a nivel mental. Si los niños se tomaran en serio que Santa Claus está en todos lados, observando a cada niño y niña en el mundo para ver si se portan bien o mal, la idea sería tan escabrosa como un teólogo medieval intentando comprender a Dios como alguien que pone etiquetas en cada uno de los pecadores del mundo y que conoce los pensamientos secretos de cada persona.

Hay formas reconfortantes para sortear el dilema y cualquier ansiedad posible que surja. Para cada idea que un ser humano haya tenido existen ideas infinitas por venir. Cuando me doy cuenta de esto me siento optimista —en el ojo de mi mente se abren visiones de creatividad ilimitada—. Pero yo sé que sólo estoy usando una imagen; no estoy observando de forma directa la realidad de la conciencia. En el poema "Burnt Norton" de T. S. Eliot hay un pasaje inquietante en el cual un ave nos conmina a correr a través de la reja de un jardín hacia "nuestro primer mundo", sólo para que el ave nos advierta después: "Vete, vete, vete, dijo el ave: la humanidad / No puede soportar demasiada realidad".

La noción de que los humanos no podemos soportar una sacudida total de la realidad es radical y sombría, como si una especie de sobrecarga hiciera explotar nuestros fusibles. Yo no estoy de acuerdo. Nuestro primer mundo no es el Jardín del Edén, aunque ésa es la metáfora que Eliot usa en el poema. Nuestro primer mundo es la conciencia pura, la cual podemos llamar "pura" porque no contiene nada. El espacio abierto entre los pensamientos tampoco contiene nada, excepto el potencial para el siguiente pensamiento, y el siguiente, y el siguiente. Al parecer una especie de nada, el hueco entre los pensamientos en realidad es la "sustancia" de lo que está hecho un pensamiento. La mente es el juego de la conciencia una vez que ésta comienza a hacer cosas.

Yo consideraría que las formas extraterrestres serían seres superiores sólo si comprendieran "todo, siempre y en todas partes". Sin eso, nosotros mismos no podemos entrar en la metarrealidad. El juego de la conciencia está detrás de toda creación. Pienso que esto es como el "Génesis ahora", la aparición constante de la novedad en cada dimensión —mente, cuerpo, cerebro y universo— que nos da la experiencia de ser humanos.

"Todo, siempre y en todas partes" es la verdadera historia de la creación. Por sí misma nos dice quiénes somos y por qué estamos aquí. Más allá de las narrativas ofrecidas por un narrador, ya sean los rabinos de 1000 a. e. C compilando la Biblia hebrea, los creadores de los mitos de la Grecia de Homero, o los teóricos modernos afirmando la existencia de un sinfín de universos posibles, *algo* hace que la creación suceda. Ese *algo* es el aquí y el ahora. No tiene historia en el sentido convencional. Es contenido, como un coreógrafo parado tras bambalinas, para inventar de forma invisible lo que el universo danzante está haciendo.

El mejor sistema de respaldo

La conciencia no está jugando *con* el universo. La conciencia *es* el universo. Juega al convertirse en un átomo de helio o en una galaxia. El cambio de la forma nunca se detiene. Cuando te sientes contento o triste estás experimentando dos modelos de conciencia contrastantes. Pero como también eres consciente, al igual que tu cerebro, sólo puede haber una conclusión. La creación es conciencia experimentándose a sí misma. Como si se hiciera toda la joyería de oro en el mundo, las formas en la creación cambian, pero el oro —la "sustancia" esencial de la creación— sigue siendo el mismo. En la búsqueda de la humanidad por la Verdad con V mayúscula, esta verdad cumple los requisitos por sí misma.

¿La Verdad con V mayúscula es apasionante, fascinante o simplemente abrumadora? Cuando la gente escucha sobre la conciencia su visión del mundo no queda hecha añicos. No se sienten maravillados mientras la Verdad los inunda. De hecho, la persona promedio muestra completa indiferencia (en mi experiencia) y desecha esos pensamientos de su mente. La oportunidad de acceder a la metarrealidad no le llega a la gente como algo urgente o necesario. He reflexionado sobre cuál es el motivo de ello, y se reduce a una serie de mecanismos de respaldo contra fallas. Un sistema de respaldo evita desastres como que todo un sistema se apague o que suceda lo impensable, como en el lanzamiento accidental de misiles balísticos armados con cabezas nucleares. Existen fuertes sistemas de respaldo para prevenir este tipo de catástrofes.

En el caso de la mente humana, el sistema de respaldo protege a la realidad virtual de no ser desmantelada. Resulta extraño que la mente deba ser protegida de su propio potencial infinito. Imagina que eres un estudiante de arte y el primer día de clases el maestro equipa tu cráneo con electrodos que llenarán tu cerebro con todas las pinturas que han existido y que existirán. Tú aceptas con reticencia, y de pronto la realidad total del arte se vierte dentro de tu cráneo, desde las primeras pinturas rupestres en adelante, cubriendo miles de años. Con toda seguridad esta experiencia sería insoportable, pero también sería inútil. No puedes enseñarles a artistas en ciernes mostrándoles todas las obras de arte. Es como si pidieras un vaso de agua y te dijeran que debes tragarte toda el agua de los Grandes Lagos. En otras palabras, el desenvolvimiento lento de la mente a lo largo del tiempo es un sistema de respaldo. En una secuencia lineal, el evento A es seguido por el evento B, que es seguido por el evento C.

Sin embargo, este proceso lineal no es real: es un mecanismo instalado en la conciencia humana. Podemos discutir si nuestros ancestros lo instalaron en la prehistoria o si fue instalado por la fuerza de la evolución. Pero no hay duda de que consideramos que este sistema de respaldo es necesario para sobrevivir. Una evidencia es lo difícil que fue convencer a la gente común y corriente de que el tiempo es relativo. Aunque el concepto surgió con la teoría de la relatividad especial de Einstein en 1905, la noción del tiempo que se desvía de una línea recta de una forma inamovible parecía incomprensible. Veinte o 30 años más tarde se veía como cierto tipo de magia. El filósofo británico Bertrand Russell, que en 1925 escribió un pequeño libro titulado *El ABC de la relatividad*, anunció públicamente, con una falta de modestia típica en él, que él era una de las únicas tres personas en el mundo que comprendían lo que era la relatividad.

La teoría evolucionaria de Einstein no alteró la vida cotidiana; la relatividad pudo ser hecha a un lado en su propia jaula caótica. (Pero existen aplicaciones prácticas. Por ejemplo, los satélites de GPS que orbitan la Tierra deben tomar en cuenta efectos relativistas. Si no lo hicieran, el GPS de tu auto estaría desfasado por una fracción de segundo y por ello no te daría una localización exacta de dónde estás.)

Una vez que aceptas el constructo humano del tiempo que se desenvuelve en una línea recta, naturalmente se deduce que existe causa y efecto. El Big Bang condujo a la creación del planeta Tierra hace unos 10 000 millones de años, lo cual a su vez condujo a la creación del ADN, luego los seres humanos, después la civilización, después la ciudad de Nueva York, más tarde el nacimiento de un nuevo bebé en un hospital de Nueva York esta mañana. El camino en reversa no puede ser cierto: el nacimiento de un bebé en Nueva York no puede derivar en el Big Bang. Eso desafiaría la causa y el efecto.

Este sistema de respaldo es tan convincente que no podemos aceptar fácilmente que es artificial. Pero la relatividad no fue el último o el único fallo. La física moderna ha creado modelos matemáticos del universo en los que todo sucede de forma simultánea al nivel más sutil de la creación, donde el tiempo se disuelve en lo atemporal y el cosmos entero es una sola partícula subatómica. Pero estos modelos son exóticos, incluso en la física cuántica, que de por sí es bastante exótica. Nadie espera que estas nociones salgan a la luz en la vida cotidiana. Sin nuestros sistemas de respaldo nos ponemos muy ansiosos.

Todos estamos bastante cómodos con las ilusiones que hemos protegido con nuestros mecanismos de respaldo. Vemos el universo como un teatro de espacio y tiempo en el cual los objetos y la gente andan por todos lados. Nuestros cuerpos son objetos. Nuestra mente es producto de una impresionante máquina de pensar llamada cerebro, otro objeto. Marvin Minsky, del MIT, uno de los padres de la inteligencia artificial, definió a los seres humanos como "nada más que máquinas de carne que llevan una computadora en la cabeza" —una expresión despiadada de lo que la mayoría de la gente supone que es verdad—.

Pero también hay respaldos personales que cada uno de nosotros construimos. Estos respaldos personales han sido apodados "como deben ser las cosas". Algunas personas deben estar a cargo; otras deben ganar, y otras nunca deben comenzar una discusión. ¿Acaso existe una explicación racional detrás de "cómo deben ser las cosas"? No: estos mecanismos psicológicos existen como formas de autodefensa. Nos dan una sensación de seguridad, e incluso un incidente que parece menor puede detonar una gran alarma. En *Verdugo del amor*, un libro publicado en 1989 por Irvin Yalom, profesor de Psiquiatría de Stanford, el autor describe a una mujer de mediana edad que llama Elva, quien ha sido víctima del robo de su bolsa afuera de un restaurante. El crimen fue fortuito, y aunque perdió 300 dólares, no había nada en la bolsa que no pudiera ser remplazado. La mayoría de la gente sentiría conmoción ante un asalto así y después continuaría con su vida. Pero Elva no podía: "Junto con su bolsa y sus 300 dólares, le fue robada una ilusión a Elva: la ilusión de ser especial".

Al haber vivido con relativo privilegio, Elva asumía que era inmune a este tipo de disrupción —repetía una y otra vez: "Nunca pensé que esto me pasaría a mí"—. Pero le había sucedido y la pérdida de la ilusión exigía un precio terrible: "El asalto cambió todo. Había desaparecido la comodidad, la suavidad en su vida; se había terminado la seguridad. Su casa siempre le había encantado con sus almohadas, jardines, cobijas y alfombras mullidas. Ahora veía cerraduras, puertas, alarmas contra robo y teléfonos".

Elva estaba constantemente ansiosa, y el tiempo no la hacía sentir que su vida volvía a ser normal. Como Yalom lo explica: "Su visión del mundo estaba fracturada [...] Había perdido la fe en la benevolencia, en su invulnerabilidad personal. Se sentía desnuda, ordinaria, desprotegida".

Ser víctima de un crimen destruye las fronteras personales, porque el crimen es una invasión personal. En este caso, Elva no podía reparar sus fronteras. Entró en un colapso existencial, perseguida por la máxima amenaza: la muerte. Era un temor que ella nunca había enfrentado, y sin embargo la muerte la había tocado íntimamente cuando su esposo murió. Era una pérdida que en realidad nunca había aceptado y se convirtió en el tema clave que Yalom trabajó con ella en terapia.

Elva resultó ser una paciente extraordinaria, y con el tiempo "ella se movió de una postura de desamparo hacia una de confianza", un cambio que Yalom considera no sólo transformativo, sino redentor. Elva, quien alguna vez pensó que había creado la historia perfecta, aprendió a estar *consciente* de la muerte sin temerle.

Es fútil creer que puedes crear una historia perfecta, que para la mayoría de la gente es la noción de una vida perfecta. Las historias siempre son interrumpidas por eventos no deseados. Y las historias se vuelven redes enredadas incluso cuando parece que van bien, porque las fuerzas inconscientes —ansiedad, depresión, enojo, celos, soledad— pueden surgir en cualquier momento. Aunque Yalom no usa el término *respaldo*, uno puede ver que la sensación de Elva de estar a salvo y protegida era un respaldo emocional. Le había funcionado bien por mucho tiempo, hasta que descubrió que en realidad era endeble y poco confiable.

Todos nosotros hemos creado nuestra propia versión de respaldos. Como con casi todos los constructos mentales, a menudo no nos damos cuenta de lo que hemos hecho y a veces nuestro mecanismo parece ser tan inconsciente que está totalmente fuera de control. Un buen ejemplo de esto son las fobias. La gente que teme a las arañas no será capaz de tocar una araña pequeña, incluso inofensiva. Si estiran la mano e intentan tocar una araña, el miedo surgirá y se volverá más extremo conforme la mano se acerque a ella. La próxima etapa es que tiemblen violentamente, presenten un sudor frío, muestren signos de pánico y tengan la sensación de estar a punto de desmayarse.

Las fobias ofrecen una evidencia perversa sobre la creatividad de la conciencia, porque la ansiedad puede enfocarse en cualquier cosa. En el sitio de internet llamado The Phobia List (La lista de las fobias) puedes encontrar un catálogo en orden alfabético de las fobias especificadas en la literatura psiquiátrica. No se ofrece un número total de fobias —ya que constantemente se añaden nuevas referencias—, pero tan sólo bajo la letra A hay 65 entradas, incluyendo la *aulofobia* (el miedo a las flautas). No todas las letras están tan llenas como la A; bajo la G, por ejemplo, sólo hay 19 fobias enlistadas, incluyendo algunas al parecer tontas, como la *geniofobia* (miedo a las barbillas) y unas bastante serias como la *genofobia*, que es un temor al sexo. No existe un consenso sobre el motivo por el cual aparecen las fobias, aunque psiquiátricamente están categorizadas como una forma de desorden de ansiedad, y el elemento común entre todas es el temor excesivo. Además de las fobias específicas, existen fobias sociales que implican situaciones en las que la persona teme lo que piensen los demás, y una clase completa de agorafobias, en las que la gente entra en pánico porque siente que está en una situación de la cual no puede escapar.

La gente que sufre de fobias no necesariamente tuvo una mala experiencia con el objeto que teme —por lo regular no la ha tenido—, pero hará todo lo que esté en sus manos para evitar dicho objeto una vez que ha surgido la fobia. Las fobias le parecen algo extraño a cualquier persona que no las sufra, en parte porque evitar el objeto o situación temida puede conducir a un comportamiento extraño, como con los agorafóbicos, cuyo temor a los espacios abiertos evita que dejen sus casas por años. También resulta extraño que el miedo —que pone a la mente y al cuerpo en una alerta elevada y que es una protección efectiva cuando el peligro real se presenta— se vuelva contraproducente en las fobias. Estar en alerta elevada porque escuchas una flauta o ves la barbilla de una persona no tienen ningún valor para la supervivencia.

Sin embargo, los respaldos normales que apenas percibimos tienen un punto de quiebre, y cuando éste se alcanza ocurre una severa dislocación. Por ejemplo, entrar en conmoción deja a la víctima de un accidente de auto, un incendio o un crimen completamente indefensa. La mirada aturdida y la incapacidad para tomar decisiones, que son síntomas de una conmoción, podrían ser vistos como lo opuesto a la respuesta de lucha o huida. En la lucha o huida se libera un flujo de hormonas del estrés, y bajo su influencia el cerebro inferior está totalmente a cargo —un soldado huyendo de una batalla presa del pánico no se puede obligar a sí mismo conscientemente a no huir hasta que el estallido de adrenalina se apague y el cerebro superior pueda volver a tomar decisiones conscientes—. (Podemos ver la misma respuesta en una situación trivial, como cuando un mago callejero nos muestra una ilusión. Cuando el mago adivina la carta correcta o saca una moneda detrás de la oreja de alguien, es bastante común que la persona dé un brinco hacia atrás o se aparte alarmada; el cerebro inferior reacciona al truco como si fuera una amenaza.) La conmoción es involuntaria y parecería que no tiene valor para la protección de uno mismo.

Al juntarlos, estos diversos sistemas de respaldo son esenciales para el modelo del yo, la visión de la realidad que te dice qué es real *para ti*. Sin duda la realidad personal tiene sus rarezas, y no existen dos personas que habiten el mismo modelo del yo. Pero a nivel colectivo compartimos la realidad virtual, con sus características universalmente aceptadas sobre el tiempo, el espacio, la materia y la energía. Estas características están tan arraigadas que nos sentimos "en casa" mientras el espacio, el tiempo, la materia y la energía no entren en caos. Pero saber que éstos son constructos mentales no significa que la realidad entre en caos. Implica adquirir conciencia de uno mismo, que por sí sola nos puede decir qué sucede realmente.

Entrando y saliendo

Ni un solo individuo creó la experiencia humana del espacio, tiempo, materia y energía —fueron creadas en nuestra conciencia colectiva, la cual se remonta hasta el surgimiento del *Homo sapiens* y seguramente antes de eso—. No podemos seguir un rastro de huellas sobre los pasos que le dieron la conciencia de sí mismo al ser humano, que es la característica única de nuestra especie. Nuestros genes contienen la evidencia de cada forma de vida, incluyendo las bacterias, que han contribuido a nuestra conformación física, pero no existen rastros físicos que nos digan cómo experimentaban su vida nuestros ancestros.

La herencia más importante de nuestra especie es invisible. Nos conectamos con este legado en la infancia temprana, absorbiendo la configuración entera de la realidad virtual. Una vez que un niño pequeño aprende que existe el tiempo, a continuación aprenderá las reglas del tiempo, y no hay vuelta atrás. Como analogía, una vez que aprendes a leer a los seis o siete años, no puedes volver al estado de analfabeta. Las letras en una página no pueden volverse marcas negras sin significado. De igual manera, una vez que tú y tu cerebro se han adaptado a las reglas del tiempo, parecería imposible vivir como si el tiempo no existiera. Un día, una hora, un minuto, un segundo —T. S. Eliot lamentaba esta disección de la vida en pedacitos de tiempo en otro poema, "The Love Song of J. Alfred Prufrock"—. El tiempo se ha convertido en el enemigo psicológico de Prufrock:

Porque ya a todos los he conocido, conocido a todos:
He conocido las noches, las mañanas y las tardes,
he medido mi vida con cucharitas de café.

Hacer que se vuelva un hábito dividir la vida en unidades de tiempo no significa que el tiempo humano sea más real que otra versión. No tenemos idea de cómo otras especies de conciencia experimentan el tiempo y el espacio. ¿Acaso la pesada tortuga de las Galápagos siente que se mueve despacio o la liebre siente que corre rápido sobre una pradera? Podríamos especular que los animales viven en el momento presente, reaccionando a los instintos que les dicen que ahora es el momento para comer, dormir o cazar. Pero el "momento presente" no existe para una criatura que no tiene un concepto del tiempo.

La naturaleza nos brinda biorritmos que están impresos en nuestros genes, como el ritmo circadiano (diario) para despertar y dormir. Pero eso no responde el acertijo de cómo existe el tiempo, en primer lugar. El movimiento del océano tiene una calibración oportuna que está sintonizada finamente a lo largo de miles de kilómetros, y nadie puede explicarla. Por ejemplo, un pequeño pájaro playero conocido como playero rojizo (*Calidris canutus rufa*) migra cada año desde la Tierra del Fuego, en la punta más al sur de Sudamérica, a sus terrenos para el apareamiento en el Ártico canadiense. A lo largo de su vida, el playero rojizo vuela alrededor de 390 000 kilómetros, una distancia mayor que la que existe entre la Tierra y la Luna.

Parece inexplicable el motivo por el cual las aves cruzan de un hemisferio a otro para aparearse, pero el playero rojizo encarna un misterio específico. Debido a que necesita alimento a lo largo de su inmenso viaje, el ave se detiene en mayo en las playas de la bahía de Delaware, haciendo que su llegada coincida con un evento primordial. Entre las lunas llenas de mayo y junio, hordas de cangrejos herradura emergen de las aguas poco profundas del mar para poner sus huevos. Una hembra pone entre 60 000 y 120 000 huevos en un solo desove. Con una edad de 450 millones de años, o bien 200 millones de años antes que los dinosaurios, la especie del cangrejo herradura parece una concha dura y redonda de tortuga con cola puntiaguda (de hecho no es un cangrejo, sino que es pariente muy cercano de la araña y el escorpión).

En el lapso de dos semanas los huevos romperán su cascarón, así que la ventana de tiempo es muy breve para que los playeros rojizos se den un banquete con ellos. Sin embargo, cada año, la urgencia para migrar se siente a 15 000 kilómetros de la Antártida. La luna llena en mayo puede caer en cualquiera de los 31 días del mes, y el playero rojizo debe comenzar su viaje desde la Tierra del Fuego en febrero. ¿Cómo fue que la naturaleza sincronizó la Luna, el ciclo de apareamiento de un fósil viviente en el mar y un pájaro diminuto que tiene la ruta migratoria más larga de la Tierra? En el caso del playero rojizo, la sincronía de alguna manera tiene sus raíces en su ADN, y surge con cambios fisiológicos tremendos. Antes de migrar, los músculos de las alas del ave se expanden, mientras que los músculos de sus piernas se encogen. Debido a que los huevos del cangrejo herradura son suaves y fáciles de digerir, el estómago del playero rojizo se encoge antes de que el ave parta. También se encoge su buche, que tiene fuerza para moler el alimento duro que el ave come en invierno.

En otras palabras, el ADN del playero rojizo sabe de antemano cada detalle del futuro. Ya que su terreno de apareamiento en el Ártico está vacío, una tundra expuesta y sin fuentes de alimento, las aves duplican su peso con grasa durante el festín frenético de huevos de cangrejo herradura en Delaware, que dura de 10 a 14 días. Si falla cualquier elemento en este ciclo sincronizado la supervivencia se ve amenazada. (Por desgracia, esto ha sucedido. Los playeros rojizos están en peligro de extinción por diversos motivos, y uno de los principales es la drástica disminución de cangrejos herradura por las aguas costeras dañadas.)

Los seres humanos no están atados al instinto en lo referente al tiempo, aunque nuestro ADN de alguna forma sabe cómo empatar la pubertad y los ciclos menstruales, por ejemplo. Las células están programadas para morir en cierto momento, un proceso conocido como *apoptosis*. Una célula típica sólo puede dividirse unas 50 veces antes de morir (el llamado límite de Hayflick) y el proceso puede ser medido científicamente en el laboratorio. Pero en definitiva es por completo misterioso. Las células son fábricas químicas dentro de una membrana suave y permeable. Cuando dos moléculas se encuentran las reacciones químicas suceden al instante; no hay titubeo, retraso, postergación ni vuelta atrás. Entonces, ¿cómo es que una colección de reacciones químicas, cada una atada al instante actual, adquiere la habilidad para eventos futuros? La pregunta es tan básica que casi nadie la formula.

Imagina un juego de billar, en el cual las bolas que representan los átomos y las moléculas deben chocar dentro de una célula del corazón o del hígado. Después de que rompes la formación, el resto es algo mecánico. Cuando las bolas de billar chocan entre sí, deben separarse unas de otras al instante, y hacia donde viajan después está determinado por las leyes del movimiento de Newton. Como dicta una de estas leyes, una vez que una bola es golpeada o choca contra otra, debe viajar en línea recta hasta que algo la detenga. No parece suceder nada anormal conforme se desarrolla el juego. Pero cuando regresas al salón de billar al día siguiente, las bolas otra vez están acomodadas en un motón, listas para el primer golpe. Este comportamiento sería extraordinario en las bolas de billar, pero tu ADN anticipa incontables eventos, al controlar la liberación programada de hormonas, por ejemplo, anticipándose a la necesidad de refrescar los detonantes químicos que entran en una célula cerebral con cada pensamiento, y organizando cientos de biorritmos sincronizados con precisión absoluta, a menos que interfiramos en ellos (al quedarnos despiertos por la noche, por ejemplo, o al tomar suplementos hormonales).

No podemos entrar en la experiencia del tiempo que tienen otras especies. Pero dado que el tiempo es tan variable y maleable, podemos decir que está construido de forma distinta por el ADN de cada ser viviente. Por ello, no es necesaria una gran imaginación para decir que el tiempo es un constructo para empezar. Como el ADN consiste en átomos que interactúan al instante, algo externo al átomo debe estar haciendo toda esta cadencia y sincronización precisas. El único candidato viable para ello es la conciencia. Después de todo, no puedes manipular el tiempo a menos que sepas que el tiempo existe.

Vivir en un universo creativo

Si el tiempo es un constructo, también lo son otras cosas que consideramos esenciales para el universo. Nuestra experiencia de la materia y la energía es muy específica para nuestra especie. ¿Acaso una termita mordisqueando la tierra a lo largo del marco de madera de una casa experimenta la madera como algo duro? ¿Acaso un topo que está confinado debajo de la tierra durante toda su vida en un túnel apenas lo suficientemente ancho para arrastrarse experimenta el espacio como apretado?

Para nuestra especie de conciencia, el tiempo, el espacio, la materia y la energía son experiencias maleables, vinculadas a nuestra creatividad. Es decir que pueden expandirse y contraerse de diversas formas, como lo explicó Einstein con un chiste: "Pon tu mano sobre una estufa caliente durante un minuto y parecerá una hora. Eso es la relatividad". Pero de hecho estaba tocando de lado el asunto central del tiempo: ¿es relativo sólo porque los humanos lo dicen? Para la gente que teme la experiencia, estar sentado en la silla del dentista disloca el tiempo; no sabría decir qué tanto tiempo pasó, pero sí que cada minuto fue desagradable. Esto no altera las manecillas del reloj en el consultorio del dentista, ¿así que cuál versión es real, la experiencia personal o la del dispositivo mecánico?

Parecerá extraño, pero la experiencia humana es lo que vuelve al tiempo real, no los relojes. Para entender cómo creamos la experiencia del tiempo —junto con el espacio, la materia y la energía— debes dejar de aceptar que éstas son cosas fijas. La teoría actual del universo nos ayuda con esto, porque después de que Einstein demostró que la materia se puede convertir en energía ($E = m^2$), se abrió la puerta a otras transformaciones. Un físico posterior, el estadounidense Richard Feynman, incluso demostró matemáticamente cómo se puede expresar la posición de un electrón moviéndose hacia atrás en el tiempo. Esto es como si te preguntaran dónde vives y tú respondieras: "Vivo en la calle Maple número 63, aunque a veces vivo en febrero pasado. Tú escoge". Nuestra noción estable sobre causa y efecto ha sido desmantelada en experimentos en "causación inversa", en los que un evento en el futuro afecta lo que sucede hoy.

Pero la transformación máxima sucede cuando el campo de partículas virtuales muta en partículas físicas. Esto es comúnmente conocido como "algo de la nada". Las partículas virtuales son invisibles y no tienen lugar en el tiempo y el espacio, pero son totalmente necesarias para el universo físico. Es como invertir las historias de fantasmas, en las que el fantasma viene primero y la persona viva después. Si observas tu mano y comienzas a reducirla a niveles cada vez más finos de lo físico, muy pronto se convierte en una red titilante de moléculas. Estas moléculas no son tan sólidas como tu mano, y al siguiente nivel hacia abajo llegas a una congregación de átomos que apenas son físicos, ya que en un 99.9999% son espacio vacío. Éste es último nivel en el cual la existencia física pende de un hilo. Al nivel de las partículas subatómicas, existen algunas que entran y salen de la existencia de forma titilante, como los quarks, los gluones y otras partículas exóticas del mundo cuántico que cambian de ser virtuales a ser intactas en nuestro universo físico. Sacar algo a partir de la nada está sucediendo todo el tiempo en tu mano y en todos los demás objetos físicos.

Así que el asunto crucial no es que lo físico sólido sea una ilusión. Nadie puede discutirlo —no podríamos existir sin creer esa idea de seguridad psicológica de que el mundo no desaparecerá mañana en una nube de vapor subatómico—. El tema crucial radica en si la conciencia, y en particular la conciencia humana, es la fuerza creativa detrás de "algo a partir de la nada".

Ser humano se despliega en el tiempo y el espacio. Tu certificado de nacimiento testifica la fecha de tu nacimiento y la ciudad donde naciste. Ningún certificado de nacimiento dice: "Fecha de nacimiento: Eternidad; Lugar de nacimiento: Todas partes". La suposición del sentido común es que el tiempo y el espacio simplemente existen "allá fuera" como parte del mundo natural. Sin embargo, para evolucionar a metahumano tenemos que dejar de pensar en la creación en términos inamovibles. La realidad debe ser reconstruida para explicar el rol que juega la conciencia. Sólo hay dos niveles de realidad. Un nivel es la conciencia pura sin límites, que es un campo de potencial. El otro nivel es la conciencia en su estado agitado (usando una frase de la física de las partículas), el cual llamamos universo.

Todos los estados excitados vibran con energía. La materia vibra con energía física, la mente con energía mental. El cuerpo es un estado excitado; también lo es el cerebro, ya que es parte del cuerpo, así como la mente conforme piensa. Incluso cuando una roca parece una roca y una neurona parece una neurona, lo cual las hace completamente distintas, las dos son modos excitados de la conciencia.

Esto es conocimiento práctico. Cuando sabes, por ejemplo, que el tiempo es sólo un estado excitado de la conciencia, puedes ver por qué el tiempo es tan maleable. No tiene otra opción que ser fluido y flexible como la mente. Manipulamos el tiempo para conformar nuestras necesidades humanas. Algunos periodos son largos, como la vida del universo, mientras que otros son cortos, como los milisegundos que tarda una señal en saltar de una célula nerviosa a la siguiente. Estos periodos pueden ser extremadamente estables: es muy probable que los átomos de hidrógeno existan hasta la muerte del universo, mientras que un pensamiento es estable sólo mientras dura, y es transitorio y efímero. El hecho de que la actividad mental pase tan rápido puede conducir a un error. Podríamos suponer que la conciencia tiene horarios, pero no es así. La conciencia puede ser rápida o lenta, grande o pequeña, aleatoria o predecible, y así sucesivamente.

Al ser la fuente de "algo a partir de la nada", la conciencia no está limitada por su propia creación, así como una persona con un vocabulario de 30 000 palabras no está atada a 30 000 pensamientos. La conciencia, que se combina y reforma todo el tiempo, se dicta a sí misma si será tan pequeña como un quark o inmensa como el universo. Este hecho ayuda a disipar una de las objeciones más obstinadas a la realidad basada en la conciencia. Nosotros no vemos a nuestra mente crear árboles, montañas, planetas y estrellas. Los escépticos dirían que la escala es incorrecta. Cuando tienes miedo y tu corazón empieza a palpitar con rapidez, un evento mental —tu miedo— detona los químicos de tu cuerpo. La escala es molecular, es decir, muy pequeña. Sin embargo, moverte hacia una montaña con tu mente no puede suceder, porque es una escala muy grande.

De cualquier manera, esta objeción es inválida, porque la conciencia no respeta los límites de la escala. Imagina que te despiertas de una pesadilla y le dices a tu amigo que 100 hombres con armas te estaban persiguiendo por la calle. Y que tu amigo te dijera: "Te creo que un hombre te estuviera persiguiendo por la calle, pero 100 es demasiado como para ser creíble". Este comentario demostraría ignorancia acerca de cómo funcionan los sueños. Los sueños no están limitados por lo grande y lo pequeño. Un ratón persiguiéndote por la calle durante una pesadilla es lo mismo que si el Ejército Rojo invadiera tu ciudad. En un sueño, una hoja de pasto puede temblar, seguido por la explosión de un planeta.

Aceptamos estas anomalías en los sueños porque estamos acostumbrados a levantarnos y volver al mundo físico y sus limitaciones. La conciencia está configurada para que algunas cosas sean libres de andar por ahí tan sólo por pensar, como los químicos cerebrales que van y vienen en sincronía con nuestros pensamientos, mientras que otras cosas no se mueven al pensar. Ésa es la configuración del universo humano. No sabemos los límites de la configuración hasta que los probamos. Uno debe ponderar si Jesús tenía una comprensión parecida en la mente cuando les declaró a sus discípulos: "En verdad os digo, cualquiera que le diga a esta montaña 'levántate y lánzate al mar', y no lo duda en su corazón, sino que cree que lo que dice sucederá, se le concederá" (Marcos 11:23).

Ya sea que aceptes esas palabras como parte del Evangelio o como metáfora, como una verdad literal o una enseñanza vívida, la noción de mover montaña con tu mente suena como algo sobrenatural, y por lo tanto irrelevante para la vida cotidiana. El problema no es que lo sobrenatural sea igual a imposible. El problema, hasta ahora, es que la ciencia no puede explicar lo que llamamos "natural". Dejar a la conciencia fuera de las explicaciones científicas estándar la condena al fracaso. La mente no puede ser explicada con químicos cerebrales haciendo malabares, y cuando la ciencia declara que no existe otra explicación, ya no estamos en el mundo de la credibilidad, estamos en el mundo de "cómo deben ser las cosas".

Como sea, una vez que la realidad virtual ha sido desmantelada, no hay vuelta atrás. No puedes ver a través de una ilusión y creer en ella al mismo tiempo. Un mago no puede sentarse entre la audiencia y ser engañado por sus propios trucos. Y, aun así, eso es exactamente lo que hacemos. Ponemos nuestra fe en el mundo físico, mientras que sabemos muy bien que es ilusorio.

En vez de aceptar con pasividad el mundo del sentido común, la metarrealidad nos ofrece una alternativa: ver todo en el universo como modos cambiantes de conciencia. Un árbol, por ejemplo, está confeccionado para ajustar nuestras respuestas humanas a él. Cualquier cualidad de un árbol puede ser extraída de su lugar asignado y reasignada para ajustarse a un esquema diferente, no humano. El color del árbol no existe para alguien con ceguera al color. La solidez de un árbol no existe para un neutrino, una partícula subatómica que puede atravesar a toda velocidad la Tierra como si pasara por el espacio exterior. El peso de un árbol no existe si lo transfieres a la Estación Espacial Internacional. La duración de la vida de un árbol desaparece cuando se compara con la duración de la vida de los protones en el núcleo de cada molécula, que toma miles de millones de años en terminar.

Todo adquiere su "realidad" desde el modo de conciencia que se le aplique. Cuando duermes desaparece todo el mundo físico y *para ti* ya no existe. Todavía existe en términos colectivos, mantenido en su lugar por las reglas de la realidad virtual. Pero cuando duermes sales de la realidad virtual y experimentas un mundo diferente, que no es la inconsciencia vacía que la mayoría de la gente cree que es. Es posible experimentar el sueño profundo como conciencia pura sin excitación —en efecto, así es como siglos de swamis, yoguis y otras versiones de metahumano lo experimentan—. El concepto budista de Nirvana es más cercano al sueño profundo que el estado de vigilia ordinario, porque el Nirvana reconecta a la persona con la conciencia pura.

Soñar es un modo de conciencia en el que las excitaciones mentales son sutiles. Y, aun así, se trata de otro mundo en el que no aplican las reglas de la realidad virtual. En los sueños, los objetos desafían mágicamente las leyes ordinarias de la física —una locomotora puede volar, el edificio Empire State puede desaparecer en una nube de humo—. No hay motivo para reducir estos dos modos de conciencia, dormir y soñar, a una posición inferior comparada con estar despierto. Si podemos ver el mundo como un sueño lúcido, ¿por qué considerar que los sueños que experimentas en la noche son menos reales o irreales?

La gente ciega supone que las cosas físicas duras son más reales que cosas sutiles como los pensamientos, la imaginación y los sueños. Pero tus impulsos sutiles determinan cómo opera tu realidad personal. He dado un ejemplo —las fobias— en el que una persona puede levantar pesas de 50 kilos en el gimnasio, pero puede ser incapaz de levantar una araña con la mano; el miedo paraliza sus músculos. No importa qué tan ligero sea el objeto temido. Pero también necesitamos ejemplos positivos de cómo las intenciones sutiles de una persona pueden alterar su realidad personal.

Recuerda nuestro ejemplo de usar un aparato de realidad virtual para simular la experiencia de estar parado en la viga de un rascacielos suspendida en el aire (página 48). Una persona parada a salvo en el suelo, debido a la ilusión del dispositivo de realidad virtual se siente mareada y débil, y experimenta una poderosa amenaza de caer. Esto indica que nuestro sentido del equilibrio puede ser manipulado conscientemente de varias formas. Los equilibristas han separado su sentido del equilibrio de cualquier sentimiento de amenaza o peligro. Para alguien que está parado en el suelo mirando hacia arriba el peligro es bastante real (tu corazón puede acelerarse tan sólo con observar un acto de circo riesgoso, aunque no lo experimentes en carne propia).

En el modelo evolutivo aceptado, todos los rasgos que heredamos tienen un valor para la supervivencia. Por obvias razones, nuestros ancestros necesitaban un sentido de equilibrio al cazar y luchar con otras criaturas. Pero todo el tiempo vamos más allá de la supervivencia y jugamos con nuestra herencia evolutiva sólo porque queremos. Caminar en la cuerda floja no tiene un valor para la supervivencia, y dado que implica un peligro considerable, a menos que estés muy bien entrenado, tiene un valor negativo para la supervivencia.

Los bebés temen caerse desde una edad muy temprana, y no pueden aprender a caminar sin probar el estado precario entre caerse y mantenerse sobre sus pies. Es claro que el miedo a caer al final pierde. Los equilibristas van un paso más allá al ignorar la evolución cuando desconectan el miedo a caer del sentido del equilibrio. Esta capacidad para ignorar la evolución es, de hecho, un rasgo evolutivo superior.

El poder de la conciencia permite que los temerarios vuelen ala delta o realicen escalada libre en rocas muy escarpadas, usando cualquier tipo de explicación —búsqueda de emociones fuertes, una motivación para lograr lo imposible, rivalidad competitiva y simplemente sin motivo alguno— ajeno a la situación de vida o muerte. Sólo el *Homo sapiens* convierte en diversión la toma de riesgos extrema. Nosotros elegimos nuestros propios motivos, y la realidad personal se mueve con nuestras intenciones. Sería terrible encontrarte en un callejón oscuro y enfrentar a un asaltante con un cuchillo, pero alguien con apendicitis, arterias coronarias tapadas o un tumor se somete voluntariamente a la violencia controlada de los cirujanos que operan con navajas. Una vez que la conciencia interpreta la situación de una forma específica, la realidad de la situación se ajusta a lo que la conciencia haya decidido.

La realidad virtual que nos rodea permanentemente es un constructo que se adapta a tantos motivos, intenciones, decisiones e interpretaciones, que ya hemos perdido la cuenta de todos ellos.

* * *

Este capítulo ha buceado en aguas profundas, y algunos temas son complejos. Pero su propósito es simple: cerrar el hueco entre la ilusión y la realidad. Nadie se va a evaporar. El mundo lógico estará ahí mañana para saludarte cuando despiertes. Y, aun así, todo está enredado en una ilusión, lo que hace que el mundo lógico sea inestable en su centro. Al probar los límites del tiempo, el espacio, la materia y la energía, probamos nuestro propio poder creativo. Mover una montaña con tu mente no es nada comparado con mover el mundo entero, que es nuestra meta máxima.

6

LA EXISTENCIA Y LA CONCIENCIA SON LO MISMO

Tengo recuerdos muy vívidos de cuando era niño en la India y asistía a escuelas de misioneros católicos. El Antiguo Testamento no era algo ligero para leer: me dejó el recuerdo de pecado, guerras, leyes, lamentos y plagas. Pero existe un verso muy al principio, después de los siete días de la creación, en el que Dios "estaba caminando en el Jardín en la frescura del día" (Génesis 3:8). Dios todavía estaba en buenos términos con Adán y Eva y, en mi imaginación, el momento era perfecto para sostener una conversación casual. No ocurre nada. De hecho, Adán y Eva al principio no estaban ahí, ya que se habían escondido de Dios por vergüenza ante su desnudez. Pero en la conversación que yo imaginé, le preguntarían a Dios algo crucial: "¿Por qué lo hiciste? ¿Por qué creaste el mundo?".

Dios respondería, un poco avergonzado: "No hubo ninguna razón. Sólo tenía que hacerlo. No pude evitarlo".

La cosmología moderna no tiene una mejor respuesta que ésa. El universo se crea a sí mismo. Existe sólo porque tiene que existir. Desde el Big Bang, todo se ha desarrollado por su propia voluntad, motivado por las fuerzas naturales. Nosotros casi no hicimos nada. Los físicos han calculado que al principio el equilibrio entre creación y destrucción era muy delicado.

La destrucción casi triunfa, porque todo, excepto la más diminuta fracción de masa y energía primarias, se colapsó en sí mismo, regresando al estado vacío, como se le conoce. Tan sólo una parte en mil millones escapó de las garras de la destrucción —una metáfora de la gravedad, la fuerza que provocó el colapso de todo lo demás—, pero una milmillonésima parte de la creación fue suficiente para permitir que se formaran millones de estrellas y galaxias. (Pero esto no sucedió rápido. Tomó 800 millones de años para que la estrella más antigua se formara a partir de polvo interestelar.)

Un universo que se crea a sí mismo es nuestra versión, con mucha parafernalia, de la noción del siglo XVIII de Dios como un relojero cósmico que le dio cuerda al universo naciente, lo echó a andar y se fue, dejando que el universo operara de forma mecánica. Pero la autocreación es un asunto complicado. ¿Quién o qué inició el proceso? El creador del creador no era un problema para los rabinos judíos antiguos: por medio de la fe aceptaban que siempre había existido Dios. Encontrar un agente similar fuera de la fe ha demostrado ser imposible.

En este libro argumento que la conciencia es el único autocreador viable, que se convierte a sí misma en mente, cuerpo, cerebro y universo. Es una desviación radical de las explicaciones físicas del cosmos. Así como en el libro del Génesis, la conciencia crea porque tiene que hacerlo. Sólo necesita existir para iniciarlo todo. (¿De dónde proviene la existencia? No tenemos que preocuparnos por eso porque, si existiera la no existencia, entonces no podría ser no existencia.)

Sólo porque existe, la conciencia pura genera la realidad como la conocemos. Las escrituras hindúes antiguas hablan de una miríada de mundos girando hacia la creación como motas de polvo flotando en un rayo de sol. Pero en el mismo rayo de sol también vemos innumerables pensamientos, sentimientos, sensaciones e imágenes, el contenido entero de la mente humana. Al enfrentarse con esta sobrecarga abrumadora, nuestra mente tiene que generar un mundo tolerable para poder habitarlo —un mundo humano— y la realidad virtual que creamos era inevitable.

Pero no era suficiente reducir la abundante multiplicidad de la realidad en bruto. El mundo humano contiene significado. ¿De dónde proviene? Siempre estuvo ahí, como un rasgo primario de metarrealidad. La conciencia pura creó un universo lleno de significado. Todo lo que podemos decir sobre el ser humano —nuestra alegría, amor, inteligencia y potencial infinito— no necesita al creador. Esas cualidades vienen con la existencia, desde el primer instante. Sin llantas, un coche no es un coche. Sin la humanidad, el cosmos no es un cosmos con el cual nos pudiéramos relacionar, o incluso habitar.

El universo fue creado para nosotros porque no existe otra alternativa. La creación no puede ser total a menos que nosotros seamos totales. Una vez que este secreto es revelado, el metahumano puede liberarse de la duda de sí mismo, la confusión y la tristeza, que son los nietos de la ilusión.

Una creación especial

La conciencia pura no puede ser entrevistada, como si se hablara con Dios, ni siquiera en una conversación imaginaria. Pero siempre ha sido viable la noción de la creación de sí misma. Podemos aceptar sin duda alguna que el *Homo sapiens* creó su propia versión de la realidad. Todavía estamos en ella, y no hay señales de que vaya a detenerse. No tiene sentido declarar que nuestros ancestros remotos de alguna manera aprendieron a ser creativos. La creatividad es intrínseca a nosotros, como respirar.

De cierta forma hemos adoptado viejos hábitos a los que se había acostumbrado la conciencia. Todas las formas de vida están envueltas en la creación de sí mismas, pero también están satisfechas con que la creación las envuelva. El ancestro de todos los mamíferos era una criatura tipo musaraña llamada *Juramaia* que vivía en los helechos de los árboles cerca de lagos de agua fresca hace 160 millones de años. El descubrimiento de esta criatura en China en 2011 llevó a datar al ancestro de todos los mamíferos "verdaderos" 35 millones de años más temprano. (Una verdadera especie mamífera es aquella en la que el feto es alimentado por una placenta en el útero. Esto abarca 95% de los mamíferos, y la porción restante son marsupiales como las comadrejas y los canguros que dan a luz a bebés diminutos que terminan de madurar dentro de la bolsa de la madre.)

La *Juramaia* no sabía que sería algo más que una musaraña, y al ver su esqueleto de 13 centímetros pensarías que sólo las musarañas modernas descienden de ella, no todos los mamíferos verdaderos. No hay rastro visible de perros, gatos, murciélagos o ballenas. Fue necesaria una gran cantidad de inferencias para sugerir que la *Juramaia* tenía una placenta, ya que no existen tejidos preservados en los fósiles. Pero no se necesita adivinar cuando se sabe que una placenta era la clave. Una vez que apareció, una característica única nunca antes vista, se abrió una puerta. Lo que entró a través de ella no fue la *Juramaia*, que eventualmente se extinguió, sino la creación propia. Un hábito imparable dio un salto hacia delante. Desde entonces, los mamíferos verdaderos podrían ser pequeños, grandes o mamuts. Podrían nadar, caminar, arrastrarse, excavar o volar. Nada era inamovible ni permanente, excepto la placenta. La naturaleza dio un salto creativo sin precedentes, con apenas un indicio en todas las formas de vida anteriores de que este nuevo tipo de nacimiento era posible.

Esto pone sobre la mesa una segunda idea equivocada, que la evolución se trata de progreso. La creatividad no necesita progresar; ya está completa. Cada forma de vida es un acto creativo completo. En el caso de la *Juramaia*, una criatura diminuta tipo musaraña, no era mejor que lo que vino antes. Los marsupiales podrían haber gobernado la Tierra —se convirtieron en los únicos mamíferos nativos de Australia—. Mucho antes, los huevos evolucionaron y siguieron rompiendo el cascarón, justo como lo hacían en los tiempos de los dinosaurios. Dar a luz a un ser vivo no era algo mejor —hoy en día algunos tiburones ponen huevos mientras que otros dan a luz a bebés vivos—. No existe una línea recta en la progresión de las primeras formas de vida hasta nosotros. Microbios de 1 000 millones de años de edad, animales unicelulares y algas verdiazules continúan existiendo porque su adaptación a la Tierra fue perfecta en su propia manera. Sin la necesidad imparable de crear, no había razón para que la vida primitiva dejara su zona de confort segura.

La autocreación es una pista fuerte de que la conciencia no necesita nada fuera de sí misma para seguir expandiéndose sin parar. A la larga, el *Homo sapiens* entró en otra puerta, la que le abrió la conciencia de sí mismo. Podemos hacer cualquier cosa que deseemos con nuestro potencial, pero sin importar cómo cambie la civilización, es imposible ser humano sin ser consciente. La única cuestión es el nivel de conciencia que elijamos adoptar. El metahumano está más cerca de lo que imaginamos, es sólo un nivel más alto de conciencia.

La conciencia y la existencia no han sido creadas. Ésa es la formulación más simple de la verdad. Al no haber sido creadas significa que simplemente *son*. Sin tener que dar una razón, sin la necesidad de una historia de la creación, la configuración primigenia de ser humanos es que estamos aquí. Existimos porque existe la conciencia. De todos los secretos de la metarrealidad, éste es el que toma más tiempo para asimilar. A primera vista, la existencia no es un tema. Nadie en una sociedad universitaria crítica como la Oxford Union discutiría el tema de la no existencia. No habría sociedades críticas si no existiéramos —el punto parece tonto, incluso infantil—. Pero si estar aquí es suficiente para producir todo en la creación por medio de un proceso consciente, *eso* es una gran noticia.

La existencia y la conciencia no pueden ser separadas. No es que sean la una para la otra, como el calor y el fuego o el agua y lo mojado. Son la misma cosa. Descartes declaró *Cogito ergo sum*, "Pienso, luego existo". Es más preciso decirlo al revés: Soy, luego pienso.

Pero, de cualquier forma, buscar una relación de causa-efecto es retórica. Existir y pensar son la misma cosa. Una no causa la otra. Y el no poder ver este hecho conduce a muchas ideas equivocadas. Por ejemplo, si insistes en que la mente necesita una causa, estás atorado intentando darle una historia de creación. Si eres una persona moderna secular, pronto quedarás atrapado en el error de creer que el cerebro creó la mente. Para un psicólogo del desarrollo no hay duda de que el cerebro crea la mente, y la neurociencia coincide con ello. Conforme surgen las historias de la creación, ésta se encuentra apuntalada por la fisiología, pero el desarrollo infantil también ofrece suficiente evidencia para derrumbar esta historia.

El cerebro en expansión

Si observamos las últimas etapas del feto en el útero, el cerebro es el principal foco de desarrollo, el último órgano que adquiere su configuración final —pero eso todavía no sucederá—. Al momento del nacimiento, el cerebro del bebé rebosa un potencial de crecimiento sin usar. La parte más grande del cerebro humano es el *cerebrum*, o telencéfalo (incluyendo a los hemisferios cerebrales), responsable del pensamiento y otras funciones superiores, y para empezar la evolución les ha dado a los bebés un enorme *cerebrum*, motivo por el cual la cabeza de los recién nacidos es tan grande, en los límites de lo que puede atravesar el canal del nacimiento. En un feto natural llevado a término, durante el último trimestre el cerebro se triplica en peso, de 100 gramos al final del segundo trimestre, a 300 gramos al nacer.

En cierto sentido, todos los bebés nacen prematuros y entran al "cuarto trimestre" el día en que nacen, porque el cerebro continúa con su crecimiento acelerado fuera del vientre materno. Durante los primeros tres meses de vida, el cerebro de un recién nacido crece tanto como 1% al día, y se expande 64% durante los primeros 90 días, después de lo cual la tasa de crecimiento se reduce a un promedio de 0.4% al día. Durante la fase de rápido crecimiento, 60% de la energía consumida por un bebé es usado por el cerebro. Esta gran escala o visión macroscópica muestra que un recién nacido ya tiene todas las células cerebrales para toda una vida —de hecho, tiene demasiadas—. El número de células de un recién nacido son alrededor del doble de las de un adulto, aunque el cerebro del recién nacido pese la mitad. Conforme crece a su tamaño completo, lo cual toma tres años, el cerebro del bebé desecha sus conexiones más débiles (un proceso técnicamente conocido como "poda sináptica"). Es como clasificar un ático lleno hasta el tope de cosas que necesitas y cosas inútiles de las que puedes prescindir.

Aquí comenzamos a ver el misterio de la singularidad, porque la poda sináptica es diferente en cada bebé. De alguna manera el cerebro se deshace de lo que no necesitará *para ese individuo único*. Un prodigio musical que necesita habilidades motoras excepcionales para tocar el piano a nivel de virtuoso quizá no necesite capacidades matemáticas avanzadas o habilidades para el lenguaje articulado. Un escultor con una capacidad altamente desarrollada para visualizar objetos en el espacio tridimensional podría arreglárselas sin las habilidades para las relaciones con el fin de encontrar la pareja correcta. Las combinaciones son infinitas y, para emparejarlas, los miles de millones de conexiones sinápticas del cerebro son suficientes. Aun así, una célula cerebral no tiene precognición de que será o no necesaria, de acuerdo con eventos en el futuro lejano. La poda sináptica no es aleatoria. Sólo hace sentido si una perspectiva superior que está más allá del tiempo está manejando el proceso.

Por ejemplo, un estudio conducido por investigadores de la Universidad de Washington descubrió que áreas específicas del cerebro que controlan los aspectos físicos del habla (el área de Broca y el cerebelo) se activan en los bebés de siete meses en anticipación para aprender a hablar. Esto es evidencia de mirar hacia el futuro y de encender de antemano los interruptores cerebrales necesarios. Un bebé de siete meses no sabe que un día hablará, pero el *Homo sapiens* lo sabe, porque somos una especie de conciencia. Nuestra especie se comunica por medio de la palabra hablada, y cada uno de los bebés hereda esa capacidad.

Esto es distinto a heredar la necesidad física de mudar los dientes de leche por los de adulto, que está vinculada al crecimiento de la mandíbula, o la necesidad de atravesar la pubertad, que hace posible que transmitamos nuestros genes por medio de la reproducción sexual. El habla es una adquisición mental, una herramienta excelente para saber lo que alguien más está pensando.

Si la comprensión del cerebro nos permitiera entender la mente, llevaríamos la delantera en el juego. Pero la noción de que "el cerebro crea la mente" siempre ha sido una falacia. Para que una célula sepa cualquier cosa no puede obtener el conocimiento de los átomos y las moléculas. Los átomos y las moléculas no saben que el habla será necesaria. Sólo la conciencia es capaz de dar una explicación válida, porque la conciencia es el elemento sabio en cada célula, cada forma de vida y cada persona.

Dado que vivimos en la era dorada de la neurociencia, uno pensaría que algún día habrá un manual del usuario para la mente. Pero ese día nunca llegará. Nuestra visión está bloqueada por el error de igualar la mente y el cerebro. Incluso el hecho de que el cerebro contiene miles de millones de conexiones es carente de sentido en términos de la mente, al igual que medir cada frecuencia de la luz visible sería carente de sentido para explicar cómo Leonardo da Vinci pintó la *Mona Lisa*. La vida no tendría sentido si el cerebro estuviera a cargo, porque el cerebro en sí mismo no tiene sentido. La mística que lo rodea al asignarle pensamientos, sentimientos y sensaciones a conjuntos de neuronas no tiene base alguna. Si un neurocientífico dijera: "Ese *quarterback* está fuera de su cerebro" o "Me gustaría comprar esa casa, pero mi cerebro no se decide", nadie dudaría que la palabra que intenta decir es *mente*.

Sin embargo, es muy difícil sacar a los neurocientíficos de su creencia de que "el cerebro crea la mente". En la sala de urgencias, un electroencefalograma revela cuando la víctima de un accidente automovilístico fatal tiene muerte cerebral, punto en el que ya no hay mente. ¿Acaso no es obvio que la mente vivía ahí, debajo de la dura protección del cráneo? Para nada. Imagina que nunca has visto a un pianista y que no tienes idea de cómo funciona un piano. Entras a una sala de conciertos y hay un piano que toca por sí mismo el vals del *Danubio azul*. Puedes ver cómo las teclas suben y bajan, y los martillos golpean las cuerdas. La materia prima de la cual está hecho el instrumento —madera, acero, fieltro y marfil— puede ser estudiada al nivel atómico. No encontrarás en ninguna parte el talento para la música. Sin embargo, en la neurociencia y en la vida cotidiana decimos que el cerebro, que también es un instrumento físico, piensa, siente, ve y hace todo lo demás que sucede en la mente. Suponemos esto sin la más mínima prueba de que la materia prima dentro de una célula —básicamente hidrógeno, oxígeno, carbono y nitrógeno— puede amar u odiar las coles de Bruselas, disfrutar los valses de Viena, enamorarse y demás. El hecho de que el cerebro está en actividad todo el tiempo no nos confirma que una mente está detrás de ello o por qué cada mente es *única en cualquier momento dado.*

Resulta fácil encontrar el origen de la mente cuando pones primero la conciencia. No es complicado hacerlo. Naturalmente confiamos en la mente porque nuestra existencia está vinculada a ella. Usamos nuestra mente de muchas maneras que no se encienden en un escaneo cerebral y que no requieren una actividad cerebral discernible. ¿Puedes reconocer el rostro de tu pareja en una multitud? Sí, al instante, pero no atraviesas un proceso que requiera actividad cerebral para lograrlo. Tu cerebro no pasa un fichero mental hasta encontrar la imagen almacenada del rostro correcto para elegirlo, así como se les pide a los testigos de un crimen elegir fotos de asaltantes en el cuartel de la policía. El reconocimiento sucede en la mente sin quemar calorías en el cerebro, y a menos que el cerebro esté quemando calorías, no está funcionando.

De la misma forma, eliges palabras sin buscarlas en un diccionario almacenado en el cerebro. Y una vez que te aprendes las calles de una nueva ciudad, puedes lidiar con ellas sin consultar un mapa, ya sea en papel o en tu cerebro. Las cosas aprendidas simplemente ahí están. También lo contrario es verdad. Si alguien te pregunta el significado de *hidrocéfalo* o *ratatouille*, y no conoces la palabra, no necesitas repasar todo tu vocabulario para encontrar las palabras, sino que de inmediato sabes que no las conoces. Pero una computadora de alta velocidad debe consultar su memoria almacenada antes de decir: "No tiene lógica".

Hace algunos años conocí a un prodigio de las matemáticas que es un profesor retirado y que había comenzado a publicar en las principales revistas de matemáticas a los 12 años de edad, y asistió a Princeton a los 16. Terminó su doctorado en Harvard mientras todavía era un estudiante universitario. Los prodigios como él son extraordinarios, y un comentario en una entrevista con este genio matemático se me quedó grabado en la mente. Cuando le preguntaron en qué se diferenciaba su proceso mental del de otras personas, él dijo que no pensaba para resolver un problema matemático; se planteaba el problema a sí mismo, permitía que incubara en él y esperaba que la respuesta correcta surgiera de pronto.

Él había desarrollado esta confianza absoluta desde muy temprano en su vida y todavía la tiene. ¿Deberíamos considerar a los genios como excepcionales, del todo separados de la norma? Para nada. Hasta cierto punto todos hemos experimentado el poder de la intuición, que puede ser definida como la mente saltando a una conclusión sin tener que pensar en todos los pasos a lo largo del camino. Cuando la gente dice cosas intuitivas, como: "Yo supe que él era el hombre con quien me casaría en cuanto lo miré", o bien: "Supe que sería piloto de avión desde que tenía cinco años", no llegó a dicha certeza pensándolo. En todo tipo de actividades, la mente confía en el elemento sabedor innato en la conciencia. Este hecho debe ser comprendido antes de poder aventurarnos en la posibilidad metahumana de usar nuestro potencial completo. La puerta se cierra si "el cerebro crea la mente" porque lo que nos hace humanos —amor, compasión, creatividad, discernimiento— está más allá del cerebro.

Podemos respaldar esto volviendo al cerebro del infante. Al nacer, un escaneo cerebral indicaría que el cerebro del bebé está sumamente activo, pero nadie afirmaría que un recién nacido está pensando, no de la forma en que los adultos forman las palabras en su cabeza. Cuando un bebé llora, está diciendo de forma no articulada que tiene hambre, cansancio, miedo, que necesita ser cambiado de ropa y demás. La madre elige una de estas posibilidades y actúa en consecuencia una vez que precisa lo que quiere su bebé. No suponemos que el bebé sabe nada más allá de su incomodidad.

En cierto punto inicia el pensamiento, y la vida de un infante se basa en la mente. Surge el pensamiento en palabras y la formación de ideas. Pero incluso si estuvieras presente en el instante exacto en el que un bebé dice su primera palabra, e incluso si pudieras mapear este momento como un evento en un escaneo cerebral, el nacimiento del lenguaje no se encuentra en el cerebro. De alguna manera, puramente en la conciencia, el pensamiento surge, conectado a un significado.

Al principio el uso de palabras es como un perico repitiendo lo que escucha. *Gu gu* no significa nada. *Mamá* es quizá una palabra que repite el bebé por insistencia de la madre. Pero entonces sucede un silencioso *ah*. Mamá es el concepto que se vincula a una persona, y sólo una persona en todo el mundo. Luego se da una aceleración del habla, y para su segundo cumpleaños los infantes entran en lo que los expertos llaman "una explosión de significados". (Éste también parece ser el punto en el que se queda corto el ADN del chimpancé, aunque sea 98% igual al ADN del ser humano. El *Homo sapiens* es único en desarrollar miles de millones de nuevas conexiones neurológicas durante los dos primeros años de vida.) Un niño de dos años típico sabe alrededor de 100 palabras; a los dos años y medio ha aumentado a alrededor de 300.

Mientras tanto, sucede un cambio que es mucho más significativo que adquirir un vocabulario: los infantes comienzan a decir cosas que *nunca han escuchado antes*, formando nuevas oraciones propias. Nadie nos enseña a hacer esto, y aun así la computadora más avanzada está muy lejos del niño promedio de tres o cuatro años. Se puede programar una computadora para inventar un número infinito de oraciones que nunca antes hayan sido dichas, pero la computadora no sabe lo que está haciendo. El proceso es totalmente mecánico: una laptop que dice "te amo" no lo dice porque lo siente.

El significado no puede estallar a partir de lo que carece de sentido, justo como las oraciones que tienen sentido no pueden surgir tan sólo de lanzar una sopa de letras al aire. La conciencia se desdobla como mente, cuerpo y cerebro, cada proceso gobernado por el significado y el propósito. (En los últimos años un famoso eslogan motivacional enuncia "la vida motivada por un propósito". Pero no podemos evitar ser impulsados por un propósito desde el nacimiento, de otra manera, seríamos estúpidos.) Quizá no seamos capaces de articular el significado de la vida, pero estamos seguros de que existe un significado y estamos diseñados para desear llegar a más.

La conciencia es un campo de significado. Lo sabemos pesar de nosotros mismos. En un experimento se les dijo a los participantes que se les haría una prueba de audición en la que debían escuchar grabaciones de oraciones dichas en voz muy baja. Aun con una buena audición era difícil descifrar lo que se musitaba en las cintas, pero se les pidió a los participantes decir lo más que pudieran escuchar.

Los participantes no sabían que cada uno estaba escuchando una secuencia de sílabas sin sentido, y a ninguno se le ocurrió esa posibilidad. Sin importar qué tan baja o ininteligible fuera la voz, los participantes escucharon —o supusieron que escucharon— oraciones con sentido. Pero incluso antes de que surgiera el lenguaje, los animales le daban sentido a su entorno, aprendiendo a reconocer los alimentos comestibles, las amenazas potenciales, una pareja deseable y a sus propias crías. Podríamos llamar a esto reconocimiento instintivo, pero no cambia el hecho de que el significado era inevitable. Incluso una amiba unicelular que se traga a otra criatura unicelular distingue el alimento de lo que no lo es. Nada, ni siquiera la fuerza de la evolución, creó el significado a partir del caos —es un hecho en el universo—.

El campo mental tiene la capacidad de convertirse en un campo minado, dependiendo del tipo de mente que desarrolle un niño. La gente que se oculta de su propio mundo interno, que con obediencia da forma a su vida de acuerdo con las normas sociales, lo hace para evitarse problemas. Pero esconderse del lado oscuro de la mente no elimina la amenaza. Una visión trágica de la vida pende sobre nosotros después de la impensable carnicería del siglo xx, cuando murió un estimado de 100 millones de personas como resultado de la guerra y el genocidio.

La explosión cognitiva que los antropólogos conjeturan que sucedió en la prehistoria, un salto que reveló el mundo de la conciencia de uno mismo, se repite con la explosión cognitiva de cada bebé conforme aprende a pensar y hablar. El cerebro del infante se adapta a la visión del mundo que se le impone. El potencial infinito se reduce de formas demasiado limitantes y contraproducentes. El escritor inglés Aldous Huxley adoptó una visión parecida hace décadas. Escribió largamente en contra del uso del cerebro como "válvula reguladora" que restringe la mente. He aquí una de las declaraciones más poderosas de Huxley al respecto:

Cada uno de nosotros es potencialmente Mente Total. Pero en la medida en que somos animales, nuestro objetivo es sobrevivir a toda costa. Para que la supervivencia biológica sea posible, la Mente Total debe ser canalizada por la válvula reguladora del cerebro y el sistema nervioso. Lo que sale del otro extremo es un mísero chorrito del tipo de conciencia que nos ayudará a mantenernos vivos sobre la superficie de este planeta en particular.

En otras palabras, Huxley contrasta el campo ilimitado de la conciencia con la muy limitada perspectiva que toma la mente cotidiana. Su punto central, que la "válvula reguladora" del cerebro era necesaria para nuestra supervivencia, ha ganado respaldo en la actualidad de parte de varios partidarios de la psicología evolutiva. Pero yo he estado argumentando que la conciencia nunca pierde su potencial infinito, sin importar lo que nos suceda dentro de la realidad virtual. Culpar al cerebro por nuestra existencia imperfecta apunta hacia la dirección errónea. El cerebro es otro modo de la conciencia. Su potencial no es inherentemente limitado. Revisemos con mayor profundidad por qué esto es así, ya que, para fines prácticos, no será posible acceder a la metarrealidad a menos que el cerebro se libre de su estrechez y nos conduzca hasta ahí.

La Mente Total y las drogas psicodélicas

El primer requisito es abrir la válvula reguladora del cerebro, lo cual ha estado sucediendo por un camino sorprendente. Una nueva ola de interés médico rodea el valor potencial de las drogas psicodélicas, la cual ha sido estimulada por una revisión minuciosa y sensible de un tema que alguna vez fue tabú, en el recuento personal de Michael Pollan titulado *Cómo cambiar tu mente*. Para que resurgieran los alucinógenos hubo una propuesta para que salieran de la oscuridad. El LSD, los hongos y la mescalina tuvieron sus mejores días en la década de 1960 y acabaron siendo muy mal vistos. Dejando de lado diversas leyes antidrogas motivadas por el temor, un investigador médico que estudiara los psicodélicos se enfrentaba al riesgo de la censura, quizá una que terminara con su carrera. Al menos, ese tipo de investigación no era tomada en serio y se hacía a un lado de inmediato.

La visión general de los psicodélicos ha sido, hasta hace poco, que son potencialmente inseguros y médicamente inútiles. Todo eso está cambiando. Lo que ha cambiado esta sabiduría convencional es un conocimiento más profundo y una mejor comprensión del cerebro. En particular, el área del cerebro que parece provocar el efecto que altera la mente con el LSD y compañía es la llamada *red neuronal por defecto* (RND), una colección de regiones en el cerebro superior que organiza y regula una amplia gama de actividad cerebral. La RND filtra el flujo de información que nos bombardea todos los días, y selecciona y controla nuestra respuesta hacia el mundo. Es la ubicación fisiológica para la edición de la realidad de la que hemos estado hablando en este libro. Una implicación inquietante de la RND es que nuestro cerebro evolucionó físicamente para convertirse en la válvula reguladora de la que habla Huxley. El LSD sacude temporalmente la RND, pero cuando termina el viaje volvemos al *statu quo* del cerebro.

Sin duda la RND sirve a una función totalmente necesaria. En vez de sentirse abrumado por un torrente de estímulos caóticos, un cerebro estable nos ayuda a enfrentar la vida con un equilibrio de buen juicio, experiencia e interés en uno mismo. La RND ha sido llamada la red del "yo", porque funciona en el cerebro de igual forma en que el ego funciona en la psicología, reprimiendo los impulsos irracionales y manteniéndolos a raya mientras organiza un ser adulto equilibrado.

La RND se empieza a desarrollar hasta los cinco años de edad, lo cual coincide con la etapa en que los niños se enorgullecen de que "ya no son bebés". Esto implica muchas cosas: no hacer berrinches ni llorar por cualquier cosa; demostrar más valentía, independencia y control de sí mismos; el deseo de ser útiles al ayudar a otros, y defender sus propios gustos e inclinaciones. Se necesita bastante control interior para un cambio tan complejo en el comportamiento, y la RND maneja casi todo ello.

Pero este cambio no es del todo bueno y positivo. Desde la perspectiva de Huxley, la Mente Total se reduce en beneficio de la supervivencia animal en bruto. Desde el punto de vista médico se conjetura que, aunque la RND es totalmente necesaria para no estar viajando todo el tiempo en medio de un torbellino nebuloso de imágenes y sonidos, tiene una desventaja. Con el tiempo sus respuestas automáticas (es decir, por defecto) se vuelven condicionadas y rígidas. Por una parte, esto puede ser la causa de la terquedad y la intolerancia asociada al envejecimiento, mientras que por otra parte podría haber una conexión con desórdenes como ansiedad, depresión y adicción. Éstas se vuelven respuestas condicionadas que sólo podrán ser eliminadas hasta que la RND deje de controlarlas tan severamente.

Uno de los recuentos más minuciosos de transformación personal en psicodélicos es *Trip*, las memorias publicadas en 2018 del escritor estadounidense Tao Lin, hijo de padres taiwaneses que nació en Florida en 1983. Lin se había sentido desmoralizado desde hacía mucho tiempo. Cómo él lo dice: "La vida me parecía desoladora, como lo había sido constantemente desde que tenía 13 o 14 años. Estaba crónicamente no fascinado con la existencia, la cual [...] no se sentía maravillosa o profunda, sino tediosa, incómoda e inquietante".

Aislado, llevando una vida estilo ermitaño y cuya soledad se agravaba por lo que Lin llama su adicción a internet y su celular, encontró los psicodélicos después de ver en YouTube durante 30 horas sin cesar los soliloquios de Terence McKenna, un defensor apasionado del viaje con drogas psicodélicas que murió en el año 2000.

A Lin le atrajo el mensaje de que estas drogas podían aumentar su imaginación y acercarlo a la naturaleza.

Lin tiene una historia compleja que contar; durante uno de sus viajes se ve a sí mismo siendo lanzado desde un cañón hacia la Vía Láctea, y pondera "todo tipo de ideas sobre qué es la realidad, qué es el lenguaje, qué es el ser, qué es el espacio y tiempo tridimensional". Esto recuerda lo que reporta la gente que vive experiencias cerca de la muerte o extracorporales. En todos estos casos, el modelo del ser deja de ser la visión por defecto de la realidad o, en términos neurológicos, la RND.

Al liberar al cerebro del control de la RND, los psicodélicos permiten una apertura para alterar la función cerebral en personas con trastornos del estado de ánimo y demás. La RND fue descubierta hasta 2001 por el investigador Michael Richie por medio de resonancias magnéticas. Por primera vez, los investigadores pudieron ver que las partes interconectadas de la RND se encendían cuando le pedían a una persona, por ejemplo, que eligiera adjetivos que la describieran. Para un neurocientífico, el flujo de sangre hacia la RND que acompaña a esta tarea demuestra, en efecto, que el yo es una función cerebral —tu RND sabe quién eres porque creó tus respuestas por defecto cuando piensas sobre ti mismo—.

El aumento y la disminución del flujo sanguíneo es un indicador útil en la investigación cerebral, porque son patrones de actividad eléctrica, pero de todas formas no son una medida de la mente, sólo su espejo físico. Los psicodélicos cambian el patrón del flujo sanguíneo de formas inusuales. Pollan cita un estudio en el que 19 sujetos que sufrían depresión mejoraron después de tomar psilocibina, el activo ingrediente en los hongos alucinógenos, cuando se mostraron resistentes a la terapia de medicamentos convencionales. Los investigadores descubrieron que disminuyó el flujo sanguíneo hacia la amígdala (el centro emocional del cerebro), pero esto no explica por qué los sujetos también reportaron haber tenido experiencias místicas profundas.

Muchas personas se muestran escépticas ante estos descubrimientos. Un problema es que no hay forma de darle un placebo a un grupo de control que simule los efectos reales de la droga alucinógena. (De hecho, nadie sabe por qué nuestro cuerpo evolucionó a tener receptores para los psicodélicos, ya que nuestros ancestros más remotos con seguridad no los encontraban a menudo.) Pero la investigación principal sobre psicodélicos parece indicar que estas sustancias reducen la actividad de la RND, y la apagan temporalmente. En conjunto con el apagado de la RND, la persona que toma estas drogas siente que el ego se disuelve, así como la experiencia normal de la mente, el cuerpo, el cerebro y el mundo. Esto enfatiza el punto de que la mente, el cuerpo, el cerebro y el mundo son sumamente maleables en la percepción humana. Estamos entregados al proceso de mantenerlos intactos cada momento de vigilia, y los psicodélicos aflojan ese control.

Para Pollan, la experiencia fue una revelación. Llegó a reconocer la "endeblez y relatividad de mi propia conciencia por defecto". Su investigación exhaustiva y objetiva —que implicó ingerir todo un espectro de drogas que alteran la mente, pero también indagar en cada recoveco y grieta de la investigación médica— lo condujo a tener la esperanza de que su uso se extendería a las personas saludables normales (aunque conserva un temor prudente hacia los malviajes). Él deseaba que el viaje psicodélico fuera considerado más que una "experiencia con las drogas". Desde su punto de vista, el primer paso sería tener la guía de alguien que pudiera explicar el significado de un viaje después de que terminara, si es que tenía significado alguno (no todos están de acuerdo en que siempre lo hay).

* * *

¿Dónde nos deja esto? Nadie lo sabe realmente, y las revistas científicas respetadas rechazan a manera de rutina las investigaciones sobre psicodélicos. Debería leerse el libro de Pollan para conocer la historia completa sobre el uso de "microdosis", en la cual se toma una cantidad diminuta de un psicodélico de forma cotidiana, la suficiente para aflojar el control de la RND, pero sin alterar el pensamiento normal. La esperanza es que, en vez de alterar la mente de manera drástica y meterla en un viaje, el método de la microdosis permitirá que la conciencia de uno mismo observe y reflexione sobre nuevas posibilidades a las que una persona no puede acceder bajo condiciones normales.

No hay duda de que, desde un punto de vista meta, los psicodélicos debilitan o disuelven los constructos mentales que mantienen intacta la realidad virtual. Algunas personas sienten que al viajar con psicodélicos acceden a la Mente Total. Esto sonaba muy deseable para Huxley, quien fue un campeón precursor de los viajes psicodélicos guiados hacia la conciencia expandida; ésta era su meta final. Pero para volverse respetables, los psicodélicos han tenido que superar su imagen *hippie*, y los escaneos cerebrales han demostrado ser la clave para ello. Sin embargo, la respetabilidad derivada de los escaneos cerebrales también tiene un defecto.

Para un neurocientífico, la RND es como el adulto en la habitación, una región cerebral que mantiene a raya nuestros impulsos más salvajes y primitivos. Por consiguiente, un grupo especializado de células se ha hecho cargo de la función exacta que Freud asignó al ego. Es típico de nuestra época que la psiquiatría dependa mucho de los fármacos para combatir la ansiedad y la depresión, remplazando años de terapia en la que el paciente habla, la cual es cara y exige mucho tiempo. Dado que la psiquiatría se ha convertido en una materia sobre moléculas que van y vienen en el cerebro, lo mismo ha sucedido con todo acerca de la mente. Pero la noción de que "el cerebro crea la mente" es tan errónea aquí como en todos lados.

La falacia atraviesa claramente en la RND, porque si en verdad controla el acto de equilibrio que es la mente adulta, ¿quién le otorgó esa capacidad? ¿Cómo aprendió los beneficios de la adultez en primer lugar? La primera respuesta que viene a la mente es que la RND surgió como un mecanismo de supervivencia, pero no existe prueba de ello; es tan sólo una amplia generalización que proviene de los recursos darwinianos. Innumerables personas funcionan bien en sociedad sin molestarse en volverse adultos maduros. Los investigadores tratan a la RND como si fuera un agente con intenciones flexibles y buen juicio. Atribuir estas cualidades a las células cerebrales es una forma de pensamiento mágico. Los puñados de químicos no comprenden cómo funciona la vida; sólo la conciencia lo puede entender.

Después de probar varias drogas distintas, Michael Pollan tuvo su experiencia más profunda sin ellas. Le enseñaron a entrar en estado de trance simplemente al respirar con rapidez y escuchar el tamborileo rítmico de percusiones. Su reacción fue: "¿En dónde había estado *eso* toda mi vida?". Estaba en la Mente Total.

Todas las drogas tienen efectos secundarios, algunos de ellos impredecibles, pero los inconvenientes de los psicodélicos son únicos. Si juegas con las cuerdas de un piano, la música comienza a sonar distorsionada. Entrar a las áreas más sensibles del cerebro superior implica un riesgo similar, pero mi objetivo no es alarmar con base en el miedo y la superstición, sino lo contrario. La Mente Total contiene la gama completa del potencial humano, y se puede acceder a ella de forma natural por medio del yoga, la meditación y diversas prácticas contemplativas. Estas prácticas también provocan cambios cerebrales benéficos, y lo logran por medio del mecanismo más natural de todos: la mente aprendiendo a conocerse a sí misma.

Ahora es el momento para que los psicodélicos salgan de las sombras y nos den una imagen equilibrada de lo que está en juego y también de lo que está en riesgo. La sensación repentina de que podemos volar puede ser una ilusión fatal si intentamos hacerlo saltando desde un edificio alto, como ya ha sucedido más de una vez. Las percepciones que uno tiene durante un viaje con alguna droga a menudo resultan ser ininteligibles al regresar al estado de vigilia normal. El panorama general va más allá de los psicodélicos. En el epílogo de su libro, Pollan incentiva a la "diversidad neural". Pero para mí, el efecto de alteración mental del LSD rinde frutos sólo si conduce a la conciencia de uno mismo. Una droga te puede mostrar lo que se encuentra más allá de la mente limitada; sólo la conciencia de ti mismo te permite habitar la Mente Total de forma permanente.

Lo opuesto a la conciencia de uno mismo es la visión mecanicista de que un ser humano es una marioneta del cerebro, un subordinado de la actividad neural. Si es que los psicodélicos tienen usos médicos, deberíamos alegrarnos. Pero es verdadera la noción de Huxley de que la Mente Total es el tema central.

Lo que nos separa de la Mente Total —o metarrealidad— es el velo más fino. Tan sólo es necesario el pensamiento más simple. Descubrí esto recientemente cuando estaba haciendo la postura del árbol con un instructor de yoga. La postura del árbol requiere de un equilibrio delicado al estar parado en un solo pie, y cada vez la hago mejor, pero de pronto esa mañana comencé a tambalearme. De inmediato el instructor dijo: "¿En qué estás pensando ahora?". Fue la pregunta correcta, porque yo había perdido mi estado mental claro y abierto por un pensamiento que me distrajo (sobre los beneficios médicos de los psicodélicos, casualmente). Para hacer mucho más en la vida que tan sólo sostener una postura de yoga se requiere un estado mental claro y abierto, despejado de pensamientos fortuitos. Esta claridad es como se siente la Mente Total. Es como se siente la libertad. Es la puerta al metahumano.

En la segunda parte haremos todo de forma personal al mostrar cómo cada persona puede experimentar el cambio hacia la Mente Total. Sólo es posible el despertar colectivo cuando los individuos despiertan, y no hay nada más urgente que eso. A manera de puente, permíteme enfatizar lo extraordinario que es despertar, así como lo impredecible que es.

Despertar nos hace más humanos y más reales al mismo tiempo, porque somos la especie de conciencia destinada —y diseñada— a conocer nuestra fuente por completo. Si una sola visión puede unir a la raza humana, es ésta.

SEGUNDA PARTE

Despertar

7

PONER LA EXPERIENCIA PRIMERO

La cultura popular ha asimilado el remate de un viejo chiste. Como yo lo escuché por primera vez, el chiste involucra a un citadino perdido que detiene su auto en una carretera rural para preguntarle a un granjero cómo llegar a cierto pueblo. El granjero se rasca la cabeza con una mirada de confusión y responde: "Lo siento, señor, pero no puede llegar ahí desde aquí".

¿Por qué nos hace reír este chiste? El humor radica en el hecho de que puedes llegar a donde sea en el mapa desde cualquier otro lugar. Pero si el citadino le hubiera preguntado al granjero cómo llegar a la metarrealidad habría obtenido la misma respuesta, sólo que esta vez no habría sido chistosa, al menos no para mí.

No puedes llegar a la metarrealidad aferrándote a la realidad virtual. La razón de esto ha sido expresada de varias formas desde que el *Homo sapiens* se dio cuenta de que existe una dimensión de la vida más allá de lo cotidiano. Estar atorado en la realidad virtual es como estar bajo un hechizo hipnótico, y no podemos romper el hechizo mientras nos tenga hipnotizados —no existe un hipnotista cerca para tronar los dedos y romper el hechizo—. O somos como soñadores cautivos por las ilusiones del sueño, y no podemos despertar mientras el sueño dure —no hay nadie junto a nuestra cama para sacudirnos y despertarnos—.

Los hechizos, los sueños, los encantamientos, la magia y la brujería, los dioses traviesos: cada cultura ha inventado versiones de la misma idea, que la realidad es engañosa. "No puedes llegar ahí desde aquí" mientras estés enredado en un truco completo y abarcador de la mente. Por ello, descubrir cómo despertar ha sido un asunto misterioso. Hasta ahora.

La vida continúa por medio del conocimiento y la experiencia, y la primera parte se trató acerca del conocimiento de la metarrealidad. ¿Entonces de dónde provendrá la experiencia? ¿Por qué no indagamos sobre ella primero? Es fácil ser impaciente (el sexo masculino, en particular, es conocido por no leer el manual ni pedir direcciones cuando está perdido), pero en este caso el conocimiento y la experiencia no pueden ser separados. No puedes saltar a la parte honda de una alberca y al mismo tiempo descubrir cómo nadar. La conciencia debe ser reestructurada desde cero; las percepciones deben cambiar; las interpretaciones deben ser abandonadas. Nada puede permanecer igual al saltar de lo humano a lo metahumano.

Aunque la realidad virtual sea tan amplia, existe una fisura, que es la experiencia misma. ¿Qué es una experiencia? Navegar por el Atlántico en una lancha individual es muy diferente de escalar los Alpes, manejar al trabajo u hornear un pay de manzana, así que el rostro de la experiencia cambia constantemente. Pero en esencia cada experiencia es la misma cosa: un evento consciente. Si cometes el error de basar tus experiencias en el mundo físico, no podrás despertar del hechizo/sueño/ilusión porque el mundo físico *es* el hechizo/sueño/ilusión.

Experimentar el mundo

La única forma de romper el hechizo es revertir la explicación normal de cómo funcionan las cosas. Con esto me refiero a poner la *experiencia* primero. La explicación normal es poner las *cosas* primero, lo que hace el sentido común. ¿Acaso las estrellas no existieron antes de que nosotros llegáramos a observarlas en el cielo nocturno? Sin la Tierra, que existía en un estado primordial antes de que comenzara la vida, no estaríamos aquí. O eso dicta el sentido común.

Pero revertir la explicación también tiene sentido. Digamos que es de mañana y estás leyendo con una taza de café junto a ti. Una "taza de café" puede significar un objeto físico inamovible, por el momento, en el tiempo y el espacio. He escrito "taza de café" entre comillas porque de hecho te estás relacionando con un objeto así llamado. En realidad, estás experimentando una fusión de sensaciones. Tus ojos ven el color, la luz y la sombra, que tú percibes como la taza. Tu nariz detecta el aroma del café, tu mano siente el calor del café en la taza, tu lengua percibe su sabor.

¿Qué sucede si eliminas todas estas experiencias? No hay taza de café. Ésta es una conclusión simple y lógica, pero si quieres reforzar el hechizo/sueño/ilusión esta conclusión es intolerable. Una taza de café simplemente está ahí, en el espacio y el tiempo, como una cosa física. Dejaremos de lado la explicación cuántica que disuelve las cosas físicas, incluyendo el universo entero, en estados virtuales invisibles. Nuestra meta aquí es diferente. El motivo por el cual hago desaparecer una taza de café no es para demostrar que nunca estuvo ahí. Es para poner la experiencia primero. Lo que llamamos un árbol, una nube, una montaña, una estrella o una taza de café existe *solamente* como una experiencia. Una vez que aceptas este hecho, el camino hacia el metahumano está libre y despejado.

Pero no hace mucho bien encogerse de hombros y decir: "De acuerdo, lo acepto". Las palabras son huecas a menos que exista una comprensión y entiendas el punto. La experiencia es como conocemos cualquier cosa. Si existe una realidad más allá de la conciencia humana, por definición nunca la conoceremos. En la física contemporánea se habla mucho de la materia y la energía "oscura" (lo cual Menas Kafatos y yo discutimos ampliamente en *You Are the Universe*). Si algunas teorías son verdaderas, la materia y energía oscuras existen fuera de las fronteras del universo físico. En el mundo oscuro podría haber "sustancia" que no sea de origen atómico, que no emita fotones ni electrones, y que quizá no tenga relación alguna con nuestra versión del tiempo y el espacio.

Digamos que estas conjeturas son ciertas (hay una probabilidad de que no lo sean, pero no entraremos en las razones técnicas aquí). ¿Acaso la materia y la energía oscuras, al ser totalmente ajenas a la experiencia humana, sin tener nada en común con la "sustancia" que constituye el cerebro humano, califican como reales pero imposibles de experimentar? Para tal caso, nadie puede experimentar el Big Bang porque antecede a los átomos y las moléculas. Nadie puede entrar a un agujero negro para experimentarlo, dado que la gravedad extrema dentro y alrededor del agujero negro desintegra la materia y despedaza toda la "sustancia" ordinaria, incluyendo el tiempo y el espacio.

Para cualquiera que acepte el universo tal como aparece, poner la experiencia primero suena absurdo, pero no lo es. La materia y la energía oscuras son conocidas por medio de la experiencia, al igual que el Big Bang, los agujeros negros y todas las demás cosas extrañas de la física. En todos estos casos la experiencia es indirecta, formulada en ecuaciones matemáticas, la colección de rastros de partículas subatómicas fugaces y la información recibida por radiotelescopios y demás. Pero no importa qué tan indirecta, *sigue siendo una experiencia*.

Alguien tiene que ver algo, aunque sólo sea una hoja de papel llena de números. Alguien tiene que escuchar a otro científico hablando o leer sus palabras. Es innegable el hecho de que incluso la ciencia más exótica ocurre como una experiencia consciente. Empareja el campo de juego con la experiencia cotidiana, porque un niño de primero de primaria que aprende el alfabeto está teniendo la misma experiencia que un físico leyendo un artículo científico sobre la gravedad cuántica.

Como una especie específica de conciencia, el *Homo sapiens* construyó su versión de la realidad a partir de las experiencias cotidianas y construyó todo desde ahí. Humanizamos la realidad virtual de acuerdo con nuestras experiencias. A nosotros nos quema la piel una roca caliente bajo el sol del desierto, pero un reptil la encuentra cómoda. La medianoche más oscura nos asusta, pero en ella los murciélagos se sienten en casa, justo como las alturas heladas son lugares perfectos para los nidos de águila y el océano es respirable para los peces.

Pero no estamos destinados a estar aprisionados en nuestras experiencias. Les damos forma y las moldeamos con una libertad extraordinaria. El cuerpo se ve como un objeto inamovible, pero podemos matarlo de hambre o engordarlo, crecer los músculos o volverlos flácidos. El asunto es qué tan maleable es la "rigidez" de las cosas. Yo lo veo como un proceso de derretimiento. Cuando los bloques de hielo se rompen en la primavera, no se derriten de inmediato. Hay una transición de un río congelado a uno que fluye. Lo mismo sucede en la manera en que experimentamos el mundo físico. En vez de ser un gran bloque congelado, se reduce a las experiencias más diminutas, como un acantilado que por los fuertes golpes de mar con el tiempo se reduce a finos granos de arena. Los cinco sentidos están exquisitamente sintonizados para percibir eventos fugaces y efímeros. He guardado en la mente un descubrimiento pequeño, pero impactante: la retina humana puede detectar un solo fotón de luz, pero hace poco esta pieza aislada de información se expandió de una forma bastante sorprendente.

El quantum se vuelve humano

Sin haber logrado una atención popular generalizada por los medios de comunicación masiva, las investigaciones han verificado que al menos cuatro de nuestros cinco sentidos son capaces de experimentar directamente el mundo cuántico, sin el uso de instrumentos científicos sofisticados. Los descubrimientos esenciales, que provienen de laboratorios universitarios importantes, pueden ser resumidos brevemente.

VISTA: El ojo humano, como acabo de mencionar, puede detectar un solo fotón. Ésta es la unidad de luz más pequeña en el universo, y nuestra capacidad de detectar un fotón ha inspirado a los investigadores a explorar si pueden indagar el mundo cuántico a simple vista.

OÍDO: El oído interno es tan sensible que puede detectar vibraciones menores al diámetro de un átomo. Puede distinguir sonidos que están a sólo 10 millonésimas de segundo.

OLFATO: Antes se estimaba que el sistema olfativo humano podía detectar 10 000 olores distintos, pero las últimas investigaciones sugieren que el olfato es un sentido cuántico que puede distinguir un billón de olores diferentes.

TACTO: Podemos detectar sensaciones táctiles desde una milmillonésima de metro.

GUSTO: Este sentido no ha sido rastreado a nivel cuántico, pero se sabe que la lengua humana detecta los cinco sabores (dulce, salado, ácido, amargo y umami) a nivel molecular. El gusto necesita del olfato para distinguir a un nivel más fino, así que incluso el gusto, cuando se combina con el olfato, está implicado en la detección cuántica.

¿Por qué la evolución nos dio esta microsensibilidad? Para responder esta pregunta debes apreciar el enorme salto que han dado las nuevas investigaciones. Antes se pensaba que los cinco sentidos operaban a nivel molecular, como el gusto. Para notar la diferencia entre salado y dulce, por ejemplo, los receptores en tus papilas gustativas están diseñadas para pegarse a las moléculas específicas de cada sabor. Físicamente, la visión aceptada ha sido que interactuamos con el mundo por medio de una miríada de receptores similares en la membrana externa de las células. Estos receptores han sido descritos como cerraduras en las que entran moléculas muy específicas (las llaves). Para oler una rosa, por ejemplo, las moléculas de su olor flotan a través del aire y entran en los receptores de células olfativas en la nariz. Dado que este proceso sucede a nivel molecular, incluso los organismos primitivos son microsensibles físicamente.

El sentido más antiguo es el tacto, que evolucionó en un organismo unicelular que respondía a ser tocado, como la amiba, así como algunas plantas; la dionea atrapamoscas cierra sus hojas en forma de mandíbula sobre su presa cuando un insecto toca los pelos sensibles dispuestos a lo largo de las hojas. Pero a pesar de ser el sentido más antiguo, el tacto todavía no se comprende del todo. Las cámaras y los dispositivos de escucha pueden duplicar la sensibilidad de nuestros ojos y orejas, pero podemos notar la diferencia entre la madera, el metal y el vidrio al tocarlos, más allá de lo que los ingenieros puedan hacer de forma artificial. Apenas hace poco, investigadores de la Universidad de California, en San Diego, demostraron que nuestros dedos pueden sentir hasta una sola molécula.

Formaron un grupo de 15 personas y les dieron tres piezas delgadas de silicón para que las tocaran. Les preguntaron cuál de ellas se sentía distinta a las otras dos. Las piezas eran idénticas excepto por la capa superior, cuyo grosor era de una sola molécula. Una superficie tenía una capa superior oxidada que era en su mayoría oxígeno, la otra estaba cubierta con una sustancia parecida al teflón. Los participantes eligieron la pieza distinta 71% de las veces.

Sin embargo, incluso las moléculas son enormes comparadas con el quantum, y la sensibilidad del ojo a un quantum de luz condujo a los científicos a considerar los otros cuatro sentidos. Ahora parece que todo el cuerpo es un detector cuántico. A primera vista es extraordinario —en efecto expande la percepción humana más allá de lo que antes se creía—. Pero a un nivel más profundo, estos descubrimientos indican cómo diseñamos y controlamos los constructos de la realidad virtual. A lo largo de los detectores cuánticos del cuerpo estamos constantemente entretejidos en el universo al nivel más delicado. Nuestro cuerpo no recibe simplemente la información en bruto del mundo "allá fuera", sino que participa de las entrañas en las que la mente y la materia se mezclan.

Llegar al meollo de cómo vemos, escuchamos, tocamos, saboreamos y olemos físicamente no explica para qué son los cinco sentidos. Anteriormente (página 23), comparé la respuesta de la retina a la luz con un contador Geiger que cliquea cada vez que es bombardeado con partículas beta y rayos gamma. Pero un contador Geiger no experimenta el mundo como nosotros. La sensibilidad de nuestros detectores cuánticos indica qué tan finamente calibradas son nuestras experiencias. Previamente, nuestra sintonía a nivel molecular condujo a proezas extraordinarias de la percepción ante los descubrimientos cuánticos recientes.

Las narices profesionales en la industria del perfume van mucho más allá del sentido ordinario del olfato, al ser capaces de distinguir docenas de aromas de rosa distintos, por ejemplo, pero los expertos no necesariamente tienen nervios olfativos superrefinados o más nervios que nosotros. Han entrenado su conciencia de los aromas. Lo mismo sucede con los catadores de vino en el área del gusto y tiradores en el área de la vista. Estas personas quizás empiezan con sentidos más agudos que la persona promedio, pero un catador o un tirador no necesitan una profusión de receptores celulares. Con un rango normal de receptores, los catadores afilan su percepción, la cual es mental.

Los llamados supercatadores tienen 30 papilas gustativas en un área específica de la lengua, comparados con los catadores promedio que tienen entre 15 y 30 papilas gustativas en la misma área, mientras que los llamados no catadores (un término más apropiado sería *catadores opacos*) tienen menos de 15. Los catadores promedio pueden mejorar su discernimiento del vino usando más sus narices, prestando mayor atención y probar despacio el sabor. Ciertamente es relevante que entre los 40 y 60 años de edad comenzamos a perder papilas gustativas y las restantes se encogen. Pero eso no es suficiente para explicar por qué la gente mayor a menudo pierde interés en la comida. Puede haber una pérdida general de interés en la vida, o sentirse solos y no deseados. El simple hecho de que algunos bebés nazcan sin el sentido del gusto, pero tengan un apetito saludable al crecer, señala el componente mental que domina nuestra existencia sensorial.

La información derivada de las mediciones de cómo funciona el ojo, el oído o la lengua no dice nada sobre nuestra experiencia real: cómo se ve un atardecer, cómo suena la música y cómo sabe el chocolate. La ciencia se trata de medir la vida y todas sus *cantidades*, grandes y pequeñas. La experiencia se trata de la vida en todas sus *cualidades*, las cuales no pueden ser contadas. La pregunta "¿cuántas unidades de belleza experimentaste hoy?" no tiene sentido. La belleza se experimenta subjetivamente, y nadie lo puede negar. Pero cada percepción también se experimenta subjetivamente, y ahí es donde sucede el enorme hueco que mencioné antes. Existe una disparidad total entre la medición de longitudes de onda de la luz y las cualidades de la luz, en particular los colores.

El color es creado en la conciencia al cruzar el hueco entre la cantidad y la calidad. En este cruce tiene lugar un truco mágico en el cual las vibraciones cuánticas se transforman no sólo en colores, sino en todo lo que es percibido por los sentidos. Sería conveniente que las nuevas investigaciones explicaran cómo sucede dicho truco, pero no lo hacen. Precisar los cinco sentidos a nivel cuántico es como tener el sentido del oído de un perro, que va mucho más allá del oído humano. Si de pronto te despertaras y escucharas el mundo como lo oye un perro, esto no explicaría la música o el habla, ni nada acerca de la escucha como una experiencia. No escucha el oído; escucha la mente.

Pero por lo menos tenemos una pista importante sobre el truco de magia que convierte los eventos cuánticos en experiencias humanas. Al llevar la percepción a nivel cuántico podemos decir —o suponer fuertemente— que vivimos al nivel en que la naturaleza transforma la realidad virtual en el mundo físico sólido. Aquí estoy usando la palabra *virtual* de una forma específica. En la física existe una casa a medio camino donde las partículas son invisibles y no tienen una ubicación fija.

Esta casa a medio camino era necesaria debido al famoso principio de incertidumbre, que dice que las partículas son el colapso de las ondas de energía. Las ondas se extienden infinitamente en todas direcciones; las partículas existen en un lugar en el tiempo y el espacio. Una partícula virtual abarca los dos estados. Todavía no ha asumido del todo la forma de una partícula, pero tampoco es una onda que se extiende en todas direcciones.

Es muy importante saber, como ya lo sabemos ahora, que la experiencia humana no tiene que esperar a que el mundo físico aparezca; somos capaces de percibir el nacimiento de las partículas, físicamente hablando. Estoy siendo bastante literal. Por décadas, la función del "colapso de las ondas" ha sido discutida acaloradamente en la física. El punto principal de la controversia es que la teoría cuántica estándar sostiene que se necesita un observador para provocar el colapso. Este punto exaspera a algunos físicos y desconcierta a casi todo el mundo. En la vida cotidiana se da por hecho que observar algo es un acto pasivo. "Mira, pero no lo toques", les decimos a nuestros hijos. Pero al nivel cuántico ver es igual a tocar. Una partícula deja de ser incierta cuando un observador está presente. La función de onda colapsa y, *voilà*, se detecta una partícula.

Espero que esta explicación abreviada tenga sentido; entrar en los detalles implica una serie de complicaciones. Basta decir que los investigadores están considerando con seriedad si este efecto misterioso en el quantum, conocido como el "efecto del observador", puede ser explicado por medio de la detección cuántica. Si tus ojos interactúan físicamente con el quantum, ello nos ayuda a comprender que la observación nunca fue pasiva. Hemos estado participando en el lugar donde la realidad virtual tiene una oportunidad de crear la realidad física.

Cómo la mente les da a las cosas
la esencia de cosas

Los nuevos descubrimientos no explican el truco de magia que sucede en el hueco entre la cantidad —cosas que pueden ser medidas y contadas— y las cualidades, las imágenes, los sonidos, los sabores, las texturas y los olores que experimentamos como seres humanos. Es apasionante humanizar el quantum, pero los seres humanos no experimentamos el mundo a través de un nivel microscópico de diferencias, aunque teóricamente podríamos hacerlo. En cambio, agrupamos las experiencias de acuerdo con conceptos útiles como el color. El rojo es rojo, no cada vibración diferente en las longitudes de onda entre los 630 y los 700 nanómetros (un nanómetro es una milmillonésima de metro).

Asimismo, lo dulce es dulce, no la interacción molecular entre las moléculas del azúcar y los receptores en la lengua. Estamos tan acostumbrados al proceso aglomerado que no nos sorprendemos a nosotros mismos haciendo nada. Pero constantemente tomamos experiencias efímeras y las metemos en posiciones preestablecidas, convirtiendo la discontinuidad en continuidad, y volviendo sólido lo que de hecho es fluido.

El término técnico de lo que sucede es *reificación* —darles a las experiencias inmateriales la "esencia de cosas"—. Esta transformación es tan convincente que la roca se ve sólida y pesada cuando, de hecho, tu mente la cosificó —has creado solidez y peso en tu propia conciencia—. Esto constituye otra conclusión escandalosa para cualquiera que busque reforzar y reafirmar el hechizo/sueño/ilusión. Pero no puedes derretir la "esencia de cosa" del mundo físico a menos que derribes el proceso que lo creó. Estoy indeciso con respecto a usar cualquier tipo de jerga, pero tenemos que indagar sobre cómo funciona la reificación o cosificación.

La definición de *cosificar* es "volver algo más concreto o real". La imagen mental del dinero se cosifica en un billete de un dólar, que puedes doblar y meter en tu cartera. La "crianza" se cosifica cuando decides tener un bebé que puedes sostener entre tus brazos. Lo que resulta impactante es que la realidad virtual le debe su existencia por completo a la cosificación.

La red de conexiones que enreda todo en el hechizo/sueño/ilusión con todo lo demás se reduce a la mente, porque las conexiones son hechas por la mente. Ningún objeto es una cosa física, pura y simple. "Objeto" y "cosa" y "física" son hebras de una red mental.

A la gente le resulta relativamente fácil aceptar que una pieza de papel moneda es una forma cosificada de un concepto (dinero), pero se resiste cuando le dicen que lo mismo sucede con el cuerpo, el cerebro y el universo. La clave es revertir todo el proceso de cosificación al traer los objetos físicos más cerca de la realidad. Los huesos de tu brazo, como los ves ahora, son sólidos y fijos; es difícil aceptar que son fluidos y maleables. Pero, de hecho, todos los objetos físicos son procesos en movimiento. Los huesos no son la excepción; constantemente intercambian una oleada de oxígeno y calcio a nivel molecular. Cada célula ósea es una actividad de vida en movimiento. Si usas zapatos que no te quedan, los huesos de tus piernas se doblarán poco a poco para adaptarse a tu caminar disparejo.

El hecho de que un proceso sea lento o rápido no afecta la realidad esencial de que las cosas son procesos. Los huesos rotos sanan más despacio que un dedo cortado, pero el mismo hecho de que la sanación suceda es evidencia de que el cuerpo es un proceso. El cáncer de hueso es mucho más temido porque es muy doloroso, pero en su estado saludable normal, los nervios conectan tus huesos con el cerebro y después con el mundo exterior. Al agrupar todas las sensaciones fugaces que experimentas ahora mismo parece que tienes un cuerpo inalterable, pero en realidad tu cuerpo hoy no es el cuerpo que tenías cuando eras un bebé recién nacido, un niño o un adolescente; ni siquiera es el mismo cuerpo que tenías ayer o hace cinco minutos.

Por lo tanto, es sorprendentemente fácil revertir el hábito de pensamiento que cosifica el cuerpo, convirtiendo una miríada de procesos interconectados en una cosa. Este giro nos ayuda a volver al origen de la creación, en la conciencia misma. Cuando logras dominar el giro puedes deshacer cualquier cosa en la realidad virtual al rastrearla de vuelta al genio creativo de la mente. Esto es lo que significa derretir la "esencia de cosa": los objetos son reducidos a un nivel de conciencia donde podemos comenzar a experimentar el proceso creativo. Conforme te acercas más a la conciencia pura, el proceso de descongelamiento se vuelve más fácil y rápido. Y cuando la "esencia de cosa" pierde su terquedad, la experiencia se transforma en algo fluido, flexible y maleable. Es crítica la realidad del "ser verdadero" porque, tal como están las cosas, todo mundo tiene un ser lleno de contradicciones. El ser con el que te has estado identificando te mantiene en el hechizo/sueño/ilusión. El ser verdadero te lleva de la ilusión a la realidad.

Tres versiones del ser

El ser verdadero está escondido detrás de varias capas de disfraz. Las capas son tan gruesas que nadie puede definir con seguridad qué es el ser. "Ser" es una ficción conveniente que aglomera un revoltijo de creencias, experiencias, condicionamientos viejos y opiniones de segunda mano. Este problema es mucho más grande de lo que imaginas. Para casi todas las personas existe un hueco muy grande entre "ser tú mismo" y "conocerte a ti mismo". Lo primero se considera como algo deseable. Cuando eres capaz de ser tú mismo te sientes natural y relajado, sin pretensiones ni defensas. Conocerte a ti mismo es un asunto diferente. Un siglo después de que Freud descubrió la mente inconsciente, ésta se ha identificado con el lado oscuro de la naturaleza humana. Reprimimos nuestra compulsión al enojo, ansiedad, envidia, inseguridad e incluso violencia. Por supuesto que no te puedes llevar con otras personas si dices todo lo que piensas o si actúas cada impulso que sientas.

Pero aún hay más. Cuando el mundo interno se identifica con el lado oscuro, la gente no quiere mirar ahí dentro. Le disgusta y teme lo que encuentra o lo que puede encontrar. Nos identificamos con la personalidad del ego, que presenta al ser que queremos que el mundo vea, e ignoramos la oportunidad de explorar lo que podría ser un yo más profundo. A la larga, un sinnúmero de personas termina creyendo que su personalidad del ego es su yo real. Pero poseemos otros dos seres, y no son de temer. De hecho, son las fuentes más ricas de plenitud humana.

El primero es el ser inconsciente. Aunque de forma rutinaria guardamos las emociones e impulsos negativos en el inconsciente para que no estén a la vista, toda la historia es mucho más positiva. El ser inconsciente es creativo y sensible. Cuando entras a una habitación en la que dos personas han estado discutiendo o alguien estaba llorando, lo sientes silenciosamente "en el aire". De hecho, lo estás percibiendo por medio de tu ser inconsciente. Al nivel que está por debajo de la conciencia cotidiana percibes constantemente tu entorno. También tienes el poder de la intuición en tu ser inconsciente. Llegas a momentos de iluminación cuando el ser inconsciente revela algo de lo que tú y tu mente consciente no se habían dado cuenta.

Conforme vas madurando, comienzas a valorar aquello que está arraigado en el inconsciente. Te sientes confiado, autosuficiente y seguro de lo que sabes. Sabes cómo hacer ciertas cosas —cocinar, manejar, calcular el saldo de tu chequera, encontrar un buen restaurante—. Pero a un nivel más profundo tienes una sensación de calma que es difícil explicar. Debido a que tu ser inconsciente presta atención a todas tus experiencias de vida, destila la esencia de tu vida en la experiencia de satisfacción interior, que con el tiempo se vuelve una parte natural de quien eres. Te conoces a ti mismo como un conjunto de valores, propósitos y logros. Hay innumerables personas que no llegan a esta etapa, y no conocen la experiencia de la satisfacción interna. Y tampoco puede ser inculcada, ya que suceden muchas cosas ocultas en el inconsciente.

T. S. Eliot me viene a la mente de nuevo. En 1925 escribió "Los hombres huecos", un poema que a los jóvenes de preparatoria les encantaba recitar, porque la adolescencia está marcada por temores ocultos. Comienza así:

Somos los hombres huecos
somos los hombres disecados
inclinados unos con otros
la cabeza llena de paja. ¡Qué pena!
Nuestras voces secas, cuando
susurramos juntos
son silenciosas y sinsentido
como el viento sobre el pasto seco.

Al escribirlo en 1925, Eliot exploró uno de nuestros temores más profundos, que la vida se puede volver sinsentido y estar afligidos por la muerte y la nada —el máximo vacío—. En tiempos de gran peligro y horror, como en las dos guerras mundiales del siglo xx, el pavor a perder todo el significado se siente muy real. Pero el ser inconsciente, al aprovechar las reservas del significado infinito, recrea el mundo en una nueva imagen, una que es llevadera a pesar del terror y el horror del pasado.

Y sin embargo, hay otro ser más, y es incluso más valioso —llamémoslo el "ser verdadero"—. Éste es un nivel de conciencia muy cercano a nuestra fuente en la conciencia pura. La conciencia pura es silenciosa y quieta. Tiene el potencial de la actividad mental antes de que surja cualquier actividad. Yo la identifico con la experiencia más simple de todas, el "yo soy" puro de la existencia. Ésta es la experiencia más simple porque no requiere pensamiento. Tú sabes que existes; eso es todo. Conforme el silencio quieto de "yo soy" comienza a vibrar en pensamientos, imágenes, sentimientos y sensaciones, los primeros movimientos son muy débiles y sutiles. Son sumamente fluidos y maleables, por lo cual los deseos e intenciones que provienen de nuestra fuente más profunda no están distorsionados por todos los deseos más vulgares del ego. "Quiero paz" es un deseo más sutil y fino que "quiero un Porsche".

Al nivel del ser verdadero, todo deseo de cambio alcanza su meta, porque sólo así "yo soy" es suficiente para brindar satisfacción total. Ninguna gratificación externa se compara con esto. A primera vista parece extraño que la mente en su nivel más sutil debería estar más satisfecha que la mente en niveles más superficiales. Para la gran mayoría de la gente la vida se trata de perseguir deseos mundanos. De la misma manera, estar quietos y en silencio resulta muy incómodo para muchos. Nos quejamos de que "no hay nada que hacer". Pero la quietud puede liberar nuevas realidades. La clave es que la conciencia pura contiene recursos infinitos de creatividad, dicha, inteligencia, amor y conciencia. Al vivir cerca de la fuente tienes acceso a este potencial infinito que te permite ser un genuino cocreador de la realidad.

He puesto a estos seres —la personalidad del ego, el ser inconsciente y el ser verdadero— en categorías separadas sólo para describirlos. En la vida cotidiana recurrimos a los tres. Cuando la conciencia surge desde su fuente, cualquier impulso tiene un componente inconsciente y eventualmente un componente del ego. Un ejemplo común es la amistad que se convierte en amor romántico. Dos amigos interactúan en gran medida en el nivel del ego, lo que significa que presentan su imagen pública el uno al otro. Pero conforme la amistad se estrecha, el inconsciente se revela a sí mismo con más intimidad, y a veces, si las dos personas se sienten lo suficientemente seguras, el verdadero centro de la amistad, que es el amor, se revela a sí mismo. Ésa parece ser la meta final, pero al nivel del ser verdadero no se necesita otra persona. "Yo soy" ya tiene la cualidad del amor, y vibra en los bordes de la conciencia pura.

A lo que esto se reduce es que el ser con el que te identificas es simplemente *el ser del que eres consciente*. No hay un ser inalterable, así como no hay un cuerpo inmutable. Pelear por tu lugar en la fila de la oficina de correos evoca a la personalidad del ego. Sentir ternura hacia un bebé evoca a la personalidad inconsciente. Sentir que tú importas en el gran esquema de las cosas evoca al ser verdadero.

En cierto punto, el ser verdadero domina la escena, y cuando sucede este cambio, el mundo también cambia. El mundo se siente duro, inamovible, terco e inflexible si tú eres todo eso. A la personalidad del ego le parece más fácil resistir que aceptar, aferrarse en vez de soltar. Así que ser duro, inamovible, terco e inflexible no es algo raro, y tampoco lo es ver el mundo de la misma manera. Si alguien explora más a fondo y comienza a identificarse con el ser inconsciente, entonces el mundo parece hermoso, fresco, renovado y lleno de luz. Esto también es un reflejo del estado de conciencia de la persona. Observa la luz brillante de las pinturas de los impresionistas franceses y verás hacia dónde conduce a los pintores este estado de conciencia.

Pero debes ir más profundo para ver el mundo en completa pureza. Este estado, conocido generalmente como "iluminación", representa el contacto directo con la metarrealidad. Dado que nuestra vida cotidiana está dominada por los deseos, necesidades y demandas del ego, no es posible concebir lo que se siente experimentar la realidad como un estado constante. Déjame darte un ejemplo sorprendente con el pensamiento y enseñanzas de Krishna Menon, que nació en 1883 en el estado de Kerala, al sur de la India. Aunque toda su vida fue un desconocido —Menon murió en 1959—, ha llegado a ser considerado como extremadamente importante entre los buscadores espirituales que desean investigar la experiencia de la iluminación (contraria a la veneración de gurús y maestros espirituales, la cual tiene un componente religioso mayor).

La naturaleza inflexible de su conciencia puede deducirse al leer las respuestas que Krishna Menon (conocido más tarde por sus seguidores como Sri Atmananda) dio cuando le presentaron las preguntas. Una y otra vez regresaba todos los temas a una pregunta esencial: ¿qué es la realidad? He aquí algunos ejemplos sucintos:

> *Sobre el placer y el dolor.* Siento placer en un momento y dolor en otro. Pero soy inmutable todo el tiempo. Porque mi placer y mi dolor no son parte de mi naturaleza verdadera.
>
> *¿Cómo se relacionan los objetos físicos con los pensamientos?* La pregunta surge del supuesto de que los objetos existen independientes de los pensamientos. Eso nunca es el caso. Sin el pensamiento no existe el objeto.
>
> *¿Deberíamos seguir a un Dios personal?* Yo digo que no, porque un Dios personal no es nada más que un concepto. La verdad está más allá de todos los conceptos.

Esta certeza tan sólida se siente liberadora y audaz al mismo tiempo. Pero es claro que Menon no hablaba sólo para atraer la atención a sí mismo; hablaba desde la perspectiva del ser verdadero, una vez que la personalidad del ego y la mente fragmentada que ésta crea han sido abandonadas. Esto se evidencia en otra pregunta y respuesta.

P: ¿La realidad es indivisible?

R: La realidad es sólo una y no puede ser afectada por calidad o grado de ninguna forma. La realidad es puramente subjetiva. Yo soy el único sujeto y todo el resto son objetos. La diversidad puede ser diversidad solamente a través de mí, el "Uno".

Tienes que alcanzar el final de esta respuesta para descubrir que, lejos de ser una expresión de solipsismo ("Yo soy el único sujeto y todo el resto son objetos"), el punto de vista de Menon refleja su sentido de la totalidad (el Uno). Esta forma de hablar recuerda a una tradición hindú de hace miles de años, conocida como Advaita, que en sánscrito significa "no-dos". También podríamos llamarla la perspectiva de la mente total, porque el propósito primario de Advaita (y del metahumano) es lograr que la gente se identifique con la conciencia como un todo, y no con sus productos fragmentados.

He llegado al punto en que dudo en adoptar un lenguaje espiritual, y prefiero ver el viaje interno como un escape de la ilusión hacia la realidad. La pregunta sigue ahí: si Menon, junto con otros que son llamados iluminados, son tan excepcionales, ¿están muy lejos de la norma? Yo digo que no. El proceso de despertar es natural; cualquiera puede hacerlo. La prueba de esto se encuentra ante nuestros ojos. Diario seguimos la guía de la personalidad del ego, el ser inconsciente y el ser verdadero en una especie de revoltijo. Pero el solo hecho de que el ser verdadero nos hable en momentos de amor, alegría, creatividad y renovación, aunque sólo sea de forma intermitente, indica que estamos en contacto con la metarrealidad. Al saber que existe la conexión, todo el proceso de despertar puede ser explorado de manera organizada. Cómo se hace esto es el tema del siguiente capítulo en nuestro viaje.

8

IR MÁS ALLÁ DE TODAS LAS HISTORIAS

Si la metarrealidad es "todo, siempre y en todas partes", entonces ocurre un hecho asombroso. No hay ninguna historia que podamos contar al respecto. Todos los elementos de una historia —inicio, argumento, varios personajes y final— no tienen cabida. Sin embargo, todo lo demás en el mundo está organizado alrededor de estos elementos. Tú eres un personaje en tu propia historia, la cual tuvo su comienzo en el nacimiento y su final en la muerte, y todo tipo de giros en la trama y personajes incidentales a lo largo del camino. El prospecto de renunciar a tu historia es impensable, pero es totalmente necesario para experimentar la metarrealidad. Incluso también debemos renunciar a historias místicas, religiosas y espirituales, porque éstas convierten a la conciencia pura en algo que no es, ya sea que ese algo es el Dios del Viejo Testamento, el Nirvana o un panteón de dioses y diosas. Yo valoro que éstas han sido una luz de guía durante siglos. Los mensajeros aislados siempre han existido para señalar otro mundo, y traen con ellos historias inspiradoras.

En sus representaciones de la Virgen y el Niño, Leonardo da Vinci siguió la historia tradicional de que san Juan siendo niño fue compañero de Jesús en su infancia. Leonardo (y otros pintores renacentistas) lo muestra señalando enigmáticamente hacia lo alto con un dedo, y con una sonrisa beatífica en su rostro. *El cielo, ¿no puedes verlo? Ahí está*, dice su sonrisa.

Aquellos que despiertan ven el mundo trascendente de forma directa. El marco de tiempo de la eternidad se vuelve natural y se siente como un flujo continuo. Buda una vez dijo (en una traducción de Sogyal Rinpoche): "Esta existencia nuestra es tan transitoria como las nubes de otoño. Observar el nacimiento y la muerte de los seres es como mirar los movimientos de una danza. Una vida es como el destello de un relámpago en el cielo, lanzándose como un torrente que desciende de una montaña escarpada".

En todas las tradiciones espirituales, este tipo de mensajes han atraído a los creyentes al mundo trascendental, pero todos ellos han fracasado en convencer a la persona promedio de que ir más allá debería ser el centro de la vida cotidiana. En ningún punto de la historia se hizo viral el despertar. En algún lugar de la evolución de la conciencia el *Homo sapiens* se enfrentó con una encrucijada en el camino. Colectivamente podríamos habernos identificado con el ser verdadero o bien podríamos habernos identificado con "Yo", la personalidad del ego. Obviamente, tomamos el segundo camino. La metarrealidad no nos abandonó; nosotros la abandonamos a ella.

Esto marcó toda la diferencia sobre cómo nos vemos a nosotros mismos. El ser verdadero está conectado a su fuente en la conciencia pura. La personalidad del ego tiene su fuente sólo en las historias que imagina y que cree. La gente moderna ha desechado la mitología, y muchos rechazan la religión organizada. Pero en todos los niveles nuestra vida sigue siendo moldeada por historias que han sido inventadas por la imaginación humana. El otro camino, que conducía al ser verdadero, ganó reputación por ser místico (es decir, desapegado de la vida real), y una vez que esto sucedió, sólo un grupo variopinto de santos, eruditos, poetas, artistas y profetas siguieron ese camino.

Encontrar la metarrealidad es una tarea imposible hasta que cuestionas tu propia historia. Debes asumir el reto de forma personal, porque el metahumano es sólo real si es real *para ti*. Si estás plenamente consciente de lo que te está sucediendo aquí y ahora, has ido más allá de todas las historias. El hábito de añadir algo a tu historia constantemente es sólo eso, un hábito. Por sí mismo, el momento presente no tiene historia, tan sólo es. ¿Por qué lo embellecemos con nuestra historia? Porque el momento presente no es satisfactorio por sí mismo, sino hasta que es enriquecido por el ser verdadero. Una computadora es inútil hasta que la conectas, y aunque ya usamos nuestra mente para todo, perdemos mucho tiempo en la fantasía, las distracciones, la evasión, la negación, la procrastinación, el juicio a uno mismo, y muchas cosas más. Cada historia contiene estos elementos no deseables. Permanecer conectado al ser verdadero en cada momento trae a nuestra conciencia la plenitud de la vida.

El metahumano podría ser llamado una nueva historia, otra ficción añadida al estante de la biblioteca, pero pienso que no sería un nombre apropiado. Cuando despiertas, el elemento de la ficción se extrae. Como parte del hechizo/sueño/ilusión, nuestras historias personales no son posibles sin el elemento ficticio. Para empezar, la realidad virtual es una ficción. Cualquier cosa basada en ella participa de la irrealidad. Podríamos compadecernos de nuestros ancestros por su apego a los mitos, supersticiones y creencias religiosas no demostradas. Pero si estamos inmersos en una historia mejor que la suya, de todas formas es una historia. Las generaciones futuras no creerán nuestra historia más de lo que nosotros creemos en Zeus, las brujas y el corazón como la sede de la inteligencia humana en vez del cerebro (ésta era una creencia persistente en la medicina de la antigua Grecia y Roma).

Este capítulo se trata de un parteaguas en el que dejamos de contarnos historias a nosotros mismos, porque ya no las necesitamos para defendernos de la dura realidad ni para darle sentido a un mundo caótico. En la metarrealidad vas más allá del peligro y el desorden. El ser verdadero te da una postura imperturbable en la realidad, y en ese punto tu vida encuentra propósito y significado desde la fuente, y no de una ficción improvisada.

Aferrarse a las historias

Los seres humanos se enorgullecen de ser contadores de historias, y nuestra historia tiene un hueco porque antes de que surgiera la escritura no hay ningún registro de los tiempos más antiguos. ¿Podemos imaginar tantas historias perdidas? Hace unos 45 000 años la gente que reconoceríamos como *Homo sapiens* modernos comenzó a migrar hacia el norte desde África. Todos ellos eran cazadores-recolectores. Muchas generaciones antes de la agricultura, la extracción de metales y moradas fijas fueron heraldos del surgimiento de la civilización, y la vida hace 45 000 años ya era demasiado compleja para arreglárselas sin historias. En la mente humana, el fuego debía provenir de alguna parte, la lluvia era impredecible por algún motivo, y las cosas que hoy damos por hecho, como un pollo saliendo de un huevo, planteaban un gran misterio. La mitología no surgió como fantasía, sino como la mejor forma de explicar la naturaleza, dada la vida que llevaba la gente. Asignarle un significado a cualquier cosa y a todas las cosas es el hilo que nos conecta con los primeros humanos. Las historias explican cómo funciona la vida y por ella satisfacen una necesidad que está tejida en la estructura de ser humano.

Todavía vivimos a partir de historias, y lo que perturba nuestra historia personal a menudo se rechaza de inmediato o se lucha contra ello intensamente. (Observa cómo los abusadores sexuales más culpables salen a la luz con el movimiento de #MeToo, abusadores que niegan de forma rotunda haber cometido cualquier tipo de ofensa.) Ya hemos discutido sobre la manera en que el ego crea la ilusión de estar separados y solos. "Yo" necesita una buena historia para sentirse seguro, importante, aceptable socialmente y valioso. Al buscar sentirse seguras, las personas desean pertenecer a algo más grande que ellas mismas —una tribu, una religión, una raza, una nación—, pero para ser aceptadas por cualquiera de estos grupos primero debes aceptar su historia. Sin pensar en la libertad que están perdiendo, la gente acepta una historia de segunda mano y aislada. Tú sabes al instante quién es "nosotros" y quién es "ellos". Y aun así, sin importar qué tan convincente sea la historia, siempre serás "ellos" para la gente que está embebida en otra historia. La seguridad que encuentras en algo más grande que tú mismo se desmorona cuando "ellos" se convierten en una amenaza, incluso un enemigo de tu propia supervivencia.

Las historias surgen de necesidades tan básicas que parece imposible ir más allá de cualquier historia. Una historia consiste en cualquier cosa que la mente humana pueda imaginar, lo que conduce a opciones infinitas. Pero podemos simplificar el asunto. Las historias son acerca del apego. Pensamos "Yo soy X", y entonces nos aferramos a X como parte de nuestra identidad.

X puede ser el grupo más grande (tribu, raza, nación, religión) antes mencionado. "Yo soy estadounidense" tiene un mayor poder sobre las personas, al igual que "Yo soy francés", "Yo soy judío" o "Yo soy blanco". Pero al ver esto, lo cual la mayoría de la gente ve, sólo estamos rascando la superficie. Cualquier versión de "Yo soy X" puede conducir a aferrarse y apegarse. "Yo soy un fanático de los Patriots" o "Yo soy de clase media alta" crea apegos pasionales. Al mismo tiempo, las historias se vuelven más potentes por aquello que excluyen. Para cada "Yo soy X" hay el mismo número de posibilidades de "Yo no soy Y". Si eres estadounidense, no eres de ninguna otra nacionalidad, y hay cientos de ellas. Si eres católico, excluyes todas las demás creencias religiosas, y así sucesivamente.

¿Qué tiene esto de malo? Si las historias fueran tomadas a la ligera, de la misma forma en que experimentamos *El Hobbit* o *El gran Gatsby*, divertirnos por un rato antes de seguir adelante, no habría problemas. La historia no es la responsable, sino tu apego a ella. El apego falsifica la experiencia al congelarla en su sitio. El peso del pasado se convierte en una carga. El momento presente se pierde en la maraña de la memoria, las creencias y los viejos condicionamientos. ¿Cuántas personas mayores desean ser jóvenes de nuevo? ¿Cuántos remordimientos albergamos y nos negamos a soltarlos? Estos apegos existen en la vida diaria de todos, sin contar la miseria y la violencia creadas por cualquier mentalidad del tipo "nosotros contra ellos".

La separación de una persona de una historia preciada es el tema central de uno de los *bestsellers* más populares de la década de 1980: *La nueva psicología del amor,* de M. Scott Peck. El libro comienza con una frase fascinante: "La vida es difícil". De inmediato, Peck se explaya sobre lo que quiere decir: "Ésta es una gran verdad, una de las más grandes verdades. Es una gran verdad porque una vez que vemos esta verdad, la trascendemos [... y] el hecho de que la vida es difícil ya no importa".

En otras palabras, estamos escuchando el llamado a ir más allá. Pero Peck, que era psiquiatra, sabía que sólo porque una verdad es grande no significa que la gente pueda enfrentarla, sino al contrario. Desde su punto de vista, después de años de tratar pacientes en terapia, el mayor obstáculo que enfrentaban sus pacientes para mejorar era su rechazo a tomar responsabilidad. ¿Por qué? "No podemos resolver los problemas de la vida si no es resolviéndolos", escribe Peck. Pero este hecho "al parecer está más allá de la comprensión de gran parte de la raza humana [...] Muchos, muchísimos, buscan evitar el dolor de sus problemas al decirse a sí mismos: 'Este problema fue causado por otras personas, o por circunstancias sociales fuera de mi control, y por ello otras personas deben resolverme este problema'".

Peck ofrece ejemplos vívidos para ilustrar este punto, como el caso de una mujer que acababa de intentar cortarse las venas. Era esposa de un militar en la isla Okinawa, en el Pacífico, donde el joven Peck era un psiquiatra del ejército.

En la sala de urgencias le preguntó a la mujer, quien había logrado hacerse sólo heridas superficiales, por qué quería suicidarse. Ella dijo que todo se reducía a vivir en "esta tonta isla". Peck no estuvo satisfecho con su respuesta, así que comenzó un diálogo que sería cómico si la mujer no se sintiera tan miserable e infeliz. El diálogo entre él y su paciente se puede resumir de la siguiente manera:

PECK: ¿Por qué es tan doloroso para ti vivir en Okinawa?

PACIENTE: No tengo amigos y estoy sola todo el tiempo.

PECK: ¿Por qué no tienes amigos?

PACIENTE: Vivo a las afueras, en el pueblo, y nadie habla inglés.

PECK: ¿Por qué no manejas al centro y encuentras algunos amigos?

PACIENTE: Porque mi esposo necesita el coche para ir a trabajar.

PECK: Podrías llevarlo al trabajo.

PACIENTE: Es un coche de velocidades. Yo sólo sé manejar automáticos.

PECK: Podrías aprender a manejar un coche de velocidades.

PACIENTE: ¿Está loco? En estos caminos no se puede.

Lo que hace que esta escena sea trágica y cómica al mismo tiempo es que la mujer, a pesar de su terquedad absurda, tenía un sufrimiento genuino; estuvo llorando la mayor parte de la conversación. Todos creemos en nuestra historia, casi a cualquier costo. Desde la perspectiva de un terapeuta, esta mujer estaba eludiendo cualquier esperanza de mejorar al exhibir todos los signos clásicos de negación. ¿Quiénes de nosotros no hemos cerrado los ojos cuando era demasiado difícil enfrentar una situación? La vida sería mucho más fácil si nuestros problemas tuvieran soluciones claras y simples, pero no las tienen.

La negación es sólo un elemento en el panorama general, el cual es que vivimos a través de historias. En esencia la negación es ignorar cualquier cosa que perturbe tu historia o la contradiga. Incluso la persona más saludable psicológicamente ignora una parte enorme de la realidad. Si vemos, de una vez por todas, que nuestro apego a las historias es lo que queremos superar, reconocemos que hay personas que han hecho justamente eso. Su mundo interno no está repleto de bagaje del pasado. No defienden "Yo soy X" como si su supervivencia dependiera de ello. En cambio, viven en el presente sin esfuerzo alguno. El asunto real no es si existe este tipo de personas; el asunto real es por qué las hemos ignorado por tanto tiempo.

Los que han despertado

Los estados de conciencia que han sido considerados místicos en Occidente por mucho tiempo —si no son falsos— existen a todo nuestro alrededor, afectando a la gente ordinaria que casi siempre mantiene sus experiencias en privado. Hace unos años conocí al doctor Jeffery Martin, un investigador social con doctorado que había conducido una investigación innovadora sobre la conciencia superior. Sus estudios eran revolucionarios por un solo descubrimiento básico: muchas más personas están despiertas de lo que uno podría suponer.

Martin les dio voz. Después de obtener su doctorado en la Escuela de Educación de Harvard, comenzó a publicar sus descubrimientos, que indicaban la prevalencia de la iluminación como un estado natural de conciencia, al cual muchas personas ya habían accedido. La investigación de Martin comenzó cuando él publicó un cuestionario en línea pidiendo respuestas de personas que él pensaba que estaban iluminadas.

Para su sorpresa, obtuvo más de 2 500 respuestas, y de todas ellas Martin entrevistó intensamente a unos 50 sujetos. Al principio era difícil encontrar un lenguaje común. Sentir que eres iluminado es algo personal, y también te separa de la sociedad normal. Los sujetos de Martin habían sido sensibilizados por ser marginados, a menudo habían sido estigmatizados en su adolescencia por ser diferentes. También sabían en su interior que no eran normales de acuerdo con los estándares sociales a su alrededor. Para muchos, revelar su estado mental inusual los había conducido a cosas como ser enviados al psiquiatra, ser medicados e incluso ser internados en un hospital psiquiátrico.

Sin embargo, muy al inicio, Martin se dio cuenta de que sin importar lo diferente que era cada uno de sus sujetos, sus experiencias eran continuas. No había sólo un estado de iluminación, sino más bien un proceso gradual. Para encontrar un terreno común y para adaptarse al modelo aceptado de cómo debe ser una investigación doctoral en psicología, dejó el cargado término *iluminación* y en su lugar adoptó la complicada etiqueta de *experiencia no simbólica persistente*. Cuando alguien comienza a tener este tipo de experiencias

IR MÁS ALLÁ DE TODAS LAS HISTORIAS 223

"hay un cambio en lo que se siente ser tú", afirma Martin. "Te alejas de un sentido individual de ser, que es considerado normal, hacia otra cosa."

No fue fácil definir qué es esa "otra cosa", porque estas personas provenían de entornos muy diferentes y estaban influidas por diversos factores culturales. Sin embargo, Martin pudo identificar áreas específicas que parecían destacarse como marcadores de una conciencia elevada.

Generalmente estas personas decían que habían perdido el sentido de ser seres separados, no tenían una noción persistente de identidad personal. Al ponerse en los zapatos de sus sujetos, Martin comenta: "Yo estaría diciendo: 'Aquí no hay un Jeffery hablándote'. Eso es literalmente lo que ellos me decían".

Otra experiencia común fue una reducción dramática en el pensamiento. "De hecho —dice Martin—, a menudo reportaban que no tenían pensamientos." Esto no era una verdad literal, como Martin descubrió cuando investigó más extensamente, pero como informe personal, no tener pensamiento alguno es sorprendente. Otra experiencia común fue un sentido de unidad, totalidad e integridad. Este estado de totalidad, dice Martin, condujo a una tremenda sensación de libertad personal. "Con esto viene una pérdida del miedo, una pérdida de la identificación con una historia personal." Muchos de ellos sentían que su cuerpo ya no estaba limitado por la piel, sino extendido más allá del cuerpo físico.

Así que ahora podemos tener un perfil objetivo del cambio hacia la conciencia superior en la vida cotidiana, el estado del metahumano. El despertar personal no es raro, y de acuerdo con aquellos que lo han experimentado, su despertar los llevó a una amplia gama de posibilidades. Las implicaciones de la naturaleza humana son intrigantes, comenzando con lo que se siente no defender "yo, mí y mío".

La fuente de tanto enojo, miedo, avaricia y envidia está arraigada en la inseguridad del ego y sus demandas infinitas.

Al ponernos en sus zapatos, estas personas despiertas no mantienen una historia en su mente sobre lo que le está sucediendo a "mí". Cuando piensan sobre sí mismos, "mí" se desvanece en cuanto lo notan. Lo mismo sucede para sus emociones, que son menos y más espontáneas. Cuando surge la ira, se desvanece casi de inmediato. Las emociones siguen siendo positivas y negativas, pero rara vez, si acaso, son extremas. Los sujetos de Martin podían sentirse irritados cuando algo malo sucedía en el trabajo, pero no llevaban el estrés con ellos después de eso y nunca se convertía en una frustración furiosa. Sentían una paz interna que podía ser interrumpida, pero que regresaba bastante pronto. En pocas palabras, estas personas eran muy buenas para soltar.

Para ordenar sus descubrimientos, Martin dividió el estado de despertar en diversas "locaciones" como etapas separadas del despertar, de acuerdo con su intensidad. Sus sujetos consideraban el despertar como un cambio definitivo, lo cual para algunos ocurriría tan pronto como seis meses antes, y para otros hasta 40 años. Una vez que llegaron a la Locación 1, como Martin llama a la etapa inicial del despertar, la gente por lo regular seguía progresando y rara vez regresaba o se adelantaba. En otras palabras, estaban experimentando la evolución personal, y el proceso no mostraba perspectivas de detenerse. Como Martin describió su actitud, ellos "aceptaban que su transición inicial era sólo el comienzo de un proceso que parecía ser capaz de desenvolverse, y profundizar, sin fin; una aventura interminable". Todo sucedía internamente, y para muchos de ellos el cambio no era algo que definirían como espiritual. Era tan sólo la forma en que se experimentaban a sí mismos.

"Si te sientas en una habitación llena de individuos y un pequeño porcentaje pertenece a este estado alterado de sí mismos —dice Martin—, no podrías identificarlos. En todas las apariencias externas son como tú y como yo."

Entonces, ¿quiénes son exactamente estas personas? Al principio, antes de que la investigación de Martin comenzara a expandirse a muchas universidades y países, su sujeto típico era el hombre blanco de Estados Unidos o Europa. Martin se decepcionó al descubrir que las mujeres, por razones desconocidas, no tenían deseos de participar como iluminadas ni de discutir sobre sus experiencias de "despertar". Los entornos religiosos eran diversos, abarcando creencias de Oriente y Occidente, aunque la mayoría de los sujetos había realizado algún tipo de práctica espiritual —deseaban entrar en un estado superior de conciencia—. Curiosamente, alrededor de 14% no había hecho nada por el estilo. Habían entrado de forma espontánea a la conciencia superior o, más típicamente, por casualidad.

La base de la investigación de Martin se ha extendido a más de 1 000 sujetos, lo que significa que debemos preguntarnos a nosotros mismos si la conciencia "normal" no es para nada un estado fijo sino un espectro, y la conciencia evoluciona mucho más lejos de lo que cualquiera hubiera pronosticado con anterioridad. Por lo menos, la conciencia superior se ha vuelto mucho menos tóxica. Ya no es la provincia de sadhus y yoguis en los Himalayas.

Cuando nos comunicamos por correo electrónico y después nos conocimos en persona, acepté por qué Martin, por motivos académicos, debía permanecer neutral. Pero desde hace siglos el despertar se ha asociado con dicha, por ejemplo, o con la comunicación con seres superiores como los ángeles, o con sentir una presencia divina. ¿Acaso todo eso estaba ausente cuando la gente moderna despertaba? Martin me aseguró que los fenómenos "externos" estaban presentes, pero que se vio obligado a no mencionarlos en su tesis doctoral. Descubrió que la dimensión espiritual de algunos de sus sujetos también se había abierto. Algunas de las personas que examinó reportaban una conciencia abierta, clara y calmada asociada con el budismo. Pero otras no tenían idea de qué hacer con su estado de conciencia.

En reportes posteriores, Martin nota que un pequeño número de sus sujetos tuvo experiencias que desafiaban las explicaciones normales.

> [Un pequeño número] experimenta una sensación de dicha profunda a lo largo de todo su cuerpo, incluso durante momentos que podrían ser físicamente dolorosos. Para algunos esto implica tolerancias al dolor al parecer infinitas. Algunos han reportado experiencias que deberían haber implicado niveles terribles de dolor, pero sólo resultaron en dicha. Otras personas que experimentan la dicha constante descubren que pueden alcanzar sus límites. Reportan un umbral, único para cada individuo, por encima del cual se experimenta el dolor.

Resulta que, conforme profundizó en su investigación, Martin descubrió cada vez más singularidad entre estas personas. Más allá de la Locación 4 unos cuantos progresaban hasta llegar a la Locación 9, por ejemplo. Martin afirma que en esa locación la gente "diría algo como 'se siente como si el universo mirara a través de estos ojos' ". Pero hablando de forma general, todos sus sujetos estaban asombrados por el alto nivel de bienestar que experimentaban, y esto creció conforme avanzaban en el espectro. Paradójicamente, en la Locación 4, todas las emociones desaparecieron, incluso el amor, el cual Martin asocia con un cambio mayor —desaparece el ser que fue construido por medio de una historia continua (él lo llama el Cambio Narrativo), junto con las emociones socialmente definidas—. Después de la Locación 4, las emociones comienzan a regresar de forma distinta, basadas en los cimientos del bienestar continuo. Pero incluso antes de que regresen, los sujetos de Martin reportaron que no extrañaban la experiencia de las emociones, porque en la libertad habían encontrado el nivel más alto de bienestar.

Enseñar a la gente cómo despertar

Martin había hecho lo que él consideraba "el descubrimiento fundamental de que éstos eran estados psicológicos que habían sido identificados y adoptados por miles de años por diversas culturas y sistemas de creencias". En el ambiente actual, en el que la conciencia es un campo de crecimiento exponencial, el verdadero problema no es el escepticismo. En una encuesta se demostró que un tercio de los adultos estadounidenses cree en cosas que son consideradas ampliamente como alternativas o New Age, desde la reencarnación y lo paranormal, hasta aplicaciones médicas a las que se ha opuesto desde hace mucho tiempo la medicina convencional. (De acuerdo con varias fuentes, entre un tercio y 38% de los adultos estadounidenses usan la medicina alternativa. Esto incluye a los 30 millones de personas, por ejemplo, que visitan al quiropráctico cada año.)

Martin no era el único que decía que la conciencia superior no era "inherentemente espiritual o religiosa, o limitada a una cierta cultura o población". Dada su inclinación hacia lo académico y técnico, decidió poner su información a trabajar. Filtró las técnicas que sus sujetos consideraran las más poderosas para que lograran llevar a una conciencia superior, y las organizó en un curso de Buscadores de 15 semanas. Lo fascinante es que los estudiantes serían gente ordinaria que, por algún motivo, se sentía atraída hacia el curso.

Tres participantes se reunieron en el sitio de internet Reality Sandwich para reportar su experiencia: Catherine, una consultora de negocios y liderazgo de París; Paul, uno de los dueños y gerente de un centro de jardines en Gales, y Rebekah, una fotógrafa semirretirada de Texas.

Cada uno tenía motivos diferentes para tomar el curso. Paul describió un periodo de dificultades personales. "Me había vuelto desconectado, desilusionado, debido a asuntos físicos y materiales, sobre todo. Yo tuve una crianza muy espiritual, pero parecía haber perdido la trama en su conjunto." Su estado general "no era suicida, pero sí lo más bajo que podía estar".

Catherine había escuchado sobre la investigación de Martin y estaba interesada en la posibilidad de estados superiores de conciencia. En particular le interesó que estos estados podían ser descritos especialmente: "No es sólo nirvana todo el día. Mi objetivo era atravesar la experiencia y alcanzar estados más altos de bienestar y calma".

Rebekah no tenía experiencias previas. "No sabía qué esperar, sólo estaba abierta a lo que fuera." Pero había escuchado acerca de los proyectos de investigación de Martin y dijo: "Confiaba en lo científico de los proyectos". También sabía lo que deseaba obtener del curso. "Mi meta era la evolución espiritual. ¿Cómo puedo elevar mi conciencia a un nivel superior?".

Los métodos que les fueron presentados a los tres eran sumamente intensivos, sumaban de dos a tres horas al día, las cuales se esperaba que mantuvieran cuando volvieran a su vida cotidiana. La instrucción consistía en un video semanal acerca de lo que harían los participantes la siguiente semana. Antes del siguiente video, como Catherine lo describe, "haces un resumen de la semana. ¿Cómo te sientes? ¿Qué te ha sucedido? ¿Cuántas veces al día realizaste las diferentes actividades?". Había meditación y también un grupo de discusión. Algunos ejercicios venían directo de la terapia estándar, como escribir y perdonar a la gente de tu pasado que te ha lastimado.

Pero en el corazón del curso estaba la investigación de Martin de ocho años sobre la gente que se consideraba a sí misma iluminada. Le dio a cada uno un cuestionario sobre qué prácticas les parecían más útiles en su viaje, lo que derivó en una enorme cantidad de información. "Revisamos todo eso, y sólo un puñado de cosas sobresalió. Algunas de ellas cruzaban todas las tradiciones, como, por ejemplo, una práctica de meditación basada en un mantra." Otras técnicas eran más específicas. Por ejemplo, dice Martin, él adoptó un "método estilo conciencia directa. Esto implica poner tu atención en la conciencia misma. Eso suena simple, pero es bastante complicado, como estoy seguro de que te lo diría toda esta gente".

A partir de la retroalimentación de los estudiantes, él aprendió rápido que ciertas prácticas funcionaban mejor que otras para cada persona. Además, mezclaba las técnicas: "No todo son prácticas antiguas. También incluimos algunos de los ejercicios de referencia de la psicología positiva". De forma general, el curso tenía dos objetivos: aumentar el bienestar lo más pronto posible y profundizar la conciencia. El éxito resultante suena como algo extraordinario: "Más de 70% de los participantes que completaron el curso reporta tener formas persistentes de una experiencia de 'despertar', y 100% dice que es más feliz que antes de que comenzara el curso, incluso aquellos que se calificaron como 'muy infelices' al inicio del curso".

Paul, el gerente del centro de jardines, casi suicida, ofrece su testimonio personal al respecto: "Fue soltar la pereza; eso fue lo más grande que noté. Las nimiedades se iban, las preocupaciones y ansiedades del día a día estaban desapareciendo a una velocidad maravillosa.

Eso fue lo que resonó inicialmente para mí. La falta de miedo, de preocupación, de ansiedad. Eso fue el impacto más grande para mí al principio".

¿Así que tenemos una respuesta final? ¿El metahumano se ha vuelto algo accesible por medio de un coctel de psicoterapia, terapia de grupo, autoayuda, meditación y un programa tan personalizado como una rutina de ejercicios en el gimnasio? No existe una respuesta clara y simple. Muchísimas personas encuentran demasiados caminos para despertar. La investigación de Martin es sólo una versión de una tendencia para hacer de la mente una especie de proyecto tecno, y aunque él afirma que 70% de los participantes que experimentaron alguna forma de despertar continuó teniendo la experiencia, sólo el tiempo lo dirá. Sólo a las pocas personas dedicadas les atraerá realizar un cambio intensivo en su estilo de vida que incluya varias horas de práctica al día.

El misterio del despertar incluye al 14% en las encuestas de Martin que despertaron espontáneamente. Un día, sin advertencia alguna, se encontraron completamente conscientes de sí mismos o se deslizaron hacia ese estado con el tiempo, pero sin esfuerzo. Ya hemos hablado de un fenómeno similar, el síndrome del genio repentino (ver página 100), y existen casos raros en que la gente descubre de pronto que recuerda absolutamente todo lo que ha sucedido en su vida (un fenómeno conocido como "memoria autobiográfica superior"). Este tipo de personas pueden reunirse y hablar de cosas como: "¿Cuál fue el mejor martes de tu vida?", o recordar la canción de una serie de televisión que sólo se transmitió unas cuantas veces en la década de 1970.

En todos estos casos, la conciencia de una persona no acepta las limitaciones impuestas como normales. Bajo hipnosis, la gente ordinaria puede destapar recuerdos que de otra manera no podría recuperar, como conocer el número de rosales en un jardín de su infancia o cuántos escalones había para bajar al sótano en la casa de sus padres. ¿Es normal recordar u olvidar? Las dos, por supuesto. La información en bruto no filtrada nos bombardea en olas demasiado abrumadoras como para absorberlas, así que olvidamos y recordamos de forma selectiva. El punto de despertar es eliminar algunas barreras creadas por la memoria y otras barreras creadas por el olvido. La felicidad está bloqueada si sigues recordando y repitiendo dolores antiguos, pero eso es tan efectivo como si olvidas lo feliz que fuiste alguna vez —es cuestión de perspectiva—. Incluso se puede decir que la realidad virtual nos hace olvidar que debemos recordar quiénes somos realmente.

En su concepción más universal, la iluminación es simplemente la conciencia de uno mismo expandida. Vamos más allá de las historias, más allá de límites establecidos, más allá del constructo endeble de "Yo" y, al hacerlo, la conciencia se expande sin esfuerzo. Se expande naturalmente, por su propia voluntad, porque, para empezar, las historias, las fronteras y las limitaciones eran artificiales.

9

EL CAMINO DIRECTO

Los guías de la humanidad que nos conminan a emprender un cambio radical usan muchas tácticas, incluyendo la promesa religiosa de la paz eterna y la felicidad ilimitada, ya sea aquí o en la vida después de la muerte. Las zanahorias son el anzuelo, pero también está el palo, la persistencia del sufrimiento actual y el temor del sufrimiento que vendrá. El palo no hace que la gente cambie, porque incluso la amenaza máxima, el sufrimiento interminable en el fuego y el azufre, no puede competir con los impulsos de deseo y el comportamiento temerario que conllevan. La zanahoria no es mucho mejor. ¿Por qué deberíamos creer en recompensas divinas? Cualquiera puede darse cuenta de que muy a menudo la virtud no es recompensada, mientras que el pecado sí lo es. A los soldados les dicen que Dios está de su lado, lo cual ofrece una justificación divina para ir a la guerra. Pero, al mismo tiempo, instar a los soldados a aniquilar al enemigo contradice la enseñanza de que Dios prohíbe matar.

Cuando se utiliza a Dios para justificar el asesinato y condenarlo al mismo tiempo, estamos casi demasiado dentro del hechizo/sueño/ ilusión como para ser rescatados. Cada religión ha intentado volver más extravagantes las recompensas de la salvación, la redención, la iluminación, el despertar o como quieras llamarlo. Considera la parábola de la Casa en Llamas, que aparece en una escritura budista antigua, la Sutra del Loto.

La casa de un hombre rico está en llamas y, para su consternación, sus hijos se niegan a salir. Están tan absortos jugando con sus juguetes que ignoran las llamas a su alrededor. Frenéticamente, el hombre rico busca una solución, y se le ocurre una. Les dice a sus hijos que afuera de la casa les esperan mejores juguetes. Lo que más deseaban sus hijos era una carretilla jalada por una cabra, lo cual los habría hecho felices, pero una recompensa mucho más espléndida sería una carretilla con joyas incrustadas jalada por dos terneros blancos como la nieve.

Esta zanahoria, como la promesa de un banquete celestial preparado por Dios con Cristo sentado a la cabecera de la mesa, demuestra qué tan lejos irán las religiones para ganar adeptos. Pero, para muchos, estas promesas desorbitadas han perdido su poder de inspirar devoción. No pienso que la gente secular moderna sea menos fiel, sino que simplemente ha cambiado su fe en la religión hacia la ciencia. El hechizo/sueño/ilusión continúa cambiando. En las sociedades prósperas la mayoría de la gente vive en una ilusión mejorada repleta de las maravillas de la tecnología. ¿Por qué deberían renunciar a ello? Con exasperación auténtica, el gran poeta persa Rumi observa a la humanidad y le suplica: "¡Por qué se quedan en la prisión cuando la puerta está totalmente abierta!". La respuesta honesta es que nos gusta estar aquí. Se requirió una creatividad enorme para concebir el estado actual de nuestro sueño colectivo. Pero la clave no es la riqueza y el confort. A un nivel muy profundo, los humanos aceptamos tener una vida con mucho drama. El drama está motivado por los opuestos enfrentados de placer y dolor, deseo y repulsión, bien y mal, luz y oscuridad, nosotros contra ellos, mi Dios contra tu Dios, y así sucesivamente.

No hay señales de que el drama terminará algún día. Las amenazas más extremas, como el cambio climático global, sólo lo exacerban. Y con respecto a las nuevas zanahorias, dudo que el despertar pueda competir con ir al cielo o encontrar una carretilla con joyas incrustadas. Debe existir una forma de alcanzar al metahumano que no sea zanahoria ni palo. Esa forma sí existe; se conoce como el "camino directo". No ofrece castigo ni recompensa. ¿Qué más hay? Totalidad. A primera vista esta respuesta no es muy tentadora. Estamos muy acostumbrados al sistema de recompensas y castigos infligidos por la guerra de los opuestos. Pero la totalidad es sanadora, supera las heridas de la separación y del ser dividido. La totalidad es imperturbable y eterna. Es lo único que nadie ni nada te puede quitar, ni siquiera la muerte.

No quiero que estas cosas parezcan otro conjunto de recompensas. El camino directo no es una táctica furtiva para disfrazar al cielo con un nuevo vestuario. La realidad ya es total, y no necesita que los seres humanos la validemos. La totalidad es completamente real. El camino directo existe para mostrar el camino a la misma realidad. Si tiene éxito, el resultado será impredecible. La realidad está confrontada por el aquí y el ahora, en medio del cambio constante. El aquí y el ahora no puede ser retratado ni descrito. Pero al terminar la guerra de los opuestos la totalidad borra una realidad falsa: ninguna recompensa que podamos imaginar se compara con esto.

El camino directo, también conocido como el método directo, busca cambiar el sentido del ser de una persona. En vez de "Yo soy X", que nos obliga a identificarnos con partes y pedazos de la experiencia, nos sentimos satisfechos con "Yo soy". Esto es más que un giro semántico. "Yo soy" significa que te identificas con la existencia, y como la existencia contiene el potencial infinito de la conciencia, tú también lo contienes. El cambio a "Yo soy" involucra cada aspecto de la vida, y esto presenta un problema potencial. ¿Qué aspectos deberíamos confrontar primero: el cuerpo, la mente, el cerebro, la psicología, las relaciones, las creencias, o bien los hábitos y los viejos condicionamientos? No está claro que deberíamos darle prioridad a cualquiera de los anteriores, ni siquiera confrontarlos.

El camino directo no nos pide que pensemos en nuestros problemas a nivel intelectual o que analicemos los prospectos para el cambio interno. De hecho, el camino directo bordea todas las formas ordinarias de vernos y pensarnos a nosotros mismos. Para empezar, éstas fueron las que nos metieron en problemas. Las formas ordinarias de ver y de pensar están totalmente adaptadas a la realidad virtual. Debemos encontrar una forma distinta.

En mi experiencia, la palabra *directo* es complicada. Implica algo que sucede de inmediato, pero asistir a la universidad durante cuatro años es el camino directo para obtener una licenciatura, y cuatro años no es algo inmediato. *Directo* también implica algo fácil, eficiente, sin obstáculos. Esto aplica, por ejemplo, cuando se entrega un paquete *directamente* a tu casa. No tienes que tomarte la molestia ni gastar para manejar hasta la fábrica para obtener lo que contenga el paquete. Pero un sherpa liderando una travesía hacia la cima del Everest es justo lo opuesto: el camino puede ser directo, pero es arduo y está lleno de obstáculos.

Los orígenes del camino directo pueden ser rastreados a la India védica y la antigua Grecia, en los que el tema de despertar era ampliamente discutido. Concibieron muchas respuestas y formas de alcanzar la meta. Una encuesta detallada de todos estos caminos podría derivar en más confusión que nunca, porque los desacuerdos abundan entre los diversos enfoques. Se han soñado atajos, como aceptar a Cristo como el Hijo de Dios, una sola decisión que redime todos los pecados y abre las puertas del cielo. Eso es lo más directo posible. Por otra parte, un monje tibetano o budista, o un hindú devoto, pueden pasar su vida renunciando al mundo para vivir en un *ashram* en el bosque o en la cueva de una montaña. Esta opción presenta el prospecto de un viaje interno largo y difícil.

En este libro he estado describiendo la versión más simple y poderosa (creo) de un atajo, que es intercambiar la ilusión por la realidad. Defino *directo* como fácil, eficiente y natural. No hay necesidad de algo arduo y lleno de obstáculos. Insisto en un camino indoloro, porque he visto demasiado de lo opuesto. Algunas personas pasan años sintiéndose frustradas y decepcionadas, esforzándose por alcanzar alguna meta espiritual que permanece fuera de su alcance. Lo que desconcierta a la gente es que todo el proyecto espiritual se enreda en ideas erróneas y expectativas destinadas al fracaso. Permíteme enlistar los obstáculos que es más probable encontrar:

1. Confundir la meta por una especie de mejoría personal, al abandonar tu viejo ser imperfecto por uno nuevo y brillante.
2. Asumir que ya sabes cuál es la meta.
3. Esperar que una conciencia superior resuelva todos tus problemas.
4. Esforzarse y luchar para llegar rápido a alguna parte.
5. Seguir un método claro y directo, por lo regular respaldado por alguna autoridad espiritual famosa.
6. Esperar ser considerado con respeto, reverencia o devoción como un ser superior.
7. Ser sacudido por las altas y bajas de los éxitos y fracasos momentáneos.

Dudo que cualquiera que honestamente haya emprendido un viaje interior sea inmune a algunos o todos estos obstáculos. Existe un enorme hueco entre el lugar donde te encuentras hoy (que depende por completo de la mente activa) y la realidad que debes revelar. El despertar no es lo doloroso, sino los obstáculos. Están creados por la personalidad del ego que cree, equivocadamente, que merece su parte de los dulces que están a punto de caer del cielo.

Si te enfocas en tu experiencia aquí y ahora, el ego es irrelevante, y muchas distracciones pueden evitarse. Piensa sobre la crianza. Los padres atraviesan todo tipo de problemas, preocupaciones, crisis cotidianas y discusiones con sus hijos, pero sin duda ellos saben que los aman. En el camino directo constantemente refuerzas tu propósito, lo cual mantiene las distracciones a raya. Los antiguos vedas declaraban que todos estamos definidos por nuestros deseos más profundos. El deseo conduce a los pensamientos, los pensamientos derivan en palabras y acciones, y las acciones llevan a la satisfacción del deseo. Así que, de una forma muy básica, el deseo es todo lo que necesitas. Si tu deseo más profundo es despertar, escapar de la ilusión, revelar la realidad, y finalmente conocer quién eres en realidad, el mensaje se comunica. Tu deseo más profundo activa un nivel de conciencia que te llevará hasta la meta.

Aunque suene extraño, el camino directo es válido sólo si conduce al lugar donde ya estás. Cada uno de nosotros ya es un ser consciente y creativo. Ya estamos en un estado de totalidad, a pesar de nuestra lealtad a los constructos mentales que imponen todo tipo de limitaciones sobre nosotros. El único cambio necesario es un cambio de identidad, y aun así ningún cambio es tan trascendental como ése. Una vez que te *das cuenta* de que estás completo, la transformación del humano al metahumano ya ha ocurrido.

El mensaje secreto de la naturaleza

Lo que hace que ya seamos completos es que la naturaleza es un todo, y nosotros somos parte de la naturaleza. Este razonamiento es totalmente sólido, pero para mucha gente es difícil aceptarlo. La física moderna sostiene que el universo opera como un todo, y cada partícula subatómica está entretejida en el entramado cósmico. Pero el método de la ciencia es subdividir la naturaleza en partes cada vez más pequeñas, y conforme la investigación alcanza niveles más sutiles de la existencia, el todo se pierde de vista. Esto es más que sólo un fallo técnico. Una cuestión crucial está en juego. ¿Acaso el todo controla las partes, o es lo contrario, no hay un todo si no es por la acumulación de las partes? Un coche nuevo es una cosa completa; lo vemos como una sola imagen y nos referimos a él con una palabra. Pero con la misma facilidad podemos ver un coche como lo ve un mecánico, como un conjunto de partes: carburador, eje de transmisión, caja de velocidades y demás. Con poco o ningún esfuerzo, tu mente puede cambiar de un punto de vista a otro.

Lo mismo sucede con la manera en que te ves a ti mismo. En el espejo apareces como una cosa entera, un cuerpo; te refieres a ti mismo con una sola palabra, tu nombre. Pero si de pronto sientes un dolor agudo en la zona del apéndice vas rápido al doctor —una especie de mecánico automotor para tejidos y órganos— y te conviertes en un conjunto de partes. Tienes la opción de verte como un todo o como un conjunto de partes. Pero si lo pensamos, ¿qué es en esencia la totalidad? Es difícil imaginar una pregunta más desconcertante que ésta. Pero sin una respuesta es imposible vivir en la totalidad. Por fortuna, la naturaleza presenta algunas pistas ineludibles, de vuelta a la primera aparición de la vida sobre la Tierra. La vida comenzó hace 3 800 millones de años cuando el ARN apareció y tuvo la capacidad de dividirse y replicarse; 1 000 millones de años después aparecieron en la escena las células sin membranas exteriores, y si brincamos a 1 000 millones de años más tarde, los organismos unicelulares evolucionaron en organismos pluricelulares.

El salto a los organismos pluricelulares no fue debido a una necesidad física, sino que fue un avance creativo, uno impresionante. Por casi 3 000 millones de años, los organismos unicelulares prosperaban, mutando en nuevas especies en una cinta transportadora interminable (que todavía sigue existiendo en medio del océano, donde millones, quizá miles de millones de criaturas unicelulares desconocidas flotan en la superficie). Las formas de vida restringidas a una sola célula, o virus y bacterias incluso más primitivos, sobrepasan por mucho, en una proporción de 100 a 1, las formas de vida pluricelulares. El ADN ha logrado la capacidad de repeler peligros ambientales y se burla de la muerte. Tres billones de amibas, algas verde-azul y hongos simples que pueblan la Tierra hoy en día son clones de un ancestro, el cual murió como un objeto físico, pero es casi tan inmortal como un paquete de conocimiento dentro del ADN.

Con esta exitosa empresa que no mostraba señales de declinar, no había motivo para arriesgar la vida pluricelular, excepto uno: la exuberancia pura de la creatividad. El desafío básico en la creación de la vida pluricelular era cómo reproducir un organismo complejo cuyas partes movibles no son las mismas. La tarea era como entregarle a alguien el manubrio de una bicicleta de carreras y pedirle que construyera una bicicleta entera a partir de esa pieza, con el reto añadido de que nadie había visto una bicicleta antes. En tu cuerpo, dos células madre pueden estar en animación suspendida por meses o años, mezcladas con células totalmente formadas. Cuando una célula madre se detona hacia la actividad, se convierte específicamente en una célula sanguínea, cerebral, del hígado o cutánea, y no en una célula humana genérica. Las últimas células genéricas en el desarrollo humano desaparecieron en el vientre materno para la quinta semana del embarazo, cuando una bola de células genéricas (el cigoto) procedió a la etapa del embrión.

El embrión inicial no se parece para nada a un cuerpo humano en miniatura, pero su apariencia amorfa y rosada es engañosa. Conforme el cigoto emergía de un óvulo fertilizado, y después pasó de dos células a cuatro, a ocho, a 16 y así sucesivamente, el ADN ganaba tiempo. Con una sincronía precisa se enviaron nuevas instrucciones que alteraron el destino del embrión, acercándolo más a la forma humana. A cada nueva célula se le dio su propia identidad separada por medio de un conjunto asombrosamente complejo de señales químicas, el cual es incluso más extraordinario que el ADN por sí mismo. Estamos muy lejos de ser capaces de explicar cómo una célula comprende lo que debe hacer, pero sabemos el esquema general. En las siguientes semanas del desarrollo embrionario no sólo una célula cerebral se volverá distinta de una célula del hígado, sino que cada célula cerebral viaja a una locación específica, se engancha con células similares que han hecho el mismo viaje y emprende una empresa conjunta: crear un cerebro. Lo mismo sucede con cada célula del hígado.

Este proceso, conocido como "diferenciación celular", ha sido estudiado minuciosamente. Es fascinante observar la llamada migración neuronal, en la cual a las células cerebrales nacientes, que viajan desde su lugar de nacimiento, se les brindan caminos escurridizos para deslizarse y alcanzar la región del cerebro que se necesite para desarrollar la visión, la respuesta de lucha o huida, las emociones, el pensamiento superior y demás. (Estoy ofreciendo una imagen simplificada, ya que la migración neuronal tiene múltiples etapas y es extremadamente compleja.) La célula parece una bolsa blanda de agua y químicos solubles, pero de hecho es el almacén de cada pedacito de conocimiento que pertenece a la historia de la vida en la Tierra.

La creación se ve como un proceso que se desenvuelve paso a paso, pedazo a pedazo, pero detrás de su apariencia una realidad crea, gobierna y controla todo. Dividir la vida en las partes que la componen —los pedazos y las partes físicas— es algo totalmente artificial. Ya sea que volvamos atrás 3 000 millones de años o al momento en que fuiste concebido en el vientre de tu madre, el mismo mensaje oculto está presente. El todo está contenido en las partes. Sin el todo, las partes no tienen sentido.

La autorregulación: pegamento de la existencia

Si el todo crea, gobierna y controla las partes, ¿podemos observar cuando lo hace? La ciencia no niega que el universo opera como un todo, pero los científicos siguen insistiendo en que gracias a las fuerzas físicas todo está pegado. Como sucede con todo en la realidad virtual, se ha inventado una historia para satisfacer la creencia de que el universo *debe* ser físico. El pegamento que en realidad hace que todo esté unido para nada es físico. Consiste en la *autorregulación*, o la capacidad que tiene cada sistema de permanecer intacto en su propio mundo.

La autorregulación es el motivo por el cual las células cerebrales saben que no deben ser células del hígado o del corazón. La autorregulación es el motivo por el cual tu cuerpo no se convierte en una nube de átomos de hidrógeno, carbono, oxígeno y nitrógeno. La autorregulación no tiene propiedades físicas —no es materia ni energía— porque es una cualidad de la totalidad misma. Para mostrar la exquisita delicadeza de este pegamento invisible, considera cómo es que el aumento de sólo unos cuantos grados en la temperatura del océano conduce a la destrucción de arrecifes de coral en todo el mundo. (También hay otros motivos, incluyendo la contaminación del agua, depredadores y enfermedades.) El fenómeno se conoce como "ola marina de calor"; estas olas atacaron la Gran Barrera de Coral de Australia en 1998 y 2002, pero sólo ocasionaron un daño limitado.

Cuando la temperatura del agua se eleva repentinamente, un arrecife emprende su autodestrucción por medio de la "decoloración del coral" —los corales, que para sobrevivir tienen una dependencia simbiótica con las algas que viven dentro de ellos, se estresan y expulsan el alga, la cual también le daba al coral sus colores brillantes—. Cuando el alga se va, el coral se blanquea y muere. Durante nueve meses en 2016 sucedió la repentina muerte de enormes porciones de la Gran Barrera de Coral, cuando una ola marina de calor afectó tres cuartas partes de los arrecifes del mundo (estas olas de calor habían comenzado a intensificarse desde 2014). "Perdimos 30% de los corales en el periodo de nueve meses entre marzo y noviembre de 2016", dijo un vocero del grupo de estudio que monitorea el arrecife. En 2017 hubo más olas marinas de calor, las cuales afectaron todas las partes de la Gran Barrera de Coral, incluyendo secciones centrales que habían logrado resistir la destrucción previa. Los corales de crecimiento más rápido pueden reconstituirse en 10 o 12 años, pero las olas marinas de calor de fuerza destructiva regresan cada seis años, en promedio.

Todo esto ha sido provocado por nuestro fracaso en evitar que las temperaturas del océano se eleven 2 °C desde la época preindustrial, o desde hace unos 100 años. Un cambio mínimo en la temperatura que apenas podrías percibir al meter la mano en agua tibia fue lo suficiente para inclinar el equilibrio de un sistema complejo de autorregulación que data de hace 535 millones de años. Pero la lección va mucho más allá. Un arrecife de coral es un megasistema que envuelve sistemas más pequeños: todos los tipos de peces y otras criaturas marinas, organismos unicelulares más abajo en la cadena alimentaria, las células que son la base de la vida y el ADN mismo. Cada sistema tiene sus propias reglas de autorregulación. Construyen sus propios límites para la supervivencia. Pero cuando se ven desde el megasistema, abarcando a toda la comunidad del arrecife, la totalidad domina por encima de la separación.

Podemos aplicar esta lección a nuestro cuerpo. Cuando acurrucas a un bebé, su piel cálida y suave se siente bien, pero si la temperatura empieza a bajar es signo de una amenaza potencial. Partiendo de una temperatura corporal normal, que es entre 36.5 y 37.5 °C, comenzamos a sentir frío a los 36 °C y la hipotermia comienza a partir de los 35 °C, la misma pequeña variación que amenaza al coral.

Si la temperatura corporal de una persona baja a 32 °C se declara una emergencia médica, y surgen diversos síntomas como delirio y alucinaciones. Debajo de 31 °C el cuerpo entra en coma. El latido irregular del corazón amenaza con la muerte, la cual ocurre con seguridad entre los 23 y 24 °C. En cualquier momento dado, aunque seamos saludables, estamos a apenas 15 grados de la muerte, menos que los cambios de temperatura durante un día de verano en las Montañas Rocallosas. ¿Cómo podemos estar bajo control? La pregunta básica quizá se respondió en la era de los dinosaurios. La especulación actual es que, a diferencia de los reptiles, los dinosaurios eran animales de sangre caliente.

Una vez más esto fue un salto creativo sin necesidad física apremiante. Las criaturas de sangre fría habían existido por más de 1 000 millones de años, tanto unicelulares como pluricelulares. Respiraron, se alimentaron, expulsaron desechos, se reprodujeron y sobrevivieron la severidad de los embates del medio ambiente. Todo esto sucedió, y sigue sucediendo, sin un elemento clave: convertir en calor algo de la energía contenida en el alimento, suficiente energía para mantener la temperatura interna del cuerpo lo bastante alta de forma constante para la supervivencia, incluso cuando la temperatura externa bajaba demasiado.

La autorregulación se encuentra en todos los niveles de la naturaleza, comenzando con el átomo, que se mantiene intacto sin correr como un juguete de cuerda ni deshacerse en sus partes más pequeñas (electrones, protones y neutrones). Esto basta para demostrar que la autorregulación es como opera la totalidad sin la necesidad de la materia o la energía como su pegamento. Aún más, en un sistema complejo como el cuerpo humano, cada célula sabe que debe vivir para el todo, no para sí misma solamente. Las células que optan por ser egoístas y se multiplican con desenfreno son cancerígenas, y la recompensa por su división rampante es su muerte y la muerte del cuerpo. Las células normales y saludables hacen de todo —comer, expulsar desechos, reproducirse, sanar y morir— y su meta principal es la supervivencia de todo el cuerpo, no la supervivencia individual.

El sentido del ser

La discusión sobre la autorregulación nos da un punto de apoyo sobre cómo funciona la totalidad. He estado insistiendo en que todo en la creación de hecho es un modo de conciencia. Una célula es un modo de conciencia, trayendo consigo todas cualidades de la conciencia, incluyendo el saber. Es literalmente verdad que una célula cerebral sabe que es una célula cerebral. La autorregulación no es un proceso mecánico. Surge de un sentido del ser. Como persona, tienes un sentido del ser que abarca cientos de sistemas de autorregulación, al igual que un arrecife de coral. Tú eres la totalidad que necesitan las partes para existir. Podemos llamar a esto una "teoría de arriba abajo", porque no puede haber autorregulación sin que el universo entero tenga un sentido del ser desde el principio. El todo crea, controla y gobierna cada evento.

Lo opuesto a ello es una teoría de abajo hacia arriba, la visión científica convencional de que las partes se unen para ensamblar el todo. Sin embargo, la autorregulación nunca fue creada físicamente. Es parte de como funciona la conciencia. Pero solo vamos a la mitad de camino en nuestras investigaciones. Hasta ahora la discusión es más que suficiente para demostrar que eres una maravilla de autorregulación, en lo que respecta al cuerpo. Pero despertar se trata de la mente y, como todos lo saben, nuestros pensamientos pueden llegar a ser salvajes al grado de la locura, y como sea, el siguiente pensamiento que tenga cualquier persona es totalmente impredecible. Podrías pensar en nosotros como pasajeros indisciplinados, manejando por la vida en un vehículo ensamblado a la perfección, con el cuerpo operando como un todo mientras que la mente deambula con temeridad de un pensamiento, sentimiento, sensación y emoción al siguiente.

El camino directo está basado en que la realidad es una cosa, una totalidad que podemos vivir en lo cotidiano. Es muy disparatado creer que vivimos con una mente total. La mente de todos parece una pila inútil de impulsos misceláneos aventados en un montón, del cual nos esforzamos para extraer un comportamiento razonable y socialmente aceptable. Esta disparidad entre un cuerpo exquisitamente regulado y una mente temeraria no regulada no ha pasado desapercibida por la neurociencia y ha generado un misterio desconcertante. De acuerdo con la neurociencia, los pensamientos son creados por las células cerebrales. Las células cerebrales operan por medio de las leyes inmutables del electromagnetismo, las cuales no dejan espacio para maniobrar. Los impulsos eléctricos y las reacciones químicas no tienen libre albedrío. Se comportan de la misma forma en una célula cerebral que como lo harían en la pila de una linterna o en la corriente de una casa. Entonces, ¿cómo fue que esta configuración inmutable y determinista derivó en la libertad de pensamiento?

Una respuesta, que suena peculiar, pero que es sostenida por muchos, da cuenta de que no tenemos libertad de pensamiento. Sólo pensamos que la tenemos (lo cual no constituiría un pensamiento libre, pero dejémoslo así). La agitación de la actividad cerebral es tan compleja, afirma la teoría, que no podemos descubrir de dónde proviene cualquier pensamiento particular. Pero dado que *debe* venir de la actividad cerebral, un pensamiento es tan determinado como las reacciones electroquímicas que lo producen. Esta hipótesis casi se salta la imprevisibilidad total de nuestros pensamientos y sentimientos. Si no tienes un ojo que todo lo ve que pueda mirar los 100 000 millones de células cerebrales, por supuesto que tus pensamientos parecerán impredecibles. Sólo una supercomputadora podría procesar semejante montaña de información, y si la tecnología de la informática sigue expandiéndose a un índice exponencial, muy pronto existirá ese ojo que lo ve todo.

Desde este punto de vista, la inteligencia artificial (IA) es superior al cerebro humano, no sólo porque procesa más información, sino porque está libre de fallas como la depresión, la ansiedad, un coeficiente intelectual bajo, las emociones caprichosas y el olvido. Nunca debemos subestimar la tecnología, o eso dice esta forma de pensar. Anticipándose al surgimiento de la IA como algo casi divino, Anthony Levandowski, conocido en Silicon Valley por su contribución a los autos sin conductor y como un visionario pionero en la IA, obtuvo la atención de los medios en 2017 al fundar la primera iglesia de inteligencia artificial, la cual nombró Way of the Future (Camino del Futuro). Levandowski está en busca de adeptos y prevé una divinidad de inteligencia artificial no como algo ridículo sino inevitable.

Como le dijo a un entrevistador de la revista *Wired*: "No es un dios en el sentido de que crea relámpagos o provoca huracanes. Pero si existe algo mil millones de veces más inteligente que el humano más inteligente, ¿cómo lo llamarías?". Lo que salva a Camino del Futuro de ser una parodia es el impacto enorme que la inteligencia artificial tendrá en todos lados. El entrevistador de *Wired* escribe: "Levandowski cree que viene un cambio, un cambio que transformará todos los aspectos de la existencia humana y que afectará el empleo, el esparcimiento, la religión, la economía y posiblemente decidirá nuestra supervivencia como especie".

Todo mundo es libre de preocuparse por un futuro hueco y deshumanizado con la inteligencia artificial, poblado por dioses falsos, pero otros escenarios del fin del mundo podrían suceder primero. Es casi seguro que se invente una supercomputadora con alcance global como arma de superhackeo (o que se convierta a sí misma en un arma), capaz de hacer un daño inmenso, desde inhabilitar las defensas de seguridad hasta arruinar el sistema bancario. Por desgracia, este tipo de ataques ya está en movimiento todos los días.

De cualquier manera, lo *artificial* en la IA evita que las computadoras estén vivas y sean conscientes: la velocidad, la memoria y la complejidad aumentadas sólo mejoran la imitación del pensamiento. La imitación no es pensamiento en sí mismo. Una computadora nunca tendrá un sentido del ser, que es un rasgo primario de la conciencia. Después de todo, gracias a nuestro sentido del ser creamos las computadoras. "Yo puedo pensar" es parte de ser consciente de uno mismo. Una vez que te dices a ti mismo: "Yo puedo pensar", tienes un motivo para construir una máquina que imite el pensamiento.

El sentido del ser te dice que tú eres tú. Te dice que estás vivo, pensando, sintiendo, deseando, soñando y demás. Ningún proceso físico creó tu sentido del ser. Lo posees como un rasgo intrínseco. Imagina que estás sentado en la oscuridad viendo una película que te tiene totalmente cautivado. Tal vez tus ojos están pegados a la escena de una persecución: tus oídos están atestados del sonido de balazos, llantas rechinando y sirenas de patrullas de policía. En ese momento no sientes el peso de tu cuerpo ni la sensación del asiento que estás ocupando. No percibes tu respiración: no es probable que percibas la temperatura del cine. Como estás absorto en la película, te has rendido ante su encanto. Pero como no estás pensando en tu cuerpo ni en tu entorno, y quizá no haya pensamientos cruzando tu mente, ¿acaso estás tan cautivado que *tú* desapareces? No.

Tú estás presente sin importar qué tan emocionante se vuelva la película, y lo mismo sucede con la película cotidiana por la que caminas como en un sueño lúcido. Puedes sustraer todo de tu experiencia, excepto tu sentido del ser. En un día típico, las experiencias que percibes son una minúscula fracción de los estímulos sensoriales que recibes. Recordarás algunas cosas o ninguna, pero seguramente no lo recordarás todo. La mayoría de las experiencias es fugaz y desaparece, por lo cual no las notas. Pero no puedes abandonar el sentido del ser. Ponerlo fuera de tu mente no lo altera, distorsiona ni destruye. Como un corcho que sube flotando a la superficie, éste siempre regresará.

Inesperadamente, de pronto volvemos al camino directo. Tu sentido del ser es lo que hace que ya estés completo. Todo lo que existe "allá fuera" o "aquí dentro" está unido por tu sentido del ser porque es el común denominador en cada experiencia. Una vez que te das cuenta de esto, puedes identificarte con tu sentido del ser y entonces el camino directo ha logrado su objetivo.

Pasar la prueba "¿Y qué?"

Por más que esta discusión haya sido muy interesante, "¿y qué?". ¿Por qué tú y yo deberíamos tomarnos la molestia de seguir el camino directo? Al ver su vida, la mayoría de la gente se siente más o menos feliz con las decisiones que ha tomado. O eso dicen las encuestas, que década tras década descubren que cuando le hacen a la gente la simple pregunta "¿Eres feliz?", más de 70% dice que sí. En las noticias aparecen historias que nombran los países más felices del mundo —el último candidato es Dinamarca— y en correspondencia existen países infelices, que resultan ser los que son muy pobres, afligidos por la guerra y los conflictos, y donde la gente debe luchar por adquirir las necesidades básicas de la vida.

El camino directo y todo lo demás de lo que hemos estado hablando —despertar, iluminación, totalidad, el ser verdadero, metarrealidad— confronta la prueba "¿Y qué?". Tomamos decisiones basándonos en si son lo suficientemente importantes en nuestra vida. Pero esto no es una medida confiable de lo que es benéfico. Los cosméticos y la moda les importan lo bastante a millones de personas, tanto como el futbol virtual y añadir más armas a su colección les importan a otros millones de personas. "¿Y qué?" es muy personal e impredecible, pero también es implacable. Hasta que algo sea lo suficientemente importante no cambiaremos la forma de vida a la que estamos acostumbrados.

He aquí mi respuesta a "¿Y qué?" aplicada al camino directo. De una forma muy real, convertirse en metahumano implica eliminar todo lo que no es necesario para nuestra especie. Este proceso ya está en movimiento en partes. El mundo moderno ha erradicado —o está en el proceso de hacerlo— muchas cosas sin las cuales el *Homo sapiens* puede vivir. A juzgar por cómo en el corazón de todas las culturas antiguas yace la creencia en Dios o los dioses, en un momento dado habría parecido imposible sobrevivir sin la religión. Pero existen millones de personas que han adoptado una visión del mundo secular, han puesto su fe en la ciencia y viven sin un sentido de pérdida en ausencia de la religión.

Podemos discutir por siempre si la religión es buena o mala para la sociedad, y sobre cualquier otra cosa que esté cambiando. Pero desde el punto de vista metahumano es esencial eliminar todas las cosas que el *Homo sapiens* ya no necesita. La ilusión se está diluyendo, por así decirlo. Los constructos mentales como la guerra y la pobreza ya no son considerados hechos de vida que la humanidad deba aceptar. ¿Entonces por qué no nos deshacemos de toda la ilusión? ¿Por qué no simplemente, completamente, y con la menor incomodidad posible?

Una vez que eliminas todo lo que no es real, lo que queda debe ser real. El camino directo concuerda con esta noción. Sostiene que sólo una cosa es real si desaparece todo lo irreal: el sentido del ser. Cada vida tiene sus propias prioridades. El sufrimiento de una persona puede estar arraigado en la pobreza, mientras que el de otra persona está arraigado en la enfermedad, una mala relación o la soledad de la vejez.

Nada es más enredado y caótico que la realidad virtual. El proceso de desmantelar todas las causas de sufrimiento es demasiado complejo como para descifrarlo con antelación. La única respuesta realista es permitir que la ilusión se disuelva con tan poco esfuerzo como con el que fue creada. Esto es de lo que se trata el camino directo; esto es lo que lo separa de cualquier otro esquema para el mejoramiento de la existencia humana.

Parece demasiado bueno para ser verdad que los grilletes creados por la mente simplemente desaparecerán por su propia voluntad.

Eso es exactamente lo que Rumi quería decir cuando declaró que la puerta de la cárcel está abierta. Dado que ya somos libres, no se necesita esfuerzo alguno para liberarse. Eres libre en el momento en que basas tu vida en una cosa: tu sentido del ser.

Tal como están las cosas, el sentido del ser está casi totalmente ignorado. La película de Woody Allen de 1983, *Zelig*, representa al personaje homónimo como una especie de fantasma histórico. Aunque Leonard Zelig era totalmente insignificante, era un camaleón humano. Tenía la capacidad de fundirse por completo en su entorno. La película se desarrolla en las décadas de 1920 y 1930, y el novelista F. Scott Fitzgerald es el primero en darse cuenta de las maravillosas transformaciones de Zelig. En una fiesta al estilo *El gran Gatsby*, Zelig está en la sala hablando con un acento bostoniano refinado y sosteniendo valores republicanos, y después, en la cocina, se presenta como un hombre común con ideas democráticas.

De alguna manera Zelig es todos y nadie, todas partes y ninguna. Ésa es una parábola del sentido del ser. Está presente en todas las experiencias, pero se funde en el entorno hasta ser invisible —hasta que empiezas a prestarle atención—. Entonces el sentido del ser, aunque parezca improbable, toma el escenario central.

El primer paso es comenzar a percibir tu sentido del ser. Imagina un círculo de debate en el cual una parte está defendiendo una postura controversial en el conflicto de Medio Oriente, el derecho a abortar o el racismo. Obsérvate a ti mismo ponerte de pie y decir un argumento elocuente apoyando una de las partes. Digamos que te opones con vehemencia al racismo, crees en la solución de dos Estados para los palestinos y apoyas el derecho de la mujer a practicarse un aborto.

Ahora colócate en la parte opuesta y articula el mismo argumento contrario para cada tema. Tal vez ayudaría si la posición contraria es indignante —podrías verte a ti mismo defendiendo la necesidad de prohibir todos los abortos o de apoyar a los terroristas que niegan el derecho de existencia de Israel—. Aunque tendrás resistencia en abandonar el lado en el que crees, los polemistas lo hacen todo el tiempo. Cambian la perspectiva de estar a favor para estar en contra con la mano en la cintura. Esta capacidad de cambiar de perspectiva va más allá de cualquier conjunto de creencias. Podemos ponernos cualquier abrigo que queramos usar. Pero ya sea que defiendas ideas que amas o ideas que odias, *tú* siempre estás presente. Tu sentido del ser es independiente de cualquier cosa que digas o hagas.

Siguiente ejemplo: toma cualquier objeto común y corriente de tu casa y tócalo. ¿Eres tú quien lo tocó? Cualquiera diría que sí en automático. Observa el mismo objeto. ¿Eres tú quien lo ve? Una vez más, sí. No hay ningún momento en la historia de la humanidad en el cual la respuesta sería distinta. Lo que sigue cambiando es nuestro modelo mental de lo que significa tocar y ver un objeto. En la prehistoria, antes del surgimiento del lenguaje, no había explicación para el hecho de ver y tocar. En una era de fe, cuando la carne muerta, el cuerpo, estaba animada por el alma, Dios era el que hacía posible esa sensación. Ahora, la experiencia de ver y tocar se adscribe al sistema nervioso central y la actividad del cerebro al recibir datos sensoriales del mundo "allá fuera".

Pero si no te molestas con ninguna de estas explicaciones, sólo hay un ser teniendo una experiencia. Puedes modificar este ejercicio de otras formas. En la escuela de medicina se les enseña a los estudiantes que las sensaciones corporales llegan al cerebro por medio de una red de nervios aferentes que corren por todo el cuerpo. Si tocas tu mano o levantas el brazo, las señales de los nervios aferentes son responsables de que sientas la experiencia. Cada señal es como un corredor inca que se apresura desde una región remota de los Andes para ver al emperador en la ciudad real de Cuzco. La información de los nervios aferentes fluye constantemente, ¿entonces por qué no sentimos el peso, la posición y el calor de cada extremidad? Siéntate en tu silla y permite que tu atención viaje desde la coronilla hasta la nariz, luego al corazón, luego a las puntas de los dedos del pie.

Si te pregunto: "¿Quién está viajando de una sensación a otra?", con seguridad responderás: "Yo". El ser selecciona aquello a lo que desea prestarle atención. Por lo tanto, el ser no está limitado por la actividad del sistema nervioso. Está presente sin importar qué células nerviosas estén encendidas.

Un ejemplo final: si cierras los ojos y ves el color azul, esta experiencia está sucediendo en tu conciencia. Si abres los ojos y miras el azul del cielo, ¿dónde está lo azul? Sigue estando en tu conciencia. La experiencia del azul "aquí dentro" y del azul "allá fuera" sucede en el mismo lugar. Cuando tomas, hueles o escuchas un objeto, puedes recordar esas sensaciones. ¿Las sensaciones viajaron del mundo exterior a tu mundo interior? Suponemos así fue. Estar sentado alrededor de una fogata cálida y ver sus flamas titilantes es distinto a recordar las flamas cálidas y titilantes. Pero las dos experiencias suceden en la conciencia. Escuchar un estallido en tu cabeza y escuchar el escape de un coche tronar en la calle son dos experiencias distintas, pero comparten el hecho innegable de que ambas suceden en la conciencia.

Si la conciencia está presente tanto dentro como fuera, ésta es independiente del espacio. De la misma forma, la fogata junto a la cual te sentaste pudo haber sucedido en la infancia, mientras que el recuerdo de ella sucede ahora mismo. Dado que la conciencia estaba registrando la fogata en ese entonces y ahora es independiente del tiempo. Cuando te das cuenta de que la conciencia no está limitada por el tiempo y el espacio, entonces tú —*el tú real que es pura conciencia*— no debe estar limitado por el tiempo y el espacio. A donde sea que vaya tu conciencia, tu sentido del ser está presente; los dos están fusionados. El ser está presente en todo, pero no nos damos cuenta de esto porque, al igual que Zelig, el ser sabe cómo fundirse a la perfección en cada situación.

Pienso que la mayoría de las personas, con un poco de reflexión, pueden aceptar que tienen un sentido del ser que las sigue a todos lados, como una sombra invisible. Pero para pasar por completo la prueba "¿Y qué?" el sentido del ser no puede ser un simple testigo. Parte del concepto de Woody Allen era que, si miras de cerca, Zelig aparece en fotografías de eventos cruciales como una inauguración presidencial, pero esto no lo convertía en alguien importante. De forma similar, percibirte a ti mismo en cada experiencia no la pone en el escenario central. El camino directo saca el sentido del ser a la luz. Lo que se necesita ahora es descubrir la enorme diferencia que genera este modesto logro.

El salto del humano al metahumano, el cambio de la realidad virtual a la realidad "real", está contenido por completo en el acto de percibir el ser. No el ego, que quiere monopolizar los reflectores y afirmar que él y sólo él es el ser. La personalidad del ego no puede evitar contener el sentido del ser —toda experiencia lo contiene—. El ego bloquea nuestra visión. Está atado a la realidad virtual y sigue atrayendo. Nuestra atención a todas partes *excepto* al sentido del ser.

Como veremos en la tercera parte, una vez que te deshagas de todas las cosas que en realidad no necesitas tu ego puede ser descartado también, pero no tu sentido del ser. Cuando las cargas y las tonterías innecesarias del hechizo/sueño/ilusión se eliminan, el sentido del ser no monopoliza los reflectores. Al ser lo único en ti que es atemporal y eterno no tiene que hacer nada. Simplemente es un faro de conciencia pura que brilla constantemente cada segundo de tu existencia. Irónicamente, a todo lo demás en tu vida se le dificulta mucho más pasar la prueba "¿Y qué?".

TERCERA PARTE

Ser metahumano

10

LIBERAR TU CUERPO

Como ya hemos visto, la conciencia está en todas partes, siempre y en todo. Si eso es verdad, entonces tú estás en todas partes, siempre y en todo. Pero en tu vida cotidiana, incluso si estás completamente convencido de esto, estás siendo guiado en la dirección opuesta. Has soportado toda una vida de entrenamiento y condicionamiento que te dice que eres una persona solitaria sentada a solas en una habitación. En vez de siempre, la duración de tu vida es muy limitada y está enmarcada por dos eventos: el nacimiento y la muerte. En vez de todo, eres un amasijo de cosas muy específicas, comenzando con tu nombre, género, estado civil, trabajo y demás.

La realidad virtual que queremos desmantelar está hecha de muchas partes movibles que ocupan sus propios compartimentos. Una parte es el cuerpo, otra la mente, el mundo y las demás personas. Estas partes se establecieron para que la vida se pueda manejar una pieza a la vez. Asistes a la universidad para tu mente, al gimnasio para tu cuerpo, a una cita amorosa para establecer una relación, al trabajo para llevar dinero a casa.

Desde el punto de vista metahumano, cualquier división de la vida en partes y pedazos sólo apoya la ilusión. La totalidad es la totalidad, no un conjunto de partes. Para decirlo de otra forma, la vida sólo sucede una vez, aquí y ahora. La razón por la que nos aferramos a la realidad virtual es que la perspectiva del "todo a la vez, aquí y ahora" es demasiado abrumadora.

Después de ponderar cómo presentar esta verdad de una forma práctica y cercana concluí que el camino directo debe comenzar con el cuerpo, no con la mente. Mi razonamiento es que el cuerpo es lo que reprime a la mayoría de las personas. Se experimentan a sí mismas encerradas en un cuerpo. Aceptan la realidad del nacimiento, la enfermedad, el envejecimiento y la muerte. Buscan placer físico y se encogen ante el dolor físico. Mientras éstas sean las precondiciones de tu vida cotidiana, no puedes ser metahumano. Tu cuerpo no lo aceptará. Una célula del hígado, del corazón o del cerebro no puede gritar: "¿Estás loco?". Pero sí parece una locura abandonar el cuerpo como un objeto físico, y este acto de locura hace que tu cuerpo sea el lugar perfecto para comenzar. Si puedes ver más allá del cuerpo como un paquete de carne y hueso, y transformarlo en un modo de la conciencia, todo lo demás se acomoda de forma natural.

La anatomía de la conciencia

Si nos hemos atrapado a nosotros mismos dentro de una ilusión, el cuerpo debe ser parte integral de eso, y lo es. Tu cuerpo es tu historia en forma física. Conforme tu historia creció a lo largo de los años, las cosas que pensaste, dijiste e hiciste requirieron un enorme despliegue de actividad cerebral. Aprender a caminar fue un triunfo del equilibrio, la vista y la coordinación motriz, entonces cuando de pequeño armaste este rompecabezas complejo, tu cuerpo recordó todo lo que aprendiste y lo guardó para toda la vida, para así poder seguir hacia algo nuevo. Tu cerebro ha almacenado una enorme variedad de habilidades, desde hablar y escribir hasta andar en bicicleta, hacer cuentas y bailar un vals. Estos logros mentales están encarnados en ti físicamente.

Sin embargo, en cuanto esto se señala caemos en el riesgo de volver a separar lo "mental" y lo "físico", lo que nos lleva directo de regreso a la ilusión. Cuando los bebés aprenden a caminar no están bajo dicha ilusión. Conforme se tambalean, se caen, se levantan de nuevo y siguen intentando, la experiencia se adecua a la descripción holística antes mencionada: todo sucede simultáneamente, aquí y ahora. Lo mismo sucede con cualquier habilidad que puedas nombrar: aprenderla no fue algo mental o físico. Estaba sucediendo en una sola dimensión: la conciencia.

Hay tantas formas en que ponemos en oposición la mente y el cuerpo que hablar de cada una sería imposible. El camino directo ni siquiera requiere la pequeña discusión por la que acabamos de pasar. En cambio, experimenta el cuerpo *en la conciencia*. Cuando haces eso la división entre lo mental y lo físico regresa a la autenticidad de un bebé que está aprendiendo a caminar. Regresas al ser como el agente de toda la experiencia, fusionando el pensamiento y la acción. En este caso cualquier acción se devuelve a la totalidad, que es donde ocurre.

Para empezar, simplemente ábrete a la idea de que tu cuerpo no es un objeto físico dentro del cual resides. Semejante punto de vista es sólo un hábito de pensamiento, aunque sea un hábito persistente. Te guiaré a través de un ejercicio que te dará la experiencia directa de vivir, no en un cuerpo físico, sino en la conciencia. (Este ejercicio y los siguientes son mucho más fáciles de realizar si alguien te los lee en voz alta. Es mucho mejor si puedes encontrar a alguien que te acompañe, para intercambiar los roles de lector y participante.)

Ejercicio: El cuerpo en la conciencia

El primer ejercicio implica los siguientes pasos:

PASO 1: Ser consciente de tu cuerpo.
PASO 2: Ser consciente de algunos procesos corporales.
PASO 3: Ser consciente del cuerpo como un espacio interno.
PASO 4: Expandir el espacio interno más allá de la piel.
PASO 5: Descansar en la totalidad.

Cada paso es una progresión natural del anterior y una experiencia simple y directa. No tienes que memorizar las instrucciones, sino sólo vivir el ejercicio como una experiencia.

PASO 1: SER CONSCIENTE DE TU CUERPO

Siéntate en silencio con los ojos cerrados. Permite que las sensaciones corporales sean el centro de tu atención para que puedas sentir tu cuerpo. No es necesario que intentes detener tus pensamientos; son irrelevantes. No importa qué sensaciones percibas. Tan sólo permanece con tu cuerpo.

PASO 2: SER CONSCIENTE DE ALGUNOS
PROCESOS CORPORALES

Sé consciente de tu respiración al inhalar y exhalar. Disminuye un poco el ritmo de tu respiración y luego aceléralo un poco. Mueve tu atención al centro de tu pecho y sé consciente del latido de tu corazón. Realiza algunas respiraciones suaves y profundas y siente cómo el latido de tu corazón disminuye conforme te relajas. Revisa si puedes sentir tu pulso en alguna parte; muchas personas lo sienten en la punta de los dedos, en la frente o dentro de las orejas, por ejemplo.

PASO 3: SER CONSCIENTE DEL CUERPO
COMO UN ESPACIO INTERNO

Ahora mueve tu atención al interior de tu cuerpo. Siente tu cabeza como un espacio vacío, y comienza a descender a lo largo de tu cuerpo por el pecho, el estómago, el abdomen, las piernas y los pies, haciendo una pausa en cada lugar para experimentar tus órganos internos como un espacio en el que tu conciencia se mueve con libertad. Si quieres también puedes experimentar tu respiración como la expansión y relajación del espacio en tu pecho, el latido del corazón como una pulsación constante del espacio en tu pecho.

PASO 4: EXPANDIR EL ESPACIO INTERNO
MÁS ALLÁ DE LA PIEL

Una vez que sentiste el interior de tu cuerpo como un espacio vacío en el que ocurren los procesos corporales, lleva tu atención a lo largo de toda tu piel. Deambula por las sensaciones en tu cabeza, sintiendo los contornos del rostro, el cuero cabelludo y las orejas. Ve más abajo y permite que tu conciencia vaya a todas partes del cuerpo —garganta, brazos, manos y pies— conforme las sensaciones lleguen a ti.

Ahora levanta tu conciencia levemente por encima de tu piel y con suavidad permite que se expanda más allá de los contornos de tu cuerpo. Algunas personas pueden hacer esto con facilidad, pero otras necesitan evocar una imagen; puedes ver tu espacio interno bañado de luz y observar la luz expandirse hasta que llene la habitación. O puedes visualizar el espacio interno alrededor de tu corazón como una esfera, una pelota redonda que se expande un poco más cada vez que inhalas, observándola volverse más grande hasta abarcar toda la habitación.

PASO 5: DESCANSAR EN LA TOTALIDAD

Ya que hayas atravesado los pasos previos descansa en silencio por un minuto o dos. Permite que la experiencia del cuerpo esté aquí y ahora.

Lo que hizo este ejercicio fue multiplicar. Te liberaste de estar atrapado dentro de una cosa al sustituir la experiencia de tu cuerpo como procesos y sensaciones. Dado que tu experiencia fue consciente, estos procesos y sensaciones se movieron hacia donde suceden en realidad, tu conciencia. Entonces te abriste a la experiencia de tu cuerpo como un espacio interno —en sánscrito este espacio se llama *Chit Akash*, o espacio mental—. Dado que todo en la vida sucede en el espacio mental, tú expandiste el espacio hasta que ya no hubo frontera entre "aquí dentro" y "allá afuera".

Quizá te sorprenda haber logrado todas estas cosas, y como es probable que la experiencia haya sido inusual para ti, fácilmente podrás volver al hábito de sentir que tu cuerpo es un objeto físico en el que resides, como un ratón escondiéndose en las paredes de una casa o un conejo en su madriguera. Pero por lo menos ahora puedes ver que existe una alternativa al viejo hábito. El viejo hábito no te servirá para liberarte de tu cuerpo.

Para romper el viejo hábito —un proceso que yo llamo "descongelamiento", como lo dije anteriormente— tómate un tiempo, una o dos veces al día, y repite este ejercicio. Cuando te acostumbres a él todo fluye de forma natural y suave. Todos somos de mente práctica, entonces ¿qué beneficios tiene este ejercicio sobre la vida cotidiana?

- Puedes hacerlo cuando te sientas estresado.
- Puedes hacerlo para aliviar la tensión corporal u otras sensaciones desagradables y dolorosas.

- También sirve para ayudar a aliviar los pensamientos de preocupación y ansiedad.
- Puedes centrarte a ti mismo con este ejercicio cada vez que te sientas distraído y disperso.

Varias prácticas de yoga y budismo zen ponen al cuerpo bajo control por medio de una conciencia totalmente enfocada. Por ejemplo, cuando sentiste el latido de tu corazón y tu respiración, tomaste el primer paso para controlar ambos procesos simultáneamente por medio del nervio vago, uno de los 10 nervios craneales que se extienden desde el cerebro hasta el resto del sistema nervioso central.

El nervio vago es un vagabundo que traza su curso como la línea troncal de un sistema telefónico antiguo del cerebro al cuello, que baja por el pecho, pasa por el corazón y se extiende hasta al abdomen. Es el nervio craneal más largo y sus fibras envían y reciben información sensorial. La mayoría de las sensaciones que experimentaste en el ejercicio que acabas de realizar fue canalizada a través del nervio vago.

Puedes aprovechar este conocimiento de forma práctica por medio de la "respiración vagal", que consiste en inhalar a la cuenta de cuatro, sostener la respiración a la cuenta de dos, y exhalar a la cuenta de cuatro. Este simple ritmo de 4-2-4 es fácil para un adulto saludable normal, y nadie debería tratar de forzarlo al punto de quedarse sin aliento o sentirse incómodo. Para la gran sorpresa de los investigadores médicos la respiración vagal es la mejor forma de reducir el estrés, en particular los signos inmediatos de la respiración irregular, aumento en el ritmo cardiaco y tensión muscular.

Resulta que el estrés crónico de bajo nivel es más importante y penetrante que el estrés agudo. En la vida moderna, vivir en un estado de estrés crónico de bajo nivel es tan común que se acepta como algo normal. Pero tu cuerpo para nada lo experimenta como normal; los inicios de la cardiopatía, la hipertensión, los desórdenes digestivos y del sueño, y quizás algunos tipos de cáncer, pueden originarse por el estrés crónico.

No es accidental que la ubicación de estos desórdenes sea paralela al curso del nervio vago, que sirve para comunicar el estrés al corazón, el estómago, el tracto digestivo y luego al resto del cuerpo conforme el nervio vago se ramifica. La respiración vagal regresa el estado corporal al equilibrio y alivia la tensión. Así que, si no te has dado cuenta de que todo lo físico y lo mental sucede en la conciencia —lo que significa que nuestro cuerpo sucede en la conciencia—, he aquí una pista indudable.

Aceptamos que una capacidad como caminar y andar en bicicleta es permanente una vez que se aprende. Sin embargo, a un nivel más básico, nuestros ancestros homínidos aprendieron y absorbieron hace millones de años los biorritmos que sustentan la mente-cuerpo como un todo. La vida moderna nos empuja a desaprenderlos, como lo atestigua el gran número de personas con desórdenes digestivos y del sueño. Las dos funciones son controladas por medio de biorritmos innatos. Cuando tu cuerpo ha olvidado cómo expresar un biorritmo, el efecto es como una trompeta o un violín tocando una pieza musical distinta a la de la orquesta: toda la sinfonía se arruina.

La respiración vagal puede acabar siendo muy útil más allá de su habilidad para normalizar el ritmo cardiaco, disminuir la presión sanguínea y hacer que la respiración sea más regular. Es una buena práctica para realizar en la cama justo antes de dormir. El insomnio leve o moderado se puede reducir o sanar por completo. El estrés general disminuye, incluyendo los pensamientos estresantes y la mente que piensa sin cesar, que innumerables personas experimentan cuando intentan dormir.

He entrado en cierto detalle (todo el tema se trata a profundidad en *El yo sanador*, libro del que soy coautor con Rudy Tanzi) para enfatizar que un mapa físico del sistema nervioso, el funcionamiento del nervio vago, que interviene conscientemente en su actividad, y percibir los resultados directamente son todos *una misma cosa*. El camino directo nos conduce a esa cosa que, con el tiempo, terminará por completo el estado de separación y nos permitirá descansar en la totalidad, que es la realidad.

Tu cuerpo, tu historia

Cuando comienzas a experimentar tu cuerpo en la conciencia, empieza a suceder la transformación. Estás saliendo de la separación entre la mente y el cuerpo y te diriges hacia la totalidad. Necesitas ser completo para ser quien eres en realidad. El camino directo es experiencial.

Conforme experimentas tu cuerpo en la conciencia, tomas un descanso de tu historia. Parece que es algo modesto, un momento o dos sin hacer nada, pero estando aquí. Y aun así no hay otra forma de desmantelar tu historia que sea tan directa. Millones de personas se benefician con la terapia y al caminar por el sendero espiritual, aunque eventualmente todos debemos enfrentar el hecho de que *todo* lo que hacemos, incluso en el nombre de la sanación y la espiritualidad, tiene un lugar dentro de nuestra historia. Como resultado podemos tener vistazos de la totalidad —a menudo son muy hermosos e inspiradores—, pero no nos llevan a la metarrealidad como nuestro hogar.

Ahora eres tu propia historia —es inevitable— y esto te mantiene atrapado en la separación. La palabra *separación* tal vez no te venga a la mente; quizás incluso no la consideres un problema. Para ilustrarlo, considera las siguientes frases que todos hemos dicho o escuchado:

Odio mi cuerpo.
Eres tan viejo como tú crees que eres.
La juventud está desperdiciada en los jóvenes.
Yo solía tener una figura perfecta.

Las afirmaciones expresan distintos sentimientos, pero cada una refleja la separación de la mente y el cuerpo. "Odio mi cuerpo" proviene de alguien que se siente atrapado en lo físico. La persona se lamenta de lo que le ha hecho a su cuerpo, o lo que su cuerpo le ha hecho a ella. El estado de separación es evidente. "Yo" juega el papel de la víctima y "el cuerpo" es el culpable.

"Eres tan viejo como tú crees que eres" es mucho más optimista, ya que afirma que la mente puede superar el deterioro de la edad. Aunque, como todos sabemos, en parte esto es una fantasía. Envejecer es un proceso inexorable. Es mucho mejor tener una actitud positiva hacia el envejecimiento que una negativa —la sociedad se beneficia de la "nueva tercera edad", que ve cada etapa de la vida como vigorosa, productiva y saludable—. Pero un pensamiento o una creencia no son lo mismo que el estado de ser consciente. "Eres tan viejo como tú crees que eres" no puede sustituir al ser verdadero. Cuando el envejecimiento se establece en tu sentido del ser como una etapa permanente, no presenta ninguna amenaza porque te identificas con lo atemporal (hablaremos sobre lo que significa el estado atemporal en la siguiente sección). De todas formas, una buena actitud hacia el proceso de envejecimiento te deja atrapado en tu historia.

Oscar Wilde bromeaba con que "la juventud está desperdiciada en los jóvenes", lo que le da cierto ingenio al triste deseo que tiene mucha gente: si tan sólo pudiera retroceder en el tiempo, viviría mi vida mucho mejor. El lamento por el pasado está dentro de la historia de todos, y la base para este lamento (y su opuesto, que es la nostalgia) es que el paso del tiempo tiene poder sobre nosotros. "Yo solía tener una figura perfecta" es lo mismo que la autoestima y sentirse atractivo.

Estos ejemplos de cómo la mente se siente separada y diferente del cuerpo podrían desarrollarse hasta el infinito. El cuerpo está sujeto a todo tipo de juicios, y aun así el proceso subyacente, que ames u odies tu cuerpo, no ha sido examinado detenidamente. Este proceso subyacente es la forma inevitable en que tu cuerpo ha asimilado cada detalle de tu historia de vida y ahora la refleja. Estar atrapado en tu historia y estar atrapado en tu cuerpo es la misma cosa. Tu cerebro ha sido moldeado cada minuto desde que naciste, y ha comunicado todo lo que experimentas a los 50 billones de células, que a cambio pasan los mensajes a tu ADN.

Entonces, la totalidad no sólo es un cambio mental. Es una revolución en la mente-cuerpo que deshace el pasado, que comienza en el cerebro, pero llega a liberar cada célula e influye en la actividad genética en cada célula. Para ver cómo ocurre esa revolución permíteme ir al corazón de cada historia, que es el tiempo.

Cómo ser atemporal

En tu infancia había un periodo en el cual tu experiencia era original y auténtica. Eras demasiado pequeño para interpretar el mundo por ti mismo. Todo tu desarrollo estaba ocupado con lo básico, como caminar, hablar, explorar el mundo y demás. Llamemos a esto el periodo de prehistoria de la vida de una persona. William Blake dividió un grupo de poemas en "canciones de inocencia" y "canciones de experiencia", que eran una narrativa no bíblica de Caer de la Gracia Divina. Al igual que los románticos que lo seguirían y que lo idolatraban, Blake creía que la Caída no les ocurrió a Adán y Eva, sino que les sucedía a los niños al perder su inocencia. La caída era una experiencia repetida de generación en generación.

Lo que Blake veía en la inocencia era una perspectiva del mundo fresca, simple, lírica y alegre. El tono está plasmado en una de las canciones de inocencia más famosas, "El cordero", en la que puedes sustituir por la palabra infante cuando dice cordero:

> Corderito, ¿quién te hizo?
> ¿Sabes quién te hizo?
> Quien te dio la vida y te procuró alimento,
> junto al arroyo y sobre el prado;
> te dio abrigo placentero,
> las ropas más suaves de lana brillante;
> y te dio esa voz tan tierna,
> que a todos los valles regocija.

En contraste con esta visión de un Edén de la infancia, las canciones de experiencia son más amargas y oscuras, y reflejan las dificultades que Blake conocía de primera mano y que vio a su alrededor en el Londres del siglo XVIII. Un famoso poema, "Un árbol venenoso", reinventa la historia del pecado original como el lado oscuro de la naturaleza humana, en un verso que podría ser una canción infantil:

> Estaba enojado con mi amigo:
> le confesé mi ira, mi ira terminó.
> Estaba enojado con mi enemigo:
> me quedé callado, mi ira creció.

Y la regué con miedos,
noche y día con mis lágrimas:
y la asoleé con sonrisas,
y con suaves tretas y ardides.

Y creció de día y de noche
hasta volverse una manzana brillante.
Y mi enemigo contempló su resplandor
y supo que era mía.

Y en mi jardín la robó
cuando el velo de la noche había caído.
En la mañana miré con alegría
a mi enemigo tendido bajo el árbol.

Incluso sin el beneficio de la visión de Blake, todos hemos experimentado la transformación de la inocencia a la experiencia. Sólo fue necesario el tiempo. No necesitamos nada más cuando íbamos aprendiendo la interpretación estándar del mundo que aceptaban todos a nuestro alrededor. Un bebé jamás se aburre. Observa el mundo con asombro. Las horas no le pesan; las fechas límite no hacen que el bebé se apresure a lo largo de sus días. No busca distracciones para escapar de sí mismo.

Blake era un visionario y vio la posibilidad de liberación del estado de caída, el cual llamaba "inocencia organizada". Es una frase brillante porque implica que la experiencia de una persona puede ser tan original, auténtica y pura como la de un bebé mientras conservamos la mente organizada, una mente que debemos tener para llevar a cabo las funciones de adultos (las cuales incluyen la tarea de cuidar a los bebés). Regresar a la inocencia significa abrazar valores como el amor y la creatividad, que se vuelven más valiosos cuando llegamos a la madurez. Pero los años de madurez hacen que sea cada vez más difícil viajar de vuelta a la inocencia. Para todas las incontables personas que anhelan lo que se siente enamorarse por primera vez, encontramos una forma de volver.

El responsable no es la experiencia, porque la experiencia puede seguir siendo alegre y auténtica en cualquier momento de la vida. El culpable está oculto en la textura de nuestra vida: el tiempo. Líneas atrás dije que la integración al mundo interpretado (es decir, el hechizo, sueño, ilusión) sólo necesitaba tiempo, nada más. De la misma manera, escapar de las garras del tiempo es la única salida. Lejos de ser una noción mística, puedes ser atemporal en este instante; de hecho ésa es la única manera.

Para la mayoría de la gente las palabras *atemporal* y *eterno* significan casi lo mismo. Para los religiosos creyentes de la tradición cristiana y musulmana el cielo es eterno, un lugar donde el tiempo perdura siempre. Para los no religiosos el tiempo termina con la muerte física. Sin embargo, en ambos casos el tiempo ordinario del reloj ha terminado. Pero existen problemas con estos conceptos, y si profundizamos en el tema, el tiempo es muy diferente a lo que aceptamos de forma casual.

La física tiene mucho que decir acerca del tiempo, gracias al concepto revolucionario de Einstein de que el tiempo no es constante, sino que varía de acuerdo con la situación. Viajar con una velocidad cercana a la luz o acercarse a la masiva fuerza de gravedad de un agujero negro tendrá un impacto drástico en la forma en que pasa el tiempo. Pero dejemos de lado la relatividad para considerar cómo funciona el tiempo en términos humanos, aquí y ahora. Por lo regular cada uno de nosotros experimenta tres estados del tiempo: el tiempo que pasa en el reloj cuando estamos despiertos, el tiempo como parte de la ilusión de tener un sueño y la ausencia de tiempo cuando estamos dormidos, pero no soñamos. Esto nos dice que el tiempo está vinculado a nuestro estado de vigilia.

Damos por hecho que una especie de tiempo —el que miden los relojes— es el tiempo real, pero eso no es verdad. Las tres relaciones con el tiempo —despierto, soñando y durmiendo— sólo se conocen como experiencias personales. El tiempo no existe fuera de la conciencia humana. No existe un reloj absoluto "allá fuera" en el universo. Muchos cosmólogos discutirían que el tiempo, como lo conocemos en nuestro estado de vigilia, entró al universo únicamente en el Big Bang. Lo que hubo antes del Big Bang quizás era inconcebible, porque "antes del Big Bang" no significa nada si el tiempo nació en el instante en que nació el cosmos. Si vas al nivel más fino de la naturaleza, al estado de vacío del cual emergió el campo cuántico, las cualidades de la existencia cotidiana, como la vista, el sonido, el sabor, el tacto y el olor, ya no existen, y también hay un punto evanescente donde desaparece la tridimensionalidad, junto con el tiempo mismo.

Lo que yace más allá del horizonte cuántico es una cuestión puramente conjetural. El estado precreado del universo puede ser moldeado casi de cualquier forma que elijas, como ser multidimensional, infinitamente dimensional o no dimensional. Así que debe aceptarse que el tiempo surgió de lo atemporal y no sólo en el Big Bang. Todo en el universo físico entra y sale de la existencia a un veloz ritmo de excitación aquí y ahora. Lo atemporal está con nosotros cada segundo de nuestra vida.

Pero algo suena raro en esa frase, porque lo atemporal no puede ser medido usando un reloj, así que no tiene sentido decir que lo atemporal está con nosotros "cada segundo". Entonces, lo atemporal está con nosotros, punto. Este mundo es atemporal. No es necesario esperar la muerte o ver el cielo para demostrar que la eternidad es real.

Una vez que reconoces que lo atemporal está con nosotros, naturalmente surge una pregunta: ¿cómo se relaciona lo atemporal con el tiempo del reloj? La respuesta es que no están relacionados. Lo atemporal es absoluto, y como no puede ser medido por los relojes, no tiene existencia relativa. Qué extraño. Lo atemporal está con nosotros, pero no podemos relacionarnos con ello. ¿Entonces de qué sirve lo atemporal?

Para responder estas preguntas tenemos que retroceder un poco. El tiempo del reloj no tiene una posición privilegiada en la realidad. No hay motivo por el cual debiera ser elevado al tiempo del sueño o a la ausencia de tiempo en el dormir sin soñar. El tiempo del reloj es sólo una cualidad de la vida cotidiana, como otras cualidades que conocemos, como colores, sabores, olores, etcétera. Los fotones, partículas de luz, no tienen brillo sin nuestra percepción del brillo; los fotones son invisibles e incoloros. Asimismo, el tiempo es un artefacto de la experiencia humana. Fuera de nuestra percepción no podemos conocer nada acerca del tiempo. Esto parece contradecir la piedra angular de la ciencia, que sostiene que "por supuesto" existía un universo físico antes de que la vida evolucionara en la Tierra, lo que significa que "por supuesto" había tiempo, miles de millones de años de tiempo.

Aquí llegamos a una encrucijada en el camino, porque ya sea que aceptas que el tiempo, como lo registra el cerebro humano, es real por sí mismo, o afirmas que al depender del cerebro humano el tiempo es creado en la conciencia. La segunda posición es por mucho la más fuerte, aunque pocas personas creen en ella. En nuestra conciencia constantemente convertimos lo atemporal en la experiencia del tiempo; no hay forma de negar esto. Debido a que esa transformación no puede suceder "dentro" del tiempo, algo más debe estar pasando. Para tener una idea de ese "algo" observemos el momento presente, el ahora, el presente inmediato.

Todas las experiencias suceden en el ahora. Incluso recordar el pasado o anticipar el futuro es un evento del momento-presente. Las células cerebrales, que físicamente procesan la conversión de lo atemporal en tiempo, funcionan sólo en el presente. No tienen otra opción, ya que las señales eléctricas y químicas que corren por las células cerebrales ocurren sólo aquí y ahora. Si el momento presente es el único tiempo real que podemos conocer en el estado de vigilia, ¿por qué es tan elusivo? Puedes usar un reloj finamente calibrado como un reloj atómico para predecir cuándo llegará el siguiente segundo, milisegundo o billonésima de segundo, pero eso no es lo mismo que predecir el ahora. El momento presente, como experiencia, es totalmente impredecible. Si pudiera ser pronosticado conocerías por anticipado tu siguiente pensamiento, lo cual es imposible.

Como ya lo hablamos, el momento presente siempre es elusivo porque el instante que registras ya sea como una sensación, una imagen, un sentimiento o un pensamiento, ya desapareció. Así que resumamos estas ideas. El ahora, el lugar donde todos vivimos, puede ser descrito como:

- El punto de unión donde lo atemporal se convierte en tiempo.
- El único tiempo "real" que conocemos en la vigilia.
- Un fenómeno totalmente impredecible.
- Un fenómeno totalmente elusivo.

Ahora, si todas estas características están descritas de forma correcta, resulta que nos hemos estado engañando al creer que el tiempo es una cuestión de tictac en el reloj. De alguna manera misteriosa cada uno de nosotros ocupa un mundo atemporal, y para producir un mundo de cuatro dimensiones para vivir en él, lo construimos mentalmente. Es decir, creamos el mundo en la conciencia primero y sobre todo. La realidad, incluyendo el tiempo ordinario del reloj, también está construida en la conciencia.

No debemos caer en la trampa y decir que la mente crea la realidad. La mente es un vehículo para la experiencia de pensamiento activo y, al igual que el tiempo y el espacio, debe tener una fuente más allá de algo tan pasajero y escurridizo como los pensamientos. Si confiáramos en nuestra mente sería lo equivalente a irnos a dormir con la muerte. Durante el sueño la mente consciente abandona el mundo de los objetos físicos y el tiempo del reloj. Pero cuando despertamos en la mañana, regresan los objetos sólidos y el tiempo del reloj. Estaban guardados a la espera, por así decirlo, por la conciencia, incluso durante las ocho horas al día en que la mente pensante estaba fuera de servicio.

Si el camino directo busca llevarnos más allá de la ilusión que aceptamos como real, debe ofrecer la experiencia de ser atemporal. En su estado más completo, la experiencia atemporal es simple, natural y sin esfuerzo —es el sentido del ser, que yace sigilosamente en todas las experiencias—. Sólo estamos ahí parcialmente. El ejercicio en este capítulo, que te permite experimentar tu cuerpo en la conciencia, descongela un aspecto de la ilusión. Esta discusión sobre ser atemporal descongela otro aspecto. En ambos casos, conforme lo físico y el tiempo del reloj comienzan a soltar su control, te das cuenta de que hay otra forma de vivir: ser metahumano.

Cuando comienzas a ser metahumano, existes en la fuente atemporal del ser. Es un enorme paso saber que lo atemporal está con nosotros, más allá de cualquier creencia en el nacimiento y la muerte, la edad y la decadencia. Las cosas aparecen y desaparecen en nuestros sueños cuando estamos durmiendo. No las extrañamos porque sabemos que los sueños son una ilusión. Lo que importa no es que las cosas aparezcan y desaparezcan, sino que no confundas el sueño con la realidad.

Descubrir que lo mismo sucede con nuestro sueño despierto nos libera del temor a la muerte. El metahumano es mucho más que esto. Al ser libres de la ilusión podemos ser libres del temor. Al final, despertar conduce a la libertad absoluta. No sólo llevamos nuestra vida cotidiana. Navegamos en el campo de las posibilidades infinitas.

11

RECUPERAR LA MENTE TOTAL

Imagina que estás en una cabaña en el bosque que está junto a un pequeño lago. El sol te despierta muy temprano, y cuando caminas hacia el lago bajo la luz pálida del amanecer, el agua está totalmente inmóvil. La superficie es serena y parece un espejo. Sientes la necesidad de levantar una piedra y aventarla al lago. La piedra cae dentro, las ondas se extienden a lo largo del agua y, conforme el anillo de ondas se amplía, éstas desaparecen hasta que no queda nada más que la superficie inmóvil del lago. Regresó a lo que era antes de que llegaras a perturbarlo.

En esta modesta experiencia se refleja toda la historia de la mente humana. Sólo se necesita ver la escena en reversa, como si pusieras una película hacia atrás. La superficie del lago está perfectamente quieta. Un débil anillo de ondas perturba el agua y el anillo comienza a encogerse. De repente una roca sale del agua y vuela hacia tu mano.

Así es como la mente humana se ve desde la perspectiva de la metarrealidad. Es conciencia pura, quieta y serena. Una actividad leve comienza a moverla, tan leve que debes estar en silencio y muy alerta para notarla. Pero esta actividad —llámala una vibración en la conciencia— se vuelve más urgente hasta que algo completamente formado entra en la existencia: una sensación, una imagen, un sentimiento o un pensamiento.

En la vida cotidiana una miríada de eventos mentales entra en la existencia, y éstos son tan constantes y atrayentes que nunca experimentamos la superficie inmóvil del lago, que es conciencia pura. El camino directo busca recuperar esta experiencia, porque un estado inmóvil y sereno de conciencia es *mente total*. La mente total contiene el potencial infinito que es único del *Homo sapiens*. Como sucede con muchas cosas de la metarrealidad, la mente total es aquí y ahora. Para poder aventar una piedra al lago primero debes tener un lago, y también debes tener un lago para que la piedra salga de él. Los dos procesos suceden en el cosmos cuando cada partícula subatómica surge del vacío cuántico y desaparece en él. Asimismo, tus pensamientos surgen del silencio, se desenvuelven en el aire el tiempo necesario para ser detectados, y después desaparecen en el mismo lugar de donde nacieron.

Si la mente total ya es aquí y ahora, ¿por qué necesitamos recuperarla? La respuesta que se ofrece en este libro es que la metarrealidad yace más allá de las ilusiones de la realidad virtual, que nos embauca aparentando ser real. No hay duda alguna de que la mente total es real, como lo busca demostrar el camino directo. Pero siento que se requiere algo más. Si la actividad mental fuera justo como piedras saliendo de un lago, cada pensamiento naturalmente moriría de todas formas, y la mente volvería sin esfuerzo a su estado sereno. En otras palabras, no habría interrupciones, caprichos o tormentas de confusión que alboroten el lago.

Por desgracia nuestra mente no está conectada suavemente a la conciencia pura. Nuestra mente es un revoltijo confuso y caótico, y algunas tradiciones orientales la han descrito de forma vívida como si fuera un mono. Cada pensamiento se une a la tormenta de otros pensamientos sin regresar al estado quieto y sereno. Ser humano es cabalgar en la tormenta. Cuando eras niño y aprendiste a hablar y poner los pensamientos en palabras, tu mente estaba desatada. "Yo", alimentado por la agenda del ego, comenzó la interminable tarea de aceptar A y rechazar B. Incluso los niños de dos o tres años quieren lo que quieren: juguetes que puedan llamar "míos", atención de su madre, su comida favorita, historias que desean escuchar una y otra vez. El rechazo también es parte vital de la agenda del ego. Un niño de dos o tres años avienta algunos juguetes al piso, rechaza los besos y abrazos, se niega a comer ciertos alimentos, etcétera.

Hay una caricatura famosa de Carol Rose y E. B. White que muestra a una mamá y su hija sentadas a la mesa durante la cena. El pie de imagen dice así:

MAMÁ: "Es brócoli, mi amor".
HIJA: "Yo digo que es espinaca y que no me la voy a comer".

Si los niños hablaran con voces de adultos, ¡así hablarían!

Desde la perspectiva del metahumano ninguna agenda del ego es una necesidad. ¿Por qué tomarse la molestia de construir un ser cuando ya *eres* el ser? La única necesidad real es estar aquí y ahora y permitir que la vida se desenvuelva.

Debido a que nuestros pensamientos no desaparecen en la calma pura y quieta es que surge un obstáculo. Los pensamientos interfieren con nuestra capacidad de estar aquí ahora. Cada pensamiento genera un nuevo pensamiento, cada sensación una nueva sensación. Esta actividad mental interminable nos distrae tanto que no podemos ver nuestra fuente ni tocarla o sentir su presencia. Deshacernos de la interferencia mental se ha convertido en un trabajo duro. La imagen de vivir años en un monasterio de budismo zen o la imagen de estar sentado en posición de loto en una cueva del Himalaya son parte de la cultura popular y representan qué tan arduo es acallar la mente. El camino directo corta por el camino del trabajo duro de una forma simple, como lo ilustra el siguiente ejercicio.

Ejercicio: Ojos abiertos, sin pensamientos

Este ejercicio se reserva para el momento en que te despiertas en la mañana. Cuando abres los ojos y antes de salir de la cama, tu mente comienza su día. Estás predeterminado a comenzar de inmediato tu rutina habitual. Comienzas a pensar acerca de lo que tienes que hacer ese día, y muy pronto has reiniciado tu historia personal —tu mente está entrenada para echarse a andar en automático, como una computadora cuyo *software* está listo para las instrucciones al instante en que se enciende la máquina—.

No obstante hay un pequeño intervalo antes de que tu historia reinicie. Por unos segundos estás despierto, pero no te has enganchado al mundo. Puedes extender estos segundos en una experiencia consciente. Te digo cómo hacerlo.

Vete a dormir con la intención de que realizarás los siguientes pasos en cuanto despiertes a la mañana siguiente:

Paso 1: Cuando te des cuenta de que estás despierto, abre los ojos.

Paso 2: Observa fijamente el techo sin enfocarte en nada en particular.

Paso 3: Intenta mantener los ojos abiertos. Enfócate sólo en esto.

Este ejercicio le tiende una trampa a la conciencia serena. Cada paso es importante en la secuencia. La noche anterior, cuando te vayas a dormir, define una intención; esto pone el ejercicio al inicio de tu agenda mental en la mañana. Abrir los ojos y mirar el techo te distrae de comenzar a pensar. Pero enfocar tu atención en mantener los ojos abiertos es un verdadero secreto. Tu cerebro despierta por la mañana en oleadas, alternando la vigilia y el sueño, y por eso te despiertas sintiéndote todavía un poco adormilado.

Al enfocar tu atención en mantener los ojos abiertos tu cerebro no tiene otra opción que bloquear el pensamiento. El esfuerzo por estar despierto lo tiene totalmente ocupado. (Puedes lograr lo mismo al ver un punto azul en tu imaginación y fijar en él tu atención.)

Cuando domines los pasos de este ejercicio te encontrarás en el estado de "ojos abiertos, sin pensamientos". Mientras estás recostado, percibe cómo se siente. Muy pocas personas han estado despiertas sin pensar por más de unos cuantos segundos. Con la práctica puedes sostener este ejercicio hasta por un minuto. Es muy significativo estar quieto, en silencio, calmado y alerta sin un ego que defender o una historia que construir. Cuanto más consciente seas de lo significativa que es esta experiencia, más comprensión tendrás sobre tu ser verdadero. El ejercicio no tiene un fin en sí mismo, sino que sólo es un punto de partida.

Existen variantes para llegar al mismo estado de "ojos abiertos, sin pensamientos". Por ejemplo, en la meditación, la mente se asienta en un estado de quietud en reposo, y cuando abres los ojos al final de la meditación, la relajación mental persiste. Aquí la mente coordina una respuesta cerebral, la tendencia natural a volver a la conciencia pura si existe la oportunidad de hacerlo. El propósito de un mantra, si practicas la medicación con mantras, es darle a la mente un sonido sin significado para que se ocupe de él, lo que te ayuda a dejar de enfocarte en lo que intentan decirte tus pensamientos. Conforme el mantra regresa a la mente se vuelve más leve y sutil, lo que permite que entres con facilidad a la mente serena. Al principio, cuando sales de la meditación, estar con "ojos abiertos, sin pensamientos" es breve, porque estás muy acostumbrado a saltar de regreso a tu propia historia. Pero con el tiempo hay una expansión, y "ojos abiertos sin pensamientos" se vuelve un estado estable las 24 horas del día.

En un punto, una persona se considera completamente despierta. En el ejercicio matutino que acabo de presentar, "ojos abiertos, sin pensamientos", está en blanco. Pero no así la experiencia de estar despierto por completo. La actividad mental surge —la piedra que sale del lago—, mientras que el estado sereno permanece. El silencio y la actividad se experimentan como una sola cosa: conciencia moviéndose dentro de sí misma. La experiencia de "ojos abiertos, sin pensamientos" al principio es modesta, aunque abre el camino para transformar la forma en que usamos nuestra mente.

He enfatizado que la mayoría de la gente no abandona sus historias, sin importar cuánto dolor y sufrimiento causen, porque su instinto natural es aferrarse a ellas. Si no eres una esposa golpeada por su marido que se niega a abandonarlo, un gay con temor a salir del clóset, un adicto al opio incapaz de dejar el vicio, o cualquier otra persona atrapada en un dolor profundo, no puedes comprender qué tan terribles pueden ser las consecuencias de aferrarse a algo. Las historias pueden convertirse en un estado de desesperanza, y ese estado desafía lo mejor que la medicina y la psicoterapia pueden hacer para ayudar.

Debido a que nos aferramos a nuestras historias, ¿el camino directo realmente puede ofrecer una salida? Estamos de acuerdo con que tú, yo y todos los demás estamos atorados en nuestra historia. *Atorado* es una palabra que resume el viejo condicionamiento que evita que generemos los cambios que deseamos en nuestra vida. Se puede aprender mucho de todas las formas en que se ha fracasado al intentar desatorarse. Considera el Nuevo Testamento, en el cual Jesús de Nazaret aparece como una de las figuras espirituales en la historia registrada. La historia del Hijo de Dios, que predica la paz en el mundo y que es crucificado por ello, constituye un drama que ha transfigurado Occidente durante dos milenios.

Pero es desconcertante que lo que enseña el Nuevo Testamento a menudo es imposible de alcanzar. "Amar a tu prójimo como a ti mismo" claramente va en contra de cómo opera la naturaleza humana (y habría sido terrible seguir esa enseñanza ante el nazismo, en una época en la que muchos judíos tenían vecinos que se unían al partido nazi, o en Bosnia donde los vecindarios mezclados con musulmanes y cristianos se volvieron campos de batalla basados en la religión). "Poner la otra mejilla" suena algo masoquista, excepto para un cristiano plenamente confirmado; pedirles a los abusadores que victimicen a los indefensos todavía más. Pero no es una crítica dirigida a una fe —todas las tradiciones espirituales han naufragado en el mismo obstáculo—. La naturaleza humana está enamorada del drama que ha creado, y entre más crudo sea el contraste entre el bien y el mal, más nos aferramos a nuestra historia. Si la raza humana está esperando el día en que triunfe el bien o el mal, el único desenlace predecible es que el drama está diseñado para durar una eternidad.

Naturalmente la mayoría de la gente se aferra al drama a un nivel más leve. Con excepción de esas épocas en que las fuerzas inconscientes hacen erupción y toda una nación, o el mundo entero, es arrastrada al borde de la catástrofe —a veces cayendo en el abismo—, la vida cotidiana está atorada en las necesidades, los deseos, los deberes y las demandas. El resultado es el mismo si te ahogas en una tina o en el mar.

Pero no debes sufrir la miseria para experimentar estar separado. Tu calidad de vida puede ser buena o mala —la vida generalmente conlleva ambas—, la situación se reduce al mismo meollo del asunto: atorado es atorado. El drama se perpetúa a sí mismo. Incluso nuestro deseo de escapar del hechizo/sueño/ilusión se vuelve parte de la historia. Una experiencia transitoria como la de "ojos cerrados, sin pensamientos" o la relajación pacífica de la meditación es como disparar una cerbatana contra un tanque. El *momentum* de nuestro drama colectivo ha demostrado ser imparable.

Si la mente total no existiera, nadie podría haberla inventado. Todos estamos demasiado atorados para ver más allá de la historia en la cual estamos enredados. Pero la mente total sí existe; por lo tanto debe tener una forma de revelarse a sí misma. En los Vedas se dice que el dios Shiva tiene múltiples formas de mostrarse como es y de disfrazarse. Vale la pena saberlo. Por cada impulso de amor existe un impulso de temor. Por cada momento de claridad existe un momento de confusión. El truco es no preferir el amor y la claridad por encima del miedo y la confusión, porque es inevitable que el péndulo regrese.

El truco es evocar la fuente de amor y claridad, acercarte a ella gradualmente y al final hacerla tuya. (El Nuevo Testamento tenía más posibilidades de ser práctico si Jesús hubiera enseñado: "Intenta amar a tu prójimo como a ti mismo" y "Ve si poner la otra mejilla ayuda a romper el ciclo de las represalias".) La única esperanza para escapar de las trampas de la mente condicionada es usar su mejor naturaleza como un hilo, siguiéndolo día con día hasta que tu historia se desvanezca. Entonces se vuelve natural vivir en la totalidad.

Un deseo de eliminar el deseo

El ciclo interminable del bien y el mal, el placer y el dolor, la felicidad y la tristeza, es como una hoguera que se alimenta a sí misma. Pero, así como la mente es activa y bulliciosa en la superficie, y serena en sus honduras, así también es la vida. El drama lo es todo, pero sólo a su nivel. Cuando tienes una experiencia modesta como la de "ojos abiertos, sin pensamientos", la interferencia de la actividad mental cesa de forma temporal. Lo que remplaza es algo más que la quietud. En lo que se refiere a negociar las demandas de la vida cotidiana, por sí misma una mente en silencio no es mejor que un coche si se apaga el motor. Debe haber algo atractivo dentro de la experiencia del silencio.

Este algo existe en la forma de una leve presencia, que ya hemos encontrado como el sentido del ser. Cuando el sentido del ser está sobre nosotros somos naturales, relajados, libres y presentes. Pero se nos escapa de las manos mantener este sentimiento de presencia. Creo que es justo decir que los vislumbres del ser verdadero que generan experiencias de amor, alegría, paz, seguridad y autoestima son lo único que ha dado luz a la condición humana. Existe un deseo natural de ampliar estas experiencias. En retribución, el ser verdadero tiene el poder de la atracción (conocido en sánscrito como *Swarupa*, la atracción del Ser).

Al ser silencioso y en gran medida inadvertido, el sentido del ser no puede desatorarnos por sí mismo. Si has realizado meditación con mantras, la práctica de atención plena o de conciencia enfocada, las cuales son técnicas valiosas para sacar a flote el sentido del ser, ya sabes con qué necedad la mente regresa a los asuntos de siempre. Puedes entrenarte con esfuerzo para desplegar cualquier atributo espiritual —gentileza amorosa, perdón, atención constante a Dios—, pero el sentido del ser no puede ser entrenado. Simplemente *es*. El esfuerzo no sólo es inútil sino también dañino. Este concepto fue expresado por el venerable maestro espiritual J. Krishnamurti cuando dijo: "¿Puedes disciplinar tu mente para ser libre?". Ése es el tema. No importa lo bien que entrenemos nuestra mente, incluyendo todos los tipos de entrenamiento espiritual, la libertad es un estado en el que la disciplina es totalmente ajena.

Yo tenía eso en mente cuando dije que el camino directo debe ser fácil, eficiente y espontáneo. Si quieres estar aquí y ahora, que es el estado del metahumano, primero debes dejar de intentarlo. El sentido del ser llega a nuestra conciencia y de hecho su presencia puede ser muy fuerte. Se puede convertir en un estado de éxtasis, un amorío con lo divino, como en este apasionado clamor de Rumi:

> Oh, Dios, ¡he descubierto el amor!
> ¡Qué maravilloso, qué bondadoso, qué hermoso es!…
> Ofrezco mis saludos
> Al espíritu de la pasión que infundió y agitó este universo entero
> Y todo lo que contiene

La experiencia usual de la presencia es placentera y con mucha menos pasión. Pero Rumi nos da una pista cuando señala el poder del deseo. En su caso, el deseo es una intoxicación del amor divino. Todos tenemos deseos, y gracias a la fuerza del deseo nos levantamos todas las mañanas con la voluntad de ver qué nos depara el día. Si el día nos trae momentos de despertar, entonces el deseo nos ha servido para desatorarnos.

Ya que el sentido del ser simplemente *es* no lo puedes desear directamente. Eso sería como decir: "Desearía existir". En cambio, lo que sucede es que engañas al deseo para lograr que vaya a donde tú quieres. (Como dijo un amigo, hackeas espiritualmente la materialidad.) En el budismo esto se dice así: "Usa una espina para sacar otra espina, y después tira las dos espinas". Esa enseñanza es famosa y ha generado muchos comentarios. Suena tan simple como remover una astilla del dedo picándola con una aguja. El equivalente mental enfrenta dificultades. Y como usaremos el deseo para ir más allá del deseo, se deben explicar un poco estas dificultades.

Originalmente Buda se refiere a las astillas como un dolor profundo que no puede ser sanado. Una de las fuentes más hondas de dolor es el miedo a la violencia, del cual Buda habla con franqueza. "El miedo nace de armarse uno mismo. ¡Mira cuánta gente teme! Te contaré sobre el temor espantoso que me sacudió por completo. Ver criaturas apaleándose unas a otras como peces en aguas poco profundas, ¡tan hostiles entre ellas! Al ver esto, tuve miedo" (Sutta Nipata).

Podemos inclinarnos para escuchar cuál fue la escapatoria de Buda ante el temor, la cual invocó la imagen de la espina. Continúa: "Al ver a la gente enfrascada en el conflicto me sentí completamente desconsolado. Pero después discerní una espina, difícil de ver, incrustada muy dentro de mi corazón. Es sólo cuando esta espina pincha a alguien, que la persona corre como loca en todas direcciones. Así que si se extrae la espina, la persona ya no corre sino que se apacigua".

En la forma pura, experimentar la espina del dolor en el corazón incentiva a la persona a encontrar paz interior. La enseñanza es hermosa, pero, como las enseñanzas del Nuevo Testamento, contradice la naturaleza humana. Cuando la gente está enfrascada en el conflicto, está motivada para aumentarlo, ya sea ignorando el dolor de su corazón o bien, más probable, como señal de que deben seguir luchando. (Para dar crédito a las culturas budistas en Asia la enseñanza de la paz ha resultado en menos conflictos violentos a lo largo del tiempo, un récord que otras religiones podrían envidiar. Sin embargo la violencia budista en contra de los musulmanes en Burma demuestra que la religión no es inmune a la violencia.)

La frase "Una espina saca otra espina" puede usarse de manera más psicológica como una táctica de sanación. La meta es sustituir pensamientos negativos y autodestructivos con otros positivos y para el bienestar personal. Bajo el nombre de terapia cognitiva, este enfoque se basa en la racionalidad para superar las emociones. Por ejemplo, una paciente se puede quejar de que nada le sale bien jamás, que sin importar qué tan duro lo intente todo termina en fracaso y decepción. Obviamente existe una fuerte carga emocional detrás del pensamiento derrotista. Cuando esto se vuelve un hábito, en una situación difícil el primer pensamiento que viene a la mente automáticamente es: "Nada va a funcionar. Lo sé".

El resultado usual es, en efecto, que nada bueno sucede. Difícilmente podría haber un mejor ejemplo de una profecía que se cumple. Un terapeuta cognitivo usaría un nuevo pensamiento para eliminar el viejo (la espina que saca la espina) al señalar que hay cosas buenas que le han sucedido al paciente. La vida no ha sido una serie de fracasos interminable. Por ello, el curso racional es pensar: "Esta situación puede terminar bien o mal. Nadie lo sabe, así que tengo la oportunidad de hacer lo mejor para obtener un buen resultado". No es fácil remplazar el pesimismo con optimismo, ya que las emociones son más profundas que la razón, y decirte a ti mismo que algo bueno *puede* pasar da paso libre al pesimismo. Con práctica y guía, la negatividad habitual puede ser suavizada, pero la naturaleza humana no se ha vuelto pacífica y plena por medio del uso de la razón.

Finalmente está la segunda parte de la enseñanza con la cual lidiar. "Usa una espina para sacar otra espina, *y después tira las dos espinas.*" En el proceso de superar una enfermedad, tomas la medicina por el tiempo necesario para mejorar y después la tiras. Pero lo mismo es todavía más misterioso cuando se trata de la mente. Por ejemplo, si usas pensamientos positivos para remplazar los negativos, sigues enfatizando que eres un pensador positivo, tan enganchado a tu historia como alguien pesimista. Sin duda es mejor creer en la luz del sol que en la sombra. Escapar de la ilusión es otra cosa.

Tirar las dos espinas significa que todo el escenario de dolor y placer, bien y mal, luz y oscuridad, se desecha. Éste es el mensaje esencial de Buda. El diagnóstico es certero, y la imagen de ser sanado —vivir más allá del control del drama— es inspiradora. El desafío que tiene el camino directo es cómo hacer de la inspiración una realidad viviente.

Despejar el camino para el ser

La respuesta, como yo la concibo, es usar el deseo como la espina, porque todos hemos experimentado su naturaleza doble. El deseo demanda ser satisfecho. Si el deseo es lo bastante fuerte, como en la atracción pasional sexual, es suficiente para enloquecer a la gente. La espina causa dolor porque nunca es suficiente tener un momento de satisfacción —el siguiente deseo llega con una nueva demanda de ser satisfecho—. ¿Cuál es la otra espina, la que terminará el dolor? La satisfacción misma. Los moralistas que predican en contra del deseo, que lo llaman obra del Diablo o, en términos freudianos, obra del ello, ven con un solo ojo. El deseo es tan hermoso como traicionero. La atracción sexual conduce a relaciones amorosas duraderas, y no sólo abuso sexual.

No creo que alguien pueda negar esta verdad evidente, y podemos recurrir a ella usando la espina del deseo para eliminar la espina del deseo. Pero ¿el deseo de qué? Si las tradiciones espirituales han sostenido el deseo de amor, paz, gracia divina, perdón y un boleto al cielo o al Nirvana, sólo para fracasar, ¿qué es lo que queda? La única respuesta que se me ocurre es el deseo de ser real. Básicamente eso, y sólo eso, es lo que ofrece el sentido del ser. No hay palo ni zanahoria, sólo la promesa de que puedes estar aquí y ahora, que es como puedes experimentar la realidad libre de toda ilusión.

En términos prácticos, la mente no puede aprender de golpe lo que es ser real. El camino directo es eso, un camino: toma tiempo. La vida ofrece todos los motivos imaginables para renunciar al camino. El deseo nos tienta para que llevemos nuestro interés a cualquier otra parte; la vieja historia es muy insistente. Pero puedes cultivar un interés en volverte real. No es necesariamente más difícil que cultivar un interés por el vino, por coleccionar timbres postales o por las novelas rusas. Sólo se necesita curiosidad y el destello del deseo (al cual se refieren en la tradición hindú como la chispa que incendia todo el bosque; la necesidad de escapar de la ilusión eventualmente destruirá la ilusión).

El camino directo es único porque no estamos siendo enseñados por el amor, la paz, la compasión o cualquier otra cualidad deseable que pueda traer nuestra vida. Estamos siendo enseñados por la existencia misma. Sólo funcionará saber qué es lo que yace en el corazón de la existencia. Contrario a lo que dice Hamlet, "ser o no ser", no es la cuestión. "Ser" es la cuestión, por sí misma. Si lo preguntas todos los días, tu ser verdadero te escuchará y después te presentará respuestas fascinantes y en constante cambio. Al estar comprometido con descubrir qué significa estar aquí, transformas tu mente, de su viejo condicionamiento a un vehículo que puede alcanzar el más allá. La mente condicionada ha decidido con firmeza lo que significa existir, y justo por eso nos atoramos.

Para desatorarnos de una vez por todas el camino directo se enfrenta con un problema práctico, el cual se ha descrito en textos hindúes antiguos como "separar el agua de la leche". En otras palabras, la realidad cotidiana mezcla lo real y lo irreal para que sean inseparables. Esto es obvio cuando observas el cerebro, que presenta la realidad virtual sólo porque la realidad "real" nos vuelve conscientes. La peor película jamás realizada se proyecta en la pantalla con el mismo proyector que una película clásica de cine de arte. Diversas versiones del camino directo nos enseñan que somos como niños mirando marionetas de sombras en la pared. Creemos en estas imágenes de manera tan absoluta que la verdad se nos escapa —las sombras no pueden existir sin la luz que las hace visibles—. La realidad virtual sólo existe gracias a la metarrealidad.

Suena fácil separar la luz de las sombras, y el camino directo lo demuestra. Lo único que necesitas hacer es llevar el sentido del ser a tu atención. En términos prácticos, nada es más fácil o natural. En cualquier momento del día cierra los ojos, respira profundo unas cuantas veces para lograr un estado de relajación y centra tu atención en tu corazón (o en tu respiración). Dada la complejidad elaborada de la religión, suena extraño que el viaje espiritual completo sea sólo esto: relajarte y ser consciente de ti mismo.

Al hacer esto, sutilmente permites que la "atracción del ser" se vuelva una experiencia real. Si tu intención es más seria, aprender a meditar o comprometerte con el yoga intensifica la experiencia de sentir el ser —los mantras y las posturas de yoga (*asanas*) fueron creados para brindar distintos sabores o colores del ser—. Ya estamos equipados para este proceso. Conforme los niños crecen, por ejemplo, aprenden a identificar las gamas de la emoción: la hostilidad, la indignación, la irritación y el odio. Cuando conectas esas etiquetas con un sentimiento interno es natural decir: "No estoy enojado, sólo frustrado" o "No te acerques a él, es un resentido".

Las gamas en la conciencia también pueden sentirse, pero no tienen etiquetas. Cuando experimentas el sentido del ser como se indica arriba, vas más allá de los pensamientos y sentimientos que pueden ser etiquetados. Ninguno de ellos, incluso el pensamiento más amoroso y el sentimiento más espiritual, es la base de la realidad. Sólo el sentido del ser es irreductible. No puedes ir más allá de él ni convertirlo en algo más básico. La actividad mental se desvanece en una especie de nada —la mente quieta—. De acuerdo con el camino directo, ésta es la fuente de todo "aquí dentro" y "allá fuera". Pero aquí está la parte complicada. ¿Acaso "todo" es práctico? Si alguien te mostrara una pieza de papel en blanco y te dijera: "Aquí están todos los libros", o un lienzo en blanco y dijera: "Aquí están todas las pinturas", esa declaración no te ayudaría a escribir un libro o a pintar un cuadro. Lo que tú quieres es escribir un libro, no todos los libros, y pintar un cuadro, no todos los cuadros.

Asimismo suena inútil decir que la realidad es "siempre, todo y en todas partes". Estamos acostumbrados a lo específico. Para bien o para mal, vivimos nuestra vida en *este* momento, en *esta* ubicación. Podría parecer irremediablemente vago decirle a alguien, como yo lo he estado haciendo: "Sé aquí y ahora". ¿Dónde más podríamos estar, en Marte? Pero una vida basada en lo específico es engañosa porque el hechizo/sueño/ilusión contiene miles de cosas específicas, tantas que no puedes lidiar con ellas o escapar de su sujeción. Cuando yo era niño y vivía en la India escuchaba versiones simples de lo que significa despertar a la realidad. En un cuento, un pez está frenético por la sed, y se mueve de un lado a otro para encontrar un trago de agua. Incluso a los cuatro años de edad un niño se ríe por el pez tonto que no se da cuenta de que está rodeado de agua. Sólo cuando creces comprendes la seriedad de la paradoja.

Una vez que tienes la experiencia de percibirte a ti mismo, lo cual está disponible para cada uno de nosotros en nuestros momentos de más calma, puedes usar tu silencio interno para transformar tu mundo, un día a la vez. Esto se logra al observar tus nociones equivocadas de la realidad y rechazarlas. Como un físico que clasifica todos los objetos en el mundo subatómico que no son los elementos constitutivos irreductibles del universo, tú examinas tus creencias fundamentales y las ordenas en el camino para llegar a tu fuente verdadera.

Esta tarea se facilita por dos cualidades invaluables de la mente: entendimiento e intuición. Son guías confiables cuando el pensamiento racional falla. Son confiables incluso cuando las emociones fallan. Cuando la gente habla de momentos eureka, el entendimiento y la intuición han atravesado un problema enredado para ir directo hacia la verdad. En estos momentos, cuando la luz nace de pronto, exclamamos: "Lo sabía, sólo sabía que éste era el camino". La belleza de un entendimiento es que se justifica a sí mismo. Simplemente lo sabes.

El sentido del ser es sereno y tan sutil que pocas personas se molestan en notarlo, pero dentro del ser hay cosas que simplemente sabemos. El camino directo nos pide sacar a la luz estas partes de conocimiento para que puedan apreciarse. El héroe aturdido en una comedia romántica por lo regular pelea con la mujer de su vida hasta que se da cuenta —ella lo supo todo el tiempo— de que la ama. Hemos visto esta trama cientos de veces, pero nos sigue encantando porque el entendimiento, el momento de "ahora lo entiendo", trae claridad y a menudo también placer.

Tener entendimientos sobre una relación o sobre un problema matemático difícil o el próximo capítulo de un libro que estás escribiendo es algo bastante específico. Pedir entendimiento de cómo funciona la vida es lo más inespecífico posible. El camino directo nos ayuda al simplificar las creencias equivocadas que debemos superar para despertar. De hecho, sólo hay un puñado de creencias erróneas a considerar:

CREENCIA EQUIVOCADA: Estoy separado y solo.
REALIDAD: El ser separado sólo es un constructo mental.

CREENCIA EQUIVOCADA: Éste es mi cuerpo.
REALIDAD: El cuerpo es parte del juego de la conciencia, que es universal, no personal.

CREENCIA EQUIVOCADA: El mundo físico es la base de la realidad.
REALIDAD: El mundo físico es una apariencia que adopta el juego de la conciencia.

CREENCIA EQUIVOCADA: Mi vida está limitada por el tiempo y el espacio.
REALIDAD: Todos vivimos en el ahora eterno, que es ilimitado.

En este punto del libro ninguna de estas equivocaciones es una sorpresa. Ahora necesitamos superarlas, lo que conduce al procedimiento de poner las cosas en orden de la siguiente manera: en cualquier momento, cuando tengas una experiencia que valga la pena ver, haz una pausa y di para ti mismo: "Éste es el juego de la conciencia". Para que la declaración se asimile, es mejor tener un sentido del ser junto con ella. Pero esa parte no es necesaria. Nadie puede separar el agua de la leche (incluso un centrifugador sólo separa los sólidos de los líquidos), así que se les debe permitir separarse a sí mismas.

Éste es un proceso simple y fácil, pero requiere paciencia. Al recordarte a ti mismo que cualquier experiencia es el juego de la conciencia, llevas la realidad a la mente. No discutes contigo mismo (ni con nadie más); no intentas ser bueno, sabio o mejor que los demás. No te rindes y tampoco luchas. En vez de eso te sientas por un momento en la intersección de la conciencia y la realidad, en un momento de reflexión. La experiencia a la mano es la vida en *este* momento, en *este* lugar. Al recordarte de forma consciente lo que es verdad, permites que la atracción del ser te traiga de vuelta a casa.

Debido a que no podríamos soportar que nos sacaran de pronto de la mente condicionada, el juego de la conciencia no insiste en nada. La vida se mueve como un río entre sus riberas. Cuando dices: "Éste es el juego de la conciencia", no estás deteniendo el río ni intentas dirigirlo. Estás sentado en la ribera observando cómo fluye el río. No sé si mencionar que esta postura se conoce como *atestiguar*, porque al escuchar la palabra mucha gente intenta atestiguar o se frustra si no atestigua lo que quiere. Lo comprendo. Suena tentador atestiguar con calma y desapego la muerte de un ser querido, en vez de estar conectado a la pena.

El río sigue su propio curso sin importar cuánto deseemos que se mueva de forma distinta —a veces se mueve hacia la pena, la tristeza, el dolor y el sufrimiento—. Después se sigue moviendo. Eso no es simplemente tristeza, sino que es el flujo inexorable que nos lleva a la libertad. Sólo debemos permitirla, en vez de luchar contra ella. Cada lucha es tan sólo otro aspecto del río, un pequeño remolino que no tiene significancia en el río que llega al mar. *Permitir* es una de las palabras clave en las descripciones del camino directo, pero es otra palabra que dudo mencionar. La gente acabará por intentar permitir, y se frustrará por no estar permitiendo cuando lo desea, y así sucesivamente.

En su forma pura, el camino directo sólo está experimentando el sentido del ser y permitiendo que haga su trabajo sin interferencia.

Pero hay otra etapa en la que el silencio y el fluir y la experiencia de "estar aquí ahora" está terminada. No son la meta, sólo una plataforma para saltar a la siguiente etapa. Con la siguiente etapa ya no eres testigo del flujo, sino que tú *eres* el flujo. El juego de la conciencia y el ser se funden en uno solo. Krishnamurti llamaba a esta fusión "la primera y última libertad", una frase hermosa. Para hacer que sea más que hermosa, tienes que experimentarla. Comencemos.

Vamos a dar un vuelco al cosmos y todo lo que contiene.

12

CONCIENCIA SIN ELECCIÓN

El *Homo sapiens* es la única especie que debe tratar de ser feliz. Entre todos los misterios que rodean al ser humano, éste es uno de los más inextricables. Durante siglos nuestra lucha contra los enemigos de la felicidad —violencia, ansiedad, desesperación y depresión— ha sido el precio que pagamos por ser conscientes. Suponemos, pero no lo sabemos de cierto, que otras criaturas no experimentan estos estados. Cuando un lobo viejo ya no puede correr con la manada se recuesta para morir, vencido por la edad y los crudos elementos de la naturaleza. A cualquier edad, un ser humano puede ser cálido, estar seguro y físicamente sano, pero en el interior se ha rendido ante la vida.

Entre más investigues la naturaleza humana, más difícil parece intentar ser feliz. Sigmund Freud, que dedicó toda su vida a investigar qué mueve a las personas, terminó sus días en Londres en 1939 como refugiado después de que Hitler integró a Austria bajo el régimen alemán en 1938. En 1933, cuando Hitler subió al poder por primera vez, los escritos de Freud fueron prohibidos, y como era judío estaba en riesgo.

Le escribió con amargura lo siguiente a un discípulo suyo que estaba en Inglaterra: "Qué progreso estamos haciendo. En la Edad Media me hubieran quemado. Ahora se contentan con quemar mis libros". Freud insistió en quedarse en Viena, y finalmente lo persuadieron de huir en la primavera de 1938, cuando la Gestapo arrestó e interrogó a su hija Anna. Después de pagar un exorbitante impuesto de "huida", por el cual los nazis les quitaban dinero y joyas a los judíos sin piedad, el fundador del psicoanálisis se fue a Inglaterra en un estado de tristeza pesimista, preguntándose, mientras el miedo y el terror florecían como una flor venenosa, si era demasiado pedir evitar que los humanos cometieran asesinato.

El psicoanálisis casi ha desaparecido de la escena, y ha sido remplazado por terapias con medicamentos para los desórdenes mentales. Sin embargo en el botiquín no existe una pastilla para la felicidad. En tiempos de paz relativa, la gente se contenta con una especie de felicidad superficial, y encuentra el amor y el placer cuando aparecen y hacen lo posible por no enredarse en lo malo.

El intento de remodelar la naturaleza humana al demostrar qué nos mueve no ha tenido éxito. El camino directo se trata de algo distinto, descubrir qué es esencial en nuestra vida. El dolor y el sufrimiento no son esenciales. Son parte del drama que hemos construido —una parte muy necia—, pero el drama puede dejarse atrás. Existe un nivel de conciencia que trasciende el dolor y el sufrimiento. La gran sabiduría del camino directo es que todo depende de tu nivel de conciencia porque todo *es* un nivel de conciencia. La metarrealidad está junto a la realidad cotidiana, a sólo un nivel de conciencia de distancia. (La teología cristiana enseña que el cielo es donde el alma encuentra la dicha eterna, pero hace mucho los teólogos abandonaron la noción de que el cielo es un lugar físico, a pesar de las imágenes que llevamos en nuestra cabeza de ángeles sentados en las nubes tocando arpas, o de corderos saltando en praderas verdes —ésa es una de las descripciones más comunes de la gente que regresa de una experiencia cercana a la muerte y que afirman haber visto el cielo—. La *Enciclopedia católica* define el cielo como un estado del ser que se obtiene por la gracia. Para mí, *estado del ser* y *estado de conciencia* son sinónimos.)

Hasta ahora hemos tomado el camino directo a través de dos ámbitos de la conciencia: el cuerpo y la mente activa. Podrías suponer que el viaje ya no tiene a dónde ir. ¿Qué más hay en la vida más allá de lo físico y lo mental? De hecho hay algo más profundo, un departamento de la existencia que hace que las cosas resulten como resultan —bueno o malo, exitoso o un fracaso, un sueño satisfecho o un sueño negado—. Aquí descubrimos que todo sucede por un motivo, pero ese motivo es muy distinto de las historias que nos contamos a nosotros mismos. La conciencia pura organiza cada evento, incluyendo cada evento posible. Lo ve y lo sabe todo. Desde este punto de vista todo sucede por una razón porque hay sólo una cosa.

Aun así, las partes de la vida que tanto nos esforzamos por tener bien —el trabajo, la familia, las relaciones, la moral, la religión, las leyes, la política— no son expresiones de una sola cosa. Son constructos compartimentalizados. Lo que sucede en uno de ellos, en otro puede ser ajeno o incluso un anatema. Va en contra de la ley tomar una vida, pero los líderes políticos pueden obtener una popularidad masiva al comenzar una guerra y tomar una enorme cantidad de vidas. La naturaleza ignora los compartimentos en cada nivel. Una célula se desarrolla como una sola cosa, no como una colección de partes. Come, respira, fabrica proteínas y enzimas, divide y expresa el conocimiento comprimido en la doble hélice del ADN. Para una célula, éstos no son compartimentos descritos en un libro de texto de medicina —las partes no importan—. Lo que importa es la vida de la célula, que es una sola cosa.

¿Podemos devolver la vida humana a una sola cosa? Y si podemos hacerlo, ¿eso resolverá el problema del dolor y el sufrimiento? El camino directo afirma que es posible. La única cosa, en lo referente a los seres humanos, es la conciencia pura, pero etiquetarla nos lleva más lejos de una sola cosa, y no nos acerca. El gran misterio de la conciencia pura es que no tiene nada que pueda ser formulado, convertido en una buena manera de existir ni que traiga felicidad.

Por ejemplo, en la tradición hindú la conciencia pura es eterna, consciente y dichosa (*Sat Chit Ananda* en sánscrito). Esta formulación llevó a alguien a pensar: "Ah, la dicha es la clave. ¿Qué es la felicidad sino dicha?". Con base en ello, la frase "sigue tu dicha" se volvió muy popular. Cuando se ponía en práctica tenía la ventaja de llevar a la gente hacia dentro, diciéndole que la forma en que se sentía acerca de su vida era más importante que las recompensas externas. Pero "sigue tu dicha" es inútil si no puedes encontrarla, en primer lugar, o si te ha afectado una tragedia o un desastre natural. Y es peor que inútil si eres blanco de una persecución maligna e imparable.

El camino directo no se basa en formulaciones o ideas fijas acerca de cómo vivir. Al ser confrontado por el misterio de ser humano, dice: "Permite que el misterio se resuelva a sí mismo. Estás aquí para observar cómo sucede. En ese papel, tú estás viviendo la expresión del misterio". Esto es lo más cerca que alguien ha estado de vivir una sola cosa al igual que las células, que es uno mismo. Cuando se destila a su esencia, el camino directo nos pide a ti y a mí dedicar nuestra vida al conocimiento de que nosotros, en nosotros mismos, somos el misterio de la vida conforme ésta se desenvuelve.

Son palabras hermosas, pero ¿qué haremos cuando nos levantemos de la cama mañana temprano? Las acciones y los pensamientos que ocupan nuestros días no son un problema. Mañana temprano saldrás de la cama y harás lo que quieras o lo que debas hacer. Si te siguieran con una cámara de video quizá no detectarían nada especial sobre tu existencia diaria; podría parecer una existencia típica que lleva una persona que nunca ha escuchado sobre el camino directo.

Pero en el interior, aquello a lo que has dedicado tu vida será muy diferente. En todas las culturas en las que la gente ha investigado seriamente una cosa (una filosofía conocida como "monismo"), estaba presente la misma dedicación. Ya sea que haya surgido en India, Persia, Grecia o China, el monismo llevó a la mente lejos de los incontables detalles de la vida hacia una sola cosa. De eso se trata este capítulo. A pesar de lo fascinante de la diversidad, la infinita variedad de cosas que contiene el universo físico, el misterio no ofrece solución alguna ahí.

Cuando reduces la vida a lo que es verdaderamente esencial, la diversidad disminuye y la unidad aumenta. Tu conciencia comienza a remodelarse alrededor de una cosa. Despertar es una cosa; la iluminación es una cosa; permitir que el misterio de la existencia se despliegue a través de ti es una cosa. Sin embargo, estas descripciones son limitadas. Lo que realmente buscamos es la experiencia de una sola cosa. Cuando se logra, se da todo lo demás, no sólo el fin del sufrimiento, sino el acceso al potencial infinito que desea expresarse a través de nosotros.

Éste es el estado que yo llamo "conciencia sin elección". Es el opuesto de la lucha. En vez de siempre hacer, practicas el arte de no hacer. En vez de intentar decidir si X te hará más feliz que Y, permites que la opción suceda por sí misma. Cuando escuchamos sobre las ventajas de soltar, vivir en el presente y permitir que la vida fluya, en el estado de conciencia sin elección estas posibilidades se vuelven reales.

La conciencia sin elección es la etapa final del despertar. Te lleva a un lugar en el cual quieres hacer lo mejor para ti. En este estado el dolor y el sufrimiento terminan porque no tienen ninguna relación con la vida que vives conscientemente. El poeta místico Kabir vio la situación con claridad.

Pregunté a mi corazón,
¿cuál es tu destino?
No hay viajero delante de ti
ni siquiera un camino.
¿Cómo puedes llegar ahí,
y dónde te quedarás?

En el imaginario de Kabir, el camino son las etapas de salir, caminar y llegar, que es como todos vivimos. Comenzamos una acción, ya sea una pequeña como sacar el jugo de naranja del refrigerador, o una grande como casarse o encontrar un trabajo. La acción comienza, sucede y termina. Kabir ve que el corazón —palabra que usa para decir alma— no puede encontrar la plenitud de esta forma. En cambio ve otro camino:

Sé fuerte, corazón mío.
Aparta tus adornos,
y quédate donde estás
en ti mismo.

Veamos si podemos lograr justamente eso.

El arte de no hacer

La conciencia sin elección suena extraña en el mundo moderno, en el cual la vida se ve únicamente como una serie de elecciones, y se piensa que la felicidad se alcanza al tomar buenas decisiones en vez de malas. Es difícil darnos cuenta de que las mejores decisiones se toman a sí mismas. La lógica detrás de no hacer es simple: una cosa no tiene nada que hacer excepto ser ella misma. Por ello, no tenemos nada que hacer, excepto ser nosotros mismos. Ésta es la esencia de no hacer.

No es una idea nueva. En la enseñanza taoísta de la China antigua no hacer es *Wu wei*. El concepto nació hace cinco o siete siglos a. e. C. En el budismo la enseñanza se encuentra en un sutra de la siguiente manera: "Se puede acceder directo a la felicidad en la meditación al abstenerse de la actividad mental consciente". En el cristianismo el salto de fe que se originó con el filósofo danés Søren Kierkegaard fue su intento por llevar a cabo el concepto central del Sermón de la Montaña, que todas las cosas pueden ser dejadas a la Providencia. En un salto de fe, un creyente permite que Dios se haga cargo, la máxima prueba de confianza.

La ausencia de lucha es común a todas las enseñanzas de no hacer, pero el paso de los siglos no la ha hecho menos misteriosa. No hacer tiene sentido para la mente lógica. Claro que tenemos muchas cosas que hacer —apenas si encontramos las suficientes horas en el día para lograrlas—. Pero ¿qué hiciste hoy para producir nuevos glóbulos rojos, el recubrimiento de tu estómago y la capa externa de tu piel? Éstas son partes de tu anatomía que deben ser renovadas constantemente porque la vida de las células de la sangre, el estómago y la piel dura sólo unas pocas semanas o meses.

En el mismo sentido, ¿qué vas a hacer hoy para cambiar oxígeno por dióxido de carbono en tus pulmones, sin el cual la vida se extingue en cuestión de minutos? La vasta proporción de tu vida física ya se hace cargo de sí misma. La existencia se divide entre cosas que hacemos y cosas que se hacen cargo de sí mismas. Por lo tanto, una parte de ti ya vive sin tomar decisiones. Para comenzar a ver el valor de la conciencia sin elección deja de asignarle tanta importancia a tus decisiones cotidianas, que en su mayoría están gobernadas por el hábito. A la larga el hábito evita que encuentres la renovación. Peor aún, mientras estás envuelto en la realidad virtual puedes caer presa del sentimiento de que la vida es increíblemente injusta. Puedes ser inteligente, tener todo tipo de talentos, ambicioso y celebrado por tus logros, pero no hay garantía de que no sufrirás el destino de Mozart.

A finales del verano de 1791 Mozart fue a Praga, donde una de sus óperas era el centro de las festividades para el emperador austriaco. Mozart comenzó a sentirse enfermo, pero regresó a Viena y el 30 de septiembre asistió a la premier de *La flauta mágica*, una de sus grandes obras maestras.

Para entonces su salud había dado un vuelco alarmante; tenía hinchazón, vómito y un dolor severo. Su esposa y su médico hicieron todo lo posible para sanarlo, mientras la mente de Mozart se abocó en escribir una nueva comisión para un réquiem, el cual nunca terminó. Fue en vano que se ocupara de lleno a su genio musical, porque el 5 de diciembre a medianoche Wolfgang Amadeus Mozart, la mente musical más preciada, murió de causas aún desconocidas a la edad de 35 años. Hacia el final de su vida hubo escenas desgarradoras en las que se sentaba en la cama para cantar tonadas de *La flauta mágica* con sus amigos. Pocas personas que aman la música clásica no consideran que la muerte de Mozart fue una gran pérdida.

No cuento esta historia —que alcanzó a muchas personas no devotas de la música clásica gracias a la película *Amadeus* de 1984— para lamentar la muerte o especular acerca de lo que la medicina moderna podría haber hecho para salvar la vida de Mozart. (Se han conjeturado casi 20 causas de muerte, incluyendo fiebre reumática, falla renal y envenenamiento de la sangre. La mayoría son infecciones que hoy en día se curan con antibióticos.) Tan sólo deseo señalar que el más grande entre nosotros también es controlado por causas invisibles. El drama al que nos aferramos tan sólo hace lo suyo, en sus propios términos. El hechizo/sueño/ilusión genera de forma misteriosa eventos impredecibles que no pueden ser desentrañados.

¿Cómo superamos la sensación de que estamos indefensos ante el azar o el destino invisible? Sin duda hay momentos en que se revelan las conexiones ocultas. La noción de sincronicidad se ha vuelto popular por describir un tipo especial de coincidencia. Piensas en el nombre de una persona, y unos minutos después esa persona llama. Quieres leer cierto libro y, sin avisar, un amigo te lleva el libro. *Sincronicidad* se define como una coincidencia significativa, distinta de las coincidencias aleatorias que no significan nada, como ver el mismo coche que el tuyo junto a ti en un semáforo.

La metarrealidad tiene una manera de enviarnos mensajes de vez en cuando que contradicen nuestras visiones inamovibles. La sincronicidad es un tipo de mensaje. Te dice: "Tu mundo está desorganizado, pero en realidad no lo está". En un vistazo fugaz observamos que la inteligencia superior puede organizar eventos para que el significado brote inesperadamente. Aún más, una experiencia sincrónica desafía nuestra concepción limitada de causa y efecto. En vez de que A cause B, las dos engranan de forma invisible. Si piensas en una palabra y al minuto siguiente alguien en la televisión dice la misma palabra, tú no creaste la coincidencia. Pero *algo* la creó.

Puedes sentir tu cuerpo físico y escuchar tus pensamientos, pero eso que organiza todos los eventos no puede ser percibido. De todas formas está aquí y ahora. El siguiente ejercicio te mostrará lo que quiero decir.

Ejercicio: Todavía estoy aquí

Donde sea que estés ahora, mira la habitación y haz un inventario de lo que contiene. Observa los muebles, los adornos, los libros, incluso las ventanas y la vista al exterior.

Ahora cierra los ojos y ve la habitación mentalmente. Comienza por eliminar su contenido. (Puedes abrir los ojos para refrescar tu memoria si lo necesitas.) ¡Observa cómo desaparecen los muebles! Y ya no existen. Elimina de la habitación todos los libros y adornos, y luego las ventanas y la vista al exterior. Te quedarás parado en una caja vacía. Si tienes una imagen mental de tu cuerpo parado en la habitación, también haz que desaparezca.

Con un último trazo elimina el techo, las paredes y el suelo. Estarás parado en un espacio sin objetos. Es difícil tener una imagen de la nada, así que tal vez veas luz blanca o negrura total. Después de quitar todo date cuenta de que tú todavía estás aquí.

Ahora revierte el proceso. Vuelve a traer el piso, las paredes, el techo. Reinstala los muebles, los adornos, los libros. Coloca de nuevo la ventana y la vista al exterior. Date cuenta de qué tú todavía estás aquí. Nada con respecto a la habitación, ya sea llena o vacía, te cambió.

Para demostrar que sigues aquí intenta deshacerte de ti mismo. Obsérvate a ti mismo parado en la habitación cuando está llena o el espacio que queda cuando la habitación ha desaparecido. En cualquiera de los dos estados, ¿puedes deshacerte de ti mismo? No. "Todavía estoy aquí" es intocable, porque tú eres la única cosa.

Este ejercicio te ayuda a recordar tu estatus verdadero. Si te encuentras en un lugar concurrido, lleno de distracciones o estrés, haz un inventario de todo lo que ves. Cierra los ojos y vacía el lugar hasta que no haya objetos, personas o la habitación. Conforme llegas al vacío, tú sigues aquí. Esto te brinda un sentimiento de autosuficiencia dichosa. Saber que eres imperecedero, *en este mismo instante*, es la máxima validación de que estás aquí ahora.

Has descubierto tu ser. Después de eso todo lo que digas, hagas o pienses es una sombra que pasa. Simplemente al ser has dominado el arte de no hacer. La siguiente etapa es permitir que esa sola cosa te demuestre de lo que es capaz.

Inmortalidad práctica

Cuando te ves a ti mismo como el punto inmóvil alrededor del cual todo se mueve te encuentras en un estado especial de conciencia. Podemos llamarlo el estado de *inmortalidad práctica*. Existen incontables personas que ya viven así, si son parte de una religión que cree en un dios personal. Al creer que Dios los está observando y juzgando, los creyentes devotos basan su vida en un ser inmortal. La máxima recompensa de este ser es ir al cielo, donde el creyente logra unirse a la inmortalidad.

En las sociedades dominadas por la religión tradicional las reglas de la moralidad tienden a ser rígidas y estrechas. Las religiones dogmáticas determinan una serie de reglas y afirman: "Si quieres saber lo que Dios quiere, obedece estas reglas". Las reglas pueden ser tan básicas como los 10 mandamientos y la Regla Dorada, o tan complejas como los cientos de instrucciones diarias que pertenecen a la vida de un brahmán ortodoxo del hinduismo. Pero vivir regido por las reglas depende de creer que existe una comunicación directa entre Dios y quien sea que dicta las reglas aquí en la Tierra. Las religiones tienden a estar de acuerdo en lo que constituye una vida devota (es decir, intentar agradar a Dios y obedecer las reglas), pero disienten sobre en qué mensajero confiar.

El camino directo no propone esa especie de inmortalidad práctica. Hay cero reglas y mandatos. En cambio, hay un camino cuyo destino es despertar. Una vez que estás en el camino debes comunicarte tú mismo con la inmortalidad, lo mejor que puedas. Moisés, Jesús y Buda no van a ayudarte (aunque, como no hay reglas, si quieres seguir una religión es tu decisión). Para comenzar a comunicarte con la inmortalidad el primer paso es creer que puedes hacerlo, lo cual no es fácil.

A lo largo de nuestra vida entera a todos nos han enseñado cómo vivir en el estado de inmortalidad práctica. Todo está calibrado de acuerdo con cómo encaja entre el nacimiento y la muerte. La gente que le exprime más placer a la vida domina muchas habilidades, trabaja duro y disfruta a todo lo que da, viaja a muchas partes, acumula dinero y posesiones; estas personas son las ganadoras en el esquema de la mortalidad práctica. Pero en su esencia más básica, todos vivimos a la sombra de la mortalidad. Esto se puede ver en nuestra adoración por la juventud, nuestra obsesión por evitar el envejecimiento, nuestro temor de que nuestro cuerpo resulte herido. La protección del cuerpo es central al volverse rico —el dinero ofrece una forma sustituta de invulnerabilidad—. Los ricos y poderosos se acercan a ser invulnerables a las dificultades de la vida. (Pero nada es más falso que decir: "Es mejor morir rico que pobre". El fin es el fin, sin importar cuánto dinero acumules y malgastes.)

En este contexto, ¿cómo puedes creer que te puedes comunicar con la inmortalidad, y mucho menos convertirla en una forma de vida? Todo lo que necesitas es el entendimiento de lo que ya estás haciendo. La totalidad —la cosa única de la que hemos estado hablando— es inmortal. Se comunica con la vida mortal al surgir en el mundo físico como tiempo, espacio, materia y energía. La física no tiene problema con esa aseveración. El estado precreado o vacío cuántico no está limitado por el tiempo y el espacio. No contiene materia y energía, sino sólo el potencial para la materia y energía.

El camino directo traslada este hecho básico a algo profundamente humano. Cuando realizas el ejercicio de este capítulo de vaciar una habitación hasta que quede un espacio en blanco, preparas el escenario para llenar otra vez la habitación con lo que tú desees. Como símbolo de la creatividad humana, el ejercicio es simple, pero cuando miras a tu alrededor te das cuenta de que el mundo ha sido construido de la misma manera. Colores, texturas, sabores, olores y demás, todos son símbolos de una cualidad que los seres humanos deseaban tener en la realidad virtual.

Perseveramos en este proyecto tomando una posibilidad, sacándola de su estado potencial para después hacerla real. Amamos a los perros por sus rasgos humanos —lealtad, amistad, obediencia, etcétera—, mientras que, en cambio, por medio de una especie de transferencia u ósmosis, el lobo siberiano primigenio, del cual provienen todos los perros domesticados, ha llevado a cabo una transformación revolucionaria. Los seres humanos seleccionamos conscientemente los rasgos que consideramos deseables y excluimos los que no deseamos ver. Los ojos adorables son un rasgo muy deseable, y un cachorro de labrador de ocho semanas de forma instintiva mira los ojos de su dueño, formando un vínculo que reconocemos al instante. (Por otra parte los lobos siguen teniendo una mirada salvaje y sin conexión con los humanos.) El perro es una creación humana en la carne y también en nuestra imaginación creativa.

La hibridación de perros y gatos, como la manipulación de los genes del maíz y el trigo para resistir las plagas, es manipulación física, pero la fuerza detrás de ella, la imaginación, no lo es. Usar nuestra imaginación es una forma en la que tú y yo y todos los demás vivimos el misterio. Nadie creó la imaginación, así como nadie creó la creatividad. Nadie creó la evolución tampoco. Cuando te acercas más a la fuente, donde la conciencia y toda su diversidad comienzan a estrecharse a una sola cosa, es evidente que el ser humano depende de contactar el mundo inmortal constantemente, no sólo cada día sino cada segundo.

La diversidad es un espectáculo deslumbrante. Siete mil millones de personas con la capacidad de ver millones de colores, escribir incontables melodías, decir combinaciones infinitas de palabras y perseguir sueños y obsesiones interminables: todo este panorama es la diversidad. Ser humano no puede ser confinado a una serie de reglas, ya sean entregadas por una autoridad divina o creadas por legisladores y agentes humanos.

Lo que nos hace humanos es invisible e imposible de codificar. Para ser humano debes saber cómo poner atención. Debes comprender lo que significa recordar algo, guardarlo en tu mente y volver a ello cuando sea que lo necesites. Debes ser capaz de llevar a cabo una intención. Estas cosas son tan básicas que apenas las notamos, pero muy a menudo las instrucciones básicas se han desviado.

La mente promedio es *inquieta*, es incapaz de quedarse inmóvil por más de un momento.

La mente promedio es *superficial*, es incapaz de ver por debajo de la superficie de la interminable actividad mental.

La mente promedio *no tiene un propósito*, es incapaz de hacer que sus intenciones fructifiquen de una forma significativa.

Estos tres problemas están interconectados, y ocasionan la lucha que la mayoría de las personas conoce muy bien. Si fuera natural que la mente humana sea inquieta, superficial y sin propósito, sería inútil hablar de metahumano como algo más que un ideal hueco. Pero, en realidad, por naturaleza la mente es relajada. Es capaz de profundizar en su propia conciencia y puede encontrar un propósito superior.

La inmortalidad práctica saca esta verdad a la luz, y nos dice qué es normal y natural en nuestra vida mental.

Cuando estás en contacto con una cosa, otras cosas básicas se vuelven claras. No puedes ser humano sin la capacidad de crear símbolos y reconocer su significado. Un símbolo rojo de alto les dice a los coches que se detengan en una intersección. *Rojo* no tiene ninguna conexión con *alto* hasta que los seres humanos le asignaron ese significado. La palabra *árbol* simboliza una clase de plantas altas con troncos de madera, pero la conexión es totalmente arbitraria. Se dice *arbre* en francés; *baum* en alemán. Pero al haber creado un símbolo podemos estar atrapados en él, al igual que las banderas atrapan a las personas en el nacionalismo, el dinero en la avaricia y los rituales religiosos en dogmatismo.

La libertad para crear símbolos sin estar regidos por ellos es parte de la inmortalidad práctica. Los sufís dicen que todo en el mundo es simbólico, lo cual creo que es verdad. Si intentas develar todo lo que implica la palabra *amor*, por ejemplo, el hilo de significado te conducirá en todas las direcciones. "Yo amo X" puede ser asignado a todos los deseos, necesidades y sueños. Lo opuesto del amor, que es el odio o el miedo, se vuelve símbolo de lo no deseable.

Como parte de ir más allá de nuestra historia es necesario dejar de ser presa del encanto de los símbolos. Puedes comenzar a ver que son como dinero falso. *Amor* puede ser la palabra que se use para justificar la violencia doméstica, los celos obsesivos, el acoso o atacar a alguien que desea a la misma persona que tú. Esta condición escurridiza aflige a una palabra como *paz*, que puede ser usada por un país que vende armas de destrucción masiva en el nombre de mantener la paz entre las naciones o para calmar a los tiranos y evitar que asesinen a su propia gente.

La máxima razón de la inmortalidad práctica es la misma que la del no hacer. Permites que la totalidad se desenvuelva por sí misma. Dejas de forzar, luchar e interferir. Es una pena que las enseñanzas de no hacer, ya sea en el budismo, el taoísmo o el cristianismo, hayan adquirido la reputación de ser místicas. Si la gente tan sólo dejara de forzar, que no es para nada místico, la vida cotidiana mejoraría inmensamente. Si dejamos de hacer muchas cosas que son malas para nosotros, el no hacer se convertiría en una forma de vida que todos querrían seguir.

¿Y por qué no lo hacemos? Porque todo lo que implica la inmortalidad práctica —poner atención, usar nuestra intención para lograr algo, satisfacer un propósito, soltar nuestra historia, terminar la tiranía de los símbolos— depende de un estado de conciencia al cual debemos llegar. La realidad virtual se trata de historias y símbolos. La metarrealidad, no. Por eso se necesita un camino para llegar de un estado de conciencia a otro distinto. Lo que nos enseña la conciencia sin elección es que el camino no se trata de lo que piensas, dices o haces. Desenvuelves tu potencial, que no es cuestión de pensar, decir o hacer. Sucede por sí mismo.

La verdad es que nadie tiene que preocuparse por comunicarse con lo inmortal, porque lo inmortal se comunica constantemente con nosotros. No nos dejará ir, jamás. Nadie inventó la atención, el amor, la inteligencia, la creatividad y la evolución. Y aun así esas cosas están aquí, ahora y siempre. Nunca nos sueltan, sin importar qué tan mal las usemos. Una cosa siempre nos tiene en mente, y por ello nosotros la tenemos en mente. Ninguna de las dos partes tiene opción.

13

UNA VIDA

Cuando estamos completos, todo el mundo se vuelve completo. Eso sería un cambio maravilloso porque, como están las cosas, nosotros estamos divididos y también lo está el mundo. El estado de las cosas va más allá de los conflictos interminables que aparecen en las noticias. Existe una fractura profunda en el núcleo de ser humano. Nos llamamos a nosotros mismos mamíferos, y aun así la mayoría de la gente cree que tiene un alma. Nos colocamos aparte de la naturaleza, y la explotamos sin considerar las consecuencias. Como cuidadores del planeta también somos su peor amenaza.

Pero ya se ha encendido un cambio en la conciencia colectiva. Uno de los signos más alentadores de esto parece trivial, un video en línea de un pulpo agradecido, que ya ha sido visto por 12 millones de espectadores. Comienza en una playa en Portugal donde un hombre, Pei Yan Heng, camina por la arena. Detecta un pequeño pulpo varado fuera del agua. Pei saca su celular para filmar a la criatura. Se presume que el pulpo fue lanzado a la orilla por una gran ola, y se ve seco y a punto de morir. Con un gesto amable Pi recoge al pulpo en un vaso de plástico, lo lleva de vuelta al agua y lo libera.

De inmediato el pulpo comienza a revivir. Sus ocho brazos se extienden (los expertos dicen que *tentáculo* no es el término correcto), y su color cambia a uno más saludable. Por lo regular el pulpo es tímido y se escabulle de cualquier amenaza que se le acerque, lo cual es una táctica necesaria para un animal de cuerpo abolsado y blando. Pero en vez de huir, el pulpo que fue salvado se acercó a las botas de Pei y las rodeó con dos de sus brazos, y se quedó ahí por varios segundos antes de alejarse aprisa. Pronto el "pulpo agradecido" entró en la cultura popular cuando el video se hizo viral. Podrías suponer que éste fue un ejemplo del sentimentalismo humano, pero no hay prueba de que el pulpo rescatado *no haya* estado agradecido. ¿Hay alguna forma de saberlo?

La respuesta convencional es que no. Puede ser un no rotundo o un no suave. El no rotundo sostiene que sólo los seres humanos somos conscientes. El no suave sostiene que los seres humanos somos las únicas criaturas totalmente conscientes. Esto deja poco espacio para maniobrar para los mamíferos de grandes cerebros, como los marsupiales, los elefantes y los grandes simios. El no suave es la fuente de la creación, el camino al sí —un pulpo *puede* sentir gratitud— está abierto.

Sin embargo, desde la perspectiva del metahumano, nada es ajeno. Existe sólo una realidad, gobernada por una conciencia. También, sólo hay una vida, a pesar de nuestras distinciones entre chimpancés inteligentes, lagartos estúpidos y bacterias totalmente inconscientes. En este momento en que la Tierra está en peligro es necesario evolucionar al metahumano, por el bien de todas las cosas vivientes.

Una vida, y sólo una vida

En un artículo publicado en enero de 2014 en la revista *Scientific American*, el muy apreciado neurocientífico Christof Koch abrió brecha en contra de la posición del "no" al preguntar si la conciencia es universal. Es muy persuasivo cuando señala que la inteligencia animal no es primitiva. No sólo eso, sino también que no está correlacionada con el tamaño del cerebro o con poseer un sistema nervioso. "Las abejas pueden volar varios kilómetros y regresar a su panal, lo cual es un desempeño de navegación extraordinario", señala Koch (yo añadiría que no sólo extraordinario, sino algo que los seres humanos perdidos en el bosque son incapaces de hacer). "Y un aroma que entra al panal puede detonar que las abejas regresen al sitio donde encontraron este olor previamente."

Koch relaciona este rasgo, llamado *memoria asociativa*, con el momento famoso de la literatura francesa que se centra en una galleta llamada magdalena. La novela enorme de siete volúmenes titulada *À la recherche du temps perdu* (*En busca del tiempo perdido*), de Marcel Proust, comienza con un flujo de la memoria provocado cuando el narrador moja una magdalena en una taza de té, lo cual es un gesto de su infancia. Koch también adscribe estas experiencias de memoria asociativa a las abejas, que es una forma más modesta de la vida de los insectos. Pero podemos encontrar una enorme cantidad de ejemplos. Hablando de las abejas, Koch señala lo siguiente:

> Son capaces de reconocer rostros específicos en fotografías, pueden comunicar a sus hermanas la localización y la calidad de las fuentes de alimentos por medio de un bamboleo y pueden navegar por laberintos complejos con la ayuda de señales que almacenan en la memoria a corto plazo (por ejemplo, "al llegar a una bifurcación, toman la salida que está marcada por el color a la entrada").

Koch afirma que el resultado es que la conciencia no puede aislarse de maneras arbitrarias sólo porque una forma de vida se ve demasiado simple a nivel biológico como para ser consciente. Con los brazos bien abiertos, declara: "Todas las especies —abejas, pulpos, cuervos, urracas, pericos, atunes, ratones, ballenas, perros, gatos y changos— son capaces de comportamientos sofisticados, aprendidos y no estereotipados". Esto nos lleva muy lejos del "no", sólo los seres humanos son conscientes, y nos acerca al "sí", la conciencia es universal.

El pulpo agradecido estaba actuando un gesto humano. Ver esto no es sentimentalismo ni fantasía. Koch cree que si no estuviéramos tan prejuiciados, veríamos que constantemente los animales se comportan de formas que serían llamadas conscientes si la misma actividad fuera realizada por una persona. La mirada de amor de un perro hacia su amo, su angustia si su dueño está ausente y la tristeza que siente si su dueño muere son rasgos conscientes que expresa otra forma de vida, aunque es difícil superar nuestro prejuicio porque le sirve a nuestro egoísmo. El *Homo sapiens* lleva consigo la cacería antigua. Matamos y comemos muchísimos animales, y para no tener cargo de conciencia los vemos como formas inferiores de vida, privadas de mente, voluntad y libertad de elección.

Todo lo que hace que otras formas de vida nos parezcan ajenas es arbitrario. Ninguna criatura se ve más extraña que un pulpo. Entre las 300 especies de pulpo, que aparecieron hace al menos 295 millones de años, de acuerdo con los fósiles más antiguos, los tipos más grandes se parecen a los pequeños porque tienen dos ojos, ocho brazos y una boca donde se unen los brazos. Al ampliarlo a una escala mayor, como en el pulpo del Pacífico, que puede alcanzar un peso de hasta 270 kilos, y con brazos de una longitud de entre cuatro a nueve metros, esos ocho brazos y esa boca enorme se ven monstruosos. Pero como el *Tyrannosaurus rex* o el gran tiburón blanco, el pulpo gigante del Pacífico no es un monstruo ante sus propios ojos. En el juego de la conciencia el pulpo ocupa el mismo estatus cósmico que el *Homo sapiens*. Está vivo y es consciente de sí mismo y de su entorno.

Existe evidencia abundante que apoya esta afirmación. En su libro publicado en 2015, *The Soul of an Octopus* (*El alma de un pulpo*), la naturalista Sy Montgomery cierra la brecha entre las personas y los moluscos de manera sorprendente. En una sección que comienza: "Los pulpos se dan cuenta de que los humanos también son individuos", relata con qué claridad un pulpo puede hacer amigos y enemigos. En el ejemplo más leve, en el acuario de Seattle se le asignó a un cuidador alimentar a los pulpos, mientras que otro los tocaba con un palo puntiagudo. Después de una semana, al ver a làs dos personas la mayoría de los pulpos se acercaba a quien los alimentaba.

Pero su capacidad de relacionarse con humanos específicos se vuelve mucho más misteriosa. Una voluntaria en el acuario de Nueva Inglaterra sin razón aparente se ganó el desprecio de un pulpo en particular llamado Truman. Cada vez que ella se acercaba al tanque, Truman usaba su sifón (un canal junto a la cabeza del pulpo que lo impulsa a través del agua) para mojarla con un chorro de agua de mar fría. La voluntaria se fue a la universidad, pero regresó meses después de visita. Truman, que no había mojado a nadie en su ausencia, de inmediato la empapó con un chorro de su sifón en cuanto la vio.

Montgomery relata a profundidad el comportamiento idiosincrático de los pulpos en cautiverio llamados Athena, Octavia, Kali y otros, casi como personas individuales. Su argumento para su similitud con los seres humanos es básicamente físico. Escribe que, después de todo, compartimos las mismas neuronas y neurotransmisores. Pero aunque los pulpos tienen un complejo sistema nervioso inusual para un invertebrado, su anatomía no se parece al sistema nervioso humano. La mayoría de las neuronas del pulpo están localizadas en sus ocho brazos, y no en su cerebro. Cada brazo puede moverse, tocar y saborear (las ventosas a lo largo de cada brazo son sitios para el sentido del gusto) de forma independiente, sin la necesidad de derivarlo al cerebro.

La anatomía no puede explicar cómo los pulpos reconocen a la gente y recuerdan su rostro. Un pulpo al que le molestaba la luz en la noche porque perturbaba su sueño lanzó un chorro de agua al foco, que se apagó por un corto circuito. La disección del sistema nervioso de un pulpo no explica cómo fue concebida esta táctica (en su estado salvaje los pulpos no echan chorros de agua en la superficie del mar). Parecería ser un acto de inteligencia creativa.

Mi postura es que la existencia es consciente; por lo tanto, la habilidad de ningún animal es extraordinaria (excepto desde nuestro punto de vista parcial), porque cada forma de vida expresa rasgos que pertenecen a la conciencia pura. Estos rasgos despiertan, por así decirlo, y emergen al mundo físico de acuerdo con la historia evolutiva de cada criatura. El pulpo agradecido no estaba siendo como un humano. Podríamos decir con justicia que cuando estamos agradecidos estamos siendo como los pulpos. Las dos visiones son parciales.

Este libro ha estado hablando de despertar, pero estar despierto no es el fin; más adelante se encuentra la conciencia cósmica. Estoy usando el término al igual que otros usan *iluminación suprema* (conocida en sánscrito como *Paramatma*). Si el metahumano es el estado despierto, piénsalo como si cruzaras un umbral. Hay un vasto territorio por explorar más allá.

Conciencia cósmica

La conciencia cósmica no le da un poquito de sí misma a una amiba, más a las abejas, todavía más a los pulpos, y finalmente el gran premio al *Homo sapiens*. En un holograma, un fragmento de una imagen láser se puede usar para proyectar toda la imagen —con tan sólo la sonrisa de la *Mona Lisa*, toda la pintura se puede proyectar—. La tecnología hológrafa incluso puede simular una estatua o una persona viva en 3D a partir de una imagen láser en dos dimensiones. La conciencia cósmica hace esto a una escala enorme —el universo entero— usando *simplemente* la posibilidad de un cosmos. Por lo tanto, no es del todo verdad que algo sea creado de la nada. El universo físico saltó de una concepción en la conciencia cósmica que se desenvuelve en forma material. La conciencia pura no es "nada".

Los seres humanos heredamos esta capacidad. Si yo digo: "Imagina la Torre Eiffel" o "Ve la Estatua de la Libertad en tu imaginación", con sólo escuchar el nombre de estos monumentos los ves en su totalidad. Un nombre no tiene tres dimensiones; de hecho, no tiene dimensiones ya que sólo es una etiqueta verbal para un concepto. La Estatua de la Libertad es el concepto de la libertad transformado en una obra de arte. Pero libertad también puede producir manifestaciones completamente diferentes, como las guerras revolucionarias o los movimientos antibélicos. Los conceptos están constantemente moldeando y remodelando eventos, civilizaciones y el mundo humano en general.

Estás viviendo en un mundo que consiste en ideas que se presentan en tres dimensiones. Como siempre, las grandes mentes llegaron ahí antes que nosotros. Hace más de 2 000 años Platón afirmó que todo en el mundo se origina en ideas universales abstractas, a las cuales llamó "formas". Dos milenios después Werner Heisenberg afirma: "Creo que la física moderna definitivamente se decidió en favor de Platón. De hecho las unidades de materia más pequeñas no son objetos físicos en el sentido ordinario; son formas, ideas que sólo en lenguaje matemático pueden expresarse sin ambigüedad".

Si las piezas fundamentales de la materia y la energía son conceptuales, entonces el universo mismo también está surgiendo de un conjunto de ideas o formas. Este particular conjunto de ideas que se convirtió en nuestro universo y hogar podría tener otras variaciones, algunas de las cuales serían inconcebibles para la mente humana. Una característica del multiverso, si es que existe, es que miles de millones de otros universos podrían estar operando bajo leyes de la naturaleza totalmente distintas a las nuestras. Una ley de la naturaleza es simplemente un modelo matemático, y los modelos matemáticos son conceptos.

Permíteme interrumpir con una nota personal. Cuando me encontré por primera vez con el quantum, lo cual derivó en un libro, *Sanación cuántica*, yo estaba maravillado de que la física fuera acorde con los profundos entendimientos de India. *Maya*, la palabra en sánscrito que usualmente se traduce como "ilusión", se refiere a la realidad virtual, y la doctrina de Maya sostiene que la ilusión es sólo un concepto. Los paralelos eran todavía más profundos. Heisenberg afirmaba que la naturaleza exhibe un fenómeno de acuerdo con las preguntas que formulemos con respecto a ella; en otras palabras, el observador extrae del campo cuántico las cualidades de tiempo, espacio, materia y energía. En la India antigua Maya se origina por medio de la participación de los humanos en busca de la confirmación de nuestras creencias internas. En ambos casos la naturaleza nos muestra lo que queremos ver.

Me entusiasmó la perspectiva de que el camino interior de los antiguos y el camino exterior de la ciencia moderna hubieran llegado a la misma realidad. Así que fue una conmoción para mí descubrir que en gran medida la física moderna les ha dado la espalda a los iluminados pioneros cuánticos. Como me lo dijo un profesor de Cal Tech: "Mis estudiantes universitarios saben más sobre física que lo que Einstein supo jamás". Este avance en el conocimiento técnico ha sido tremendo, pero ¿acaso justifica desechar lo que entendieron los pioneros cuánticos acerca de la realidad?

Einstein al menos reconoció el peligro cuando señaló: "Tanta gente hoy en día —e incluso científicos profesionales— me parece como alguien que ha visto miles de árboles, pero nunca ha visto un bosque". Para corregir esta miopía, Einstein propugnó que los científicos adquirieran un amplio conocimiento sobre filosofía, la cual consideraba la marca de un "verdadero buscador de la verdad". Es una pena que en el siglo XXI se ven cada vez menos bosques que nunca, mientras la ciencia se vuelve más especializada y fragmentada. Puedes dedicar una carrera entera en física enfocándote en un solo concepto como la inflación eterna o una sola partícula elemental, como el bosón de Higgs.

La conciencia cósmica suena como algo muy alejado de la forma en que usamos nuestra mente en la vida cotidiana. No obstante, en la realidad la mente de cada persona proyecta la conciencia cósmica todo el tiempo. Tu mente es un fragmento de la conciencia cósmica, pero, como en un holograma, un fragmento es suficiente para proyectar el todo. El siguiente ejercicio te ayudará a llevar este entendimiento a casa.

Ejercicio: Navegar por el universo

Cierra los ojos e imagina que estás parado en una playa, observando las olas. Cuando ya tengas esta imagen clara en tu imaginación, comienza a transformar las olas de varias maneras. Observa cómo se vuelven más grandes, creciendo hasta ser las olas monstruosas que montan los surfistas de clase mundial. Observa cómo se encogen hasta ser muy pequeñitas. Haz que las olas se tornen de diferentes colores: rojas, moradas o naranja neón. Colócate a ti mismo sobre las olas, equilibrándote sin tabla de surf mientras te deslizas hasta la orilla. Si lo deseas puedes inventar tus propias transformaciones. Quizás una sirena surge de las olas, cantando una canción. Ya tienes una idea.

Reflexiona sobre lo que estaba sucediendo cuando hiciste estos cambios creativos a las olas. No hojeaste un catálogo de posibilidades. En cambio, fuiste libre para dejar volar tu imaginación. Si dos personas hubieran hecho este ejercicio se les habrían ocurrido decisiones creativas distintas. Las posibilidades son ilimitadas y no están limitadas por ninguna regla. Nada te impide convertir el océano Pacífico en una gelatina rosa. No tiene sentido afirmar que estas posibilidades creativas están almacenadas en los átomos y moléculas de tus células cerebrales. Tomaste decisiones conscientes sin precedente, construyendo una cadena única de pensamientos creativos.

Pero incluso si todos los 7 000 millones de personas sobre el planeta realizaran este ejercicio, estarían haciendo una sola cosa: transformar la posibilidad en realidad. Esta sola cosa está sucediendo todo el tiempo, y es suficiente para crear el universo. En la primavera de 1940 uno de los físicos más visionarios de los tiempos modernos, John Wheeler, le llamó por teléfono a otro físico visionario, Richard Feynman.

"Feynman —exclamó Wheeler—, ya sé por qué todos los electrones tienen la misma carga y la misma masa." "¿Por qué?" "¡Porque todos son el mismo electrón!"

Esta noción desconcertante, que se conoce como el universo de un único electrón, cayó en la imaginación de Feynman, aunque, como él recuerda, no la tomó con la suficiente seriedad al principio. Cuando miramos el mundo físico existe una cantidad enorme de electrones —cada segundo, billones de ellos envían cargas eléctricas por la corriente de tu casa—. Cada electrón traza un camino en el tiempo y el espacio, conocido como línea de universo.

Wheeler propuso que un solo electrón podía zigzaguear por todas partes, creando una maraña de líneas de universo. Es una alternativa fascinante a muchos electrones creando muchas líneas de universo. Ahora traduzcamos esto a términos humanos. En vez de muchos electrones, sustituye muchos observadores, cada uno con sus propios ojos. Sin embargo, esos miles de millones de observadores expresan la capacidad de observar, que es una sola cosa. Así que es enteramente plausible que habitemos un "universo de un observador". Es como decir: "Todos los humanos inhalan aire" sin tener que contar cuántos humanos están respirando. Ésta es la perspectiva de la conciencia cósmica. No elegí por accidente la imagen de las olas golpeando la orilla. Los videntes hindúes antiguos señalaban el mar y decían: "Cada ola es un afloramiento del mar sin ser diferentes de él. No te dejes engañar por tu ego individual. Eres un afloramiento de la conciencia cósmica sin ser diferente de ella".

El *Homo sapiens* es la única criatura que puede elegir qué perspectiva tomar. Podemos ser olas separadas de un océano. La única diferencia entre un universo de un solo electrón y un universo de muchos electrones es nuestra perspectiva. Los dos son tan reales como decidamos que lo sean. O para decirlo de forma más enfática, los dos son *sólo* tan reales como decidamos que lo sean. Al estar parados en el pivote de tomar esta decisión, estamos parados en el pivote de la creación. Sólo una cosa está sucediendo: la posibilidad se vuelve realidad. John Wheeler también dijo que vivimos en un universo participativo. Yo sólo estoy desarrollando la misma idea. Un universo participativo ofrece opciones infinitas; la única cosa que no puedes decidir es *no* participar.

Cuando estás en el juego, depende de ti cómo jugar. Los seres humanos pueden contemplar la creación y explicarla de cualquier forma que elijan. ¿Por qué hay virus de gripa, elefantes, secuoyas y ratones en el mundo? Algunos dirían que Dios los creó a propósito, mientras que otros creen que surgieron del vacío cuántico por medio de un proceso fortuito que tomó miles de millones de años en dar fruto. La explicación más radical es que el *Homo sapiens* añadió todo lo que deseábamos a nuestra realidad virtual. Cada explicación es tan sólo una historia diferente. Más allá de las historias, la conciencia cósmica está creando desde su interior. Las historias son poscreación; la conciencia cósmica es precreación.

La causa sin causa

Nuestro papel como creadores de la realidad impone una pesada carga si lo vemos desde el punto de vista de las limitaciones humanas. Durante muchos siglos todo habría sido dejado en las manos de Dios. Por ejemplo, la mente medieval hizo de Dios el origen de todo en el cielo y en la tierra; Tomás de Aquino, el mayor teólogo medieval, presentaba a Dios como el primer motor (*primum mobile* en latín). Sólo Dios tenía el conocimiento para crear el universo.

Como la perfección es un atributo divino, Dios debe de haber echado a andar la creación en un movimiento perfecto, mientras que en el mundo caído todo lo que está en movimiento, incluso un corazón latiendo y las olas crecientes del mar, es una representación imperfecta de la obra de Dios. Cuando Adán y Eva cayeron, también lo hizo la naturaleza. Los primeros humanos fueron expulsados de un mundo natural perfecto a uno imperfecto. El Jardín del Edén dio lugar a un salvajismo hostil.

En la *Divina comedia*, que es considerada como la reflexión más completa de la cosmología medieval en literatura, Dante logró una imagen visual de la perfección divina para que sus lectores pudieran asirla. Como lo describe el sitio de internet Danteworlds: "En el Primum Mobile (primer motor) —la esfera más veloz y remota que imparte movilidad a las otras esferas— Dante ve nueve anillos ardientes girando alrededor de un punto central de luz intensa".

Estos nueve anillos ardientes son niveles angélicos, porque en la visión religiosa del mundo de Dante debían existir seres perfectos asignados para mantener la creación en curso. De otra forma Dios habría tenido que estar dirigiendo todo, lo que es una imposibilidad porque por definición era el Motor Inmóvil. (*Él* es un uso arcaico e incorrecto en hebreo, pero recurro al término masculino por conveniencia, ya que *él/ella/eso* es engorroso.) Al referirse a Dios, la mente del cristiano medieval no podía violar —ni escapar— la perfección divina.

Esa obsesión sobrevive hoy en día, pero con un disfraz distinto. Sin una creación perfecta con la cual soñar, nos quedamos con nuestras propias imperfecciones. Nos sentimos tan perplejos y confundidos como Adán y Eva bíblicos. Nos sentimos culpables por depredar el planeta, pero no podemos ayudarnos a nosotros mismos, aunque la naturaleza se derrumbe ante nuestros ojos.

Este libro ha propuesto que la creación se desenvuelve a partir de la conciencia pura. No existe un artista divino con una imagen en mente. Solamente hay creación evolucionando sin final. El proceso no contiene la trama de nadie; abarca todas las tramas. No tiene moralidad. Para la imaginación humana, la tragedia es tan fascinante como la comedia, y por ello seguimos creando ambas. (Shakespeare presentaba el panorama completo a su audiencia parado en el patio del Globe Theatre, y Hollywood hace que continúe el espectáculo.)

La evolución de la conciencia es la única explicación para la creación que lo une todo. Tiene la ventaja de no poseer límites. Lo milagroso está en el campo de juego al mismo nivel que lo mundano. En este punto me la voy a jugar. Si entras a YouTube y escribes cuatro palabras en la barra de búsqueda, "Hostia levitando en Lourdes", puedes ver un milagro que ocurrió en Lourdes, Francia, y fue filmado. Como lo explica un comentarista en línea informado:

> En 1999, durante una misa celebrada por el cardenal Billé, después arzobispo de Lyon, la hostia comenzó a levitar justo por encima de la pátina [el plato usado para la eucaristía] desde el momento de la Epíclesis hasta la elevación. El prodigio fue filmado para transmisión y un video de ese momento está circulando por todo internet. En ese momento los obispos franceses decidieron mantenerlo en silencio. Recientemente llamó la atención de un cardenal en la Curia, quien se dio a la tarea de verificar el origen del video y le preguntó al actual arzobispo de Lyon cuál era la postura de los obispos franceses. Este cardenal en turno lo pasó al Santo Padre. A él le preocupa que ciertos obispos se apresuraron a descartar algo que parece ser un signo auténtico.

El video existente es borroso, pero muestra lo que describe el comentarista. Durante esta misa se usó una hostia grande, como del tamaño de un plato extendido. La levitación, que dura varios minutos, termina con la elevación de la hostia, cuando el arzobispo la levanta para mostrarla a la congregación. La levitación, si eso es lo que estamos viendo, mantiene la hostia en el aire entre tres y cinco centímetros.

Yo no sé quién está en posición de dictaminar si la filmación es real o un engaño digital ingenioso, pero para mí el asunto no se trata de milagros. Se trata de aquello que los seres humanos están dispuestos a permitir en la imagen aceptable de la realidad. A la fecha millones de personas han visto el video de la hostia levitando y sus respuestas cubren todo el espectro. La mayoría de la gente que conozco de momento se impresiona; otros cuestionan las imágenes borrosas. Unos cuantos adoptan una expresión extraña en el rostro, como si Horacio y Hamlet acabaran de decir: "Hay más cosas en el cielo y en la tierra, Horacio, / de las que han sido soñadas en tu filosofía".

Podrías decir que Hamlet está acusando a su amigo de no soñar lo suficiente. Los milagros son recordatorios parecidos. La hostia levitando podrá ser explicada algún día; después de todo, en la física teórica existe la antigravedad. Podría ser expuesta como un fraude o tan sólo hundirse en la pila de recuerdos olvidados. Incluso así, algo importante sucedió. Se permitió que un poco de extrañeza entrara en nuestro sueño colectivo. Sólo se necesita una chispa para incendiar todo un bosque.

El tiempo para despertar nunca es demasiado breve. Despertar te lleva más allá de las fronteras del tiempo. Aunque no es difícil sentir la presión del desastre conforme más se acerca. Existe algo así como una tormenta tan poderosa que sólo sucede una vez cada 500 años pero, según los cálculos de los meteorólogos, sucedieron 26 tormentas de este tipo en la década pasada. Si vamos a convertir la conciencia cósmica en materia, no podemos usar lentes color de rosa. Esas tormentas, y la miseria humana que provocan, fueron permitidas para entrar en la realidad virtual. Muchas cosas han entrado en la realidad virtual para hacer que la vida sea una pesadilla.

La persona promedio no está preparada para aceptar la responsabilidad del hechizo/sueño/ilusión en el que estamos atrapados. La acumulación de gases invernadero puede explicarse como castigo divino, o como el resultado de una serie de eventos muy desafortunados, o como la imperfección humana que echa a perder una cosa más. La autodestrucción es parte de nuestra naturaleza, pero la creación de uno mismo es infinitamente más poderosa. Al despertar, los metahumanos pueden hacer bien lo que los humanos han hecho mal. Despertar le sucede sólo a una persona a la vez. La realidad no es una quiniela. Es un universo de un jugador, y tú y yo bastamos para mover la creación misma.

UN MES PARA DESPERTAR:

31 lecciones metahumanas

Un propósito de este libro es desmitificar el proceso de despertar. El camino directo debe ser fácil y natural. La única incertidumbre es el tiempo —todas las personas que quieren alcanzar una conciencia superior comienzan en un lugar distinto, y esto hace una diferencia—. En mi propia experiencia he descubierto que el deseo es un incentivo importante, sin importar desde dónde comiences. Si verdaderamente quieres algo —aprender un nuevo idioma, cocina francesa, escalar en roca— el proceso se vuelve disfrutable. Cuanto mejor aprendas, más disfrutable es.

Pero a diferencia de esas cosas, despertar no es una habilidad. No tiene un conjunto de reglas o lineamientos. Incluso la búsqueda de un maestro está llena de tropiezos. ¿Cómo te demuestra un maestro que ha despertado? Sin embargo, todas las culturas que creen en la conciencia superior a lo largo del tiempo han desarrollado un escenario para este tipo de aprendizaje, como un *ashram* en la India o un monasterio budista zen.

Estos escenarios encajan en el contexto de cada cultura. Pero si no perteneces a la cultura y estás viendo estos escenarios desde fuera, los *ashrams* y los monasterios te parecen extraños y exóticos. Aun así, no hay prueba de que sea obligatorio un escenario especial.

Después de todo, el proceso de despertar se trata de la conciencia de uno mismo. Nadie te puede enseñar a ser consciente de ti mismo. No es necesario. La conciencia ya incluye la conciencia de uno mismo. En este libro he estado afirmando que la existencia *es* conciencia. En otras palabras, naciste con las herramientas para volverte más consciente de ti mismo. Es sólo cuestión de que las apliques.

En el proceso de despertar no se requiere un estilo de vida especial. Vives como lo haces ahora, al ser consciente del mundo "allá fuera" y el mundo "aquí dentro". Lo único nuevo es que te vinculas con los dos mundos usando nuevos supuestos. Supones que eres un todo al nivel del ser verdadero. Supones que el ser verdadero ofrece una mejor forma de vida, una forma más consciente, pero también más creativa, abierta, relajada, receptiva y libre.

Las suposiciones no son lo mismo que la verdad o los hechos. Deben ser puestas a prueba, lo cual es el propósito de esta sección. Se te pide que experimentes en ti mismo, que durante un mes te dediques cada día a descubrir si el camino directo funciona. Es un tiempo afortunado para buscar la conciencia superior. Al estar despojada de los adornos de la religión y la bruma del misterio, la conciencia ha entrado en una nueva fase y ahora es un tema de investigación completamente desarrollado, estudiado por psicólogos, psicoterapeutas, biólogos, filósofos, neurocientíficos e incluso físicos.

De hecho, esta explosión en el interés por la conciencia es un mejor escenario que los *ashrams* y monasterios tradicionales. Puedes estar totalmente enganchado en la vida cotidiana al tiempo que enfocas tu atención más profunda en despertar. Es un poco extraño que alguien deba aprender a despertar, pero es el resultado de vivir tanto tiempo con la mente condicionada. Al estar convencida de que el hechizo/sueño/ilusión es real, nuestra mente se adapta a él. El despertar sucede al desmantelar el condicionamiento que nos mantiene atrapados en constructos mentales. Llegamos al estado de despertar cuando esos constructos comienzan a desvanecerse.

Llegar ahí es impredecible y totalmente personal. Es mejor hacerlo con una mente abierta y sin expectativas. Tan sólo adopta la actitud de que despertar es real; otras personas lo han hecho a lo largo de muchos siglos, y el único requerimiento es la conciencia de uno mismo.

Un plan diario

Las lecciones en esta sección están diseñadas para ser lo más flexibles posible. Primero presento un axioma o entendimiento del día. Después, una explicación breve y al final un ejercicio. Lee por lo menos una vez el axioma y la explicación, aunque es mejor que las leas varias veces a lo largo del día, para que lleves tu atención de vuelta al tema del día. Los ejercicios deben ser realizados las veces necesarias para que sientas que en verdad lo asimilaste —de una a tres veces a lo largo del día bastarán—. Finalmente, he dejado espacio para que escribas acerca de tu experiencia. Sería todavía mejor si llevaras un diario aparte, destinado a tu despertar.

¿Un mes es tiempo suficiente para despertar por completo? Sinceramente, lo dudo, pero se sabe de algunas personas que abren los ojos en la mañana, miran a su alrededor y saben con certeza que han despertado. Otras personas cambian de forma gradual y se deslizan hacia la conciencia superior casi sin notar que el cambio ha tenido lugar: a lo largo de los años se convirtió en su segunda naturaleza. Es muy probable que aproveches al máximo si repites estas lecciones y vuelves a ellas cuando sientas el deseo de reconectarte con el proceso de aprendizaje. Hay grados de despertar, así como hay niveles en el aprendizaje de un nuevo idioma, de la cocina francesa o de la escalada en roca. Parte del proceso es reforzar tu estado despierto.

Las lecciones son más largas conforme avanza el mes, no porque sean más difíciles, sino porque hay más cosas que ver. Todas las lecciones tienen la misma facilidad.

Sé abierto, fluido y flexible con respecto a la idea de llegar ahí. La belleza del camino directo es que cada lección a lo largo del camino tiene sus propios logros, sus propios momentos eureka y sus propios placeres. Con este espíritu, permite que comience el despertar.

DÍA 1

··· ———— ···

La experiencia cotidiana de la realidad comienza con las percepciones:
sonidos, colores, formas, texturas, sabores y olores.

Se supone que despertar debe ser fácil. Pero es importante saber dónde comenzar. No hay mejor lugar para empezar que donde estás en este momento. De hecho, vamos a acabar teniendo problemas si fingimos que hay otro punto de inicio. Estás experimentando la vida como es, un flujo de experiencias que comienza con los cinco sentidos.

PARA HOY

Contacta con lo básico. Siéntate por un momento y permanece con tu experiencia más simple de luz, calor, los olores que flotan hacia ti, el sabor de la comida. Relájate en la experiencia. Sólo observa. Cuanto más te puedas relajar, más fácil será despertar. Relajarte en el momento es la clave. En un estado relajado tu actividad mental se calma, y entonces puedes observar tu experiencia de formal natural.

TU EXPERIENCIA: _____

_____

_____

_____

_____

_____

DÍA 2

••• ——————— •••

El rango de la experiencia humana es un ancho de banda estrecho
de sensaciones en bruto.

Los cinco sentidos son nuestra ventana a la realidad, pero la apertura es una rendija, no un ventanal. La frase "ver es creer" por lo regular aplica a una pequeña fracción de la información en bruto que bombardea el ojo cada segundo. Lo mismo sucede con los otros cuatro sentidos. Conspiran para entregar un ancho de banda estrecho de la realidad. Expandir el ancho de banda y aumentar nuestra percepción son un motivo para despertar.

PARA HOY

Conéctate con la estrechez de tu sentido de la realidad. Ahueca tus manos, colócalas sobre tus orejas y percibe cómo el mundo se amortigua. Ponte lentes oscuros y observa el mundo volverse borroso. Apaga las luces en la noche y con cuidado, con pasos pequeños, intenta caminar por una habitación en tu casa que conozcas muy bien. Cuando retires las manos de tus orejas quítate los lentes oscuros y enciende las luces, tu conciencia de todo a tu alrededor se expande. Despertar expande la realidad aún más.

TU EXPERIENCIA: _____

_____

_____

_____

_____

_____

DÍA 3

••• ——————— •••

Todos los organismos biológicos tienen su propio y único ancho
de banda de experiencia sensorial.

La experiencia nos define a todos, y como estamos sintonizados sólo en un ancho de banda de la realidad —llámalo el Canal del Yo— nuestra identidad también es estrecha. Otros seres vivientes están sintonizados en diferentes anchos de banda, lo que les da una existencia que apenas podemos imaginar, pero los humanos podemos cambiar el canal a voluntad. La realidad es tan estrecha como nuestra conciencia. Cuando despiertas estás sintonizado con el ancho de banda completo. Entonces la realidad es ilimitada.

PARA HOY

Tómate un momento para escuchar las aves cantar. Cada ave cuenta una historia. El canto de las aves comunica información de los padres a los polluelos, anuncia los límites del territorio, atrae a una pareja, advierte del peligro e identifica a qué especie pertenece el ave. Date cuenta de que no comprendes absolutamente nada del Canal de las Aves. Si es invierno y no escuchas aves, entonces considera a un perro olisqueando el aire. El olfato de un perro puede saber quién caminó por ahí, qué había en los zapatos de esa persona y cuándo ocurrió el incidente. Observa que tu olfato no reúne nada de la información que se percibe en el Canal de los Perros.

TU EXPERIENCIA: _____

_____

_____

_____

DÍA 4

··· ———————— ···

Nuestro cuerpo físico también es una percepción sensorial.

El Canal del Yo te dice que tienes un cuerpo. El cuerpo que ves y sientes, las sensaciones que atraviesan el sistema nervioso, los sitios de placer y dolor: todas estas señales son transmitidas por el Canal del Yo. El cuerpo no es una cosa; es una confederación de percepciones. Tu mente une estas percepciones fragmentadas en una imagen coherente en el tiempo y el espacio. Si tu mente no hiciera eso, el Canal del Yo sólo estaría transmitiendo ruido.

PARA HOY

Tómate un momento para percibir tu cuerpo directamente. Cierra los ojos y siéntate en silencio. Permite que tu atención se mueva de sensación a sensación. Eleva los brazos y siente su peso. Frota unos contra otros los dedos de tus manos y siente su suavidad y la textura de la piel. Escucha tu respiración y el latido de tu corazón. No importa cuántas señales percibas, o si tu cuerpo se siente bien o no. Has contactado con el cuerpo real que tienes. La experiencia del cuerpo *es* el cuerpo. Todo lo demás es interferencia mental. Cuando despiertes, aceptarás y disfrutarás la experiencia del cuerpo mismo, que es maravillosa.

TU EXPERIENCIA: _____

_____

_____

_____

_____

DÍA 5

• • • ——————— • • •

Por sí misma, cada experiencia perceptual es una sensación única, fugaz, inasible y momentánea. Nuestros sentidos toman instantáneas de la realidad.

La vida nos da un flujo constante de percepciones por las cuales nos guiamos. Los cinco sentidos son los canales a través de los cuales todo fluye. Pero no es como un flujo continuo del agua de un grifo. Las sensaciones son mucho más como lluvia, que cae una gota a la vez. Le damos sentido a la vida usando pensamientos y sensaciones fugaces. Ignoramos lo efímera que es cada percepción: cada sensación comienza a disiparse en cuanto la notamos. Cada pensamiento ya ha desaparecido en el momento en que se registra. Al despertar, dejamos de ignorar lo que en realidad está sucediendo todo el tiempo. Desaparece la necesidad de convertir las sensaciones fugaces en una película en marcha o en una historia.

PARA HOY

Coloca un grano de azúcar o sal sobre tu lengua. Observa cómo el sabor empieza a disminuir después de la primera sensación fuerte. Pon atención a cómo tus glándulas salivales pronto reaccionan y cómo tu garganta quiere tragar. Esto te pone en contacto con lo breve y temporal que es la experiencia. Pero ahí viene lo bueno. Intenta tragar lo que está en tu lengua antes de que pongas el azúcar o la sal sobre ella. No puedes hacerlo. Ese sabor, el cual quizá no notaste cuando ocurrió, ha desaparecido para siempre. Las percepciones fugaces son la textura de la vida.

TU EXPERIENCIA: _____

_____

_____

_____

_____

_____

DÍA 6

*La única constante en cada foto instantánea de la percepción
es la presencia del ser y de la conciencia.*

Las fotografías instantáneas no se toman a sí mismas, debe haber un fotógrafo detrás de la cámara. Sin importar cuántos miles de fotos tome un fotógrafo profesional, él es la constante detrás del lente. Su trabajo es mirar, ordenar el escenario, colocar las luces, enfocar y decidir si la imagen lo satisface. Tú haces lo mismo con la realidad. Tus sentidos te brindan fotos instantáneas de información en bruto, la cual cambia de formas interminables. La única constante eres tú, viendo, ordenando y convirtiendo las explosiones aleatorias de percepción en algo con lo que te puedes identificar. Casi todo esto sucede en automático, pero cuando despiertas puedes ver lo que estás haciendo. Entonces tienes mucha más libertad para crear.

PARA HOY

Vuelve a conectarte con las unidades básicas de la experiencia. Siéntate por un momento y permanece con tu experiencia más simple de la luz, el calor, los olores que flotan hasta ti, el sabor en tu boca. Relájate y entra en la experiencia. Observa cada sensación de forma espontánea, hacia donde se mueva tu atención. Cuanto más seas capaz de relajarte, más fácil será despertar. En sí mismo, despertar es un estado totalmente relajado y espontáneo, abierto a lo que sea que suceda aquí y ahora.

TU EXPERIENCIA: _____

_____

_____

_____

DÍA 7

··· ———————— ···

La sucesión de instantáneas perceptuales crea un sentido de continuidad,
al igual que una película se crea de la secuencia rápida de imágenes.

Cuando la invención de las imágenes animadas reveló que nuestros ojos pueden ser engañados al encadenar una serie de instantáneas a 24 cuadros por segundo, también se reveló una verdad más profunda de la realidad. El cerebro humano funciona por el disparo de las neuronas. Cada disparo es una explosión de energía, seguido por una pausa, y después la siguiente explosión. Las explosiones se deslizan a la realidad en partes de información provenientes de los cinco sentidos. Cuando un tren pasa a toda velocidad junto a ti, no lo ves en movimiento. Ves estallidos de información en tu cerebro que dan la ilusión de movimiento. Igualmente, no escuchas sonidos continuos.

La continuidad de tu vida es una ilusión necesaria. Tenemos que ver el mundo en movimiento para poder vivir en movimiento, y no en trozos congelados de sensaciones. En este momento estás experimentando imágenes e historias creadas en tu mente por medio del mismo proceso de montaje. Cuando despiertas, estas imágenes e historias serán vistas por lo que son en realidad: constructos artificiales de la mente. Vivirás desde la realidad "real" que está más allá de las películas y las historias: la conciencia misma.

PARA HOY

Siéntate frente a una imagen en movimiento de tu televisión o computadora; puede ser cualquier cosa, desde gente caminando hasta las noticias o un evento deportivo. Enfócate en algo que cruce la pantalla de izquierda a derecha. En realidad no hay una persona cruzando la pantalla; ni un solo fotón de luz cruza la pantalla. Al concatenar estos estallidos en una secuencia, se crea la ilusión de movimiento. Ahora date cuenta de lo difícil que es ver el proceso actual sucediendo ante tus ojos. Tu mente debe ver movimiento porque, desde que naciste, el mundo ha sido una serie de imágenes en movimiento: así de condicionado estás para aceptar una ilusión como la realidad.

TU EXPERIENCIA: _____

_____

_____

_____

_____

_____

DÍA 8

••• ———— •••

El cuerpo físico y la apariencia del mundo físico son creados en la mente
como constructos de sensaciones intermitentes y efímeras.

En la vida cotidiana no investigamos cómo la mente crea un mundo tridimensional a partir de fragmentos de sensaciones aleatorios y sin sentido. Comenzando con el mundo simple que experimenta un bebé, todo se va volviendo cada vez más complicado. Un recién nacido no puede enfocarse en su mano, que él ve como una cosa amorfa y rosada flotando en el aire. Con el tiempo, la masa amorfa se convierte en una mano pegada al cuerpo; adquiere un nombre; desarrolla muchas capacidades. La medicina la estudia, desde cada músculo hasta cada célula.

Esta construcción del contenido ocurre en la mente y es creada por la mente. Una mano vacía no tiene ninguna historia que decir; no tiene capacidades ya desarrolladas. Todo aquello en lo que una mano se puede convertir cuando le pertenece a un pintor, escultor, actor de circo, chef o soldador dotado es creado por la mente. Lo mismo sucede para el cuerpo entero y el mundo físico. Construimos la realidad virtual para poder tener las imágenes e historias que son necesarias para ser humano.

PARA HOY

Toma una hoja tamaño carta y haz un agujero en el centro. Si sostienes la hoja cerca del ojo puedes ver toda la habitación a través del agujero: ésta es tu imagen mental de la habitación. Ahora sostén la hoja de papel a unos centímetros de tu ojo, hasta que veas sólo partes de objetos que te resulten familiares: tan sólo partes de lámparas, sillas, ventanas y demás. Intenta caminar por la habitación viendo solamente estos fragmentos a través del agujero. Es muy difícil. Al no contar con la imagen que crea tu mente, la habitación es un revoltijo de imágenes fragmentadas. Reflexiona en la manera en que has usado la mente para construir el mundo tridimensional familiar que aceptas al pie de la letra.

TU EXPERIENCIA: _____

_____

_____

_____

_____

DÍA 9

• • • ━━━━━━ • • •

La apariencia del cuerpo y del mundo son actividades en la conciencia —verbos, no sustantivos— que cambian de forma constante y rápida.

Cuando entras a una habitación, vas al trabajo o das un paseo al aire libre, los objetos que ves aparecen ante ti como inamovibles y estables, pero no lo son. Tu cerebro constantemente se está disparando para mantener la ilusión de la estabilidad. Tus cinco sentidos cooperan al convertir los fotones en imágenes y las vibraciones del aire en sonidos que puedas reconocer. En otras palabras, constantemente estás creando el mundo. Un proceso siempre cambiante e interminable sucede en tu conciencia. Por lo tanto, el mundo exterior es un proceso siempre cambiante e interminable disfrazado de objetos inamovibles y estables. Al despertar ves a través de la máscara de la materia y te reconectas con el proceso creativo que genera el mundo.

PARA HOY

Observa la fotografía de un amigo, un miembro de tu familia o una celebridad. Ahora voltéala de cabeza. Ya no puedes reconocer el rostro. Tu cerebro se ha trabado, ya que está condicionado a reconocer los rostros solamente cuando se ven al derecho. Hubo un proceso para reconocer el rostro; el rostro en sí mismo no tiene sentido. O imagina colocar una foto en un tornamesa y hacerla girar (puedes intentar hacerlo en una bandeja giratoria o en un tocadiscos). Observa que no puedes darle sentido a la foto mientras da vueltas. El mundo en movimiento no tiene ninguna realidad hasta que la mente la convierte en un mundo humano. El cambio constante adquiere la ilusión de estabilidad e inmutabilidad.

TU EXPERIENCIA: _____

_____

_____

_____

_____

DÍA 10

••• ———————— •••

El constructo mental del cuerpo y del mundo es producto
de siglos de condicionamiento.

En la vida cotidiana aceptamos el mundo como viene. Los árboles, las montañas, las nubes y el cielo simplemente están ahí. Pero son solamente el escenario de la realidad virtual. Todo en el mundo más allá de la información en bruto está arraigado en la mitología, la historia, la religión, la filosofía, la cultura, la economía y el lenguaje. La sensación desnuda está revestida con este condicionamiento complejo. Como resultado, el cuerpo y el mundo que percibimos han sido interpretados de antemano. Existen como extensiones del drama humano. Al despertar, te sales del drama para ser quien eres realmente. Ves que la realidad virtual es un objeto de segunda mano, con el cual ya no tienes que conformarte.

PARA HOY

Éste es un ejercicio simple en la percepción. Contempla la letra *A*. Cuando posaste tu mirada en ella viste un signo simple hecho con tres líneas por una pluma. Pero esas líneas no tienen un significado inherente, como lo podrás comprobar si volteas la *A* de cabeza. El significado de la *A* está insertado en ella. Es un significado antiguo que proviene del alfabeto fenicio. Está mezclado con la letra hebrea *aleph*, que representa el principio, la creación y Dios. La *A* es sinónimo de uno, el cual connota la individualidad y el inicio de la aritmética. La *A* es una calificación deseable en la escuela, y si obtienes suficientes *Aes* es muy probable que te conviertas en alguien bien educado y termines siendo próspero.*

———————

* En algunos países A equivale a 10. *(N. de la T.)*

Si una sola letra del alfabeto conlleva tanta historia e implicaciones, imagina qué complejo es el entramado del mundo humano. Heredamos una enorme cantidad de significados que sostienen el mundo, pero que también se convierten en una carga. (Piensa en todos los problemas que ha causado otra letra del alfabeto, I.)*

TU EXPERIENCIA: _____

_____

_____

_____

_____

_____

---

* *I* en inglés, significa *yo* en español. (*N. de la T.*)

DÍA 11

La mente misma no es otra cosa que conciencia condicionada.

Cada uno de nosotros nació en un mundo interpretado. Las generaciones anteriores pasaron su vida entera dándole un significado humano a todo. Como recién nacido creces aprendiendo lo básico, y una vez que puedes navegar el mundo —caminar, hablar, tomar decisiones de vida, formar relaciones— encuentras tu lugar en la realidad virtual. En algún punto te gustaría tener tus propias experiencias únicas. "Quiero ser yo" es un incentivo poderoso.

Pero la única forma de tener una experiencia es usando la mente, y la mente de todos está totalmente condicionada. No tenía otra opción. Al aprender lo básico, cada uno de nosotros sacrificó "quiero ser yo" en el nombre de "quiero encajar". En ello están implicadas más cosas que la presión social. Las reglas de la realidad virtual requieren que aceptemos un conjunto compartido de imágenes, historias, creencias y hábitos. Al despertar, logras ser tú mismo más allá de las reglas. La realidad "real" siempre es nueva y original.

PARA HOY

Hoy, el desafío es que tengas un pensamiento totalmente tuyo. Este pensamiento no puede ser un eco de nada que hayas escuchado decir a alguien o nada que hayas leído en un libro. No puede ser formulado en una frase conocida. No debe salir de la memoria, porque entonces sólo estarías repitiendo el pasado. Al enfrentarte a este simple desafío puedes ver qué tan atrapado te tiene la mente condicionada. Hay rutas de escape comprobadas, como la imaginación y la fantasía, que sortean las reglas al no coincidir con la realidad. Hay otra ruta de escape, despertar, que te permite estar aquí ahora. En el ahora eterno la mente condicionada no tiene lugar.

TU EXPERIENCIA: _____

_____

_____

_____

_____

_____

DÍA 12

••• ——————— •••

La realidad virtual es una red de relaciones.

El mundo físico se trata por completo de relaciones. Hemos creado historias alrededor de ellas. Un árbol de Navidad cuenta una historia; el árbol en el que están colgados los adornos se relaciona con otros árboles de hojas perennes, lo que conduce al reino vegetal y los orígenes de la vida. No hay nada en el mundo que pueda ser visto sin estar insertado en relaciones que se extienden en todas direcciones. Esta red de relaciones es la red invisible que lo une todo. Al estar enredados dentro de la red creamos historias interminables en una película en marcha.

Pero ¿cómo te sales de la red? Los humanos sueñan con un reino como el cielo que permite que el mundo relativo desaparezca para siempre. El cielo puede ser un sueño, pero un mundo más allá no lo es. Al despertar te encuentras a ti mismo en ese mundo, que es la conciencia misma. Más allá de todas las cosas creadas está el vientre de la creación.

PARA HOY

Permite que tu mirada vague por la habitación y elige un objeto al azar. Ahora, de forma rápida y sucesiva, durante 30 segundos piensa en todas las palabras posibles que se relacionen con ese objeto. Digamos que elegiste una lámpara de mesa. Algunas palabras vinculadas con una lámpara de mesa son: *luz, luciérnaga, antorcha, Estatua de la Libertad, lámpara junto a la puerta dorada, libertad, inmigrantes, Alemania, nazismo, Hitler, Segunda Guerra Mundial,* y demás. Observa que el flujo de palabras se desenvuelve por sí mismo, yendo en cada una y todas las direcciones. Con un simple ejercicio de asociación de palabras, has tejido un hilo de la red que crea el mundo conocido.

TU EXPERIENCIA: _____

_____

_____

_____

DÍA 13

La mente nos ha enredado en una realidad virtual de nuestra propia creación.

En los mitos acerca de la creación alrededor del mundo, Dios o los dioses están aparte, mirando hacia abajo al mundo que han creado. Pero los humanos creamos la realidad virtual y después entramos en ella. El propósito de la realidad virtual fue permitirnos un doble rol, tanto como autores de nuestras propias historias como actores que las interpretamos. Los dos roles son creados por la mente y mantenerlos separados resulta confuso. Cuando surge un problema la gente se pregunta a sí misma: "¿Me hice esto a mí mismo?", y no puede responder.

Al estar enredados en la realidad virtual, nos parece más fácil seguir la corriente y fingir que jugamos un rol, el actor. Pero el rol del autor es mucho más importante. Por desgracia, en gran medida ha sido olvidado. La vida ya es muy confusa. Al despertar ves con claridad tu rol en el proceso creativo. Ya no estás indefenso ni eres una víctima, más de lo que Romeo y Julieta son víctimas de Shakespeare. Ellos cobraron vida en la conciencia de su autor, al igual que tú cobras vida todos los días en la tuya.

PARA HOY

Regresa al centro creativo de las cosas. La próxima vez que ordenes comida o pidas ver algo en una tienda, enmarca la situación de esta manera: yo tuve el pensamiento que puso en movimiento esta situación. Yo puse el pensamiento en palabras. Las palabras provocaron que otra persona emprendiera una nueva acción. Esa acción da pie a otra acción realizada por los cocineros en la cocina (o el fabricante que llevó los productos a una tienda), que están ganándose la vida para crear sus propias historias, y la suma de todas esas historias es la historia humana. Por lo tanto, en cada momento, mis pensamientos están en el centro creativo de la historia.

Esto es más que una nueva forma de enmarcar la actividad común y corriente. Es la verdad. Tú eres el centro creativo de las cosas, por siempre.

TU EXPERIENCIA: _____

_____

_____

_____

_____

_____

DÍA 14

••• ———— •••

El cuerpo, la mente y el mundo, cuando son vistos directamente
y sin interpretación, son una sola actividad.

Aunque nos ocupemos con mil cosas al día, nos resulta natural ver el mundo como una sola cosa. Para un creyente devoto, la cosa única es la creación de Dios. Para la mayoría de los científicos, la cosa única es el universo físico. Pero éstas son respuestas condicionadas. Los creyentes no pueden consultar a Dios para confirmar su creencia, y los científicos no pueden confirmar de dónde provienen el espacio, la materia y la energía. ¿Qué pasaría si miras el mundo directamente, sin una respuesta condicionada? Verías que la cosa única es la conciencia que se modifica a sí misma constantemente. El cuerpo, la mente y el mundo son experiencias en la conciencia. Esto puede ser verificado. La experiencia es la piedra angular de la realidad. Cuando despiertas, se convierte en la única piedra angular que necesitas. Te unes al juego de la conciencia y te deleitas en ella.

PARA HOY

El juego de la conciencia abarca toda la creación. Hoy puedes unirte al juego como una experiencia disfrutable. Tómate un momento para hacer algo que te haga feliz: puede ser comer con un amigo, apreciar los árboles y el cielo, observar a los niños en los juegos del parque. Si tu placer proviene de comer helado a medianoche, eso está muy bien. Lo que sea que estés haciendo, relájate en tu disfrute y obsérvalo. El placer es la forma más fácil de estar aquí y ahora. Tan sólo al notar tu placer ya te has puesto a ti mismo en el juego eterno de la conciencia.

TU EXPERIENCIA: _____

_____

_____

_____

_____

DÍA 15

Cuando se examina de cerca, no existe mundo externo o cuerpo físico independiente de nuestras percepciones.

Estamos tan acostumbrados a vivir con un ser dividido que es un paso muy grande ver más allá de él. El ser dividido te dice que vives en dos mundos, uno "aquí dentro" y otro "allá fuera". Pero si la realidad es una sola cosa, esta visión está equivocada. La conciencia es la única cosa. Se desenvuelve como una realidad. Al saber esto, tienes terreno firme sobre el cual pararte: tu propia conciencia. La mente condicionada corrompe y distorsiona la conciencia. Colorea tus percepciones y te obliga a aceptar la división entre el mundo interno y el externo. Despertar clarifica la verdad. Todos los mundos se experimentan en la conciencia. No hay necesidad de demostrar o no demostrar la existencia del mundo físico. Estás aquí ahora, y eso es suficiente.

PARA HOY

No es difícil fundir el mundo interno y el mundo externo en uno solo. Busca una foto de ti mismo; puede ser tu licencia de conducir o una foto tomada con el celular. Sostén tu foto con la mano y mírate en el espejo. Después mírate en la foto, y finalmente, mírate a ti mismo en tu imaginación. Moverte de ver tu cuerpo físico reflejado en un espejo, luego capturado en una foto y al final dentro de tu mente, cada una fue una experiencia en la conciencia. Con base en ello, no fueron tres experiencias distintas. Fue una experiencia siendo modificada de tres maneras. Todo en la vida se encuentra en el mismo terreno, como experiencias que son conciencia modificada.

TU EXPERIENCIA: _____
_____
_____
_____
_____

DÍA 16

··· ———————— ···

Ya que no hay un mundo físico independiente, la realidad cotidiana es un sueño lúcido sucediendo en el ahora vívido.

Los sueños no están hechos del mismo material. Algunos sueños son vagos, apenas más vívidos que tener un recuerdo fugaz cuando estás despierto. En el extremo opuesto están los llamados sueños lúcidos. Cuando estás teniendo un sueño lúcido no tienes idea de que es un sueño. Estás totalmente inmerso en él, y cuando despiertas es difícil reconocer que el sueño no era real. Asimismo, la realidad virtual es una experiencia de inmersión total. Existen pocas claves para sugerir que no estás del todo despierto.

Por ese motivo, los destellos de claridad, los momentos de alegría, las inspiraciones creativas y la experiencia de la meditación son momentos preciosos. Sugieren que estás inmerso en un sueño lúcido vívido. El despertar sucederá como una sorpresa —para muchas personas es una conmoción darse cuenta de que han estado dormidos toda su vida—. Cada momento que pasó fue como experimentar el ahora vívido. Pero una vez despierto, el ahora se convierte en una ventana hacia la conciencia pura. Lo que importa es que estás totalmente despierto a ella.

PARA HOY

Los momentos en que ves a través del hechizo/sueño/realidad a menudo suceden espontáneamente —llegan de sorpresa—. No hay una forma establecida de provocar esos destellos; lo más cerca que puedes llegar es por medio de la meditación. De todas formas, hoy puedes preparar el terreno para la semilla de la experiencia de la metarrealidad. En cualquier momento mira a tu alrededor, sonríete a ti mismo y di: "Imagina que todo esto es un sueño y yo soy el que lo sueña". La sonrisa es importante. Es como esperar la Navidad cuando eres niño. Sabes que algo bueno está en camino y, al recordártelo, abres el camino.

TU EXPERIENCIA: _____

_____

_____

_____

_____

_____

DÍA 17

••• ———— •••

El ahora no es un momento en el tiempo que pueda ser asido y guardado.
El ahora es el vaivén de la conciencia.

Si quieres saber quién ejecuta las reglas de la realidad virtual, un buen lugar para empezar es el reloj. El tictac del tiempo del reloj se desliza en la vida en segmentos de segundos, minutos y horas. Una vez que te identificas con el tiempo del reloj, tu vida pasa en segundos, minutos y horas. Este tipo de existencia es mecánico y rutinario. Hoy día, liberarte de la realidad virtual se ha convertido en un estado de conciencia, sin embargo esto no es tarea sencilla. Cuando despiertas, el ahora es una presencia; es la experiencia ininterrumpida de estar aquí.

Cuando experimentas esta presencia eres testigo de cómo la corriente de la conciencia brinda una secuencia de sensaciones y percepciones fugaces. Dividir esta corriente de actividad en segundos, minutos y horas es un constructo mental. Cuando estás despierto le prestas más atención a la presencia de la conciencia que a los eventos efímeros que suceden en la mente.

PARA HOY

La actividad mental es muy pegajosa. Tú tienes una participación en los pensamientos, imágenes y sentimientos que pasan por tu mente. Pero no es necesario que tengas una participación en esos pensamientos, sensaciones, imágenes y sentimientos. Imagina que estás sentado en un tren suburbano, viendo por la ventana. Conforme el paisaje pasa ante tus ojos, no lo ves eligiendo cada edificio, árbol, coche o persona. Es tan sólo el paisaje. Si notas algo que destaque, esto pasa tan rápido como las cosas que no notas. Ahora sustituye las ventanas por tus ojos. Estás sentado detrás de ellos, observando el paisaje. Cuando adoptas esta posición, que se conoce como "atestiguamiento", te aproximas por un momento al estado permanente de estar despierto.

TU EXPERIENCIA: _____
_____
_____
_____
_____

DÍA 18

••• ———————— •••

El tiempo del reloj rebana lo atemporal y le da principios y finales. Como
resultado, existe el nacimiento, el envejecimiento y la muerte.

Toda la realidad virtual, desde el átomo hasta el cuerpo humano y el
universo, es un proceso atemporal congelado en el tiempo. Si dices:
"Yo nací en 1961" o "La junta comienza a las tres en punto", estás haciendo lo mismo: congelar un proceso fluido constante en un inicio,
que automáticamente conlleva una mitad y un final. El comienzo, la
mitad y el final son constructos mentales. ¿Cuál es la mitad del azul?
¿Qué fue lo último que sucedió anoche antes de que el tiempo comenzara? Cuando despiertas, estar aquí es continuo —de hecho, siempre
ha sido continuo, hasta que fueron inventados el inicio, la mitad y el
final—. Sentirás un gran alivio al desechar esos conceptos. No sólo
descubrirás que estás viviendo en el ahora, sino que el nacimiento,
el envejecimiento y la muerte se volverán irrelevantes.

PARA HOY
Para salir del tiempo del reloj y entrar en lo atemporal, tómate un momento y observa un color, digamos el azul del cielo. Intenta ver más
allá del azul. Realmente inténtalo. Te darás cuenta de que es inútil
llevar tu mente ahí. La actividad mental es irrelevante. Y tampoco
importa si de hecho puedes ver más allá del azul. Al no permitir que
tu mente interfiera escapaste del tiempo del reloj, y el único lugar en
el que puedes estar es atemporal. De forma similar, intenta imaginar
un tiempo en el que tú no existías. Esto también hará que la mente
pensante deje de interferir. Experimentarás el no tiempo cuando no
existías. ¿Acaso hay una mejor definición de eternidad?

TU EXPERIENCIA: _____

_____

_____

_____

_____

_____

DÍA 19

• • • ———— • • •

La realidad es la actividad interminable de la conciencia
modificándose a sí misma.

Si alguien llegara y te dijera: "Quiero estar aquí ahora. ¿Dónde está sucediendo?", te sentirías confundido. "Ahora" no es un lugar en el mapa. Las conexiones cerebrales pueden ser mapeadas en sus locaciones precisas, pero no existe un arriba, abajo, frente y vuelta de la conciencia. El ahora es continuo porque la conciencia es continua. Sólo en la realidad virtual hay limitaciones impuestas como inicios y finales, o nacimiento y muerte. Al experimentarla de forma directa, la realidad fluye como un río. Pero tienes que imaginar que es un río que fluye en un círculo, sin comenzar en las montañas y desembocar en el mar.

Cuando estás despierto, incluso es demasiado limitado describir la conciencia como un flujo. La conciencia no necesita ser activa. Conforme sucede la actividad está en todas partes. Fuera de la meditación o de momentos inesperados de silencio, la mente participa de forma constante en el vaivén de la conciencia conforme se modifica a sí misma. Más allá del alboroto constante de actividad, la conciencia es silenciosa, pura, ilimitada y sin la necesidad de hacer nada. En cuanto despiertas te identificas con la conciencia pura, y disfrutas la calma y la seguridad que brinda.

PARA HOY

La conciencia silenciosa siempre está contigo, esperando a que la percibas. Siéntate en un lugar tranquilo y di para ti mismo: "Yo soy _____", llena el espacio en blanco con tu nombre completo. Con una breve pausa entre las dos palabras, di para ti mismo las siguientes frases: "Yo soy [primer nombre]", después: "Yo soy", luego: "Soy", y al final ningún pensamiento. Sin etiquetas con las cuales identificarse la mente está en silencio. Cuando experimentas este estado, aunque sea sólo un momento, has encontrado tu identidad real. El ego emerge de la actividad mental; tu ser verdadero surge de la conciencia silenciosa.

TU EXPERIENCIA: _____

_____

_____

_____

_____

_____

DÍA 20

El tiempo es sólo un tipo de limitación. También lo son el espacio,
la materia y la energía. La conciencia misma no tiene limitaciones.

Ahora, el despertar es más claro que en el pasado, cuando se consideraba que el proceso era tan misterioso que se veía totalmente paradójico. Como lo dice una metáfora antigua, querer despertar es como ser un pez sediento. El pez tiene sed sólo porque no se da cuenta de que está rodeado por el océano. Asimismo, una persona que busca despertar no se da cuenta de que el infinito océano de la conciencia está en todas partes y en cada momento.

La limitación comienza en la mente pero se refleja en el tiempo, el espacio, la materia y la energía. Este efecto de reflejo se mantiene vigente en el sueño y en la vigilia. La diferencia es que cuando despiertas el universo físico se ve por lo que es realmente, el juego de la conciencia. La conciencia no tiene forma ni fronteras. Estar más allá de las etiquetas y los pensamientos es inconcebible. Y también es quien realmente eres.

PARA HOY

Levanta la mano y muévela en varias posiciones, y en cada posición haz un gesto que signifique algo. Representa el papel de un policía que dirige el tránsito, un maestro que señala el pizarrón, un amante acariciando la mejilla de su amada, un chef batiendo huevos para un omelette, lo que puedas imaginar. Reflexiona sobre cómo tu mano llevó a cabo lo que fuera que tu imaginación quiso representar. La mente y la materia fueron apariencias diferentes de la misma conciencia. Asimismo, tu realidad personal consiste en la acción de la mente para coordinar el tiempo, el espacio, la materia y la energía.

Expresan las mismas posibilidades limitadas que la imaginación humana.

TU EXPERIENCIA: _____
_____
_____
_____
_____
_____

DÍA 21

••• ———————— •••

La realidad virtual surgió de la necesidad humana de vivir
en la limitación. Esta necesidad inició el proceso que creó
la mente condicionada.

La limitación es parte de la realidad virtual, y parece algo totalmente convincente y necesario. No puedes volar como un ave; no puedes ser rico con desear que así fuera; si te atropellase un coche, estarías lastimado seriamente o muerto. He dicho que la mente condicionada edita la realidad para que ésta sirva a las necesidades humanas. El infinito se vuelve finito. Estamos confinados por realidades severas. De hecho no tiene nada de malo editar el infinito en lo finito —después de todo, no puedes tener pensamientos infinitos de golpe, aunque tengas la capacidad de tener pensamientos infinitos—.

El problema es que hemos olvidado que nosotros hicimos esta edición. La realidad virtual no es un hecho; fue manufacturada. La configuración es finita, y así como no puedes tener pensamientos infinitos de golpe, físicamente los humanos no pueden hacer todo de golpe, decir todo de golpe o desear todo de golpe. La configuración de la realidad virtual le conviene al ser que pensamos que tenemos —y que debemos tener—.

Cuando despiertas, la imagen se revierte. Te das cuenta de que la realidad virtual es un constructo. Al despertar te liberas de la mente condicionada, el ser limitado y las limitaciones de la realidad virtual creadas por la mente. En la libertad sigues sin poder volar, volverte rico con sólo desearlo o evitar ser herido si te atropella un coche. Por otra parte, no es lo mejor declarar que todo es posible. Despertar te lleva por encima de un umbral. Lo que espera del otro lado es un nuevo y vasto territorio de posibilidades.

PARA HOY

Siéntate por un momento y comienza a pensar en todas las cosas que quisieras hacer o ser, que son imposibles. Quizá te gustaría ser fabulosamente rico o increíblemente atractivo o ser joven otra vez: el cielo es el límite. Conforme cada cosa te venga a la mente, haz una pausa y di para ti mismo: "¿Por qué no? ¿Por qué esto es imposible?". Espera una respuesta y permite que ésta se desarrolle, diciéndote todos los motivos por los cuales no puedes tener o ser lo que tú quieres.

Ahora pregúntate: "¿Quién dice que no puedo?". No hay una buena respuesta a esta pregunta. Las cosas son imposibles no porque alguien lo diga. Son imposibles porque toda la configuración de la realidad virtual lo dice. Todas las limitaciones están incrustadas en la realidad virtual. Cuando alguien dice que algo es imposible, tan sólo está sosteniendo la realidad virtual. ¿Quién dice que debes seguir el lineamiento? Nadie, ni siquiera tú mismo. Cuando asimilas esto comienzas a vislumbrar qué tan libre eres en realidad.

TU EXPERIENCIA: _____

_____

_____

_____

_____

DÍA 22

••• ———————— •••

Cuando se edita la conciencia infinita, aparecen la forma y el fenómeno (es decir, cosas que podemos ver, escuchar, tocar, saborear, oler y sobre las cuales pensar).

Para los propósitos de la vida cotidiana, el infinito necesitaba ser editado. Todos estamos de acuerdo con eso, pero olvidamos que no había un reglamento o un conjunto de lineamientos para editar la realidad. Las únicas reglas son impuestas por uno mismo. La conciencia pura se desarrolló en el universo físico, imponiendo sobre su creación el tiempo, el espacio, la materia y la energía. Pero la conciencia pura no creía que debía hacer las cosas de esta manera. La física moderna ha planteado que existen miles de millones de universos con otras configuraciones.

Al nivel de la conciencia pura, nunca hubo duda de que las reglas son autoimpuestas. Heredamos esta certeza. El arte y la cultura expresan la certeza de que la mente humana puede construir cualquier escenario, mientras que también acepta el escenario del universo físico. Esto hace que parezca que la vida tiene dos compartimentos: el mental, que es ilimitado, y el físico, que es limitado. Pero ése es un error. Una casa no está separada del deseo de construir una casa y del conocimiento de cómo hacerlo. Lo mental y lo físico son aspectos de una cosa: la inteligencia creativa que juega. Cuando despiertes verás cómo funciona la inteligencia creativa y, con fascinación y curiosidad, te convertirás en un cocreador de la realidad.

PARA HOY

Para volverte consciente de cómo se desenvuelve la inteligencia creativa, comienza con un objeto pequeño. Ya sea un clavo, un arete o las llaves de tu coche, estas cosas son ideas que tomaron una forma física. Ahora piensa en algo más grande, el edificio Empire State o el puente Golden Gate. También son ideas que tomaron una forma física. ¿Acaso importa que un arete sea diminuto y que el Golden Gate sea inmenso? No. La inteligencia creativa no es grande ni pequeña. No es dura ni suave, aquí pero no allá, visible o invisible. La capacidad de crear se contiene a sí misma por completo, y no respeta limitación alguna de estados ni formas. La creatividad sólo se necesita a sí misma. Sin la inteligencia creativa, los estados, las formas y los eventos no podrían surgir.

Ahora mírate en el espejo y di para ti mismo: "Soy creatividad infinita que ha tomado una forma". Deja de identificarte con la forma y comienza a identificarte con la creatividad. Así es como despiertas.

TU EXPERIENCIA: _____

_____

_____

_____

_____

_____

DÍA 23

Cada forma y fenómeno son una sola cosa: la modificación de lo que no tiene forma, lo infinito reducido a lo finito, conciencia pura a la que se le da un comienzo, un punto medio y un final.

El mundo recompensa a los grandes pensadores y les da un lugar en la historia. En comparación con Albert Einstein o Leonardo da Vinci, todo mundo se siente como un pensador menor. Pero un gran pensador no es necesariamente el pensador más grande. El pensador más grande ve que la realidad es una cosa; la creación, un proceso. Eso es la imagen completa en una sola visión, lo cual se convierte en tu realidad al despertar.

La imagen completa se vuelve clara cuando la mente deja de nublar constantemente tu visión con pensamientos, sensaciones, imágenes y sentimientos que interfieren. Éstos representan el estira y afloja entre tú y el exterior. Cuando despiertas desaparecen los patrones de interferencia. Aceptas como un hecho natural que el infinito, la conciencia pura sin forma, es la fuente de todas las cosas. Darte cuenta de esto es natural porque te ves a ti mismo como una expresión de una sola cosa, no de un revoltijo de actividad mental y física.

PARA HOY

Si ves un objeto en el mundo exterior, lo ves desde el exterior. La totalidad —la única cosa— no tiene afuera. Tampoco tiene adentro. Por lo tanto, no puedes verla. Como tú *eres* la totalidad, ni siquiera puedes relacionarte con ella de diversas maneras, como aceptarla o rechazarla, participar en ella un día y salirte al siguiente. Cuando despiertas sabes que eres la única cosa. Incluso cuando ahora puedes dejar de relacionarte con ella falsamente.

Hoy practica no tener ninguna actitud hacia tu mente. Permite que los pensamientos lleguen y se vayan, y cuando estés tentado a formar una actitud hacia lo que sucede, no lo hagas. No digas que un pensamiento es bueno y el otro malo. No asignes etiquetas como inteligente, tonto, positivo o negativo. La mente no es ninguna de esas cosas. Es el flujo de actividad que proviene del absoluto. Etiquetar la mente es como decir que la totalidad es buena, mala, positiva, negativa y demás. Claramente, la totalidad está más allá de todas las etiquetas. Al igual que tu conciencia. Al no juzgar tus pensamientos comienzas a adoptar el estado abierto y sin juicio de estar despierto.

TU EXPERIENCIA: _____

_____

_____

_____

_____

_____

DÍA 24

••• ———— •••

Sólo la conciencia es real. Incluso cuando juega el rol de observador y observado, incluso cuando crea mundos "allá fuera" y "aquí dentro", su propia naturaleza es inmutable.

La conciencia existe. Todo lo demás es una experiencia pasajera. Estas dos oraciones han sido dichas una y otra vez durante siglos. Este hecho demuestra, por lo menos, que los seres humanos contemplaban la realidad y les parecía misteriosa. ¿Cómo surgió el cambio a partir de lo inmutable? ¿Cómo Uno se convirtió en Muchos? El misterio se formuló de distintas e incontables maneras. Preguntar: "¿Qué había antes de que el tiempo comenzara?", como lo hace la cosmología moderna, es sólo una variante medieval a la pregunta: "¿Qué existía antes de Dios?".

La respuesta está contenida en la pregunta. Lo que había primero siempre ha estado aquí. El cambio es sólo una máscara de lo inmutable. Cuando los seres humanos vimos el misterio, vimos nuestra propia naturaleza. Somos creadores y creados, Uno y Muchos, experiencia cambiante y conciencia inmutable. Nada de esto debe ser demostrado ni examinado. Si aceptas o no tu naturaleza verdadera no afecta en nada a tu naturaleza verdadera. Sigue siendo. Cuando despiertas ves tu naturaleza verdadera con claridad, y entonces comienza una nueva vida.

PARA HOY

Tómate unos momentos y permite que tu mente deambule por algunas cosas que puedas recordar de tu pasado —recuerdos de tu infancia temprana, tus padres, cumpleaños, la escuela, tu primer beso, algunas cosas tristes y demás—. No importa lo que decidas ver. Ahora reflexiona sobre aquello que tienen en común. Tú estuviste ahí. Tú eres lo inmutable en medio del cambio. Ahora conoces tu naturaleza verdadera. Todo lo demás es un escaparate.

TU EXPERIENCIA: _____

_____

_____

_____

_____

_____

DÍA 25

••• ———————— •••

El sufrimiento humano es inherente a la realidad virtual. No existe
en la conciencia misma.

Cuando sufres y te sientes infeliz, ansioso, deprimido o desesperado tu sufrimiento se siente totalmente real. Estás experimentando algo que es un hecho, se siente como un hecho, arraigado en el dolor físico y la angustia mental. Pero la realidad virtual, nuestro hechizo/sueño/ilusión, es un constructo. El sufrimiento está insertado en el constructo, y por ello se siente como algo inevitable. Las creencias acerca del sufrimiento, ya sea que se originen en la doctrina del pecado, del karma o de las teorías médicas modernas, refuerzan la realidad virtual.

Despertar no garantiza que nunca más habrá dolor físico o días tristes. La mente condicionada es terca, y nuestro cuerpo ha sido bombardeado constantemente con señales de la mente condicionada. Las sombras del condicionamiento continúan cayendo (siempre recordando que las sombras pueden ser livianas y también pesadas). Al despertar abandonas tu lealtad hacia la mente condicionada, y desde ese instante comienza a desaparecer y a soltarte. Ves que la liberación del sufrimiento es posible y natural. El sufrimiento no existe en la conciencia misma, la cual es tu verdadera naturaleza.

PARA HOY

Cuando la gente sufre —por ejemplo, cuando se siente deprimida o es diagnosticada con una enfermedad mortal— existe la tentación de culparse a sí misma. "¿Por qué me hice esto a mí mismo?" es una pregunta que se plantea a partir del remordimiento, y el remordimiento está listo para culpar. La mejor respuesta es que tu sufrimiento es parte de la realidad virtual. Tú aceptaste la realidad virtual, por lo cual es inevitable tu participación en el dolor y el sufrimiento. No significa que estés condenado; algunas personas evitan el sufrimiento grave. Pero tu participación es un trato cerrado, sin importar quién seas o lo que te suceda, a menos que hagas un cambio.

Para terminar el sufrimiento rompe el trato. Cuando despiertas, el contrato se anula por completo. Hoy puedes preparar el camino hacia el despertar al no creer en el dolor y el sufrimiento como algo predestinado e inevitable. Recuerda algunas experiencias que consideres de sufrimiento —podrían incluir momentos de dolor, pérdida, enfermedad, traición, fracaso, humillación y demás—. Tú eres la misma conciencia que atravesó el sufrimiento, pero también el no sufrimiento; que experimentó el dolor, pero también el placer; que perdió, pero que también ganó. En cada opuesto has experimentado ambos polos. Por lo tanto, no eres ninguno de ellos.

Eres la conciencia inmutable que atestigua el cambio, la pantalla sobre la cual toda la experiencia evoluciona, sin ser una experiencia. Esta verdad contiene todo el secreto para terminar con el sufrimiento.

TU EXPERIENCIA: _____

_____

_____

_____

_____

_____

DÍA 26

• • • ———————— • • •

El sufrimiento continúa porque nos aferramos a la memoria y nos sujetamos a la experiencia. Es una ilusión creer que el ahora puede asirse o que es posible aferrarnos a la realidad.

La verdad parece fría cuando no hay nada que puedas hacer al respecto. La gente siente la verdad de que la vida conlleva sufrimiento, y odia sentirse indefensa ante dicha verdad. El resultado es un gran conflicto interior. Por una parte, pretendemos aceptar que la vida implica sufrimiento. Por la otra, luchamos por evitar la sensación de indefensión. La medicina moderna acaba con parte de la confusión y la lucha. Conforme se van conquistando las enfermedades, los seres humanos se sienten más poderosos y hacen a un lado el sufrimiento, por el momento.

El sufrimiento en la forma de angustia mental no ha sido aliviado, y tampoco el temor a la enfermedad y el envejecimiento, o el pavor a la muerte. La historia de la civilización tecnológica moderna es el mejoramiento de la realidad virtual. (Así como el descubrimiento de nuevas formas de muerte mecanizada es un deterioro de la realidad virtual.) El sufrimiento continúa porque queremos aferrarnos a las buenas experiencias y al recuerdo de días mejores. Siempre y cuando la juventud, la salud y la felicidad estén arraigadas en el tiempo, y que los buenos tiempos sean preferibles a los malos, no podremos evitar el sufrimiento. Aferrarnos a la realidad virtual significa que el sufrimiento es parte del constructo.

Cuando despiertas no intentas aferrarte o asirte a nada. No almacenas los buenos recuerdos y separas los malos. Lo único que hay es ser aquí ahora. En el ahora no hay nada a lo cual asirse o aferrarse.

Cuando ya no te aferras has cortado tu conexión con la realidad virtual. Entonces el sufrimiento ya no se aferra a ti.

PARA HOY

Cuando alguien te dice que sueltes y dejes de aferrarte, ¿su consejo te ayuda en realidad? Los resentimientos, afrentas, heridas y enojos más persistentes se están aferrando a ti, no al revés. Después de un divorcio amargo, perder un trabajo o ser traicionado por un amigo, nadie despierta pensando: "Ahora tengo algo a lo que realmente me quiero aferrar". En cambio, el enojo y el resentimiento regresan por su propia voluntad, y duran tanto como decidan durar, no lo que tú deseas que duren.

A lo que te estás aferrando en realidad no es a los malos recuerdos, viejos rencores y sentimientos de dolor. Te estás aferrando a la realidad virtual. Al despertar, sueltas tu lealtad hacia ella, y entonces lo malo deja de aferrarse a ti. Piensa en algo que te haga sentir muy enojado o resentido. Cuando lo tengas en la mente, suéltalo. No podrás hacerlo si es que todavía se está aferrando a ti. En realidad, estás donde estás. Este lugar está lleno de cosas malas que alguna vez sucedieron, dolores y resentimientos que se encuentran en distintas etapas: fuertemente aferradas, comenzando a soltar o casi disipadas por completo. La realidad virtual está configurada de manera que, estés donde estés, experimentes aquello que se aferra a ti como si fueran percebes en el casco de un barco. Ver esto te da la sensación de desapego, lo cual es signo de que estás despertando.

TU EXPERIENCIA: _____

_____

_____

_____

DÍA 27

... ——————— ...

El sufrimiento termina cuando ya no tememos la impermanencia.
Mientras sigamos participando en la ilusión, sufriremos.

Los niños están impacientes por explorar el mundo, y les fascina ver cómo todo cambia. Pero al mismo tiempo, un niño desea la seguridad y la confianza de su hogar. El cambio se vuelve amenazante cuando no hay nadie en casa que prometa confianza y seguridad. Una forma de mantener la ansiedad a raya es pretender que "yo", la personalidad del ego, es estable y confiable. "Yo" participa en el mundo, algo que mantener. El ego se construye a sí mismo por medio de todo tipo de formas de aferrarse —el placer, la fantasía, el idealismo, el condicionamiento desgastado, los viejos recuerdos y las creencias falsas—.

Todas esas cosas son impermanentes, así que no sirve construir un ser con base en ellas. El temor al cambio sólo desaparece cuando basas tu vida en el ser verdadero. Conforme despiertas sucede naturalmente la transición del ego al ser verdadero.

PARA HOY

La mejor forma de sentirte seguro es cuando das por hecho tu seguridad sin preocuparte por ella. Piensa en los comerciales que ves en la televisión que anuncian seguros, medicamentos, asilos y alarmas contra robo. Ofrecen consuelo, primero, al presentar el temor de que no estás a salvo. La táctica funciona porque en realidad no damos por hecho nuestra seguridad personal; en cambio, sólo hacemos a un lado la ansiedad para no verla.

Para percibir lo real y firme que se siente la seguridad, deja de leer por un segundo. Después vuelve a leer, y detente una vez más. En la pausa entre la lectura de estas palabras, diste por hecho que sabías leer. No existe una ansiedad subyacente acerca de esto —lo sabes de cierto— y lo mismo sucede con docenas de cosas que sabes hacer. Así es como se siente cuando estás completamente seguro sin ocultar la ansiedad subyacente. Cuando despiertes, darás por hecho que siempre has existido y que siempre existirás. Con base en ello, una vez más eres como un niño, libre de explorar el mundo y a salvo del temor porque siempre estás en casa, dentro de ti mismo.

TU EXPERIENCIA: _____

_____

_____

_____

_____

_____

DÍA 28

••• —————— •••

La libertad es el estado natural de la existencia, saber que somos
conscientes aquí y ahora.

La realidad virtual no es confiable en lo que se refiere a la felicidad duradera, la seguridad, la plenitud, el amor y otras cosas que apreciamos. Algunas personas disfrutan muy pocas de esas cosas, e incluso si tenemos más de nuestra justa porción, tememos la posibilidad de perderla. No es buena idea confiar en lo no fiable. No aceptarías un trabajo de un patrón que te diga que todos los días echará un volado para decidir si te quedas o si te despide. Pero nos aferramos a la realidad virtual sin garantía de que las cosas van a funcionar. Esto es una forma de esclavitud —la peor forma, ya que la creencia ampliamente aceptada es que no hay alternativa—.

La libertad real no es algo que te esfuerces por alcanzar, que esperes que suceda ni que sientas poco probable ganarla. La libertad es nuestro estado natural si no nos aprisionamos a nosotros mismos. Al despertar ya no te sientes atado a la realidad virtual. Los constructos mentales pierden su control sobre ti y eventualmente desaparecen por completo. Estar aquí ahora es lo mismo que la libertad total, porque el ahora ha desaparecido antes de que pueda reclamarte nada. Tú existes y eres consciente, eso basta para liberarte.

PARA HOY

Todos nosotros tenemos nuestra propia versión de lo que se siente ser libre y su opuesto, lo que se siente estar atrapado, cercado y sofocado. Pero estos conceptos disfrazan la realidad, que es que nuestro sentido de libertad siempre está limitado por su opuesto. El retiro nos libera de las demandas del trabajo; que los hijos se vayan a la universidad nos libera de tenerlos bajo nuestro techo. Pero nuestra libertad está constreñida a tener un trabajo y a convertirnos en padres.

La verdadera libertad no está regida por su opuesto. Para demostrarte esto a ti mismo, piensa un momento y describe lo que estabas haciendo a las 7:37 de la noche el martes pasado. ¿Qué pensamientos te vinieron a la mente? ¿Qué palabras dijiste? Incluso si retienes algo memorable, toma cierto esfuerzo recordarlo. Eres libre del martes pasado a las 7:37 de la noche porque no hay un apego a ello. Un momento del ahora se ha ido y desaparecido. El momento en que comenzaste a leer esta lección se ha ido y desaparecido. Tu relación con el ahora es experimentarlo, extraer lo que tiene que dar y continuar. Éste es el estado de no hacer y no apego, que se convierte en nuestro estado natural cuando despertamos.

TU EXPERIENCIA: _____
_____
_____
_____
_____

DÍA 29

··· ———— ···

Al conocernos a nosotros mismos como seres atemporales, podemos vivir conscientemente. Podemos ser quienes somos realmente: una especie de conciencia creando el universo humano.

"Yo", la personalidad del ego, subyuga la sustancia de la creación todos los días, convirtiendo nuevas ideas en realidad. A esto lo llamamos *progreso*, y lo es —de cierta forma—. Las ideas que volvemos realidad tienen una agenda y un pasado. Brotan en un contexto que las acepta o las rechaza. La mente condicionada no tiene otra opción que responder a todo tipo de limitaciones externas. Una vez que un deseo, esperanza o sueño se las arregla para volverse realidad, nos aferramos a lo que hemos creado. Ignoramos la ruina inevitable de todas las cosas —un día las cosas que hemos construido serán reliquias como el Partenón o las pirámides de Egipto—.

La creación duradera debe ser construida sobre lo atemporal. Eso no es posible con las cosas físicas, y dado que los objetos físicos representan ideas, incluso las ideas no pueden durar realmente ante los estragos de tiempo. En lo atemporal, lo que permanece no es una idea o una cosa, sino la creatividad misma. La "sustancia" de la creación es nuestra propia conciencia y su capacidad infinita de crear. Al despertar creas a partir de ser un creador, no a partir de las ideas y cosas que te rodean. Tú estás más allá de las cosas y las ideas, un ser consciente de dimensión atemporal.

PARA HOY

Atemporal es un concepto que se siente muy lejos de la vida cotidiana, pero se acerca cuando te das cuenta de lo que es el tiempo. El tiempo es el proceso de creación y destrucción. Por lo tanto, si tú no te identificas con la creación ni con la destrucción, estás en lo atemporal. Tienes la opción de cambiar tu lealtad hacia lo atemporal cada vez que lo desees. Detente un momento y mira alrededor de la habitación. Cuando vuelvas a leer esta página, todo lo que miraste está en proceso de decaer, disolverse y disiparse. Pero ¿acaso el tiempo se llevó el momento presente? No, sólo se llevó las cosas que notaste en el momento presente. El momento presente se renueva a sí mismo constantemente. Representa lo atemporal que persiste en la actividad del tiempo. Cuando estás despierto, lo atemporal precede a todo lo demás. Este cambio te permite celebrar la creación sin sentir ansiedad por la muerte de las cosas.

TU EXPERIENCIA: _____

_____

_____

_____

_____

_____

DÍA 30

Al saber que somos libres, el futuro de la humanidad puede ir más allá del nacimiento, de la muerte y todas las historias que suceden en medio.

Si pudieras aterrizar en cualquier momento de la historia, podrías buscar a personas que ya hayan despertado. Siempre serán una minoría, y quizás una fracción diminuta de una minoría. Pero contar narices no es como funciona el despertar. Si quieres saber si los seres humanos pueden nadar, sólo necesitas encontrar un ejemplo. De forma similar, una persona despierta te dice que despertar es posible y, más aún, que todos somos parte del proceso. Despertar no se aprende; no es un comportamiento adquirido. Es un estado en el que todos nosotros ya existimos. Lo único que sucede cuando despiertas es que te das cuenta de quién eres en realidad. La humanidad ya es libre, de lo contrario no estaríamos aquí como seres conscientes. Sólo las historias que nos decimos a nosotros mismos bloquean nuestra visión de nuestra verdadera naturaleza.

Este patrón de interferencia, como una imagen borrosa en la televisión, no afecta la realidad. El transmisor sigue enviando una imagen clara, incluso si tu receptor no la recibe. Cuando despiertas, tanto la señal como el receptor son claros y están en sintonía. Los pensamientos y los sentimientos van y vienen sin crear interferencia. Esto es lo que significa estar en el mundo sin ser del mundo.

PARA HOY

Puedes estar en la pobreza por dos motivos: ya sea que en verdad eres pobre, o eres rico pero no lo sabes. En relación con el potencial infinito que es nuestra naturaleza verdadera, nos sentimos limitados en nuestra vida cotidiana. ¿Entonces cuál es verdad? ¿Estamos limitados o no sabemos que somos ilimitados? La respuesta no se encuentra al observar las condiciones sobre el terreno. La persona más rica, más inteligente, más talentosa y más feliz puede llevar una vida muy limitada. La respuesta sólo se encuentra en tu propia conciencia.

Siéntate por un momento e intenta pensar un pensamiento prohibido. Podría ser algo que te hayas negado a considerar por algún motivo —por ser demasiado vergonzoso, indignante, antisocial, degradante o cualquier otra cosa prohibida—. En el instante en que se te ocurre ese pensamiento, deja de ser prohibido. No puedes limitar el pensamiento, y dado que los pensamientos brotan de la conciencia silenciosa, no puedes limitar la posibilidad de que nacerá cualquier pensamiento. Dado que tu vida entera —y la vida de la humanidad— está basada en la conciencia, tú también eres ilimitado. Puedes dejar de creer todas esas historias sobre el nacimiento, la muerte y todo lo que sucede en medio. Saber que eres ilimitado significa que ninguna historia puede limitar tus posibilidades.

TU EXPERIENCIA: _____

_____

_____

_____

_____

_____

DÍA 31

Puedes disfrutar la película mientras al mismo tiempo sabes que tú la creaste. Éste es el estado despierto.

El mundo cotidiano opera por medio de opuestos. En cada experiencia existe un polo negativo y un polo positivo. Para navegar por la vida, la gente intenta asir el polo positivo, pero este esfuerzo nunca la libera del espectro de que el polo negativo también llegará un día de éstos. La polaridad máxima es el apego y el desapego. Los buscadores espirituales aprenden que el desapego es positivo, porque el apego (es decir, estar atorado, aferrado, creyendo la ilusión) deriva en dolor y sufrimiento.

En un lugar donde siempre llueve es difícil dejar de usar la palabra *mojado*. En un mundo gobernado por los opuestos es difícil usar una palabra como *desapego*. Pero en el panorama general no hay apego ni desapego. Cada uno depende del otro; por lo tanto, cada uno conduce al otro. Las rupturas difíciles muestran lo difícil que es desapegarse de algo (o alguien) a lo que estás profundamente apegado. Pero tenemos que relacionarnos; de eso se trata todo el mundo relativo.

En el estado despierto las cosas cambian. Sabes que creaste la película, así que puedes disfrutarla sin creértela. Los directores aman las películas que hacen. Pero cuando la miran no se la pasan recordándose a sí mismos que crearon la película. Dan por hecho que son sus creadores. Asimismo, cuando estás despierto sabes que tú creaste la película en la que vives, pero no te obsesionas con eso. Estás demasiado ocupado con estar inmerso en el ahora. Ser un creador está en el fondo de tu conciencia, y este conocimiento tras bambalinas es suficiente.

PARA HOY

Justo ahora hay cosas a las que estás apegado y cosas a las que no. Si eres padre o madre de un niño pequeño, por ejemplo, le permites a tu hijo cierta libertad mientras que entras en escena cuando es necesario. Esta alternancia entre mantenerte alejado o involucrarte es la tarea cotidiana de ser padre o madre. En el fondo de tu mente sabes que eres un padre o madre; éste es tu estatus, y no necesitas sacarlo a relucir todo el tiempo.

Ahora piensa en la manera en que te crías a ti mismo. De la misma forma, algunas veces te dejas ir y otras veces entras en escena para monitorear tu comportamiento. Es imposible soltarte todo el tiempo, y es igualmente imposible refrenarte todo el tiempo. No importa en qué modo estés, en el fondo de tu mente se encuentra tu sentido del ser. Siéntate en silencio por un momento y experimenta tu sentido del ser. ¿Acaso no ha estado ahí siempre, en las buenas y en las malas? Tu sentido del ser está en el fondo de tu mente siempre, y no hay necesidad de sacarlo a relucir todo el tiempo.

Cuando despiertas, el sentido del ser se aproxima a primera vista. Con asombro experimentas que todo surge de tu sentido del ser —todos los pensamientos, palabras, acciones, el mundo exterior e interior—. Darte cuenta de esto no puede estar exento de maravilla y asombro. Pero a la larga el sentido del ser, al darse cuenta de lo infinito que es, se retira una vez más al fondo de tu mente. Dos personas pueden comprar palomitas en el cine, y sólo una de ellas es una persona rica. Las dos comieron la misma bolsa de palomitas y pagaron lo mismo por ella. Pero aquel que sabe que es rico tiene un conjunto de posibilidades muy distinto en el fondo de su mente. Esto es lo que se siente estar despierto, saber que cada pequeña acción está respaldada por posibilidades infinitas.

TU EXPERIENCIA: _____

_____

_____

_____

_____

_____

PARA TODOS LOS DÍAS

••• ──────── •••

Despertar siempre es en el ahora. No hay un tiempo en el calendario
para que te des cuenta de que tú eres quien sueña, y que no eres el sueño.

Ha pasado un mes de despertar. Has emprendido el viaje que va de
aquí hacia allá. Como no hay disonancia entre aquí y allá, un mes fue
suficiente para completar el viaje. Pero en otro marco de referencia,
el tiempo nunca es suficiente. Sólo cuando lo atemporal es tu parque
de diversiones ya no importa ir "desde aquí hasta allá". El ahora envuelve por completo todos los principios, puntos medios y finales.

Pero estar aquí ahora nunca fue la meta, como lo puede ser convertirte en una mejor persona o criar bien a tus hijos o ganar un mi-
llón de dólares. No puedes comparar el ahora con nada, porque todos
los ahoras ya se han perdido para siempre. Lo que cambia conforme
despiertas es sutil pero de suma importancia. Ya no hay un viaje de
ningún tipo. No un viaje externo ni uno interno. Ningún sueño que
alcanzar, ningún temor del cual escapar. El pasado ya no está lleno
de remordimientos ni el futuro acecha con amenazas. El lado fantas-
mal de la vida se ha disipado, y esas cosas eran fantasmas.

PARA CADA DÍA

En momentos al azar, cuando te den ganas, detente y mira a tu alrededor. Di para ti mismo: "Muchas cosas están sucediendo. Muchas
cosas han estado sucediendo. Yo estoy aquí, y eso es lo que importa".
Conforme despiertas, estas palabras significan algo distinto para ti.
Se expandirán para abarcar cada vez más y más. Al estar aquí te estás
uniendo a la danza cósmica. Valora la danza por lo que es hoy. La
parte cósmica tocará a tu puerta cuando estés listo.

TU EXPERIENCIA: _____
_____
_____
_____
_____
_____

PALABRAS FINALES

A pesar de nuestros 7 000 millones de historias, estamos unidos en una sola vida. El destino del planeta depende de que nos demos cuenta de este hecho. Una vez que lo hagamos, la raza humana puede evolucionar a metahumana. ¿Qué tan cerca estamos de ello en este momento? La respuesta no es clara. La vida nunca se tranquiliza lo suficiente. Si hubiera existido un diario en la Roma antigua, la Francia medieval o el Londres de Shakespeare, veríamos el mismo drama. Los mejores aspectos de la naturaleza humana siempre están precariamente equilibrados con los peores aspectos. Nosotros somos las únicas criaturas capaces de autocompasión, y las únicas criaturas que sienten que la merecen.

En vez de enfocarnos en cómo se comportan los humanos, cómo se comportan los animales e incluso cómo se comportan los quarks y los bosones, deberíamos preguntarnos cómo se comporta la conciencia. La conciencia lo une todo. Todos los objetos, ya sean una célula cerebral, un acantilado de piedra caliza o un cuchillo prehistórico hecho de pedernal, representan la mente en movimiento. El juego de la conciencia es infinito, pero hay una unidad manteniendo unido el juego.

Si las ideas densas y complicadas en este libro te han desconcertado, te comprendo. Lo último que quiero hacer —o que podría hacer— es obligar a nadie a aceptar nada de lo que yo diga. Pero es crítico despertar a la vida que compartimos. Si te consideras una persona moderna, entonces vives y te comportas como lo hace el mundo moderno. Es motivo de orgullo que el mundo moderno ha sido muy exitoso al acumular conocimiento, un hecho a la vez. No han pasado ni siquiera dos décadas desde el momento en que se contó el número de genes humanos y se mapeó el genoma humano entero. En la siguiente década se mapearán los billones de conexiones cerebrales a través de un esfuerzo científico enorme y concertado.

Así que debe ser impactante cuando lees en este libro que todo lo que puedes contar, medir, calcular y reducir a datos es parte de una ilusión envolvente. Quizá sea todavía más estremecedora mi afirmación de que todo lo que puedas percibir, imaginar o pensar en palabras habita la misma ilusión. No soy un enemigo de la ilusión. Creo que las personas tienen derecho de mejorarla todo lo que quieran, y siento pena por aquellos cuya porción de la ilusión está tan deteriorada que están sufriendo.

Pero sólo despertar permite que la unidad de una sola vida sea experimentada de forma directa. De otra manera, el mundo siempre sería un choque de opuestos, fundamentado en la certeza de que los seres humanos somos capaces de lo mejor y lo peor. Pero lo que nos hace capaces de escuchar nuestros demonios un día y bendecir a los ángeles al siguiente no es en realidad la naturaleza humana. Es el estado de separación que seguimos reforzando, generación tras generación.

No preveo que el *Homo sapiens* dé un salto colectivo en su evolución, pero sé que puede hacerlo. Nuestra evolución cambió del mundo físico al mental hace decenas de miles de años, aun cuando los primeros humanos estaban desnudos y eran vulnerables, llevando una existencia tan llena de amenazas como cualquier animal atrapado en la lucha entre presa y depredador. Es un misterio total cómo llegamos a la conciencia de nosotros mismos. Una vez que lo hicimos, o que lo hicieron nuestros ancestros homínidos, la mente estuvo presta para triunfar en todos los aspectos de la vida. Pero la mente activa no es lo mismo que la conciencia. Un pensamiento, sentimiento o sensación es como una ola que sube y baja; la conciencia es el océano.

Esta analogía se remonta a miles de años atrás en la India, y no puedo recordar cuándo fue la primera vez que la escuché de niño. Las palabras parecían como un cliché, de la misma forma en que "Amarás a tu prójimo" y "Ser o no ser, ésa es la cuestión", se sienten como un cliché. La repetición drena el significado, incluso de los dichos más profundos.

Sopesé este obstáculo y decidí que el camino directo debe brindar un pequeño despertar todos los días; despertar no debería tenerse como la máxima recompensa al final del camino espiritual. En mi propia vida aspiro a tres tipos de experiencia. Si una de ellas sucede hoy, he alcanzado un pequeño despertar. Si suceden dos o las tres, el pequeño despertar se magnifica. Éstas son las tres experiencias:

- Veo la realidad con mayor claridad.
- Me siento menos atrapado en los hábitos, la memoria, las creencias desgastadas y los viejos condicionamientos.
- Dejo de aferrarme a las expectativas y recompensas externas.

¿Cómo se aplicarían estas experiencias en tu vida?

VES LA REALIDAD CON MAYOR CLARIDAD

Ésta es la experiencia de percibir con la mirada fresca. Renuncias a formas viejas de interpretar el mundo a tu alrededor y tu propia vida. La interpretación es inherente a la percepción. Es inevitable que le des nombre a todo, que tengas opiniones, que recurras a experiencias del pasado y que lances juicios sobre lo que está sucediendo. El mundo ha sido interpretado por ti desde que eras un infante, y aun así tienes control sobre esto ahora que eres un adulto. El mundo no tiene que cambiar. Si percibes frescura y renovación, si despiertas con una sensación de optimismo y te sientes abierto a lo desconocido, entonces cada día es un mundo. No tienes que intentar vivir en el momento presente, porque no podrás escapar del momento presente. Te atraerá sin resistencia, porque todo ahí está por ganar y nada que perder cuando una persona vive aquí y ahora, en vez de repetir el pasado y anticipar el futuro.

TE SIENTES MENOS ATORADO EN LOS HÁBITOS, LA MEMORIA, LAS CREENCIAS DESGASTADAS Y LOS VIEJOS CONDICIONAMIENTOS

Ésta es la sensación de desatorarte. La realidad virtual sería perfectamente aceptable si la gente se sintiera libre de alterarla de acuerdo con sus propios deseos. Pero gran parte de la vida está más allá de nuestro control, lo que conduce a la sensación de estar atrapados, confinados, limitados e incluso sofocados. Yo agrupo estos sentimientos en la palabra *atorarse*. Al desatorarte te desenredas de la complicada red tejida por la personalidad del ego. Esta red se ha vuelto pegajosa a través del proceso de identificación. Cada vez que dices "Yo soy X" estás más lejos de poder decir "Yo soy". Como ya vimos, X puede ser cualquier cosa: tu nombre, tu trabajo, tu estado civil, tu raza, tu religión, tu nacionalidad. Éstas y muchas más cosas se convierten en tu historia personal. "Yo soy" va más allá de todas las historias.

DEJAS DE AFERRARTE A LAS EXPECTATIVAS
Y RECOMPENSAS EXTERNAS

Ésta es la experiencia de convertirte en ti mismo. La personalidad del ego constantemente está al acecho de recompensas externas para validar lo que vale. Si le preguntas a la gente: "¿Qué preferirías ser: feliz sólo por existir o rico?", su respuesta es obvia. La necesidad de recompensas externas, no sólo de dinero sino también de estatus, el vecindario adecuado, un coche nuevo, la aprobación social y más, alimenta nuestra dependencia sobre ellas. Con el tiempo la personalidad del ego se ha vuelto una fuerza dominante, incluso cuando alguien se considera a sí mismo sin ambiciones y espiritual —las bancas del frente en las iglesias se sienten mejor que las de la última fila—. Pero el ego es una guía falsa porque la plenitud total que promete siempre está más allá del horizonte. Vivir con expectativas va de la mano con la necesidad de recompensas externas —siempre hay un mítico sobresalto de placer o triunfo o riqueza, el gran marcador que de una vez por todas hará que nuestra vida valga la pena—. Para cortar las cuerdas necesitas sentir que la ausencia de recompensas externas no es dolorosa, porque existen recompensas internas. La más grande es la libertad de ser tú mismo.

Como resultado de estas tres experiencias, despertar se convierte en tu vida, poco a poco, y después, casi sin saberlo, estás participando en la vida única, que es real, radiante y total.

Como todos podemos tener pequeños despertares, el futuro de nuestra especie no tiene que ser un proyecto enorme marcado por las turbulencias de la guerra y la paz, la revolución y el retroceso, lograr la grandeza y perderla de nuevo, o jugar los roles de opresor y oprimido. Una persona a la vez puede despertar a la realidad. Eso será suficiente. El misterio de ser humano ha sido ocultado de cada uno de nosotros, y quizá por ello sigue siendo tan seductor. Nunca hemos dejado de ser una especie que se crea a sí misma. Si podemos crear un mundo de alturas gloriosas sin estar despiertos del todo, imagina lo que podríamos hacer con los ojos bien abiertos.

AGRADECIMIENTOS

Experimento gratitud cada vez que se termina un nuevo libro debido a la generosa y productiva relación que tengo con mi editorial. Comenzando por Gina Centrello, presidente y editora de Penguin Random House, quien ha mostrado una lealtad inquebrantable hacia mí. Gracias.

En Harmony Books, gozo de una relación de confianza con mi perspicaz editor, Gary Jansen, que sin cansancio me brinda sugerencias para mejorar el manuscrito. No sé cuántas veces Gary ha guiado mi escritura en la dirección correcta —un autor no podría pedir más—. Además, deseo reconocer el apoyo de todos los que en Harmony Books dedicaron su tiempo, creatividad y pasión a este libro, incluyendo a Aaron Wehner, Diana Baroni, Tammy Blake, Christina Foley, Molly Breitbart, Marysarah Quinn, Patricia Shaw, Jessie Bright, Sarah Horgan, Heather Williamson y Ashley Hong. Y un agradecimiento especial para Rachel Berkowitz, en el departamento de derechos internacionales, quien ha sido imprescindible para ayudarme a difundir mi obra alrededor del mundo. El público no tiene idea de lo dedicado que debe ser un equipo en una casa editorial y lo mucho que aman los libros y sirven a los escritores. Muchas gracias.

Un agradecimiento especial a Poonacha Machaiah, innovador con inspiración, buen amigo y sabio guía.

Finalmente, agradezco a todos cerca de casa, comenzando con Carolyn Rangel, cuya calidez, dedicación y paciencia la han convertido en alguien invaluable desde hace muchos años —eres muy especial—. También lo son los equipos en el Centro Chopra en California, el equipo de HomeBase en Nueva York: Paulette Cole, Marc Nadeau, Teana David, Sara McDonald y Kendall Mar-Horstman.

Los colaboradores más nuevos en mi vida son los miembros del equipo del podcast *Infinite Potential*: Jan Cohen, David Shadrack Smith, Julie Magruder y los amigos de Cadence 13 —gracias por permitirme estar conectado al mundo digital a lo largo de un nuevo camino tan productivo—. Mientras *Metahumano* se estaba escribiendo, el consejo directivo de la Fundación Chopra enfrentó un año de nuevos retos, y los directivos se adaptaron a ello, mostrando gran apoyo y orientación, así que expreso mi profundo agradecimiento a Alice Walton, Matthew Harris, Ray Chambers, François Ferre, Fred Matser, Paul Johnson y Ajay Gupta, junto con los "exploradores" que están en el camino de despertar la conciencia. También quiero darle la bienvenida a Tonia O'Connor, CEO de Chopra Global.

Mi familia ha crecido a lo largo de los años, ha atravesado muchos cambios y sigue siendo una fuente de calidez y alegría amorosas: Rita, Mallika, Sumant, Gotham, Candice, Krishan, Tara, Leela y Geeta, los guardo en mi corazón por siempre.

Metahumano de Deepak Chopra
se terminó de imprimir en junio de 2020
en los talleres de
Litográfica Ingramex S.A. de C.V.,
Centeno 162-1, Col. Granjas Esmeralda, C.P. 09810,
Ciudad de México.